FOR A
MISSIONARY REFORM
OF THE CHURCH

FOR A MISSIONARY REFORM OF THE CHURCH

THE *CIVILTÀ CATTOLICA* SEMINAR

EDITED BY
Antonio Spadaro, SJ, and Carlos María Galli

FOREWORD BY
Massimo Faggioli

TRANSLATED BY
Demetrio S. Yocum

Paulist Press
New York / Mahwah, NJ

Cover image: Photo copyright by *L' Osservatore Romano*
Cover and book design by Lynn Else

Library of Congress Control Number: 2017951005

ISBN 978-0-8091-5348-0 (paperback)
ISBN 978-1-58768-714-3 (e-book)

Published by Paulist Press
997 Macarthur Boulevard
Mahwah, NJ 07430

www.paulistpress.com

Printed and bound in the
United States of America

CONTENTS

FOREWORD

It is a great honor to introduce the English version of this volume edited by Antonio Spadaro, SJ, and Carlos María Galli, which Paulist Press courageously decided to translate and publish for the English-speaking readership, because this book is much more than the usual collection of essays presented at an academic conference. It is the contribution of a group of theologians to Pope Francis's vision of Church reform, having in mind the necessity of translating the theological and pastoral insights of Jorge Mario Bergoglio into ecclesiological and canonical language and in the concrete ecclesial praxis for the future of the Church in terms of pastoral and missionary reform.

These essays are grounded in the awareness that Pope Francis's pontificate represents a shift in the Catholic discourse on the idea of *reform* and on the progress toward *reforms* in the Church. In this sense, the volume gives voice to the sense of urgency for a Church trying to develop a theologically sound set of concrete transformations for the transition from a Eurocentric and clergy-driven paradigm to a truly global Catholic Church. At the same time, these essays interpret a realistic and therefore humble understanding of Church reform as a long-term process, where academic theology, lived ecclesiology of the people of God, and ecclesiastical structures are interrelated in a circularity between ongoing theological-spiritual growth on the one side, and on the other side an institutional makeup that today still reflects the social and political structures of medieval European Christendom—which for the papacy still means a form of government typical of European monarchies in the early modern period.

The volume collects thirty essays that are the final product of one week of discussions, and fruit of lifelong research projects of each of the participants. There are different ways of approaching such a volume. One way is to read the essays individually, as separate contributions for which each author is individually responsible, where each author reacts and interacts with Francis's pontificate and with the theological and ecclesial situation today in a different way, though in dialogue with the other authors.

A second way of reading these essays is to look at the volume more systematically, with essays covering four areas: (1) theology of reform in light of Church history and of Francis's pontificate; (2) reform of Church structures *in capite,* that is, reform of the papacy and of the central government of the Catholic Church; (3) reform of Church structures at the diocesan and interdiocesan level; (4) Church reform in terms of a new understanding of the Church as local, pastoral, ecumenical, and inculturated.

There is also a third way of reading this volume. The thirty essays can be read also a twelve-step program for the process of Church reform:

1. understanding the theological and historical roots of the reform of the Church
2. conversion to missionary holiness
3. renewal of the communion of the people of God
4. reforms in order to become a more synodal Church
5. conversion of the papacy
6. changes in the Roman Curia *semper reformanda*
7. better articulation of the relationship between *communio ecclesiarum* and *collegium episcoporum*—communion of the churches and episcopal collegiality (the relationship of the bishop with his diocese; reform of the selection and appointment of bishops)
8. theological and canonical reevaluation of diocesan churches
9. theological and canonical reevaluation of the particular churches (interdiocesan particular churches; review of national bishops' conferences; promotion of plenary councils, and of regional and continental bishops' conferences)
10. changes in the participation of the lay faithful (men and women)

11. fostering ecumenical unity among Christians and Church reform
12. transformation of structures toward a more inculturated, poor, and merciful Church.

There is, finally, a fourth way of reading the thirty essays of the volume: as the tip of the iceberg of a global, intellectual, and spiritual ongoing conversation in the whole Catholic Church about its future form, a conversation in which what takes place in Rome reflects the conversation taking place globally today. This book is a tangible example of the "Francis effect" on the Catholic Church.

The *Civiltà Cattolica* seminar was an act of dialogue with the pontificate of Pope Francis, and an acknowledgment that with the pontificate of Francis the reception of the Second Vatican Council and the reform of the Church have entered a new phase. This volume aims to be a joint effort of Catholic theologians coming from all over the world with different backgrounds and perspectives in accompanying and supporting Francis's reforms. As coeditor Fr. Spadaro emphasizes in the opening essay, the task of the reformer is to start or accompany historical processes: reforming means opening open processes, not gaining power spaces. In this sense, this volume must be read with a very realistic sense about the obstacles against Church reform in the entirety of Church history until today. At the same time, the authors share a belief in the crucial role of theology for the Church as a communion and as an institution, especially in time of reform.

This volume can be read therefore also as an act of reading Francis's pontificate, and an encouragement to look at Francis in the context of a vision of reform but also in the context of the history of the Church Jorge Mario Bergoglio comes from. From the essay by the coeditor Carlos María Galli, it is clear that Francis cannot be understood without the history of the Catholic Church in Latin America in the twentieth century: the reception of Vatican II as "the council of the people of God"; the CELAM conferences of Medellin (1968), of Santo Domingo (1992), and especially of Aparecida (2007); and the ecclesiological shift of a Church in dialogue with the whole world, the people, and its cultural expressions in a missionary perspective (especially the conciliar documents *Lumen Gentium*, *Gaudium et Spes*, and *Ad Gentes*).

Two key ideas emerge from these reflections as typical of Francis's pontificate in light of an ecclesiology of reform: the first is of *pastoral conversion*. Francis maintains that the Second Vatican Council reread the gospel in the light of contemporary culture, and that this dynamic is absolutely irreversible: "Each particular Church, as a portion of the Catholic Church under the leadership of its bishop, is likewise called to missionary conversion.... To make this missionary impulse ever more focused, generous and fruitful, I encourage each particular Church to undertake a resolute process of discernment, purification and reform" (*Evangelii Gaudium* 30). Just like Vatican II was a reform council, Francis's pontificate is programmatically about Church reform in terms of *pastoral and missionary conversion*: "I want to emphasize that what I am trying to express here has a programmatic significance and important consequences. I hope that all communities will devote the necessary effort to advancing along the path of a pastoral and missionary conversion which cannot leave things as they presently are. 'Mere administration' can no longer be enough. Throughout the world, let us be 'permanently in a state of mission'" (*Evangelii Gaudium* 25).

The second key idea is of *synodality*, that is, of a Catholic Church that acts in a synodal way, less centered on institutional power monarchically structured and relying more on consultation and listening to the people of God on some critical issues in some critical moments in the life of the Church. Synodality was a theological insight already part of the theological culture of Vatican II, but was not fully expressed by the Council and indeed until a few years ago was not really part of the official language of theology, nor of the magisterium. Today synodality plays a very important part in Francis's ecclesiology, and therefore in his idea of Church reform, as we have seen from the speech he gave on the fiftieth anniversary of the institution of the Bishops' Synod on October 17, 2017 (just two weeks after the conclusion of the *Civiltà Cattolica* seminar). That speech is the papal *magna carta* for synodality in the Catholic Church, and certainly this volume must be read in the context of the new emphasis of papal magisterium on *synodality of the whole Church* (based on the ecclesiology of the *sensus fidei* of the whole people of God) together with and not separated from *collegiality between the pope and the college of bishops*.

The importance of the translation of this volume for English-speaking readers lies in the fact that the essays here published contain, in my opinion as a European Catholic theologian working in America since 2009, three different kinds of challenges or stimuli for the very vital part of the global Catholic communion that is embedded in Anglo-Saxon culture.

The first challenge is about Vatican II and the reform of the Church and reforms in the Church. All the essays of the volume are based on the assumption of the importance of Vatican II for the Catholic Church, for the pontificate of Francis, and for the future of the Church. The essays in this volume approach Vatican II in a way similar to Francis's, that is, taking the Second Vatican Council as part of the great Catholic tradition without submitting it to a magisterial hermeneutics driven by a particular interpretation of what happened *after* Vatican II in a particular area of the life of the Church in a particular country. Francis's pontificate is not a new chapter in the history of the battle for meaning around Vatican II.

A second stimulus is given by the assumption in these essays that theological discourse, the life of the Church, and the institutional dimension of the Church must have a lively and continued conversation between themselves; they do not have the luxury to act in a totally independent and separated way from the other levels. On the one side, the institutionalist and traditionalist ecclesiologies carry some responsibilities in separating one level from the other to shield the institution from the potential for institutional change that is always a product of theological reflection and of the lived experience of Catholics. On the other side, the postmodern tendency to deconstruct Church history and Catholic theology in a series of narrower fields of "Catholic studies" defined by the identitarian quest (gender, race, ethnic-national background, local versus global, etc.) may weaken theology from being capable of interacting with the institution and push toward reforms urgently needed for the future of the Catholic communion. This volume aspires to propose reforms that include and take seriously, but try to look beyond, the fragmentation of the Catholic discourse in the Northern Hemisphere today.

A third kind of challenge has to do with the particular relationship between Francis's pontificate and the English-speaking Catholic world. The English translation of this book is important not because the book is an act of "interpretation" of the pontificate (it is not), but rather because it is an example of interaction with this pontificate by a diverse group of scholars looking at Francis and his potential for a Church reform, without submitting the pontificate to the scrutiny of a particular theological agenda. Francis's repeated invitations to de-ideologize Catholic discourse and praxis resonated particularly with the polarized English-speaking Church: the reforms proposed here embrace Francis's invitation to imagine the reform of the Church on the basis of the Catholic tradition, of theology, and of pastoral experience escaping the temptation to turn the *ecclesia semper reformanda* into a short-lived ideological platform.

The essays in this book advance different proposals for a complex and demanding set of practical and concrete reforms: reform of the way of structuring ordained ministry; a tangibly new role for the laity and women in the Church; a reform of the central government of the Church; a new relationship between theology and canon law. But Francis's path toward reform is not merely bureaucratic, minimized toward a streamlining of procedures or rationalization of resources:

> The renewal of structures demanded by pastoral conversion can only be understood in this light: as part of an effort to make them more mission-oriented, to make ordinary pastoral activity on every level more inclusive and open, to inspire in pastoral workers a constant desire to go forth and in this way to elicit a positive response from all those whom Jesus summons to friendship with himself. (*Evangelii Gaudium* 27)

This reform is not just *in membris*, aimed at a reform of local practices, but also *in capite*, for the center of the institutional Church:

> Since I am called to put into practice what I ask of others, I too must think about a conversion of the papacy. It

> is my duty, as the Bishop of Rome, to be open to suggestions which can help make the exercise of my ministry more faithful to the meaning which Jesus Christ wished to give it and to the present needs of evangelization. (*Evangelii Gaudium* 32)

The objective of this text is to present an articulated set of concrete stimuli and proposals for the deepening and continuation of the reform of the Catholic Church. It does not contain final conclusions shared by all authors, who wrote under their own individual responsibility. But the volume, as a whole, sets out from the idea of *Ecclesia semper reformanda,* which expresses the need for a permanent renewal and the demand for reform at a given moment. It covers *both* the reform of personal and communal Christian life *and* the transformation of ecclesial structures.

Massimo Faggioli
Villanova University (Philadelphia)
June 15, 2017

PREFACE

A Missionary Reform of the Church

See, I am making all things new. (Rev 21:5)

The Exchange during the Study Seminar

From September 28 to October 2, 2015, a seminar was held in Rome at the headquarters of the Jesuit magazine *La Civiltà Cattolica*. The participants were thirty men and women ecclesiologists, historians, ecumenists, canonists, and pastoral experts from thirteen countries: Argentina, Belgium, Brazil, Canada, Chile, the Philippines, France, Germany, Italy, Netherlands, Congo, Democratic Republic, Spain, and the United States.

The theme of the seminar—which was held in the year marking the fiftieth anniversary of the closing of Vatican II—was "The reform and reforms in the Church." The seminar developed the issue of the *Ecclesia semper reformanda* ("The Church must always be reformed"), considering the renewal called for by the Second Vatican Council in its vital and structural aspects, and in its doctrine of the Church. In addition to paper presentations, every day there were three periods of dialogue among the participants that allowed real and open exchange.

The purpose of the seminar was to offer humble and honest contributions inspired by the processes that the Church is experiencing now under the guidance of Pope Francis. The Bishop of Rome in the encyclical *Laudato Si'* wrote that he addressed his first exhortation *Evangelii Gaudium* "to all the members of the

Church with the aim of encouraging ongoing missionary renewal" (*LS* 3).

An unofficial initiative of men and women theologians, both lay and ordained, the seminar was organized by the Jesuit magazine *La Civiltà Cattolica*. The realization of the event, in its simple and essential format, was made possible thanks to the contribution of four foundations.

The topics discussed were rich and complex. After introductory remarks on the vision that Pope Francis has of the reform of the Church in light of his experience as a Jesuit and in light of his pastoral ecclesiology rooted in the Latin American tradition, the seminar covered the following topics: (1) the renewal of the Church in the Second Vatican Council; (2) the lessons of history about the reform of the Church; (3) the synodal communion as the key of life and renewal of the people of God; (4) the reforms of the universal Church and the particular Churches; (5) Christian unity and the reform of the Church; (6) reflections for a more poor, fraternal, and inculturated Church.

The seminar included a reflection on the sources of permanent renewal of the Church and expressed some common indications on how to deepen and institutionalize the various reforms of the Church. The seminar also collected criteria for action and concrete proposals for reform.

Those who attended the seminar include the following (in order of intervention): Antonio Spadaro, SJ (Italy), Carlos María Galli (Argentina), Hermann Pottmeyer (Germany), John O'Malley, SJ (United States), Andrea Riccardi (Italy), Giancarlo Pani, SJ (Italy), Angelo Maffeis (Italy), Hervé Legrand, OP (France), Dario Vitali (Italy), Alphonse Borras (Belgium), Gilles Routhier (Canada), Silvia Scatena (Italy), Severino Dianich (Italy), Salvador Pié-Ninot (Spain), Myriam Wijlens (Netherlands), Massimo Faggioli (United States), Carlos Schickendantz (Chile), William Henn, OFMCap (United States), Piero Coda (Italy), Joseph Famerée, SCI (Belgium), Peter de Mey (Belgium), Jorge Scampini, OP (Argentina), Juan Carlos Scannone, SJ (Argentina), Diego Fares, SJ (Argentina), Serena Noceti (Italy), Mario De França Miranda, SJ (Brazil), Léonard Santedi Kinkupu (DRC), José Mario C. Francisco, SJ (Philippines), Mary Melone, SFA (Italy), Msgr. Víctor Manuel Fernández (Argentina).

Participants included six lay people; twelve religious; eleven diocesan priests; and an archbishop rector of a university. Some of the esteemed participants are specialists in more than one church discipline. Regarding the topic at hand, it should be noted that there were twelve ecclesiologists; five church historians; eight ecumenists; three canonists; and six professors of spiritual and pastoral theology. Further, eighteen have produced studies on the Second Vatican Council and eleven on evangelization and inculturation.

The ad hoc organizing committee was formed by a group of Argentine Jesuit professors and writers of *La Civiltà Cattolica*. The committee decided that the thirty participants would participate by delivering keynote lectures or interventions in different sessions. Among the topics that they were required to address are these: think, in dialogue, about the reform and reforms *in* and *of* the Catholic Church; combine theological and philosophical contributions, especially in ecclesiology, church history, spirituality, canon law, and pastoral theology; consider reform movements and institutional reforms in the second millennium, especially in the thirteenth, sixteenth, nineteenth, and twentieth centuries; provide theological and institutional bases to ground, illuminate, or accompany pending reforms inspired by the Second Vatican Council; develop ecclesiological formulations in view of canonical formulas and legal formulations that give substance to theological ideas; analyze institutional macroreforms in the name of the missionary transformation of the Church and of the current challenges of globalization; rethink the Church's synodal communion, starting from God's people, the college of bishops, and the Bishop of Rome; consider the implications of the "conversion of the papacy" (*EG* 32) and of the role of Catholicism in the face of various ecumenical dialogues to promote the unity of the churches; expand on some of the points of Pope Francis's magisterium on reform to help discern the processes in place and, above all, forms of future institutionalization.

From our agenda were excluded issues and specific reforms that are being dealt with in other ecclesial organizations such as the C9 and the Synod of Bishops: for example, the reform of the institutions and the economy of the Roman curia; the synodal process on marriage and the family in the present world; the custody of creation, along with the option for the poor; the study topics of the international theological commission; and the formation of priests-pastors.

The working *method* we adopted was that of an open and well-founded dialogue to clarify the issues in a theoretical and practical manner. The quality of the interventions led to rich and prolonged exchanges, during which everyone expressed themselves freely and affably. Discussions were not driven by hasty consensus nor have statements been issued. There has been an efficient translation service, coordination, and synthesis. Each question was initiated starting with its corresponding *status quaestionis*; and after the theoretical developments, participants offered some propositional outlines and recommendations for the medium and long term.

A Proposal of Proposals

The richness of the texts, presented originally in Italian, English, or Spanish, offers an interesting range of views on the reform and the reforms in the Church. In this context, the organizing committee, chaired by Carlos María Galli, proposed to the participants to publish a volume of all their papers to share their thoughts with a wider audience and motivate others to think about different issues related to ecclesial renewal. It is in our interest that other colleagues in the theological community and other members of the Church are inspired to make their contribution, in freedom and communion, to the reform of the Church in accordance with the Spirit and the gospel, in line with the Second Vatican Council, and under the impulse of Francis's pontificate.

This collective work considers, from many different perspectives, the central question of the permanent and current *reform* or *renewal* of the Catholic Church. It investigates the issues at a disciplinary or interdisciplinary level because of the complexity they present. It seeks to discern some possible reforms for the present life of the Church. The thirty contributions offer an in-depth look at principles, criteria, guidelines, and stimuli to create, shed light, or accompany reforms both in the attitudes and in the institutions of the people of God. In several chapters, the authors advance their personal proposals to study or promote concrete changes in the lives of the local churches, the regional realities, and the universal Church.

Our work follows the itinerary of reflection, articulated in six sections (and an introduction), which shaped the basic structure of the seminar. The *theological logic* of this general scheme allows the contextualization of the reflections of the various collaborators. Readers can quickly consult the section headings and chapters in the table of contents that precedes this preface, and can read, in more detail, the internal structure of each chapter in the general index at the end of the volume.

To begin with, the authors of the thirty contributions have made significant efforts for which we, as editors, are very grateful. They have responded generously to our invitation, sent in the middle of 2014, even though they were busy amid their many activities. They have devoted much of their time for the preparation of their interventions, for the shared experience and work during those four days. They have shared their thoughts with openness and frankness in dialogue and discussion with others; they have rigorously worked at correcting, translating, and editing their writings; and they have encouraged us to promote common paths of ecclesial renewal. We thank them publicly for their personal contributions and for sharing their knowledge in this collective process. All have delivered texts that are strong, articulate, creative, and open, written with honesty and earnestness. And each chapter, of course, is under the sole responsibility of its author.

To our readers—especially bishops, theologians, and pastoral representatives—we offer this work as an *ordered collection of independent proposals* that share a love of the Church, the Second Vatican Council, and of Francis's papacy. We want it to be read with the same spirit that has marked its beginning, development, and purpose: *create a varied set of different theological contributions of the highest level to think about the reforms of and within the Church.*

As editors, we have considered whether to include a final chapter, after the thirty contributions; some colleagues have contributed their opinion to this common discernment. In the end, we preferred not to add a chapter with expressed propositions, taken from the previous chapters, to avoid giving the impression that they were the conclusions of the group. A common text would have required greater collective effort to combine the various positions on so many themes and from different theologies, horizons, positions, and sensitivities.

The Ecclesial Reform through Missionary Conversion

The terms *reforma* and *reformatio* appear for the first time at the Council of Vienne (1312). Since then, several councils have proposed reforms that have seen the involvement of the laity, religious, and clergy, especially bishops and the Bishop of Rome. From the Council of Constance (1414–1418), which put an end to the Western Schism, there arose the inclusive formula *ecclesia sit reformata in fide et moribus, in capite et in membris* (reform in faith and practice, in head and members). On the eve of the Lutheran protest, Lateran V (1512–1517) promoted a reform of the Church of the Renaissance "in its head and members." The popes who followed summoned subsequent sessions of the Council of Trent, which had its ups and downs, since it dealt at the same time with doctrine and reform. Trent promoted a pastoral reform to restore *cura animarum* of the Christian people, starting from the duty to preach the word of God. The First Vatican Council (1869–1870) dealt with the issue of faith in relation to reason and that of the papacy in the Church, but was unable to develop a comprehensive ecclesiology or to grasp the incipient ferments of renewal.

In the heart of the twentieth century, the Second Vatican Council gathered the fruits of the different processes of renewal, among which were the biblical (*Dei Verbum*), liturgical (*Sacrosanctum Concilium*), ecclesiological (*Lumen Gentium*), missionary (*Ad Gentes*), pastoral (*Gaudium et Spes*), and ecumenical (*Unitatis Redintegratio*) movements. This renewal is based on the "living tradition" (*DV* 12), which combines creative fidelity to Catholic doctrine with its aggiornamento to draw *nova et vetera* (new and old things) from the treasure of the Gospels (Matt 13:51). Continuity in renewal and renewal in continuity form the tradition of the people of God and connect the teachings of Vatican II with the Council of Trent and Vatican I (*DV* 1).

The popes and the conciliar documents have been able to

grasp the newness of God for this historic moment of the Church. Already in 1959, John XXIII described the Council as "a new Pentecost," because any type of reform is the work of the Spirit. And while Paul VI spoke of a "new reform" (*Ecclesiam Suam* 39; 46ff.) or of a "Church renewal" (*ES* 12; 55), the conciliar documents have promoted its reform (*LG* 4) or renewal (*UR* 4).

In the exhortation *Evangelii Gaudium,* Pope Francis has made the conciliar proposal his own. He has stated that

> the Second Vatican Council presented ecclesial conversion as openness to a constant self-renewal born of fidelity to Jesus Christ: "Every renewal of the Church essentially consists in an increase of fidelity to her own calling....Christ summons the Church as she goes her pilgrim way...to that continual reformation of which she always has need, in so far as she is a human institution here on earth."' (*EG* 26)

Here we find two of the words that John XXIII used to express renewal: fidelity and aggiornamento. And Francis has said, "For me, the great revolution is to go to the roots, recognize them and see what those roots have to say to us today."[1]

There are two words that condense the conciliar process of renewal of the Church: the neologism *ressourcement,* which expresses the traditional idea of reform understood as a return *ad fontes* (return to the sources) to illuminate current situations and deal with the Church's problems; the term *aggiornamento,* which implies a renewal starting from the current situation, means that the Church does not just give and teach, but receives and learns from the world (*Gaudium et Spes* 44) in an admirable mutual exchange (*GS* 40). The renewal brought about by the Spirit is stimulated by the process in which the people of God try to discern the true signs of God's presence (*GS* 4; 11). Reform must pay close attention to the cultural context in which the Church is immersed.

The concept of reform urges the Church to conform dynamically to the *forma Christi,* with the risk, however, of being reduced to its mere formal character. It requires the establishment of an *a quo* point from which to start, namely from its mistakes, but does not clearly identify the *ad quem* term, that is, the direction to follow. Each process must be understood always. For this reason, the reform needs subjects open to the Spirit and able to go out of oneself, in opposition to focusing on oneself in the forms of self-referentiality. Those who are closed in themselves are unable to withstand the process of reform; this leads to "the absolute priority" (*EG* 179) of going out of oneself. Reform requires the audacity—*parrhesia*—to go out, despite the dangers of incurring in accidents and loss of comfort, which leads to "being confined" (*EG* 49).

The reform of the Church focuses on a missionary dream capable of renewing everything:

> I dream of a "missionary option", that is, a missionary impulse capable of transforming everything....The renewal of structures demanded by pastoral conversion can only be understood in this light: as part of an effort to make them more mission-oriented, to make ordinary pastoral activity on every level more inclusive and open, to inspire in pastoral workers a constant desire to go forth and in this way to elicit a positive response from all those whom Jesus summons to friendship with himself. As John Paul II once said to the Bishops of Oceania: "All renewal in the Church must have mission as its goal if it is not to fall prey to a kind of ecclesial introversion." (*EG* 27)

A Theology of Synodal Reform

This collective volume is a work of people who are dedicated to theology and belong to numerous academic institutions. Therein lies both its value and its limit. The pastoral ministry of theology thinks faith in the service of the word of God in the Church. It is only one thread in the fabric of the various processes that renew Christian life and the proclamation of the gospel. A more comprehensive task involves listening to voices of different members of God's people; increasing the exchanges in the theological community; finding new formulations with experts in canon law and sharing the discernment of the authorities that govern the Church in the name of Christ, the Good Shepherd. With simplicity and responsibility, we offer our work to the Church, which we deeply love. We wish to rediscover the novelty of Jesus, who renews through his Spirit the journey of God's people.

The different contributions in this volume can be considered, without wanting to minimize their wide-ranging content nor indicate a reductive simplification, contributions for a renewed theology of the synodality of the Church in its process of ongoing renewal. This formulation is from Pope Francis's speech given on the fiftieth anniversary of the institution of the Synod of Bishops.

> What the Lord is asking of us is already in some sense present in the very word *synod*. Journeying together—laity, pastors, the Bishop of Rome—is an easy concept to put into words, but not so easy to put into practice....A synodal Church is a Church which listens, which realizes that listening "is more than simply hearing" (EG 171). It is a mutual listening in which everyone has something to learn. The faithful people, the college of bishops, the Bishop of Rome: all listening to each other, and all listening to the Holy Spirit, the "Spirit of truth" (John 14:17), in order to know what he "says to the Churches" (Rev 2:7).[2]

Paraphrasing this eloquent papal formulation, we can say that what the Lord truly wants to reform his Church in our time is, in a sense, found in the neologism *synodality*. To promote a synodal church implies renewing institutions to express an attitude of love, communion, listening, dialogue, initiative, hospitality, mutual exchange, cooperation, and participation among people and communities. *The reform of the Church is the synodal reform of the local churches and the whole Church*.

Synodality is the participatory and dynamic expression of the communal and pilgrim character of the Church, the sacrament of the kingdom of God in history toward its eschatological fullness. In the above address, Francis has made a great contribution to this topic. His teaching not only exceeds the vision of a pyramid structure of the Church, but proposes, through the ecclesiology of the

Council, *a synodal Church as an inverted pyramid* that integrates the people of God, the College of Bishops, and the Successor of Peter. Synodality provides the context for interpreting the apostolic authority as a power to serve the people of God (*LG* 18; 24).

The Revolution of Mercy

Many of the reforms of the Church were inspired by a return to evangelical poverty and a renewed commitment to the poor. The reformist movements in the thirteenth, sixteenth, nineteenth, and twentieth centuries were marked by communion with the poor Christ; the conversion to the word of God and its preaching; a supportive community life; being rooted in the new suburban areas; the identification with the excluded, that is, with the "lesser" brothers and sisters of Jesus (Matt 25:40); and by new institutional forms to create works of mercy.

Love for the poor is born of faith in Christ, who "became poor, so that by his poverty you might become rich." (2 Cor 8:9). On September 11, 1962, John XXIII spoke of the "Church embracing everyone, but [that] above all wishes to be the Church of the Poor." In inaugurating the Council, with the opening speech *Gaudet Mater Ecclesia*, he asked that the Church become "a loving mother of all, benign, patient, full of mercy and goodness." In the closing speech of the Council, Pope Paul VI said that the old story of the Good Samaritan was "the paradigm for the Council's spirituality." John Paul II expressed the option of the Church for the poor (*CA* 57), and Benedict XVI showed that "in the brethren we find Jesus himself, and in Jesus we find God" (*DCE* 15). Today, Francis promotes a reform based on the gospel and from the outskirts of poverty. *The reform of the Church means to carry out the evangelical and evangelizing revolution of tenderness*.

In 1950, Yves Congar indicated as a first condition for real reform the pastoral purpose and the primacy of love.[3] Jesus began the "revolution of tenderness" (*EG* 88) that transforms mercy in the backbone that sustains life, missionary work, and Church renewal. The Easter cross reveals "the tender mercy of our God" (Luke 1:78). Passionate and compassionate love characterizes "the Church of love," the Samaritan Church that ought to be a mother with an open heart to witness the loving humanity of our God. In the Year of the Jubilee of Mercy we would like to renew the desire to be merciful as the Father is merciful.

The reforms of and amidst the people of God, receiving impetus through the Holy Spirit, grow by synodal processes oriented toward the expansion of the kingdom of God ushered in by the Passover of the dead and risen Christ. They require a strong historical awareness and a keen sense of time and opportunity. In any process, it is possible to take small steps forward, but with maximum hopes. The pilgrim Church and the reforming processes leverage the theological virtue of hope, which makes possible what is arduous, and the virtues pertaining to the sphere of strength: perseverance, patience, magnanimity, and courage. They also demand great prudence and even greater mercy (*EG* 44).

"May the God of hope" (Rom 15:13), "the God of love" (2 Cor 13:11)—because "God is love" (1 John 4:8)—support us, guide us, and accompany us in this ongoing process of renewal.

Carlos María Galli
Antonio Spadaro, SJ

NOTES

1. H. Cymerman, "Entrevista al Popa Francisco," in *L'Osservatore Romano,* Spanish ed., June 20, 2014, 6.

2. Address of His Holiness Pope Francis, Ceremony Commemorating the 50th Anniversary of the Institution of the Synod of Bishops, Paul VI Audience Hall, Saturday, October 17, 2015: http://w2.vatican.va/content/francesco/en/speeches/2015/october/documents/papa-francesco_20151017_50-anniversario-sinodo.html.

3. See Y. Congar, *Vera e falsa riforma nella Chiesa* (Milan: Jaca Book, 1972), 231–352. Translated by Paul Philibert, OP, as *True and False Reform in the Church* (Collegeville, MN: Liturgical Press, 2011).

ABBREVIATIONS

Sources

AAS	*Acta Apostolicae Sedis*, Rome, 1909–
Acta	*Synodalia Acta Synodalia Sacrosancti Concilii Oecumenici Vaticani II*, Vatican City, 1970–1980
ASS	*Acta Sanctae Sedis*, Rome, 1865–1908
CT	Görres-Gesellschaft, ed., *Concilium Tridentinum. Diariorum, actorum, epistularum, tractatuum*, Freiburg i. Br., 1901–
COD	G. Alberigo et al., eds., *Conciliorum Oecumenicorum Decreta*, Bologna, 1991
DH	H. Denzinger, *Enchiridion symbolorum, definitionum et declarationum de rebus fidei et morum*, edited by Peter Hunermann, Bologna, 2009
EE	*Enchiridion delle encicliche* (1740–2005), 8 vols., Bologna 1994ff.
EV	*Enchiridion Vaticanum*, 29 + 3 vols., Bologna, 1976ff.
Mansi	J. D. Mansi, ed., *Sacrorum Conciliorum...nova et amplissima collectio*, Florence-Venice, 1758ff.
FAPA	G. Rosales and C. G. Arévalo, eds., *For All the Peoples of Asia*, 3 vols., Quezon City, 1992ff.
PG	J. P. Migne, ed., *Patrologiae cursus completes...Series graeca et orientalis*, Paris, 1857–1886
PL	J. P. Migne, ed., *Patrologiae cursus completes...Series latina*, Paris, 1844–1864
WA	*D. Martin Luthers Werke. Kritische Gesamtausgabe*, 120 vols., Weimar, 1883–2009

Documents of Vatican II and from the Holy See

AA	Second Vatican Council, Decree *Apostolicam Actuositatem*, November 18, 1965
AG	Second Vatican Council, Decree *Ad Gentes*, December 7, 1965
ApS	Congregation for Bishops, Directory *Apostolorum Successores*, February 22, 2004
CA	John Paul II, Encyclical *Centesimus Annus*, May 1, 1991
CD	Second Vatican Council, Decree *Christus Dominus*, October 28, 1965
ChL	John Paul II, Apostolic Exhortation *Christifideles Laici*, December 30, 1988
CIC	*Codex Iuris Canonici* (Code of Canon Law), promulgated by Pope John Paul II, Vatican City, 1983
DCE	Benedict XVI, Encyclical *Deus Caritas Est*, December 25, 2005
DGC	Congregation for the Clergy, *General Directory for Catechesis*, August 15, 1997
DV	Second Vatican Council, Dogmatic Constitution *Dei Verbum*, November 18, 1965
EG	Francis, Apostolic Exhortation *Evangelii Gaudium*, November 24, 2013
EN	Paul VI, Apostolic Exhortation *Evangelii Nuntiandi*, December 8, 1975
ES	Paul VI, Encyclical *Ecclesiam Suam*, August 6, 1964
GD	Paul VI, Apostolic Exhortation *Gaudete in Domino*, May 9, 1975
GE	Second Vatican Council, Declaration *Gravissimum Educationis*, October 28, 1965
GS	Second Vatican Council, Pastoral Constitution *Gaudium et Spes*, December 7, 1965
LF	Francis, Encyclical *Lumen Fidei*, June 29, 2013

LG	Second Vatican Council, Dogmatic Constitution *Lumen Gentium*, November 21, 1964
LS	Francis, Encyclical *Laudato Si'*, May 24, 2015
NA	Second Vatican Council, Declaration *Nostra Aetate*, October 28, 1965
NMI	John Paul II, Apostolic Letter *Novo Millennio Ineunte*, January 6, 2001
OE	Second Vatican Council, Decree *Orientalium Ecclesiarum*, November 21, 1964
OT	Second Vatican Council, Decree *Optatam Totius*, October 28, 1965
PG	John Paul II, Apostolic Exhortation *Pastores Gregis*, October 16, 2003
PO	Second Vatican Council, Decree *Presbyterorum Ordinis*, December 7, 1965
RH	John Paul II, Encyclical *Redemptor Hominis*, March 4, 1979
RM	John Paul II, Encyclical *Redemptoris Missio*, December 7, 1990
SC	Second Vatican Council, Constitution *Sacrosanctum Concilium*, December 4, 1963
SDA	Congregation for Bishops–Congregation for the Evangelization of Peoples, Instruction *De Synodis Dioecesanis Agendis*, 1997
UR	Second Vatican Council, Decree *Unitatis Redintegratio*, November 21, 1964
UUS	John Paul II, Encyclical *Ut Unum Sint*, May 25, 1995

Other Abbreviations

CELAM	Consejo Episcopal Latinoamericano (Bishops' Conference of Latin American nations)
DA	Fifth General Conference of the Bishops of Latin American and the Caribbean, *Documento di Aparecida*, June 29, 2007

DP	Third General Conference of the Bishops of Latin American and the Caribbean, *Documento di Puebla*, March 23, 1979
DR	Joint International Commission for the Theological Dialogue between the Roman Catholic Church and the Orthodox Church, *Documento di Ravenna*, October 13, 2007
DSD	Fourth General Conference of the Bishops of Latin American and the Carribean, *Documento di Santo Domingo*, October 28, 1992
Sp. Ex.	Ignatius of Loyola, *Spiritual Exercises*, 1548
FABC	Federation of Asian Bishops' Conferences

I

THE RENEWAL OF THE CHURCH TODAY, IN LIGHT OF THE SECOND VATICAN COUNCIL

1

THE REFORM OF THE CHURCH ACCORDING TO POPE FRANCIS

The Ignatian Roots

Antonio Spadaro, SJ

On August 15, 1537, Ignatius of Loyola and his first six companions vowed in Montmartre (Paris) to "spend their lives in the service of souls" (*Autobiography*, 85). For twenty years Christianity had been torn by the insurgence against the Church of Rome, started in 1517 by Luther, with the publication of the famous 95 Theses against the papal indulgences. Luther died in 1546, just months after the Council of Trent was inaugurated.

From the beginning of the Council, some Jesuits were present as theology experts. We have a letter in which Ignatius gives instructions to his confreres about how to behave at the council.[1] The interesting thing is that he does not enter at all into doctrinal and theological issues, but is concerned about the living testimony that the Jesuits would give while there. This already gives us an idea of how Ignatius intended the reform of the Church. For him, it was not so much a matter of reforming the structure, as of reforming the people from within. For example, he recommends that, following in his own path, they go visit the sick in hospitals, "confessing and consoling the poor, bringing some material help if possible, and having them pray [for the council]."[2]

The Election of Pope Marcellus II

After the death of Julius III, on April 9, 1555, Marcello Cervini, cardinal of the Basilica di Santa Croce, was elected pope. He had been one of the papal legates at the Council of Trent, where he had the chance to get to know the Jesuit theologians. Cervini argued that the reform of the Church could not only be founded on the removal of some abuses, but had to be radical, that is, it had to start from the "self-renewal of the pope and the Curia." But he also saw clearly that this self-renewal had to go hand in hand with an incisive conciliar reform. "The world cannot be disappointed by the reform that was expected by the Council," he wrote to his trustee Maffei, "or the last error will be worse than the first." On his election, Ignatius, in letters addressed to the whole Society of Jesus, revealed his thinking on what he intended the reform of the Church to be.[3]

From these letters, we can infer that Ignatius's desire was to have a pope who had done the entire *Spiritual Exercises*. It may well be that at the Council of Trent the then Cardinal Marcello Cervini, being in contact with the Jesuits Laínez and Salmerón, had come to know, and maybe even done the *Exercises*, at least in part. In any case, his disposition was perfectly in accordance with them.

Ignatius was convinced that, starting from the "reform of one's own life," and keeping one's eyes fixed on the poor and humiliated Christ, one could not but necessarily achieve a structural reform of the Church.

Ignatius and Pope Francis

Pope Francis is a Jesuit pope and his idea of the reform of the Church corresponds to that of Ignatius. The reform is indeed a spiritual process that also affects, by connaturality, the ecclesial structure as the litmus paper changes color naturally, because it modifies the level of acidity or alkalinity of the liquid in which it is immersed. One of the great inspirations of Bergoglio is the Jesuit St. Peter Faber, who Michel de Certeau simply characterized as the "reformed priest," for whom the inner experience, the dogmatic expression, and structural reform are intimately connected. Pope Francis is inspired by this kind of reform.[4]

But to what extent does Francis have clear this Ignatian root in his way of examining himself, even as pope?

On the afternoon of August 19, 2013, I went for the first time to the room of Pope Francis at the Casa St. Martha. We agreed on that day for an interview, which later appeared in *La Civiltà Cattolica* and other Jesuit magazines.[5] The first question I asked was not among the ones I had previously prepared in my notes: "Who is Jorge Mario Bergoglio?"

He, I remember, stared at me in silence. I thought at that moment that I had gone too far. He gave me a quick nod to let me know that he would answer, and then said slowly, "I do not know what might be the most fitting definition....I am a sinner. This is the most accurate definition. It is not a figure of speech, a literary genre. I am a sinner." Francis, still reflecting, profoundly, said, "Yes, a sinner; but the best summary, the one that comes more from the inside and I feel most true real, is this: 'I am a sinner on whom the Lord has looked upon.'"

Hearing these words, I realized that the pope had given me a twofold answer. The first is what he expressed: he perceives himself as a redeemed sinner. But, talking to me, a Jesuit like him, he replied by defining himself in light of his spirituality and his choice of life as a Jesuit. In fact, in 1974, Fr. Jorge Mario Bergoglio participated in the XXXII General Congregation of the Society of Jesus. The second decree issued by that world assembly of representatives of the Order begins with the question, "What does it mean to be a Jesuit?" The answer is, "It means to recognize oneself as a sinner, but called by God to be a companion of Jesus Christ, as Ignatius was." Thus, Pope Francis revealed to me something about himself in light of a charisma that touches deeply his identity.

Ignatian spirituality is therefore the "dark chamber" of deep, or we could say "chemical," elaboration of Bergoglio's experiences as bishop first, and then as pope. Francis is a product of the *Spiritual*

Exercises, and his vision of Church reform is rooted in the reform of life that is the outcome of the *Exercises*.

A Reformer Is One Who Emptied Himself

If we read what Francis has said of the Jesuits, we understand why he feels that he ought to "empty himself." In his homily at the Church of the *Gesù*, Rome, on January 3, 2014, he said,

> The heart of Christ is the heart of a God who, out of love, "emptied" himself. Each one of us, as Jesuits, who follow Jesus should be ready to empty himself. We are called to this humility: to be "emptied" beings. To be men who are not centered on themselves because the center of the Society is Christ and his Church. And God is the *Deus semper maior*, the God who always surprises us. And if the God of surprises is not at the centre, the Society becomes disorientated. Because of this, to be a Jesuit means to be a person of incomplete thought, of open thought: because he thinks always looking to the horizon which is the ever greater glory of God, who ceaselessly surprises us. And this is the restlessness of our inner abyss. This holy and beautiful restlessness![16]

The Society of Jesus was founded by Ignatius of Loyola and his first companions. After emptying themselves of their projects, they put themselves at the service of the pope, to be sent anywhere in the world where there was more urgent need of them. This immediate availability for the pope, which is expressed in the fourth vow of obedience, is motivated by the fact that the pope is the one who has the most universal vision and knows the needs of the *Ecclesia universa*, wherever they arise. The reform, for Francis, is rooted in this emptying of self. If it were not so, if it were only an idea, an aspirational project, the fruit of one's own desires, even if good, it would become yet another ideology of change.

The Nonideological Discernment

The spirituality of Ignatius of Loyola is a historic spirituality, connected to the dynamics of history. Better yet, it is what drives history and organizes and gives shape to an institution. The spiritual ministry of Ignatius is institutionalized in the service to the Church, giving shape to the Society of Jesus and its ability to dialogue with culture and history.

This is in fact the background against which a more complex picture emerges, which is of paramount importance to understand Bergoglio's way of proceeding during his pontificate. He observes that in Ignatius's life is found the internal coherence of his project. But what is exactly Ignatius's "project"? A theoretical vision ready to be applied to reality, to force it in its parameters? An abstraction to be applied to reality?

Nothing of the kind. "His project is not a planning of functions, nor an assortment of possibilities. His project consists in making explicit and concrete what he had experienced in his inner world," as Bergoglio has put it.[7] In light of this, the question about what Pope Francis's "program" is does not make sense. The pope has no clear and distinct ideas to apply to reality, but he proceeds based on his spiritual experience and prayer that he shares in dialogue and in consultation with others.

This procedure is called "discernment": it is the discernment of God's will in our daily lives. Although it is fulfilled within the heart, the inner self, its raw material is always the echo that daily reality reverberates in that intimacy. It is an inner attitude that drives us to be open to dialogue, to the encounter with others, to finding God wherever he wants to be found, not only in narrow, or well-delimited and restricted, confines. In this regard, Pope Francis asked the American bishops,

> Do not be afraid to set out on that "exodus" which is necessary for all authentic dialogue. Otherwise, we fail to understand the thinking of others, or to realize deep down that the brother or sister we wish to reach and redeem, with the power and the closeness of love,

> counts more than their positions, distant as they may be from what we hold as true and certain.[8]

Our actions and decisions, therefore, must be accompanied by a careful, thoughtful, and prayerful reading of the signs of the times. For Bergoglio, the world is always on the move: the ordinary perspective, with its measures for classifying what is important and what is not, does not work. The life of the spirit is guided by other principles.

And we cannot practice discernment on ideas, even ideas of reform, but on what is real, on histories, on the concrete history of the Church. For Francis, realities are always more important than ideas (see *EG* 231–33). Therefore, the starting point is always historical and means first to recognize that *Dios trabaja y labora por mí en todas cosas criadas sobre la haz de la tierra* (God works and labors for me in all things created on the face of the earth, *Sp. Ex.* 236) and that the world is God's "the construction site."

An Open and Historical Process

The task of the reformer is therefore to initiate or accompany historic processes. This is one of the fundamental principles of Bergoglio's vision: time is greater than space (*EG* 222–25). To reform means to start open processes and to not "cut heads" or conquer spaces of power. It is with this same spirit of discernment that Ignatius and his first companions faced the challenge of the Reformation.

The pope has very clear the context, the initial situation: he is informed, and listens to the opinion of others; he is firmly rooted in the present. However, the road that he intends to take is for him really open, it is not a theoretical "road map": the path opens walking. In fact, his project is a lived spiritual experience that takes shape step by step and that is expressed in concrete terms, into action. It is not a vision that reflects ideas and concepts, but a life that reflects "times, places, and persons," and, therefore, not ideological abstractions. So that inner vision does not impose itself on history trying to organize it according to its own coordinates, but interacts with reality: it fits into the history of man, it takes place over time.

Francis is the pope of processes, of "exercises." A superior, in his own words, should be "a leader of processes and not a mere administrator."[9] This is, from his viewpoint, the form of true "spiritual government."[10] Bergoglio's pontificate and his willingness to reform are not and will not be only of the "administrative" type, but are intended to inspire and accompany processes: some may be fast and dazzling, others extremely slow.

The process is therefore truly open: only God knows when it will end and its outcome. It is other and far more than a human project, and is "more than our expectations."[11] Even if they are the pope's. In *Meditaciones para religiosos*—a series of reflections written when Bergoglio was provincial of the Argentine Jesuits—he explains the dynamics of the process with spiritual and practical understanding. He uses a very effective image from the gospel: "We are encouraged to build the city, but perhaps we need to tear down the model we were drawing in our head. We must take courage and let God chisel our face, even if this means smoothing out some of our tics that we thought were gestures."[12] The *pars destruens*, which consists in doing away with the "model," is functional for leaving the chisel in the hands of God. Here is another interesting example for understanding Francis's vision.

Another remarkable example is the movement given to the entire Church with the III Extraordinary General Assembly of the Synod of Bishops. The event was thought as a process set in motion by an extensive questionnaire addressed to all the people of God; it then converged into the extraordinary synod and opened a year of reflection before it reconverged in an ordinary assembly of the same synod. But the dynamics of *parresía*, clarity, and freedom of expression and listening in which the process was experienced, initiated in the entire Church a dynamic that has also frightened many. Yet, it is precisely in the distant eighties that Bergoglio established his confidence in processes, thus expressing a radical trust in the Holy Spirit: the wisdom of discernment "implies surrendering to God's will, and this in turn means to stop controlling processes with purely human criteria."[13] And again: "In the course of processes, to wait means to believe that God is greater than ourselves, that God is the same Spirit who governs us" (*Sp. Ex.* 365), and the "'Master' who allows the seed to grow."[14]

The pope lives a constant dynamic of discernment, which opens him to the future. It opens him also to the future of the reform of the Church, which is not a project, but an exercise of the spirit that does not see only in white and black, as those who always want to fight "battles." Bergoglio sees shades and stages: he seeks to recognize the presence of the Spirit in our human and cultural reality; the seed already planted of its presence in the events, feelings, desires, and the deep tensions in our hearts and in social, cultural, and spiritual contexts. And the seed is not the tree: it is often buried and thus invisible to a careless eye. This is what was expressed by the XXXIV General Congregation of the Society of Jesus, which took place in 1995: "In exercising their priestly ministry, the Jesuits try to see what God has already done in the lives of individuals, societies and cultures, and to discern how God will continue that work" (no. 177).

It is an interior attitude that drives us to be open inwardly to dialogue, encounter, finding God wherever he wants to be found and not only in narrow or well-defined and restricted confines. It does not fear the contradictions in our lives but faces them with courage. It is not an intellectual knowledge, but one that integrates the values of the heart and mind.[15] The actions and decisions, therefore, should be rooted deeply inside, and must be accompanied by a careful, meditative, and prayerful reading of the signs of the times, which are everywhere.[16]

A Careful Process to Find the Greatest in the Tiniest

The principle that sums up this evolutionary view is this motto: *Non coerceri a maximo, contineri tamen a minimo, divinum est*, which can be translated as, "Not to be limited by the greatest and yet to be contained in the tiniest—this is the divine." The motto is part of a long literary epitaph composed by an anonymous Jesuit in honor of Ignatius of Loyola. Hölderlin liked it so much that he affixed it as a motto to his *Hyperion*. And we know how much Bergoglio loves Hölderlin's work, so much so that he cited the German poet in the original two days after his election as he greeted the cardinals in the Clementine Hall.

What does Pope Francis mean by citing this epitaph? That within the horizon of the kingdom of God the infinitesimal can be infinitely large while infinity instead can be a cage. It seems a paradox, but not for God who became man. The great reform project is realized in the slightest gesture, the little step: God is hidden in what is small and what is growing, even if we are incapable of seeing it. It's a thought that has accompanied Bergoglio at least since the years in which he was provincial superior, as documented in an essay entitled *Conducir en lo grande y en lo pequeño*, perhaps one of his most significant, given that the pope cited it several times during the interview with me.[17]

The perception of the divine enclosed in the smallest space and not restricted in the larger one is therefore a fundamental criterion. Without it you will have "the charlatan priest, who in his comings and goings shows the inability to get established in God and in the concrete history with which he is bound"; or we will have the "elaboration of grand plans without any attention to the concrete mediations that will make them possible."[18] That ironic epitaph becomes the principle of a pastoral action, but also of leadership and assessment of reality.

A Process That Faces Limitations, Conflicts, and Problems

But Bergoglio never speaks of a heroic and sublime aspiration far from the daily passing of time. He is not a "maximalist." He does not believe in a rigid idealism, nor in "ethicism" or spiritual "abstractionism."[19] The spiritual path has nothing to do with a pseudomysticism that promotes tales invented by our anxious and impure hearts. The real inner journey involves taking charge of our age, of our poverty, the history that belongs to us. For this reason, limits, conflicts, and problems are an integral part of our spiritual journey.

Rather, along the journey it is necessary "not to mistreat the limits."[20] With this expression Bergoglio want to alert us against the aggression of idealism,

> which is always tempted to project on reality the ideal scheme, without taking into account the limits of that

> reality (whatever they may be). This danger can also appear at the ascetic level: by mistreating limits by excess (demanding in an absolutistic manner) or by defect (giving in, not setting limits that should be placed).[21]

The relationship between desire and limit is advantageous, realistic, humanizing: it highlights our smallness, and opens us to the greatness "ever greater" of God. Bergoglio writes,

> The figure of a guide who is not afraid to set limits and, at the same time, relies on the dynamic of hope expressed in his waiting for the Lord's intervention in the processes, is, for the members of an institution, the image of a strong man, who is the head of something that is not his own, but of "his Lord," the image of a man who is not intimidated by the horizon of large projects, yet does not complain by despising the small things.[22]

Indeed, God helps us to accept our limits, because he "communicates in a *limited* way"; thus, we must "accept the limits of our pastoral expression (so distant from the notion of the one who has the solution to all the world's problems, who knows neither waiting nor hardship, and who lives driven by frenzy and delusions)."[23]

We do not even need to be afraid of conflicts, which sometimes disturb and frighten us. Talking to superiors of the male religious orders in November of 2013, Pope Francis used a beautiful image: "We need to caress conflicts." But for Bergoglio the distinctive trait of the Society of Jesus is "make possible the harmonization of contradictions."[24] He then makes a quick list of contradictions:

> We Jesuits have been contemplatives and men of action; of discernment and obedience; men of "consolidated" works as well as of missions that seemed almost incursions; men who devote themselves to what they do with total commitment and, conversely, with great generosity (men equally Jesuits when shaping peoples and when all they had to call home was a simple cart: so were our missionaries).[25]

Contradictions are part of a fruitful history. And indeed, so are problems. So much so that it is not always appropriate to resolve them, writes Bergoglio. A problem may not always need to be solved immediately, on the spot. There is a discernment that involves history and verifies times and moments.[26] Sometimes a problem can be solved without wanting to face it immediately. It is therefore necessary to understand the processes taking place, even giving up the things of the moment. A real temptation is to "want to separate the wheat and the weeds prematurely."[27] These are important words to understand Francis's vision of the timing of the reforming process.

A Process That Deals with Temptations

But temptations and the struggle against them are part of this process as well. The reform process for Bergoglio is a competitive process. The pope has a "militant" vision of reality. This dramatic quality comes from St. Ignatius of Loyola and his *Spiritual Exercises,* especially from his meditation "on the two flags" (*Sp. Ex.* 136–48), which[28] should be read carefully. Ignatius depicts a battlefield in which are contrasted "Christ, our supreme master and lord" and "Lucifer, the mortal enemy of our human nature." For Bergoglio, there is an inevitable dimension of belligerency in the Christian *modus vivendi*. "The Christian life is a battlefield,"[29] so to speak, and "our faith is revolutionary, and foundational in itself. It is a *fighting faith*."[30]

But pay attention: yes, we cannot be naive, and yet—writes Bergoglio, perhaps once again breaking down stereotypes—we need to have "the combative tenderness that appears in the seriousness of a child who makes the sign of the cross and in the depths of the soul of an elderly person reciting his or her prayers: this is faith, this is the vaccine against the spirit of defeat."[31] "Discernment is an instrument of struggle."[32] Actually, "when, following the Lord, there is lack of fight or vigilance, often emerges a latent temptation of idolatry: to make the gifts of the Lord, or the Lord himself, an object reducible to our selfish categories."[33] To not accept the military character of our vocation implies, for fear of the conflict, to apply "all sorts of adjustments and scrambles…all to gain some kind of peace. Which in reality means, provided that no contradiction appears. The result? Men and women who know nothing of true peace, but live like cowards or, if you will, the peace of the grave."[34]

The temptation often lurks in the institutions. "The evil spirit," writes Bergoglio, "is smart enough to know that his battle becomes really difficult and that he has little chance of winning when faced with men and women and communities where the dominant feature is the wisdom of the Spirit." In this case it acts trying to tempt under the appearance of good. The subtlety of the "Enemy's" argument becomes extreme, because those tempted think that they have to act for the good of the Church. The greater subtlety is to

> make us believe that the Church is being distorted and try to convince us that, therefore, we must save it, perhaps even in spite of itself. It is a constant temptation and present under an infinite number of different masks, but which ultimately have all something in common: a lack of faith in the power of God who always dwells in his Church.[35]

From here also,

> the sterile clashes with the hierarchy, the devastating conflicts between "factions" (for example, "progressive" or "reactionary") within the Church....In short, all those things which we "absolutize" what is secondary, when, seduced by "a great throne of fire and smoke" (Sp. Ex. 140), we end up giving more importance to the single parts than to the whole.[36]

The temptation under the appearance of good, with its nets and chains, has the effect of pulling the Church away from reality, from history, which is one of its most disastrous and pervasive effects. We experience it when figures arise who seem to want to replace the pope to defend doctrine, or when they sow uncertainty and confusion, even letting us believe that orthodoxy is in danger. We are not referring here to specific scandals, which are obvious temptations that need to be identified, but the subtle temptations *sub specie boni* (under the appearance of good). They

> generate distortion, because the almost superstitious attachment of many sectors of the Church to some *scientific tools of analysis of reality* is truly blinded; because the pretense of *possessing the Spirit* in many charismatic movements is blinded; because the need *to situate oneself within the confines of critical doubt* is blinded; because the *opium of nostalgia*, so characteristic of the traditionalists, which distracts us from the creativity of a faithful memory is blinded; because the *individualism of those who trace an ideal ethics program* without having the courage to embrace the reality that moves forward with its possibilities is blinded.[37]

The result is that pastors or spiritual or theological *elites*—either "progressive" or "conservative"—create an isolated consciousness from that of the "faithful people of God." Thus, Bergoglio invites us to ask ourselves a few questions: "What am I defending with my isolation? Pastoral autocracy? An exquisite role that makes me 'a sheep whisperer,' instead of a shepherd? In pastoral reality, people want religion to bring them closer to God, priests to be shepherds, and not tyrants, or dandies lost in following the latest fashion trends."[38] We find in these words the same images that Bergoglio today uses as pope when he rails against the "spiritual worldliness" of the Church, which is his last and deepest temptation that needs to be fought to the last breath.

The Ministers of the Church and Their Formation

Pope Francis understands that the reform of the Church he speaks about requires a broad and profound formation, especially of pastors. In this sense, it is also in line with the profound need, which the Society of Jesus always perceives as a mission, to train the clergy and pastors. From a certain picture of the Church come also its ministers.[39] They must be persons "unafraid of going forth into their night…able to dialogue with those disciples who, having left Jerusalem behind, are wandering aimlessly, alone, with their own disappointment, disillusioned." It is therefore necessary to train merciful people, whose heart can become "part of a world of 'wounded' persons in need of understanding, forgiveness, love."[40]

Today the Church needs ministers "able to step into the night without being overcome by the darkness and losing their bearings; able to listen to people's dreams without being seduced and to share their disappointments without losing hope and becoming bitter; able to sympathize with the brokenness of others without losing their own strength and identity."[41]

This ability to go down into the night, touching the shadow of others, is very important. It presupposes great fortitude, but also humility and inner freedom in being put into question. The pastor should not be too inflexible or self-confident: "The great leaders of the people of God, like Moses, have always left room for doubt," said Bergoglio some time ago. Moses, for example, is the perfect example of the humble leader, who before God does nothing but "gather into himself with his doubts, with the intimate experience of darkness, not knowing how to act. And then slowly he is purified from all this." Actually, Bergoglio says that when someone "has the answers to all the questions, that is the proof that God is not with him."[42] Pope Francis recalled again the figure of Moses while speaking to the US Congress, in Washington, on September 23, 2015.

The priest must be exposed to the people of God. It is this people who can go out of himself and who can be stirred in the "depths of his priestly heart."[43] This vision of God's minister, who has a heart capable of great empathy, has deep roots in Bergoglio's spirituality. This is the reformed priest. We can find in a work written at the beginning of the Society of Jesus, which Bergoglio knows well and commented on, expressions that help us to understand these roots. It is a text in which the Jesuit Fr. Pedro de Ribadeneira, a contemporary of the founder, speaks of "how St. Ignatius governed."

In this text, quoted by the then Fr. Bergoglio in his meditation for Jesuit superiors, it is written,

> It is very necessary that the one dealing with our neighbors in order to cure them should be like a good physician—they should neither be frightened at the neighbor's illnesses nor be repelled by their wounds. They should accept with great patience and gentleness

> the neighbor's weaknesses and importunities. To this end, they should regard our neighbors, not as children of Adam, and vessels of frail glass or clay, but as images of God, purchased by the blood of Jesus Christ. For themselves they should take care to use the aids they have, and dispose themselves through good works to receive the Lord's grace or grow in it. He it is in whom they must hope: that since He has called them to so high a ministry, He will make them a worthy themselves and place it in the goodness of the same Lord who has called them and made them a member of this religious order. (5.12)[44]

It is precisely this attitude that Ignatius required from *el que trata con para los prójimos curarlos* (he who deals with his neighbors to heal them) that for Bergoglio must be the characteristic of every sacred ministry.

From the need for this attitude, Pope Francis derives the need for a thorough review "of the structures in place for the formation and preparation of the clergy and the laity of the Church"[45] in a pastoral perspective. In particular, the then Cardinal Bergoglio had devoted a reflection on priestly formation at the plenary session of the Pontifical Commission for Latin America, February 18, 2009, recalling that the image of the Good Shepherd is "the *analogatum princeps* of all formation." In a very important text of September 11, 2008, entitled *El mensaje de Aparecida a los presbíteros*, Bergoglio wrote that the faithful people of God want "shepherds" and not "state clerics": teachers of life who teach by being close, becoming neighbors, sharing the life of their flock, and not as "amateurs" who discuss unimportant matters. Training must shape this kind of teacher-pastors—writes Bergoglio—capable of saying, as the Jesuit St. Albert Hurtado, "My Mass is my life and my life is one prolonged Mass."

The Bishops, the Church Structures, and Missionary Work

This strong missionary exhortation is not linked only to "acts," that is specific things to do or initiatives to be pursued, but has a paradigmatic value in the sense that it leads to "setting in a missionary key all the day-to-day activities of the Particular Churches" and thus leads, as a direct consequence, to a "whole process of reforming ecclesial structures." For the pope, this "'change of structures… will not be," as many actually expect, "the result of reviewing an organizational flow chart."[46] This would lead to an inert reorganization. The change must be linked to the dynamics of missionary work, it must be linked to current challenges.

Thus, even image of the bishop is transformed. This is the portrait that Pope Francis offers us talking with the bishops responsible of CELAM, the Episcopal Council of Latin America and the Caribbean:

> Bishops must be pastors, close to people, fathers and brothers, and gentle, patient and merciful. Men who love poverty, both interior poverty, as freedom before the Lord, and exterior poverty, as simplicity and austerity of life. Men who do not think and behave like "princes." Men who are not ambitious, who are married to one church without having their eyes on another. Men capable of watching over the flock entrusted to them and protecting everything that keeps it together: guarding their people out of concern for the dangers which could threaten them, but above all instilling hope: so that light will shine in people's hearts. Men capable of supporting with love and patience God's dealings with his people. The Bishop has to be among his people in three ways: in front of them, pointing the way; among them, keeping them together and preventing them from being scattered; and behind them, ensuring that no one is left behind, but also, and primarily, so that the flock itself can sniff out new paths.[47]

More recently, the pope reiterated this vision while addressing the US bishops: "We are bishops of the Church, shepherds appointed by God to feed his flock. Our greatest joy is to be shepherds, and only shepherds." And he continued,

> I know that you face many challenges, and that the field in which you sow is unyielding and that there is always the temptation to give in to fear, to lick one's wounds, to think back on bygone times and to devise harsh responses to fierce opposition.
>
> And yet we are promoters of the culture of encounter. We are living sacraments of the embrace between God's riches and our poverty. We are witnesses of the abasement and the condescension of God who anticipates in love our every response.
>
> Dialogue is our method, not as a shrewd strategy but out of fidelity to the One who never wearies of visiting the marketplace, even at the eleventh hour, to propose his offer of love (Matt 20:1–16).
>
> The path ahead, then, is dialogue among yourselves, dialogue in your presbyterates, dialogue with lay persons, dialogue with families, dialogue with society. I cannot ever tire of encouraging you to dialogue fearlessly. The richer the heritage which you are called to share with parrhesia, the more eloquent should be the humility with which you should offer it. Do not be afraid to set out on that "exodus" which is necessary for all authentic dialogue. Otherwise, we fail to understand the thinking of others, or to realize deep down that the brother or sister we wish to reach and redeem, with the power and the closeness of love, counts more than their positions, distant as they may be from what we hold as true and certain. Harsh and divisive language does not befit the tongue of a pastor, it has no place in his heart; although it may momentarily seem to win the day, only the enduring allure of goodness and love remains truly convincing.[48]

The Bishops' Conference as an ecclesial structure is called upon to better understand itself in light of the image of Church that the pope proposes. In fact, as Francis told the Brazilian bishops, "Communion is a fabric to be woven with patience and perseverance, one which gradually 'draws together the stitches' to make a more extensive and thick cover. A threadbare cover will not provide warmth."[49] And to the American bishops he reiterated, "Only a Church which can gather around the family fire remains able to attract others."[50]

To build a church that "provides warmth"—thus a Church with "a more extensive and thick cover"—we must go back to the method experienced in 2007 at Aparecida, which was able to gather diversity to set in motion vital dynamic forces. On that occasion, there was no document issued as *Instrumentum laboris*. Aparecida promoted the participation of local churches as a path to preparation. Thus, the initial work consisted in "pooling the concerns expressed by the bishops as they considered the new period of history we are living and the need to renew the life of discipleship and mission with which Christ founded the Church."[51]

Emmaus, after all, is precisely the illustration of this method: the disciples return to Jerusalem to recount their experience of their encounter with the Risen One, but they also become aware of the experiences of their brethren. Inspired by Emmaus, here is a "definition" of episcopal conference provided by Pope Francis: "a vital space for enabling such an exchange of testimonies about encounters with the Risen One."[52] Therefore, the local and regional elements must be enhanced in relation to the central bureaucracy, thereby increasing collegiality and solidarity. Obviously, what the pope said to the bishops of Brazil must be extended to the Church in general. This is the portrait of the Church that Pope Bergoglio has in mind.

Tension between Spirit and Institution

To conclude, it must be said that, for Pope Francis, the reform of the Church is experiencing a strong and fruitful dialectic tension between Spirit and institution. In his apostolic exhortation *Evangelii Gaudium* he wrote, "The Church has to accept this unruly freedom of the word, which accomplishes what it wills in ways that surpass our calculations and ways of thinking." (*EG* 22). There is a dialectical and intraecclesial tension in Francis's remark regarding Spirit and institution: one never denies the other, but the former must animate the latter in an effective, incisive way to counter the "ecclesial introversion" (*EG* 27)—as St. John Paul II called it—which is always a great temptation.

The pope also wrote, "I do not want a Church concerned with being at the center and which then ends by being caught up in a web of obsessions and procedures." (*EG* 49). He then says that the Church is a "people of pilgrims and evangelizers, transcending any institutional expression, however necessary" (*EG* 111).

Finally, worth noting is this fruitful tension between the Church as a "pilgrim people" and as "institution," which reflects two of Pope Francis's favorite definitions of the Church, as it is also evident in the interview he gave to *La Civiltà Cattolica*: the "pilgrim people of God" (*Lumen Gentium*) and "Holy Mother the Hierarchical Church" (Saint Ignatius of Loyola). The reform of the Church, for Francis, is basically this: to ensure that the Holy Mother the Hierarchical Church is always the pilgrim people of God.

NOTES

1. See *Monumenta Ignatiana, Epp*. 1:386–389. Quotations are from the Italian edition: Ignazio di Loyola, *Gli scritti*, a cura dei Gesuiti della Provincia Italiana, Adp (Rome, 2007), 1017–19. The numbering of the letters follows this edition.

2. Ibid., 387.

3. They are quoted and commented extensively in E. Cattaneo, "La riforma della Chiesa secondo sant'Ignazio di Loyola," in *La Civiltà Cattolica* 2013/IV: 341–451.

4. The edition, ed. by M. de Certeau, is P. Favre, *Mémorial* (Paris: Desclée de Brouwer, 1960).

5. A. Spadaro, "Intervista a Papa Francesco," in *La Civiltà Cattolica* 2013/III: 449–77. English translation: "A Big Heart Open to God: An Interview with Pope Francis," *America*, September 30, 2013, https://www.americamagazine.org/faith/2013/09/30/big-heart-open-god-interview-pope-francis.

6. Homily of Pope Francis at Church of the Gesù, January 3, 2014, http://w2.vatican.va/content/francesco/en/homilies/2014/documents/papa-francesco_20140103_omelia-santissimo-nome-gesu.html.

7. J. M. Bergoglio, *Chi sono i gesuiti* (Bologna: EMI, 2014), 20.

8. Pope Francis, Meeting with the Bishops of the United States of America, September 23, 2015: http://w2.vatican.va/content/francesco/en/speeches/2015/september/documents/papa-francesco_20150923_usa-vescovi.html.

9. J. M. Bergoglio, *Nel cuore di ogni padre. Alle radici della mia spiritualità* (Milan: Rizzoli, 2014), 88.

10. Ibid., 90.

11. Ibid., 81.

12. Ibid., 274.

13. Ibid., 94.

14. Ibid., 96.

15. See ibid., 130.

16. See ibid., 229.

17. See ibid., 91–102.

18. Ibid., 156.

19. Ibid., 37.

20. Ibid., 97.

21. Ibid., 95.

22. Ibid., 96–97.

23. Ibid., 132.

24. Ibid., 83.

25. Ibid., 84.

26. See ibid.

27. Ibid., 129.

28. See ibid., 162–69.

29. Ibid., 194.

30. Ibid., 128.

31. Ibid., 129.

32. Ibid., 165.

33. Ibid.

34. Ibid., 189.

35. Ibid., 22.

36. Ibid., 36.

37. Ibid., 107. Emphasis added.

38. Ibid., 179.

39. This topic was developed in D. Fares, "La figura del vescovo in Papa Francesco," in *La Civiltà Cattolica* 2014/II: 433–49 and, more broadly, in Fares, *Il profumo del pastore* (Milan: Àncora, 2015).

40. Pope Francis, Meeting with the Bishops of Brazil, July 28, 2013: https://w2.vatican.va/content/francesco/en/speeches/2013/july/documents/papa-francesco_20130727_gmg-episcopato-brasile.html.

41. Ibid.

42. J. Bergoglio and A. Skorka, *Il cielo e la terra. Il pensiero di papa Francesco sulla famiglia, la fede e la missione della Chiesa nel XXI secolo*, ed. Diego F. Rosemberg (Milan: Mondadori, 2013), 39–40.

43. Pope Francis, Chrism Mass, Saint Peter's Basilica, March 28, 2013: http://w2.vatican.va/content/francesco/en/homilies/2013/documents/papa-francesco_20130328_messa-crismale.html.

44. English tran.: "Writings on Jesuit Spirituality II by Jorge Mario Bergoglio, SJ," trans. and ed. Philip Endean, SJ *Studies in the Spirituality of Jesuits* 45, no. 4 (2013): 25.

45. Pope Francis, Meeting with the Bishops of Brazil.

46. Pope Francis, Address to the CELAM Leadership, July 28, 2013: https://w2.vatican.va/content/francesco/en/speeches/2013/july/documents/papa-francesco_20130728_gmg-celam-rio.html.

47. Ibid.

48. Pope Francis, Meeting with the Bishops of the United States of America, September 23, 2015.

49. Pope Francis, Meeting with the Bishops of Brazil.

50. Pope Francis, Meeting with the Bishops of the United States of America.

51. Pope Francis, Address to the CELAM Leadership.

52. Pope Francis, Meeting with the Bishops of Brazil.

2

THE MISSIONARY REFORM OF THE CHURCH ACCORDING TO FRANCIS

The Ecclesiology of the Evangelizing People of God

Carlos María Galli

This essay examines Pope Francis's ecclesiological teaching, which supports and sustains his project of reform of the Church in line with the gospel as interpreted by Vatican II for the contemporary world. His Argentine and Latin American ecclesial experience, his attentive reading of many works by great authors, his original thought presented in spiritual and pastoral texts, are the foundation of the pastoral ecclesiology that Francis has developed in the programmatic exhortation *Evangelii Gaudium* and in various oral and written testimonies of his papal magisterium.

Thus, my contribution intends to trace a discursive path in six stages. The starting point is the novelty represented by the first Bishop of Rome who comes from a church of the Southern Hemisphere. This section is followed by the development of four major themes of Francis's ecclesiology: the radical reform of the Church that springs from the joyful newness of the gospel of Jesus Christ;

the revolution animated by the tenderness of a God who is rich in mercy; the renewal born from the conciliar ecclesiology of the evangelizing people of God; and the reform led by the paradigm of missionary conversion. Our journey ends on a little-known and little-studied topic: the search for a new ecclesial form for a communion in differences that will allow to overcome oppositions, tensions, and conflicts.

The Spirit of God Breathes New Life in the Church from the South of the World

1. We live in a unique *kairós* (time) because the Southern, Latin American, and Argentine Church has given to the *Catholica* its first successor of Peter. The Holy Spirit "blows where it chooses" (John 3:8) and has blown as "the rush of a violent wind" (Acts 2:2). Since 2012, we have been using an image created by Cardinal Walter Kasper: a *southerly wind blows*.[1] In 2013, Francis was elected when the peripheries of the world appeared in the heart of the eternal city.[2] He represents the arrival of the South in the heart of the Church and, as shown by his presence at the United Nations, the voice of the *Global South* at the center of the world.

> Francis is the first pope who comes from the Southern hemisphere or, as he said, from the end of the world. The encounter between the conciliar reception of the South with that of the West has provoked an *earthquake*, as is the case with underground movements of tectonic plaques. Some things that were poorly built collapsed almost overnight. Those with solid foundations have resisted; and it is on these foundations that a new building can rise.[3]

2. *With Francis the Latin American Church brings to completion its first entry into global history*. In 1973, the Uruguayan historian Methol Alberto Ferré, a friend of Jorge Bergoglio, wrote,

> What the Church will do in Latin America will have a tremendous role in the Third World. And at the same time, Latin America can have a decisive influence on the fate of the Church in Europe. Latin America and its church have a great opportunity, and I believe that through our church the fate of the global church is at stake. The possibility of global renewal of the Church passes through Latin America and this is a serious responsibility for us.[4]

That same year, a collection of texts was published by the Argentinean Eduardo Pironio, bishop and then president of CELAM (Episcopal Council of Latin America and the Caribbean), who spoke of the providential time of the pilgrim Church in Latin America.[5] In 1974, the Swiss missiologist Walter Bühlmann published his work *Es kommt die dritte Kirche* because he realized that the time had come for the churches of Latin America, Africa, and Asia.[6] Today, we say that these churches have crossed the threshold and are in the heart of the house of God.

3. *The Church has grown and grows in the Southern Hemisphere.* Sixty-eight percent of Catholics live in Africa, Latin America, Asia, and Oceania. In the last hundred years there has been a reversal in the composition of Catholicism. In 1910, 70% of baptized Catholics lived in the North (65% in Europe) and 30% in the South (24% in Latin America). In 2010, 32% lived in the North (24% in Europe, 8% in North America) and 68% in the Southern continents: 39% in Latin America, 16% in Africa, 12% in Asia, 1% in Oceania. The largest increase occurred in Africa and Asia.[7]

4. Karl Rahner interpreted Vatican II, which gathered together bishops from all continents, as the passage to a Church truly (*wirklich*) global, a *Welt-Kirche* (World Church).[8] At Vatican I there were few Latin Americans; at Vatican II they represented 22 percent of the Council. Not long before, Yves Congar called for a *new balance* between the communion of the churches of the first millennium and the universal Church of the second.[9] We would like to extend his observation to the cultural setting of the Church:[10] after a first millennium marked by the Eastern churches and a second led by the Western church, a third millennium is emerging revitalized by churches in the South, in a crosscultural catholicity presided in

charity by the Church of Rome and characterized by a polycentric spiritual and structural dynamic.

5. Since 1955, the Church of Latin America has formed its regional "body," which brings together twenty-two dioceses coordinated by the Latin American Episcopal Council—CELAM, which recently turned sixty.[11] Regionalism is an original feature of our church, the only plural ecclesial community on a continental scale that ran a *regional, collegiate, inculturated and creative reception of the Council.* It received *Gaudium et Spes* via the encyclical *Populorum Progressio* at the Second General Conference of Medellín (1968); conciliar pastorality, mediated by the theology of evangelization of *Evangelii Nuntiandi* in Puebla (1979); and the horizon of a new evangelization proposed by John Paul II in Santo Domingo (1992). On its own initiative, the V Conference of Aparecida (2007) began a new phase of the people of God people through *a continental and permanent missionary movement.* Francis embodies typical features of the "Latin American and Caribbean Church" (*DA* 100). Bergoglio participated in the conference in Aparecida and was president of the commission in charge of drafting the final document, which is cited twenty times in *Evangelii Gaudium*. With Francis, the dynamics of missionary conversion promoted by the Latin American periphery bears its contribution to the reform of the whole Church. This confirms what was said by Yves Congar in 1950: *reform initiatives come from the peripheries.*[12]

6. *The Latin American and Caribbean region is the most urbanized in the world.* Here eight out of ten live in urban areas; the majority live in new suburban and poor neighborhoods. For this reason, our church, since 1965, has been thinking about a new pastoral plan for large urban areas (*DA* 509–19), particularly in Mexico, Brazil, Argentina, and Colombia. In the book *Dios vive en la ciudad* (God lives in the city) we show that Bergoglio was the first archbishop of Buenos Aires actually from Buenos Aires.[13] He is the first pope born in a big city of the twentieth century because in 1936, the year he was born into an Italian immigrant family, the city already had 2.4 million inhabitants (880,000 foreigners and 1.6 million natives) and already in 1947 it had reached three million. He is a *glocal* pope who experiences in a new way the fact of being bishop of the city and shepherd of the entire world,[14] who

considers the bipolar tension between globalization and localization (*EG* 234),[15] which presents the new pastoral challenges of urban cultures.[16]

7. This pontificate has its roots in both the singular figure of the Jesuit Jorge Mario Bergoglio and in the Latin American Church and in the Aparecida project; and, in its interpenetration with the incipient but promising Argentine theology. Francis is a missionary *shepherd* and wise *pastoralist*. Before becoming bishop, as director of the Colegio Màximo of the Society of Jesus (1979–1985), he founded and was the first pastor of the *Patriarca San José* parish in the diocese of San Miguel, in Buenos Aires. There he fostered a diffused evangelization and created chapels in peripheral neighborhoods. At the same time, he taught pastoral theology and commented on the exhortation *Evangelii Nuntiandi* of Paul VI at the Jesuit Faculty of Theology.

The Radical Reform of the Church Based on the Joyful Novelty of the Gospel

1. Francis encourages the reform of the Church starting from the "eternal newness of the Gospel" or "the original freshness of the Gospel" (*EG* 11). He points out the absolute novelty of Christ who renews the human being (*EG* 11–13) and makes all things new (Acts 21:5; Rev 14:6; Heb 13:8). He says that "the Second Vatican Council presented ecclesial conversion as openness to a constant self-renewal born of fidelity to Jesus Christ" (*EG* 26; *UR* 6). A reform aspires to renew the Church, starting from its evangelical roots to be more faithful to Christ. In an interview the pope said, "For me, the great revolution is to go to the roots, to recognize them and see what those roots have to say today."[17] In the encyclical *Laudato Si'* he affirms that he wrote the apostolic exhortation *Evangelii Gaudium* addressing the "members of the Church with the aim of encouraging ongoing missionary renewal" (*LS* 3).

2. The joy of the gospel is a source of the reform for a new ecclesial stage (*EG* 1). The title of the exhortation expresses the

joy that is derived from receiving and giving the good news, which is Jesus Christ (Mark 1:1). He is the source of the messianic joy (*EG* 5, 21). In the encyclical *Lumen Fidei* (*LF*), Francis showed "the joy of faith" (*LF* 47) that, with its beauty, illuminates the path of life, even amid the dark night (*LF* 57). His smiling face reflects God's own smile.

3. The pope announces a "time of evangelization and joy of evangelizing," parallel to the "time of mercy." And this announcement is like a unifying thread that starts from the speech with which St. John XXIII inaugurated the council, *Gaudet Mater Ecclesia*, and reaches up to *Evangelii Gaudium*, passing by the conciliar constitution *Gaudium et Spes* and Paul VI's exhortation *Gaudete in Domino*. Francis has a deep devotion to Paul VI, whom he beatified; he admires his exhortations of 1975: *Gaudete in Domino* and *Evangelii Nuntiandi*. The title of his exhortation of 2013 brings together two words from both titles. Francis cites *Evangelii Nuntiandi* fifteen times, and on this solid foundation he communicates his vision of the proclamation of the gospel. At the diocesan convention in Rome ("A People Who Generates Its Children, Communities and Families in the Great Stages of Christian Initiation," June 16, 2014) he said that *Evangelii Nuntiandi* "to this day it is the most important post-Conciliar pastoral document, which hasn't been surpassed.... That Apostolic Exhortation is a great source of inspiration.... It is a wealth of resources for pastoral life.... And is truly the pastoral testament of the great Paul VI."[18]

4. Paul VI called to preserve "the delightful and comforting joy of evangelizing" (*EN* 80). Bergoglio has thought and written much about the joy of evangelization.[19] As a member on the editorial committee of the *Aparecida Document* (*AD*) in 2007, we can testify that Cardinal Bergoglio wanted to mention that phrase in the conclusion (*DA* 552). He then cited it three times in his oral intervention at the consistory of 2013. The first note of *Evangelii Gaudium* quotes *Gaudete in Domino* (*GD* 22 in *EG* 3). That document was "a hymn to the divine joy" (*GD* 2, 22), because "in the same God all is joy because everything is a gift," as Paul VI said in the conclusion.

5. Francis innovates by focusing on the joy of evangelizing and not only on the joy of believing. The title of the second section of his apostolic exhortation, preceding nos. 14–18, states, "The

Delightful and Comforting Joy of Evangelizing" (*EG* 14–18). "The Gospel joy which enlivens the community of disciples is a missionary joy" (*EG* 21). This joy comes from love; the missionary joy is the fruit of the gift of evangelizing love. "This joy is a sign that the Gospel has been proclaimed and is bearing fruit. Yet the drive to go forth and give, to go out from ourselves, to keep pressing forward in our sowing of the good seed, remains ever present" (*EG* 21).

The Revolution of the Merciful Tenderness of God as Love

1. The reform of the Church is a historic change to live and communicate in a more transparent way the love of God reflected in the face of Christ.[20] The God "rich in mercy" (Eph 2:4) surprises with the initiative of his love and gives impetus to a renewed proclamation of the gospel (see *EG* 112).

> The Church which "goes forth" is a community of missionary disciples who take the first step, who are involved and supportive, who bear fruit and rejoice. An evangelizing community knows that the Lord has taken the initiative, he has loved us first (cf. 1 John 4:19), and therefore we can move forward, boldly take the initiative, go out to others, seek those who have fallen away, stand at the crossroads and welcome the outcast. Such a community has an endless desire to show mercy, the fruit of its own experience of the power of the Father's infinite mercy. (*EG* 24)

2. The root (*radix*) of the reform is "the heart of Christ's message" (*EG* 34), which is expressed in the founding and essential *kerygma* of the salvific, pascal, and trinitarian love of God. "The kerygma is trinitarian. The fire of the Spirit is given in the form of tongues and leads us to believe in Jesus Christ who, by his death and resurrection, reveals and communicates to us the Father's infinite mercy" (*EG* 164).

The kerygmatic announcement is centered on God's merciful love. This trinitarian christocentricity is in the footprint of Paul VI (*EN* 26), John Paul II (*DCG* 99–100), and Benedict XVI (*DCE* 1). Francis says, "Where your synthesis is, there lies your heart" (*EG* 143). Since 2005, we like to sum up the faith and theology in two biblical texts. The first, which is John's, announces that God is love (1 John 4:8). The second, of St. Paul, teaches that "the greatest of these is love" (1 Cor 13:13).

3. Francis proclaims the revolution of the tenderness of God begun with the incarnation of God's Word. In his Christmas messages in Buenos Aires, Bergoglio used to say, staring at the image of the Child Jesus in his hands, that God is tenderness. With John XXIII, Francis symbolizes "the Church of love"[21] that becomes tenderness through caresses, embraces, and kisses. The Church is a community of faith, hope, and charity, but today it must communicate faith through a new creativity in love in order to sustain hope. The pope proclaims the *time of the mercy of God* who comes near to heal the wounds of our suffering humanity (*EG* 3, 44, 47).[22] "True faith in the incarnate Son of God is inseparable from self-giving, from membership in the community, from service, from reconciliation with others. The Son of God, by becoming flesh, summoned us to the revolution of tenderness" (*EG* 88).

4. "The tender mercy of our God" (Luke 1:78) come to us through *the maternal tenderness of the Church*. Francisco speaks of the Mother Church following the Latin patristic tradition and contemporary ecclesiology.[23] He likes feminine images of the Church: wife, spouse, mother, widow. The Church is a mother with an open heart (*EG* 46–49). The pope follows the *Spiritual Exercises* of Saint Ignatius Loyola who speaks of "our Holy, Hierarchical Mother Church" (*Sp. Ex.* 353, 363), thus stressing the pastoral maternity of the people of God. The Church is a mother who opens the doors of her home not only to welcome in more children, but for those who are in it to go out and meet all those outside (*EG* 46). In Buenos Aires, Bergoglio used to invite to *callejar* to stroll around, because when the Christian community goes out, people come in. Recalling that expression, Francis insists that he prefers an itinerant Church that is "bringing Jesus to every street" (*EG* 106), even if at times it "bruised, hurting, and dirty," rather

than a Church that is frightened, choked, and sick, one caught up "in a web of obsessions and procedures" (*EG* 49).

5. *Mercy is a hermeneutical principle of the current pontificate.* Francis evangelizes by what he is, says, and does. The combination of the expression of his face, the message of his words, and the strength of his actions is the reason for his credibility. One in seven people in the world do not live where they were born. On the island of Lampedusa, the pope has showed the world a Samaritan Church that cares for refugees. Today he calls on all the Church and the entire world to open doors to them. At the school of Jesus, his gestures are signs of the love of God and the coming of the kingdom. These actions have a real and symbolic effectiveness: they do not solve the structural dramas, but indicate the direction for change.

6. Francis and "Good Pope" John XXIII reflect the tenderness of the Good Shepherd.[24] Both have responded to the Lord, saying, "I was in prison and you visited me" (Matt 25:36). On Christmas of 1958, John XXIII visited Rome's Regina Coeli prison; on Holy Thursday of 2013, Francis washed the feet of incarcerated juveniles. On October 11, 1962, celebrating the inauguration of the Council, Pope John XXIII invited us to use the medicine of mercy and let go of the rod of severity; on March 17, 2013, in his first Angelus message, Francis said that God is merciful and never tires of forgiving. In his radio message of September 11, 1962, John XXIII said that the Church should be, in the underdeveloped countries, "the Church of everyone, but especially the Church of the poor"; before reporters, on March 20, 2013, Francis expressed his desire for "a poor Church, and for the poor."

7. A source of the theology of mercy of *Evangelii Gaudium* is the *Summa Theologiae* of St. Thomas Aquinas, quoted seventeen times.[25] Here we can find his teachings on the new law of grace of the Holy Spirit and on the organic structure of the virtues centered on love, and on their exterior fruit, mercy. This Thomist inspiration is a feature of the Argentine way of doing theology: cross-fertilizing between classical tradition and contemporary reflection.[26] As stated in *EG* 37,

> Saint Thomas Aquinas taught that the Church's moral teaching has its own "hierarchy," in the virtues and in

> the acts which proceed from them. What counts above all else is "faith working through love" (Gal 5:6). Works of love directed to one's neighbour are the most perfect external manifestation of the interior grace of the Spirit: "The foundation of the New Law is in the grace of the Holy Spirit, who is manifested in the faith which works through love." Thomas thus explains that, as far as external works are concerned, mercy is the greatest of all the virtues: "In itself mercy is the greatest of the virtues, since all the others revolve around it and, more than this, it makes up for their deficiencies. This is particular to the superior virtue, and as such it is proper to God to have mercy, through which his omnipotence is manifested to the greatest degree."

8. Christianity is the religion of mercy: "The compendium of the Christian religion consists in mercy, as regards external works."[27] Inspired by the words of Jesus (Matt 25:31–46)—cited several times by Francis (*EG* 179, 197, 209)—the Christian religion has fostered the practice of the works of mercy and created *a culture of mercy*. Mercy is the root of divine action, which is attributed to God in the highest degree.[28] It is the compassion of the heart facing the sufferings of others.[29] It is *the historical form of love* because in the history of us human beings we always suffer ailments and afflictions.[30] God loves us with the affection of a love that binds us and unites us to him as if we were one with him, and saves us through an efficacious mercy that effectively heals our spiritual and physical sufferings.[31]

9. Mercy expresses the depth of God's being as love. Jesus' paschal cross reveals that God's love is stronger than sin, death, evil. In the bull *Misericordiae Vultus*, Francis calls us to rediscover the face of mercy in Jesus who tenderly heals the wounds of our fragile condition, and to touch the "suffering flesh of others" in which we touch "the wounds of the Lord."

> Sometimes we are tempted to be that kind of Christian who keeps the Lord's wounds at arm's length. Yet Jesus wants us to touch human misery, to touch the suffering flesh of others...and instead enter into the reality of

other people's lives and know the power of tenderness." (*EG* 270)

Mercy is the master beam that sustains life, mission, and the reform of the Church.[32]

A Reform Starting from the Conciliar Theology of the Evangelizing People of God

1. If Vatican II was, as Karl Rahner put it, "the beginning of a beginning," *the pontificate of Francis is a new beginning of that initiation of reform promoted by the Council.* With the current pope, the reception of the Council and the reform of the Church—not just the curia—have entered a new phase. The decisive question is the interpretation of the meaning of reform. In a well-crafted expression, Cardinal Kasper has said that the pope is certainly interested in continuity, but in the *continuity of conciliar reform.*[33] Francis argues that the Council provided a rereading of the gospel in light of contemporary culture and that this dynamic is absolutely irreversible.

2. "Vatican II is, par excellence, the Council of the People of God."[34] The notion of the people of God, present 184 times in the conciliar documents,[35] is developed in the second chapter of *Lumen Gentium.*[36] In an interview for *La Civiltà Cattolica*, Francis expressed his preference for that idea, as confirmed in *Evangelii Gaudium* (*EG* 119).

> The image of the church I like is that of the holy, faithful people of God. This is the definition I often use, and then there is that image from the Second Vatican Council's "Dogmatic Constitution on the Church" (No. 12). Belonging to a people has a strong theological value. In the history of salvation, God has saved a people. There is no full identity without belonging to a people. No one is saved alone, as an isolated individual, but God attracts us looking at the complex web of relationships that take

> place in the human community. God enters into this dynamic, this participation in the web of human relationships. The people itself constitutes a subject. And the church is the people of God on the journey through history, with joys and sorrows.[37]

3. With Francis we assist at a *twofold return of the people of God*.[38] On the one hand, the Christian people bursts on the scene in a new way, as seen in St. Peter's Square and during the pope's apostolic journeys. This "legitimacy from the bottom up," starting from the affection and support of believers—and of many people of other faiths and good will—adds to the "legitimacy from the top," conferred by the Spirit through the pope's election and guidance in his ministry. On the other, with Francis resurfaces the theology of the people of God, which reinstates its centrality given to it by Vatican II, a centrality that since 1985 had been buried in the documents of the papal magisterium. Francis today shares some ideas of the so-called *Argentine theology of the people*.[39] That evocative expression, however, can be simplistic if the word *people* refers only to the civilian community. For us, there are two similar meanings of the word *people*: an ecclesial and civilian one, which are as strongly dissimilar as they are alike. We prefer to say that Francis takes, enriches, and universalizes *the Argentine theology of God's people, along with the people(s) and the popular pastoral care*, because it includes an ecclesiology, a theology of culture and history, and a pastoral theology.

4. This theology understands the *world*, of which the Council speaks about, through the realities of the *people* and its *culture*. It has considered the people as a collective historical subject and a hermeneutical tool to read the signs of the times. It has favored an analogic understanding of the category of the incarnation to understand the presence of God's people among the civilian people. It has sustained that which is popular through a theological concept borrowed from the ecclesiology of Vatican II. If the "body of Christ" expresses the christological and eucharistic reality of the Church, the "pilgrim people of God" expresses its sociohistorical dimension. "With *Lumen Gentium* we mainly adopt the notion of the People of God as inserted in history and walking with the people in history."[40] Our theology has dedicated its reflections to

the relations between the people of God and the cultures of the peoples.[41]

5. Although "there are many nations there is but one people of God" (*LG* 13b). "The People of God is incarnate in the peoples of the earth, each of which has its own culture." (*EG* 115). The section titled "A People of Many Faces" (*EG* 115–18) develops the image of the face in an ecclesiological sense to support the intercultural richness of the Church. "In the diversity of peoples who experience the gift of God, each in accordance with its own culture, the Church expresses her genuine catholicity and shows forth the 'beauty of her varied face'" (*EG* 116; *NMI* 40).

6. The faculty of theology of Buenos Aires, which in 2015 celebrated its first centenary,[42] has been a *pioneer* in commenting on the constitution *Lumen Gentium*, starting in 1965.[43] Already it showed the unity between the first two chapters of *LG*,[44] based on the macro-categories of *mystery* and *people*. The "mystery of the holy Church" (*LG* 5) is realized in history in the form of "a people" (*LG* 9), as Lucio Gera said in one of the best commentaries to the first chapter of the constitution of the Church ever written.[45] This binomial is the foundation of what we call the systematic—or ecclesio-logical—architecture of *LG*.[46] In 1989, in a report presented to the Theological-Pastoral CELAM team, we showed that the Argentine reception of the notion of the people of God was original and was not subjected to reductive interpretations neither in the line of a "democratic" nor of a "popular" Church.[47]

7. *The Argentine trend is little known in Europe*. The larger European public has known only the works of the most famous Latin American theologians, with only one exception: the recognition given by the great exponents of German theology. In 1974, Peter Hünermann, who had ties with Argentina through his teacher Bernard Welte, came across the work of Gera and argued that it is time to think about the relationship between the Church and the people in terms of identity and difference.[48] In 1978, Karl Lehmann, member of the International Theological Commission, acknowledged in the field of liberation theology an independent and valuable current, originally identified with Argentina, that emphasized people's culture and religion.[49] In his book on Pope Francis, Walter Kasper devotes a chapter to the "People-of-God ecclesiology understood concretely"; more recently he said that

"for Pope Francis center stage is occupied by the Church as the pilgrim People of God."[50] The great novelty of his pontificate includes the smaller novelty of a wider dissemination of our theology.

8. Francis combines *Lumen Gentium, Gaudium et Spes,* and *Ad Gentes* because the people of God and its mission in the world cannot be separated. *The pilgrim people of God is the subject of evangelization in history*. This people "a mystery rooted in the Trinity, yet she exists concretely in history as a people of pilgrims and evangelizers, transcending any institutional expression" (*EG* 111). "The entire people of God proclaims the Gospel" (*EG* 111–34) and "all the members of the People of God have become missionary disciples" (*EG* 119–21). The pope follows the logic of chapter 2 of *LG*, which culminates with the mission of the people of God, because the last redaction of this document included a paragraph on missionary work (*LG* 17). In 1965, *Ad Gentes* proclaimed, "The pilgrim Church is missionary by her very nature" (*AG* 2).[51] The *Aparecida Document* cites this text at the beginning of its pastoral section (*AD* 347).

9. When the Bishop of Rome says, "pray for me," he recognizes that the believing and praying subjectivity of the Christian people sustains his ministry. Argentine theology has contributed to *reevaluate popular piety as an expression of an inculturated Catholic faith* (*PD* 444, *SD* 36) both at Puebla (1979) and at Aparecida (2007). *Evangelii Gaudium* (115 and 122) recalls several times the *Puebla Document*, because its chapter "Evangelization and Popular Religiosity" (*PD* 444–69) has become a classic on the subject, quoted by the same *Catechism of the Catholic Church* (CCC 1674–76). *Evangelii gaudium* cites also the *Aparecida Document* (*EG* 98, 102–4, 106) and its beautiful section on popular spirituality (*EG* 124). Aparecida spoke of "popular spirituality or mysticism" (*AD* 262–63) because it configures "a true experience of theological love" (*AD* 263).

Francis understands popular Catholic piety from the relationship between the people of God and cultures. "Genuine forms of popular religiosity are incarnate, since they are born of the incarnation of Christian faith in popular culture" (*EG* 90). Popular piety is the peculiar way of living the faith practiced by most Catholics in a particular cultural form. "Each portion of the people of God, by translating the gift of God into its own life and in accordance with its own genius, bears witness to the faith it has received and enriches it with new and eloquent expressions" (*EG* 122).

10. In Latin America there is a hermeneutical circle between the notion of people of God and the popular Catholic reality; the latter is a living experience of believers and that notion sheds light on it in a supple way. Such experience urges us to do theology embracing the *sensus fidei fidelium*. Popular piety is an active evangelizing power (*EG* 126) and a *locus theologicus* to think about faith. "Expressions of popular piety have much to teach us; for those who are capable of reading them, they are a *locus theologicus* which demands our attention, especially at a time when we are looking to the new evangelization" (*EG* 126). Since 1974, Bergoglio has spoken of infallibility *in credendo* of the holy people of God (*LG* 12). If the magisterium and theology teach *what* we believe, popular piety shows *how* it is, for example, the love for the Virgin Mary.[52] The wisdom of faith of the baptized knows by love (*EG* 119).

This leads to a concrete way to put an inculturated theology into practice.[53] In 1996, I participated with John C. Scannone at a meeting in Vallendar, Germany, called by the Latin American Episcopal Council and the Congregation for the Doctrine of the Faith, and presided over by Cardinal Joseph Ratzinger. The sixteen participants developed a document and approved this proposition: *we must continue on the path of inculturation of the theological reflection, so it becomes fully Catholic and fully Latin American*.[54]

11. The maternal love for the simple faith of the holy people is visible when Francis asks for more stress on the "*credere in Deum* than on *credere Deum*" (*EG* 124). According to the Augustinian and Thomist theology of the act of faith (*ST* II–II, 2, 2),[55] the *credere in Deum*—the orientation or predisposition to God as the ultimate and blessed goal of life—sustained in the *credere Deum*—the trusting abandon in God as witness and guarantor of truth—takes precedence over the *credere Deum*, namely over the believing knowledge of God's revelation and his salvific plan. The faith by which we surrender ourselves to God (*fides qua*) supports the reflected understanding of its content (*fides quae*). The *credere in Deum* is perfected in the *amare Deum*, the love that unites us with God and with our neighbors in God. The knowledge of faith is nestled between trusting assent and loving surrender. Therefore,

pastoral care should focus more on faith becoming filial piety and fraternal love rather than on the conceptual development of its contents (*EG* 124), without neglecting its value because of the circularity that exists between intelligence and will in the act of faith. This pastoral reinterpretation of the theology of faith is common to Argentine theologians and pastoralists of several generations.[56]

A Reform Guided by the Paradigm of Missionary Conversion

1. *Reform is the missionary conversion—personal, communitarian, structural—of all the people of God and of all in the people of God.* Francis's program is "the reform of the Church in her missionary outreach" (*EG* 17) A Church that "goes forth" (*EG* 20–24) is decentered because it is centered in Christ for her conversion and in the human being for missionary work. Since the disciples share their lives with Jesus' person, message, work, Passover, and mission, the conversion to Jesus will lead them to participate in his mission. This is the figure of the missionary disciple. After the canonization of Peter Faber, Francis said, "Only if one is centered in God can go to the peripheries of the world."[57]

2. The first chapter of his exhortation establishes a "pastoral conversion" (*EG* 25–33) or a "missionary conversion" (*EG* 30). These inclusive formulas synthetize the proposals of Aparecida on pastoral conversion and missionary renewal (*AD* 365–72). This program calls for a reform of church structures "to become more mission-oriented" (*EG* 27), including the conversion of the papacy and the central government of the Church (*EG* 32). The *Ecclesia semper reformanda* is an *Ecclesia in statu conversionis*, and an *Ecclesia in statu missionis*.

3. For Francis the "missionary outreach is *paradigmatic for all the Church's activity*." (*EG* 15). The mission is the paradigm: "I dream of a 'missionary option,' that is, a missionary impulse capable of transforming everything.…The renewal of structures demanded by pastoral conversion can only be understood in this light: as part of an effort to make them more mission-oriented" (*EG* 27). Here the pope applies his distinction between paradigmatic and

programmatic mission. The former implies undertaking missionary work as the key to the life of the Church and the reform of the structures of the ordinary pastoral care in a missionary key. It points to the style of a Church permanently in movement and going forth. The latter includes the symbolic gestures, the concrete plans, and the specific events of an openly missionary character.[58]

4. *A new evangelical and missionary reform of the Church involves long processes*. The pope encourages the Church to be "concerned about initiating processes rather than possessing spaces" (*EG* 223). The dynamics of missionary reform must permeate the historical form of the Church. In 2007, we introduced the *Aparecida Document* privately to the Standing Committee of the Argentine Episcopate and publicly in a press conference with Cardinal Bergoglio. Knowing well Latin American pastoral history, we affirmed that the missionary project of Aparecida, if it is constantly updated, would affect the entire twenty-first century. The significance of that fifth Conference of the Latin American Episcopate has grown because the pope employs some of its ideas and relaunches them in his own reforming program. But he does not intend to export a Latin American model; what he wants instead for each church to take on the mission in an inculturated way in its own time and place. Otherwise we fall into another form of pastoral centralism.

5. *The reform of the people of God from its head to its members includes the "return" of various ecclesial issues*: the *sensus fidei* of all believers; the initiatives of local churches; the structures of collegiality and synodality; the ecumenical and interreligious dialogue; the permanent mission to all the peripheries of the world; the place of the poor in the Church; a renewed look at the family as domestic church; the call to theologians to be children of their people, believers and prophets, to think by praying and to pray by thinking,[59] along with a more respectful institutional treatment toward them; the fight against clericalism and centralism; the fraternal bonds of ordained ministers with all the faithful, men and women, because "lay people are, put simply, the vast majority of the people of God. The minority—ordained ministers—are at their service" (*EG* 102). And the reforms of the attitudes and structures in the Roman curia can focus on the commission of cardinals (the so-called G-9); the secretariats of the economy and communication; the stimulus that encourages participatory processes; *pro tempore* appointments to

cut at the root of "careerism" (*EG* 277); the changes in congregations for the choice of bishops; a new *ratio* for priestly formation to promote the model of pastor; the appointment of cardinals coming from the most suffering churches in the world; and so on.

6. *Reforms are achieved through synodal processes animated by the utopia of the kingdom of God inaugurated with the Passover of Jesus Christ,* which requires a keen sense of *time*. We live in the tension between the contingent situation and the broader horizon of the "utopian future as the final cause which draws us to itself" (*EG* 222).[60] The pilgrimage in time demands the theological virtue of hope and virtues that fall into the sphere of strength: perseverance, patience, magnanimity, courage (*parrēsìa*); much prudence and even more mercy (*EG* 44). Francis leads us in this direction:

a) the mission embodied in possibilities and limits, human, temporal and expressive (*EG* 34–45);
b) the art of accompanying individuals and communities in processes of growth (*EG* 169–73);
c) the priority given to time (*EG* 222–25)—"God's messenger" (*EG* 171)—which is a mystery traversed by the tension between the desire for fullness and reality of the limit.

7. *Nomen est omen*. The first Jesuit pope has chosen the name of the Poverello of Assisi. In Assisi, he recalled the union of St. Francis with Jesus, who made him an *alter Christus*, and his dedication to the evangelic mission: "Repair my house." He also stressed three main points: the love of the poor, starting from Francis's embrace of "Lady Poverty"; the charisma of peacemaking, condensed in the motto "Peace and all good"; the union with all creation expressed in the *Canticle of Creatures*.[61] The name Francis responds symbolically to three current dramas: poverty, peace, and creation. The fourth chapter of *Evangelii Gaudium* faces the issues of the poor (*EG* 186–216) and peace (*EG* 217–58). *Laudato Si'* reflects the charism of St. Francis (*LS* 10–12) and considers the correlation between the cry of the poor and the cry of the earth (*LS* 2).

8. *Francis promotes an evangelical and evangelizing reform from the peripheries of poverty*. Starting from the heart of God he wants a poorer Church, and one for the poor. The profound link that unifies

all the currents of liberation theology is the preferential option for the poor. Francis embraces this evangelical and Latin American emphasis in his reflection on "the poor in the heart of God and the Church" (*EG* 186–216). Examining the ecclesial tradition, we believe that this section of the exhortation represents *the best example of a papal document on Christ, the Church and the poor.*[62]

A Reform for Communion That Overcomes Tensions and Oppositions

1. Some *attitudes* proposed by Francis for the reform of the Church are the following: the centrality of love in an evangelizing key (*EG* 10, 121, 156); communion as harmony of differences in the totality (*EG* 117, 228, 237); patience with processes and limits (*EG* 24, 44, 223); renewal starting from the evangelical *kērygma* as experienced in the ecclesial tradition (*EG* 26, 116, 164). Some of these attitudes bear some similarity to the four conditions defined by Congar in 1950 to carry out a true Catholic reform: the primacy of charity and pastoral purpose; remaining in the communion of the Catholic totality; patience to avoid problems and delays; a return to the original tradition to avoid superficial adaptations.[63]

2. The integration of the parts into a whole and the overcoming of conflicts to reach unity are two of the principles employed by the pope for "the growth of a peaceful and multifaceted culture of encounter" (*EG* 220). These principles help to overcome the binary tensions in society and build peace. They are the following: time is greater space; unity prevails over conflict; *realities are more important than ideas*; the whole is greater than the part.

> I would now like to set forth these four specific principles which can guide the development of life in society and the building of a people where differences are harmonized within a shared pursuit. I do so out of the conviction that their application can be a genuine path to peace within each nation and in the entire world. (*EG* 221)

3. The second principle states, *Unity prevails over conflict* (*EG* 226–30). Conflict is a reality that must be acknowledged (*EG* 226) to "resolve it and to make it a link in the chain of a new process" (*EG* 227) to "build communion amid disagreement" (*EG* 228). The "unity brought by the Spirit can harmonize every diversity" (*EG* 230), especially the "fragmentation and breakdown" affecting personal interiority and social coexistence (*EG* 229). Here we can notice the influence of two thinkers: Ismael Quiles, SJ, whose philosophy was centered on the unity of the person (*EG* 229n183), and Romano Guardini, whose observation helps to discern the human fullness of an age (*EG* 224n182). *Laudato Si'* cites Guardini when it analyzes the global technocratic paradigm (*LS* 101–36). The fact that Francis is inspired by Guardini is known by some and begins to be recognized by others.[64] We will now examine his theory of opposites to understand the anthropology of the pope, and above all, the ecclesiology underlying his way to discern, lead, and reform the Church.

4. In the twentieth century, several theologians and philosophers reflected on ways to *overcome the conflicts* in the human family and people of God.

a) Regarding the first area, we will mention only the philosophical contributions of three Jesuits. Gaston Fessard understood the conflictuality of history starting from the *three Pauline dialectics*—male/female, slave/free, Jew/Gentile—and their overcoming through fraternal and differentiating—not separating—unity of Christ and his Church (Gal 3:28).[65] Bernard Lonergan has shown the *integration of dialectical opposites* through a full conversion to overcoming horizons and common foundations.[66] Juan Carlos Scannone has developed the *analectical* method that, in the three-dimensionality of the analogy, contains and transcends the dialectic two-dimensionality, thus helping to discern possible forms of freedom, justice, and unity in the events of history.[67]

b) In the ecclesiological context, we find the *great theologians of the twentieth century*—Henri de Lubac,[68] Hans Urs von Balthasar,[69] Yves Congar,[70] two thinkers of the following generation—Alberto Methol Ferré,[71] Peter

> Hünermann[72]—and the binomial Romano Guardini–Jorge Mario Bergoglio. Francis has read Guardini, de Lubac, von Balthasar, Fessard, Congar, Methol, Scannone, and many others. Here I will just briefly outline the thought of Guardini and Francis.

5. Romano Guardini proposed a reform of the Church in accordance with its origins,[73] and, as philosopher, he outlined a theory of opposites that helped him understand certain aspects of the mystery of the Church. In 1922, he wrote that the human being acquires the sense of totality in the Church,[74] because it broadens the horizons of the individual, reality, and mystery.[75] The polar opposition between the particular and the universal is expressed in the union between the personal and the communal. These are opposite—not conflicting—realities because opposites are the interior forms of concrete living, that is, of the human being and human communities, including the Church in its human reality.[76] In 1988, not knowing that Bergolio in Buenos Aires was working on his doctoral thesis on cultural mediation in Guardini, I wrote, while at Tübingen, Germany, a complete study on the first ecclesiology of Guardini, comparing it with those of Karl Adam and Johannes Pinsk.[77]

Guardini's early essay on polar oppositions (1925) analyzes *the dialectical rhythm* internally running through all reality. Opposition is a fundamental feature of human life.[78] *Der Gegensatz* outlines a theory of polar oppositions present in the human community.[79] It develops a systematic typology of oppositions in themselves and in their mutual relations. It organizes them in categorical oppositions and transcendental ones. The first are divided into two series: intraempirical (fullness/form, act/structure, individuality/totality) and transempirical (production/disposal, originality/rule, immanence/transcendence). The transcendental ones form opposites as such: unity/plurality, and likeness/distinction.[80] To these opposites, Guardini adds another at the vital level: measure/rhythm; and another in the epistemological field: intuition/concept. Guardini defines opposition as the link between two realities that reject but connect each other, and at a deeper level, presuppose each other and cannot be reduced to each other. It is a unique form of constraint that keeps in tension a relative inclusion and a relative exclusion, combining effectively the pairs of transcendental opposites.[81]

Guardini analyzed several series of opposites and their cross-links to account for the richness of human life. His theory of *Weltanschauung* expresses the art of knowing the realities in their correlations and in the totality of the world. The nuances of realities can be grasped by means of symbols and concrete concepts—unlike the abstract ones—that is, by means of those who proceed through an articulated succession of dialectical propositions. Hence, Guardini closely links his metaphysics of opposition to a theory of knowledge of the concrete.[82]

6. Jorge Mario Bergoglio has envisioned *a path of communion to overcome binary oppositions maintaining differences and accepting tensions*. He has updated and completed Romano Guardini's theory on the superior unity that integrates opposites in tension. Since 2013, Francis has been proposing and teaching *a social anthropology of the people and an ecclesiology of the people of God based on the ability to overcome binary oppositions in every community*. His social philosophy manifests itself in the second principle underpinning a culture of encounter.

> This requires acknowledging a principle indispensable to the building of friendship in society: namely, that unity is greater than conflict. Solidarity, in its deepest and most challenging sense, thus becomes a way of making history in a life setting where conflicts, tensions and oppositions can achieve a diversified and life-giving unity. This is not to opt for a kind of syncretism, or for the absorption of one into the other, but rather for a resolution which takes place on a higher plane and preserves what is valid and useful on both sides. (*EG* 228)

In 1989, Bergoglio developed this theme in an essay of political anthropology in a pastoral key.[83] He used a method inspired by Guardini and cited some of his works like *Der Gegensatz* and *Das Ende Der Neuezeit*; he formulated some of the bipolarities present in contemporary culture; he promoted an anthropology that integrates the individual and the community through solidarity; and he explained the ontology underlying his proposal.

Like Guardini, Francis proposed a phenomenological-dialectical method free from Hegelian resonances, and he understood the dynamic interaction between opposing realities, while capturing both the rhythm of life and the unity of being. He also offered a formulation of solidarity that paved the way for the text just cited from *Evangelii Gaudium* and transforms conflicts in the forms of a multiform unity.[84]

This anthropology helps to think of plural unity in a people and the world. The fourth principle of Francis is this: the whole is greater than the part (*EG* 234–37). And its symbol is the polyhedron:

> Here our model is not the sphere, which is no greater than its parts, where every point is equidistant from the centre, and there are no differences between them. Instead, it is the polyhedron, which reflects the convergence of all its parts, each of which preserves its distinctiveness....It is the convergence of peoples who, within the universal order, maintain their own individuality; it is the sum total of persons within a society which pursues the common good, which truly has a place for everyone. (*EG* 236)

7. Francis's *ecclesiology* proposes *a reform of the Church animated by the Spirit who achieves the harmony of differences* by considering the newness of the gospel at the center of its tradition. The people of God is animated by the Holy Spirit, who gives *harmony* amid tensions because it is the bond of love in the Trinity and the link of communion in the Church (*EG* 40, 117, 130–31, 220, 242, 254). "He builds up the communion and harmony of the people of God. The same Spirit is that harmony, just as he is the bond of love between the Father and the Son" (*EG* 117). The Spirit is the source of the profound peace within the strong ecclesial tensions. The reform seeks to integrate all truth and virtue in the organic and "hierarchizied" unity given by the gospel of charity (*EG* 34–40). The *kerygma* proclaims the essential nucleus from which each component of Christian life must find "a fitting sense of proportion" (*EG* 38).

> All revealed truths derive from the same divine source and are to be believed with the same faith, yet some of them are more important for giving direct expression to the heart of the Gospel. In this basic core, what shines forth is the beauty of the saving love of God made manifest in Jesus Christ who died and rose from the dead. (*EG* 36)

8. These inclusive categories help to think different realities of life and of the ecclesial reform, and cooperate to delineate, along with other contributions, a speculative ecclesiology.[85] Theology is called to integrate bipolarities in ecclesiological notions. For Ghislain Lafont the conciliar model of structured communion creates a balance in "the binomial terms *body-people*."[86] For Hermann Pottmeyer the notions of body, communion, or sacrament are categories used in a *predicative* or *attributive* sense, while that of people of God indicates the *subject* (*Träger*) and, as *subjective concept*, "it remains irreplaceable."[87] As for us, we are seeking to integrate the concepts of *populus*, *communio*, and *missio* reflecting on the mystery/sacrament of communion of the missionary people of God in, from, and for the world.[88] The Church is the communion *of* the missionary people of God in history, or the mystery *of the* pilgrim people of God as universal sacrament of salvation.

9. *The Ppople of God is the Church "in" the world* (*GS* 40). In this relationship, there is "no ontological dualism...but dialectical unity."[89] There is no monism because they are two communities formally different. Nor is there dualism because they are two communities "materially" identified with human beings, who may or may not be subjects of both according to different modalities. In our opinion, there is *a dialectic-speculative union* in which real duality is maintained and superseded in a similarly real, mystical, and superior unity. One consequence of this is clear: *we cannot think of the Church without the world and the world without the Church*. In his message to our faculty of theology in Buenos Aires for its centenary, Francis said that one of the great contributions made by Vatican II is the union between theology and pastoral care, and between faith and life. "I dare say that it has revolutionized to some extent the statute of theology, the way of doing and thinking of a believer."[90]

10. A theology of the union of opposites is symbolized in the plural *polyhedron* reflecting the plural unity of the national and international community. Similarly, this symbol may also reflect the universal unity of faith embodied in the diversities of cultures. It is a figure of the multiform face of the one people of God inculturated in many peoples of the world.

> We would not do justice to the logic of the incarnation if we thought of Christianity as monocultural and monotonous. While it is true that some cultures have been closely associated with the preaching of the Gospel and the development of Christian thought, the revealed message is not identified with any of them; its content is transcultural. (*EG* 117)

11. The same logic allows the pope not only to overcome the hierarchization of the pyramidal image of the Church, but to think, in line with conciliar ecclesiology, of a *synodal Church as an inverted pyramid* in which the people of God, the College of Bishops, and the successor of Peter are integrated.

> *Synodality*, as a constitutive element of the Church, offers us the most appropriate interpretive framework for understanding the hierarchical ministry itself. If we understand, as Saint John Chrysostom says, that "Church and Synod are synonymous," inasmuch as the Church is nothing other than the "journeying together" of God's flock along the paths of history towards the encounter with Christ the Lord, then we understand too that, within the Church, no one can be "raised up" higher than others. On the contrary, in the Church, it is necessary that each person "lower" himself or herself, so as to serve our brothers and sisters along the way.
>
> Jesus founded the Church by setting at her head the Apostolic College, in which the Apostle Peter is the "rock" (cf. Mt 16:18), the one who must confirm his brethren in the faith (cf. Lk 22:32). But in this Church, as in an inverted pyramid, the top is located beneath the base. Consequently, those who exercise authority

> are called "ministers," because, in the original meaning of the word, they are the least of all. It is in serving the people of God that each bishop becomes, for that portion of the flock entrusted to him, *vicarius Christi*, the vicar of that Jesus who at the Last Supper bent down to wash the feet of the Apostles (cf. Jn 13:1–15). And in a similar perspective, the Successor of Peter is nothing else if not the *servus servorum Dei*.
>
> Let us never forget this! For the disciples of Jesus, yesterday, today and always, the only authority is the authority of service, the only power is the power of the cross. As the Master tells us: "You know that the rulers of the Gentiles lord it over them, and their great men exercise authority over them. It shall not be so among you; but whoever would be great among you must be your servant, and whoever would be first among you must be your slave" (Matt 20:25–27). *It shall not be so among you*: in this expression we touch the heart of the mystery of the Church, and we receive the enlightenment necessary to understand our hierarchical service.[91]

12. *The reflection on the reform of the real Church must discern conflicts and tensions to think the union of opposites in the truth of an including and inclusive catholicity.*

Divisions, paradoxes, and tensions exist and challenge us: mystery and history; tradition and reform; ressourcement and aggiornamento; conversion and mission; Church and world; people and hierarchy; person and community; love and truth; holiness and sin; fullness, limit, and path; time and space; guide, accompaniment, formation; heart and structure; freedom and justice; mercy and justice; *sensus fidei* and magisterium; incarnation and transcendence; unity and plurality; universality and particularity; identity and otherness; equality and difference; union, division, and reconciliation; dialogue and proclamation; charism and institution; synodality and authority; episcopal collegiality and Petrine primacy; laity and clergy; globalization and localization; inculturation and interculturality; center and periphery; poverty and inclusion; service and power; and many other binary realities that determine overarching mediations with regard to reflection and action.

Here we seek new creative historical figures of the mystery of communion of the missionary people of God so it may become a transparent sacrament of the kingdom of God in the human family.

13. With the same all-encompassing gaze, we contemplate Mary, who is Mother and Model of the Church. Her profound love accompanies the pilgrim and evangelizing people of God. Pope Francis has cited the story of *Nican Mopohua* (*EG* 286) on the mystery of Our Lady of Guadalupe, Mother of America. From her we learn the "Marian 'style' to the Church's work of evangelization...the revolutionary nature of love and tenderness" (*EG* 288). That style includes humility, proximity, encounter, affection, gift, service, joy. Mary is the Dawn of the Morning of the gospel and the Evening Star of the first and the new evangelization (*EN* 81; *EG* 287).

NOTES

1. See W. Kasper, *Chiesa cattolica. Essenza–realtà–missione.* (Brescia: Queriniana, 2012), 46; C. M. Galli, "En la Iglesia está soplando el Viento del Sur," in *Hacia una nueva evangelización,* by Consejo Episcopal Latinoamericano (Bogotá: CELAM, 2012), 161–260.

2. See M. Faggioli, *Papa Francesco e la Chiesa-Mondo* (Rome: Armando, 2014), 19–26. Translated as *Pope Francis: Tradition in Transition* (New York: Paulist Press, 2015).

3. W. Kasper, "El Vaticano II: intención, recepción, futuro," *Teología* 117 (2015): 95–115, at 113.

4. A. Methol Ferré, "Marco histórico de la Iglesia latinoamericana," *Sedoi* 4 (1974): 1–12, esp. 11 (passim); see also the more recent A. Methol Ferré and A. Metalli, *La América Latina del siglo XXI* (Buenos Aires: Edhasa, 2006), 59–82.

5. See E. Pironio, *Escritos pastorals.* (Madrid: BAC, 1973), 3–10 and 205–27.

6. See W. Bühlmann, *La tercera iglesia a las puertas* (Madrid: Paulinas, 1977[2]), 157–96.

7. See "Annuario Pontificio 2014 y Annuarium Statisticum Ecclesiae 2012," *L'Osservatore Romano* (Spanish ed.), August 8, 2014, 4. (Unless otherwise specified, the weekly edition of the *L'Osservatore Romano* refers to the Spanish edition [N.d.R.]).

8. See K. Rahner, "Una interpretación teológica a fondo del Concilio Vaticano II," *Razón y Fe* 200 (1979): 183–95.

9. See Y. M. Congar, "Dalla comunione delle Chiese ad una ecclesiologia della Chiesa universale," in *L'episcopato e la Chiesa universal*, ed. Y. M. Congar and B. D. Dupuy (Rome: Edizioni Paoline, 1965), 279–322. Originally published as *L'Épiscopat et l'Église universelle* (Paris: Cerf, 1962).

10. See M. De França Miranda, *A Igreja que somos nós* (São Paulo: Paulinas, 2013), 148–56.

11. See L. Ortiz, "El CELAM como servicio de comunión a las Iglesias particulares," *Medellín* 162 (2015): 209–13.

12. "Altogether, initiatives and novelty come especially from the periphery, from the Church at her frontiers": Y. M. Congar, *Vera e falsa riforma della Chiesa* (Milan: Jaca Book, 1995), 211. Translated by Paul Philibert as *True and False Reform in the Church* (Collegeville, MN: Liturgical Press, 2011). Originally published as *Vraie et fausse réforme dans l'Église* (Paris: Cerf, 1950).

13. See C. M. Galli, *Dio vive in città. Verso una nuova pastorale urbana alla luce del Documento di Aparecida e del progetto missionario di Francesco* (Vatican City: Libreria Editrice Vaticana, 2014), 315ff.

14. See A. Riccardi, *La sorpresa del Papa Francisco* (Buenos Aires: Agape, 2014), 185–215. Originally published as *La sorpresa di papa Francesco. Crisi e futuro della Chiesa* (Milan: Mondadori, 2013).

15. See J. M. Bergoglio, *Nosotros como ciudadanos, nosotros como pueblo* (Buenos Aires: Claretiana, 2013).

16. See C. M. Galli, "El Pueblo de Dios en las culturas urbanas a la luz de *Evangelii gaudium*," in *Evangelización en las culturas urbanas*, by Consejo Episcopal Latinoamericano (Bogotá: CELAM, 2015), 105–42.

17. H. Cymerman, "Entrevista al Papa Francisco," *L'Osservatore Romano*, June 20, 2014, 6.

18. Pope Francis, "A People Who Generates Its Children, Communities and Families in the Great Stages of Christian Initiation," June 16, 2014. https://w2.vatican.va/content/francesco/en/speeches/2014/june/documents/papa-francesco_20140616_apertura-convegno-diocesano.html.

19. See J. M. Bergolio, *Meditaciones para religiosos* (Buenos Aires: Ediciones Diego de Torres, 1982), 63. The text dates back to February 8, 1978. See also *Mente abierta, corazón creyente* (Buenos Aires: Claretiana, 2013), 17–25. Translated by Joseph Owens as *Open Mind, Faithful Heart: Reflections on Following Jesus* (New York: Crossroad, 2013).

20. See C. M. Galli, "El amor y la alegría en *Evangelii gaudium*," in *La caridad y la alegría: paradigmas del Evangelio. XXIII Semana Argentina de Teología*, by Sociedad Argentina De Teología (Buenos Aires: Agape, 2015), 65–103.

21. See G. Lafont, *L'Église en travail de réforme. Imaginer l'Église catholique* II (Paris: Cerf, 2011), 145–68.

22. See Francis, "Tiempo de misericordia," *L'Osservatore Romano*, March 14, 2014, 4ff.

23. See Y. M. Congar, "Au lecteur," in *Ecclesia Mater chez les Péres des trois premiers siècles*, by K. Delahaye (Paris: Cerf, 1964), 7–32. H. de Lubac, "La maternidad de la Iglesia," in *Las iglesias particulares en la Iglesia universal* (Salamanca: Sígueme, 1974), 143–231; H. U. von Balthasar, "La maternidad envolvente de la Iglesia," in *El complejo antirromano. Integración del Papado en la Iglesia universal* (Madrid: BAC, 1981, 185–229.

24. See J. Aiello and C. M. Galli, *San Juan XXIII, la Iglesia de la ternura* (Buenos Aires: Agape, 2014), 77–85.

25. In the text, extended citations recur three times (*EG* 37, 43, 171) and with fourteen references in footnotes (*EG* 35, 40, 44, 48, 93, 105, 117, 133, 166, 191).

26. See W. Kasper, *La misericordia. Clave del Evangelio y de la vida Cristiana* (Santander: Sal Terrae, 2013).

27. "Summa religionis christianae in misericordia consistit quantum ad exteriora opera": Thomas Aquinas, *Summa Theologiae* II–II, q. 30, a. 4, ad 2.

28. See ibid., I, q. 21, a. 3 e 4.

29. See ibid., II–II, q. 30, a. 1, ad 2.

30. See J. Sobrino, *El principio-misericordia. Bajar de la cruz a los pueblos crucificados* (Santander: Sal Terrae, 1992).

31. See *Summa Theologiae* II–II, q. 27, a. 2 e I, q. 21, a. 3.

32. See W. Kasper, *Papa Francesco—la rivoluzione della tenerezza e dell'amore. Radici teologiche e prospettive pastorali* (Brescia: Queriniana, 2015), 49–56, translated by William Madges as *Pope Francis' Revolution of Tenderness and Love: Theological and Pastoral Perspectives* (New York: Paulist Press, 2015); F. Torralba Roselló, *La revolución de la ternura* (Lleida: Milenio, 2014), 167–93; J. Erbacher, *Papst Franziskus. Aufbruch und Neuanfang* (Munich: Pattloch, 2013), 112–30.

33. Kasper, "El Vaticano II," 113.

34. D. Vitali, *Popolo di Dio* (Assisi: Cittadella, 2013), 119.

35. See J. Deretz and A. Nocent, *Konkordanz der Konzilstexte* (Graz: Styria, 1968), 579–585; M. Keller, *Volk Gottes als Kirchenbegriff. Eine Untersuchung zum neueren Verständnis* (Zurich: Benzinger, 1970), 237–46.

36. See Istituto per le Scienze Religiose, Indices Verborum et locutionum decretorum Concilii Vaticani II, III: *Constitutio dogmatica de Ecclesia "Lumen gentium"* (Florence: Vallecchi, 1968), 179ff.

37. Antonio Spadaro, "A Big Heart Open to God: An Interview with Pope Francis" *America*, Sept. 30, 2013.

38. See C. M. Galli, "El 'retorno' del 'Pueblo de Dios'. Un concepto-símbolo de la eclesiología del Concilio a Francisco," in *La Eclesiología del Concilio Vaticano II. Memoria, Reforma y Profecía*, by V. R. Azcuy, J. C. Caamaño, and C. M. Galli (Buenos Aires: Agape, 2015), 405–71; Azcuy, Caamaño, and Galli, "Il ritorno del Popolo di Dio. Ecclesiologia argentina e riforma della Chiesa," *Il Regno—Attualità* (5/2015): 294–300; Azcuy, Caamaño, and Galli, "Lectura teológica del texto de *Evangelii gaudium* en el contexto del ministerio pastoral del Papa Francisco," *Medellín* 158 (2014): 47–88.

39. See J. C. Scannone, *Le pape du peuple. Bergoglio raconté par son confrère théologien, jésuite et argentin. Entretiens avec Bernadette Sauvaget* (Paris: Cerf, 2015), 45–77; Scannone, "Papa Francesco e la teologia del popolo," *La Civiltà Cattolica* (2014/I): 571–90; Scannone, "El Papa Francisco: ¿teólogo del pueblo?," *Criterio* 2414 (2015): 44–46.

40. L. Gera, San Miguel. "Una promesa escondida," *Voces* 17 (1990): 6–20, at 16; see J. C. Scannone, "Lucio Gera: un teologo 'dal' popolo," *La Civiltà Cattolica* (2015/I): 539–50.

41. See C. M. Galli, "Aproximación al 'pensar' teológico de Lucio Gera," in *Presente y futuro de la teología en Argentina. Homenaje a Lucio Gera*, ed. R. Ferrara and C. M. Galli (Buenos Aires: Paulinas, 1997), 75–103; Galli, "Epílogo. Interpretación, valoración y actualización del pensamiento teológico de Lucio Gera in 'Del Preconcilio a la Conferencia de Puebla' (1956–1981)," in *Escritos teológico-pastorales de Lucio Gera, I: Del Preconcilio a la Conferencia de Puebla (1956–1981)*, ed. V. Azcuy, C. M. Galli, and M. González (Buenos Aires: Agape–Facultad de Teología UCA, 2006), 867–924; "Lucio Gera, buen pastor y maestro en teología," in L. Gera, *Meditaciones sacerdotales*, ed. V. Azcuy, J. Caamaño, and C. M. Galli (Buenos Aires: Agape, 2015), 15–43.

42. See C. M. Galli, "La recepción del Concilio Vaticano II en nuestra incipiente tradición teológica argentina (1962–2005)," in *100 años de la Facultad de Teología. Memoria, presente, future*, ed. J. Caamaño, G. Durán, F. Ortega, and F. Tavelli (Buenos Aires: Fundación Teología y Cultura–Agape, 2015), 341–87.

43. See R. Ferrara, L. Gera, et al., "Lumen gentium. Comentario de la Constitución conciliar sobre la Iglesia," *Teología* 7 (1965): 127–53, and 8 (1966): 3–105.

44. See F. Geremia, *I primi due capitoli della Lumen Gentium* (Rome: Marianum, 1971), 152.

45. See L. Gera, "El Misterio de la Iglesia," in Ferrara and Gera, "Lumen gentium," 45–106.

46. See C. M. Galli, "La encarnación del Pueblo de Dios en la Iglesia y en la eclesiología latinoamericanas," *Sedoi* 125 (1994): 1–147, at 11, where we present both the different ecclesiology of Medellín and Puebla and those of L. Gera, R. Muñoz, L. Boff, and J. C. Scannone.

47. See C. M. Galli, "La Iglesia como Pueblo de Dios," in *Eclesiología. Tendencias actuals*, by Consejo Episcopal Latinoamericano (Bogotá: CELAM, 1990), 91–152, esp. 113–21; "La recepción latinoamericana de la teología conciliar del Pueblo de Dios," *Medellín* 86 (1996): 69–119, esp. 83–106.

48. See P. Hünermann, "Evangelium der Freiheit. Zur Physiognomie lateinamerikanischer Theologie," in *Gott im Aufbruch. Die Provokation der lateinamerikanischen Theologie*, ed. P. Hünermann and G. Fischer (Freiburg: Herder, 1974), 11–24, at 19.

49. See K. Lehmann, "Problemas metodológicos y hermenéuticos de la teología de la liberación," in *Teología de la liberación*, by Comisión Teológica Internacional (Madrid: Edica, 1978), 3–42, n. 92. Originally published as "Methodologisch-hermeneutische Probleme der Theologie der Befreiung," in *Theologie der Befreiung* by, Internationale Theologienkommission (Einsiedeln: Johannes Verlag, 1977), 9–44.

50. See respectively Kasper, *Papa Francesco—la rivoluzione della tenerezza* (*Pope Francis' Revolution of Tenderness and Love*), 57–69; "El Vaticano II," 114.

51. See Y. M. Congar, "La Missione e le missioni nelle prospettive del Concilio Vaticano II," *Sacra Doctrina* 11 (1966) 5–13; J. Ratzinger, "La mission d'après les autres textes conciliaires," in *L'activité missionnaire de l'Église. Decret 'Ad gentes,'* ed. J. Schütte (Paris: Cerf, 1967), 121–47.

52. See Bergoglio, *Meditaciones para religiosos*, 47.

53. See C. M. Galli, *De amar la sabiduría a creer y esperar en la Sabiduría del Amor. Inteligencia de la fe, profecía de la esperanza, sabiduría del amor* (Buenos Aires: Facultad de Teología-Guadalupe, 2012), 18–20, 32–41, 103–8.

54. Consejo Episcopal Latinoamericano, *El futuro de la reflexión teológica en América Latina* (Bogotá: CELAM, 1996), 367.

55. See *Summa Theologiae* II–II, q. 2, a. 2.

56. See R. Ferrara, "Fidei infusio y revelación en Santo Tomás de Aquino: *Summa theologiae* I–II q. 100 a. 4 ad 1^{m}," *Teología* 23/24 (1974): 24–32; R. Tello, *La nueva evangelización* (Buenos Aires: Agape, 2008), 47–52; E. Bianchi, *Pobres en este mundo, ricos en la fe. La fe de los pobres de América Latina según Rafael Tello* (Buenos Aires: Agape, 2012), 167–232.

57. Pope Francis, Holy Mass on the Liturgical Memorial of the Most Holy Name of Jesus, January 3, 2014.

58. Pontificia Commissione per l'America Latina, *Riflessioni sulla nuova evangelizzazione in America Latina: sfide e priorità* (Vatican City: Libreria Editrice Vaticana, 2012); J. M. Bergoglio, "Carta del Sr. Arzobispo con motivo del inicio de la Misión Bautismal en Buenos Aires," *Boletín Eclesiástico* 524 (2010): 456–60.

59. See Francis, Video Message to Participants in an International Theological Congress Held at the Pontifical Catholic University of Argentina, September 3, 2015: https://w2.vatican.va/content/francesco/en/messages/pont-messages/2015/documents/papa-francesco_20150903_videomessaggio-teologia-buenos-aires.html.

60. See J. M. Bergoglio, *La nación por construir. Utopía, pensamento y compromise* (Buenos Aires: Claretiana, 2005).

61. Pope Francis, Homily, Pastoral Visit to Assisi, October 4, 2013.

62. See C. M. Galli, "Los pobres en el corazón de Dios y del Pueblo de Dios. Del "Pacto de las Cata- cumbas" a la Evangelii gaudium de Francisco," in *El Pacto de las Catacumbas. La misión de los pobres en la Iglesia*, ed. X. Pikaza and J. Antunes Da Silva (Estella: Editorial Verbo Divino, 2015), 259–96.

63. See Congar, *Vraie et fausse réforme dans l'Église*, 231–352.

64. See D. Fares, *Papa Francesco è come un bambù. Alle radici della cultura dell'incontro*, preface by Antonio Spadaro (Milan: Àncora, 2014), 11–35, translated as *The Heart of Pope Francis: How a New Culture of Encounter Is Changing the Church and the World* (New York: Crossroad, 2015); Kasper, *Pope Francis' Revolution of Tenderness and Love*, 34ff.

65. See G. Fessard, "Dialogue théologique avec Hegel," *Hegel Studien* 11 (1974): 231–48 (these are the Stuttgarter Hegel-Tage 1970, ed. by H. G. Gadamer); "Esquisse pour une analyse chrétienne de la societé," *Communio* V (1980): 18–28.

66. See B. J. F. Lonergan, *Método en Teología* (Salamanca: Sígueme, 1994), 229–65. Originally published as *Method in Theology* (New York: Herder, 1972).

67. See J. C. Scannone, *Discernimiento filosófico de la acción y pasión históricas. Planteo para el mundo global desde América Latina* (Barcelona: Anthropos, 2009), 15–62.

68. See H. de Lubac, *Paradoxes suivis de Nouveaux Paradoxes* (Paris: Seuil, 1955); *Paradoja y misterio de la Iglesia, Sígueme* (Salamanca, 1967).

69. See H. U. von Balthasar, *Cattolico* (Milan: Jaca Book, 1977); *La verdad es sinfónica* (Madrid: Encuentro, 1979). Translated as *Truth Is Symphonic: Aspects of Christian Pluralism* (San Francisco: Ignatius, 1987).

70. See Congar, *Vraie et fausse réforme dans l'Église*; "Propiedades esenciales de la Iglesia," in *Mysterium Salutis. Manual de teología como historia de*

la salvación IV/1, ed. J. Feiner and M. Löhrer (Madrid: Cristiandad, 1973), 371–546, originally published as *Mysterium Salutis* (Paris: Cerf, 1970).

71. See A. Methol Ferré, "Actualidad de la Iglesia en América Latina," in *Conflicto social y compromiso cristiano en América Latina*, by Consejo Episcopal Latinoamericano (Bogotá: CELAM, 1976), 201–31; Methol Ferré and Metalli, *La América Latina del siglo XXI*, 59–82, 123–49.

72. See P. Hünermann, "Konkretion und Geist. Der qualitative Sprung im Verständnis von Weltkirche," *Theologische Quartalschrift* 165 (1985): 216–27.

73. See H. U. Von Balthasar, *Romano Guardini. Riforma dalle origini* (Milan: Jaca Book, 1970), 17–39. Translated as *Romano Guardini: Reform from the Source* (San Francisco: Ignatius Press, 2010).

74. R. Guardini, *Von Sinn der Kirche* (Mainz: Grünewald, 1933[3]), 96. Translated by Ada Lane as *The Church and the Catholic* (London: Sheed & Ward, 1935).

75. R. Guardini, *Cristianismo y Sociedad* (Salamanca: Sígueme, 1982), 25ff.

76. See Guardini, *Von Sinn der Kirche*, 33–51.

77. See C. M. Galli, "Tres precursores de la eclesiología conciliar del Pueblo de Dios," *Teología* 52 (1988): 171–203. A later analysis, brief and with a philosophical character, is in the work of X. Tilliette, *L'Église des philosophes. De Nicolas de Cuse à Gabriel Marcel* (Paris: Cerf, 2006), 244–49.

78. See R. Guardini, *Der Gegensatz. Versuche zu einer Philosophie des Lebendig Konkreten* (1925), afterword by H.-B. Gerl (Mainz: Grünewald, 1985), 169–74.

79. See ibid., 152–67.

80. See ibid., 80–88.

81. See ibid., 50, 126, 131.

82. See ibid., 39, 136, 180; see also 185–201.

83. See J. Bergoglio, "Necesidad de una antropología política: una cuestión pastoral," *Stromata* 45 (1989): 173–89.

84. See ibid., 188.

85. See C. M. Galli, "Claves de la eclesiología conciliar y postconciliar desde la bipolaridad Lumen Gentium—Gaudium et spes. Síntesis panorámica y mediación especulativa," in *A cuarenta años del Concilio Vaticano II: recepción y actualidad*, ed. Sociedad Argentina De Teología (Buenos Aires: San Benito, 2006), 49–107, esp. 85–97.

86. G. Lafont, *Imaginer l'Église catholique* (Paris: Cerf, 1995), 119; see 7–16, 81–86, 112–37, 263–79. Translated as *Imagining the Catholic Church: Structured Communion in the Spirit* (Collegeville, MN: Liturgical Press, 2000).

87. See H. J. Pottmeyer, "Dal sinodo del 1985 al grande Giubileo dell'anno 2000," in *Il Concilio Vaticano II. Recezione e attualità alla luce del Giubileo*, ed. R. Fisichella (Cinisello Balsamo: San Paolo, 2000), 11–25, at 22.

88. We explain our dialectical-speculative ecclesiology in C. M. Galli, "La complexio oppositorum entre la Iglesia y el mundo. Ensayo de eclesiología especulativa a partir de la paradoja de los opuestos," in AA.VV., *Moral, verdad y vida, en la tradición de santo Tomás de Aquino*. (Tucumán: Editorial UNSTA, 2008), 135–78.

89. G. Thils, *L'après-Vatican II. Un nouvel âge de l'Eglise?* (Louvain: Éditions de la *Revue Theólogique* de Louvain, 1985), 76.

90. Pope Francis, Video Message to Participants in an International Theological Congress Held at the Pontifical Catholic University of Argentina.

91. Pope Francis, Ceremony Commemorating the 50th Anniversary of the Institution of the Synod of Bishops; Paul VI Audience Hall; Saturday, October 17, 2015: http://w2.vatican.va/content/francesco/en/speeches/2015/october/documents/papa-francesco_20151017_50-anniversario-sinodo.html.

3

THE CHURCH ON ITS PILGRIM WAY TO ARISE AS THE PEOPLE OF GOD

Hermann J. Pottmeyer

The reform *of* the Church and the reforms *within* the Church at the service of a pastoral plan good for all times: this was the purpose of the popes and of the fathers of Vatican II. *Aggiornamento* (bringing up to date) was the term coined for this purpose by Pope John XXIII. We cannot properly understand the Council if we only see it as characterized by a conflict between opponents and advocates of reform. The desire for reform was not part of the discussion. There were, of course, different ideas on how to assess the contemporary world.[1] Moreover, it also discussed what was binding and unchanging in the Church, and what in it was instead bound by time and change, and therefore whether it needed to be reformed. These two issues concern many people to this day, and help to create a kind of polarization in the Church. One can understand, therefore, the relevance of a hermeneutic of reform that addresses these problems and tries to enlighten them. The Council itself practiced the hermeneutic of reform and its documents should be interpreted in this light.[2]

The Hermeneutic of Reform

In effect, it was Pope Benedict XVI who spoke of a hermeneutic of reform, in his Christmas message to the curia on December 22, 2005, referring to the discussion on the Council interpretations. "The church," said the pope, "is a subject which increases in time and develops, yet always remaining the same, the one subject of the journeying People of God." The nature of true reform consists "in this combination of continuity and discontinuity at different levels." The task of the hermeneutic of reform is to identify and distinguish these levels.[3]

That this distinction is complex was explained by the Council in these terms: the Church forms "one complex reality which coalesces from a divine and a human element" (*LG* 8). Precisely in this "growing together" of the divine and the human element lies the difficulty to distinguish between them, that is, to distinguish between the nature and the permanent task on the one hand, and their temporal and historical configuration, which possibly needs an update, on the other. The "divine element" always appears incarnate in a human form, and it can be all too easily confused with it, or vice versa.

Regarding the historical form, the "human element" of the Church, the Council says, "Christ summons the Church to continual reformation as she sojourns here on earth. The Church is always in need of this, in so far as she is an institution of men here on earth" (*UR* 6). For as such it "has the appearance of this world which is passing and she herself dwells among creatures who groan and travail in pain "(*LG* 48).

It is beyond dispute that the judgment as to what is forever binding, and what needs to be reformed, must be oriented on the word of God. And indeed, the texts of the last Council are based largely on the Bible. This was possible thanks to the intensive research by the biblical sciences in the decades that preceded the Council. Biblical science has proved of great importance for the hermeneutic of reform: it helps to distinguish "truth which God wanted put into sacred writings (5) for the sake of salvation" (*DV* 11), from those aspects that remain conditioned by time.

We bring here an example, to show how difficult it is to distinguish between binding traditions and constraints that are subject to time. This difficulty appeared in all its magnitude during Vatican II on the topic of collegiality. A sizeable number of the Council fathers were of the mind that the doctrine of collegiality was irreconcilable with the dogma of Vatican I on the primacy of the successor of Peter.[4] On the contrary, the majority of the Council fathers and theologians believed that the doctrine of collegiality of the episcopal ministry was founded on the Bible and that it remained doctrine and practice of the Church until the nineteenth century. Based on its theory of the continuing evolution of the dogmas, the minority argued that only in the nineteenth century had the Church come to full recognition of the primacy of the pope. Since this dispute between the Council fathers could not be solved, Paul VI found himself compelled to add the *Nota explicativa praevia* (preliminary note of explanation) to the Constitution *Lumen Gentium*. It allowed the minority to ascertain that the dogma of Vatican I had been considered, and that the centralized guidance of the universal Church had been assured.

Only after Vatican II did the study of Vatican I intensify.[5] It was thus noted that Vatican I did not intend to deny and reject the traditional doctrine of collegiality, but rather to consider it a binding tradition and practice of the Church. The spiritual and temporal needs of the nineteenth-century Church, and the desire to strengthen the position of the pope, ensured the diffusion after Vatican I of a maximalist interpretation of the two dogmas of primacy and infallibility of the pope, which claimed for the latter an internal and external sovereignty.

Thus, we know now that during Vatican II the minority was reading the dogmas of Vatican I through the lens of a maximalist interpretation, and confounded them with a form of primacy linked to the historical situation. This fact gives us the ability to operate an update on the relationship between primacy and collegiality. The dogma of Vatican I is no longer an obstacle.

The direction in which the reform plans of most of the Council fathers of Vatican II moved can be inferred by their reaction to the first schema of the Constitution on the Church. The first schema is mentioned in the first chapter, the "Nature of the Church Militant."[6] It was the nineteenth-century image of the Church: the Church as a hierarchical institution, as *societas perfecta*, which, facing the errors of the times, was trying to defend itself from the outside even against the loss of its spiritual, social, and political power in Europe that it had enjoyed until then. The criticism that the Council fathers moved against this schema spoke of triumphalism, clericalism, and legalism. They demanded that instead of that, the constitution should reveal the spirit of the gospel, a missionary spirit, and the spirit of service.

The Mystery of the Church

That is precisely what we read in the first chapter of *Lumen Gentium*, titled "The Mystery of the Church."[7] From the beginning, it clearly establishes a difference from a triumphalist conception. Not the Church, but Christ is the "light of the nations." And the primary task of the Church is not to give security to herself, but to carry out its mission. "The Church is in Christ like a sacrament or as a sign and instrument both of a very closely knit union with God and of the unity of the whole human race" (*LG* 1). The Church as a sacrament for the salvation of the world is a dominant theme that runs through many of the Council documents (*LG* 1, 9, 48, 49; *GS* 45; *SC* 26; *AG* 1, 5). The goal of the Council was a missionary pastoral plan.

Several times it is pointed out that the mission of the Church does not justify any claim to power. "The Church...is not set up to seek earthly glory, but to proclaim, even by its own example, humility and self-sacrifice" (*LG* 8). The Council thus wanted to do away with such a specific image of the Church, the one that still characterized the first schema of the Constitution.

The origins of the Church belong to its mystery. The Church is founded on the action of the triune God and it is his image. Thus, the Church has been seen as "a people made one with the unity of the Father, the Son and the Holy Spirit." (*LG* 4). The reference to the trinitarian unity of God opens the view on the unity of Church in its multiplicity—as opposed to a centralized uniqueness. In its unfolding is made manifest the work of the Father, of the Son made man, and of the Holy Spirit: the Church is the people of God, the Body of Christ, and temple of the Holy Spirit.

Finally, the place in salvation history of the Church belongs to its mystery. The Church is "the kingdom of Christ now present in mystery" (*LG* 3); "on earth, the initial budding forth of that kingdom" (*LG* 5). The Church, therefore, is not an end in itself, but a sacrament of God's kingdom and his coming. The Church is the call of God addressed to all men.

In what follows—and in explicit contrast to the first schema and its legalism—a series of biblical images are applied to the Church. In addition, her sacramental nature is emphasized: sacramental, because it "form one complex reality which coalesces from a divine and a human element." Therefore, the Church "by no weak analogy, it is compared to the mystery of the incarnate Word" (*LG* 8). The "divine element" of the Church is perpetually incarnate in a human and historical figure, which must continually turn to the word and example of Jesus Christ.

The mystery of the Church aside, the discourse on the complex reality of the Church leads to its existence and its configuration in the world, which corresponds to *LG*'s second chapter, the one on the people of God. The Church, understood as the people of God on the way toward the full realization of God's kingdom, became the characteristic pattern of conciliar ecclesiology. The idea of the complex reality of the Church, which is the foundation of the hermeneutic of reform, rightly constitutes the element that connects the two chapters. The people of God must in fact face two challenges: the fidelity to its mystery, and pastoral care in the contemporary world.

The Church in the Modern World

Essentially, the Second Vatican Council, as it has rarely happened in those councils that preceded it, dealt with the social context of its time. This transpired in the Pastoral Constitution on the Church in the Modern World: *Gaudium et Spes*. The Dogmatic Constitution on the Church and the Pastoral Constitution are closely tied together. The world today is both the historical site of which the Church is a part, and the recipient of its mission. And in this sense the analysis of the contemporary world is part of the hermeneutic of reform that the Council has followed. The Council fathers rejected the first schema also for the fact that it adhered to an anachronistic and Eurocentric image of society and the Church. In the meantime, the Church has found herself in a globalized and pluralistic world, where faith and the Church are no longer part of the public order and the dominant power. This society is no longer centered on the principle of tradition, but on the principle of self-determination.[8]

The hermeneutic of reform came into operation also in relation to the right to self-determination. The Council made a distinction between the right to freedom and self-determination intended as autonomous, or as theonomous. If, as usual, it refused the first, it however proclaimed the second. "For this Gospel," as in the Pastoral Constitution, "announces and proclaims the freedom of the sons of God, and repudiates all the bondage which ultimately results from sin (cf. Rom 8:14–17); it has a sacred reverence for the dignity of conscience and its freedom of choice" (*GS* 41). Indeed, the Council considered that the development of the right to freedom, understood as theonomous, is a "sign of the times" (*GS* 4, 11), showing the coming of the kingdom of God in our history. On this basis, the Council declared itself in favor of freedom of religion and of the "autonomy of earthly affairs" (*GS* 36). Moreover, Paul VI gave visible signs testifying to this evolution.[9] He deposed the tiara and abolished the papal court, that is, the symbols of the monarchical form of authority of the Church. The introduction of age limits for bishops and curial officials was no less important a break with the past. The internationalization of the Curia was a response to the increasing globalization of the Church.

Anyone today who reflects on the reform of the Church cannot avoid analyzing the world and society of today, as did the Council.[10] To that end, theology and the Church need the help offered by the humanities, and social and historical sciences. These help to identify those aspects of the historical figure of the Church and the way in which she exercises her authority that prevent the Church from reaching the people of today with its message.

Why, after the Council, did a certain disappointment emerge from the fact that its attempts and its reform projects produced only limited effects? Here we must mention two realities that have emerged after the Council. On the one hand, there was the postconciliar crisis that John XXIII had expected, thanks to his knowledge of the history of the Church. Many Catholics began to doubt the truth of their faith, because they were no longer able to distinguish between the usual historical form of the Church, which was changing, and the permanent truth of its message. In addition, thousands of priests and religious left their ministries or their communities. The other reality was represented by the so-called youth revolt, which broke out immediately after the Council. Young people rebelled against the supposed authoritarian faith of their parents, asking for the democratization in all fields, even in the Church. Their rebellion was accompanied by the so-called sexual revolution, brought about in part by the introduction of an effective contraceptive pill. In 1968, the encyclical *Humanae Vitae* was issued, which led many Catholics to take a critical view of the magisterial authority and of the Church's ethics on marriage and sexuality.

Even today, sexuality and marriage are spheres in which the faithful are making a stronger claim for their self-determination before the Church's magisterium. But the need for self-determination is not only limited to this field. In democratic and pluralistic societies, in which tradition and obedience are no longer the motivations that drive behavior, the Church must increasingly take into account the understanding and personal conviction of her faithful, and to strengthen the reasons for gratitude and love of God, so that the faithful can welcome her message and norms. Evangelization has thus become even more demanding. However, in the history of Christianity this kind of motivation is not completely unknown: in the words of a German bishop, our world has become no longer un-Christian, but more proto-Christian.

It was only expected that the break with the different traditions and the need for self-determination, often shrouded in a claim to autonomy, would cause a reaction. Authoritative voices in the Church warn against any adjustment to the contemporary world. This has led to a polarization between the members of the various local churches, especially in the Western world. It can also be noted that in the Church, now become global, particular churches have emerged where the need for self-determination does not have the same relevance as in Europe and the United States. All this was also made clear at the last synod of bishops and, significantly, in the sphere of sexual and marriage morals.

The Church at a Crossroads

Faced with this situation, there are two alternatives. As a first reaction, one is tempted to correct the bias with a forced centrist interventionism, to ensure the unity of the Church. The alternative could consist in assuming once again the task of aggiornamento, remaining faithful to the Council. The lament of the Bishops' Conferences, during the pontificate of John Paul II, on a centralism that was regaining strength is an indication that the first alternative was already in place. Certainly, Pope John Paul II accepted and further explored in many ways the requests of Vatican II. But, because of his frequent absence from Rome, the Roman curia felt entitled to remedy the polarization itself, that is, with more directives and control. Today many are asking whether a forced centralism is not paralyzing the Church just like the dangers she intends to fight.

Many signs point to the belief that Pope Francis intends to choose the second alternative, and to reconnect to the reform attempts of the Council and Paul VI. His giving more power to the Synod of Bishops is one example. Centralism characterizes a style of government from top to bottom that emphasizes the authority of the leader and is inspired by the principles and rules that the government must instill and control so they are observed. Pope Francis made it clear, however, that he wants to make room for dialogue from the bottom up, taking account of the people with their concerns and problems so that pastoral care does not fall on deaf ears. By doing so he is reconnecting with a fundamental intent of the Council, which thought of an aggiornamento of pastoral care.

Pope Francis knows well that he cannot carry out his plan without the cooperation of the Roman curia. In his openly critical speech of December 22, 2014, he called on the curia to take a new course. The real responsible parties who decide an aggiornamento together with the pope, however, are not the members of the curia, but the bishops as successors of the apostles and leaders of their local churches. Through them, even local churches and their members, each with their own voice, take on a role, and can make their voices heard.

An influential model in this respect can be considered the so-called Apostolic Council (Acts 15:1–33), which decided on the first aggiornamento of the Church.[11] In addition to the apostles, even the *leaders* participated in the decision, thus including the whole community. In this sense, Vatican II has repeatedly argued that pastors must consider the advice and assistance of "those who live in the world, [who] are versed in different institutions and specialties, and grasp their innermost significance" (*GS* 44). Following the model of the Apostolic Council, Pope Francis, in preparing the last synod of bishops, called for the inclusion of the local churches and their members as well.

In synods and councils, the *communio fidelium* and the *communio eccelesiarum* become particularly visible. To emphasize even more the important dual role of the bishops, as successors of the apostles and as leaders and spokespersons of their local churches, it is only appropriate that episcopal ordination no longer be a requirement to take on certain positions in the curia.

The apostolic council is an influential model for making decisions on the aggiornamento of the Church, from another point of view. As it was then in Jerusalem, a decision of that kind is a largely spiritual event. To reach a decision requires the prayer of the whole Church, so it can be inspired and can discern God's will, which the Holy Spirit makes manifest. We can ask ourselves whether the consultation of the faithful before the last synod of bishops took place following precisely this model and these criteria.

Church as the People of God

But let us return to the Council. After the first chapter on the mystery of the Church, the second chapter of *Lumen Gentium* deals with the Church as the people of God. This chapter, as the previous one, is a reaction to the first schema of the Constitution on the Church. The latter regarded the Church as an institution primarily structured hierarchically. In its place, the main theme of *Lumen Gentium* becomes what is common to all members of the Church and makes them jointly responsible subjects of its mission. And this has also changed the usual concept of the people of God. This expression no longer defines the faithful as separate from the hierarchy, but the Church in its totality.[12]

This passage of the Council can be truly considered a *re-volution*, better yet, a *re-volutio* in the original sense of the term, and in two ways. On the one hand, the Council turned to the concept of the Church as God's people that we find in the testimonies of the Bible and of the early Church. On the other, the Council has sought to reformulate the structure of the Church to put her back on her feet. Over the centuries, in fact, the Church was biased in favor of the hierarchy and the laity had become mere recipients of the mediation of salvation wrought by ordained ministers. Instead, for the Council the whole people of God is responsible for evangelization.

Finally, of this holy *re-volution* of the Council, the option for the poor has an eminent part. The Church is sent in a special way to the needy and the oppressed. It must carry out this mission in following Jesus, "in poverty and persecution" (*LG* 8; cf. *GS* 42; *CD* 13; *PO* 6; *AA* 8; *AG* 12; *UR* 12).

After all, it was not only the testimony of the Bible and of the early Church to lead the Council to this *re-volution*. There was also the realization that in a society in which the Church as an institution has lost its authority, it is also the testimony of the laity that reaches and persuades people. In his apostolic exhortation *Evangelii Nuntiandi*, still relevant today, Paul VI said, "Modern man listens more willingly to witnesses than to teachers, and if he does listen to teachers, it is because they are witnesses" (*EN* 41).

People of God as *Communio Fidelium*

As for the chapter of *Lumen Gentium* on the people of God, it is worth noting not only the fact that it is placed before the chapter on the hierarchy; it also develops a theology of the people of God that justifies this precedence. It is the trinitarian mystery of the Church, described in the first chapter, that now grounds and creates in the second the communion and sharing of the mission among the members of God's people: the essential configuration of the people of God as *communio fidelium*, as well as the common priesthood, and the gifts of the Spirit in God's people.

The Council established the *communio* of the people of God on the Trinity; actually, it sees *aliquam similitudinem* (a certain similarity; *LG* 24) between the trinitarian *communio* of God and God's people understood as *communio fidelium*. The Church is in fact *de unitate Patris et Filii et Spiritus Sancti plebs adunata* (a people made one with the unity of the Father, the Son ,and the Holy Spirit; *LG* 4), *a Christo in communionem vitae, caritatis, et veritatis constituta* (established by Christ as a communion of life, charity, and truth, *LG* 9), and in *Spiritu sancto congregata* (*CD* 11). Thus, the Synod of Bishops in 1985 saw in the nature of the Church as communion a "fundamental idea of the Council's documents" (II C 1). And this means that the more the Church lives of its *communio* with the Father through Jesus Christ in the Holy Spirit, the more it gains the possibility of becoming a *communio fidelium* in its heart and figure. In short: the maturing of the people of God toward *communio* is ultimately a spiritual challenge. That was the intention that John Paul II indicated as the program of the Great Jubilee of 2000, in his apostolic exhortation *Tertio Millennio Adveniente* of 1994.

There are some who have wanted to replace the expression *people of God* with *communio* as the fundamental concept of the Church. However, we must adhere to the people of God as a basic concept to indicate the Church as the acting agent that is supported by many individual agents. Instead *communio* designates their joint participation and their way of feeling, that is, as a trait of God's people.

One element of their joint participation is the common priesthood, which gives all members of the Body of Christ the right to participate in the activity and the priestly task of the Church, basing it on the ministry of Christ (*LG* 9). While retaining the distinction between "common priesthood" and "ministerial priesthood," the priesthood no longer divides God's people into two classes, as was characteristic for a long time for the Catholic Church. For the Council, all members of God's people form a "priestly community" (*LG* 11), in which "all share a true equality with regard to the dignity and to the activity common to all the faithful for the building up of the Body of Christ" (*LG* 32). The ministerial priesthood is at the service of the common priesthood. These statements are shaped by the spirit of the holy revolution undertaken by Vatican II. They shift the weights and in doing so change the figure of the Church, without ever denying a single dogma of the Church. This is an example of the hermeneutic of reform that the Council has put into practice.

The traits of a holy *re-volution* become evident even in the way the Council founded the Church as the people of God in a pneumatological sense (*LG* 12). For centuries, the hierarchy and its magisterium claimed for itself a monopoly on the possession of the Spirit. Charisms were mainly attributed to religious orders. Of course, it is wrong to say that the Council has operated a sort of "democratization" of the possession of the Spirit, as some so-called liberals are inclined to think. However, it is interesting to note that the Council explicitly attributes to the people of God, as a whole, and to its *sensus fidei*, infallibility *in credendo* (in belief). And that is intended by the Council not only in a passive sense, but also in a clearly active one, that is, as an industrious safekeeping, a living testimony, and an ever-deeper understanding of the faith. In his apostolic exhortation *Novo Millennio Ineunte*, John Paul II exhorted the bishops, citing Paulinus of Nola, "Let us listen to what all the faithful say, because in every one of them the Spirit of God breathes" (no. 45).

The Holy Spirit gives to the faithful "of every rank"—as the Council underlined—"charisms, whether they be the more outstanding or the more simple and widely diffused" (*LG* 12). With John Paul II, we may wonder if this spiritual capital is valued and used enough, when it comes to the aggiornamento of the Church. There were women like Catherine of Siena, Teresa of Avila, and Hildegard of Bingen who, with their charisms, sparked reforms in the Church. Are there also large numbers women today who, with their guidance and initiative, and assuming positions of responsibility, could contribute to the aggiornamento of the Church? The Council on this point opened the door.

The People of God as *Communion Ecclesiarum*

The *communio fidelium* is lived concretely in local churches. *Communio* as an essential feature of the people of God is expressed in structural terms in the *communio ecclesiarum*. The third chapter of *Lumen Gentium* clearly says that the *communio ecclesiarum* belongs to the fundamental structure of the people of God: "This Church of Christ is truly present in all legitimate local congregations of the faithful which, united with their pastors, are themselves called churches in the New Testament" (*LG* 26). And "in and from which churches comes into being the one and only Catholic Church" (*LG* 23). Unfortunately, the *communio ecclesiarum* in the third chapter of *Lumen Gentium* is only a secondary theme compared to the *communio hierarchica*.

The same is not true regarding the second chapter, in the context of an ecclesiology of the people of God. Here it is noted that the coexistence of local churches so different among themselves, and with their own traditions, is an enrichment for the entire Church. It is in fact stated that

> in virtue of this catholicity each individual part contributes through its special gifts to the good of the other parts and of the whole Church. Through the common sharing of gifts and through the common effort to attain fullness in unity, the whole and each of the parts receive increase....Moreover, within the Church particular Churches hold a rightful place; these Churches retain their own traditions, without in any way opposing the primacy of the Chair of Peter, which presides over the whole assembly of charity and protects legitimate differences, while at the same time assuring that such differences do not hinder unity but rather contribute toward it. (*LG* 13)

The task mentioned here—that is, to find the right balance between the necessary unity and a possible multiplicity—is not new. In a Church that has become global and that sees itself as the people of God, this task is posed with an urgency that is both new and greater. Today it is an important aspect of the aggiornamento. The question is to include in this issue a policy that so far has been mainly Eurocentric and more centristic, and turn it into a policy that considers the wider cultural diversity and the diversity of pastoral challenges in the local churches. As indicated in the quote above, the Council considered that a wider variety represented an opportunity rather than a threat to unity, and precisely as an opportunity for *plenitudo in unitate*.

To achieve this goal, we must expand the powers of the episcopal conferences.[13] Forcing an entire linguistic area to translate the language of the liturgy as dictated by Rome, as was the case for the English-speaking world, is an indication of centralism.

To dismantle centralism, we must also restructure the primacy of the successor of Peter, still understood in a monarchical sense, turning it into a primacy of communion.[14] A step in this direction was the proposal of Joseph Ratzinger, who asked to clarify the Petrine and patriarchal functions of the Bishop of Rome. In fact, as Ratzinger said, "The unitary canonical law, the unitary liturgy, the unified assignment of episcopal sees by Rome—are all things that are not necessarily tied to primacy as such, but derive from this close conjunction of two different offices," the Petrine and the patriarchal.[15] The same Ratzinger, as Pope Benedict XVI, took a step forward in this direction when in 2006 he eliminated the designation *Occidentis Patriarca* from the official papal titles. The role of new patriarchal spaces, in which reciprocal horizontal connections are expressed—another proposal from Ratzinger—is safeguarded today in a certain sense by the continental episcopal conferences, albeit without the necessary authority.

The Reception of *Lumen Gentium* in Pope Francis's Exhortation *Evangelii Gaudium*

To define and understand the Church as the people of God: do we find this element of Vatican II in Pope Francis' apostolic exhortation *Evangelii Gaudium*? In this document, the pope has traced the guidelines and intent of his pontificate. The theme of the exhortation—"The Proclamation of the Gospel in Today's World"—was suggested to him by the Synod of Bishops, and he followed this advice in an entirely personal and original way. Above all, it is striking that the exhortation is dictated by the experience of a pastor of souls and bishop. Contrary to the gloomy tone found in some local churches, its main theme is that faith and proclamation of the gospel are sources of joy and happiness.

Recalling *Lumen Gentium*, Pope Francis in his exhortation speaks of "the reform of the Church in her missionary outreach"—the "the Church, understood as the entire People of God which evangelizes" (*EG* 17). In fact, here we find a really timely synthesis of the conciliar ecclesiology of the people of God, when the pope writes about the Church as

> the agent of evangelization, is more than an organic and hierarchical institution; she is first and foremost a people advancing on its pilgrim way towards God. She is certainly a mystery rooted in the Trinity, yet she exists concretely in history as a people of pilgrims and evangelizers, transcending any institutional expression, however necessary. (*EG* 111)

What is paradigmatic here is the distinction between the permanent nature of the Church and its historical form—the distinction that is dealt with by the hermeneutic of reform.

Other themes from *Lumen Gentium* that are relevant to Francis are the Church as a sacrament of salvation (*EG* 112); the faithful as subjects of evangelization, with its own *sensus fidei* and charisms (*EG* 119, 130); and the people of God as "communion and mission" (*EG* 23). It is his concern to grant more space in the Church to the cultural diversity of the peoples (*EG* 115–18): "When properly understood, cultural diversity is not a threat to Church unity" (*EG* 117).

A fundamental purpose of the exhortation is to realize "renewal of structures demanded by pastoral conversion" (*EG* 27). "The Second Vatican Council presented ecclesial conversion as openness to a constant self-renewal born of fidelity to Jesus Chris" (*EG* 26). In fact—as the pope said—there may be structures that could endanger a dynamic of evangelization; among these, even "the papacy and the central structures of the universal Church" are no exception. From the day when John Paul II asked for help to exercise his leadership in a form more suited to the contemporary world, "we have made little progress" (*EG* 32).

Regarding the desire of the Council—as stated by Pope Francis—for the episcopal conferences to assume the tasks of the ancient patriarchal churches, "this desire has not been fully realized." In conclusion, the pope says, "Excessive centralization, rather than proving helpful, complicates the Church's life and her missionary outreach" (*EG* 32).

In short: in *Evangelii Gaudium* Pope Francis not only acknowledges the assertion of *Lumen Gentium* of the Church as the people of God, but his exhortation reflects the spirit of the Council as well, the spirit that invites us all on a journey.

To conclude, as a guideline of our reflections on what the Council has to say today regarding this journey that we must undertake, we chose the hermeneutic of reform. It is not only the key to understanding how the same Council understood the task of aggiornamento. The Church today should also orient itself toward it in her quest to find her true face as the people of God. Faced with the difficult distinction between the "divine element," which must remain firm in the Church, and its human configuration, we must not recoil even today from the discussion, to determine the extent to which we can and should reach a reform. But even this is part of the Church as the people of God on its pilgrim way. On one thing, however, there can be no doubt, something that was very precious to the Second Vatican Council: the *communio* among the members of the people of God can only increase to the extent that their *communio* with the triune God increases as well.

NOTES

1. See F. X. Kaufmann and A. Zingerle, eds., *Vatikanum II und Modernisierung. Historische, theologische und soziologische Perspektiven* (Paderborn: Schöningh, 1996).

2. G. Routhier, "Sull'interpretazione del Vaticano II. L'ermeneutica della riforma, compito per la teologia," *La Rivista del Clero Italiano* 11 (2011): 744–59 and 827–41; Chr. Theobald, "L'herméneutique de réforme implique-t-elle une réforme de l'herméneutique?," *Recherches de science religieuse* 100 (2012): 65–84; J.-H. Tück, "Die Verbindlichkeit des Konzils. Die Hermeneutik der Reform als Interpretationsschlüssel," in *Erinnerung an die Zukunft. Das Zweite Vatikanische Konzil*, ed. J.-H. Tück (Freiburg: Herder, 2012), 85–104.

3. Benedict XVI, Address to the Roman Curia, December 22, 2005: http://w2.vatican.va/content/benedict-xvi/en/speeches/2005/december/documents/hf_ben_xvi_spe_20051222_roman-curia.html.

4. See H. J. Pottmeyer, "Recent Discussions on Primacy in Relation to Vatican I," in *Il ministero petrino. Cattolici e ortodossi in dialogo*, ed. W. Kasper (Rome: Città Nuova, 2004), 227–47. Translated by the Staff of the Pontifical Council for Promoting Christian Unity as *The Petrine Ministry: Catholics and Orthodox in Dialogue* (New York: Newman Press, 2005).

5. See K. L. Schatz, *Vaticanum I 1869–1870*, 3 vols. (Paderborn: Schöningh, 1992–1994).

6. See G. Philips, "Die Geschichte der Dogmatischen Konstitution über die Kirche 'Lumen gentium,'" in *Lexikon für Theologie und Kirche. Das Zweite Vatikanische Konzil. Dokumente und Kommentare*, vol. 1 (Freiburg: Herder, 1966), 139–41.

7. See K. Rahner, *Kommentar zu Artikel* 18–27, in *Lexikon für Theologie und Kirche*, 1:210–46.

8. See P. Hünermann, ed., *Das Zweite Vatikanische Konzil und die Zeichen der Zeit heute* (Freiburg: Herder, 2006).

9. P. Hebblethwaite, *Paul VI: The First Modern Pope* (New York: Paulist Press, 1993).

10. See F.-X. Kaufmann, *Quale futuro per il cristianesimo?* (Brescia: Queriniana, 2002). Originally published as *Wie überlebt das Christentum* (Freiburg: Herder, 2000).

11. See H. Söding, "Das Apostelkonzil als Paradebeispiel kirchlicher Konfliktlösung. Anspruch, Wirklichkeit und Wirkung," in *Dialogprozesse in der katholischen Kirche. Begründungen—Voraussetzungen—Formen*, ed. J. Wiemeyer (Paderborn Schöningh, 2013), 25–34.

12. See H. J. Pottmeyer, "Dal sinodo del 1985 al grande Giubileo dell'anno 2000," in *Il Concilio Vaticano II. Recezione e attualità alla luce del Giubileo*, ed. R. Fisichella (Cinisello Balsamo: San Paolo, 2000), 11–25.

13. See H. Müller and H. J. Pottmeyer, *Die Bischofskonferenz. Theologischer und juridischer Status* (Düsseldorf: Patmos, 1989).

14. See H. J. Pottmeyer, *Il ruolo del papato nel terzo millennio* (Brescia: Queriniana, 2002).

15. J. Ratzinger, *Il nuovo popolo di Dio. Questioni ecclesiologiche* (Brescia: Queriniana, 1992^4), 155ff. Originally published as *Das neue Volk Gottes* (Düsseldorf: Patmos, 1969), 142. See H. J. Pottmeyer, "Primato—collegialità episcopale nella ecclesiologia di Joseph Ratzinger" in *Primato e collegialità. "Partecipi della sollecitudine per tutte le Chiese,"* ed. R. La Delfa (Rome: Città Nuova, 2008), 71–90.

II

THE LESSONS OF HISTORY ABOUT THE REFORM OF THE CHURCH

4

REFORM IN THE LIFE OF THE CHURCH

The Council of Trent and Vatican II

John W. O'Malley, SJ

Today anyone with even the slightest knowledge of the Christian Church knows that in its long history it has undergone significant changes in its organization, in its theological styles, in the forms by which it has exercised its authority, and in many other ways. Change endangers identity, but it is also a condition for maintaining it by acting as a remedy for ossification and irrelevance.

Change has occurred in the Church in two basic ways, either as a result of events or developments over which the Church had virtually no control, or within the Church itself as the result of deliberate decisions taken by leaders of the community. Many of the most radical changes came as a result of the first alternative. Few events had a more lasting and profound impact on the Church than Emperor Constantine's edict of toleration and his subsequent actions granting Christianity a favored place in his empire. Other examples abound. But in recent history perhaps the most telling and most troubling for our conference on Church reform is the radical shift in historical consciousness with which we all live today.

We are thus reminded of two things: first, that the Church has very imperfect control over the course of its history, and, second, that the deliberate decisions taken within the Church in view of reform do not occur in a vacuum but are often a reaction to changes occurring "outside" the Church. In such cases the decisions are often an unacknowledged form of aggiornamento.

In this book, we are concerned with that second alternative, deliberate decisions. Reform is traditionally defined as *mutatio in melius*, that is, change as a presumed improvement on the status quo. Lateran Council IV, 1215, provided a succinct norm for when such changes should be undertaken, namely, when called for by "urgent necessity or evident utility" (*urgens necessitas vel evidens utilitas*).

We are focused on reforms enacted by official, hierarchical Church leadership, that is, by the Bishop of Rome and by other bishops, especially when gathered in council. I have organized what I have to say about such reform into four periods; (1) the first millennium, (2) the Latin Middle Ages, (3) the Council of Trent and its aftermath, and (4) Vatican II to the present. During the second and third periods, the popes moved from being the most aggressive agents of reform, to being considered the chief obstacle to reform, to presiding over a Church supposedly not needing reform. With Vatican II reform again surged to the surface. I look both at what happened during these periods and at what the understandings of reform were that were used to justify what happened. Until Vatican II those understandings changed comparatively little.[1]

From the earliest centuries well into the modern era, deliberate decisions of substance rested in the hands of councils or synods, words traditionally used synonymously, which includes of course the hundreds upon hundreds of local councils/synods.[2] Although they were in communion with the Holy See, they functioned independently of it and made decisions binding on the local Church. From a historical viewpoint, traditional Church governance was synodal governance.

As early as the second century at least fifty councils/synods were held in Palestine, North Africa, Rome, Gaul, and elsewhere. The Council of Trent, we recall, prescribed that bishops hold annual synods and that metropolitans hold triennial synods of their province, a provision Carlo Borromeo carried out in such a thorough fashion as to influence the whole Church. In the young United

States between 1829 and 1886, the bishops held in Baltimore twenty diocesan, provincial, and plenary councils—an average of about one every three years but none after 1886. With the definitions of primacy and infallibility, synods lost their vitality and, despite the Code of 1917 requiring bishops to hold one at least every ten years (#356), ever fewer took place.

As Gerhard Ladner showed many decades ago, reform within the Christian tradition has to be understood in the context of the conversion of heart and the reform of life propounded in the New Testament.[3] Nonetheless, the immediate vehicle for dealing with problems within the Christian community were the legislative and judicial institutions of the Roman Empire. By the second century, bishops had adopted and adapted these institutions for their own purposes in the form of local councils and then with Nicaea in 325 in the form of a Church-wide council.

Although each of these councils/synods had its own specific characteristics, every one of them can be defined as a meeting principally of bishops who are gathered in Christ's name to make decisions binding on the Church. From the beginning bishops enjoyed the determinative voice in councils, but also from the beginning until Vatican I the laity played important, often crucial roles. A striking instance of lay participation is the Fourth Lateran Council. When Pope Innocent III convoked it, he insisted on the broadest possible participation. Present at the council, therefore, were four hundred bishops, eight hundred abbots and superiors of other religious bodies, envoys of the emperor and the kings of France, England, Hungary, Jerusalem, and Cyprus. A number of counts and their vassals came in person. In speaking of these persons as laity, I am of course using a modern shorthand because the sharp distinction between the two orders that we make today took a long time to develop.

Church reforms have had different magnitudes.[4] The simplest is reform within a system without significant alteration of the system itself, as with the many reforms of the Roman curia since 1588. More comprehensive is reform by replacing one system with another, yet within the boundaries of a larger system. When in 1588 Pope Sixtus V replaced the consistorial mode of the Roman curia's operation with fifteen Congregations, with a cardinal heading each of them, he created a new system that would operate like a modern bureaucracy, the system we have today.[5] Yet his system did not challenge the system in place since the Gregorian Reform of the eleventh century, when the cardinals began to assume a leadership role in central governance.

The most radical is a replacement, at least inchoately, of one comprehensive system or paradigm with a new comprehensive system/paradigm. Although the Gregorian reformers certainly did not formulate their reform in this manner, they in effect strove to replace with another system the feudal and familial relationships upon which early medieval society rested. The alternate name for the Gregorian Reform, the Investiture Controversy, itself suggests a confrontation of systems.

The Gregorian system was characterized by strong centralized authority and rationalized procedures based upon ancient legal texts that overrode feudal customs. The Gregorian reformers, in the name of restoring an older and more authentic paradigm of Church order, created a new paradigm or system whose defining center was papal authority. The Gregorian Reform is the great watershed in the history of the Western Church.

The best proof of the radical nature of what the Gregorians attempted is the fierce resistance their efforts met, which led to civil war in Germany, the invasion of Italy by imperial troops, and the death in ignominious exile of the greatest protagonist of the Reform, Pope Saint Gregory VII himself. We can take as axiomatic that the degree of resistance a change sparks is in direct proportion to its challenge to the system in possession.

But there is a quite specific reason the Gregorian Reform is crucial to the problem of Church reform as it developed in the West. The Gregorian Reform can be said to begin with Emperor Henry III's intervention in the Synod of Sutri in 1043 and with his subsequent appointments of the bishop of Rome. By means of these interventions, the emperor rescued the papacy from the disarray and moral morass into which it had wallowed for well over a century. He set in motion the series of reforming popes that began in earnest with his cousin, Pope Saint Leo IX, the first of the Gregorian reformers.

Events soon forced the reformers to undertake a reform of papal elections, and in so doing they provided their reform with an institutional grounding that ensured its future. A decree by Pope

Nicholas II in 1059 for the first time put the election into the hands of cardinals, primarily the bishops of the nearby sees such as Ostia and Palestrina. For a long time, these bishops had been quasi-incardinated into the diocese of Rome, in that they often presided at liturgical ceremonies in the great basilicas of the city.

The decree of 1059 transformed this essentially liturgical and politically inert body of clergy into one of the most powerful forces in the Church by placing the election of the pope in its hands. From its ranks, moreover, most popes would in the future be elected. The decree also transformed the Roman curia, which in time came to be dominated by the cardinals. The cardinals' influence increased as they helped increase the influence of the popes. The decree rationalized the election process, and it at the same time created a body whose interests and fortunes were tied to what had become the central, even if only implicit, tenet of the Gregorian movement, enhancement of papal authority.

The First Millennium

But let us first look at reform in the first millennium, which was reform undertaken by councils. I have space to speak only of those recognized as ecumenical. They are important for five reasons: First, they were convoked by laypersons, one of whom was a woman, the Empress Irene. Second, the bishops of Rome, though always especially honored, played roles ranging from marginal to important but never determinative.

Third, in them we find clear beginnings of official Church reform as a Church-wide concern, even though the words *reform* and *reformation* never occur in them. Nicaea I, for instance, speaks of the need to "amputate" and "cut off" certain customs that have sprung up. Constantinople I speaks of the need of some Churches for "emendation," which seems to refer to a restoration of doctrinal health in areas touched by heresy. Chalcedon speaks of the need for "correction" in certain provinces of the failure to hold regular synods.

The fourth reason these councils are important is because behind such metaphors lay an important presupposition about reform, which consists not only in some form of reinstatement of a normative past but a past transmitted unchanged as it passes through the vicissitudes of history. Except in the case of heretics or local bad custom, there is no suggestion of discontinuity between past and present. In this view of history, the Church is a kind of unchanging substance that sails through the sea of history without being affected by it. As we all know, this presupposition would persist in Catholicism, though with ever-diminishing credibility, at least into the twentieth century.

The fifth reason these councils are important is because they betray so clearly that they are operating as legislative and judicial bodies, operating as the ecclesiastical equivalent of the correlative institutions of the Roman Empire. If the so-called Council of Jerusalem (Acts 15) served as biblical justification for councils, the Roman Senate provided the implicit model for how the councils actually functioned.

It seems clear that when Constantine convoked Nicaea, he conceived of it as somehow the ecclesiastical equivalent of the Senate, whose function was to secure public order in the empire. Like the Senate, the council exercised its judicial function by hearing the case against Arius and rendering judgment on him for the high ecclesiastical crime of propagating heresy. From this time forward councils reformed doctrine simply by condemning deviations from its authentic form and by imposing penalties on the offending parties.

The Council of Nicaea exercised the Senate's legislative function by passing laws prescribing or proscribing certain public behavior, especially of clerics. The laws generally included penalties for nonobservance, often an anathema. Thus, with Nicaea was set the model to which all councils conformed down to Vatican II. Although of course the remote goal of councils was the good of souls, their immediate goal was proper public order in the Church in both doctrine and discipline.

The Latin Middle Ages

Constantinople IV (late ninth century), was the last of the Eastern, Greek councils recognized by the West. The next council thus recognized, Lateran I, held in Rome and convoked by the pope, did not meet not until two and a half centuries later, in 1123. The propelling force behind the ultimate emergence of the popes as the conveners was the Gregorian Reform. The religious and cultural alienation between East and West had grown during the intervening period and culminated in the Schism of 1054, an event for which the Gregorian reformers were largely responsible. From this point forward, a Western, Roman, papal Church developed as a reality virtually self-contained and markedly distinct from what had gone before.

The leaders of the Gregorian Reform sharpened the old idea that reform meant a retrieving of the normative past. They engaged, that is, in a naive form of ressourcement, now more explicitly articulated than in the first millennium but not more critically analyzed. They were convinced that two sacred traditions of the Church—clerical celibacy and the free election of bishops—were being seriously abused. They found those traditions in the ancient canons, genuine and forged, of the Roman Church, and they set about with utter determination to make the canons operative once again.

The reformers were at least partially responsible for the fact that the word *reformare* begins explicitly to appear in council documents and eventually become an insistent theme, a particularly Western phenomenon. They were also at least partially responsible that the belief explicitly appears that certain abuses infected almost the whole Church. That belief became explosive during the Great Western Schism, 1378 to 1418, when two, then three men claimed the papal throne.

It comes as no surprise, therefore, that demands for reform climaxed at the Council of Constance (1414–1418), convoked to resolve the Schism, and then at the Council of Basel (1431–1437), convoked still in the wake of the Schism. At Constance the seemingly all-inclusive formula took hold in the call for "reform of the Church in faith and mores, in head and members," *ecclesia sit reformata in fide et moribus, in capite et in membris.*

Although the popes of the post-Constance period were not altogether insensible to the need for reform, they heard with alarm the cry for reform of "the head," which of course meant themselves and their curia. They became increasingly defensive and even obstructive of efforts by subsequent councils to move in that direction. Whereas until the Council of Constance, popes could call upon councils to support them and their agenda, they after Constance came to fear them as if they were avenging angels.

Papal fear of reform grew, in the first place, out of the potential consequences for them if two now-strident grievances against them were heeded. The first was the scandal of papal taxes, dispensations, and other bitterly resented financial exactions, especially when the revenues seemed to support an ever more worldly seeming and ostentatious papal court.

The second was the resentment bishops felt of actions taken by the Holy See that seemed to disregard their own interests and prerogatives. It is telling in this regard that bishops at Lateran Council V (1512–1517) strongly urged the formation of a rotating congregation of bishops in Rome that would safeguard their interests. Pope Leo X and the curia cardinals at his side made sure this initiative went nowhere.[6]

But what the popes feared most was the specter that, as at Constance, a council might depose them, which in turn rested on the principle that the authority of councils was superior to theirs, as the Council of Constance stated in arguably a qualified way but that Basel asserted categorically. The popes were quick to try to counteract this principle. Now the issue of the precise relationship between the authority of a council duly convoked and the authority of the pope who convoked it entered Church history as a contentious and profoundly important issue still troublesome today. It deeply troubled the Council of Trent, though the decrees of the council give not the slightest hint of it.

The Council of Trent

The immediate impetus for the Council of Trent was Luther's Reformation and the demand for a "free Christian council in German lands" that almost immediately sprang up in its wake.[7] Beginning shortly after Emperor Charles V condemned Luther as an outlaw of the empire in 1521, the emperor made every effort to persuade, cajole, or force Pope Clement VII to convoke a council, but Clement, more fearful of a council than of the emperor, managed for the entire decade of his pontificate to resist the pressure.

When Paul III succeeded Clement in 1534, he made clear his determination to convoke a council and soon formed an informal and uneasy alliance with the emperor to do so.

From the very beginning, each of the two protagonists had to make compromises, which began after much haggling even over where the council would be held. They finally settled on Trent, a solution not fully satisfactory to either of them. As it turned out, neither popes nor emperors ever set foot in Trent during the council's entire eighteen-year duration, but the popes tried to control the council's course through papal legates, who presided at the council, and the emperors tried to control it through envoys (or ambassadors) to the council. Other monarchs would also send envoys with the same end in view. It was in this way, traditional in the medieval councils, that the laity—or should I say the nonclerics—played an important role in the decision-making at Trent.

Luther's challenge to the Church was twofold—doctrine and reform. Although these two challenges have characteristics special to Luther and the Reformation, they are simply a specific instance of the traditional agenda of councils, doctrine and reform, *fides et mores*, which is precisely how Trent would proceed. Luther may have set the agenda, but Paul III and Charles V were more directly responsible for the binary character of the task the bishops at Trent determined upon.

The pope and the emperor agreed in a generic way that both of Luther's challenges had to be met, but that is where the agreement ended. The pope envisaged the council as responding to the doctrinal issues raised by Luther, which he interpreted as just some old heresies in new dress that could easily be disposed of. The Lutherans were to be condemned, and with that the council could quickly conclude its business. The council was to be much more circumspect about reform, which was best handled by the pope himself, particularly when it touched upon him or his curia.

The emperor's agenda was almost diametrically opposed to the pope's. He optimistically believed that some measure of reconciliation with the Lutherans was still possible. He feared that a condemnation of Luther's teaching would seal the religious division irreparably, and he was determined to delay the council's dealing with doctrine until after it had completed its reform agenda. A practical man, Charles believed that the real problem was reform. Just as the unreformed condition of the Church had, in his analysis, caused the Lutheran crisis, a reform of the Church was the first, most urgent, and indispensable step in resolving it.

The council had to deal with this conflict of priorities within its first few weeks. It soon recognized that the two subjects were closely related, which led to the sensible solution of treating doctrine and reform in tandem. Every decision on doctrine would be accompanied by one on reform.

Doctrine and reform—put in such abstract terms the agenda sounds global and without delimitation. In fact, Trent's agenda turned out to be narrowly circumscribed, very much unlike the agenda of Vatican II. Under doctrine the council meant to treat only Protestant teachings that contradicted Catholic ones. Reform had a similarly precise focus. For the bishops at Trent "reform of the clergy and Christian people"—or, as the council also expressed it, "the reform of the Church"—meant almost exclusively reform of three offices in the Church—the papacy, the episcopacy, and the pastorate. In other words, Trent followed the tradition that generally directed reform to the clergy. The Church that was to be reformed was, then, the Church often referred to today as the institutional or hierarchical Church.

Time after time through the council's long history, the papal legates had to insist with the bishops that reform of the papacy was off limits. But the issue would not go away. During the long eighteen years of the council, the popes kept promising reforms and actually implemented a few, but not enough to satisfy critics. After the council, the popes set to work, but surely not with the thoroughness many bishops wanted.

As it turned out, therefore, the council directed its main energies toward reform of bishops and pastors, with special attention to the former. Reform of the bishops included the method of their selection, their qualifications, and similar matters. The driving motive behind the reform was pastoral effectiveness. (Trent was a pastoral council!) The first condition for such effectiveness was residence in the diocese or parish. But absenteeism was widespread. Seemingly without scruple, absentee bishops and pastors pocketed the revenue from their benefices and devoted their time and energy to other pursuits. The abuse was most glaring when individuals held multiple bishoprics or pastorates so as to collect the money from them, as did Luther's nemesis, Albert of Brandenburg, who simultaneously held, in effect, three bishoprics.

Being absent from one's diocese or parish and holding multiple, incompatible benefices was of course contrary to canon law. To do so, a papal dispensation was required. Such dispensations were not particularly difficult to obtain, but they were not given free of charge. In fact, revenue from this and similar sources formed an essential part of regular papal revenue.

Previous councils had tried both to persuade bishops to reside and to force them to do so by reinforcing legislation against multiple benefices. But the weak link in the chain was dispensations from the Roman curia. By the third period of the council, 1562–1563, many bishops, led by the Spaniards, were determined to solve the problem once and for all by proposing that residence was an obligation *jure divino*, by divine law. If by divine law, then even the pope could not dispense from it. In this way Trent's reform of the bishops touched upon papal prerogatives and the functioning of the papal curia, the forbidden subject.

Conflict over this issue brought the council to a grinding halt for ten long months, from mid-September 1562 to mid-July 1563. During that time the council was paralyzed, unable to take any effective action. The crisis was finally resolved by an uneasy compromise, which meant somewhat curtailing the stringency of *jus divinum*, while still insisting that residence was an obligation of conscience. Even without the stringency of *jus divinum*, no bishop could leave Trent still under the impression that residence was simply a regulation of canon law, more serious, perhaps, than a traffic regulation but not by much. The fierce debate of the issue had made that much clear.

Fulfillment of the Tridentine decree on residence slowly became normative and unquestioned, largely due to the example Borromeo and the other bishops like him played after the council by their good example. We are thus reminded that to be effective reforms must enlist agents wholeheartedly committed to making them a reality.

Besides insisting on residence, the council provided the bishops with a job description once they took up residency in their see. They were to preach every Sunday and holy day. They were to visit the institutions of the diocese annually or at least on a regular basis. They were to hold annual synods. They were to establish seminaries for the training of poor boys who wanted to become priests. These were traditional duties. Even the seminary was an updated form of the bishop's obligation to train his clergy. These traditional duties received new force from the council and were marshaled for the first time in an effective way.

Nonetheless, the reforms were to be accomplished principally by a restoration of an older discipline. Words indicating restoration such as *restituere* and *revocare* appear often in the council's documents, and they need to be interpreted as revitalizing the discipline or canons of an earlier age in the hope of reproducing once again the presumably better mores of that age. In the critical question of episcopal residence, the council affirmed, quite correctly, in session six that it was renewing the "ancient canons that have fallen into almost total desuetude." Because Luther accused the Church of early falling away from the authentic past, Trent insisted more frequently and explicitly than any previous council upon its continuity with it.

Once the Council of Trent ended, who was to implement its reforms? Operative during the council had been three centers of authority—the pope, the monarchs, and the bishops themselves. After the council, each of these centers claimed the right to implement it, and each could find justification in the council's documents. The bishops' instrument for doing so was their synods, as Borromeo showed so clearly. The rivalry as well as the cooperation among these three centers became a hallmark of Catholicism after the council as it had been before it. The difference was that now the council often became the focal point.

Three centuries elapsed between Trent and the next council, Vatican I. The reasons for this long interval are multiple and intertwined with political and religious developments in Western Europe. But not to be underestimated was papal apprehension about the direction a council might take.

Moreover, the mistaken persuasion grew that Trent had solved all problems, and insofar as the Church might need reform Trent had done it once and for all. Although Trent spoke freely of its decrees as reform—*de reformation*—the word *reform* gradually slipped out of usage among Catholics as inapplicable to the Church. In Vatican I it appears only once, and that is in the negative sense that the definitions of the Roman pontiff are "irreformable" (*ireformabiles*). Even at Vatican II it appears only once regarding the Church, in *Unitatits Redintegratio*. The Council preferred softer words such as *renewal* and *updating*, which suggest improvement on something already operating satisfactorily.

Pius IX, riding high on the crest of the Ultramontane movement, could dare to convoke Vatican I. The French Revolution and its repercussions in the rest of the Catholic world had had the unexpected result of virtually wiping out Gallicanism, Febronianism, Josephism, and similar phenomena that challenged papal authority. It had also generated among many Catholics the conviction that the only bulwark against the chaos and carnage that everywhere threatened was a papacy with absolute authority. The stage was set for the definitions of primacy and infallibility, definitions that in the minds of many Catholic thinkers rendered councils/synods unnecessary. The pope and his curia could—and should—handle all problems.

Vatican Council II

Although in a few quarters the persuasion that councils were a thing of the past was being discreetly questioned, it was an article of faith by the middle of the twentieth century for most bishops and theologians. In such an atmosphere, John XXIII's decision to convoke a council is even more remarkable. Just where he derived the inspiration to do so is not altogether clear, but certainly a major factor had to be his prolonged work editing the records of Carlo Borromeo's 1575 visitation of Roncalli's own diocese of Bergamo to apply the Tridentine reform legislation.[8] It was likely Borromeo's example that prompted John both as patriarch of Venice and bishop of Rome to call diocesan synods. Moreover, John's broad and direct experience of the wider world before he became patriarch of Venice–Bulgaria, Turkey, and postwar France—surely made him aware of problems and opportunities Churchmen of more circumscribed experience were not alert to.

In any case, during the almost two centuries since the French Revolution, the world, especially the Western world, had undergone political, social, economic, scientific, and cultural transformations that in their breadth, depth, and radical implications were utterly unprecedented in the history of the world. It is impossible to exaggerate how profoundly these changes shook the very foundations upon which society had previously rested.

John XXIII seems to have had a least an inkling of what was at stake, and certainly once the Council met the bishops took account of the situation as best they could and spoke of the "new era" the world had entered. In fact, one of the unique characteristics of Vatican II is its self-aware taking account of the world "outside" the Church, recognizing that the world impacts upon the Church and at the same time insisting that the Church act as partner with the world for the world's betterment—or, shall we say, for the world's reform? The encyclical *Rerum Novarum* was an early portent of such awareness that was new in being now explicit.

It is often said of Vatican II that it was special in not having to face a crisis, as did, for instance, the Council of Trent.[9] In fact, however, Vatican II met in a period of perhaps the most profound crisis in the Church's history, a crisis even more serious for being diffuse and not easily defined in a few words. For lack of a better word, we can call it the crisis of the modern world. During the nineteenth century, the Church had almost invariably assumed a negative stance toward "the modern world." By the time of Vatican II such a stance was no longer credible, as most theologians and bishops at the Council on some level realized. In this context merely tinkering with the status quo no longer sufficed as efficacious reform.

The Council was an incomparably rich and complex event that cannot be reduced to a few truisms. Nonetheless, for the purposes of this book I think we can isolate three orientations or issues at the Council that were pervasive and that are particularly pertinent for us. The first is the relationship between center and periphery, the second is the problem of change within continuity, and the third is the question of the style, mode, or "personality" of the Church. These three are intrinsically related to one another, and to speak about one invariably entails engaging the others.

The issue of center and periphery burst into the Council in the debate on the very first document, *Sacrosanctum Concilium*, which granted some autonomy to episcopal conferences, challenging the exclusive control over liturgy enjoyed by the Congregation of Rites. Along with the use of the vernacular, this provision sparked the most fire and passion in the interventions. It was a portent of what became a general principle of the Council: to balance the exclusively vertical structure of authority in the Church with horizontal norms and structures.

The Council instructed bishops, for instance, to treat their priests "as sons and friends," who "cooperate" with them in the government of the diocese especially through their "senate or council" (*CD* 27). In designating the Church as the people of God, the Council countered the designation of it as a monarchy, a word that, despite its currency before the Council, does not appear a single time in the documents of Vatican II. The vocabulary of the Council overflows with words indicating horizontal and reciprocal relationships, such as *cooperation*, *friendship*, *brothers and sisters*, and most tellingly, *dialogue*.

The lightning rod for this issue was of course the doctrine of episcopal collegiality. The minority fiercely and unrelentingly opposed it on the grounds that it contradicted the tradition enshrined in the definition of primacy in Vatican I. The vehemence and tenacity with which the minority opposed it reveals at once that a crucial principle was at stake.

Bishops of the majority argued, not always convincingly, that collegiality was an enhancement of the primacy. When viewed against the large background of history, collegiality was in essence an assault on the Ultramontane assumptions of the previous century. It was another instance of the many attempts to deal with the problem chronic since the Great Western Schism of the relationship between bishops and pope and, more specifically between council and pope. When viewed against the very largest background of history, collegiality was in essence an assault on the central assumption of the Gregorian Reform of the eleventh century.

Once the doctrine was approved, the Council had to decide on the practical form it would take. It had to decide what its institutional grounding would be in the life of the Church, lest it remain simply a beautiful idea without consequence. As is well known, before the Council was able properly to address the problem, Paul VI intervened by creating the Synod of Bishops. Faced with the papal intervention, the Council incorporated the Synod into *Christus Dominus* as if it were an expression of collegiality.

But of course it was not. As defined by Paul VI, the Synod was simply an advisory body, with no authority beyond what the pope might concede it. It was an instrument not of the episcopacy but of the primacy. Probably without realizing it, Paul radically redefined what the word *synod* had meant since the Church's earliest days. Synods were decision-making bodies. With that redefinition Vatican II's single most important reform regarding Church order had been rendered largely impotent. Nonetheless, although the minority seemingly had won the battle, a seed for potential change in the future had been sown.

A specific aspect of the relationship between center and periphery was the relationship of bishops to the Roman curia. The issue had troubled councils from Constance to Trent, including local councils. Although at Trent reform of the curia was a forbidden topic, the bishops could not be restrained from raising it, and in the end, they had some modest success. For obvious reasons, it was not an issue at Vatican I. Rather than reform of the curia, the Council's definitions of primacy and infallibility resulted in enhancing the curia's authority.

Vatican II was different from Trent in that at Trent no cardinals from the curia were present except for one to four legates. At Vatican II they were all not only present, but were in control of the Council's commissions. In the years before Vatican II opened, the curia, especially the Supreme Congregation of the Holy Office, was increasingly criticized. The criticism was discreet and muted, but during the first period of Vatican II it exploded behind the scenes because bishops believed the curia was trying to dictate to the Council and curtail its freedom. The criticism was directed especially against the Holy Office, and among themselves some bishops advocated its complete abolition. Reform of the curia was sure to reach the floor of the Council in the second period and be argued with great passion.

Paul VI diffused the tension when just before that period opened he addressed the curia. He told its members that reform was necessary, but he reassured them by saying that he himself, with their cooperation, would undertake it, an action that seems almost a replay of what happened at Trent. As he promised, Paul subsequently made changes, some important, but certainly not as far-reaching as some members of the Council thought necessary. He made changes within a system without changing the system itself, the system that had developed out of decisions taken in 1059 and 1588.

With that, we come to our second issue, change within continuity. Although Luther had made this an issue for the Council of Trent, the Council did not have to face it directly except to insist on the Church's continuity with the apostolic tradition. At Vatican II, however, it bounded to the surface at almost every turn, as we have already seen with collegiality. The first paragraph of the Council's first document, *Sacrosantum Concilium*, contains at least five words indicating change, including the word *change* itself. The paragraph is about reform, *mutatio in melius*, even though the word *reform* itself is notably absent.

The issue of change was thrust upon the Council from so many quarters that it could not fail to deal with it. It had to deal with a historical consciousness new in the history of the world. It was a consciousness or awareness that challenged some of the most basic assumptions upon which the Church had operated. Catholics had been taught that the Church did not change and was not susceptible to reform. That position no longer made sense.

Though with older roots, the new consciousness began to form in the Enlightenment, which laughed to scorn belief in a normative past and threw history's goal into an ever-brighter future. During the nineteenth and early twentieth centuries historical methods transformed all branches of sacred learning and made devastatingly clear the discrepancies in the Christian tradition between past and present. Modern philosophies of history destroyed the illusion that the past was recoverable "as it really was"—*wie es eisentlch gewesen*, to use von Ranke's famous words. Darwin's *Origin of the Species* made the stories of Adam and Eve sound like a child's fantasy. The classical worldview had collapsed.

The council dealt with the problem especially in three ways, captured in three words, ressourcement, aggiornamento, and development. Each of these had important repercussions on the idea of reform. *Ressourcement*, though a neologism, succinctly expresses the traditional idea of reform, which was a translation into the needy present of a remedy from the normative past.

Today this idea of reform, though certainly crucial, now requires a high degree of sophistication if it is to be used validly and credibly.

Aggiornamento was a new word for reform, even though updating had often but silently been operative in the history of the Church and the history of reform. What is special about it in Vatican II is that it is explicit, that it is not a rare exception but a general rule, that it betrays a greater alertness to historical and cultural differences than any previous council, and that it implicitly validates as reform a measure of accommodation or adaptation to the world. When *Gaudium et Spes* taught that the Church learns from the world, it simply took the idea a further step (*GS* 40). Can it not be said that the Church learned from the world the evil of slavery, the evil of capital punishment, and the justice of religious liberty?

Development and related words such as *growth*, *evolution*, and *progress* are utterly new to a council and are the immediate product of the nineteenth century. During the Council bishops and theologians sometimes invoked development to cover almost any kind of change, but it specifically meant the unfolding of something already present either implicitly or in germ. The minority bishops in the Council objected to it only when invoked, as in the Declaration on Religious Liberty, to justify a change that seemed not to further but to contradict the direction a teaching had been heading. In fact, development sometimes, as in this case, was a euphemism for a silent rejection of a position earlier held, which itself poses delicate questions for the theologian.

In summary, we can say that the Council did not solve the problem of change within continuity, which in fact was not the Council's task, but it addressed it and in so doing revealed its complexity. It implicitly showed that there were no simple solutions to the problem. It warns us in this conference that we cannot glibly speak of Church reform as if it were a concept without complications.

The third issue I will treat is the style of the Council and thus the style of the Church. In *Gaudet Mater Ecclesia*, with which Pope John opened the Council, he stressed in his gentle way that the Council should as far as possible formulate its decisions in positive terms. It would thus show the Church to be, in his words, "the loving mother of all, benign, patient, full of mercy and goodness."[10] He explicitly asked that the Council avoid issuing condemnations.

These innocent-sounding words led to the Council's abandoning the judicial framework of earlier councils and very much modifying the legislative, especially by eliminating the punitive aspect. As the Council did so, it created a form of discourse no previous Council had ever employed, or better said, had never employed in such a consistent, characteristic, and comprehensive way. The Council thus displaced one comprehensive system with another and in so doing substantially modified the very definition of a council. This was a major reform—effected silently and with only vague comprehension of its deep significance.

Instead of prescribing or proscribing certain behaviors, Vatican II held up ideals to be striven for. *Christus Dominus*, for instance, paints the portrait of the ideal bishop and does so in such a way as to appeal to the bishop's conscience and good will. Vatican II thus banished certain words previously characteristic of councils, most notably *anathema*, and introduced a set of words new for a council, though traditional in Christian spirituality. I refer especially to *conscience* and *holiness*.

Of course, like its predecessors, Vatican II was concerned with good public order in the Church as is clear from its treatment of collegiality, but public order was not its defining center. The center for Vatican II, I argue, was the universal call to holiness, something new for a council because the judicial-legislative model inhibited it from emerging. Once the call to holiness got articulated at length in chapter 5 of *Lumen Gentium*, it became a leitmotif of the Council, appearing in some form in almost every subsequent document. Indeed, it is possible to interpret the Council's documents as extended contemplations of the characteristics of holiness in the "modern world." The Council's style of discourse excites a desire to make those characteristics define one's very being through a process of inner conversion. Reform continues to be about reform of structures, but the Council now makes the all-important connection between such reforms and the ongoing reform of life that makes such reforms truly Christian.

According to the Council, the ideal Christians of today are actively engaged in both Church and the world, strive to be agents of reconciliation between races and religions, are committed to working for the advancement of human rights, and for the advancement of peace and justice for all, especially for the poor. They draw strength for their Christian commitment particularly from the liturgy, the sacraments, and the word of God, and, while relying on the guidance of the Church, they know that their conscience is "the secret core and sanctuary "of their being, where they are "alone with God whose voice sounds in their depth" (*GS* 16).

The new literary style projects, therefore, an image of the ideal Christian, and at the same time creates and projects an image of the ideal Church. Previous councils unwittingly and unfortunately projected an image of the Church as doctrinal watchdog and enforcer of discipline. The new literary style creates and projects a different style or mode of Church behavior—indeed, a different image of the very personality of the Church, in fulfilment of Pope John's ideal of the Church as "the loving mother of all, benign, patient, full of mercy and goodness." *Le style, c'est l'homme même*. In our case, *le style, c'est l'église même*.

Conclusion

In choosing to take the full sweep of the history of Church reform as the subject for this chapter I realized that I would for the most part be covering well-known ground. I chose it in the hope that simply reviewing the story would widen our perspective as we begin to address our task and allow us to see how some problems have been long standing while others are new with "the modern world" and therefore with Vatican II. I apologize for the outrageous generalizations the approach has forced me to make. Please believe me when I say that I know how grievously I have sinned.

The review raises many questions. I have formulated twelve, with full awareness that they are only the beginning. I have tried to pose them in a succinct and provocative way. I then add a final consideration.

1. The words *reform* and *reformation* fell out of favor with Catholics. We have been called together to examine the problem of Church reform. Is there any problem in reintroducing the term?

2. Reform entails engaging the problem of change within continuity, which as a theological problem is among the most serious in the Church. In the past, the specific problem of reform was solved by denying change and employing a naive form of ressourcement. That solution is no longer possible. Just what are the dimensions of reform today, and, to borrow from Yves Congar, is there any way of distinguishing "true" from "false" reform?
3. In the modern era Church reform seems somehow and sometimes to entail world reform. Is that true, and, if it is, is it of any particular concern for us?
4. The struggle over collegiality during and after Vatican II can be seen as simply the latest episode in the long-standing tension between bishops (councils) and the papacy. Can collegiality and the empowering of episcopal conferences be related to the ancient synodal tradition of the Church? If so, does it make any difference for Church reform, at least in the terms in which it is articulated?
5. Two factors seem required for a "successful "reform: grounding in an ongoing institution and agents wholeheartedly committed to the reform. Must we take those factors into account?
6. Reforms have had different degrees of magnitude (reform of system in place, replacing the system, etc.). So what for today?
7. With the Extraordinary Synod on the Family of last year, Pope Francis seemed to signal a desire to reinvigorate the synodal tradition. Synods/councils have been the normal agents of Church reform. Should they be so today? If so, to what extent? With today's electronic media of instantaneous communication, what are the dangers of such decentralization? How important is it to reckon with the potentially centrifugal force of that tradition? The example of the Synod of Pistoia, 1786, is well known. The Synod, which embodied principles of Febronianism and similar movements to which the

papacy was adamantly opposed, is a striking example of a synod gone wrong from a papal viewpoint.

8. The problem of how bishops are nominated begins to be explicit and contentious in the West with the Gregorian Reform and has reappeared often. Does the current system need reform, especially with a view to making the process more inclusive and more sensitive to local needs?
9. Reform of the curia has for centuries been a recurrent problem in the history of the Church. If today we address the problem as a reform of the system fundamentally in place, are there advantages of making regular programs of review by outside agencies an essential element in the reform, something that until now has been absent? Should not clear job descriptions be drawn up for major offices to ensure accountability and reduced the potential of arbitrary decisions?
10. If the time ever comes when the system itself is to be reformed (replaced), truly basic questions arise. The curia as we know it today is, as mentioned, fundamentally the product of decisions taken in 1059 and 1588 that created cardinals, organized the curia into Congregations, and put cardinals in charge of them. But is the role of the curial cardinals in the Church today really clear? Are they staff or little princes or something in between? If they are to assist the pope, is there not something exceedingly strange about the system when cardinals of the curia publicly take positions in opposition to the pope? The basic questions: *Precisely what is the curia, what is the function of the cardinals in it, and why are they there at all, especially since now they are bishops?*
11. In the past, the laity have played important roles in decision-making in the Church. Although they have sometimes abused their roles, they have also had a positive impact, as did Emperor Charles V in insisting the Council of Trent deal with Church reform. The sociopolitical situation today is so different from earlier times that it is difficult to imagine how to enable

equitable participation of the laity in the direction of the Church, but it should not be seen as an innovation or as untraditional or as an unworthy concession to modern democracy. Does not a genuine reform of the Church today require addressing the issue?

12. As I presented lay participation, I said nothing about women except to mention in passing the Empress Irene. In relationship to the Council of Trent I could have mentioned the important roles played by Queen Catherine de' Medici of France and Queen Mary of Hungary while she was governor of the Habsburg Netherlands. Women have, therefore, played roles at the highest level, but so rarely as to be statistically insignificant. Is that appropriate for today?

A Final Consideration

To be true to Vatican II, must not any reform of the Church, even if its immediate goal is reform of structures, ultimately be directed to promoting the universal call to holiness? The Council gave form to what holiness means today by in effect drawing a portrait of the ideal Christian, and in so doing it drew a portrait of the ideal Church, a Church that presents itself in word and deed to its members and to the world at large as Pope Saint John described it, "the loving mother of all, benign, patient, full of mercy and goodness."

NOTES

1. See, e.g., John W. O'Malley, "'The Hermeneutic of Reform': A Historical Analysis," *Theological Studies* 73 (2012): 517–46.

2. See, e.g., Alberto Melloni and Silvia Scatena, eds., *Synod and Synodality: Theology, History, Canon Law, and Ecumenism in New Contact* (Münster: Lit, 2005), and Jan Grootaers, *Heurs et malheurs de la "collégialité": Pontificats et Synodes face à la réception de Vatican II* (Leuven: Peeters, 2012).

3. See Gerhard B. Ladner, *The Idea of Reform: Its Impact on Christian Thought and Action in the Age of the Fathers*, rev. ed. (New York: Harper and Row, 1967).

4. See, e.g., John W. O'Malley, "Developments, Reforms, and Two Great Reformations: Towards a Historical Assessment of Vatican II," *Theological Studies* 44 (1983): 373–406.

5. See Maria Teresa Fattori, "Continuità e discontinuità nel consitoro della chiesa cattolica romana: alcuni momenti della seconda metà del XVI secolo," in Melloni and Scatena, *Synod and Synodality*, 143–72, and Josep M. Colomer and Iain McLean, "Electing Popes: Approval Balloting and Qualified-Majority Rule," *Journal of Interdisciplinary History* 29 (1998): 1–22.

6. See Nelson Minnich, "The Proposals for an Episcopal College at Lateran V," in *Ecclesia Militans: Studien zur Konzilien- und Reformationsgeschichte, Remigius Bäumer zum 70 Geburtstag gewidmet*, ed. Walter Brandmüller et al., 2 vols. (Paderborn: Ferdinand Schöningh, 1988) 1:213–32.

7. The standard history is Hubert Jedin, *Geschichte des Konzils von Trient*, 4 vols. in 5 (Freiburg i.Br.: Herder, 1949–1975). See also John W. O'Malley, *Trent: What Happened at the Council* (Cambridge, MA: Harvard University Press, 2012).

8. See Jared Wicks, "Tridentine Motivations of Pope John XXIII before and during Vatican II," *Theological Studies* 75 (2014): 847–62.

9. The standard history is Giuseppe Alberigo, ed., *History of Vatican II*, 5 vols. (Maryknoll, NY: Orbis, 1995–2006). See also John W. O'Malley, *What Happened at Vatican II* (Cambridge, MA: Harvard University Press, 2008).

10. *Acta Synodalia Sacrosancti Concilii Vaticani II*, 32 vols. (Vatican City: Typis Polyglottis Vaticanis, 1979–1999), I/1, 166–75.

5

LESSONS FROM THE REFORMS OF THE TWENTIETH CENTURY

Andrea Riccardi

Reforms and Historical Movements

Before drawing lessons from the reforms of the twentieth century, we would like to focus on both the changes in the Church that took place in the twentieth century and those that did not. After all, we do not believe that we can draw true lessons from history, precisely because each generation makes its own choices and has its own experiences. However, familiarity with history is necessary to understand the present, since Christianity—in the words of Marc Bloch—is a religion in which history plays a decisive role.[1] History, in fact, is essential to understanding the present and facing one's responsibility for the future. Historical culture, however, has had a certain decline in the world of the Church. The collapse of historical studies in ecclesiastical formation is a serious sign of disengagement from a vision of Catholicism in the history of all people, and not just of the Church.

The awareness of Christianity in history was established particularly after the Second Vatican Council. In recent decades, there has been a systematic reaction against it. On the part of the

Catholic Church, there has been a gradual withdrawal before a complex world, in which Catholicism felt in part alien and out of place. This withdrawal was inspired by a model of Christianity as a minority with strong identity and traditional characteristics in a pluralistic world, whose historical outcomes are complex and not easy to measure.[2] The historical and social reality was assessed based on the greater or lesser adherence to a set of principles and values.

A return to the study of history, in all its facets, helps us to better understand the reality of Christianity today and to assess changes and nonchanges that have occurred in the twentieth century. This is the scenario for the reforms we need today: a legacy of reforms that were imagined, accomplished, interrupted, but also—we must not forget—changes brought about by the reality of the times. For it is history itself that changes the Christian communities that live in it.

I will only briefly touch on the history of Vatican II, which is the starting point of the most significant reform processes of the twentieth century, because the subject is treated in greater detail by John O'Malley.[3] What I would like to underline is the recurring (and very significant) relationship between reforms and movements of thought and feeling that almost always accompanied the reforming events in the history of the twentieth century. It was not just a matter of reform from the top down. The reforms of the last century had behind them a movement of ideas, spirituality, theology, feelings, thoughts, and experiences: the liturgical, biblical, ecumenical movement, and—in a more limited manner—the reform that led to interreligious dialogue. More can be added to that. These movements prepared reforms and favored their reception by the people of God. Interreligious dialogue, with the notable and important exception of that between Catholics and Jews, was among the novelties of the Council, the least prepared by previous experiences, even though there were important pioneers.[4]

Pope Francis's new (and old) direction in *Evangelii Gaudium* lies precisely in connecting mission and missionary conversion with the reform of the Church, to which it gives emotional intensity and depth. The missionary conversion of the Church, as a movement led by the pope, is the ground and the direction of the reforms that should be introduced in the life of the Church.

However, one must note that this process takes place in a cultural context that is not particularly exciting for the concerns of today's Catholicism, and especially its ruling class. A drawback in certain sectors of the Church at the end of the twentieth century and beginning of the new one is the lack of ideas and vision, especially in Church leadership and in its worldview. There is also a lack of reform movements. The ruling classes' lack of vision and inability to think more broadly is also a matter of concern in view of reforms. Here it is worth recalling the words of Paul VI—a great reformer—in 1967, when he pointed out the lack of ideas:

> It must be admitted that men very often find themselves in a sad state because they do not give enough thought and consideration to these things. So we call upon men of deep thought and wisdom—Catholics and Christians, believers in God and devotees of truth and justice, all men of good will—to take as their own Christ's injunction, "Seek and you shall find." (69) Blaze the trails to mutual cooperation among men, to deeper knowledge and more widespread charity, to a way of life marked by true brotherhood, to a human society based on mutual harmony.[5]

As an example, I would like to briefly reflect on one reform of the twentieth century, that of the Roman curia. There were actually three reforms of the curia in the twentieth century: that of Pius X with the apostolic constitution *Sapienti Consilio* (which marked the end of the curia of the Papal State and of Sixtus V's order); Paul VI's *Regimini Ecclesiae* of 1967; and John Paul II's *Pastor Bonus* of 1988. There is a difference between a structural adjustment and a thoughtful and inspired reform.[6] The latter well describes Paul VI's reform of the curia, supported by the Council, which helped to advance other significant changes such as the institution of the Synod of Bishops, no longer part of the Roman curia, and more. Paul VI's reform was part of a movement of ideas and feelings, generated by the Council and shared by the world episcopate, which called for a new image for Rome and a new relationship between the government of the universal Church and the local churches.

Clearly Paul VI's curial reform depended on a balance between the centrality of Rome's initiative and the need to avoid acting in isolation, but in communion with the bishops and their conferences throughout the world, seen as essential players in such an all-embracing Catholicism. This is not the place to discuss Paul VI's reform. We may, however, draw a conclusion from it: ecclesial, intellectual, spiritual, and emotional *humus* is crucial to the reforms. Today, for us, in a reformist perspective, the *humus* is the one roused by Pope Francis, his words, his indications, and the climate he has created in today's Church.

The Geographic-Demographic Change

We must consider some changes in the twentieth-century life of the Church. The twentieth century was characterized by a vast geographic and demographic change: the growth of the Church in the Southern Hemisphere, leading to a major dislocation in the south of Catholics (and of Christianity itself).[7] At the end of the century, Europeans comprised only 26 percent of the total Catholics, a reversal of Catholicism's center of gravity, which had never occurred before in history. A similar reversal in the Anglican communion has led to deep fragmentation, in which African Anglicanism has assumed an increasingly autonomous position from the "mother" Church of England. In the Catholic world, the center (not only of the government, but of the human and financial resources) remains strongly in the North.

The Catholic growth in the Southern Hemisphere during the twentieth century tendentially reflected a missionary model of expansion from Europe, driven by the criteria of the Congregation of Propaganda Fide. The missionary expansion of the nineteenth–twentieth centuries took place with a reduced role of the states, contrary to the expansion achieved during the conquest of Latin America, in which the royal patronage played a decisive role.[8] The extension to the ends of the earth, so to speak, did not mean the introduction of a multipolarity of ecclesial subjects, but often saw Rome take on new responsibilities and a widespread presence of the pope, urged also by the new dynamics of the global world.

The driving force behind this growth was primarily the Congregation of Propaganda Fide, whose spatial and geopolitical vision—in the perspective of the history of the institutions and not as an assessment of management practices—corresponds to a ministry of the colonies in European governments of the twentieth century, with a tendency of dependency on the part of local churches, even for financial reasons: the department has always been led by Europeans (except for the Indian Diaz and Cardinal Agagianian, an Armenian who is nevertheless "more Roman than the Romans"). Even if the Propaganda's jurisdiction was later reduced in some regions, and if most of the bishops' conferences have become indigenous, Propaganda Fide itself has not yet been touched by reform. This is a decisive factor if we want a multipolar growth of the Church.

In short, it represents an immovable body that has survived many revisions—which should make us reflect. It is less and less clear why the northern churches or those of Latin America are connected to the Congregation for Bishops or other Roman dicasteries (there is now the newly created Council for Promoting the New Evangelization), while the churches of the former Third World are under the Congregation for the Evangelization of Peoples, that is, the former Propaganda Fide. Should we not—at the administrative level—equalize the treatment of all the dioceses of the world? Of course, in an increasingly vast and complex Catholicism, we should strengthen the continental perspective, as is the case of Latin America, which has a Pontifical Commission for Latin America, corresponding to the very active council of Latin American Bishops (CELAM).

Popes and Reforms

The development of Catholicism corresponds also to a growing role of the pope in a reforming sense in the history of the twentieth century. Pius XII, despite complications and contradictions, tried to implement changes from the center.[9] In the perspective of Pius XII, and starting from the center, the Jesuit Fr. Riccardo Lombardi launched a plan of ecclesial, religious, and curial reform, introducing the idea of the retirement of bishops. It was a significant effort on

Lombardi's part, of which traces are still discernible in subsequent decisions. But he was criticized by John XXIII both for his papal-centrism and how his reform project became a way to bypass the ecumenical council, thus reducing the reform to a series of practical changes only.[10]

Already on the eve of Pope Pius XII's election in 1939, however, Cardinal Celso Costantini, who had extensive experience in China and at Propaganda Fide, proposed a council. The ecumenical council objectives were—in his opinion—"renewal," the liturgy in modern languages, and the relationship with other cultures: all changes that he felt strongly about after his years in Asia.[11] His was an attempt to respond to the diversity of issues and visions present in the Catholic Church, an approach clearly different from that proposed by Lombardi.

Until Vatican II, reform initiatives imposed by reality (reforms are often a reaction to reality itself) usually occurred on the initiative of the papacy, along with its direct involvement. In the mid-twentieth century, the Latin American continental body with CELAM emerged more prominently than other continental conferences. However, after the end of the Cold War, everything—even international politics—tended to become multipolar in the global world.

From Vatican II emerged a different perspective for reform or reforms of the Church, even in Paul VI's mediating approach, that kept together the resolve to leave the action of the papacy intact and to highlight the collegiality and importance of the churches without devolution of powers. However, his approach did evolve, blocked as it was by postconciliar polarization and the crisis of the seventies.

Something should be said of Paul VI's reforming vision with respect to what appears to be specifically coming from Pope Francis, at least according to interpretations that have been given or expressions of his intentions and choices. Even though Francis often refers to Paul VI, there are significant differences between the two, due to their living in separate times and their personal traits. It has been said that Pope Francis does not have a project to address the reality of the Church, while it should be remembered that his predecessor not only had a reform project, developed during the long years of service as a member of the Roman curia at the Secretariat of State and by observing the Catholic world from the center, but also as part of a real project-oriented culture. When Paul VI was elected he already had a project to reform the curia and of the universal Church. He was convinced that the Church leadership (top positions in the curia and the bishops' conferences) should be changed through replacements that would have led certain figures close to him or in conciliar positions into office. He was also aware that only by ending governance by the preconciliar ruling class would real change be introduced.

In a historiographical perspective, and regarding the ecclesiastical elites close to Paul VI, the expression "montinians" is commonly used—and not inaccurately. Pope Montini had some clear ideas (that he had to assess against opposite postconciliar reactions) on how to change the Church. He was also convinced that change was possible with a new ruling class in the Church and in key posts in the curia. It does not seem that Pope Francis has promoted an extensive renewal of the curia, or that he doggedly promotes those close to him to key positions. It should also be noted that Montini had at his disposal the then-new retirement card for changes at the top of the curial and episcopal hierarchies.[12]

The Church of the South and the Church of the Poor

To return to the significant change to Christianity that mostly took place in the Southern Hemisphere, perhaps it is important to better understand the reality of the Christian people globally. As Philip Jenkins observes, "Christianity is spreading in a surprising way among the poor and the persecuted, while it is weakening among the rich and the wealthy."[13] The Church belongs more to the South and even more so to the world of the poor. Who are its members? The category of "people," modeled on the Council that Pope Francis constantly proposes, not only represents, in fact, the overcoming of the model of a withdrawn minority, but it is also—from a sociological point of view—an inclusive category of a stratified reality not limited by clear-cut boundaries, of the people, of believers, including the poor and the Christians in need.

Here it should be noted—among the processes triggered by the Council—how the vision of the Church of the poor remains unfinished business in the reflection, practice, and relationship between the Church, the poor, and poverty. There is a whole history on the works of the Council regarding this issue that we will not deal with here, which, however, reveal some obvious limitations and lack of development.[14] Since the sixties, the key challenges of poverty and development have caught the attention of the Church. After Vatican II—with *Populorum Progressio* in mind—the so-called social question shifted from a question of industrial societies to the reality of the relations between North and South, raising the question of development and dependence.

In more recent decades, developments and reconsiderations of the social doctrine have followed. And at the same time important structures and institutions of social intervention have increased, locally and internationally, often in contexts of significant organization of social action. This is not the problem. Nor do we want to venture into the themes of liberation theology. But the Church of the poor is not only the development of social action. Instead, what needs to be emphasized is how little developed is the reflection—and perhaps also the practice, though with notable exceptions—on the Church of the poor, where the poor are really the key part, better yet, the qualifying reality of ecclesial life. In short, the poor as a sacrament of Christ, as John Chrysostom once put it. It is not a trivial matter, and it would certainly change the Church's self-understanding. And the faith of the poor would find a new space in the Church. It would be enough to think of popular piety and its story (at times one of marginalization, if not contempt) in postconciliar Catholicism. In truth, there is an essential need to more fully understand that the Church is now, in a significant way, the people of the poor and the lowly…and it must be so even more as well as being even more recognized as such.

A deeper analysis took place—thanks to John Paul II—on the theme of martyrdom (though at times it was arbitrarily used to legitimize a certain vision of the Christian minority in the clash of civilizations and religions). Many of the faces of contemporary Christianity are those of martyrs or the lowly. Consider the Christians in the Middle East or Pakistan, to name just two examples. It is not about individual cases, but about a reality of a subjugated and suffering people. Such a condition of subjugation and persecution requires a change in the self-awareness of the Church.[15] A church of martyrs and a church of the poor: this is the humiliated Christianity of today—not all of it, but important and revealing segments of her own profound reality.

And here emerges the theme of the real and ordinary confrontation between Christians, violence, and war. It was very hard to face the two world wars and the *shô'âh*, which has highlighted the centrality of the issue of peace in all pontificates, turning them almost into ministries of peace.[16] The ministry of peace is a reality that today is linked—as it happens in the spirit of Assisi—even with interreligious dialogue. Yet, in the global world, despite the hopes of peace and the end of the Cold War, conflicts have multiplied and changed in form, and a reality of widespread violence (terrorism, mafia, drug traffickers, gangs, etc.) has dramatically expanded to the point of a "molecular civil war." It is the challenge of war, but also of widespread violence, which needs to be transformed into a pacifist mission of Christians in everyday life, that same people who Clement of Alexandria used to refer to as *eirēnikòn ghénos*.[17]

Changing the Way We Live with Others

Peace means living with others responsibly. Between the nineteenth and twentieth centuries, the Catholic position, facing a pluralistic world, was exemplified by the intransigent movement, in the words of Émile Poulat, which knew adaptations but represented a pattern, almost on the model of the *Syllabus*, with respect to secularism, laity, and socialism.[18] It had a dissenting, prophetic strand, at times violently combative, which introduced also a level of antagonism in society (even though we should not forget that even other movements were also characterized by a certain aggressiveness).

The second radical change I would like to emphasize, alongside the geographical and demographic, was, for the Church, the transition from the "intransigent" model to the *model of "cohabitation."*[19] The twentieth century was in many ways a tragic century, marked by so many hostile settings, or at least those foreign to Christianity. Let us also not forget that the twentieth century was the most secularized century in history, to the point of witnessing the creation of the first fully atheist state of Albania in 1967.

The "other"—after Vatican II—was no longer the intruder in our traditional societies to oppose (the secular, the communist, or the Protestant, and the Muslim), but someone with whom we ought to live peacefully. Then there are whole regions of the world where the "other" is the majority and Christianity the minority. The problem of the relationship with Islam was recognized by Pius XI at the end of the thirties, along with that of the "religious cultures" (as the Pope Ratti used to refer to them). Others with similar views worth mentioning here were not only known figures like Massignon, but also Fr. Fausti, a Jesuit and advocate of Islamic-Christian dialogue in the thirties, later martyred in Albania.[20]

What had happened since the thirties? The belief that, upon contact with Christianity, other religions would disappear was in question: So, what to do? A model of cohabitation was needed. And with Vatican II, the "other"—for the first time in the long history of Christianity—found a space and a theological status (not disparaged) by the Church in a Catholic perspective, with the recognition of religious freedom, and ecumenical, interreligious dialogue, as well as dialogue with nonbelievers.

In this way, non-Catholic Christians, other religions, and nonbelievers enter into the horizon as Catholic interlocutors, and not as people to fight against or to convert, but with a positive status. Structures for dialogue, both in the Roman curia (and not only in the spheres of diplomacy or the Catholic mission, appointed to handle the contact with "others") and in dioceses, were created, thus widening the horizon of Christians and their relationships.[21] To practice dialogue on the part of Catholic institutions and Catholics meant to achieve a more peaceful climate of coexistence, almost representing a "peaceful people," as it was put at the time. The religious leaders, gathered in Assisi in 1986 by Pope John Paul II, and the resulting spirit of Assisi, represent a creative and imaginative acceptance of Vatican II. There, with the support of the pope and the Church, a joint commitment of religions for peace was created, delegitimizing the connection between religion and war, and liberating gestures and attitudes of peace that come from a religious background.[22]

The complexity of the cohabitation with others gives rise, however, to processes of rejection, under the form of an apparent return to the intransigent model of the nineteenth–twentieth centuries. But these are mainly a falling back on institutions and a certain idea of truth. Dealing with an accentuated pluralism of society, the themes of relativism (with a return of elements of the modernist crisis) gain traction, which gradually push Catholicism to identify as a "minority" protected by well-defined doctrinal identity and social boundaries. It is not just a conservatism à la Lefebvre, but a trend that is widely visible in recent years, even with the spread of principles and values that are barriers to global pluralism considered invasive. In practical terms, it is a reduction of Catholicism to some models, hardly feasible in all its complex reality; yet it is a trend.

However, a constantly emerging proposal remains from time to time and from situation to situation: that of a cohesive and ideological minority in a pluralistic world, along with the rejection of the typical complex areas of contact and exchange typical of the great religious worlds and of the situations of cohabitation. But it is also a minority capable of starting cultural battles, as the many and various minorities living in hypermediatic societies do lobby on issues they care about, carving out a space for themselves. With his pastoral approach and leadership, Pope Francis has distanced himself from this model. In September 2015, he told the American bishops,

> We fail to understand the thinking of others, or to realize deep down that the brother or sister we wish to reach and redeem, with the power and the closeness of love, counts more than their positions, distant as they may be from what we hold as true and certain. Harsh and divisive language does not befit the tongue of a pastor, it has no place in his heart; although it may momentarily seem to win the day, only the enduring allure of goodness and love remains truly convincing.[23]

When it comes to living with "others," one cannot forget that, just in the last decades of the century, a different religious world emerged, that of Gilles Kepel's *La revanche de Dieu*: the magmatic Neo-Protestant movement; the rapidly growing theology of prosperity (which uses Christian codes and languages); but also non-Christian religions marked by fundamentalism, like Islam.[24] No doubt, they are actually quite different from each other. It is a world that Vatican II, dealing with interreligious dialogue and ecumenism, did not foresee, but is typical of the globalization process. At the time of the Council, the expectation was that of the affirmation of a secular world, not that of a religious world or of religious languages, as it eventually occurred in much of the world. Neo-Protestantism—to put it in general terms—represents the greatest religious growth in the twentieth century: from not a single faithful to half a billion in a century.[25] What does it mean to live in this world for the Catholic Church, which has chosen the paths of dialogue?

The Change of Globalization

History disrupts human landscapes. We would like to insist on the *change of globalization*, which is the third type of change I would like to address here. Many of the changes linked to new religious forms are connected in turn to globalization, or are reactions to it. The process of globalization places the "local" in a complex perspective, one that is different from the scenarios of the twentieth century, mostly set in national or colonial contexts. In such scenarios, Catholicism settled both in traditionally Christian countries as in other ones. Globalization enhances the role of cities—as Carlos María Galli has pointed out—but substantially reduces the national framework and the weight of national politics.[26]

If, in the twentieth century, the creation of the episcopal conferences offered a mapping of Catholic subjects, we still lack reflection on globalization, the reality in which to place the Church and the communion between churches. It is not a trifling matter, with respect to mobility, interconnections, migrations, urbanization, and the end of homogeneous population contexts. The geography of humanity and its living environment has dramatically changed.

For example, to cite one case in the Christian world besides Catholicism, globalization has dramatically challenged Orthodox national churches, not only for the diaspora of the faithful (and all the problems associated with the diversity of national jurisdiction), but also for the limited national horizons in which they are incardinated. These are all issues that the Orthodox churches must face and would partly deal with in the great pan-Orthodox council in June 2016. The issue of the pastoral care of the Orthodox in the diaspora (managed according to national affiliations) is one of the great issues that, however, is assumed to be left unresolved.

Faced with globalization, the papacy in some ways has been almost forced by the facts to expand its presence. After all, the pope—especially with John Paul II and Francis—is in fact a global *leader*, also recognized outside Catholicism, while it seems that he also meets the needs of the global world. In the complexity of a global world, Catholicism is already a global reality that is also certainly and inherently antiglobal.

The theme "Church and globalization" still gets little attention. What does inculturation in a global cultural context mean that calls into question the boundaries of cultures and civilizations, mixing them with each other? This is not a secondary question We cannot talk about reform or reforms without considering the global human *habitat*, with its anthropological, religious repercussions. Think of the megalopoles with their vast suburbs. Often, we have been slow in our understanding and our choices, because we think, we go on, and keep ruling focusing on parameters and dimensions of the past.

In the face of tumultuous movement realities such as Neo-Christianity or the various fundamentalisms, and with globalization, the mobility of messages and populations and the complexity of belonging, we should also reflect on the division of the geographical space, so typically Roman and partially modeled on the vision of a state: founded on territory (a way of living, thinking, and governing the Church), on which Catholicism is articulated (with the exception of the small Eastern Catholic churches, connected to the communities of people both in patriarchal territories and the diaspora). It is, in short, the type of geopolitics of Catholicism depicted in the *Atlas Hierarchicus*.[27] We must reflect on local and regional institutions in relation to space, not to disrupt them, but to liberate them from a self-sufficient vision and management: the dioceses and parishes.

A Christianity of the People and Its Institutions

For centuries, global and mobile entities in the Catholic world, playing a compensatory role regarding the rigidity of the system, had been orders and congregations of religious men and women. These, however, are experiencing a crisis in the last decades of the twentieth century, after reaching, in the middle of the twentieth century, the highest level of growth. Significant was also the role of religious congregations in implementing the reforms of the Council of Trent, and later in carrying out of missionary work throughout the centuries. Today, the Congregation for Institutes of Consecrated Life faces the problems of the religious world through a centralized management, which for years has proven to be rather ineffective in implementing any kind of change. Can problems be solved from the center, or is there need of a plurality and diversification of approaches? In any case, the decline of religious life, if we cannot reverse the trend, does affect the geography of Catholicism, especially that of Catholic women who found in consecrated life a particular form of expression.

The element of the "people"—insists Pope Francis—along with popular piety and much more, are not finding the space they deserve. There is a significant problem of the relationship between the institution and the dynamics of the people, a problem not easily solved, but that must be addressed and understood. Institutions and people are held together, but on what terms? The parish (Francis speaks of it profusely in *Evangelii Gaudium*), or rather the diverse types of the parish, have undergone profound changes. In its impact with globalization and urbanization, and in terms of the people, how do we articulate the space of the diocese (at times as a self-sufficient body or with the "fixation"—reasonable and understandable—to control the whole territory despite the lack of clergy, as seen in some European countries)?

The problems of the Catholic Church in the global world lead to a reflection on its leadership. The Church's ruling class has expanded to worlds and diverse cultures: it is a group of about 5,300 bishops worldwide. In a diverse world, an internationalization of the curia in the last half-century has been implemented (the twentieth century witnessed the transition from a curial staff of the Papal States to an Italian and then an international one). It has not so much been restored to the dimension of the Church of Rome, which presides in charity and participates in some way in the service of communion of its bishop, but rather the Holy See has developed on the model of an international organization, with the presence of national components, but in the mold of a common ecclesiastical culture.

Catholicism appears to be a unique example of a cohesive and worldwide institution, with an international leadership, and a common language. Here we can observe Francis's ability to speak an evangelical language comprehensible to everyone. Yet—limiting myself to the European continent and in comparison with its political elites—I must say that, compared to past generations, especially after the Council, there has been a decline of the cultural level of the episcopal conferences, as the world becomes more complex, with ever more complex signs of the times to decipher. New cultural paths have emerged, replacing a more classical culture (humanities, canon law, philosophy), which, however, did not result in a true renewal, except to overcome models of the past. This has created an ecclesiastical culture, between government and pastoral ministry, not exactly suited to dealing with changes and interpret such a complex reality, but perhaps able to govern the institutions and lead churches as minorities. This is—in my opinion—the problem of Francis's impact on the episcopal conferences and the clergy, or rather the resistance of a part of these to the pressures to go out and change (thus following his example), instead of the traditional "enthusiasm" for the pope that used to prevail among the bishops; this resistance often comes precisely from a type of ecclesiastical culture and an idea of Church management that was part of a certain type of formation.

Failure to Reform the Clergy

Francis's various interventions on clericalism in the Church, untouched through the decades, are interesting and nonformal, especially because they reveal the anxiety of clericalisms's overcoming. But how? In the twentieth century, alongside an ecclesiastical management of the Church, the laity—in various ways—found its own place, often through aggregated forms: Catholic Action, movements, and so on. But these are sectors that are neither all equal nor coincident. The problem is not to enhance a sector (the laity), but has to do with a vision of the Church that is so tied—if you will—to a vision and approach of the clergy.

This represents a serious *nonreform* in the twentieth-century Church, despite the great conciliar achievements on the priesthood of the faithful. The clergy, who—in successive waves—has been asked to provide more commitment, more spirituality, has nonetheless operated steadily within the same frameworks, characterized by its formation. We are talking about 280,000 diocesan priests and 134,800 religious ones, of which 127,800 are European and 54,100 are from the rest of the world. The problem is not only the shortage of priests (a real and dramatic fact in some countries), but it has also to do with the culture and approach represented by this category, which slows down the development of the role of women and laypeople, who are removed from the ecclesiastical culture or should be clericalized to homogenize them.

The Council of Trent, unlike Vatican II, had proposed a model of priest associated with the seminars, the parish, and catechism: the parish priest (manuals on the topic speak for themselves). In this regard, little changed with Vatican II, although there were changes in the facts. Paul VI ruled out the discussion on celibacy and reflection on a new type of clergy. Unlike Trent, we do not really have a Vatican II model of priest, but a modernized version of the classical one. Burdened and under so much pressure and subject to new demands, we have many priests under stress and struggling, subject to various demands, and often declining in number.

We can understand then how some sectors of the clergy are inclined toward delimited models of Catholicism and truth, are more defensive with respect to the complexity of the present, and capable of limiting their horizons. In short, the problem of the clergy remains a crucial point for the basic reality of Catholicism, for its dimension of people, for its leadership, and for addressing the issue of the laity and women in the Church.[28] A first problematic sign is precisely the opposition, by considerable sectors of the clergy, to Francis's message.

Conclusion

The relevant and real problem—it seems to me—is that of a Christianity that lives in history with its transformations in complex and plural societies. Consider the relentless migration toward Europe that is transforming the continent from being rigidly identitarian to a reality of hospitality and integration. In a certain sense, reform is Christianity in history. Deep down—just as Vatican II revealed it in its depths—Christianity is truly an open religious world and—I would like to add—with an intrinsic alertness to what is happening in our global society. This can be seen well in contrast with the Islamic identitarian rigidity and the intra-Islamic conflicts. The awareness of missionary work (and conversion to it) and the need to live and interpret history represent the basis for reform and reforms in a century characterized by great changes, but one in which Christianity appears to be marked by difficulties and great hopes.

NOTES

1. See M. Bloch, *Apologia della storia o mestiere di storico* (Turin: Einaudi, 1978).

2. See S. Dianich, *La Chiesa cattolica verso la sua riforma* (Brescia: Queriniana, 2014).

3. See his essay in this volume, 77–100, esp. 89–96.

4. On this subject, see my article "Da Giovanni XXIII a Paolo VI," in *Chiesa e papato*, ed. A. Riccardi and G. Alberigo (Rome: Laterza, 1990), 169–285; and also P. Rossano, "I papi, la Chiesa e il mondo delle religioni," ibid., 485–534.

5. Paul VI, encyclical letter *Populorum progressio*, March 26, 1967, no. 85.

6. See N. Del Re, *La Curia romana. Lineamenti storico-giuridici* (Rome: Edizioni di storia e letteratura, 1973); F. Jankowiak, *La Curie romaine de Pie IX à Pie X. Le gouvernement central de l'Église et la fin des États pontificaux, 1846–1914* (Rome: École française de Rome, 2007); A. Riccardi, introduction, in *Mélanges de l'École Française de Rome* 110, no. 2 (1998): 439–43, a monograph dedicated to this theme: "Les secrétaires d'État du Saint-Siège 1814–1979. Sources et méthodes."

7. See P. H. Jenkins, *La terza Chiesa. Il cristianesimo nel XXI secolo*, preface by Franco Cardini. (Rome: Fazi, 2004).

8. See S. Gruzinski, *La pensée métisse* (Paris: Fayard, 1999).

9. See A. Riccardi, ed., *Pio XII* (Rome: Laterza, 1984); Riccardi., *Il potere del papa da Pio XII a Giovanni Paolo II* (Rome: Laterza, 1993).

10. See G. Zizola, *Il microfono di Dio. Pio XII, padre Lombardi e i cattolici italiani* (Milan: A. Mondadori, 1990); R. Lombardi, *Il Concilio per una riforma nella carità* (Rome: Apes, 1961).

11. See R. Simonato, *Celso Costantini. Tra rinnovamento cattolico in Italia e le nuove missioni in Cina* (Pordenone: Concordia sette, 1985).

12. See A. Riccardi, "La Santa Sede e la Chiesa in Italia," in *Paul VI et la modernité dans l'Église. Actes du colloque organisé par l'École française de Rome* (Rome: École française de Rome, 1984), 647–72. See also F. De Giorgi, *Mons. Montini. Chiesa cattolica e scontri di civiltà nella prima metà del Novecento* (Bologna: il Mulino, 2012); *Paolo VI. Il papa del Moderno* (Brescia: Morcelliana, 2015).

13. See Jenkins, *La terza Chiesa*, 313.

14. See J. Planellas I Barnosell, *La Chiesa dei poveri. La sfida sempre attuale del Concilio Vaticano II*, preface by Armand Puig i Tarrech (Milan: F. Mondadori, 2015); G. Cottier et al., *Chiesa e povertà* (Rome: AVE, 1968); M. T. Fattori and A. Melloni, eds., *L'evento e le decisioni. Studi sulle dinamiche del Concilio Vaticano II* (Bologna: il Mulino, 1997); G. Turbanti, *Un Concilio per il mondo moderno. La redazione della costituzione pastorale "Gaudium et spes" del Vaticano II* (Bologna: il Mulino, 2000); R. De Mattei, *Il Concilio Vaticano II. Una storia mai scritta* (Turin: Lindau, 2010).

15. See A. Riccardi, *Il secolo del martirio* (Milan: Mondadori, 2000 [new ed., *Il secolo del martirio. I cristiani nel Novecento* [Milan: Oscar Mondadori, 2009]); J.-M. Di Falco, T. Radcliffe, and A. Riccardi, eds., *Il libro nero della condizione dei cristiani nel mondo* (Milan: Mondadori, 2014).

16. A. Riccardi, *Le politiche della Chiesa* (Cinisello Balsamo: San Paolo, 1997).

17. See J. Joblin, *L'Église et la guerre. Conscience, violence, pouvoir* (Paris: Desclée, 1988); see also A. Riccardi, *La pace preventiva. Speranze e ragioni in un mondo di conflitti* (Cinisello Balsamo: San Paolo, 2004).

18. É. Poulat, *Église contre bourgeoisie. Introduction au devenir du catholicisme actuel* (Paris: Berg International, 2006[2]).

19. É. Poulat, *Une Église ébranlée. Changement, conflit et continuité, de Pie XII à Jean-Paul II* (Tournai: Casterman, 1980); A. Riccardi, *Intransigenza e modernità. La Chiesa cattolica verso il terzo millennio* (Rome: Laterza, 1996).

20. On Louis Massignon, see G. Basetti Sani, *Louis Massignon 1883–1962* (Florence: Alinea, 1985); and his biography by C. Destremau and

J. Moncelon, *Massignon* (Paris: Plon, 1994); on Fr. Giovanni Fausti, see P. Pepa, *Pagine sulla dittatura. Il volto dei martiri albanesi* (Avezzano: Rindertimi; Terlizzi: Ed. Insieme, 1998).

21. See A. Riccardi, ed., *Le Chiese e gli altri. Culture, religioni, ideologie e Chiese cristiane nel Novecento* (Milan: Guerini, 2008).

22. See Comunità di Sant'Egidio, *Lo spirito di Assisi. Dalle religioni una speranza di pace* (Cinisello Balsamo: San Paolo, 2011); M. Nicolini-Zani, ed., *Insieme per pregare. Le religioni nello spirito di Assisi*, introduction by Enzo Bianchi (Magnano: Qiqajon/Comunità di Bose, 2011); C. Bonizzi, *L'icona di Assisi nel magistero di Giovanni Paolo II* (Assisi: Ed. Porziuncola, 2002).

23. Pope Francis, Meeting with the Bishops of the United States of America, Address of the Holy Father, Cathedral of Saint Matthew, Washington, DC, Wednesday, September 23, 2015.

24. Riccardi, *Le Chiese e gli altri*, 22–25; see also G. Kepel, *La revanche de Dieu* (Paris: Seuil, 1991).

25. See Jenkins, *La terza Chiesa*; W. Hollenweger, "Le Pentecôtisme avenir planétaire du christianisme?" in *Géopolitique du christianisme*, ed. B. Chélini-Pont and R. Liogier (Paris: Ellipses, 2003), 149–57.

26. See C. M. Galli, *Dio vive in città. Verso una nuova pastorale urbana* (Vatican City: Libreria Editrice Vaticana, 2014).

27. Congregatio Pro Gentium Evangelizatione, *Atlas Hierarchicus* (Vatican City: Libreria Editrice Vaticana, 2010).

28. See M. Guasco, *Storia del clero in Italia dall'Ottocento a oggi* (Rome: Laterza, 1997).

6

ECCLESIA SEMPER REFORMANDA

From the Fourteenth to the Sixteenth Century

Giancarlo Pani, SJ

The origin of the formula *Ecclesia semper reformanda*, although widespread among the Calvinists, is unknown: we do not know who the author is. Until not long ago, it was believed to be Karl Barth, who would use it, even before the fifties, in several of his books, including the famous *Kirchliche Dogmatik*.[1] But when he was asked what the origin of "his" formula was, he responded by saying that it was an old tradition of the Church.[2]

The *Encyclopédie du protestantisme* traces the formula to Calvin's *Institutio christianae religionis* (IV, 2:11ff.).[3] After the break with Rome, the Genevan reformer, inquiring about the responsibility of the papist Church, accusing it of imprisoning God's word and the sacraments, determined that it was necessary to weed out its errors in light of Scripture. This condemnation of the Church of Rome did not prevent him, however, from detecting in it the traces of the true Church, but they would have to be improved. However, the formula does not appear in Calvin's text.

The *Lexikon für Theologie und Kirche* mentions it in a few lines, only in the latest edition, stressing that it is a formula of Calvinist theology, with roots in the early seventeenth century. It also notes that the formula was restored at Vatican II.[4]

More documented is Theodor Mahlmann's "Reformation" entry in the *Historisches Wörterbuch der Philosophie* of 1992,[5] later mentioned again in the 2010 essay entitled *Ecclesia semper reformanda*. Through extensive historical research, Mahlmann traces the origin of the formula to the Dutchman Jodocus van Lodensteyns (1602–1677), a Reformed pastor of the more rigorous and committed Pietist strain, which in turn refers to an anonymous source.[6]

Some scholars have challenged the Calvinist origins of the formula, which could have also originated before the Reformation.[7] Others have argued that it echoes the already present Carthusian formula, albeit in a different sense. Their motto is well known: *Chartusia numquam reformata quia numquam deformata* (The Carthusians were never reformed because they were never deformed).

However, considering the beginning of the pontificate of Paul III in 1534, it is worth noting an unpublished memoir of a jurist from Novara, Giovan Battista Caccia, on the reform of the Church: *De fide integrand ac de ecclesia reformanda*, dedicated to Paul III, in which stand out criticisms and protests calling for a mandatory Church reform. At the beginning of the treatise, he states that "the Holy Mother Church" has changed so much that it no longer shows "a sign of her evangelical character, and there is no sign in her of humility, frugality, continence, and apostolic vigor."[8]

Ecclesia Semper Reformanda

In any case, the meaning of the formula is clear. It concisely enunciates a fact and a program. The fact is the historical present of the Church at the end of the medieval period and beginning of the modern world: there is urgent need of reform and renewal at the end of a long and troubled period. This can be interpreted variously. The gerundive *reformanda* affirms a spiritual goal that the motto presumes and revives: a need springing from the situation of the Church as a living organism. By its nature, the Church is called to a continuous purification, to regenerate its spiritual growth. It is the meaning of Romans 12:2, where Paul refers to a renewal, a spiritual progress, inner progress, precisely of its baptismal life, its crowning glory; or even of Ephesians 4:23, with the invitation to be renewed in the Spirit, to reach the fullness of Christ's body.

The gerundive of the formula may also indicate an action ordered from above, that the Church *must* perform. *Ecclesia semper reformanda* is the consequence of the word of the living God.[9] The gerundive also reinforces the spiritual inspiration that underlies and always reiterates that the "reform" is permanent, a longing for a constant spiritual regeneration that never ends. It is based on the awareness of the inability to correspond with what it "ought to be," and therefore, in the face of inevitable failure, it expresses the need to reform, in order to regain the original form of the gospel.

Reform "in Head and Members"

A similar formula—*reformatio in capite et membris*—dates to the high Middle Ages.[10] As early as the fourteenth century, the need to reform the Church became an emerging and explosive question of political relevance, acquiring an urgency hardly imaginable earlier. At the Ecumenical Council of Vienne, in France (1311–1312), a new wrinkle arises: the pope, Clement V, after developing the idea of calling the council and setting the agenda (the problem of the Templars, reform, etc.), invites the bishops to make proposals for the renewal of the Church.

The best-known document is the treatise of the bishop of Mende, Guillaume Durand the Younger (d. 1330), on how to hold the council.[11] He is the first bishop to speak of a reform of the universal Church and uses the expression that later became the historical and widely cited formula, *reformatio tam in capite quam in membris*. He envisions the function of the council to "correct and reform...the Church of God,...both in its head and in its members."[12] For the first time a theme appears that will subsequently reappear until the Council of Trent, one that would become "a real cry of alarm."[13] A term is also employed that will become epochal in the history of the Church and will constitute its historical crux: *reform*, *reformatio*. The problems that emerge are listed accurately and exemplify the same criticisms emerging in the following centuries:

> Limitations of the episcopal power, accumulation of prebends and disrespect for the obligation of residency;... neglect of the duty of preaching; very little training, greed, and low spiritual and moral levels of the clergy; excessive and abusive recourse to ecclesiastical penalties, with the far too often recourse on the part of parish priests to excommunication of hundreds of people.[14]

But the biggest novelty was that of Durand's "reform in head and members," which ended with the Gospel invitation: "Why do you see the speck in your neighbor's eye, but do not notice the log in your own eye?" (Matt 7:3).

However, even though Council of Vienne issued several decrees to reform the Church, it all came to nothing. A few years later the Great Western Schism occurred, and its serious and urgent problems sidelined Church reform.

The Following Councils

The theme of reform occurs multiple times in subsequent ecumenical councils.

The Council of Constance (1414–1418) was intended not only to eradicate the schism and restore unity in the Church, but also to reform it "in head and members."[15] The Council of Basel (1431–1449), despite the ongoing conflict between Eugene IV and the conciliarist group, had among its objectives the reform of the Church as well. A key element was the reduction of centralism and the papal fiscal system, which linked the granting of offices to the economic interests of the Roman curia. Annual payments, the Roman assets linked to office employment, were suppressed. Episcopal elections, which for a long time were exclusive to Rome, were resumed. It also intervened at the ecclesial level with the reestablishment of regular diocesan and provincial synods, as well as with various interventions aimed at the reform of the clergy and religious orders. Nothing, however was said about the sinecure system, on which the livelihood of clergy, bishops, and cardinals depended. It did not deal with the monetary interests of the conciliar fathers. John of Segovia, one of the council members and a professor at the University of Salamanca, was not wrong when he argued that there was something similar to what usually happened to justice even in the reform of the Church: "It was wanted in every other house, but not in one's own."[16]

Of Lateran V, summoned by Pope Julius II to delegitimize the *Conciliabulum* of Pisa, it is worth remembering Giles of Viterbo's inaugural address, focused on the "reform" of the Church and society. His assessment became famous: *Homines per sacra immutari fas est, non sacra homines* (Man must be changed by what is holy, not what is holy by man), which stresses that man must be transformed by religion, and not the opposite.[17] Several reform proposals were then discussed, without ever being carried out. In his history of the Council of Trent, Hubert Jedin wrote, "A great opportunity was lost."[18]

Simultaneously, in 1513, immediately after the election of Leo X, two Camaldolese monks, Paolo Giustiniani and Pietro Quirini, sent to the pope a proposal for a reform of the Church worldwide, entitled *Libellus ad Leonem X*.[19] They presented a comprehensive reform program under the aegis of the new pope. Leo X was of the Medici family; thus, his name was seen as a symbol of his mission to heal and "medicate" the Church. The two monks railed against the ills and evils of the Church: first the scandal caused by the life and behavior of the clergy and religious, then the conduct of the popes and the cardinals of the curia, who were only concerned with the interests of their families and had even reached the point of transforming the capital of Christianity into a scandalous brothel.[20] The *Libellus* clearly denounced the root of all these evils: the degradation and ignorance of the priests (many of whom were unable to read Latin liturgical texts),[21] their public and private lives, and the rampant superstition in worship.[22] The two monks also denounced the laity's lack of interest in religious instruction.

With the new scenario that emerged with the discovery of the Americas, Quirini and Giustiniani urged the Church of Rome to rethink the work of evangelization in the New World. This shows the attention of the two monks, not only to the widening of the boundaries of the gospel proclamation, but also to the new historical dimension that was about to become world history. The reference to the New World is thus even more important, as there seems to be almost no trace of it at the Council of Trent.

Positive proposals were not lacking either: it was necessary to reform theology and how it was studied, to always have the Bible and the Church fathers as reference points. The idea of making a vernacular translation of the Scriptures for use in the liturgy was original and brave, in imitation of what St. Jerome had done with the ancient Vulgate.[23] Unfortunately, there were some low points: it was assumed that force would be used, if necessary, to convert Jews and Muslims.[24]

The *Libellus* had no impact on the life of the Church, but soon after its proposals were to become reality with Luther's Reformation.

Along with Lateran V, we should recall a consistory in 1514, in which a singular episode took place. While the Council was proposing a reform of the Roman curia, Leo X granted to Albert of Brandenburg, already archbishop of Magdeburg and administrator of Halberstadt, the dispensation to add the bishopric of Mainz to the two he already possessed—a booty of ecclesiastical benefices unusual even for Germany.[25] Albert of Brandenburg was just twenty-five, and as the seat of the electorate, Mainz was politically the most important bishopric of the empire. To obtain the papal dispensation and the pallium, it was necessary to pay a considerable sum, which could be provided by selling indulgences for the reconstruction of St. Peter's Basilica. It became the spark that ignited the Reformation.[26]

Erasmus of Rotterdam

Before moving on to Martin Luther, we should remember Erasmus of Rotterdam, not only for the fact that he is traditionally seen in close contact with the Reformation (for many Catholics Erasmus laid the egg that Luther hatched),[27] but also for his decisive influence on the history of the sixteenth century.

Erasmus has been called the "prince of humanists": in him converged the currents of reform that arose in Europe in the late Middle Ages and the early modern period. These included, in particular, *devotio moderna*; Lorenzo Valla (in terms of reform, worth remembering of his is not only his *Donation of Constantine*, but also his philological study of the New Testament); Johannes Reuchlin, the first Hebraist of humanism and scholar of Jewish culture; Lefèvre d'Etaples (Faber Stapulensis) and evangelism with the publication of the first historical-critical edition of Paul's letters; John Colet and his new way of commenting on the Letter to the Romans; and Cardinal Francisco Ximenes de Cisneros and the *Polyglotta Complutensis*, where classical humanism and philological exegesis meet. With Erasmus, we reach the climax of the literary humanism that exerted a most profound influence on European cultural history. However, his attempt at cultural and ecclesial reform was squeezed between Luther's Reformation and the renewal that animated the Council of Trent.

Erasmus's masterpiece is not, as considered for centuries, the *Praise of Folly*, but the *Novum Instrumentum*, the first critical edition (ahead of its time) of the New Testament in Greek, with a Latin translation entirely rewritten and based on the original.[28] The edition included also, as introduction, the *Methodus* and the *Paraclesis id est exhortatio ad christianae philosophiae studium*. Erasmus strongly urges with all knowledge of classical rhetoric to the "holy and wholesome study of Christian philosophy" found in the Scriptures that far exceeds all pagan philosophy. The *Novum Instrumentum*, which later took the title of *Novum Testamentum*, is accompanied by an edition of patristic texts so accurate that it became the basis for many subsequent editions. All reformers would eventually treasure Erasmus's edition of the New Testament, which in the sixteenth century saw five new versions and over two hundred reprints.

It is also worth remembering the *Enchiridion militis christiani*, the manual of the Christian soldier, in which through war imagery Erasmus points out the importance of the Christian militia and aims to present Christianity as it is announced in the gospel, assimilating it to the true biblical and Christ-centered *pietas*. In other words, he wanted to offer for the reform of the Church a condensation of humanism (literary elegance, philology, rhetoric, grammar, as opposed to the "barbarism" of Scholasticism) and the *philosophia Christi*, which is based on a great familiarity with the New Testament and with the Pauline letters: "For Erasmus the man in all its fullness is the Christian formed in classical culture and transformed by the Gospel."[29]

As for the relationship between Erasmus and Luther, some have stressed their closeness, reducing or tempering the conflict that arose between them to personal matters. Emblematic of this is their controversy over free will (Erasmus's *De libero arbitrio*, Luther's *De servo arbitrio*), which reflects the deep and irreconcilable difference between the two figures. While Luther defended a certain determinism, invalidating all man's faculties, Erasmus's "Catholic" point of view seems to be simply Pelagianism.[30] Luther had tried at first to win the humanist's support, whom he later considered a skeptical theologian: he even referred to him as elusive and slippery as an eel, always able to escape from any place he wanted to.[31]

Ignatius of Loyola, on the other hand, left an unambiguous verdict against the prince of humanists: his works should not be read.[32] The reason for this is precisely Ignatius's spiritual discernment: Erasmus is a master of literary interiority cultivated with taste, a wholly human interiority, while Ignatius is a master of spiritual discernment, conversion, and Christian life. His most famous book, the *Spiritual Exercises*, are not an ascetic work to be read, but one designed to shape in the believer an evangelical life and inner conversion.

Today, it is quite remarkable that the man who had perhaps the most influence on the culture and theology of the sixteenth century had no disciples or followers, nor did he start a school. Luther's Reformation first, and later the Council of Trent, crushed him.

Martin Luther and the Reformation

Luther did not come from nowhere. In the beginning, there are the personal vicissitudes of an Augustinian monk who questions the "righteousness of God," the critical conscience of a biblical exegesis teacher facing the prevailing Scholastic theology and taking a sincere but singular stance against the preaching of indulgences for the reconstruction of St. Peter's Basilica. At a more profound level, there was the need for an encounter with the gospel and a pastoral concern for a reflection of faith. At the center, there is the question of the justification of the sinner, along with the problematic nature of the penitential practices of the times.

On the eve of All Saints Day, October 31, 1517—according to the official version—Martin Luther, a young professor at the University of Wittenberg, nailed on the church door of the castle the text of the Ninety-Five Theses on indulgences. This story gave rise to Reformation Day, which is celebrated on October 31 and commemorates the posting of the theses.

But there is historical doubt: is this is a true story, or a legend? The question is legitimate, because on the one hand, based on the answer appears the intention, no doubt sincere, of a then-unknown professor, Martin Luther, who takes to heart his vocation as theologian and questions the scandal of indulgences; and on the other, a lack of attention along with the refusal by the Church's authority to engage in a serious doctrinal reflection on the controversial issue of a will for reform.

The only document that attests to the fact is found in the introduction to the second volume of Luther's Latin works. Philip Melanchthon wrote it in 1546, a few months after the death of the reformer: "Luther wrote theses on indulgences and posted them publicly on the church which is next to the castle of Wittenberg, the eve of All Saints Day, in the year 1517."[33]

The reliability of this testimony was questioned by Erwin Iserloh, a historian of the Reformation: he pointed out that the testimony dates about thirty years later, is not supported by any previous document, and moreover, came from a witness who was not in Wittenberg at the time.[34] It is also worth considering that Melanchthon, although an intimate of Luther, was not well informed of events he had not witnessed (for example, he claimed that indulgences were preached in Wittenberg, but that never happened because of the explicit prohibition of Prince Elector Frederick the Wise, who wanted to prevent money from going abroad).[35]

The historian did not merely criticize the legendary origin of the nailing of the theses, but put in evidence the reasons why it could not have happened, at least in those terms. The point is that Luther became aware that the preachers of indulgences were not acting on their own personal initiative, but according to a precise *Instruction*, that is, an official directive of the Church. Thus, on October 31, 1517, he wrote two letters, one to his ordinary, the other to the presiding officer of the preaching of indulgences, Albert of Brandenburg, to communicate to them his pastoral concerns about the scandal of the illicit trade. This second letter has been preserved.[36] Luther frankly stated, but without defiance, that he could not remain silent in the face of such grave facts. He lamented over the reckless manner in which indulgences were presented to the people[37] and above all—and this is the essence that will cause unexpected developments—the false security that the preachers wanted to inculcate in the minds of the faithful for the salvation of their souls.[38] They preached and affirmed as an essential aspect of the indulgence itself, that once the letter of indulgence had been obtained, their hearers obtained the forgiveness of even the most serious sins, and salvation was thus assured. They also added that the souls of the deceased, to whom the indulgence was applied, were immediately released from purgatory. Discretely but firmly, Luther pointed out to the archbishop that the Christian people needed someone who could preach the gospel, prayer, and charitable works, rather than indulgences. In his view, the gospel message, "the first and only mission of every bishop," was neglected to make room for the "racket of indulgences."[39] He begged him, therefore, to revoke the *Instruction* for preachers, which was drafted in the archbishop's name but certainly without his knowledge.

At the end of the letter, the Ninety-Five Theses on indulgences make their sudden appearance. In fact, Luther suggested that if a remedy was not sought quickly, it would have been possible for someone to publicly refute the preachers of indulgences, thus proving that the *Instruction*, which bore the name of the archbishop, was baseless.[40] Therefore, Luther included in his letter a series of objections, some ironic, some sarcastic, to show the concerns of a theologian regarding the preaching of indulgences.[41] These objections dealt with the practice and theology of penance, in particular indulgences, intended as a way to reduce the temporal punishment and as a good deed. In them, Luther also criticized the treasures of the Church and the power of the pope. Finally, through them he proposed greater attention to the poor. Overall, the Ninety-Five Theses formed an exhortation to evangelical repentance and to embrace the cross of Christ.

Thus, they were presented as notes of reflection on which Luther had dwelt at length, rather than as articles of a profession of faith.

They were addressed in confidence to the religious authorities, not shouted in public as a gesture of protest. Above all, they were intended to ask for a reason, not start a debate: the scandal of indulgences had profoundly hurt him, and he needed clarification in the context of an academic debate. That is why the theses were written in Latin:[42] they were not intended for circulation, least of all for the general public. This is also the reason why the theses were not known in circles closest to Luther.[43]

After writing to the bishops, Luther waited some time for an answer that never came.[44] Then he began to talk to friends and send a few handwritten copies to known and trusted theologians: "Despised, I decided to make the theses known to the public."[45] A short time later, by January 1518, they had spread throughout Germany. It is known that they were greeted favorably by some future opponents of Luther, such as Johann Cochläus, Hieronymus Emser, and Duke George of Saxony.[46] This is the true story revealing on the one hand the conscience of a professor of theology dealing with a doctrinal problem, and on the other, the silence of the Church on a serious and pressing matter. The archbishop of Mainz did not deign to respond to Luther, but instead denounced him to Rome since the theses criticized the authority of the pope and therefore were heretical.

It thus becomes clear that the Wittenberg theses did not express any desire to break with the Church, but they articulated the doubts of a theologian, addressed to the Church, and the sincere desire to reach acceptable clarification on a matter of faith and Christian life; in essence, they demonstrated the need of a reform. As Joseph Lortz repeatedly pointed out, at that time Luther had no intention to break with the Church.[47] The breakup eventually took place, but against his original intentions.

The Roman Curia and the Princely Splendor

At this time, the state of the Roman curia was truly miserable, the *cura animarum* (care of souls) almost completely overlooked. Instead the only care was for money for lavish display and princely patronage, the luxury of the court, and for repaying debts. The corruption of offices was deplorable, the privileges of all sorts, the benefices, and all that they entailed. In 1522, the situation of the curia was articulated with clarity and sincerity in the admission of guilt by Adrian VI, the successor of Leo X, through the nuncio Francesco Chieregati, at the Nuremberg diet: "Vice has become so natural that those who are stained with it...are no longer aware of the stink of it."[48]

> We openly confess that God allows this persecution of his Church because of the sins of men, and in particular of priests and prelates....The Holy Scripture clearly teaches that the sins of the people have their origin in the sins of the clergy....We know that even in this Holy See for years many detestable things took place: abuses in ecclesiastical matters, violation of precepts; better yet, everything has changed for the worse. So it is no wonder that the disease has gone from the head to the members, from the popes to the prelates....We need to humble ourselves before God: each one should meditate on the reasons of his fall and make straight his path again.... Therefore, in our name you promise that we want to commit ourselves to the improvement of the Roman curia, from which all these evils originated: from here the disease spread, so from here health will be restored. And we consider ourselves all the more obliged, since we all ardently wish for reform.[49]

Adrian VI had the courage to make a truthful confession before the world: he frankly denounced the evils of the Church, indicating the means to find a remedy, but most importantly he reiterated that reform must start from the pope and the Roman curia.

However, the pope's initiative was not successful. His premature death, after a year of pontificate, put everything to rest. It would take the disaster of the Sack of Rome in 1527 and the expansion of the Lutheran Reformation to awaken the Church to work effectively for the convening of a council.

An Attempt at Reform before Trent: The *Consilium de Emendanda Ecclesia*

Among the works of Paul III Farnese (pope from 1534 to 1549) for the reform of the Church, worth noting is the *Consilium de emendanda ecclesia* of 1537. It is well known that for the Farnese prince, throughout his life, the advancement of his own family was one of his main concerns. As a Farnese, he behaved like a pope, and as pope he remained a Farnese. But he took on the responsibilities and problems handed down by previous pontificates. Particularly among these were a peace treaty between the Christian princes; the advance of the Turks in Europe; the concern for Luther's Reformation, which exploded in Germany and was swiftly spreading throughout Europe; the urgent need to convene a council universally demanded for years; and especially the reform of the Church. If the way in which he dealt with all these issues is debatable, ultimately more as an astute politician than as a pope and man of the Church, Paul III had the merit of having convened the Council of Trent and, before that, establishing the *Consilium de emendanda ecclesia,* which was a report for ecclesial reform. If the *Consilium* in the end did not have an immediate effect, it did pave the way to the council.

Before convening the *Consilium,* Paul III renewed the college of cardinals, which as early as the previous century had undergone a process of secularization. He appointed several cardinals who would have important roles in the Council of Trent: Gasparo Contarini, John Fisher, Giampietro Carafa (later Pope Paul IV), Marcello Cervini (later Pope Marcello II), and Giovanni Morone (who would lead the third session of the Council of Trent). It is worth mentioning Hubert Jedin's assessment of the college of cardinals: "The sixty-three cardinals who were part of the college that in the year 1545 constituted the council, taken together, were a senate of the Church of absolute worth."[50]

The *Consilium* proposed a fundamentally pastoral reform project, with the *cura animarum* as its main goal. The starting point was the realization of the worldly and scandalous life of the Church, which originated first with the papacy. Some scholars taught the pope as head of the Church was allowed everything, and therefore his will, whatever it may be, became legitimate. "From this cause, as from the famous Trojan horse, the Church of God has been inundated by such a large number of abuses and evils that, as we can see for ourselves, it is afflicted in an almost hopeless way."[51] Hence a series of abuses in establishing God's ministers: among others, the ordination of unprepared priests and abuses in the distribution of ecclesiastical benefices, first of all the bishoprics: "about which, it has become customary to favor individuals, to whom are awarded benefices, and not the flock of Christ and the Church."[52] Regarding the cardinals, the accumulation of multiple bishoprics was reported.

The Reform and Women

Within the reform processes of the Church between the fifteenth and sixteenth centuries, an important role should also be ascribed to the new opportunity given to anyone who was able to read the Bible and interpret it—therefore, also to women. From the middle of the fifteenth century, thanks to the invention of the printing press, versions of the sacred text began to be published in the vernacular. Women, hitherto excluded from direct contact with the word of God, treasured it, read it with acumen, assimilated it, and discovered something: the message of the Lord's resurrection was entrusted to Mary Magdalene, thus women also are called to proclaim the gospel. Sacred Scripture spoke of them, and to them.

The study dedicated to the Bible and women, edited by Adriana Valerio, highlighted this aspect very well.[53] The *Memoriale di Monteluce* of 1488 states that the nuns of a Perugia convent copied and translated into the vernacular not only biblical books, but also the commentaries on the sacred texts.[54] St. Catherine Vigri, in the second half of the century, anticipated some biblical themes that would be central in the sixteenth century: the Scriptures emancipate believers from blind obedience—which sometimes goes against their conscience and makes them incapable of spiritual judgment.[55] Domenica da Paradiso, though illiterate, thanks to the spread of public Bible readings in the vernacular, became a "preacher," showing excellent biblical erudition and an unusual familiarity with the sacred texts. Even before Luther, from her writings the role given to the Holy Scriptures as the basis for Church reform is clear.[56] She was the "spiritual mother" of Caterina Cybo, the protagonist of Italian evangelism.

At the beginning of the sixteenth century, there were many spiritual circles, often hosted by noblewomen, where the Bible was read and commented on. Vittoria Colonna, one of the animators of the *Ecclesia Viterbensis*, promoted in her poetry a reform of the Church from the reading and interpretation of Sacred Scripture.[57]

The *Ecclesia semper reformanda* at this point reached into the Council of Trent, a new phase in its history. Despite the previous century's experience with conciliarism and Lateran V, the council was universally considered the appropriate way to deal with theological problems and the reform of the Church. Although it would not be an easy road, as it was imagined at first, in its long trajectory of nearly twenty years, Trent marked the turning point that led to a new page in the history of the Church.

NOTES

1. K. Barth, "Die Lehre von der Versöhnung," in *Die Kirchliche Dogmatik* IV/1 (Zurich: EVZ, 1960), 770, 773, 787; but it had already apeared in *Die protestantische Theologie im 19. Jahrhundert. Ihre Vorgeschichte und ihre Geschichte* (Zurich: Evangelische Verlag, 1947), 518.

2. Theodor Mahlmann, "*Ecclesia semper reformanda*. Eine historische Aufklärung. Neue Bearbeitung," in *Hermeneutica sacra. Studien zur Auslegung der Heiligen Schrift im 16. und 17. Jahrhundert*, ed. T. Johansson, R. Kolb, and J. A. Steiger (New York: Walter de Gruyter, 2010), 388.

3. A. Birmelé, "Église," in *Encyclopédie du protestantisme*, ed. P. Gisel (Paris: Cerf, 1995), 490.

4. M. Kehl, "Ecclesia," in *Lexikon für Theologie und Kirche*, ed. W. Kasper (Freiburg: Herder, 1995^3), 437. See also *LG* 9 ("*Ecclesia puri canda*") and *UR* 6 ("*Ecclesia…vocatur a Christo ad perennem reformationem*").

5. T. Mahlmann, "Reformation," in *Historisches Wörterbuch der Philosophie* (Basel: Schwabe, 1992), 8:416–27.

6. More precisely, he refers to a "geleerd Man": see "*Ecclesia semper reformanda*," 423–25.

7. See G. Bárczay, *Ecclesia semper reformanda. Eine Untersuchung zum Kirchenbegriff des 19. Jahrhunderts* (Zurich: EVZ, 1960), 19n37.

8. I. B. Cacia, *De de integranda ac de ecclesia reformanda ad Paulum III*, in Cod. Vat. 3659, *f.* i^v. See L. Von Pastor, *Storia dei Papi dalla fine del Medioevo*, vol. 5, *Paolo III (1534–1549)* (Rome: Desclée, 1931), 89ff.

9. See Bárczay, *Ecclesia semper reformanda*, 21.

10. K. A. Frech, *Reform an Haupt und Gliedern. Untersuchung zur Entwicklung und Verwendung der Formulierung im Hoch- und Spätmittelalter* (Frankfurt: Lang, 1992), 366.

11. G. Durantis, *Tractatus de modo generalis concilii celebrandi et corruptelis in ecclesia reformandis* (Lyon 1531; repr., London, 1964).

12. Ibid., tit. I, p. I.

13. See K. Schatz, *Storia dei Concili. La Chiesa nei suoi punti focali* (Bologna: EDB, 2012), 113.

14. Ibid., 113ff.

15. Ibid., 131.

16. Ibid., 142.

17. Cf. J. W. O'Malley, "Egidio da Viterbo and Renaissance Rome," in *Egidio da Viterbo, O.S.A. e il suo tempo. Atti del V Convegno dell'Istituto storico agostiniano* (Rome: Analecta Augustiniana, 1983), 77ff.

18. H. Jedin, *Storia del Concilio di Trento*, vol.1, *La lotta per il Concilio* (Brescia: Morcelliana, 1973^2), 157.

19. *Il Libellus ad Leonem* was published by J. B. Mittarelli and A. Costadoni in the *Annales Camaldulenses Ordinis Sancti Benedicti*, IX (Venice, 1773), 612–719.

20. Ibid., 674–76. A few years before, around 1490, a text, *Epistola de miseria curatorum seu plebanorum*, appeared in Augusta, Bavaria, which knew several editions, and in which the priests warned of the possible dangers and delusions inherent in pastoral care. The epistle enumerates nine *diaboli*; among these dangers are mentioned, in addition to the collaborators of priest and concubines, even bishops who, for their privileges, are compared to rapacious wolves (ibid., 10 and 11).

21. *Libellus ad Leonem*, 676.

22. Ibid., 675.

23. The two hermits, in proposing the vernacular version of the Bible, referred to the origins of the history of Christianity and insisted on the *mos antiquorum* and the *christiana puritas* to return to the sources of the ancient Church. Even the *Epistola de miseria curatorum* insisted on the priests' duty to know the Bible (folio ij and 8r).

24. *Libellus ad Leonem*, 621ff. In any case, it was also said that no one should be forced into the faith.

25. L. Von Pastor, *Storia dei papi dalla fine del Medioevo*, vol. 4/1: *Leone* X (Rome: Desclée, 1908), 213ff.

26. G. Alberigo, "La Chiesa e l'Europa nel Cinquecento" in AA.VV., *La storia dei giubilei*, vol. 2, *1450–1575* (Rome: Giunti, 1998), 150–79.

27. The saying is found in the letters of Erasmus: P. S. Allen, *Opus epistolarum Des. Erasmi Roterodami* (Oxford: Clarendon, 1924), 5:609 and 11:21.

28. *Novum Instrumentum omne diligenter ad Erasmo roterodamo recognitum et emendatum ad graecam veritatem, Apud inclytam Germaniae Basilaeam* (Froben, 1516). The text consists of more than a thousand pages.

29. L. E. Halkin, *Erasmo*, intro. by Eugenio Garin (Rome: Laterza, 1989), 220.

30. See S. Corradino, "Vera e falsa interiorità," in *Stella Matutina* 2 (1964): 48–51.

31. WA Tischreden 1, 55, 32ff.

32. Ignazio di Loyola, *Gli scritti*, ed. Gesuiti della Provincia d'Italia (Rome: ADP, 2007), 1271: Letter to Annibale de Coudret, August 27,1553.

33. *Corpus Reformatorum* 6, C. A. Schwetschke, Halis Saxonum 1839, 161ff. At the origin of the debate on the posting of the Theses are the studies of H. Volz, *Martin Luthers Thesenanschlag und dessen Vorgeschichte* (Weimar: Böhlau, 1959); Volz tries to prove that the posting of the Theses did not occur on October 31, 1517, but the next day, on the Feast of All Saints.

34. E. Iserloh, *Lutero tra riforma cattolica e protestante*, foreword by Mario Bendiscioli (Brescia: Queriniana, 1970 [orig. ed., 1962]). Studies on the subject are numerous, but no one can dispute Isterloh's rigorous reconstruction.

35. Ibid., 125–27.

36. The letter is in the Stockholm Royal Archives.

37. Cf. WA Briefe 1, 111, 15–20. Luther claims that he had not heard the preachers of indulgences personally. Tetzel had begun preaching in March 1517 at Halle and then in April at Jüteborg, a few miles from Wittenberg, where the inhabitants had come to listen to him "like crazy" (WA Tischreden 5, 76, 14).

38. This warning is also found in Luther's earlier writings, especially in the *Dictata super Psalterium*: cf. WA 3, 417, 7ff. See *Tactatus* in WA Briefe 12, 9, 151–156.

39. "*Opera pietatis et charitatis sunt in in nitum meliora indulgentiis.... Omnium Episcoporum hoc sit officium primum et solum, vt populus Euangelium discat et Charitatem Christi*" (ibid., 1, 111, 37–41).

40. "*Si t[uae] R[evendissime] p[aternitati] placet, poterit has meas disputationes videre, vt intelligat, quam dubia res sit Indulgentiarum opinio, quam illi* [the preachers of indulgences] *vt certissimam seminant*" (ibid., 112, 66–68).

41. The date is found at the end of the letter: "*Ex Vittenberga 1517. Vigilia omnium Sanctorum*" (ibid., 112, 65ff.).

42. Cf. J. Lortz, *La Riforma in Germania*, vol. 1, *Premesse, inizio, primi risultati* (Milan: Jaca Book, 1979).

43. Lang, prior of the Augustinian convent of Erfurt, received them a few days after November 11, 1517 (WA Briefe 1, 122, 55).

44. A late *Tischrede* (of 1532) testifies that the Lutheran ordinary, Hieronymus Schulz, replied in that circumstance with the intimation of silence on indulgences since the institutions of the Church were called into question (WA Tischreden 2, 479, 6–8).

45. "*Ego contemptus edidi Disputationis scedulam*" (*Vorrede zum 1. Bande der Gesamtausgabe seiner lat. Schriften* [Wittenberg, 1545]: WA 54, 180, 12–20).

46. See Lortz, *La Riforma in Germania*, 237ff.

47. Ibid., 432–47; 489–90. See also Iserloh, *Lutero tra riforma cattolica e protestante*, 160. The historian is able to discern through Luther's words that he became a "reformer against his will": "*Nunc, quid faciam? Revocare non possum et miram mihi invidiam ex ea invulgatione video con ari: invitus venio in publicum periculosissimumque ac varium hominum iudicium, praesertim ego indoctus, stupidus ingenio, vacuus erudition*" (Letter of Presentation of the *Resolutiones* to Leo X: WA 1, 529, 3–6); "*In negotium euangelii insciens a Deo coniectus sum. Quod si praevidissem ea, quae nunc expertus sum, nullo modo passus fuissem me adigere*" (WA Tischreden 1, 601, 15–17).

48. Lortz, *La Riforma in Germania*, 94. On Adriano VI, see M. Rosa, "Adriano VI," in *Enciclopedia dei Papi*, III, *Enciclopedia Italiana* (Rome: Istituto della Enciclopedia italiana, 2000), 64–70.

49. L. Von Pastor, *Storia dei papi dalla fine del Medio Evo*, vol. 4/2, *Adriano VI e Clemente VII* (Rome: Desclée, 1929), 87ff.

50. Jedin, *Storia del Concilio di Trento*, I1:491.

51. M. Marcocchi, *La riforma cattolica. Documenti e testimonianze*, I (Brescia: Morcelliana, 1967), 480ff.

52. Ibid., 482ff.

53. A. Valerio, ed., *Donne e Bibbia. Storia ed esegesi* (Bologna: EDB, 2006).

54. *Memoriale di Monteluce* (Assisi: Porziuncola, 1983).

55. A. Vigri, *Le sette armi spirituali* (Modena: Ed. della Felce, 1963; orig. ed. 1775).

56. See her *Dialogo della mistica e scolastica teologia* (1503): see A. Valerio, *Domenica da Paradiso* (Spoleto: Centro Studi sull'Alto Medioevo, 1992).

57. A. Valerio, "La Bibbia, le donne e la crisi dell'Europa moderna," in *Donne e Bibbia nella crisi dell'Europa cattolica (Secoli XVI–XVII)*, ed. A. Valerio and M. L. Giordano (Trapani: Il pozzo di Giacobbe, 2014), 16–22.

7

ECCLESIA SEMPER REFORMANDA

The Lessons of History and the Ecumenical Meaning

Angelo Maffeis

It is often argued—not without good reason—that among the reasons that have caused the concept of reform to become suspect for the Church and Catholic theology is the memory of the ecclesial division that came after the Protestant Reformation of the sixteenth century, whose consequences are still painfully present. In the collective memory, the idea of reform is indeed spontaneously associated with the loss of the unity of the Church in the West, as mentioned also in the recent document published by the Lutheran-Roman Catholic dialogue in view of the fifth centenary anniversary of the Reformation, which will be celebrated in 2017. The document states,

> The historical remembrance has had material consequences for the relationship of the confessions to each other. For this reason, a common ecumenical remembrance of the Lutheran Reformation is both so important and at the same time so difficult. Even today, many

> Catholics associate the word "Reformation" first of all with the division of the church, while many Lutheran Christians associate the word "Reformation" chiefly with the rediscovery of the gospel, certainty of faith and freedom. It will be necessary to take both points of departure seriously in order to relate the two perspectives to each other and bring them into dialogue.[1]

Add to that the level of theological reflection, the suspicion that any reform project that wants to profoundly affect the structure of the Church would not be confined to only eliminating deformations and modifying secondary elements, but would affect what belongs to the essential and immutable constitution of the Church and could determine in this way a loss of elements that are part of the apostolic heritage of the Church.

The two aspects just mentioned are not unfounded, but they require some clarifications. It must first be pointed out that, even after the time of the Protestant Reformation, the Catholic Church continued to speak of *reformatio*, as the medieval Church had done extensively regarding the recurring reforms of monastic orders to renew ancient observance, or as happened with the pauperist movements inspired by the ideal of returning to the life of the apostolic Church, or also in relation to the desire that for the whole Church might be fulfilled *a reformatio in capite et in membris*. That the concept of reform was not banned in the Catholic Church even in the post-Reformation period is irrefutably proven by the long series of *de reformatione* decrees published by the Council of Trent, which dedicated a large part of its work precisely to establishing the criteria and rules for the renewal of Church structures and the lives of its pastors. The Council of Trent, however, delineated at the same time a fundamental distinction: the *reformatio* had to do with the institutional, the canonical, and pastoral context, while in matters of doctrine the criterion was the application of the most rigorous fidelity to what the tradition has taught.

Indeed, on this point there is a clear difference in how Luther understood the purpose of his reform of the Church and the determination of the context in which reform would have to primarily be accomplished. A passage from his *Tischreden* allows us to grasp the backbone of Luther's reform project and recognize its peculiarities:

> Doctrine and life must be distinguished. Life is bad among us, as it is among the papists, but we don't fight about life and condemn the papists on that account. Wycliffe and Huss didn't know this and attacked [the papacy] for its life. I don't scold myself into becoming good, but I fight over the Word and whether our adversaries teach it in its purity. That doctrine should be attacked—this has never before happened. This is my calling. Others have censured only life, but to treat doctrine is to strike at the most sensitive point, for surely the government and the ministry of the papists are bad. Once we've asserted this, it's easy to say and declare that the life is also bad.[2]

Luther's text mainly shows the inadequacy of an interpretation in a "moral" key of the reform of the Church and of the objectives that he was pursuing. The reformer's main concern was above all what was preached and taught in the Church, because the faith that saves and justifies before God depended on the conformity of preaching and teaching to God's word. On the contrary, false preaching—which creates a false security by promising indulgences for a cheap form of salvation, and arbitrarily imposes as necessary for salvation conditions that in reality are not—causes the decadence of the Church to the point of its complete destruction.

Precisely on this point—the determination of the context in which Church reform is required—there was a clear difference between Luther's perspective, the Lutheran churches, and the interpretation of Church reform by the Council of Trent.

Even the Tridentine fathers were aware of the decisive importance of preaching for the life of the Church. One of the first reform decrees of the Council of Trent published in session five (June 17, 1546) attributes to preaching a central position in the life of the Church and outlines a biblical training program for clerics. To encourage the knowledge and study of the Bible, the council prescribed that in churches that would benefit from the teaching of theology, the cleric in charge should also dedicate time to biblical studies; in all other churches with a large number of clerics where a similar biblical program did not exist, it must be established.[3] The bishop must then nominate qualified people, examining the candidates *de vita, moribus et scientia*.[4] The decree also insisted on the duty to preach, which is *praecipuum episcoporum munus*.[5] The same duty also applies to all those who exercise the care of souls, who must carry out this task for the salvation of the people entrusted to them, explaining to the faithful *omnibus quae scire necessarium est ad salutem*.[6]

However, preaching, which in the reform decrees appears to be the fundamental task of pastors, is not considered in the definition of the doctrine of the sacrament of orders. During the redaction of the decree on sacred orders, repeated attempts were made to integrate gospel preaching into the ordained minister's duties, but this was rejected for fear of favoring an interpretation of ecclesial ministry reduced to the function of preaching. In the draft of the *doctrina* of October 1562, preaching is recognized as belonging to the priestly functions, although its exercise is not required for all:

> It must not be denied that the *ministerium verbi* is also beneficial for the priests, who nevertheless, do not cease to be priests even though they do not exercise this function, as attested by the Apostle saying that priests who preside well are worthy of a double honor, especially those who work in word and doctrine.[7]

In the revised draft after the debate, the reference to the *ministerium verbi* disappears and all that remains is the reference to "power, transmitted to the apostles and their successors in the priesthood, to consecrate, to offer and administer his body and his blood, as well as forgive and retain sins, and to perform other things (et cetera) that are part of his task."[8] In the final text, the reference to other ministerial functions (*cetera*) is also missing and only the reference to the Eucharist and to penance remains.[9]

This example illustrates one of the problems encountered in the formulation of Catholic doctrine in a context marked by the confrontation with the positions of the Reformation: the dogmatic definition is conditioned by the fear of endorsing a Protestant position and, therefore, the reform of the ministry—which no doubt aims to have a clergy prepared for preaching and dedicated to pastoral ministry—does not find an adequate foundation in the theology of ministry elaborated by Trent. The result is the inability to propose a unified and coherent vision of the ministry, which includes the theological foundation and forms of its exercise in the Church.[10]

This attitude is also found in many other chapters of dogmatic teaching proposed by Trent. The council refused to discuss doctrinal issues or enter theological dispute with Protestant interlocutors, but it primarily interprets its role as judicial. It condemns positions deemed incompatible with the tradition of the Catholic faith and reaffirms the fundamental aspects of the traditional teaching that it considered "amputated" from the criticism advanced by the Protestant Reformation. The conciliar assembly was therefore limited in most cases to confirming what the Church had taught and practiced over the centuries—*alias ecclesia errasset*—without formulating a response to the theological challenge proposed by the reformers and with even less intention of accepting their demands of reform founded on Scripture.

Vatican II

At Vatican II, the situation was completely different. The Catholic Church could articulate a more appropriate response to the questions raised by the Protestant Reformation and embrace some of its demands. This was possible because the Reformation and the questions raised by the reformers were not in the foreground and, unlike the sixteenth century, were not perceived as a challenge that questioned the essential elements of the Catholic faith. Therefore, Vatican II formulated an *indirect* response to the Reformation, accomplished through the recovery of traditional elements of the faith that had been forgotten—the movement to return to the sources—and through the effort to adapt languages, structures, and protocols of ecclesial presence to the needs of a world in profound transformation (aggiornamento). A new appreciation of Scripture and authoritative witness of the early Church allowed the recovery of elements of faith and ecclesial practice forgotten over the centuries or censored because of the need to polemically contradict the adversaries of the moment. The study of Scripture, the authority of the Church fathers, along with a less selective and one-sided listening to the tradition of faith, thus gave credit to positions that objectively represented a reception of the reformers' demands.[11]

In the decades before Vatican II, there had been a direct confrontation between Catholic and Protestant theology. In this context, some came to accept the belief that the Catholic Church had something to learn from the Protestant Reformation and could rediscover the authentic elements of the Christian message through the testimony of the Reformed Churches. This conviction was also expressed in some interventions at Vatican II that recalled the ecumenical scope of certain disputed issues and the need to consider the views and sensitivities of other Christian traditions (see, for example, the debate on the relationship between Scripture and tradition).[12] But at the same time, the conciliar discussion reveals widespread fear that the reception of some elements of the Reformation would result in a loss of Catholic identity.

In this context, both for the deepening of the theme of tradition, as well as for the revival of the idea of reform within theology and the Catholic Church, we must recall Yves Congar's contribution. His work *Vraie et fausse réforme dans l'Église*, which appeared in the preconciliar period (1950), was the most elaborate attempt to refocus on the theme of the reform of ecclesial life. After claiming the legitimacy of Church reform—which also implies the possibility of criticism—the Dominican theologian sought to define the conditions of a reform without a schism (the primacy of charity and pastoral concern; the remaining in communion with the whole Church; patience and a renewal achieved through the return to principle and tradition and not through a mechanical adaptation to the present) and in the end discussed the questions that the Protestant version of Church reform poses to the Catholic Church. Congar particularly insisted on the criterion that tradition represents for Church reform:

> The great law of a Catholic reform will then be to begin by returning to the principles of Catholicism. We must first ask questions of the tradition, to immerse oneself

> in it again: to understand that "tradition" does not mean "routine" nor "past." No doubt, tradition comprises an aspect of the past; it is itself, in part, the treasury of texts and the realities of the Church's past; but it is certainly much more than that. It is essentially the continuity of development from the time of the initial gift and the integration of all the forms that this development has taken and presents at the moment currently. It is the presence of the principle at all stages of its development.[13]

Congar thus outlined the program of a "reform according to the principle of tradition" and a return to the sources (ressourcement) that have been adopted and applied extensively by Vatican II.

The Idea of Reform

Before proposing and introducing concrete Church reforms, Vatican II took on a somewhat risky task when it agreed to integrate the *idea of reform* in its reflection on the Church. The Church to which the word of God is entrusted, which is the place where the grace of God sanctifies the believers, enjoys a steadfastness that is the result of the action of God. Therefore, there are areas where the Church is not open to corrective human interventions or reform. On the other hand, the Church is also a historical reality that never corresponds perfectly to the unique gift given to it by God. Therefore, reform is not only possible but necessary and arises from the need for greater fidelity to her vocation. In this perspective, the Second Vatican Council can be considered an effort to renew the doctrine of the Church and ecclesial institutions, so that the Church better corresponds to the mission to which it is called.

The commitment to Church reform is also significant in the ecumenical field. The experience of the division among Christians and churches, in fact, raises with emphasis and urgency the issue of the disconnect of the historic church with the gift that it received from God and the gift of reconciliation given by Christ to humanity, which the Church must proclaim and make visible in history.

The theme is developed in the conciliar decree on ecumenism: after *UR* 4 mentions the need for all to examine "their own faithfulness to Christ's will for the Church and accordingly to undertake with vigor the task of renewal and reform," no. 6 introduces the issue of the reform of the Church and of personal conversion as essential elements of the implementation of ecumenical commitment:

> Every renewal of the Church is essentially grounded in an increase of fidelity to her own calling. Undoubtedly this is the basis of the movement toward unity. Christ summons the Church to continual reformation as she sojourns here on earth. The Church is always in need of this, in so far as she is an institution of men here on earth. Thus if, in various times and circumstances, there have been deficiencies in moral conduct or in church discipline, or even in the way that church teaching has been formulated—to be carefully distinguished from the deposit of faith itself—these can and should be set right at the opportune moment. (*UR* 6).

It should be noted that in the second chapter of the Decree on Ecumenism, the renewal of the Church, designated in the passage cited as *renovatio* and *reformatio*, is placed first in the program for the ecumenical activity of the Catholic Church and in some way constitutes an acknowledgement "of the *semper reformanda* characteristic of the essential requirements of the sixteenth-century Reformation."[14] In the effort to serve the cause of Christian unity, Catholics must not therefore think first of all the other churches, but of themselves and of what needs to be changed for the Catholic Church to be increasingly faithful to her vocation. In this way, the Catholic Church also contributes to the rapprochement between churches.[15] The following are the areas in which, according to the Decree on Ecumenism, the reform and renewal of the Church must take place:

1. In moral conduct, choices, and behaviors of individual Christians and communities
2. In ecclesiastical discipline, that is, in the form taken from the concrete life of the Church and, by extension,

in the form of its institutions, which are always historically conditioned

3. In the way of expressing doctrine, which must be distinguished from the deposit of faith

The third envisioned field, the way of expressing doctrine, proved to be one of the most promising in the ecumenical dialogue initiated and conducted by the Catholic Church after Vatican II. Therefore, in the dialogues in which the Catholic Church has participated in the last fifty years, the Tridentine scheme that proposes reform only in institutions and ecclesial discipline is impossible, but this is not so in the doctrinal field. On the contrary, all the effort made in the ecumenical dialogue to reach a consensus on the profession of the faith has led to a real "reform" of the way the doctrine of the Catholic Church has been formulated over the centuries.

The Dialogue on Justification

The Catholic-Lutheran dialogue on justification is an exemplary case of the work done to reform the way of exposing doctrine, which, as stated in *UR* 6, must be distinguished from the deposit of faith.

From the beginning, the ecumenical dialogue has found itself in the undesirable situation of seeking agreement on issues that in the past have been the subject of dispute among the churches, but needing to fulfill this task by using the language created, or at least deeply affected, by precisely the controversy it wanted to overcome. The language of the disputes, in fact, not only has affected the perception of other churches, but it has also profoundly marked the formulation that each church has given of its own faith.

The dialogue on the doctrine of justification has found itself in the same dilemma: is it possible to maintain fidelity to the testimony of faith that comes from the past and, at the same time, not be imprisoned in the controversial and exclusive formulation that the expressions of faith have received? To answer this question, ecumenical dialogue cannot avoid confronting issues that in the past have caused the separation of churches, and is therefore forced to resume the terms in which the problems were formulated when dissent manifested itself. On the other hand, dialogue has some hope of success only if it demonstrates sufficient creativity that opens the way for understanding and finds a new language for faith where in the past the positions have seemed irreconcilable.

To achieve this goal, the Catholic-Lutheran dialogue sought above all to put in touch the languages of the two ecclesial and theological traditions and to create the conditions for mutual understanding. In this venture, the results of Pauline exegesis and the contribution of historical research for the interpretation of the documents and testimonies of the ecclesial tradition have been decisive. Thanks to the resources of a more attentive hermeneutics, it has been possible to contextualize doctrines and practices, to grasp the intent behind formulas that in their immediacy appear to be irreconcilable, and to recognize the inevitable partiality that every perspective entails.

The *Joint Declaration on the Doctrine of Justification*, officially signed by the Catholic Church and the Lutheran World Federation on October 31, 1999, sums up the result of a long and complex work, carried out in various sessions, but also from the biblical, historical-dogmatic, and theological research of the second half of the twentieth century. The central claim of the document is that Catholics and Lutherans can jointly profess their faith in the justification that God gives to mankind and, on this basis, the different doctrinal positions developed by the Catholic and Lutheran traditions can be recognized as compatible. The basic consensus on the meaning of justification is formulated in the *Joint Declaration* in these terms:

> In faith we together hold the conviction that justification is the work of the triune God. The Father sent his Son into the world to save sinners. The foundation and presupposition of justification is the incarnation, death, and resurrection of Christ. Justification thus means that Christ himself is our righteousness, in which we share through the Holy Spirit in accord with the will of the Father. Together we confess: By grace alone, in faith in

> Christ's saving work and not because of any merit on our part, we are accepted by God and receive the Holy Spirit, who renews our hearts while equipping and calling us to good works.[16]

In this text and in other similar ones, the fundamental statement common to the two confessional traditions assumes a form that is closer to that of the profession of faith. The choice of this language seems to suggest that the consensus has its original place in the act by which the churches welcome in faith the gospel message proclaiming Jesus the Savior. To the biblical *message*, therefore, the churches respond with a *profession of faith* that, in the various texts of consensus on justification, takes the form of a christological and trinitarian affirmation. On this basis, the theological reflection elaborates the *doctrine* of justification, which aims to explain the way how the gift of grace reaches human beings and transforms them, and how to maintain the integrity of the profession of faith and safeguard it from the danger of deformation.

The recognition of this common basis allows a different assessment from those of the past over the differences in the doctrinal formulation of the content of faith. In the presentation of the classic themes of the sixteenth-century controversy proposed in the *Joint Declaration*, the following scheme constantly returns: a common statement of faith (*together we confess...*), shared by Catholics and Lutherans, follows the reference to the characteristic formulations of the two traditions, each of which is interpreted in the sense of the common affirmation and presented as a legitimate explanation of the same faith (*when Catholics/Lutherans say...they mean...*). What is proposed is therefore a *differentiated consensus* (or "differentiating," in a more precise definition), based on a common profession of faith that endorses various theological explanations.

Regarding the classical problem that saw the opposition, on the one hand, of a *forensic* view of justification, intended as an imputation of a justice that remains outside man, and, on the other, of an *effective* concept that interprets justification as a person's transformation, the *Joint Declaration* states,

> We confess together that God forgives sin by grace and at the same time frees human beings from sin's enslaving

power and imparts the gift of new life in Christ. When persons come by faith to share in Christ, God no longer imputes to them their sin and through the Holy Spirit effects in them an active love. These two aspects of God's gracious action are not to be separated, for persons are by faith united with Christ, who in his person is our righteousness (1 Cor 1:30): both the forgiveness of sin and the saving presence of God himself. Because Catholics and Lutherans confess this together, it is true to say that:

> When Lutherans emphasize that the righteousness of Christ is our righteousness, their intention is above all to insist that the sinner is granted righteousness before God in Christ through the declaration of forgiveness and that only in union with Christ is one's life renewed....
>
> When Catholics emphasize the renewal of the interior person through the reception of grace imparted as a gift to the believer, they wish to insist that God's forgiving grace always brings with it a gift of new life, which in the Holy Spirit becomes effective in active love.[17]

On this and on other aspects of the dispute, the agreement was reached, therefore, placing the foundations for a common affirmation of faith and explaining, in light of that statement, the respective confessional doctrines. Thus, their compatibility in principle is declared, but through a hermeneutic that intentionally explains them by the sense of the common statement and considers the instance of which the other doctrine is bearer. Catholics thus acknowledge that the fundamental concern of the Lutheran doctrine is to ensure the divine origin of justification, while Lutherans recognize that the Catholic concern is to assert the effectiveness of the justifying action in transforming the creature. The two concerns have generated forms of thought and language that can be recognized as compatible based on the common affirmation of faith and provided that they mutually recognize the legitimacy of the intention that has shaped the doctrine of other theological and ecclesial tradition.

Justification and the Church

The consensus reached on the doctrine of justification shows in a concrete case the possible application of the principle of unity in diversity. The positive result achieved on this point raises the question of whether the model of "differentiated consensus" is also applicable in other fields and, in particular, to the ecclesiological one.[18] In this regard, the situation at the Council of Trent seems to present today, but in reverse: on the doctrine of justification, ecumenical dialogue has reached an agreement, ratified by the churches, while on the understanding of the Church and, in particular, on the ecclesial structures that should be qualified as necessary, there remains a disagreement that at the moment does not appear resolvable. This raises several questions. Is it possible to reform the ecclesial institutions and the doctrine related to them? What degree of plurality is acceptable in the field of ecclesiastical institutions?

In principle, the model of differentiated consensus can also be applied to the Church and its structures. The plurality of the Christian tradition is not valid only for doctrines, but for the Church and its structures. It is also evident that the ecclesial communion reestablished among the churches cannot lead to the eradication of the different ecclesial structures that have been shaped over the centuries and that contribute to defining the ecclesial identity of these communities.

On the other hand, we cannot ignore that, in the ecclesiological field, the model of differentiated consensus is called to contend not only with different theories about the nature of the Church and its essential elements, but also with the concrete institutional realities that exist—or not—in the various Christian churches. The institution's logic, at least at first glance, does not seem to show the same flexibility of doctrine: while the latter allows to conceive different expressions of a common belief, the institutions face the dry alternative of whether they exist or not, and whether the name used to designate them in the different churches corresponds to the same reality, or whether the designation is a source of misunderstandings.

The question is particularly acute regarding the institutions that serve the ecclesial communion at the regional and universal level. For the Catholic tradition, the episcopate, as a college of local churches pastors, in which is incardinated the primatial ministry of the Bishop of Rome, is an essential tool for the universal communion of the Church in time and space. For the churches of the Reformation, however, this ecclesiological vision unduly attributes a normative character to institutions that are the result of historical processes characterized by a high degree of contingency and to which, therefore, cannot be attributed a necessary character.

To avoid being trapped by this alternative, ecumenical dialogue has resorted to the distinction between the episcopate, understood as an institution present and active in the Catholic Church and in other churches with an episcopal structure, and the function of the *episcopé*, which is a component of the ministry exercised in all churches, but has found different institutional concretizations (in a personal ministry or in synodal forms). Similarly, a distinction has been made between the ministry of the Bishop of Rome, with the theological and legal prerogatives that the Catholic tradition assigns to him, and the *Petrine function*, which is derived from the role of Peter in the early church, and is linked to the question of a ministry serving the unity of the universal Church.

This scheme presents some points of contact with the model of differentiated consensus. In fact, it connects a fundamental fact—a recognized *function* as necessary for the Church—and an institutional concretization of this function, which can take place in different forms. But with respect to the application of the model of differentiated consensus to the field of doctrine, in this case the differences seem to have a greater scope. The Catholic Church is convinced that some of the historical developments through which its ministerial structures have been formed have an irreversible character and their result, therefore, constitutes an essential element for the Church. This Catholic conviction does not necessarily imply a rejection of the model of differentiated consensus in the ecclesiological field. This model, in fact, does not claim that every difference is acceptable in principle, but recognizes as legitimate the differences that do not contradict the common affirmation of faith, and are compatible with each other.

The point then is to identify a criterion for distinguishing legitimate differences from those that compromise communion. The criterion of the compatibility of different doctrinal expressions corresponds in an ecclesiological field to the criterion of the possibility of recognizing and of working together that different ecclesial structures must exhibit. This also establishes the limit to the admissible diversity within ecclesial communion: all differences are acceptable that do not prevent the various ecclesial institutions from acting together, for example within the common exercise of *episcopḗ*, or in an ecumenical council. Totally different theological concepts of the ministry representing the Church in a conciliar assembly, or radically diverse ways of defining its ability to act and its prerogatives, would in fact deprive such an assembly of every possibility of joint action.

In terms of the ecclesiological understanding, this means that the distinction between the transcendent foundation of the Church and the multiplicity of its historical figures—sanctioned by some interpretations of the Leuenberg Agreement—is too schematic.[19] Between the foundation and the many forms, it is possible to identify a fundamental form of the Church, whereby it is possible to recognize its actual presence in the plurality of the manifestations that advance the claim to be a church, which can thus fulfill the function of criterion. This fundamental form can be easily identified with the local church, in the presence of the word and the sacraments, and of a pastoral ministry placed in their service. The same should also be possible for the forms in which the ecclesial communion is experienced at wider and universal levels than just the local one. The definition of this form can contribute to the criterion of compatibility, in the form in which it has been applied to ecclesial structures: what are the conditions required for the structures of the different churches to interact and act together? To match this criterion, the current structures of all churches must certainly change and converge with each other, giving up their claim of absoluteness. But this cannot happen without the consent around a fundamental form of the Church that carries out the function of a common criterion and reference point that supports the diversity of ecclesial forms.

Conclusions

The latest considerations regarding the need for a criterion to establish compatibility between different ecclesial forms suggest a concluding observation of the idea of ecclesial reform. It is a theme whose importance can hardly be underestimated in the ecumenical field and, more generally, in the history of the Church. In fact, it asserts that Church fidelity to its vocation cannot have the form of a rigid doctrinal system and a rigidified ecclesial institution.

The importance of the idea of reform, however, must not overlook its limits. The fundamental limit is its formal character: it says that the Church can and must change to correct its deformities and to correspond better to the will of its Lord, but it is unable to tell us exactly what is to change and in what direction this need for fidelity directs its path.

In fact, there is no reform project that is not inspired, consciously or unconsciously, by a vision of the Church and of what it is called to be. The impetus for reforming the Church that originated at Vatican II was also closely linked to an image of the Church, outlined by the Council through a rereading of the biblical testimony and the ecclesial tradition. Therefore, reform does not arise from a gesture of rupture with the past, but it intends to emphasize how tradition—in its apostolic origins, and in the most authoritative testimonies of successive centuries—attests to the nature and vocation of the Church.

NOTES

1. *From Conflict to Communion: Lutheran-Catholic Common Commemoration of the Reformation in 2017; Report of the Lutheran-Roman Catholic Commission on Unity* (Leipzig: Evangelischer Verlagsanstalt; Paderborn: Bonifatius, 2013), 13n9.

2. WA Tischreden 1, 294, 19–24. The English translation is from *The Works of Martin Luther*, vol. 54, ch. 1.160, no. 624. Luther goes on to say, "When the Word remains pure, then the life (even if there is something lacking in it) can be molded properly. Everything depends on the Word, and the pope has abolished the Word and created another one. With this I have won, and I have won nothing else than that I teach aright.

Although we are better morally, this isn't anything to fight about. It's the teaching that breaks the pope's neck."

3. See *COD* 667ff.

4. *COD* 669.

5. "In the Christian republic the preaching of the gospel is no less necessary than teaching: this is the primary task of bishops. The holy synod has established and decreed that all bishops, archbishops, primates, and all other prelates in the Church are required to preach the holy Gospel of Jesus Christ, if not legitimately prevented." (*COD* 669).

6. *COD* 669.

7. CT IX, 39.

8. Ibid., 105ff.

9. See ibid., 620.

10. On the relationship between the dogmatic doctrine of the sacrament of order and the pastoral image of the ministry at the Council of Trent and in the subsequent reception, see A. Maffeis, "La figura tridentina del prete. L'insegnamento del Concilio di Trento e la sua prima recezione," in *Ministero presbiterale in trasformazione* (Quaderni teologici del Seminario di Brescia 15) (Brescia: Morcelliana, 2005), 89–156.

11. See J. W. O'Malley, *What Happened at Vatican II* (Cambridge, MA: Belknap Press of Harvard University Press, 2010).

12. See A. Maffeis, "La parola di Dio e la chiesa. Il significato ecumenico della costituzione *Dei Verbum*," *Teologia* 31 (2006): 173–213.

13. Y. M. Congar, *Vraie et fausse réforme dans l'Église* (Cerf, Paris 1968^2), 303. Translated as *True and False Reform in the Church* (Collegeville, MN: Liturgical Press, 2011).

14. H. Roux, "Le Décret sur l'Œcuménisme 'Unitatis redintegratio,'" in *Points de vue de Théologiens protestants. Études sur les décrets du Concile Vatican II* (Paris: Cerf, 1967), 105.

15. See G. Thils, *Le décret sur l'œcuménisme. Commentaire doctrinal* (Paris: Desclée de Brouwer, 1966), 91–98; G. Cereti, *Riforma della chiesa e unità dei cristiani nell'insegnamento del Concilio Vaticano II* (Verona: Il Segno), 1985.

16. "Dichiarazione congiunta sulla dottrina della giustificazione," in *Dossier sulla giustificazione. La dichiarazione congiunta cattolico-luterana, commento e dibattito teologico*, ed. A. Maffeis (Brescia: Queriniana, 2000), 30n15. On the contemporary ecumenical debate on justification, see also Maffeis, *Giustificazione. Percorsi teologici nel dialogo tra le Chiese* (Cinisello Balsamo: San Paolo), 1998.

17. *Joint Declaration of the Doctrine of Justification* 22–24: http://www.vatican.va/roman_curia/pontifical_councils/chrstuni/documents/rc_pc_chrstuni_doc_31101999_cath-luth-joint-declaration_en.html.

18. Here I am drawing on some considerations proposed in A. Maffeis, "La situazione attuale del dialogo: ecumene del consenso e delle differenze. Una prospettiva cattolica," *Protestantesimo* 67 (2012): 15–29.

19. See Hüffmeier et al., *Die Kirche Jesu Christi. Der reformatorische Beitrag zum ökumenischen Dialog über die kirchliche Einheit* (Frankfurt: O. Lembeck, 1995); on this topic, see W. Thönissen, "Die Leuenberger Konkordie als ökumenisches Einheitsmodell? Umrisse eines katholischen Konzepts von Kirchengemeinschaft," *Catholica* 49 (1995): 1–31.

III

THE SYNODAL COMMUNION AS THE KEY TO RENEWAL OF THE PEOPLE OF GOD

8

COMMUNIO ECCLESIAE, COMMUNIO ECCLESIARUM, COLLEGIUM EPISCOPORUM

Hervé Legrand, OP

The Reception of the Third Chapter of *Lumen Gentium*

How and why have the doctrinal, pastoral, and ecumenical objectives attributed to the third chapter of the Constitution *Lumen Gentium* not been met satisfactorily? Why—and how—should we fix this?

By convening the Second Vatican Council, John XXIII set as a general program a doctrinal and, above all, a pastoral aggiornamento, required by the necessities of the time. This also implied a revision of canon law and would have allowed a rapprochement with the separated Christians.[1] Without the preliminary *vota* revealing anything, the Council fathers found themselves, quite quickly, "in collegiality" (as it was then said),[2] a theme that brought together their expectations, aroused the greatest number of interventions on their part,[3] and strongly cemented a conciliar majority.

The question of "collegiality" was aimed at improving the relationship between local churches and the whole Church, on the pastoral, ecumenical, and doctrinal levels.

On the pastoral level, most Western bishops hoped to get rid of a suffocating administrative centralization.[4] They wanted to assume their responsibilities, particularly by renewing the liturgy so the people could pray in their own language. Some also wanted to review the status of the clergy (for example, the so-called worker priests) or be associated with the great church doctrinal guidelines (see the strong criticisms of the Holy Office). In a context of decolonization, as we shall see, the bishops of young churches considered missionary adaptation and inculturation very important. The idea of a new theological and practical enhancement of regional churches, through the national episcopal conferences, with canonical jurisdiction, quickly took shape. The representatives of the Eastern Catholic churches, which are indeed particular churches, aspired to be recognized as such.[5]

The ecumenical objectives assigned to the Council by Pope John XXIII were converging with these pastoral goals. In fact, without progress on the above issues, there could not be hope for any significant rapprochement with the Orthodox, Anglican, or Lutheran churches, considering the extent to which the *communio ecclesiae,* conceived in a uniform and centralized manner, had absorbed the *communio ecclesiarum* in the Catholic Church.

For the Council fathers, this convergence of pastoral and ecumenical goals was translated into a single doctrinal task that was evident to them: to balance the ecclesiology of Vatican I. To correct the unilateralism of that Council's reception, their efforts were directed *in a special way* and almost exclusively *toward the elaboration of the concept of the college of bishops in its relation to the papal primacy* defined by Vatican I. The third chapter of the Church's Dogmatic Constitution *De Ecclesia,* its most systematic result, is focused on this.

THE THIRD CHAPTER OF *LUMEN GENTIUM* DID NOT CONSIDER HOW ITS OBJECTIVES WOULD BE MET

The third chapter of *Lumen Gentium* was not adopted without enthusiasm: it was judged as "the backbone of the entire Council," and "the center of gravity of Vatican II."[6] Yves Congar wrote in this regard,

> With this vote, one gained the feeling that that was it: Vatican II had balanced Vatican I...with a majority that had never went below 87%.[7] [Vatican II had attained its goal:] to restore to the episcopate a greater importance and initiative in the concrete government of the church, currently dominated by a certain exercise of papal primacy, one requiring the curial system and Roman centralization,[8] [and against which] stumble all the other churches which understand papal power as absolutist and monarchical.[9]

Half a century later, the *Wirkungsgeschichte* of this chapter of *Lumen Gentium* elicits very different theological evaluations, including those of the Pope Francis himself. In the apostolic exhortation *Evangelii Gaudium,* Francis notes that the three great objectives of the third chapter of the Constitution have not been met. In fact, he hopes to enhance the local diocesan churches,[10] as well as regional churches in the form of episcopal conferences[11] or even groups similar to the patriarchates of the ancient church,[12] completely reassessing the ecclesiological statute of the Roman curia.[13]

This is not the space to reconstruct this story, or search for the intellectual or moral responsibilities that are involved. We will limit ourselves instead to a brief conceptual analysis of the third chapter and the effects it has produced, which Pope Francis faces in his reform plans.

THE STRUCTURE OF UNIVERSALIST ENUNCIATION OF THE THIRD CHAPTER OF *LUMEN GENTIUM* HAS RENDERED INEFFECTIVE THE REDISCOVERY OF THE *COMMUNIO ECCLESIAE* AS *COMMUNIO ECCLESIARUM*

Focusing our analysis on the third chapter of *Lumen Gentium* is certainly not a good method and is also likely to present a very distorted picture of Vatican II, which cannot be confined to this chapter only! We are somewhat obliged to consider it a reference text, for its position in the *dogmatic* constitution of the Church and its connection with Vatican I. In fact, in the absence of any definition of faith, one of its formulations, particularly poor from a doctrinal point of view, has become the normative definition of the episcopal college, and indeed its formalization through the Code of Canon Law (336). This is the passage from *LG* 22: "Hence, one is constituted a member of the Episcopal body [of the 'college of bishops,' according to 336] in virtue of sacramental consecration and hierarchical communion with the head and members of the body."

This semblance of definition makes no mention of the fact that the newly ordained is assigned to a church. Theologians saw in it only a mere oversight,[14] but the 1983 Code turned this oversight into a norm. Because of this omission, official canonists defined, *first*, the Catholic bishop as a member of a college of which the pope is the head, and only then as one to whom the pope, without obligation, assigns a local church. This universalist conception of episcopal ordination has justified the various curial initiatives that accentuate the prerogatives of the universal Church over the local churches and bishops. It so happens that the third chapter of *Lumen Gentium* neutralizes the ecclesiological objectives it was required to pursue and that Pope Francis intends to accomplish.

THE FORMULATION OF *LG* 22 HAS IN FACT ALLOWED A DISSOCIATION BETWEEN THE *COLLEGIUM EPISCOPORUM* AND THE *COMMUNIO ECCLESIARUM*

Taken literally, the formulation of *LG* 22, reproduced in the 1983 Code, separates the correlation between the bishops and their church, more precisely between the college of bishops and the communion of churches. Allow me to insist on this formulation, theologically deficient in its literal meaning, because it probably allowed John Paul II to specifically justify the separation—unjustifiable from a doctrinal point of view—in *Apostolos Suos*: "The College of Bishops...as an essential element of the universal Church, it is a reality which precedes the office of being the head of a particular Church" (12), a statement justified in footnote 55: "Besides, as is clearly evident, there are many Bishops who are not heads of particular Churches, although they perform tasks proper to Bishops."

Such separation has weighed on the reception—better still, dominated the reception of *Lumen Gentium* by the curia—especially since it is situated in a clearly universalist perspective, made explicit in its relation to the primacy of Rome. Number 22 insists on it in two occasions: "But the college or body of bishops has no authority unless it is understood together with the Roman Pontiff, the successor of Peter as its head. The pope's power of primacy over all, both pastors and faithful, remains whole and intact." And, further on, "The order of bishops, which succeeds to the college of apostles..., is also is also the subject of supreme and full power over the universal Church, provided we understand this body together with its head the Roman Pontiff and never without this head."

In addition, the *nota explicativa praevia* (preliminary note of explanation) to the third chapter of *Lumen Gentium* recognizes a regulatory character for the patchy formulation of *LG* 22: in no. 2 it is based on it. Whatever its statute, the *nota praevia* will have a decisive influence: the idea of ecclesial communion, which is a communion of churches in the plural, has no place in it.

The *nota praevia* recognizes only the government of the Church by the pope. It is stated that his power can be exercised, "to his own discretion"—this would be the technical term—in a personal or collegial way.[15] Vatican I did not express itself in these terms, as it established as objective of the primacy the unity of the episcopate and not the daily government of the whole Church.[16] If the third chapter of *Lumen Gentium* was to correct the maximalist reception of Vatican I,[17] we must observe with J. Ratzinger that the *nota praevia* confirms an erroneous reception:

> That the exercise of this power [of the pope] is simply to his own discretion [*secundum propriam discretionem*] as he sees fit, by reason of the demands of his office [*omni tempore to placitum*] has never been expressed in this form in any document of the Church....A notion of collegiality that is reduced exclusively to the collegiality

> of the *actus stricte collegialis* on the universal Church leads to an impasse....The sense of collegiality, in fact,... is to assert and enhance the role of the churches in the Church and, if so, to promote a "particular collegiality."[18]

One could translate, implement a real *communio ecclesiarum*.

THE CURIAL INTERPRETATION OF *LUMEN GENTIUM* HAS NOT ADVANCED TOWARD A *COMMUNIO ECCLESIAE* CONCEIVED AS *COMMUNIO ECCLESIARUM*

At the promulgation of the Constitution on the Church, Karl Rahner, supported by his Scholastic orientation, gave a negative judgment on the third chapter of the document: "The Constitution brings nothing new."[19] This irritated Joseph Ratzinger, who had a patristic formation, to the point of prompting him to write that that point revealed "the serious responsibility of the commentators, and its scope is difficult to predict."[20]

Ratzinger rebuked Rahner for not considering about fifty (of sixty-one) notes that referred to those patristic and liturgical sources that for the fathers constituted an interpretive norm of that third chapter. He particularly noted Rahner's distance from tradition, accepting as original the idea of a universal college, while during the first five centuries to which *Lumen Gentium* refers, "in vain one will search for...the summary idea that the College of Bishops as such is the successor to the college of the Apostles."[21]

Ratzinger was right: the fathers of the Second Vatican Council wanted to breathe new life in the notion of *communio ecclesiae* as *communio ecclesiarum*. In order to not weigh down on our presentation and its logic, we refer to this in excursus A.[22]

To recap: because of the canonical formalization of the "definition" of the college in *LG* 22, the postconciliar disciplinary guidelines regarding the statute of local bishops and churches have increasingly given priority to the *communio ecclesiae*, which will end up absorbing the *communio ecclesiarum*.

A BRIEF OVERVIEW OF THE INCREASINGLY RIGOROUS REDUCTION OF THE *COMMUNIO ECCLESIARUM* TO THE *COMMUNIO ECCLESIAE* PURSUED DURING JOHN PAUL II'S PONTIFICATE

We resort to an unusual image: a slalom race. When you miss a gate, you obviously end up missing all subsequent ones. Conceptually, the concept of college is quite the same thing: once formalized by the Code of Canon Law, it produces a chain-like separation, perfectly coherent, but in many cases contrary to the initial objectives it was intended to achieve. Let us look at the most significant stages of this development.

1983: THE REVISED CODE WEAKENS DIOCESAN CHURCHES BY SEPARATING THEM FROM THEIR TERRITORIES, WHICH MAKES IT POSSIBLE TO REGARD THEM AS EQUAL TO OTHER SMALLER DISTRICTS, MAKING IT DIFFICULT TO UNDERSTAND THE CHURCH AS A COMMUNION OF CHURCHES

According to John XXIII, the revised Code of Canon Law would have contributed to the conciliar aggiornamento. However, in its systematics and vocabulary, for example in the strengthening of the bishops' dependence with respect to the pope, it moves away from the pastoral and ecumenical views that the fathers wished to develop in the name of collegiality.

The systematics of the 1983 Code have been aptly described as follows: "It implies the priority of the concept of a particular church over the diocesan church, of the episcopate of apostolic succession over the diocesan episcopate, and finally, of the universal Church over the particular church."[23] Its second book begins, true to *Lumen Gentium*, with the people of God and in the first part takes into consideration the status of the faithful, clergy, and laity, and, in the second part (section 1), the supreme power in the Church and the college of bishops. Thus, after having addressed the topic of bishops, it considers their dioceses, called systematically particular churches (part 2, section 2). Therefore, it establishes, from the ecclesiological point of view, who are the laypeople and the clergy, the pope and the college of bishops, the synod of bishops, the college of cardinals, the Roman curia, even the nuncios, before even establishing what a local church is! Such a systematic choice no longer allows us to think that the Church is a communion of churches.

While for *LG* dioceses are a part of the Church, the Code tends to see them as part of the universal Church, arbitrarily imposing on them the neologism *particular* Church, depriving them also of their own denomination of Catholic churches (see excursus B).[24] This choice of a term derived from the root *pars*, whether deliberate or not, goes to reinforce the universalist ecclesiology: since in Latin and the languages that derive from it, as it is in English and especially in German (*Teilkirche*), *particular*, from a lexical point of view, is the antonym of *universal*. This option thus conveys the subordination, pure and simple, of the particular churches to the universal Church, because language itself at times does our thinking for us.[25]

In addition, under the pretext of modernity, because the Code rejected the idea of locality as one of the essential characteristics of the dioceses, since this quality was not mentioned in the definition of *CD* 11, their juridical status has been downgraded by the proliferation of nondiocesan ecclesiastical districts and often by nonterritorial ones (military ordinaries, Eastern Catholics exarchates, territorial and personal prelatures, as recently for the former Anglicans,[26] etc.), which have often been assigned to bishops and legally equated to dioceses. Finally, the latter are seen as a special case of ecclesiastical districts of the universal Church, as evidenced by a *Dictionary of Ecclesiology*, published in Rome in 2010: the lemma "diocese" is absent and the entry does not even appear in the general index.[27] It thus becomes theologically difficult to attribute to the local diocesan churches a statute of subjects of law in the *communio ecclesiarum*.

Finally, *the revised Code emphasizes the authority of the Holy See over the college of bishops and over every individual bishop*. According to the doctrine of *LG* 27, the bishops are "vicars and ambassadors of Christ…nor are they to be regarded as vicars of the Roman Pontiffs." The Code does not mention this title and reserves it to the pope, "the head of the college of bishops, the Vicar of Christ, and the pastor of the universal Church on earth" (331). Thus, even for the bishops, "no appeal or recourse is permitted against a sentence or decree of the Roman Pontiff. "(can. 333, § 3). Similarly,

"It is for the Roman Pontiff, according to the needs of the Church, to select and promote the ways by which the college of bishops is to exercise its function collegially regarding the universal Church." (337, § 3). The terms of their oath of fidelity after 1987[28] and those of the most recent disciplinary documents, give them, before the pope, equivalency to a statute, in the law in force, to that of vicar general with respect to one's own bishop.[29] Returning to the initial image, here is where we end up when we miss the first gate in a slalom race.

1988: WITH PASTOR BONUS, *THE NEW JURIDICAL STATUS OF THE ROMAN CURIA CONFIRMS ITS ORDINARY VICARIAL POWERS IN THE GOVERNMENT OF THE WHOLE CHURCH*

Tested by the hard trial of the Council, the curia subsequently gained an unprecedented juridical status. The apostolic constitution *Pastor Bonus* confirms it as one of the means of the pope[30] in the daily government of the Church (see can. 349). The number of personnel more than doubled, its bishops quadrupled (about twenty in Pius XII's time, currently more than eighty—a kind of permanent synod!). Several dicasteries themselves produce their own theology and history[31] and have their documents approved by the pope in a specific form, while papal teaching has never been more abundant.[32] Thus, the doctrinal responsibility given to the whole college of bishops becomes a fiction, outside an ecumenical council.

1990: THE CODE OF CANONS OF THE EASTERN CHURCHES

Although it defines the concept of Church *sui iuris*, the Code of Canons of the Eastern Churches strengthens the process toward administrative uniformity of these churches. It amalgamates heterogeneous canonical traditions such as those of Byzantium and Ethiopia, Armenia and Syriac India. The Code is in Latin, even though the Eastern Catholics always fear Latinization.[33] Finally, the pope promulgated it alone, not with the heads of these churches,[34] and some of its provisions considerably extend papal primacy.[35]

1992: COMMUNIONIS NOTIO *TEACHES "THE CHRONOLOGICAL AND ONTOLOGICAL PRIORITY OF THE UNIVERSAL CHURCH OF ALL THE PARTICULAR CHURCHES"*

Number 9 of *Communionis Notio,* the letter of the Congregation for the Doctrine of the Faith on certain aspects of the Church intended as communion, has the clear intent of strongly relativizing the scope of *in quibus et ex quibus* of *LG* 23, that is, the axiom of the Constitution of Vatican II on the Church expressing in the clearest way the simultaneity between the Church and the churches, to reject one of the most fundamental ecclesiological orientations of the last council:

> *Ontologically,* the Church-mystery, the Church that is one and unique, precedes creation (42), and gives birth to the particular Churches as her daughters. She expresses herself in them; she is the mother and not the product of the particular Churches. From the Church, which in its origins and its first manifestation is universal, have arisen the different local Churches, as particular expressions of the one unique Church of Jesus Christ. Arising *within* and *out of* the universal Church, they have their ecclesiality in it and from it. Hence the formula of the Second Vatican Council: *The Church in and formed out of the Churches [Ecclesia in et ex Ecclesiis]* (44) [*LG*], is inseparable from this other formula: *The Churches in and formed out of the Church [Ecclesia in et ex Ecclesiis]* (45).

With this statement there is another, also unknown to the tradition, according to which the successor of Peter belongs "already to the essence of each particular Church from 'within'" (13).[36] This tends to make the Bishop of Rome a sort of universal bishop, a role that, however, Pius IX refused after Vatican I.[37]

In reality, *Communionis Notio* has not been adopted[38] because it raised numerous objections,[39] the most important of which is the assertion of the existence of the universal Church *prior* to the concrete, confessional, and sacramental processes that establish it, and *independently* of these same processes, thus cutting it off from the believers and the sacraments of faith. Such a church would necessarily be a "being of reason."[40] Nothing obliges us to postulate it in this way, not even the preexistence of the Church in God's plan, which it is difficult to see because it does not include the simultaneous nature of the Church and churches. This abstraction goes hand in hand with the idea that "the episcopal college is a reality which precedes the office of being the head of a particular church" (*AS* 12). Unlike the Church's maternal role for the faith of the faithful, or the maternity of a founding Church in relation to the one she generated, the idea of a maternity of the universal Church regarding all the local churches seems to have never been formulated.[41]

Even though it was not adopted, *Communionis Notio* served as a foundation for several other disciplinary measures that undermine the juridical status of diocesan churches and bishops in the *communio ecclesiae,* always conceived as immediately universal.[42] Among these measures, we list the two most significant ones, without getting into details, since they add nothing new conceptually. They just confirm the "missed slalom gate" principle!

1997: DE SYNODIS AGENDIS *UNDERMINES DIOCESAN SYNODS, AND DISTANCES ITSELF FROM A THEOLOGY OF THE PEOPLE OF GOD*

The Instruction on Diocesan Synods, *De synodis dioecesanis agendis,* issued jointly by the Congregations for Bishops and for the Evangelization of Peoples, excludes

> *from the synodal discussions* theses or positions—as well as proposals submitted to the Synod with the mere intention of transmitting to the Holy See "polls" in their regard—discordant with the perennial doctrine of the Church or the Magisterium or concerning material reserved to Supreme ecclesiastical authority or to other ecclesiastical authorities. (IV.4)

The local churches are therefore subjects of law only within very strict limitations. Even in the disciplinary field, in which much is permitted, they must maintain compliance with the "universal church."[43]

To justify such a measure, is it not necessary to reject the theology of the people of God affirmed in *Lumen Gentium*? In fact, the diocesan synod is no doubt an expression of them, since, under the presidency of the bishop, it brings together presbyters, deacons, religious men and women, as well as laypeople, and women speak and vote. This without mentioning that synods, in allowing the articulation of synodality and collegiality, could also contribute to a better exercise of the magisterium.

1.5.6. 1998: UNDERMINING THE MODEST JURIDICAL STATUS OF THE EPISCOPAL CONFERENCES (WITH APOSTOLOS SUOS *AND* AD TUENDAM FIDEM*), WHICH DEPRIVES THEM DE FACTO OF AUTHENTIC MAGISTERIUM*

LG 23 expected for the episcopal conferences a legitimate pluriformity in the Church, in line with the ancient patriarchates—an aspiration that their original and too-modest canonical status did not allow them to achieve. The *motu proprio* of 1998, *Apostolos Suos,* recalls that their very existence is suspended by order of the Holy See that establishes them and determines all their powers (13 and 20).[44] It also deprived them of the authentic magisterium they exercise in accordance with the can. 753 of the Latin Code, except for cases of unanimity.[45] Moreover, bishops "assembled in Episcopal Conference," are expected to "take special care to follow the magisterium of the universal Church and to communicate it opportunely to the people entrusted to them" (21). In short, they are to be repeaters of the teaching of the Holy See, which holds the strictest control on the interpretation of the Christian faith in the cultures of the entire world.[46] But such a strict control seems to go against the wish of *LG* 23, which had hoped that particular-regional churches would take shape within the *Catholica*.[47]

The Reasons for the Banned Reforms and How to Proceed

The analysis of the reception of the third chapter of *Lumen Gentium* has allowed us to see that the issues that concerned most of the

Vatican II fathers are always present. The correlation between the *collegium episcoporum* and the *communio ecclesiarum* remains very weak: the *communio ecclesiarum* has not developed much beyond the *communio episcoporum*. The juridical status of the Roman curia, which implies that of the primacy, was greatly strengthened. Let us review the reasons that justify reforms in each of these spheres.

THE REASONS FOR REFORMS

THERE ARE VERY SOLID REASONS TO REESTABLISH A CORRELATION BETWEEN THE COLLEGIUM EPISCOPORUM *AND THE* COMMUNIO ECCLESIARUM

Doctrinal Reasons

According to our Catholic faith every local church (diocese) is fully God's church, but it is not the whole church of God. In this sense, the ecclesial communion cannot but be a communion of the churches. The bishops are above all the ministers of this communion.

Therefore, the affirmation of *Apostolos Suos*, according to which "the episcopal college is a reality which precedes the office of being the head of a particular church" (*AS* 12), represents a recent innovation, as it is little substantiated. It clashes with the safer doctrinal facts on the apostolic succession and the episcopate.

For example, after the Council of Chalcedon rendered absolute ordinations null and void,[48] the Catholic Church never justified this type of ordination. When the Church multiplies them, as recently, these bishops receive the title of a titular church, like "Vegesela of Byzacena," sometimes already occupied by an Orthodox bishop.

Further, episcopal succession, so important as witness of the true faith,[49] is never established by episcopal laying on of the hands. A new bishop succeeds his predecessor in the same diocese, not the bishop who ordained him regardless of see;[50] we would not know that there was apostolic succession if not by the fact he presides over a church that has the apostolic faith. The apostolic succession—or the powers that are involved, as can be seen below—cannot be transmitted from individual to individual.[51]

Faced with the current considerable number of bishops without actual sees (48 percent), due to the multiplication of auxiliaries and emeritus bishops, we can recall that Pius IX created a commission to study whether they should participate in the First Vatican Council. The commission replied that those bishops "did not have to, but could."[52] Just as Benedict XVI is no longer pope after his resignation—no one doubts that—emeritus bishops cease to be bishops, which does not prevent them from assuming other roles in the Church.

Pastoral Reasons

The separation between the episcopate and the presidency of a church involves numerous distortions. Let us list the main ones.

The separation of a bishop from a local church dissolves the relationship between collegiality and synodality and disregards the traditional—and nonclerical—understanding of the people of God, as found in *Lumen Gentium*, citing St. Cyprian, for whom "the bishop is in the church and the church in the bishop,"[53] or St. Augustine, who said that he felt reassured to be a Christian among Christians but perceived it as a burden and a danger to be the bishop to others.[54] Pope Francis spontaneously lives this ecclesiology and praises it.[55] Instead of immediately imparting his first blessing *urbi et orbi* to the people, as was expected, he surprised the faithful by first asking for their prayers. In his address to the Latin American and Caribbean Bishops' Council (CELAM), in which he denounced clericalism, he questioned the bishops in a significant way:

> Is pastoral discernment a habitual criterion, through the use of Diocesan Councils? Do such Councils and Parish Councils, whether pastoral or financial, provide real opportunities for lay people to participate in pastoral consultation, organization and planning? The good functioning of these Councils is critical. I believe that on this score, we are far behind.[56]

LG 12 stated that the "entire [*universitas*] body of the faithful, anointed as they are by the Holy One, cannot err in matters of belief [*in credendo falli nequit*]." This is an invitation to the magisterium to account for the reception of their teachings and to consult the faithful in their elaboration. Especially of note is *LG* 37: "The latter [the spiritual leaders], on the other hand, aided by the experience of the laity, can more clearly and more incisively come to decisions regarding both spiritual and temporal matters." This means that the bishops' magisterium will be much more just as the bishops themselves will listen to the faithful, a practice that Pope Francis has observed in the two consultations prior to the synod on the family. These consultations cannot be easily renewed on a universal scale; hence the importance of diocesan synods.

Ecumenical Reasons

There is no possibility that other Christian churches will recognize the tradition in our recent understanding of collegiality. The Orthodox observer N. Nissiotis had sternly warned the fathers during Vatican II against the adoption of such a doctrine.[57] Later, however, the Joint Commission for Theological Dialogue between the Catholic Church and the Orthodox Church underlined the close bond between succession and communion, stating that the new bishop "receives from his church, which is faithful to tradition, the word he transmits."[58] The Reformed Churches hardly agree on this separation,[59] and we do not dare to think that the Anglican position is the same as ours, as J. H. Newman subtly demonstrated.[60]

In the Communio Ecclesiae, *the Particular Churches (and Not Only Diocesan) Should Be, at Different Levels, Subjects of Law and Initiative Because the Church Is Catholic and Not Simply Universal*

Doctrinal Reasons

The *communio ecclesiarum* is simultaneously a communion between dioceses and between particular-regional churches (*LG* 23 at the end), a prospect that Pope Francis intends to develop (*EG* 32). In both cases, the juridical status of the Roman curia should be reexamined.

After the promulgation of *Lumen Gentium,* the theological foundation of the particular churches has been developed in *Ad Gentes,* which has shown well how the universality of the mission required the particularity of the churches. Since the Church is Catholic, it must become particular in the cultures it encounters. From the day of Pentecost, as stated in the missionary decree, "a Church which speaks all tongues, understands and accepts all tongues in her love, and so supersedes the divisiveness of Babel" (*AG* 4). Similarly, in her mission, the Church must imitate Christ who was led "to bind Himself, in virtue of His Incarnation, to certain social and cultural conditions of those human beings among whom He dwelt" (*AG* 10). In this logic, "This congregation of the faithful, endowed with the riches of its own nation's culture, should be deeply rooted in the people" (*AG* 15). Tradition attests that the encounter of the gospel with the most diverse cultures has given rise to so many particular churches in the cultural sense of the term: Syriac, Coptic, Armenian, Greek, Latin, Georgian, Ethiopian, and Malabar, to name a few.

Nothing prevents and everything suggests putting into the third chapter of *Ad Gentes*, which wants to promote "in each major socio-cultural area," the birth of authentic "Particular Churches" (the title of the chapter). They can bear fruit, provided that "every appearance of syncretism and of false particularism will be excluded, and Christian life will be accommodated to the genius and the dispositions of each culture....Finally, the young particular churches, adorned with their own traditions, will have their own place in the ecclesiastical communion" (*AG* 22).

The perception of Vatican II, according to which the "each major socio-cultural territory" (*AG* 22) is part of the theological definition of a regional church (in the same place it talks about the collaboration between different episcopal conferences), thus remains to be developed. The reduction of divine right to relations between bishops and dioceses is not sustainable doctrinally. In principle, the Eastern Catholic Churches *sui iuris* have similar legitimacy in divine law.

The fears that such an evolution can arouse, as the solutions it will need, have been well described by J. Ratzinger, who wrote,

> Uniformity of canon law and liturgy and the appointment of bishops by Rome—all these things are not necessarily derived from the primacy as such. Therefore, it

> should be considered as a task for the future to clearly distinguish the authentic office of Peter's successor and the patriarchal office, and, where necessary, to create new patriarchates, which should no longer be considered incorporated in the Latin Church....In the not too distant future, we should think about how to give to the churches of Asia and Africa, as well as those of the East, their own form as "patriarchates" or autonomous "great churches," or whatever these *ecclesiae* in the *Ecclesia* might be called in the future.[61]

We must obviously think like him that we "will need a common and patient effort on the part of members of the hierarchy and theologians, canonists, systematic theologians, historians, and experts, who will also have to bear in mind that there is no perfectly good practice that no church can live without mutual patience."[62]

Pastoral Reasons

It seems unnecessary to repeat these, after what has been said. But we will certainly need to avoid the disadvantages.

Ecumenical Reasons

Although it is impossible to imagine the future forms of a unified Christianity, one thing is certain: the current churches will not merge with each other. Each will retain a large part of their spiritual profile. The Church will truly be Catholic as it will be able to combine diversity in unity; remaining universalist will not serve the cause of unity.[63]

The Nature of the Communio Ecclesiarum *and the Power Already Recognized to the* Collegium Episcoporum *Would Allow the Roman Curia to Be an Institution in the Service of the Pope and of the Churches*

According to the existing law (*Pastor Bonus* 3),

> The Roman Curia came into existence for this purpose, that the fruitful communion we mentioned might be strengthened and make ever more bountiful progress, rendering more effective the task of pastor of the Church which Christ entrusted to Peter and his successors, a task that has been growing and expanding from day to day.

Its disciplinary and managerial reform and the criticism of its approach are already a reality.[64] But there remains the question of its ecclesiological status, the only one that may be the theologians' responsibility.

Doctrinal Reasons

At present, the curia is a central body; and the "Supreme Pontiff usually conducts the affairs of the universal Church through the Roman Curia which performs its function in his name and by his authority for the good and service of the churches."[65] It also exercises ordinary vicarial powers for the daily government of the Church.[66] This is a maximalist interpretation of Vatican I. That Council did not say that the pope should exercise his prerogatives in terms of the daily government of the Church down to the very last detail.

So, what would prevent the pope from ceasing to be the direct head of the curia? After all, this is a fabrication even today. The curia could be put under the authority of the pope and the college of bishops, based on can. 336 of the Code of Canon Law: "The college of bishops, whose head is the Supreme Pontiff...together with its head and never without this head, is also the subject of supreme and full power over the universal Church."

According to this configuration, the pope would, like today, have his direct council (the equivalent of the so-called C-9), while the curia would also have a supervisory board responsible for its ordinary functioning that accounts for both the pope and the college of bishops, represented, for example, by the council of the

Synod of Bishops with the pope, if this institution were to be maintained and renewed.[67]

Pastoral Reasons

The curia takes upon itself matters that it cannot solve adequately, both at the universal level and in relation to the theology of local churches.[68] But it is also evident that it must be able to continue to act with real authority over the bishops. The pedophilia crisis is not, unfortunately, the only case that illustrates this need within the communion.

From the pastoral point of view, by ceasing to be unilateral, from top to bottom, communication between the curia and the bishops would be greatly improved, and the latter would feel valued in their responsibilities.

Ecumenical Reason

It is a reality against which "stumble all the other churches," as the previously mentioned Congar once wrote.

IN THE EXERCISE OF THE PRIMACY IT IS NECESSARY TO REWRITE THE SYMBOLIC FIGURE OF THE POPE'S ABSOLUTE POWER, THE CULTURAL FIGURE OF HIS GOVERNMENT, AND IN NO WAY DOGMA

Doctrinal Reasons

The definitions of Vatican I are those of an unfinished council, limited at the same time in its historical horizon and its conceptual universe. That is why the trajectory that followed it, which coincides with its maximalist reception, requires a doctrinal amendment. It would therefore be necessary to show that Vatican I did not dogmatize either the daily management of the Church by the pope, nor his absolute power. By clarifying these two points, we can seriously pave the way for the unity of all Christians.

In the modern era, the pope exercises his authority in a discretionary manner and without being questioned. No one ever, under any circumstances, for any reason, in any form can say to the pope, "Why are you doing this?" Certainly, discretionary does not mean arbitrary or despotic, but simply "according to the pope's judgment," a judgment that comes entirely from himself. This applies not only to his supreme acts of government and magisterium, but for all his acts, of any kind.

This model of authority, entirely secular, is borrowed from the Roman law in which the prince is *legibus solutus*. It was strengthened after Vatican I: witness to this is Cardinal Billot, SJ, for whom the pope is a "monarch who holds the fullness of supreme power, both legislative, judicial, and executive, regardless of any other body, be it a chamber or a senate."[69] Paul VI asked that the third chapter of *Lumen Gentium* should read that the pope was *uni Domino devinctus*: no legal constraint, outside his conscience, is imposed on the pope in the government of the Church. The theological commission refused this to him, but was later granted in the *nota praevia* and in the 1983 Code, since there is no legal determination of the authority of the bishops on the universal Church that would be outside the papal authority.

Ecumenical Reasons

The Orthodox, as is well known, usually recognize only a *primus inter pares*. Yet few theologians like J. Zizioulas have developed a theology of primacy. The position of the Reformed Church is well expressed by Melanchthon in the *Defense of the Augsburg Confession*: "But the adversaries perhaps require [a new Roman definition], that the Church be defined thus, namely, that it is the supreme outward monarchy of the whole world, in which the Roman pontiff necessarily has unquestioned power, which no one is permitted to dispute or censure [no matter whether he uses it rightly, or misuses it]."[70]

HOW TO REFORM? THE IMPORTANCE OF A PROCEDURAL METHOD

The question of the *modus procedendi* is acutely relevant. We probably need to follow Pope Francis's method: he does not cite nor interpret in detail the texts of Vatican II, except in sporadic cases.

Evangelii Gaudium includes 217 notes, of which only thirteen refer to the last Council. Without getting caught up in exegesis, he does what the Council requires. For example, through the procedure he has chosen to prepare the two sessions of the Synod on the Family, Francis ensured a reception of the theology of the people of God and of collegiality that had remained largely theoretical for fifty years. And he did it in the best way: that is, based on learning, involving not only the two hundred bishops of the synod, but *all* diocesan bishops, who received a questionnaire and who were strongly asked to work *with their diocesans, articulating in this way collegiality and synodality*, as we have mentioned.

It would be worthwhile to reflect on the advantages and disadvantages of an approach to reform similar to this preparation of a synod. In this way, we could get there more straightforwardly with a series of *motu proprio*. Our excursus C develops further this idea.[71]

Overall Conclusion

At the end of this theological path that we have proposed so far, a final reflection is required: the reforms that emerge are opposed to a model that, with a Weberian expression, we might call legal-bureaucratic. To change the paradigm in a fruitful way, the theologians' reflections must be fully open to the contributions of historians, canonists, and sociologists.

EXCURSUS A: THE THIRD CHAPTER OF *LUMEN GENTIUM* RESTORED VALUE TO THE *COMMUNIO ECCLESIAE* AS *COMMUNIO ECCLESIARUM*

The third chapter of *Lumen Gentium* includes numerous doctrinal enunciations that conceive the communion of the Church as a communion of churches, which challenges the legitimacy of the universalist ecclesiology that, nevertheless, prevailed after Vatican II.

The dioceses are portions of the whole church: this is a fundamental statement.[72] A portion has all the qualities of the whole and the addition of portions does not create mass, while a *part* cannot exist outside of its relationship with the whole and is subordinate to it.[73] Moreover, this leads away from a universalist ecclesiology to an ecclesiology of the communion of churches, which prevents the diocese from being conceived as administrative circles of the universal Church, a trend favored by John Paul II,[74] and requires treating them as subjects of law and initiative in the communion of churches. In addition, *LG* 23 explicitly teaches that the *communio ecclesiae* is a *communio ecclesiarum*: it is from them "in and from which [*in quibus et ex quibus*] churches" that "comes into being the one and only Catholic Church"—here a particular church designates the local diocesan church. This change of perspective revives the tradition that *the communion among the bishops is an expression of the communion of churches*. The *collegium episcoporum* cannot be separated from the *communio ecclesiarum*, a paramount theological perception of the tradition, which remained almost extraneous to Vatican I.[75] In the *communio ecclesiarum, LG* 23 legitimizes the incorporation of the dioceses "into several groups, organically united, which, preserving the unity of faith and the unique divine constitution of the universal Church, enjoy their own discipline, their own liturgical usage, and their own theological and spiritual heritage." Relying on the last text, Pope Francis thinks he can find in the Church the equivalent of the patriarchates of the early church (see *EG* 32). This will reinforce the catholicity of the Church, which will thus connect in a more realistic way diversity in unity and unity in diversity.

EXCURSUS B: THE SYSTEMATIC DESIGNATION OF THE DIOCESE AS PARTICULAR CHURCH WAS NOT A DOCTRINAL DECISION OF VATICAN II, BUT WAS IMPOSED BY THE EDITORS OF THE 1983 *CODE*

Contrary to a widespread opinion, designating dioceses as particular churches was not a doctrinal decision of Vatican II. Some council fathers (fifty-seven in all) asked the *Christus Dominus* preparatory commission to replace the term *diocese* with *particular church* because "the word 'diocese,' of imperial origin and of an administrative nature, conveys an ideology that is too secular."[76] There were, therefore, ethical considerations—to avoid "administrative" and "imperial" connotations—at the onset of this proposal and not just an intention to take a position on the ontological relationship between the Church and the churches.

The request was ignored:[77] *Christus Dominus* refused to resort to the category of "particularity" to define dioceses, preferring to declare, "A diocese is a portion of the people of God…it constitutes a particular church in which the one, holy, catholic, and apostolic Church of Christ is truly present and operative" (*CD* 11).

While Vatican II designates the dioceses as "local churches," the editors of the Code refused this traditional definition, on the pretext that, by containing a *portio Populi Dei*, they are no longer tied to a locality, but to universality (*sic*!).[78] Perhaps adopting a term with the root *pars* would seem to indicate that the dioceses were incomplete parts of the Church. In any case, the curial decisions, eroding the structure of dioceses not only in lexical terms, were later implemented with the particular church/universal Church combination, which has created this particular connotation.[79] The committee that drew up the Code of Canons of the Eastern Churches refused to accept this choice that Cardinal P. Felici imposed on the Code of Latin Canon Law.[80]

EXCURSUS C: TO REFORM, EVEN FROM THE GROUND UP, IN A PROCEDURAL WAY? WITH A *MOTU PROPRIO*?

Given their complexity, reforms will have to be studied in a multidisciplinary way and introduced in a procedural manner. To allow our suggestion to become an item of discussion, we provide a series of examples.

THE CORRELATION BETWEEN COMMUNIO ECCLESIARUME *AND* COLLEGIUM EPISCOPORUM *CAN ONLY BE ACHIEVED BY STRENGTHENING THE JURIDICAL STATUS OF DIOCESES AND THE INTEGRATION OF BISHOPS IN THE PEOPLE OF GOD*

* *To strengthen the juridical status of dioceses in a canonical manner.* We have demonstrated the doctrinal, pastoral, and ecumenical soundness that strengthening the dioceses as

subjects of law and initiative would have, whereas now they resemble administrative districts of the universal Church to which they are subject, sometimes in the smallest details. To do this we can

- Revitalize and strengthen diocesan councils (presbyteral, pastoral, economic), accepting a special right according to the new "patriarchates" *de jure condendo*.
- Strengthen diocesan synods, in particular. The decisive doctrinal choice of *Lumen Gentium*, treating the people of God before the episcopate, has had almost no practical realization apart from extending the right of association of the laity, a concept of secular law that almost never expresses their original rights in the communion (*iura communionis*).[81] In reality, the diocesan synod should be the place where a portion of the people of God, in the diversity of its charisms (priests, deacons, religious men and women, laymen and -women) expresses itself under the presidency of its bishop.[82] It would be important to establish for these synods a certain regularity, which, paradoxically, has disappeared in the postconciliar regulation, and allow them to put items on the agenda and to votes in free areas of interest, so that votes cast in accordance with the bishop may be the expression of a portion of the people of God.
- More importantly, they should be asked to make a list of priests who recommended for the episcopate. Current legislation prohibits, apparently for no reason, consulting diocesan groups on this issue![83]
- Verify whether the right to submit a grievance can be resumed. Theoretically always in force, it allows a diocesan bishop to suspend the pope's decision, if he considers it unfavorable to the pastoral welfare of the diocese.[84]
- Avoid the plurality of dioceses in the same territory: could a collegial episcopal government not have the meaning of communion?[85]
- Use the expression *particular church* as little as possible to designate the dioceses, especially in the context of the particular church/universal Church binomial. Reserve this terminology for the Eastern Catholic Churches and

the future "patriarchates" evoked in *LG* 23. Eliminate the term *ecclesiastical district,* which hints more at a universalist than Catholic ecclesiology.

* To strengthen the integration of bishops in the people of God:
    - Make compulsory the consecration of all bishops in their cathedral, or at least among their people. Restore a ritual dimension to their reception by the people, especially if the new ordinary has already been consecrated bishop. This symbolic act should have as much importance as the reading of the pontifical mandate.
    - Make very rare the ordinations of bishops for protocol or administrative purposes. How can one justify the ordination of an eighty-seven year old religious man or a professor of ninety-two (paradoxically both created cardinal deacons) to the episcopacy, which they will never exercise? Is it necessary to "automatically" confer the episcopate to heads of diplomatic missions of the Holy See or to many officials of the curia, when these services are actually *diakonia*? This individualistic and universalist conception of belonging to the college of bishops is recent: even on the eve of Vatican I, it was not clear to Pius IX whether the bishops lacking a see would participate in the Council.[86]
    - If, on the one hand, the auxiliary bishops should be maintained to safeguard the pastoral unity of the large cities (there are eleven auxiliaries in Mexico City), why can they not be *sedi datus*, instead of being assigned to sees that do not exist? An *episcopé* exercised in a team would be theologically conceivable, with a leader, and would preserve the diversity and unity of the church in the same city; it would also be a desirable path if Christian unity was reestablished.[87]

CONCERNING THE PARTICULAR CHURCHES *DE IURE CONDENDO*

Two observations: Is it possible that the national scale is not suitable for organizing conferences of bishops (nationalism is not an illusory phenomenon; the bishops' personal freedom will be better ensured if they are in sufficient numbers). It would be more appropriate to strengthen the continental Bishops' Conferences (CELAM, CCEE, etc.), considering their own suggestions. Their powers would be extended, not in terms of decentralization (creating mini-Vaticans on every continent), but to help the Church to be in line with Pentecost.

REGARDING THE ROMAN PRIMACY

After Vatican II, the papal authority has remained "absolute" or "purely monarchical." Pope Francis could therefore, by issuing a *motu proprio*, recognize episcopal rights that would greatly change the symbolism of absolute power and the path to Christian unity. Here are some suggestions that go in this direction, in general and modifiable terms:[88]

- The pope could make his decisions within a consistory, whose composition would be rethought (which would *ipso facto* lead to a reflection on the cardinalate), drawing on the Roman synods of antiquity or the medieval consistory, prior to the reform of Sixtus V.
- Recognize the right of the episcopal conferences (if they reach a certain number) to put questions on the agenda of the synod of bishops. Give decision-making authority to these synods in some circumstances, which has not been done so far.
- Recognize the right of consultation to bishops before an important doctrinal decision, and even require their majority decision (what type?).
- Recognize the possibility for a qualified number of bishops to request the convening of an ecumenical council.
- Develop opportunities for recourse to the Holy See, making can. 333, §3 more flexible, since according to this canon no appeal is possible against a judgment by the Roman pontiff. At least, avoid reinforcing a prohibition now extended to the decisions of the Congregation for the Doctrine of the Faith.[89]

NOTES

1. The Bull of Indiction of the Council thus specifies this goal: "Provide the premises of doctrinal clarity and of mutual charity that will make even more alive in our separated brethren the desire for the hoped-for return to unity and will smooth the way to it." John XXIII, Apostolic Constitution *Humanae Salutis* of December 25, 1961, in *AAS* 54 (1962) 9. Translated as "Pope John XXIII Convokes the Second Vatican Council," 3: https://jakomonchak.files.wordpress.com/2011/12/humanae-salutis.pdf.

2. In fact, the term never entered the vocabulary of Vatican II.

3. After the interventions regarding Mary, which practically split the assembly.

4. Paul VI's motu proprio *Pastorale Munus* (in *AAS* 56 [1964] 5–12) illustrates the subordination in which Catholic bishops were kept until then. Maximus IV, patriarch of the Melkites, commented, "Some faculties that are granted to the bishops really puzzle us: for example, the faculty granted to the bishop to keep the Holy Eucharist in his chapel;...to allow their priests to celebrate Mass two or three times on Sundays; to allow religious women to wash corporals, purificators, and palls, *prima quoque ablutio*....If truly a successor to the apostles does not have the right to allow religious women to wash purificators, what then are they allowed to do in the church of God? The excesses to which the 'pope, source of all power in the Church' has reached, show how much this theory is to be reconsidered in its foundations in view of a healthy ecclesiology." See *L'Église grecque melkite au concile. Discours et notes du patriarche Maximos IV et des prélats de son Église au concile œcuménique Vatican II* (Beirut: Dar al-Kalima, 1967), 210ff.

5. Their subjection was a source of humiliation in the eyes of the Orthodox: only six months before the announcement of the Council, the oriental patriarchs were dispensed by Pius XII from giving precedence in any circumstance to a simple delegate priest of the Holy See! See *AAS* 50 (1958): 550.

6. See Cardinal P. Eyt, "La collégialité épiscopale," in *Le deuxième concile du Vatican 1959–1965. Actes du colloque organisé par l'École française de Rome en collaboration avec l'Université de Lille* 3 (Rome: École Française de Rome, 1989), 54.

7. Y. M. Congar, *Le concile au jour le jour. Troisième session* (Paris: Cerf, 1965), 44.

8. Ibid., 37.

9. Congar, *Le concile au jour le jour. [Première session]* (Paris: Cerf, 1963), 18. Translated as Paul Murray, ed., *Receptive Ecumenism and the*

Call to Catholic Learning: Exploring a Way for Contemporary Ecumenism (Oxford: Oxford University Press, 2008), 391. The following year, this general optimism faded away: "Only the future and practice will tell what the doctrine of collegiality will bring to both the possibilities of ecumenical dialogue and the balance of papal and episcopal functions within the Catholic Church. They will also tell whether a sketch of theology of the local church, contained in *Lumen gentium* and resumed in *Ad gentes*, will have found an echo in the life of the Church, and with what ecumenical impact." (Congar, *Le concile au jour le jour. Quatrième session* [Paris: Cerf, 1966], 134).

10. He demonstrated this in the preparatory procedure of the two sessions of the Synod on the Family, sending the preparatory questionnaire to each bishop, who were asked to discuss it with their diocesans. We cannot appreciate episcopal collegiality without diocesan synodality! Has this clear message been understood everywhere?

11. *EG* 32: "Yet this desire has not been fully realized, since a juridical status of episcopal conferences which would see them as subjects of specific attributions, including genuine doctrinal authority, has not yet been sufficiently elaborated." In no. 22 of *Apostolos Suos* (1998), John Paul II removed the doctrinal authority that the Code of Canon Law of 1983 was willing to recognize them, unless they were decisions taken unanimously (the only instance of such requirement in all existing legislation).

12. *EG* 32: "The Second Vatican Council stated that, *like the ancient patriarchal Churches*, episcopal conferences are in a position 'to contribute in many and fruitful ways to the concrete realization of the collegial spirit.'" *LG* 23, to which the pope refers here, speaks of those churches that "enjoy their own discipline, their own liturgical usage, and their own theological and spiritual heritage."

13. *EG* 32: "John Paul II asked for help in finding 'a way of exercising the primacy which, while in no way renouncing what is essential to its mission, is nonetheless open to a new situation.' We have made little progress in this regard. The papacy and the central structures of the universal Church also need to hear the call to pastoral conversion."

14. The *Acta Synodalia* do not contain any intervention on this topic.

15. *Nota praevia* 3: "It is up to the judgment of the Supreme Pontiff, to whose care Christ's whole flock has been entrusted, to determine, according to the needs of the Church as they change over the course of centuries, the way in which this care may best be exercised—whether in a personal or a collegial way." *Preliminary Note of Explanation*: http://www.vatican.va/archive/hist_councils/ii_vatican_council/documents/vat-ii_const_19641121_lumen-gentium_en.html.

16. *Proemium* to the dogmatic constitution *Pastor Aeternus*: *Ut vero episcopatus ipse unus et indivisus esset* (*DH* 3051).

17. We refer here to the classical work of J.-M. R. Tillard, *L'évêque de Rome* (Paris: Cerf, 1982). Translated as *The Bishop of Rome* (Wilmington, DE: Michael Glazier, 1983).

18. See J. Ratzinger, "La collegialità episcopale dal punto di vista teologico," in *La Chiesa del Vaticano II. Studi e commenti intorno alla Costituzione dogmatica "Lumen Gentium,"* ed. G. Baraúna (Florence: Vallecchi, 1965), 756.

19. K. Rahner, "Dogmatische Konstitution über die Kirche. Kommentar zum Drittes Kapitel, Artikel 18–27," in *Lexikon für Theologie und Kirche. Das Zweite Vatikanische Konzil. Dokumente und Kommentare*, vol. 1 (Freiburg: Herder, 1966), 210ff.: "Was gesagt wird, ist weder neu noch bedeutet es gegenüber dem bisherigen Stand einen sehr erheblichen dogmengeschichtlichen Fortschritt" [What is said is neither new, nor does it imply a very considerable advance in dogmatic history].

20. See Ratzinger, "La collegialità episcopale dal punto di vista teologico."

21. Ibid., 203n27.

22. See at the end of this essay, 179–80.

23. See W. F. Rothe, "Kanonistische Anmerkungen zum Verhältnis von Universalkirche und Particularkirche," *Forum Katholische Theologie* 18 (2002): 224–32.

24. See at the end of this essay, 179–84.

25. A theologian as respected as Cardinal A. Dulles, SJ, falls into this trap when he writes, "The ontological priority of the Church universal appears to me to be almost self-evident, since the very concept of a particular church presupposes a universal Church to which it belongs, whereas the concept of the universal Church does not imply that it is made up of distinct particular churches." *Inside the Vatican* 20 (June 4, 2001): 13.

26. An idea of these complex structures appears in H. Legrand, "Episcopato, *episkopè*, Chiesa locale e comunione delle Chiese nella costituzione apostolica *Anglicanorum Coetibus*," in *La costituzione "Anglicanorum Coetibus" e l'ecumenismo*, ed. G. Ruggieri (Bologna: EDB, 2012), 63–84.

27. There are three entries for "ecclesiastical districts" (territorial, personal, Oriental). The entry for "local church," while excellent overall, does not specifically address the diocese. The bureaucratic concept of ecclesiastical district thus becomes an inclusive concept.

28. The Italian version reads, "I will always be faithful and obedient to the Holy Roman Apostolic Church and to the Supreme Pontiff, successor to Blessed Peter Apostle in the primacy and Vicar of Christ, and to his

legitimate successors....It will be my concern to promote and defend the rights and authority of the Roman Pontiffs; as well as the prerogatives of their legates and procurators. I will report to the Roman Pontiff with sincerity whenever there might be an attack on any of said officials....I will take accountability for my pastoral office and will report faithfully about the situation of the clergy and the people entrusted to me; I will also respectfully accept what I will be ordered and put it into practice with the utmost commitment." [Translator's note: the English version is different; see http://www.vatican.va/roman_curia/congregations/cfaith/documents/rc_con_cfaith_doc_19880701_professio-fidei_en.html].

29. Thus G. Bier, ordinary of canon law with the *nihil obstat* of the Holy See in Freiburg in Brisgovia, concludes his habilitation thesis: *Die Rechtsstellung des Diözesanbischofs nach dem Codex Iuris Canonici von 1983* (Forschungen zum Kirchenrechtswissenschaft, 32) (Echter: Würzburg, 2001), 376. Can. 480 states, "A vicar general and an episcopal vicar must report to the diocesan bishop concerning the more important affairs which are to be handled or have been handled, and they are never to act contrary to the intention and mind of the diocesan bishop." We have read thirteen reviews of the work; some express their surprise at the distance between the law in force and the theology, but none of them dispute the conclusion.

30. John Paul II, Apostolic Constitution *Pastor Bonus*, June 28, 1988, no. 6, in *AAS* 80 (1988): 848. John Paul II refers to Innocent III to justify himself, and uses Innocent's words to explain the situation where the pope cannot do all by himself: "Although the Lord has given us the fullness of power in the Church": see ibid., no. 3, in *AAS* 80 (1988): 844.

31. For example, the 1997 Instruction, issued in common by eight dicasteries, known as *Ecclesiae de Mysterio*, on the collaboration of lay faithful to the ministry of priests, affirms, "With regard to the administration of this sacrament [anointing of the sick], ecclesiastical legislation reiterates the theologically certain doctrine and the age-old usage of the Church which regards the priest as its only valid minister" (article 9, § 2). According to A. Chavasse, *Étude sur l'onction des infirmes dans l'Église latine, I: Du IIIe siècle à la réforme carolingienne* (Lyon: Imprimerie Nouvelle J. Gamon, 1942), the anointing was often administered by a member of the family with oil blessed by the bishop.

32. The *Teachings of John Paul II* could reach four thousand pages (1982) or five thousand pages (1988) per year.

33. Not unnecessarily: a decree of March 4, 1998, not implemented, decided on the expulsion and transfer to Ukraine of all legally married Greek-Catholic priests, active in Poland, and their replacement with celibate Latin-rite or bi-ritual priests: see *Istina* 44 (1999): 278–89.

34. The papal formula for the approval of the Acts of Vatican II could have served as a precedent: see G. Alberigo, "*Una cum patribus*. La formula conclusiva delle decisioni del Vaticano II," in *Ecclesia a Spiritu Sancto edocta: Lumen Gentium* 53. *Mélanges théologiques. Hommage à Mgr Gérard Philips* (Gembloux: Duculot, 1970), 291–319.

35. Two examples that will surprise the Orthodox. According to can. 57, §1, "The erection, restoration, modification and suppression of patriarchal Churches is reserved to the supreme authority of the Church," that is, to the pope. According to can. 1008, §1, "The Roman Pontiff is the supreme administrator and steward of all ecclesiastical goods," which is specified in §2: "Under the supreme authority of the Roman Pontiff, ownership of temporal goods of the Church belongs to that juridic person which has lawfully acquired them." Establishing a maximum value, for the transfer of a good, could have avoided a wording that will be poorly understood by Orthodox monks.

36. See Congregation for the Doctrine of the Faith, *Letter to the Bishops of the Catholic Church Understood as Communion*, May 28, 1992, in *AAS* 85 (1993): 838–50.

37. See *DH* 3112–17.

38. Of over thirty ecclesiologists who have expressed themselves on the letter *Communionis Notio*, only one is convinced, without saying why. See the list drawn up by A. Cattaneo, "La priorità della Chiesa universale sulla Chiesa particolare," *Antonianum* 77 (2002): 503–39, which we have completed in *Revue des Sciences philosophiques et théologiques* 88 (2004): 495ff. For example, see also K. McDonnell, "Walter Kasper on the Theology and the Praxis of the Bishop's Office," *Theological Studies* 63 (2002): 713.

39. For a more in-depth analysis, not possible here, see H. Legrand, "La théologie des Églises sœurs," *Revue des Sciences philosophiques et théologiques* 88 (2004): 474–80.

40. According to Cardinal H. de Lubac, "A universal Church prior to all individual churches or seen as existing in itself apart from them, is merely an abstraction." See also Lubac, *Pluralismo di Chiese o unità della Chiesa?* (Brescia: Morcelliana, 1973), 46. Translated by Kilian McDonnell, OSB, as "The Ratzinger/Kasper Debate: The Universal Church and Local Churches," *Theological Studies* 63 (2002): 245.

41. See K. Delahaye, *Per un rinnovamento della pastorale. La comunità, madre dei credenti* (Bari: Ecumenica, 1974). See also E. Lanne, "Église sœur et Église mère dans le vocabulaire de l'Église ancienne," Delahaye, *Tradition et communion des Églises. Recueil d'études* (BETL 129) (Leuven: Leuven University Press, 1997), 625–36, where the author notes that it is "only in an accommodating sense that Jerusalem is understood as the mother of the churches" (ibid., 626) and that, on the contrary, "maternity

applies to local churches founded by the apostles," and therefore not to a universal church (ibid., 636). As for the title of *mater and magistra* of all the faithful, it means something else (see Lateran Council IV, 2, 4, 5, 236, and Lyon Council II, paragraph 1). Only Clement VI in Avignon (1342–1352) claimed that "the church of Rome would institute all patriarchal, metropolitan, cathedrals and rank of every order within them. Her pastor and ruler, the Roman Pontiff, has full disposition of all churches, rank, appointments, and ecclesiastical benefits": O. Rinaldi, *Annales ecclesiastici*, ed. A. Theiner (Paris: Bar-le-duc, 1880), XXV, 350.

42. This observation does not deny at all that the pope and ecumenical councils can speak *in persona ecclesiae*.

43. SDA IV, 4, in *AAS* 89 (1997): 706–27.

44. No. 13 of John Paul II's *motu proprio* emphasizes that conferences are "really quite different from…the College of Bishops," "the binding effect of the acts of the episcopal ministry jointly exercised within Conferences of Bishops and in communion with the Apostolic See derives from the fact that the latter has constituted the former and has entrusted to them,…specific areas of competence." According to no. 20, for that joint exercise of their pastoral ministry "to be legitimate and binding on the individual Bishops, there is needed the intervention of the supreme authority of the Church which, through universal law or particular mandates, entrusts determined questions to the deliberation of the Episcopal Conference."

45. Ibid., section IV, art. 1: "In order that the doctrinal declarations of the Conference of Bishops referred to in No. 22 of the present Letter may constitute authentic magisterium and be published in the name of the Conference itself, they must be unanimously approved by the Bishops who are members, or receive the *recognitio* of the Apostolic See." This is the only case of unanimity required in current law. This measure is unusual, in that the faithful are obliged to "obey the will and the intelligence" of their diocesan bishop, but not if he is speaking in agreement with other ninety-two bishops of a conference of ninety-four members!

46. It is clearly stated: *recognitio* is to ensure that the "doctrinal response will favour communion and not harm it, and will rather prepare an eventual intervention of the universal magisterium" (22, end).

47. Such control, perhaps useful, creates a well-founded uneasiness in the bishops. According to the Instruction of the Congregation for Divine Worship, *Liturgiam Authenticam* 80, the liturgical translations of the episcopal conferences must be reviewed by Rome, "an exercise of the power of governance, which is absolutely necessary (in the absence of which the act of the Conference of Bishops entirely in no way attains legal force)"; so, as the Indonesian Msgr. F. Hadisurmata pointed out, an

intervention is required from "people who do not speak or understand our languages" (*Origins* [May 7, 1998]: 773). There was also the attempt to translate into Japanese *et cum spiritu tuo* with a term that means "with your phantom" (see *Il Regno—Attualità* [10/2014]: 321). Similarly, it took eleven years (1992–2002) and the participation of two dicasteries for the curia to regulate, in four stages, the issue of girls wishing to serve at the altar like boys at a universal level, whether they live in Montreal (Canada) or Peshawar (Pakistan); five conditions are set for access to this service.

48. *COD* 90: "The sacred synod has decreed that the ordination of those ordained without title is null, and that they cannot operate anywhere, because of the presumption of the one who ordained them." Translated by Norman P. Tanner, SJ, in *Decrees of the Ecumenical Councils*, 1:90.

49. See L. Koep, "Bischofsliste," in *Reallexikon für Antike und Christentum* (Stuttgart: Hiersemann, 1954), II, 407–15.

50. Such a conception of the succession is typical of Donatists, who associate it with the continuous succession of the imposition of the hands of orthodox bishops. Confronting them, Saint Augustine only recognizes "God as Father, the Church as a mother, and the one who has ordained him as a brother"; the rest is irrelevant, refusing even to name the one who ordained him: see S. Lancel, ed., *Actes de la Conférence de Carthage en 411* (Sources chrétiennes 224) (Paris: Cerf, 1976), 1184–86. It is clear then how little ecclesiological sense is the work of I. Perraud and A. Chapeau, titled "Généalogies et succession apostolique," *L'ami du clergé* 88 (1978): 49ff., which refers abundantly to specific national continuous successions—the Italian, the French, the Sino-Portuguese, and so on.

51. In the texts of the episcopal ordination liturgies, it is not "a matter of transmitting apostolic powers through ordination": See H. Ohme, "Bischofslisten," in *Lexikon für Theologie und Kirche*, ed. W. Kasper (Freiburg: Herder, 1998), 500. As Congar wrote, "Ordination does not transmit a portable power"; see *Oecumenica* 1 (1966): 61–80. Canon 6 of the Council of Nicea observes that power is related to the exercise of a duty in communion: "If anyone is baptized without the consent of the metropolitan, this great synod stipulates that he should not be bishop [*mè dêin êinai epískopon*]'" (*COD* 9); and can. 29 of the Council of Chalcedon stipulates that bishops rightly deposed should not even be left in the rank of priests (*COD* 101). The *episcopi vagantes*, who impose their hands on each other, are of opposite opinion. Consider the refusal of the Holy See to acknowledge the episcopal ordinations made by the archbishop of Hué, outside the Church's communion: see *AAS* 78 (1976): 623.

52. Mansi 49, 492ff.

53. Cyprian of Carthage, *Epistulae* 66, 8, 3, in *Lettere* (Rome: Città Nuova, 2006), II, 120.

54. "Where I'm terrified by what I am for you, I am given comfort by what I am with you. For you I am a bishop, with you, after all, I am a Christian. The first is the name of an office undertaken, the second a name of grace; that one means danger, this one salvation." Augustine of Hippo, *Sermones* 340, 1, in *Discorsi*, V: *273–340A su I santi* (Rome: Città Nuova, 1986), 995. Translated as *The Works of Saint Augustine (4th Release). Electronic Edition. Sermons (306–340A) on the Saints*, vol. 3/9 (Charlottesville, VA: InteLex Corporation, 2014).

55. In his address to the CELAM during the General Coordination Meeting in Rio de Janeiro on July 28, 2013, Pope Francis denounced clericalism five times in five sentences, as "a temptation very present."

56. Ibid.

57. For the orthodox theologian, this notion of collegiality "has no scriptural or historical foundation....Orthodox see the sign of a dangerous ecclesiological misconception [in the fact] that a council submits to discussion a conception of collegiality that is neither biblical nor historical and decides to adopt it": N. A. Nissiotis, "Die Ekklesiologie des Zweiten Vatikanischen Konzils in orthodoxer Sicht und ihre ökumenische Bedeutung," *Kerygma und Dogma* 10 (1964): 157ff.

58. See Joint International Commission for Theological Dialogue between the Catholic Church and the Orthodox Church, "Le mystère de l'Église et de l'eucharistie à la lumière du mystère de la Sainte Trinité," *Irénikon* 55 no. 3 (1982): 350–62.

59. As an example, see P. E. Persson, *Repraesentatio Christi. Der Amtsbegriff in der neueren römisch-katholischen Theologie* (Göttingen: Vandenhoeck und Ruprecht, 1966).

60. J. H. Newman, *Essays Critical and Historical* (London: Longmans, Green & Co., 1888[8]), 2:87: "Catholics believe their Orders are valid because they are members of the true Church; and Anglicans believe they belong to the true Church because their orders are valid."

61. See J. Ratzinger, *Il nuovo popolo di Dio. Questioni ecclesiologiche* (Brescia: Queriniana, 1971), 155ff.

62. Ibid., 155.

63. On the unfortunate fate of the note on catholicity after the Reformation, see G. Thils, *Les notes de l'Église dans l'apologétique catholique depuis la Réforme* (Gembloux: J. Duculot, 1937), especially 214–54: Most authors ended up identifying it with geographic universalism. The post-conciliar official documents clearly testify to the reduction of catholicity to universality, particularly through the frequent use of the universal

church / particular church combination. For example, the declaration *Dominus Iesus* speaks exclusively of a universal church, never of a Catholic church. Cardinal G.-M. Garrone, French translator of *Lumen gentium. Actes de Vatican II* for Bayard, and Prefect of the Congregation for Catholic Education, renders "ecclesia universa" ("the whole Church") and "ecclesia universalis" ("the universal Church") in an identical way; other translators do the same. Even in Italian editions, this confusion is frequent: in the translation of the Code of Canons of the Eastern Churches, *ecclesia universa* becomes, again, "universal Church." We have a problem here!

64. There is perhaps a first idea of how Pope Francis sees the curia in his address to the CELAM General Coordination Meeting: "The Church is an institution, but when she makes herself a 'centre,' she becomes merely functional....She becomes increasingly self-referential and loses her need to be missionary. From an "institution" she becomes a 'enterprise'. She stops being a bride and ends up being an administrator; from being a servant, she becomes an 'inspector.'" See also his amazing address to the curia on December 22, 2014, published in *AAS* 107 (2015): 44–53.

65. See Code of Canon Law 360.

66. According to can. 349, it is up to the cardinals to assist the Roman pontiff and help "in the daily care of the universal Church." For ordinary vicarious power of the curia, see *Code de droit canonique annoté* (Paris: Cerf, 1989), 250.

67. The present synod is simply a council: it has no control over its regularity, agenda, publication of its resolutions, or its composition (for example, the Special Assembly for Latin America [1997] included only 136 members elected by their peers, while the other 161 were *ex officio* members, or designated by the pope). It could easily become a more representative structure of the episcopate, without pretending to be a body of universal collegiality.

68. See above, n47.

69. L. Billot, *Tractatus de Ecclesia Christi* (Rome: Ex Typ. Polyglotta, 1900), 3:38; M. De Luca speaks of an "absolute monarchy" (*Institutiones juris ecclesiastici publici* II (Rome: Libraria Pontificia, 1901), 36–41).

70. Philip Melanchthon, *The Defense of the Augsburg Confession* (1531), in *Confessioni di fede delle Chiese cristiane*, ed. R. Fabbri (Bologna: EDB, 1996), n. 288, 167ff. Translated as *The Defense of the Augsburg Confession, Articles VII and VIII: Of the Church*, no. 23: http://bookofconcord.org/defense_6_church.php.

71. See below pp. 181–84.

72. *LG* 23 (twice) and *LG* 28, *CD* 11.

73. An image will suffice to make the concept clear: a portion of any sweet has in itself the essence of sweetness, whatever its form or size; but the essence of a car is not found in some of its parts.

74. See G. Calabrese, P. Goyret, and O. F. Piazza, eds., *Dizionario di ecclesiologia* (Rome: Città Nuova, 2010); we mentioned this earlier; see n27.

75. The proemium of *Pastor Aeternus* gives to the Roman "primacy" the objective to serve "so that the Episcopate also might be one and undivided, and so that, by means of a closely united priesthood, the multitude of the faithful might be kept secure in the oneness of faith and communion" (*DH* 3051), as if the faithful constituted a one and only great papal diocese.

76. *Acta Synodalia* III, VI, 162ff.

77. The Second Vatican Council refers to the dioceses 143 times with their usual name and only twelve times with the suggested neologism, which correspondingly refers twelve times—and rightly so—to the Eastern Catholic churches and other diocese groups with a specific identity within catholicity.

78. See *Nuntia* 23 (1986): 4: "*Ecclesia localis*, while being established in the Christian East, and especially in use among the Orthodox churches, and even though proposed by two consultative bodies, was, however, not approved, because it is hardly compatible with the definition of *populi Dei portio*..., which is not necessarily connected to a *locus* or *territorium*" (*sic*!).

79. For example, the letter of 1992 *Communionis Notio* always designates the church as universal, never as Catholic, or whole. On the influence of this binomial expression, see the quotation of Cardinal A. Dulles, above, n25.

80. See *Nuntia* 23 (1986): 4, with the asterisk.

81. Ulrich Stutz's view on the 1917 Code: "The Catholic Church is the church of the clergy and its rights are almost without exception rights of the clergy, where lay people do not have the rights of citizens, but of foreigners who are residents and protected," is mostly correct; see U. Stutz, *Der Geist der Codex iuris canonici* (*Kirchenrechtliche Abhandlungen 92–93*) (Stuttgart: Enke, 1918), 83–88.

82. When this is not possible, democratization demands are dealt with, which have no connection to the theology of the people of God.

83. Canon 377, §3, forbids consulting together the organs of a diocese: a college of consultors, cathedral chapter, etc.

84. See H.-J. Guth, *Ius remonstrandi. Das Remonstrationsrecht des Diözesanbischofs im kanonischen Recht* (Fribourg, Switzerland: Universität-

Verlag, 1999). But would it be appropriate for every single bishop to act that way?

85. See H. Legrand, "Un seul évêque par ville. Pourquoi et comment redevenir fidèle au 8e canon de Nicée? Un enjeu pour la catholicité de l'Église," *Irénikon* 77 (2004): 5–43.

86. See above, n52.

87. The question is more important than it seems; for example, the Israel-Palestine Catholic Churches, faced with the same difficult problems, do not enjoy the possibility of holding a common synod. See F. Bouwen, "Assemblée générale du synode des Églises catholiques de Terre-Sainte," *Proche-Orient Chrétien* 50 (2000): 297–308.

88. These suggestions include some of Antonio Acerbi's contributions to this issue: A. Acerbi, "Per una nuova forma di ministero petrino," in *Il ministero del papa in prospettiva ecumenica* (Milan: Vita e Pensiero, 1999), 303–38.

89. See Congregation for the Doctrine of the Faith, *Ratio agendi in doctrinarum examine*, June 29, 1997, art. 28, in *AAS* 89 (1997): 834.

9

THE CIRCULARITY BETWEEN *SENSUS FIDEI* AND MAGISTERIUM AS A CRITERION FOR THE EXERCISE OF SYNODALITY IN THE CHURCH

Dario Vitali

This contribution focuses on a matter of great relevance in the life of the Church: the circularity between *sensus fidei* and magisterium as a criterion for the exercise of synodality in the Church. This topic is not easy to explain, both because the two parts involved—*sensus fidei* and magisterium—are in asymmetric relationship, with the magisterium in clear position of control of the function of authorized interpreter of the revealed deposit, and because the very possibility of their relationship seems to be prejudiced from the very profile of the *sensus fidei*, easily associated with controversy and dissent in the Church. For many, in fact, the formula immediately evokes endless discussions, advanced after Vatican II, on the "democratization" of the Church. Although we must say that the *sensus fidei* is much more, we must recognize that this conditional reflex does not help in formulating the problem, and in any case, it obliges us to clarify the profile of a function of the intelligence of faith that is certainly recovered by the Council, but to which—beyond the statements of principle or the words of circumstance—we cannot say that it has been recognized as having an actual, and not just nominal, role in the life and conscience of the Church.

Not that there is a lack of theological literature on *sensus fidei*. For my part, I have devoted much of my efforts in the field of theology to this topic.[1] But when I try to talk about it, I find myself inevitably faced with a disheartening outcome: the theme of *sensus fidei* has not broken into ecclesial practice and awareness. Perhaps it could not be otherwise, considering on the one hand the ignorance of the people of God on a prerogative that belongs to them—a prerogative that even the leaders of the people of God generally do not know or recognize—and, on the other, the substantial silence of the magisterium on the subject from the Council to the present.[2] One can hope that, after the explicit reference to *sensus fidei* by Pope Francis in the apostolic exhortation *Evangelii Gaudium*, the tendency reverses. The theme can be found at the beginning of the third chapter, on the proclamation of the gospel (*EG* 110–74), where it becomes clear that the subject of this proclamation is "the entire people of God" (*EG* 111–34):

> In all the baptized, from first to last, the sanctifying power of the Spirit is at work, impelling us to evangelization. The people of God is holy thanks to this anointing, which makes it infallible *in credendo*. This means that it does not err in faith, even though it may not find words to explain that faith. The Spirit guides it in truth and leads it to salvation. As part of his mysterious love for humanity, God furnishes the totality of the faithful with an instinct of faith—*sensus fidei*—which helps them to discern what is truly of God. The presence of the Spirit gives Christians a certain connaturality with divine realities, and a wisdom which enables them to grasp those realities intuitively, even when they lack the wherewithal to give them precise expression. (*EG* 119)

The International Theological Commission has also recently published a very thorough text[3] that brings *sensus fidei* back to the attention of the scientific community and all the people of God. Considering these two documents, it seems the time has come to give *sensus fidei* its proper importance in the theological synthesis that has been laboriously maturing after the Second Vatican Council; without the actual recovery of this property of the *universitas fidelium,* it is unthinkable to clarify the question of the circularity between *sensus fidei* and magisterium. On the other hand, it is not enough to just put the two terms one next the other: after a process of concentration of the ecclesial mediation on the revealed deposit in the hands of the magisterium alone, recognizing the role of another subject of the intelligence of the faith is neither immediate nor automatic. Therefore, we need to show—and prove—that *sensus fidei* is not a novelty introduced by Vatican II, but the recovery and underlining of an obvious, to say the least, fact of the tradition. This is the path we want to follow in this contribution, showing how and where *sensus fidei* manifested in various periods of Church life, and when the bond with the magisterium was broken, gradually losing the active capacity of the people of God as subject of doctrinal authority. More than in a historical perspective, we prefer to approach the theme hermeneutically: in this horizon, the choice to work our way backward becomes clear, from Vatican II to the Church fathers through the intermediate stages of the controversialist theology after Trent and Scholasticism in the Middle Ages.[4] The advantage is to bring out, by contrast, how each age was confronted with an instance that has resisted all attempts to be weakened and erased from the consciousness and the life of the Church.

From Vatican II to Vatican I

At present, the difficulties affecting *sensus fidei* are the same ones that have accompanied and determined the eclipse of the people of God after Vatican II. Nor could it be otherwise, considering that the text of reference (*LG* 12a) is a foundation of the second chapter of *Lumen Gentium*, the one on the people of God:

> The holy people of God shares also in Christ's prophetic office; it spreads abroad a living witness to Him, especially by means of a life of faith and charity and by offering to God a sacrifice of praise, the tribute of lips which give praise to His name. The entire body of the faithful, anointed as they are by the Holy One, cannot err in matters of belief. They manifest this special property by means of the whole peoples' supernatural discernment in matters of faith when "from the Bishops down to the last of the lay faithful" they show universal agreement in matters of faith and morals. That discernment in matters of faith is aroused and sustained by the Spirit of truth. It is exercised under the guidance of the sacred teaching authority, in faithful and respectful obedience to which the people of God accepts that which is not just the word of men but truly the word of God. Through it, the people of God adheres unwaveringly to the faith given once and for all to the saints, penetrates it more deeply with right thinking, and applies it more fully in its life. (*LG* 12a)

The crossfire on the ecclesiology of the Council, which has animated the postconciliar debate, dragged along with it *sensus fidei*, almost as if it were the flag of a democratic idea of church, derived from the theology of the people of God, the cause, for many, of all the problems that have afflicted the ecclesial experience after the Council. This would end up causing further suspicion of a reality reduced to a claim against the power of the hierarchy in the Church and further proof of the inopportunity of an ecclesiology founded on the category of God's people.

On the positive side, it can be said that the recovery of *sensus fidei* is closely linked to the effective recovery of a theology of the people of God. This observation allows us to make a clarification on a weakness of Vatican II itself, when it speaks of *sensus fidei*: according to *LG* 12, it is evident that the subject of this infallible property is the totality of the faithful, "from the Bishops down to the last of the lay faithful." Unfortunately, the same Council indirectly creates the misunderstanding, when it introduces a reduplication of the doctrine of *sensus fidei* in *LG* 35, applying it to laypeople alone. The fact that laypeople are made witnesses of Christ, from whom they receive the "understanding of the faith [*sensus fidei*] and an attractiveness in speech so that the power of the Gospel might shine forth in their daily social and family life," does not constitute them exclusive subjects of the *sensus fidei*, which is a capacity of every baptized person and of all the baptized, regardless of their status and function, linked to the presence and action of the Spirit given in baptism. The fact that the members of the clergy are part of the *universitas fidelium*, far from emptying the function of the *sensus omnium fidelium* in favor of the magisterium, shows that Church priority is not in the exercise of functions—of service or power—but in the life of faith as a "place" of Christian salvation, and therefore also as a factor of the intelligence of the faith.

On the other hand, the same Council had asserted the importance of the life of faith even for the progress of tradition when, in *Dei Verbum*, it affirmed that, under the action of the Spirit,

> There is a growth in the understanding of the realities and the words which have been handed down. This happens through the contemplation and study made by believers, who treasure these things in their hearts (see Luke 2:19, 51) through a penetrating understanding of the spiritual realities which they experience, and through the preaching of those who have received through Episcopal succession the sure gift of truth. (*DV* 8)

The *textus prior* did not mention the third growth factor, namely the bishops, inserted later based on the consideration that even the preaching of those in the Church who are experts in the faith was the reason and cause of the progress of the tradition. Thus amended, the final text altered the original intent of the text itself, which distinctly addressed the part of the people of God in no. 8 and that of the magisterium in no. 10, not to separate and contrast, but to establish a fruitful circularity between the faithful and their pastors. If the pastors' task is to preach the gospel as "the source of all saving truth and moral teaching" (*DV* 7), it is not to exercise power over the faithful, but to enable the holy people of God to respond to revelation with the obedience of faith (*DV* 5). The first paragraph of *DV* 10 draws this circularity between the people of God and pastors, when it says,

> Sacred tradition and Sacred Scripture form one sacred deposit of the word of God, committed to the Church. Holding fast to this deposit the entire holy people united with their shepherds remain always steadfast in the teaching of the Apostles, in the common life, in the breaking of the bread and in prayers [see Acts 2:42, Greek text], so that holding to, practicing and professing the heritage of the faith, it becomes on the part of the bishops and faithful a single common effort.[5]

The significance of this passage, rarely evoked to describe the circularity between *sensus fidei* and magisterium, depends on the fact that in the texts of Vatican II, the relationship is not discussed, and, when evoked, it is always asymmetric, as in *LG* 12, where the people of God are placed "under the guidance of the sacred teaching authority, in faithful and respectful obedience." On the other hand, the theme of collegiality, and then of the *munus docendi* of bishops, is too limited to the question of primacy to consider the connection with *sensus fidei*. Moreover, it should be remembered that the discussion in aula on the hierarchical constitution of the Church preceded that on the people of God, respecting the sequence of the chapters in Philips's arrangement.[6]

From Vatican I to Trent

The *schema de ecclesia* of the Second Vatican Council resumed the *schema constitutionis secundae de ecclesia* "*Tametsi Deus*" of Vatican I, upon which the discussion in aula for the suspension *sine die* of the Council was not completed.[7] The schema contained the assertion that neither the faithful *in credendo* nor the magisterium in *docendo* "may fall into error."[8] But this statement is now residual, because the Council had already separated the two forms of infallibility, with the drafting of the *constitutio prima de ecclesia* "*Pastor Aeternus*," limited to points of primacy and infallibility. The bond between indefectibility of the Church and infallibility of the magisterium was still firmly in the *schema constitutionis de ecclesia "Supreme Pastoris*."[9] Choosing to break up the chapters on infallibility and primacy (even reversing the order, and hence the logic that governed the entire discourse) to treat separately the question of primacy resulted in the split between the indefectibility of the Church and the infallibility of the pope. Once the part related to the pope was removed, the obligation to use the theme of indefectibility fell to the choice to draw up an ad hoc dogmatic constitution; it was sufficient to say that the pope, in the exercise of his *ex cathedra* teaching, "enjoys that infallibility with which the divine Redeemer willed his Church to be endowed."[10] To the holy people of God all that was left was the *infallibilitas passiva*, a weaker version of infallibility *in credendo*: the faithful are likened to the musical instrument from which someone—the magisterium, to be more precise—draws the sound.

Yet theology before Vatican I—and we are not referring to Möhler or Newman, who made considerable contributions to the development of *sensus fidei*, but to controversialist theology—firmly maintained the unity between *sensus fidei* and magisterium. If they were not unified, the definition of the immaculate conception would be unthinkable based on the *singularis antistitum ac fidelium conspiratio*. Both Perrone's *positio*[11] and Passaglia and Schrader's study[12] on the definability of the dogma had indicated the *sensus fidelium* as sufficient evidence to establish the definition.[13] But the use of the *sensus omnium fidelium* was possible because controversialist theology placed it among the infallible *regulae fidei* in the interpretation of the revealed deposit. These *regulae* are listed among the *loci theologici*, that is, among the doctrinal authorities from which theologians can infer evidence in support of Catholic truth, as Melchor Cano (1509–1560) had systematized them in *De locis theologicis libri duodecim*.[14]

In this work, the theologian from Salamanca lists in sequence ten *loci theologici*, in descending order of importance regarding their ability to provide evidence for theological argumentation. The most important are the Scriptures and tradition, called *constitutivi*, because they are the two sources in which the truths of faith are found. Next, the five *loci theologici interpretativi*, three of which are active ecclesial subjects in the present—the Catholic Church, the councils, and the Roman Church—to which are added the

Church fathers and the Scholastic theologians, as the past authorities that have contributed to deepening the understanding of the revealed deposit. These are seven doctrinal authorities, qualified as *loci theologici proprii*, accompanied by three *loci theologici alieni*, that is, of a nature that is not theological, but useful in the dispute to provide further arguments in support of the Catholic position: reason, philosophers, and history.

The *sensus omnium fidelium* coincides with the third of the *loci theologici*, the *ecclesia catholica*, which appears immediately after Sacred Scriptures and tradition. The Church is intended here as totality of the baptized, inserted among the doctrinal authorities based on the conviction that *Ecclesia in credendo errare non potest*,[15] that *Ecclesiae fides deficere non potest*[16]: not only in the past, but also the present and future the Church cannot err in faith.[17] It may be surprising that the authority of the *universitas fidelium* is cited before that of the councils and the pope, especially when we consider the list of *loci theologici* in descending order of importance. But for the Catholic theologian Melchor Cano, in the search for evidence in favor of his thesis, after the testimonies of Sacred Scriptures and tradition, he had to first consider all the doctrines that lie on the *fidelium communis sensus*. This means that to the statements of the *sensus fidelium* are at least granted the same credit enjoyed by the rulings of the councils and the pope, because they come from an ecclesial subject placed at the same level of the other two *loci interpretativi*.

If Melchor Cano would eventually deem those rulings irrelevant on the grounds that the faithful will never be able to produce testimonies that have not already been better expressed by *pastores ac doctores*,[18] the fact remains that the *sensus omnium fidelium* retains its prominent place among the doctrinal *auctoritates*. Its value lies above all in the fact that it is distinct from the bishops gathered in council and from the pope as teacher and pastor of the universal Church. Unlike the solution developed after Vatican I, when we speak of the Church magisterium as the only subject endowed with interpretive authority, articulated into three forms of infallibility, at this stage of the history of dogma we still talk about three subjects endowed with their own infallibility.[19] That of the *universitas fidelium* is the infallibility *in credendo*, which still constitutes the assumption of the *infallibilitas in docendo*.

From Trent to the Middle Ages

Melchor Cano's proposal was conceived as a counterattack against the Reformation theses. If to the *sola Scriptura* as the only authority recognized as the foundation of theology, he opposed ten *auctoritates*, to the interpretation of Scripture by the individual believer he opposed the totality of the baptized who lived in the communion of the Church, in obedience to their legitimate pastors. It was a development of the principle, evoked at Trent based on the Lerinian canon, "that version that the Holy Mother Church has always maintained and continues to maintain."[20] The Council does not specify whether that version was maintained by the pope, or by the bishops, or by the totality of the faithful, even to avoid getting into further controversies: the subject of this faithfulness to tradition is "the Holy Mother Church."

We have here an echo of the doctrine of the infallibility of the Church, expressly supported in the Middle Ages as a completely obvious and clear fact, when the process of distinction of *auctoritates* within the Church had not yet begun, which would lead to the constitution of two distinct *cathedrae*: the *doctoralis*, proper to theologians, and the *pastoralis*, proper to bishops. Before that time, infallibility is a property of the *congregatio fidelium*, that is, of the Church as a totality of those who are bound together by faith.[21] Precisely because faith is a formal principle that justifies the existence of the Church, the totality of the faithful constituted in one body by baptism cannot be mistaken in believing: it is infallible *in credendo*. The reason for the infallibility, or indefectibility, or inerrancy of the *universitas fidelium* (the terms are not fully aligned, and therefore reveal the complexity of such property of the faithful) lies in the promise of Christ himself that "the gates of Hades will not prevail against it" (Matt 16:18) and in the gift of the Spirit, who "will guide you into all the truth" (John 16:13).

This conviction is not contradicted by the fact that it is up to the ecumenical council to determine the faith of the Church, as the bishops gathered in synod represent the universal Church. On closer inspection, it is the same infallibility of the Church that manifests itself through the discernment of her pastors. Here the tendency of medieval theology to accurately distinguish subjects and competencies emerges, as is also evident from the function attributed to the pope. To him, according to Thomas Aquinas, *spectat editio Symboli*:[22] it is his responsibility, as the ultimate and highest instance in the Church, to publish, making them binding, the deliberations of the council. In this function, the pope is infallible insofar as he is bound to the Church's faith, and preserves and defends it publicly. This condition is evident in the extreme case of the pope *a fide devius*, who then *ipso facto* ceases to be head of the Church, since he no longer personifies the faith. It is as if to say that the Middle Ages consider the question of infallibility in reversed terms compared to modernity: it is the indefectibility of the Church—the *congregatio fidelium* assisted by the Holy Spirit—that is the foundation of the infallibility of the pope, and not vice versa.[23]

What caused this change of picture, leading to the definition of papal infallibility? On closer inspection, the entire process was triggered by the change of ecclesial model that began with the Gregorian Reform. The victory of the papacy over the empire gave the Bishop of Rome a leading role on the entire Western world, which also had the effect of putting pressure on the understanding of the church in a pyramidal sense. The emphasis on the primatial function of the pope, the holder of all powers, shifted the emphasis from Rome as a local church with a universal function of service to the unity of the churches, to the universal Church—the Roman Catholic Church—under the guidance of the only Vicar of Christ, who rules directly, in the logic of *Dictatus papae*, the whole of Christianity.

This change of perspective has, however, determined that the *universitas fidelium* turned into an indistinct mass of faithful, who less and less express their faith publicly. The assertion on the infallibility of the *universitas fidelium* is not denied; but the endemic passivity of the body of the faithful frees the passage to the *auctoritates* able to preserve and convey the faith. From here, to transfer the infallibility of the Church to such *auctoritates*—the council, as it deliberates on issues *de fide et morum*, and the pope as he recognizes and publicly acknowledges the faith of the Church established in the conciliar decrees—it is a short step. This is how began the long and tormented path of clarifying the role and responsibilities of the subjects endowed with infallibility in the Church, which passes through the season of conciliarism, up to, after many tensions, reaching the radicalization of Vatican I on primacy, laboriously rebalanced by Vatican II in the third chapter of *Lumen Gentium* on the hierarchical constitution of the Church.

Along this path, the picture painted by the Middle Ages remains formally intact, but what changes is the logic that regulates the relationship between the various subjects endowed with infallibility. If Melchor Cano's vision is still based on the medieval synthesis, ordering in succession Catholic Church, councils, and Roman Church, Vatican I will fully legitimize the function of the successor of Peter as the "perpetual and visible principle and foundation of unity both of the Bishops and of the multitude of the faithful,"[24] further replaced by the dogma of infallibility *ex cathedra*. The outcome will be the passage from three subjects—the totality of the faithful, the totality of the bishops gathered in council, the pope—respectively endowed with infallibility, to a single subject, the magisterium of the Church, capable of a triple exercise of infallibility: that of the pope when he speaks *ex cathedra*; that of the ecumenical council; and that of the bishops in their sees in communion with the pope. If in the totality of the bishops we see an evolution of the Catholic Church as *regula fidei*, we must also note the reversal of the three subjects, which also manifestly reveals the pyramidal shape.[25]

From the Middle Ages to the Church Fathers

From where do the Middle Ages conjure up the idea of infallibility of the Church? Clearly from the first millennium. However, a serious question arises here, which is not so much about the sources, but the plausibility of the idea itself, expressed in terms in use for a very different model of Church. In the first millennium, the Church is with all the evidence the *corpus ecclesiarum*, born from the apostolic preaching, experiencing a long process of structuring and institutionalization, in search of a criterion of unity that safeguards the division and fragmentation of a movement that had reached "the very ends of the earth."[26] This process—very painful and marked by a lot of resistance—has led to the widespread conviction that the church *toto orbe diffusa* was the *catholica,* that is, the *communio ecclesiarum.* It is as if to say that the *catholica* is the church spread all over the world, which, however, is nothing else than the churches that make up its body and that can and must be called—each and all of them—"Catholic churches," as they manifest the catholicity of the Church. In other words, local churches recognized themselves in the universal communion of the Church, never conceived as a sum of churches, but as the ecclesial body, to which every church belongs and in which it identifies:[27] no church is self-sufficient, but lives in the totality of the Church, expressed by the *communio.*

From this ecclesiology of *communio ecclesiarum* it is natural to move to the idea of the faith of the whole Church: if the certainty of being the *catholica* resided in every church in the belief of preserving and transmitting the apostolic faith, the unity of faith was nothing more than the "most uniform consent of all Christian people."[28] The Christian peoples are nothing but the different churches spread throughout the earth, in communion with each other because for the sharing of the same apostolic faith. Against the opinions of the heretics is the *singularis conspiratio,* the *consensus omnium fidelium* that cannot be mistaken in believing, as it expresses the faith of all the churches that are the *catholica,* which is also the totality of the faithful, "from the Bishops down to the last of the lay faithful."

Since the *catholica* is the *communio ecclesiarum,* the role of both the ecumenical council and the Bishop of Rome is easily understood. In fact, in the council, the universal church is manifested, as every bishop represents his church and brings to the synodal council the faith of his holy people, which is a voice in the unanimous symphony of all the voices of the churches scattered over the face of the earth. On the other hand, the Bishop of Rome has always had the task of ratifying the acts of the council, acknowledged by all, whether it be a claim of primacy over other churches, as Rome wanted, or a necessity for the recognition on the part of all the bishops of the synodal decrees, as the East saw it. These are the terms that the Middle Ages receive and will tend to change, when the Gregorian Reform with its revolution will produce the modification of the ecclesiological model. The amendments emerging from the context of the first centuries were corrections required by the new situation, in which the gradual loss of active capacity of the *congregatio fidelium*, transformed from *plebs sancta* gathered around the bishop, "surrounded by his presbyters and his ministers"[29] in a shapeless and anonymous mass of the universal church, imposed the transfer of its prerogatives to those who had guaranteed its exercise: the council and the pope.

Based on this path, the presence and permanence of *sensus fidei* has not only been demonstrated through the centuries, but the reference model is based on the real circularity between *sensus fidei* and magisterium of the Church: the *singularis antistitum et fidelium conspiratio*, which had already been practiced when the Popes Pius IX and Pius XII were made sure of the faith of the faithful and their pastors to define the dogma of the immaculate conception and the assumption of Mary in heaven. If the *conspiratio* was possible at a time when the pyramid model of the Church was dominant, it can and must be even more so after the rediscovery by the Second Vatican Council, of the Church as the people of God.

Conclusions

Based on the demonstrated presence and strength of the *universitas fidelium* as a subject of authority in the Church, how to think and ensure the circularity between *sensus fidei* and magisterium as a criterion for the exercise of synodality in the Church?

The first step is to recognize *sensus fidei* as a function of the intelligence of the faith. History has shown its resistance irreducible to any attempt to marginalize and invalidate it: the function has always reemerged, even when it was not organic to a system of thought that conferred to the magisterium only the only active capacity to speak in the Church. Vatican II has done nothing but recover a clear fact of the tradition. The second step is to recognize that this function, fundamental to the intelligence of the faith, corresponds to a specific subject, irreducible to magisterium and theology: the totality of the baptized. In the case of the definition of the Marian dogmas, on closer inspection, the recourse to the function took place without the actual recognition of the subject; even the reference to the *sensus fidei* as a voice of dissent in the Church, widely practiced in the postconciliar Church, does not recognize the people of God as a subject, when it transforms it into an instance against the hierarchy, without feeling the need to listen to it. In either case, the risk is to use a privileged position in the Church to establish with the *universitas fidelium* an asymmetric relationship, which in fact results in the lack of consideration and failure to respect the subject itself. This is not to emphasize an ecclesial entity at the expense of others, but to put them all in their own function. Only the proper distinction of the subjects qualifies their functions, protecting them from unjustified infringing or overlapping. Respect for the other is the first rule of a relationship.

The third step is to ask whether the ecclesiological framework and ecclesial practice drawn up after the last council promote such recognition and respect, or do not tend instead to marginalize the role of the totality of the baptized. It is quite evident that the preconciliar ecclesiology reduced the totality of the faithful to an undivided mass, for its own way of understanding the Church as a pyramid, dependent on the pope's *potestas iurisdictionis*. But even the conciliar category of "people of God," if understood in generic terms, while favoring the possibility of affirming the active function of the *universitas fidelium*, in reality, is likely to result in a stalemate. A criterion of judgment of the ecclesiological models proposed by theology but also by the magisterium—think of the ecclesiology of communion—should be the substantiation of the space and the role acknowledged to the people of God in the life of the Church.

From the recognition of the subject comes the respect, and therefore the willingness to learn and listen. Here is perhaps one of the hardest obstacles to overcome, after centuries where not only the faithful had no voice, but were deemed illiterate in the faith and induced to accept asymmetric relationships of dependency that have configured an amorphous and anonymous mass rather than the people of God. Too much engrained in the pastors is the conditioned response of the "unwashed masses," the passive recipient of directives that fall from above, without the necessity of activating listening and participation processes, in which the entire Christian community is invested in ecclesial discernment.

Where and when the baptized people have no ability to think, speak, participate, and instead solely ask for spaces on the role register, the failure of believers and communities to grow is attributed to the weak presence of those who have responsibilities in the formation of theological life, in which the *sensus fidei* of each is rooted. To return to spend time to train Christians, at a time when it has become clear again that "one is not born Christian, but becomes one," is perhaps the most urgent challenge for today's Church. Only under these conditions does the truth that the Holy Spirit is bestowed to every baptized person become the principle of fruitfulness in the Church; it is true that the Spirit can speak through the simple, but the simplicity of the kingdom is the result of a long path of growth in faith that does not necessarily translate into great discourses, but in intuition, discernment, testimony, and courage in accounting for the hope of eternal life (see 1 Pet 3:15).

Not only must we believe that the Holy Spirit speaks in every baptized person, so all the people of God are prophets (see Num 11:29); we must also reaffirm with clarity and strength that the Church as a community of the baptized participates in the prophetic function of Christ (see *LG* 12). It is not enough to train Christians: we must form the Church as a listening community, docile to the voice of the Spirit. To presume that God speaks to the Church always and only through the voice of her pastors is an assertion that could rely on a logic of defending the truths of faith, entrusted to the custody of the *ecclesia docens*, to whom the *ecclesia discens* is bound to obey. But on this path, we have lost the fruitful circularity between the pastors and the people of God.

Such circularity, for pastors, is not a loss of their function. If anything, one guarantees and feeds the other, as it can be easily seen from *DV* 10:

> Sacred tradition and Sacred Scripture form one sacred deposit of the word of God, committed to the Church. Holding fast to this deposit the entire holy people united with their shepherds remain always steadfast in the teaching of the Apostles, in the common life, in the breaking of the bread and in prayers (see Acts 2, 42, Greek text), so that holding to, practicing and professing the heritage of the faith, it becomes on the part of

> the bishops and faithful a single common effort [*singularis fiat antistitum et fidelium conspiratio*].

The text recovers much of the language that the theological tradition applied to *sensus fidei,* including the formula advanced as proof of the Marian dogmas, built—as we have seen—on Augustine's text. The privileged place of this *conspiratio* is the celebration of the Eucharist where the bread of the word is broken to nourish the holy people of God; a sloppy and repetitive preaching, far from the experience of the people, cannot nourish the community in faith, to accept "that which is not just the word of men but truly the word of God. Through it, the people of God adheres unwaveringly to the faith given once and for all to the saints, penetrates it more deeply with right thinking, and applies it more fully in its life" (*LG* 12). On these actions is based and structured the ability of the people of God to "show universal agreement in matters of faith and morals" (*LG* 12).

But this may not be enough; we should choose in the Church places and forms of listening and dialogue, where Christian communities are educated in ecclesial discernment. If we do not activate processes of participation, where the faithful are not extras, but actors of discernment through a listening that really wants to recognize in their voices the voice of the Spirit, where and how can the holy people of God learn to express their consent? If Christian communities are not educated in such processes through an ecclesial pedagogy that teaches how to move from expressing one's opinion to sharing it, from spreading ideas to the patient search of consent, in the docility of all to the Spirit, how can we expect the faithful to go beyond opinions in the expression of their faith?

This does not mean to surrender the Church to the logic of public opinion. *Sensus fidei* and public opinion are irreducible, because the second proceeds from purely human logic, the first from the Spirit of truth: "But you have been anointed by the Holy One, and all of you have knowledge....But as his anointing teaches you about all things, and is true and is not a lie, and just as it has taught you, abide in him" (1 John 2:20, 27). Provided, however, that the subject of the *sensus fidei* is not reduced to a sum of people, but it is the Church itself, it is never the individual, but only and always the *universitas fidelium* that is unfailing and "cannot err in matters of belief." The ability of every believer to think and express convictions that proceed from their faith is the presupposition for realizing that "singular consensus between bishops and the faithful" not only as evidence for a doctrine to be defined, but as a style of a Church journeying through history while listening to the Spirit.

But where is or, more radically, who is this Church? A totality of the baptized that coincides *sic et simpliciter* with the universal Church is destined to repeat the patterns of the second millennium, when the *sensus fidei* has been transformed into an anonymous subject, endowed with passive infallibility, that is, delivered to the will of others—either the magisterium or the theologians—to decide the rules of the game. The first millennium refers instead to the model of the particularly unanimous agreement of the Christian peoples, able to join the faith of the Church spread throughout the world in the *communio* of the *catholica*. This is still a chapter to be written, not so much by theologians, as by the churches themselves. If we want to read the signs of the times, Pope Francis's request to the particular churches to respond to a questionnaire on the family and on the challenges it faces today is very similar to a consultation of the people of God, which evokes not only Newman's arguments in this regard, but the path chosen by Pius IX and Pius XII to define the Marian dogmas. More than by theological arguments, the path may be opened by the desire to begin a journey. The Letter to the Hebrews says that we can "make straight paths for your feet" (see Heb 12:13). On the other hand, the tradition sends again in the present the principle that "what concerns all, must be examined and approved by all."[30] This could be the rule of a synodal Church, which appreciates and values the *sensus fidei* of the holy people of God.

NOTES

1. *Sensus fidei* was the theme of my PhD thesis under the direction of Z. Alszeghy, SJ: D. Vitali, *Sensus fidelium. Una funzione di intelligenza della fede* (Brescia: Morcelliana, 1993). I further examined the topic in various articles: "*Sensus fidelium* e opinione pubblica nella Chiesa," *Gregorianum* 82, no. 4 (2001): 689–717; "*Universitas fidelium in credendo falli nequit,*" *Gregorianum* 86, no. 3 (2005): 607–28; "Il *sensus fidelium* in

Ippolito Marracci," in *L'Immacolata Madre di Dio nel Seicento. Apporti teologici e spirituali di Ippolito Marracci nel IV centenario della nascita (1604). Atti del XIV Colloquio Internazionale di Mariologia* (Rome, Santa Maria in Portico in Campitelli, February 18–21, 2004), ed. D. Carbonaro and F. Petrillo (Rome: AMI, 2006), 157–77; "La función de la Iglesia en la inteligencia de la fe," in *Romper el silenzio sobre Dios. Razón, Fe, Amor* (Santiago de Compostela: Instituto Teológico Compostelano, 2008), 155–74; "La funzione della Chiesa nell'intelligenza della fede," *Rassegna di teologia* 49, no. 1 (2008): 13–30; "Il '*sensus fidelium*' come questione teologica," *Settimana* (May 18, 2008): n. 20, 12ff.; "Il *sensus fidelium* tra modelli di interpretazione della fede e processi di partecipazione," *Rivista di Scienze Religiose* 25, no. 1 (2011): 39–55; "La totalità dei fedeli non può sbagliarsi nel credere (LG 12): il *sensus fidelium* come voce della Tradizione," *Urbaniana University Journal* 66, no. 2 (2013): 37–70; "*Sensus fidei* e Magistero," *Revista Catalana de Teologia* 39, no. 1 (2014): 97–128. I have also tried to show how *sensus fidei* enters the exercise of synodality, in "Più collegialità. Senso e portata di una richiesta," *Rivista del Clero Italiano* 95, no. 3 (2014): 182–206 and, in particular, *Verso la sinodalità* (Magnano: Qiqajon–Comunità di Bose, 2014).

2. Apart from sporadic references, the theme of *sensus fidei* before Pope Francis was dealt with in two documents, however, of opposite points of view: Pontifical Council for Social Communications, Pastoral Instruction *Communio et progressio* on the means of social communication, May 23, 1971, in *AAS* 63 (1971) 593–656; *EV* 4, 781–967: the reference here to *sensus fidei* is at no. 116 (English available at http://www.vatican.va/roman_curia/pontifical_councils/pccs/documents/rc_pc_pccs_doc_23051971_communio_en.html). The other reference, contained in a section on dissent in the Church, is available in Congregation for the Doctrine of the Faith, Instruction *Donum Veritatis* on the ecclesial vocation of the theologian, May 29, 1990, in *AAS* 82 (1990) 1550–70 (English available at http://www.vatican.va/roman_curia/congregations/cfaith/documents/rc_con_cfaith_doc_19900524_theologian-vocation_en.html); *EV* 12, 244–305: the reference here to *sensus fidei* is at no. 35.

3. Commissione Teologica Internazionale, *Il* sensus fidei *nella vita della Chiesa* (Bologna: EDB, 2014).

4. In our recent contribution to the volume of essays, C. Caltagirone and G. Pasquale, eds., *Ecclesiologia dal Vaticano II. Studi in onore di Cettina Militello* (Venice: Marcianum Press, 2016), we follow this line of development and we explain extensively why this approach should be preferred. In the following, we draw extensively on that study.

5. That the text refers to *sensus fidei* is demonstrated by the citation of the constitution *Munificentissimus Deus,* in which Pius XII in 1950—

that is, fifteen years before the promulgation of *Dei Verbum*—solemnly defined the doctrine of Mary's assumption in heaven by the "remarkable harmony between the bishops and the faithful [*singularis antistitum et fidelium conspiratio*]." This simple fact demonstrates that the doctrine of *sensus fidei* could in no way constitute a novelty for the fathers, having been used as evidence to justify and to establish the dogma of the assumption.

6. This schema was articulated into four chapters only: I) *De mysterio Ecclesiae*; II) *De constitutione hierarchica Ecclesiae, speciatim de Episcopatu*; III) *De populo Dei, speciatim de laicis*; IV) *De vocatione ad sanctitate in Ecclesia* (cf. *Acta Synodalia* II, I, 215–281).

7. Mansi 53, 308A–317A.

8. "Iam vero praecelsum hoc donum, quo Ecclesia Dei vivi columna et firmamentum veritatis est, in eo positum esse definimus, ut neque fideles universi credendo, nec ii, qui potestate docendi totam Ecclesiam praediti sunt, cum hoc munere funguntur, in errorem labi possint. Quaecumque igitur in rebus fidei et morum ubique locorum sub episcopis apostolicae sedi adhaerentibus tanquam indubitata tenentur vel traduntur, necnon quaesive ab iisdem episcopis, accedente romani Pontificis confirmatione, sive ab ipso romano Pontifice ex cathedra loquente ab omnibus tenenda et tradenda definiuntur, ea pro infallibiliter veris habenda sunt" (Mansi 53, 313A).

9. This is demonstrated by the sequence of the chapters: VIII) *De Ecclesiae indefectibilitate*; IX) *De Ecclesiae infalli- bilitate*; X) *De Ecclesiae potestate*; XI) *De Romani Pontificis primatu*. And this is the text of the eighth chapter on the indefectibility of the Church: "Declaramus insuper, Christi Ecclesiam, sive existentia sive constitutio eius spectetur, societatem esse perennem atque indefectibilem, nullamque post illam neque pleniorem neque perfectiorem salutis oeconomiam in hoc saeculo expectandum esse. Etenim cum ad finem usque mundi qui in terris peregrinantur mortales Christo auctore salvandi sint: Ecclesia ipsius, quae sola est salutis societas, ad finemusque mundi in sua constitutione immutabilis semper et immota persistet. Licet igitur Ecclesia crescat, et utinam augeatur iugiter fide et caritate, ut Christi corpus aedificetur; licet pro varia aetate sua, et pro diversitate adiunctorum, inter quae constanter militando versatur, varie sese explicet: eadem tamen in se suaque a Christo accepta constitutione immutabilis perseverat. Quare Christi Ecclesia numquam potest excidere suisproprietatibus et dotibus, sacro suo magisterio, ministerio et regimine, un Christus per corpus suum visibile perpetuo sit omnibus hominibus via, veritas et vita." For the entire schema, see the *Schema constitutionis de ecclesia "Supremi pastoris"* of Vatican I (Mansi 51, 539A–636A).

10. Vatican Council I, *Pastor Aeternus*, ch. IV (DH 3074).

11. G. Perrone, *De Immaculato B.V. Mariae conceptu an dogmatico decreto definiri possit. Disquisitio theologica* (Rome: I. B. Marini et B. Morini, 1847).

12. C. Passaglia and C. Schrader, *De Immaculato Deiparae semper Virginis conceptu*, 3 vols. (Rome: Typis sacrae congregationis de propaganda fide, 1854–1855).

13. The dependence of the Roman School on the Catholic School of Tübingen is known: authors such as Perrone, Passaglia, Schrader, and Franzelin were able to adopt Möhler's positions more or less directly. On the other hand, the two theologians of the Roman School did not introduce any novelty, since already in the seventeenth century, among the many texts written by Ippolito Marracci (1604–1675) to defend the definition of the immaculate conception, there was a study (still unpublished) on the *sensus omnium fidelium* as proof in support of the doctrine; see Carbonaro and Petrillo, *L'Immacolata Madre di Dio nel Seicento*.

14. The work was published posthumously in 1563 and had a great fortune in theology. Even after the promulgation of Leo XIII's encyclical *Aeterni Patris* (in *ASS* 12 [1879/80]: 98–114), which opened the season of neo-Thomism, the method was not abandoned but further refined in the apologetics between the two Vatican councils.

15. M. Cano, *De locis theologicis*, IV. IV. 3, *conclusio secunda*.

16. Ibid., IV. IV. 2, *conclusio prima*.

17. Cf. ibid., IV. IV. 7, *conclusio tertia*.

18. Cf. ibid., IV. IV. 9.

19. Unlike Melchor Cano, Francisco Suárez (1548–1617) does not address the question of the *loci theologici*, but that of the *regulae fidei*, that is, the authorities with infallibility in the Church, able to guarantee the preservation and transmission of the *depositum fidei*. The first five *loci* meet this characteristic: sacred Scripture and tradition as *regulae fidei constitutivae*; Catholic Church, Council, and Roman Church as *regulae fidei interpretativae*. The three *regulae fidei* with interpretive function are evidently three different subjects, with a unique and peculiar form of infallibility. On this topic, see F. Suárez, *De Incarnatione. Tractatus I de Fide theologica. Disputatio V: De regulis quibus fidei objectum infallibiliter proponitur*. After Vatican I, the definition of papal infallibility will lead to the transition to a single subject of authority, the magisterium, with three forms of infallibility: that of the pope alone, that of the bishops gathered in council, and that of bishops scattered throughout the world in communion with the pope. This results in the disappearance of the totality of the faithful, endowed only with passive infallibility, as their capacity as a subject capable of interpreting the deposit of the faith has

been transferred to their pastors. The maximalistic form of this vision essentially concentrates the three forms of exercise of infallibility in the hands of the pope: when he alone speaks *ex cathedra*, when he calls an ecumenical council, and when he summons all bishops around the world to collegiate action. This vision will affect quite significantly Vatican II's debate on collegiality, tightly centered on the roles of the pope and college of bishops.

20. See Council of Trent, *Decree Concerning the Canonical Scriptures*, of April 8, 1546 (*COD* 663); *Decree Concerning the Most Holy Sacrament of the Eucharist*, of November 11, 1551 (*COD* 693).

21. *Ecclesia est congregatio eorum qui per fidem ambulant*: Thomas Aquinas, *Summa theologiae* III, q. 8, a. 3, ad 2; *Ecclesia, secundum statum viae, est congregatio fidelium, sed, secundum statum patriae, est congregatio comprehendentium*: ibid., a. 4, ad 2.

22. *Summa theologiae* II–II, q. 1, a. 10.

23. Still in 1330, an author such as Hermann von Schildesche argued, "The Pope's decision has its foundation in the Catholic Church, which cannot err or go astray from the infallible truth, as the judgment of the head is based on the body....In such things, the pope will never give a wrong judgment or be mistaken if he is well implanted [*coaptetur*] in the body of the church." *Tractatus contra haereticos negantes immunitatem et iurisdictionem sanctae Ecclesiae*, pars II, cap. IX, ed. A. Zumkeller (Würzburg: Augustinus Verlag, 1970), 77ff. For a study on the birth of the idea of papal infallibility, see B. Tierney, *Origins of Papal Infallibility 1150–1350: A Study of the Concepts of Infallibility, Sovereignty and Tradition in the Middle Ages* (Leiden: E. J. Brill, 1972); and A. Naud, *Il Magistero incerto* (Brescia: Queriniana, 1991).

24. I Vatican Council, Dogmatic Constitution *Pastor Aeternus*, prologue (DH 3050). English trans.: Congregation for the Doctrine of Faith, the Primacy of the Successor of Peter in the Mystery of the Church, no. 4: http://www.vatican.va/roman_curia/congregations/cfaith/documents/rc_con_cfaith_doc_19981031_primato-successore-pietro_en.html.

25. However, it should be remembered that at Vatican I the definition of infallibility is based on the reference to the infallibility of the *universitas fidelium*: "The Roman Pontiff, when he speaks *ex cathedra*, that is, when, exercising the office of pastor and teacher of all Christians, he defines with his supreme apostolic authority a doctrine concerning faith or morals to be held by the universal Church, through the divine assistance promised him in St. Peter, is possessed of *that infallibility with which the divine Redeemer willed his Church to be endowed in defining doctrine concerning faith and morals*": ibid., ch. IV (*DH* 3074).

26. The stages of this process are well known: from individual churches, each with its bishop and presbyters, to the dioceses and metropolises, to patriarchs. In the second millennium, the pattern in the West is in some ways inverted: the Church is no longer the *communio ecclesiarum*, but the *ecclesia catholica romana*, with the pope as the only bishop, and bishops as pope's officials in the diocese, reduced to administrative districts of the church.

27. This is perhaps the most precise meaning of *kath 'hólu*, an adverbial expression that can be translated as "universally," "in general," and that would indicate a practice and an ecclesial consciousness characterized as "according to the whole," "according to all," emerging mainly in ecumenical councils, in which every bishop made his church present.

28. *Christianorum populorum concordissima fidei conspiratio*: Augustine of Hippo, *Epistola* 194, 7, 31, in *Opera omnia*, XXIII: *Lettere* 185–270 (Rome: Città Nuova, 1974), 290ff.

29. See *SC* 41, which resumes the model of Church emerging from the letters of Ignatius of Antioch.

30. Y. M. Congar, "Quod ad omnes tangit, ab omnibus tractari et approbari debet," *Revue d'Histoire du Droit français et étranger* 36 (1958): 210–59.

10

ECCLESIAL SYNODALITY, PARTICIPATORY PROCESSES, AND DECISION-MAKING PROCEDURES

A Canonist's Point of View

Alphonse Borras

I have been asked to write a contribution that completes and actualizes, from a canonical point of view, the ecclesiological perspective. Canonists are people of facts and not primarily of ideas, as they deal with the "real Church." Now, like any social body, the Church is threatened by inertia as she faces changes in the world and society, and as she confronts needed reforms that these changes arouse within her. Pope Francis has already warned us of the danger of the attitude that says, "We have always done it this way" (*EG* 33).

In matters of government, he evoked the principle that time is greater than space, especially in the political sphere. For this reason, he said to generate "processes of people-building" (*EG* 224).

This is true for the ecclesial field: synodality is for the most part a principle of ecclesiogenesis. Synodality builds the people of God in the sense that it molds them and, at the same time, it shapes them to "reform" them, to make them continually conform to what God wants here and now for the ecclesial body of Christ inhabited by his Spirit.

The canonical or legal practice is always a function of action,[1] and to speak of human acts is to speak of discernment and the implementation of freedom in accordance with norms and in reference to the circumstances; beyond the virtue of justice is the virtue of prudence being mobilized on the ground of law. These epistemological considerations explain the *ratio sub qua* of canon law, that is, its role in regulating ecclesial life, especially when it comes to considering the objective conditions of government reforms.

Our contribution intends to clarify first the doctrinal notion of synodality, and then examine a cluster of synodal institutions provided by the Code of Canon Law of 1983. Without exposing all the canonical provisions of these "participatory processes," according to the expression used by Pope Francis (*EG* 31b), the following reflection will focus on their decision-making procedures. In proceeding, we will see that the notion of synodality intersects with that of collegiality: the two are distinct, but they support and reinforce each other. Now, let us say from the start that the more we are "synodal," the more we are "collegial"—and vice versa. What is at play is the catholicity that we confess in the Creed and, therefore, the indispensable inculturation of the testimony of faith as well as its missionary zeal and its concern for the universal. In fact, God wants to save *all* human beings (see 2 Tim 1:9; Tit 3:5).

Preliminary Remarks

For several centuries the Latin Catholic Church has been characterized by the personal exercise of pastoral authority, to the detriment, broadly speaking (that is, in reference to "some"), of the communal one involving the community more extensively (that is to say in reference to "all"), of the whole of the baptized as Christ's ecclesial body.[2] The increase of the "personal" dimension is still reflected today, so much so that it is determined by several factors, such as the insufficient consideration of the *sensus fidelium*, the concentration of power and isolated exercise of authority, a centralized and discretionary style of government, and the opacity of regulation procedures.

These factors weigh on the ecclesial imaginary.[3] We cannot overlook here the weight of representations among the Catholic faithful. This imaginary includes the style of exercise of authority, relational practices of the faithful and the social practices that are based on the separation of clergy/laity, the permanency of the internalization of this separation, the relationship between administrators/administered, or active and passive subjects (!), the sacred vision, and the preservation of a priestly management of spiritual goods.

This ecclesial imaginary inherited from the past remains a bottleneck in the rehabilitation of the "Church subject," in double sense of the expression: the protagonism of the *ecclesia*, guided by Christ and animated by the Holy Spirit, and the quality of the active and responsible subjects of all baptized within the Church in the diversity of their charisms, vocations, services, and ministries.[4] Since they are people of facts, canonists know that representations do not change under the *automatic* effect of the current doctrines or of decrees of the authority.[5]

Doctrine and discipline—theology and canon law—undeniably affect ecclesial life. It is still necessary that the practices be increasingly permeated, in a learning that effects a slow, sometimes laborious, but always indispensable appropriation. This is where canonical regulation intervenes as mediation between a theoretically professed ecclesiology and the ecclesial experience. But it should be noted, finally, that the law in force is poorly known and unequally applied in ecclesial government. Therefore, we are personally convinced that it is not desirable to invent new institutions; it is rather imperative to make use of existing ones, while ensuring their proper canonical functioning. I am defending here an institutional sobriety: rather than creating other institutions, let us settle for the implementation of the participatory processes required by Vatican II and promulgated by the current Code. There is still so much to do on the ground in the dioceses!

Synodality, an Abstract and Plurivocal Concept

When the canonists deal with synodality, they know better than anyone else the abstract and plurivocal character of this concept, which is not found in legislative texts, but in canonical doctrine.[6] They learn this from a variety of institutional expressions. Despite this, let us first expound this notion, since theologians and canonists do not always agree on its content.[7] There would nevertheless be a consensus in seeing a Church feature arising from its communal nature. In this sense, synodality would be a quality of the *ecclesia*[8] that pertains to it as "Church-subject."[9]

ECCLESIAL SYNODALITY AND BAPTISMAL CORESPONSIBILITY

Yet, the *ecclesia* is not given outside or above the disciples of Christ. It concerns all the faithful. It consists of the participation or the convergence of all the baptized, each according to one's own condition. It is based on the baptismal coresponsibility[10] of all the faithful in the diversity and complementarity of their charisms "so that all according to their proper roles may cooperate in this common undertaking with one mind" (*LG* 30). The mission that God has entrusted to the Church so that it is realized in the world (see *LG* 31a; *CIC*, can. 204, §1), is exercised by the baptized "in keeping with their condition" (see can. 96; 204, §1; 207 and 208; cf. *LG* 32, *ChL* 24).

Does not the responsibility of everyone express the participation of everyone in a truly synodal dynamic? Etymologically, the Church is *synodal* not only in the sense of walking, or making the way together and each at one's own pace, but also in the sense of crossing the same threshold, to dwell together, thus to reunite.[11] Applied to the ecclesial reality, the concept of synodality can thus evoke the experience of a common path, or simply the fact of meeting, holding an assembly.

Coresponsibility and synodality would be like the two faces of ecclesial life. This implies that we listen to everyone to discern "what the Spirit is saying to the churches" (Rev 2:29). Coresponsibility is the fact of a Church of *subjects* (see *ChL* 15a), the synodality of the Church-*subject*. We will appreciate here the rich heuristic significance of the distinction between "Church subject" and "Church of subjects" to deal respectively with the protagonism of the *ecclesia*, and the involvement of all the faithful.

SYNODALITY IN THE STRICT SENSE AND SYNODALITY IN THE BROAD SENSE

Intuitu claritatis (for the sake of clarity), we prefer to reserve the term *synodality in the strict sense* of the internal communion to a particular Church, that is, to the communal reality of the Church that develops *in a place*, in the local or particular Church (can. 368), whose normal or habitual form is the diocese (can. 369; cf. *CD* 11, *LG* 23a). This applies by analogy, to the "parochial communion" (cf. can. 529, §2), as well as to other communities, hierarchical or associative, within the diocese. *In a sense,*[12] synodality designates this same communal reality of the mystery of the Church and refers to the communion of churches (*communio ecclesiarum*), to the Church as a whole (or *ecclesia universa* or *tota*, or even *integra*).[13]

In the ecclesiological perspective (of the mystery) of the Church as a communion of local churches, synodality therefore is intended first and foremost in its strict sense: it takes concrete account of the communion *in this place*, that is, the whole catholicity of the local Church, or, in other words, the Church that is realized *in this place* in the diversity of charisms and ministries, vocations, and states of life (see *LG* 32a). Just as coresponsibility (of the Church of subjects) is *differentiated* because of the diversity of charisms, synodality (of the Church subject) is *plural*: every baptized will play a role and may have a word to say. It is precisely catholicity that is in play in synodality.

FORMAL SYNODALITY AND INFORMAL SYNODALITY

The implementation of synodality requires the widest possible involvement of the of the baptized—the Church concerns everyone—to discern what the Spirit is saying to the Church *in this place*, in order to seek and find the will of God, so that his kingdom may come to the heart of this story tending toward its fulfillment. Now, the Spirit "speaks" through different mediations such as the listening to the Scriptures, the silence of prayer, the faithful rereading of life and of events, the signs of the times, the confrontation of points of view, the *sensus fidei*, theological reflection, the testimony of the saints, the pastoral authority, and so on.

Whoever says *discernment* says *listening*. This is fundamental, since the Spirit is given to the whole Church and no entity or mediation can appropriate it. A synodal Church is a Church that listens because she wants to discern in view of testimony. The widest possible participation in discernment *as a Church* attests to "God participating in the human adventure, and, in response, reconciled humanity in Christ, who participates in the life of God."[14]

The involvement of the baptized people is carried out in very variable ways, depending on their formalization. Alongside an *informal* synodality, resulting from mutual listening and cooperation of the baptized in the mission, there is a more *formal* practice of synodality, in formalized ways and different levels of institutionalization. Synodal practices are not limited to the synodal institutions or existing synodal procedures at a particular time in Church history. The fact remains, however, that synodality can hardly exist without institutional sites and implementation procedures. At this stage, it is not just a matter of listening but of consulting, asking for opinions.

BODY AND HEAD, SYNODALITY AND CEPHALITY

A final clarification is required in our exploration of the concept of synodality. It derives from the diversity inherent in ecclesial communion, which includes the singular function of pastoral authority. How to understand and implement the latter? Do we need to talk about a hierarchical principle—or principle of cephality—that would be articulated along with the synodal principle? If we take the traditional metaphor of the body that includes the head, the hierarchical principle of pastoral authority—at any level—is rooted in the synodal principle of which it is, precisely, the ministerial pole. In this sense, the synodal principle would therefore be sacramentally the whole ecclesial body; and the hierarchical principle would be the sacramental figure of Christ, who is the head thanks to his Spirit. There is a mutual implication between the two principles: one does not work without the other.[15] In our opinion, the synodal principle necessarily includes the synergy of the entire ecclesial body, including the head. It would then be more accurate to speak of a brotherly principle and ministerial principle, inscribing synodality in the convergence and symbiosis of the two, since one does not go *without* the other, within the organic and *symbolic* communion that is the Church.

Let us emphasize here "symbolic" because we are dealing with a reality that "holds together" (συν-βάλλειν) the ecclesial body, head included.[16] Every ecclesial community is structured, literally coheld (or contained), in this intrinsic relationship between the body and the head, the whole of the faithful and Christ, the ecclesial body and its pastor. The bond of these two components within a whole, the ecclesial body, refers to the one who founds both: God, through Christ, in the Spirit. This symbolic relationship does not subtract anything—on the contrary!—from the fundamental unity of the ecclesial body, but emphasizes its structure, which rests on a constitutive asymmetry.

By everyone's participation in the life of the Church and its mission, synodality is organic, but also symbolic and therefore asymmetrical. The ordained ministry, especially that of the pastors—bishops and priests—is structuring and not just constitutive. It signifies to the Church *in this place* that it receives itself from God and that it is not the whole Church.

APOSTOLICITY OF THE FAITH, APOSTOLIC MINISTRY, AND ECCLESIAL PRESIDENCY

The ordained ministry, especially that of the bishop, does not exist outside of a Church. It is inside the Church *in this place*, as the Church does *not* happen *without* him. It is for his rootedness in a local Church that the bishop, pastor of a people *in this place*, is in communion with the whole Church—a communion of which the communion with the college and its head is the evidence and not the cause.[17] Member of the college of bishops, the bishop inscribes his local Church in the communion of churches, presided over by the Bishop of Rome as Peter's successor. The Church's synodality *in this place* is for this reason structurally challenged to open to the communion of all churches and, through the bishop's ministry, to the episcopal collegiality.

The ordained ministry—par excellence, the episcopate—attests to the Church's profound apostolicity, namely its rooting in the apostolic faith inherited from the apostles and lived in the Spirit, in a communion both diachronic (over the centuries) and synchronic (among local churches). The sacramental investiture establishes the "apostolic" ministry in the twofold sense that this ministry is inscribed in the wake of the mission entrusted by Jesus Christ to the twelve apostles and that, for this purpose, it ensures the apostolicity of faith. The sacrament of orders gives the grace for this ministry; it irreversibly takes those whom the Church calls throughout their existence and throughout their lives, for the gift of God is without repentance.

In leading the Church—in its pastoral government—bishops and priests signify and realize the one and only priestly mediation of Christ, the head of the ecclesial body built by the Holy Spirit. They exercise in this regard a priestly ministry of presidency of the Church and her Eucharist.[18] They sacramentally represent Christ the Head, the Good Shepherd par excellence, who leads his Church into the kingdom, so that it all becomes a priestly, prophetic, and royal people.

Synodality as the quality of the *ecclesia* is truly communal, organic—plural, diverse, and complementary—and symbolic—thus asymmetrical and structured—without prejudice to the unity confessed in the Creed, which is itself correlated to the ecclesial catholicity.

Institutional Versions of Synodality

What about the formal synodiality in the provisions of the 1983 Code? Let us first look at the institutions in terms of the particular churches in the logic of what we have called synodality *in the strict sense*. We will then consider synodality in the broadest sense of the Church groupings and, then, from the papal primacy perspective.

FORMAL SYNODALITY IN THE PARTICULAR CHURCH

THE DIOCESAN SYNOD

The first synodal institution of the diocese is the diocesan synod, which the Code presents primarily (canons 460–68) in the internal organization of particular churches (canons 460–572). The *ecclesia* in this case is the diocese (can. 369).[19]

This institution, over a thousand years old, is today described in these terms: a diocesan synod is a "group of selected priests and other members of the Christian faithful of a particular church who help the diocesan bishop for the good of the whole diocesan community" (can. 460).[20] Composed of clerics and laypeople, members by right according to the Code or elected according to diocesan regulations (can. 463), this body is intended to "offer assistance to the diocesan bishop for the good of the whole diocesan community" (can. 460).[21] It is theologically based on the equality of all the baptized in the Christian dignity and ecclesial edification (can. 208; see *LG* 32c). All together, and each individually, carry the mission of the Church *in this place*.

The diocesan bishop convenes and presides over the synod (can. 462), as well as presiding over the Church *in this place* in the rich diversity of charisms and the necessary complementarity of vocations (see *LG* 32c) and gathering it in the name of Christ in the Holy Spirit (see *ChL* 22a at the end). The 2004 Directory for the Pastoral Ministry of Bishops *Apostolorum successores* adds, "In and through a Synod, the Bishop solemnly exercises the office and ministry of shepherding his flock" (no. 167, at the end). The same document defines the gathering of a diocesan synod as "*an action of episcopal governance and an event of communion*" (no. 168).

The synod expresses an original and traditional way of exercising the diocesan legislative power. The 1983 Code thus resumes the practices of the first millennium, when the bishops imposed upon themselves not to decide "without the advice of the clergy and the suffrage of the whole people."[22]

Since he is the only legislator in his diocese (can. 391; see can. 135, §2), the diocesan bishop is the only one to give "authority" to the decrees prepared by the synodal assembly (can. 466).[23] In other words, he is the only one to have a deliberative vote, the only one to decide on legislative matters. Other members, though they have only a consultative vote (can. 466), participate in the elaboration of canonical rules, for without them the decrees would never be "synodal," but would remain "episcopal."

The "advisory" nature of the diocesan synod (can. 466) means that "the Bishop remains free to accept or not the recommendations made to him by the members of the Synod" (*SDA* 2a) as well as to decide on the "the outcome of the synodal votes, the Bishop *always remains free* to determine what weigh is to be attributed to their results. Consequently, he may wish to accept the common view expressed by the members of the Synod, unless there should exist some grave obstacle to be evaluated by him 'coram Domino'" (IV, 5b).[24] The synod is not a deliberative college; such suffrage is not intended to reach a majority agreement, but to "have the possibility of *freely expressing* their opinions on the questions proposed for discussion" (IV, 5a). The "participatory process" aims, beyond a mere majority of the votes, to the widest possible consensus of the participants strictly around the legislative power of the bishop; this institution is thus a good example of cooperation of the faithful in the exercise of the power of government properly described (can. 129, §2; see can. 135, §2, and can. 391, §2).

THE PASTORAL COUNCIL

The pastoral council of the diocese is another place of synodality. It is a new institution (*CD* 27d) that concerns the diocesan *ecclesia*, since legislation provides that the whole portion of the people of God is reflected (*revera configuretur*) *in this place* (see can. 512, §2). The faithful are consulted by virtue of their baptism (can. 204, §1, and 208) and charisms that are their own, "whether they be the more outstanding or the more simple and widely diffused" (*LG* 12b), and not as experts in virtue of their knowledge or competence (can. 212, §3; see *LG* 37a).

Unlike the synod, the pastoral council is a permanent body; however, it ceases to exist when the episcopal see is vacant (see can. 513, §2). The mandatory nature of the pastoral council (can. 511: *constituatur*) is conditioned upon the evaluation of pastoral circumstances (*quatenus pastoralia adiuncta id suadeant*). The Code goes a bit further than Vatican II, which strongly recommended its creation (*CD* 27d: *valde optandum est*). The mission of the pastoral council is threefold: to study matters pertaining to pastoral activities, evaluate them, and propose practical conclusions (can. 511; cf. *CD* 27). Unfortunately, the Code did not resume the statement of its purpose as formulated by Paul VI after the last Council: to promote compliance of the diocesan life and activity with the gospel.[25] As the diocesan synod, the pastoral council *has only* a consultative vote (cf. can. 514, §1).

On the parish level, synodality can also be expressed formally through the pastoral parish council. Its constitution depends on a judgment of opportunity by the diocesan bishop, after hearing the presbyteral council (can. 536, §1). By analogy with the diocesan pastoral council, this body must reflect the diversity of the parish community, and is called upon to *give advice* to the pastor to verify the evangelical conformity of life and testimony of the parish. This body is only advisory: it participates in the making of decisions, while the responsibility for making decisions lies with the pastor (see can. 536, §1).

AND THE PRESBYTERAL COUNCIL?

I briefly mention here the presbyteral council, which does not directly concern the diocesan *ecclesia*, but the priests, or, better said, the presbytery around the bishop. This council is compulsory, unlike previous institutions. Like pastoral councils, the presbyteral council is also a new institution.[26] It is not a proper synodal institution, but a ministerial body that assists the bishop in the governance of the diocese, to promote the pastoral good of the portion of the people of God *in this place* as effectively as possible (see can. 495, §1). The bishop who presides over it is the head of the presbytery that is represented. In this perspective of the presbytery, which *is not without* the bishop, the council is referred to the episcopal ministry and the communities of the diocese; and thus, it indirectly refers to the synodality of the former and collegiality of the latter.

It is a governing body that is rather separate in relation to the episcopal function,[27] in a relationship of alterity with the bishop, while sharing with him a unity of consecration and mission (see *PO* 2). It does not ensure a collegial direction in a strictly legal sense, although its function is that of "a group" around the pastor of the diocese. Like the pastoral councils and the diocesan synod, the presbyteral council has only a consultative vote.[28]

SYNODALITY AT THE LEVEL OF GROUPINGS OF PARTICULAR CHURCHES

What can be said of the synodality in the "groupings of particular churches" (*coetus ecclesiarum*: can. 431–59), on an interdiocesan level, concretely speaking that of apostolic provinces and regions (can. 431–34), but also of episcopal conferences (can. 447–59)? Here synodality intersects with collegiality.

THE PARTICULAR COUNCILS

The "particular councils" constitute a generic category that includes the provincial council, which corresponds to a provincial council (can. 440), and the plenary council, as part of a conference of bishops (can. 439).[29] These are bodies composed of bishops—diocesan and titular (can. 443, §1) and if necessary emeriti (can. 443, §2)—who have the right to the deliberative vote. Other members have a purely consultative vote, namely vicars general and episcopal vicars, major superiors of religious institutes, rectors of Catholic universities and deans of faculties, some rectors of major seminaries, all of whom *must* be called upon to join (can. 443, §§3 and 4). Along the members with a deliberative or consultative vote, there is a third category of people who are invited as observers (can. 443).

The *ecclesia* in question in these canons exceeds, therefore, the diocesan context. The participants are the bishops of the dioceses (of all categories), pastors, and other faithful. The first have a deliberative vote, by virtue of their *episcopal ordination*, more precisely in their capacity as college of bishops (since there are, among them, bishops who do not have jurisdiction over a diocese!). In this perspective, the particular council really expresses the collegiality among bishops. The latter have *only* a consultative vote, being without episcopal ordination and, in this regard, they reflect the reality of their particular Church and express the protagonism of their respective *ecclesia*.

The dual mode of suffrage, deliberative and consultative according to the members, is symptomatic of the fact that the particular councils implement "participatory processes" involving Church *leaders*, by virtue of their episcopal ordination (and not primarily by virtue of the power of jurisdiction since not all the bishops, for example the emeriti, are endowed with it!), and some *members* of the particular churches concerned. The hierarchical or ministerial principle therefore prevails in the composition of the assemblies, but it does not rely on the power of jurisdiction, which only the diocesan and ordinary bishops of the place hold (can. 446).

The decrees issued by a particular council will not be promulgated until after their recognition (*recognitio*) by the Apostolic See. The *recognitio* can be understood as a "review" to ensure compliance with the universal canonical discipline (*ApS*, 31b, at the end). Commentators seem to attach much importance to the discretion that must surround the existence of these decrees before their *recognitio*, which is the premise required for their promulgation, and that gives them authority (see *CIC*, can. 7). Ecclesiologically, the *recognitio* has all its meaning as an act of recognition of ecclesial communion; canonically, this is expressed by the clause "so that, always without prejudice to the universal law of the Church" (can. 445 *salvo semper iure universali ecclesiae*). However, it remains problematic if it wants to be an instrument of control.

THE CONFERENCE OF BISHOPS

Since Vatican II, there have hardly ever been particular councils. Rather, on the level of the groupings of particular churches, usually the episcopal conference is the place of collegiality in the broad sense, that is, referring to the communal reality of a set of particular churches.[30] It is a "joint" operating agency of the pastoral office (*CD* 381, can. 447) on the part of the "those who preside over all the particular churches" concerned (see can. 448, §1; see can. 450).[31] Unlike the particular councils, once established, the episcopal conference is a permanent institution (can. 447). The powers of an episcopal conference are determined by can. 455: "where universal law has prescribed it or a special mandate of the Apostolic See has established it."[32]

The deliberative vote rests with the diocesan bishops (and "those who are equivalent to them in law") as well as the coadjutor bishops (can. 454, §1); auxiliary bishops and other titular bishops do not necessarily have it (can. 454, §2). Unlike the particular councils, here the simple fact of being a bishop does not therefore necessarily mean having a deliberative vote (see can. 443, §2). This body exercises over certain matters an ordinary power (see can. 131, §1), with a two-thirds majority of the prelates who possess a deliberative vote (can. 455, §2). General decrees and executive decrees thus issued do not obtain binding force until after the *recognitio* of the Holy See, the obligatory premise of their promulgation (can. 455, §2). Outside these limits and conditions, the episcopal conference cannot make binding legal decisions if not unanimously (cf. can. 455, §4).

Pope John Paul II's *motu proprio Apostolos Suos* of May 21, 1998, has restricted the doctrinal power of the authentic magisterium of the episcopal conferences by imposing the unanimous approval of the bishop member (without mandatory *recognitio*) or approval by plenary meeting by a two-third vote of the prelates possessing a *deliberative vote* (with the *recognitio* of the Holy See). The other conference decisions that have not met all the conditions cannot receive binding force except as single actions of the diocesan bishop.

THE CONTINENTAL ASSEMBLIES

The episcopal conferences are an aspiration to significant autonomy of the so-called regional churches, in this case most of the time within a nation (see can. 448, §1). But this aspiration to a broader collegiality also translates to the level of continental assemblies. These are not episcopal conferences, and thus do not have the same competence, but they have as their purpose the goal to "promote and protect the greater good" (can. 459, §1: *ad maius bonum promovendum ac tuendum*).

The episcopal conferences and continental assemblies of bishops contribute to the communion of the churches through the episcopal collegiality. In this sense, they promote the synodality of the particular churches through the heads of their churches, encouraging the protagonism of each one *in its place* and encouraging the baptismal coresponsibility of all as a function of the indispensable inculturation of the faith. These assemblies also generate processes that build a people (see *EG* 224).

To this end, we should move beyond a minimalist understanding of the episcopal collegiality that they implement; this way, it would not only be a matter of *affectus collegialis*, "a spirit of collegiality," a reductive expression opposing the strict concept of episcopal collegiality, resulting from the joint action of the college of bishops, with the Bishop of Rome and never without him. Beyond this division of "all or nothing" between an "effective" collegiality and an "affective" collegiality,[33] we must think the collegiality of these *coetus*, conferences or assemblies of bishops, as the realization of the *real*, though *partial*, achievement of collegiality.[34] Thus, the doctrinal study will allow us to overcome a simply "pastoral" consideration of these conferences and assemblies that, by its very nature, rests on a legal voluntarism. Since these *coetus* ultimately concern the particular churches through their prelates who are their members, we must restart from a theological consideration of the local Church and take seriously the communion that exists between them.

REALIZATIONS OF COLLEGIALITY AND COMMUNION OF CHURCHES

The notion of *collegium*, as indeed those of *ordo*, *corpus*, and *fraternitas*, have traditionally designated "both the union of all the bishops and particular unions within the episcopate."[35] The notion of collegiality has in fact imposed itself gradually to designate the communion of service and responsibility belonging to the ministry of bishops, who are what they should be *together*, as successors of the apostles and following in their footsteps.[36] This notion, however, has been toughened, if not limited, to the extent that, since the fifth century, the *collegium episcoporum* "already settled and legally secured"[37] lost sight of the ecclesial fellowship of the local churches, *each* of which realizes the only Church of God.

Once it became less sensitive to the intrinsic catholicity of each of them and their openness to other churches, the notion of college forgot the transversal relationships of the bishops with each other, on which the unity of communion of the whole Church (*ecclesia universa*) is founded.[38] This is not in an external relationship of the whole Church of God with particular churches, since there is rather a mutual interiority, an intrinsic reciprocity, a "perichoresis," given that the one and only Catholic Church is realized starting from the particular churches (see *LG* 23a).[39]

If we care about the rooting of the ministry of the bishops in the particular churches, over whose catholicity they preside over, we honor more completely the reality fully ecclesial of each particular Church and their true catholicity. It is through the catholicity of the Church entrusted to them that the bishops inscribe these in the *communio ecclesiarum* and, at the same time, become a sign of the communion of faith of the whole Church.

By the principle of mutual interiority of the churches entrusted to the bishops, the collegiality among neighboring churches, though "partial," refers to the whole, to both the whole Church and the whole of the college of bishops. Even partially, it effectively brings together transversally the catholicity of neighboring churches. It meets the synodality inherent in each Church *in its place*. The incidence of the ecclesiological starting point is measured according to the choice between universalist ecclesiology and ecclesiology of the communion of the churches.[40]

The doctrine of collegiality is intertwined with the doctrine of synodality, which concerns the rise of the Church *in this place*, that is, the ecclesial body of Christ as a community. The link between collegiality and synodality is rooted in the mystery of the one and only Church. As Joseph Ratzinger once wrote, "There is ultimately the collegiality of bishops because there is fraternity in the Church, and the collegiality of bishops accomplishes its meaning only if it serves this fraternity and is itself realized in this fraternity and in a fraternal sense."[41] In this perspective, the primacy of the Roman See is not suppressed. It presupposes the *communio ecclesiarum*, starting from which it must be understood and in the service of which it is exercised as "primacy of communion."[42] In it, the function of the Bishop of Rome articulates the "we" of the bishops in unity of faith and of communion.

SYNODALITY IN THE BROAD SENSE, STARTING FROM THE EXERCISE OF THE PAPAL PRIMACY

It is the Synod of Bishops we want to deal with now, especially since the Ordinary Assembly of the Synod of Bishops of 2015 was preceded by an extensive consultation throughout the Church. Let us, therefore, leave aside some questions related to the functioning of the Roman curia, which, as such, exercises a vicarious power and for this reason does not act by its own right or on its own initiative.[43]

The Synod of Bishops is

> a group of bishops who have been chosen from different regions of the world and meet together at fixed times to foster closer unity between the Roman Pontiff and bishops, to assist the Roman Pontiff with their counsel in the preservation and growth of faith and morals and in the observance and strengthening of ecclesiastical discipline, and to consider questions pertaining to the activity of the Church in the world. (can. 342)[44]

Created by Paul VI shortly before the promulgation of *Christus Dominus*, he understood it as a "council of bishops" that provides more effective help to the pope as it participates in the hierarchical communion (with him) showing that all bishops "partake of the solicitude for the universal Church" (*CD* 5). Its collegial dimension is certainly not excluded. However, it is a collaborative body with the Bishop of Rome in his primatial function. The Code leaves no doubt on this point.[45] Once Jean-Marie Roger Tillard qualified it as the "episcopal council of the Roman primacy."[46] This definition accurately describes its nature.

After half a century of existence, it must be noted that, despite its limitations, the Synod of Bishops plays a role in the pope's government and in the exercise of his magisterium. It has become a place of exchange for bishops with the pope, where they have been able to express the concerns of their colleagues in the episcopate and their concern for the whole Church. John Paul II did not hesitate to say that certainly "the synod is the instrument of collegiality," or "a way of expressing the collegiality of the bishops" for the solidarity that binds them in the episcopal ministry and the concern for the entire Church.[47] It is not so much a matter of collegial action in the strict sense, as of "in the collegial way the pastors of the local Churches express themselves"; and Wojtyla added, "The Synod expresses collegiality in a highly intense way, even while it does not equal that achieved by the Council" where the solidarity and concern are manifested "to the highest degree when all the bishops are gathered *cum Petro et sub Petro* ('with Peter and under Peter')."[48]

From the beginning, the Synod of Bishops has had an *exclusively* consultative power: its responsibility is to discuss issues and express its wishes, "but not to resolve them or issue decrees" (can. 343). And yet this same canon adds that "in certain cases" the synod of bishops can be endowed with "deliberative power" by the pope, "in which case he ratifies the decisions of the synod." The pope could thus give a deliberative value to the word of the bishops. To date, this case has never happened.

Although formally it would be nothing more than a primatial act of the pope, who would delegate this deliberative power to the bishops, such an exception could in any case mean that the bishops' concern for the entire Church is taken seriously.[49] It would give authority to make decisions in matters of ecclesial discipline[50] and that the pope would take up without having to convene an ecumenical council, which would be imposed when there is *fidei causa*.[51] The question is whether in the near future he can exercise the primacy concerned more to promote collegial acts than simply conforming to an expression of collegial spirit (*affectus collegialis*).

The practice of primatial synods poses some methodological questions for their preparation and management. Pope Francis has also said, "Perhaps it is time to change the methodology of the Synod, because the current one seems static."[52] He has already made inroads embarking on a broad consultation that will need to be evaluated.

Finally, we would have to consider the themes to address at a synod. Would it not be a gain to better identify the theme and focus it on of well-defined points that require decision-making? The rich content of the texts, in each of the phases of the synod, is certainly a real *think tank,* but it also generates frustration, or disappointment, when the time comes to (re)turn to the particular churches.

Suggestions

Our contribution has mainly centered on the *formal* synodality emerging from a set of directives of the Code of Canon Law. However, we must not neglect informal synodality, which still remains a *habitus* that needs to be encouraged, particularly by pastors, to overcome a monocratic exercise of their ministry.

Moving forward, we have established some links, *ex natura rerum*, between the notion of synodality, ecclesial catholicity, and collegiality, with its realizations: ecclesial fraternity, communion of churches, college of bishops, and the pope's primacy. The main concern underlying our path has led us to the decision-making procedures of the "participatory processes" examined. This expression borrowed from the sociology of organizations emphasizes the dynamic aspect of this act that, *in the Church*, activates its communal reality.

Let us now assess the ecclesiological extent of involvement of the faithful in this process. The communion of the *ecclesia*—at whatever level—is organic and symbolic at the same time. It is pervaded by a structuring difference, due to the ordained ministry of the pastors—bishops and priests—in the service of the ecclesial body, of which Christ is the head. By these theological assumptions, the participation of the faithful in the decision-making process cannot be "deliberative" in the sense that, in a tie vote, they would take decisions by a simple or qualified majority. The ordained ministry of the bishop and priests grant them a status of *guarantor* of the apostolicity of faith both through time, in a diachronic manner with respect to the origins, as well as in in the present, in a synchronous way.

But the absence of deliberative vote does not lead to the fact that the faithful have nothing more than an advisory vote: the consultative power in the Church is never, whatever people may say, purely consultative.[53] The current president of the Pontifical Council for the Interpretation of Legislative Texts, Francesco Coccopalmerio, once said about the parish pastoral council that the expression *votum tantum consultivum* is inadequate, if understood in accordance with civil law.[54] It is also lamentable because it denies ecclesial synodality. This reflection applies to all councils and Church meetings.

Ecclesiologically speaking, these synodal bodies cannot be reduced to *purely* advisory bodies. Their members seek *in the Church* how to respond to the will of God *here and now*; they are listening to the Spirit of God through his word that resonates in their actuality, so that the ecclesial body itself is inhabited and inspired by the same Spirit. Their voice must therefore be heard. In ecclesial communion, there is ultimately the *whole* community, in the *diversity* of its members, which is called to *give* advice. Is it not this way that "all according to their proper roles may cooperate in this common undertaking with one mind" (*LG* 30)?

To decide *in the Church*, pastors must listen to the voice of the faithful.[55] The law also stipulates that they must in some cases seek their opinion. This is done according to well-defined formalities and modalities. Pastors cannot act arbitrarily or eclectically: they must act according to the law.[56]

According to the Code, which reflects here the wisdom of the canonical tradition of government, when a superior must, in order to place acts, seek the counsel of people taken individually, the act is invalid if he fails to listen to them (can. 127, §2). Whether he consults collectively (can. 127, §1), or does so individually (§2), it is interesting for our discussion to underline what the Code says: "Although not obliged to accept their opinion even if unanimous, a superior is nonetheless not to act contrary to that opinion, especially if unanimous, without a reason which is overriding in the superior's judgment" (can. 127, §2, 2°; see can. 105 of the 1917 *CIC*). Otherwise, in general, the superior who listens to the persons whose opinions he sought for on a given question, de facto will follow their unanimous opinion (*votum concors*). He is not obliged to do so, but in general *he will*. This principle is of capital importance.

The *ecclesia* is never without the *ministerium*, the community is never without its pastor. There is no external relationship between them, but alterity in reciprocity. A council or assembly of the Church cannot make decisions that the pastor is obliged to accept.[57] Exchanges, debates, and other discussions are carried out in union with him, never without him, by working together. It is important to draw a distinction between *elaborating* a decision (*law making*) and *making* a decision (*law taking*). The elaboration of decisions is *not* done *without* the pastor, as well as he does not think *without* the contribution of all. However, the one who makes the decision is the pastor, who remains personally responsible.

We are glad to recall here what was said in the 1997 instruction on diocesan synods, to apply it in general to other synodal bodies: "In virtue of their experience and their counsel, those who participate in the Synod also collaborate actively in drawing up those declarations and decrees" (SDA, 1.2). To this view of the "Church of subjects" I would add the point of view of the "Church subject." As a subject of law, by its fundamental synodality, the *ecclesia* really participates in the elaboration of decisions concerning it. In this perspective, it would be better to say that advisory bodies *elaborate* decisions, whose final responsibility lies with the pastoral authority that *assumes* them.

Conclusion

It is important then to overcome a minimalistic view of the advisory bodies that is not sufficiently respectful of baptismal coresponsibility. In the democratic *ethos*, a better practice of collegiality will favor the credibility of a Church that listens to her faithful, anxious to give them a voice and to involve them in pastoral decisions. Greater synodality will also contribute to a better articulation of the personal exercise of pastoral authority through a communal and collegial exercise.

In terms of synodality, as in other areas of Church life, it is not all about theology alone, including the postconciliar magisterium, but about ecclesial practice. This is where canon law plays its regulatory role. Practices will change the representations, but it will take time and patience. Sometimes a significant event is enough to play a catalyst role in accelerating changes. Is this not what is happening with the pontificate of Pope Francis?

A greater synodality passes through the proper application of the canonical provisions, a proper understanding of the decision-making procedures, a fundamental trust in the people of God, associating them in the elaboration of decisions that the pastors are required to take, because the aim is "the missionary aspiration of reaching everyone" (*EG* 31).

NOTES

1. Laws, as ethics in general, concern human *action* and lie within a logic of ultimate causality: the end determines action; their language is performative. Science in general, particularly human sciences and in this case theology, concern the *being*, the nature of things, the facts to be observed and understood according to the cause-effect logic; their language is constative.

2. I refer to the recommendations of the Commission on Faith and Order of 1981, which cites the interpellation of Lausanne of 1927, later resumed in 1981 in the so-called Lima document: Foi & Constitution, *Baptême, eucharistie et ministère* (Taizé: Presses de Taizé; Paris: Centurion, 1982), part III, no. 26, pp. 64ff.

3. For the concept of social imaginary, I gratefully refer to the Canadian sociologist Charles Taylor. In the context of one of his studies on democracy, he emphasizes that the imaginary is not reduced to the perhaps too conceptual aspect of the notion of representation. The social imaginary, conveyed and fed as such by a community—which is in turn guided by it and replenishes it—includes simultaneously a mimetic aspect (music, dances, rites, relational customs, social uses, etc.), a mythical-narrative aspect (myths of foundation, great tales, fables and epics, etc.) and a discursive aspect (reasoned speech, philosophy, great political ideas, etc.). The social imaginary in the Church, as in society, is not limited, therefore, to normative and other clerical discourses: it includes relational habits, the style of exercise of authority, and other social uses that forge—and perpetuate—a representation of the clergy; see C. Taylor, "Démocratie et imaginaire social," in *Les sciences sociales en mutation*, ed. M. Wieviorka (Auxerre: Éd. Sciences humaines, 2007), 581–602.

4. I borrow the expression in its double dimension of "Church subject," the *ecclesia*, and "Church of subjects" the baptized, from H.-M. Legrand, "Le développement d'Églises-sujets. Une requête de Vatican II. Fondements théologiques et réflexions institutionnelles," in *Les Églises après Vatican II. Dynamisme et prospective. Actes du colloque international de Bologne, 1980*, ed. G. Alberigo (Paris: Beauchesne, 1981), 149–84. Originally published as "Lo sviluppo di chiese-soggetto: un'istanza del Vaticano II," in *Cristianesimo nella storia* 2 (1981): 129–64.

5. Similar reflections on civil society will be made starting from the work of a sociologist of organizations such as M. Crozier, *On ne change pas la société par décret* (Paris: Grasset, 1979). Translated as *Strategies for Change: The Future of French Society* (Cambridge, MA: MIT Press, 1982).

6. It is a concept of theological and canonical doctrine. See N. Witsch, "Synodalität," in *Lexikon für Kirchen- und Staatskirchenrecht*, ed. A. Von Campen-Hausen, I. Riedel-Spangenberger, and R. Sebott, vol. 3 (Paderborn: Schöningh, 2000), 642–44, here 642. "Lex iubet, not docet," says an old adage: canonical rules do not care to define abstract concepts, but to foresee the regulatory system of ecclesial life and its institutions.

7. Already among canonists, there are nuances that diversify the approaches. Compare, for example, M. Dortel-Claudot, "L'évêque et la synodalité dans le nouveau Code de droit canonique," in *Nouvelle revue théologique* 106 (1984): 641–57; E. Corecco, "Sinodalità," in *Nuovo dizionario di teologia*, ed. G. Barbaglio and S. Dianich (Cinisello Balsamo: Edizioni Paoline, 1991[6]), 1431–56; Witsch, "Synodalität"; M. A. Santos, "Sinodalidad" in *Diccionario general de derecho canónico*, ed. J. Otaduy, A. Viana, and J. Sedano, vol. 7 (Navarre: Universidad de Navarra, 2012), 341–45.

8. *Ecclesia* may designate different institutional entities of the ecclesial community of Christ's disciples: the particular Church, or the diocese as a Church realized in a place, a grouping of particular churches, ecclesiastical provinces or episcopal conferences, as well as the communion of all the local churches as universal Church, without forgetting, of course, the range of ecclesial communities that the faithful make up by virtue of either a creation by the competent authority—parishes, chaplains, works of charity (hospitals, prisoners, students, etc.; hierarchical communities)—or by virtue of their freedom of association—private or public associations (associative communities).

9. For some, in the perspective of the "Church subject," synodality would designate at the level of the particular Church what "conciliarity" designates at the level of the whole Church (see *communio ecclesiarum*). See G. Routhier, "La synodalité de l'Église locale," in *Studia canonica* 26 (1992): 111–61. For others, synodality would be, in terms of the relations between the faithful, what episcopal collegiality is for the bishops; it then refers to the *communio fidelium*, at the level of the local Church, or to the Church of subjects. The words *council* and *synod* have long been interchangeable: the former derived from Latin and the latter from Greek, and have often designated assemblies with various forms and purposes, held in quite different ways according to different times and places.

10. In the footsteps of Vatican II, the Code of 1983 states very sensibly that Christians "have been constituted as the people of God" and "they are called to exercise the mission which God has entrusted to the Church to fulfill in the world" (can. 204, §1; see *LG* 31a). Gilles Routhier is rather critical of the use of the concept of coresponsibility, mainly because this term does not do justice to the diversity of charisms and functions, introducing a strict equality of responsibility between the baptized; in other words, it contains "promises that cannot be really kept" (G. Routhier, *Le défi de la communion, Une relecture de Vatican II* [Montreal: Médiaspaul, 1994], 189). While agreeing in substance with our colleague in Quebec, here we retain the use of the term to speak of the baptized as active subjects in the Church, while emphasizing that this responsibility is diversified and differentiated, particularly by what we call the "structuring dissimilarity" that pervades the people of God.

11. According to the current etymology, the word comes from the Greek *synodía*, which designates a group of people who go the way together (*syn*, "with", and *hodós*, "road, away"); see for example, J. Fontbona, "La sinodalitat," in *Revista catalana de teologia* 37 (2007): 357ff. According to our colleague from Louvain-la-Neuve, Arnaud Join-Lambert, the following etymology should instead be considered: the prefix *syn-* and the word *udós*, which in classical Greek comes from the Attic dialect (with a smooth breathing!), indicates the "threshold" of the house (it would not therefore come from *hodós*, with a rough breathing). See A. Join-Lambert, *Les liturgies des synodes diocésains français 1983–1999* (Paris: Cerf, 2004), 61–65.

12. The concept of synodality can also indicate the fact that the churches come together or walk together in the same region because of their sociocultural identity and in view of the inculturation of the gospel in that place; in this perspective, it applies more widely to all local churches spread throughout the world, from East to West, walking with the Church of Rome presiding over charity (see Fontbona, "La sinodalitat," 358). On this basic synodality of the organic, plural, and diverse communion, see the brief reflections of R. Cheno, "L'unité de la réalité complexe de l'Église," in *Revue théologique de Louvain* 40 (2009): 349n33.

13. It is in this sense that the concept of synodality is often used to designate the organs of communion of the churches, especially the bishop's collegiality. This implies the inclusion of bishops in the Church that was entrusted to them by episcopal consecration (= diocese, see *LG* 21b). In this perspective, it must be rooted in the synodality of the particular Church. However, the bishop's collegiality is fully realized in the

conciliar communion, which is solemnly expressed in the ecumenical council (see *LG* 22a).

14. The expression is from Routhier, *Le défi de la communion*, 36.

15. Worth emphasizing here is the double negative "not without," which recalls Michel de Certeau, who in turn inscribes himself in Martin Heidegger's thinking (*nicht ohne*): what makes the action is what it lacks. See M. De Certeau, *La faiblesse de croire* (Paris: Seuil, 1987), 112–14 (see X–XI). These reflections fall within the consideration of the pluralist rules of Christian authorities (see ibid., 107–29, esp. 124–26).

16. Here we find the structuring dissimilarity that traverses the Church and determines significant differences: all and (among them) some, the community and (in her midst) the ministry, synodal principle and hierarchical principle, diocese and bishop, parish and parish priest. It is the intrinsic bond of reciprocity between these elements that speaks and allows to "be a sign," referring to the radical alterity of God, for Christ, in the Spirit. See L.-M. Chauvet, "Le Peuple de Dieu et ses ministères. Approche théologique," in *Prêtres diocésains* 1280 (1990): 127–55.

17. This perception of things is opposed to a universalist ecclesiology that explains the communion of churches from the communion of bishops. See W. Kasper, "L'Église comme communion. Réflexions sur l'idée directrice de l'ecclésiologie du concile Vatican II," in *La Théologie et l'Église* (Paris: Cerf, 1990), 402. Originally published as *Theologie und Kirche* (Mainz: Matthias-Grünewald-Verlag, 1987). Translated by Margaret Kohl as *Theology and Church* (New York: Crossroad, 1989).

18. For their ministry, deacons sacramentally represent the *diaconia* of Christ, to which the whole Church is called: they help the baptized to become a people of servants and show the world what it means to serve. See the new can. 1008 and 1009, §3 of the Code, concerning the sacrament of order, especially the diaconate. See A. Borras, "Les diacres d'après les nouveaux canons 1008 et 1009 § 3," in *Revue théologique de Louvain* 43 (2012): 49–78.

19. The *Code* says nothing of a similar synod in the other forms of particular churches. Is this not emblematic of the ecclesiological dimension of the diocese, which is its normal, as well as habitual, form (see can. 369)?

20. See, among others, G. Ghirlanda, "Aspetti teologici e canonici del sinodo diocesano," in *La Civiltà Cattolica* (1998/III): 480–93; N. Witsch, "Diözesansynode," in Campenhausen, Riedel-Spangenberger, and Sebott, *Lexikon für Kirchen- und Staatskirchenrecht*,1:452–53; R. Calvo Pérez, "Sínodo diocesano," in *Diccionario del Sacerdocio*, ed. Profesores De La Facultad De Teología De Burgos (Madrid: BAC, 2005), 761–67.

21. "The diocesan synod is the instrument *par excellence* for assisting the bishop in establishing the canonical ordering of the diocesan Church" (Directory for the Pastoral Ministry of Bishops "*Apostolorum Successores,*" 67a, which cites can. 460).

22. See Cyprian of Carthage, *Epsitola* 14, cited by H. Legrand, who shows well how diocesan synods are more of a return to the patristic tradition than an innovation, the only absolute innovation being the present participation of Christians in these assemblies; see H. Legrand, "Démocratisation ou communion? Une lecture théologique," in *Les synodes diocésains*, ed. H. Monceau et al. (Paris: Desclée de Brouwer, 1994), 174–76.

23. The bishop is not in an external relationship with the members of the synod. He is at most in a relationship of alterity in virtue of the symbolism of the apostolic ministry, which means that the Church comes from God through Christ in the Spirit. The sense remains the same: "coming from or originating from" means finding your own source from/in.

24. The Instruction *De synodis diocesanis agendis*, issued jointly by the Congregation for Bishops and the Congregation for the Evangelization of Peoples, could have reversed the statement in these terms: "The bishop will generally follow the commonly shared opinion of the synodal members, unless there is a serious cause that obliges his conscience, 'coram Domino', to oppose it." The 2004 *Apostolorum Successores* (no. 171) directory goes quite in this sense when it reads, after recalling the freedom of the diocesan bishop, "On the other hand, the Bishop will not dissociate himself from opinions and votes expressed by a large majority except for grave doctrinal, disciplinary or liturgical reasons." It should be added that the bishop will not wait for the outcome of the works to show his opposition, by virtue of the evangelical freedom conferred on him by his apostolic ministry.

25. See Paul VI's *motu proprio Ecclesiae sanctae*, August 6, 1966, I, 16, §1.

26. It is the distant heir to the presbytery of the Church of the first four centuries, though with functions previously devolved to the cathedral chapter (of which the Code deals with in the following chapter, canons 503–10).

27. The presbyteral council operates a decentralization of power, while the episcopal council (see can. 473, §4) forms a body with the diocesan bishop on the grounds of his vicarious participation in his power of jurisdiction (can. 473, §4, see can. 475 and 476). See A. Borras, "L'évêque diocésain, son conseil épiscopal et le conseil presbytéral au service du gouvernement du diocèse," in *Studia canonica* 49, nos. 1–2 (2015): 111–38.

28. The bishop must consult the presbyteral council "in affairs of greater importance" (*maioris momenti*: can. 500, §2), that is, on issues "concerning the Christian life of the faithful and the governance of the

diocese" (*ApS* 182d). The Code obliges the bishop to seek the opinion in seven specific cases (§461, §1, 515, §2, 531, 536, §1, 1215, §2, 1222, §2, 1263). The present Code does not cover cases in which the diocesan bishop is forced to seek the consent of the presbyteral council. As P. Valdrini recalls, "The universal legislature reserves the right to recognize cases in which the decisions of the law should be submitted to the consensus of the presbyteral council. The same holds true for particular legislators, particular councils, episcopal conferences, diocesan bishops" (P. Valdrini, "La constitution hiérarchique de l'Église," in *Droit canonique*, ed. P. Valdrini et al. [Paris: Dalloz, 1999^2], 157).

29. The particular councils take "care that provision is made for the pastoral needs of the people of God" (can. 445). They possess jurisdictional powers, especially legislative, in matters regarding the increase of the faith, organization of pastoral action, the regulation of morals, and of the common ecclesiastical discipline (can. 445, at the end).

30. Can. 447: "A conference of bishops, a permanent institution, is a group of bishops of some nation or certain territory who jointly (*coniunctim*) exercise certain pastoral functions for the Christian faithful of their territory in order to promote the greater good which the Church offers to humanity, especially through forms and programs of the apostolate fittingly adapted to the circumstances of time and place, according to the norm of law."

31. The joint aspect of their action has not received unanimous qualification from doctrine. Is this an ordinary power of governance (see can. 131, §1, attributed to the function of member of this *coetus*) and proper (see can. 131, §2, exercised on their own behalf, as members of this *coetus*)? Or is it a vicarious power of governance (see can. 131, §2, on behalf of each of the bishops in question, as heads of particular churches)? Or even a simple delegated power (see can. 131, §1, granted to the *coetus* by delegation of the members)? These issues cannot be separated from that of the nature of collegiality, depending on whether this precedes the presidency of a particular Church or is intrinsically united with the episcopal ministry.

32. The 2004 Directory *Apostolorum Successores* states that it would not be licit to extend the power of the conference, "*transferring to it the jurisdiction* and the responsibility of its members for their dioceses" since only the pope is competent to do so by issuing a special mandate (see 31ff.).

33. "The disastrous effects of these 'all or nothing' rigid positions are all too familiar regarding other ecclesiological issues. It will be enough here to mention two. 1) Before Vatican II, this was the way to think the relationship between the one and only Church and many other churches:

either they possess the whole ecclesiality of the Church of Christ, or they are not churches. 2) Similarly, it was the same for several centuries regarding the question of the members of the church: either they were full members (with all the essential, internal, and external ties) or they were not. Fortunately, today we talk about the gradual realization of ecclesiality of the Church of Christ and of different degrees in the union of the people with the Church. It seems clear to us that the dynamic nature of collegiality manifests itself in different degrees of realization": A. Antón, "Le 'status' théologique des conférences épiscopales," in *Les Conférences épiscopales. Théologie, statut canonique, avenir*, ed. H. Legrand, J. Manzanares, and A. García y García (Paris: Cerf, 1988), 275. Translated as *The Nature and Future of Episcopal Conferences* (Washington, DC: The Catholic University of America Press, 1988).

34. We refer to our study: A. Borras, "Considérations corrélatives sur l'exercice de la primauté romaine," in *Changer la papauté?*, ed. P. Tihon (Paris: Cerf, 2000), 85–120.

35. J. Ratzinger, *Le nouveau peuple de Dieu* (Paris: Aubier Montaigne, 1971), 109 (emphasis added). Note 13 on this same page as well as n8 on the previous page refer to the collective work, Y. Congar, ed., *La collégialité épiscopale. Histoire et théologie* (Paris: Cerf, 1965), esp. the chapter by J. Lécuyer, "La collégialité épiscopale," 41–57.

36. "The apostolic office is collegial. The bishops are the successors of the apostles, so they too have a collegial constitution, so that the college of bishops is the succession of the college of apostles; as each individual apostle held his function only by his association with the others who formed the apostolic community with him, so also each single bishop holds his office only in that he is part of the college, which represents the post-apostolic continuation of the college of apostles. Indeed, this argument is a sort of general compendium of the doctrine of epsicopal collegiality." (Ratzinger, *Le nouveau peuple de Dieu*, 105).

37. Ibid., 112.

38. See ibid., 107.

39. Regarding the episcopal conferences and the collegiate spirit that is realized through them, the question is precisely to know whether the mutual interiority is between the universal Church and the particular churches or between the Church of God, the one and only *catholica*, and these. The use of the "universal Church" category (as opposed to the "particular Church") leads here to denying the true catholicity of the local churches, which always requires their communion with the whole Church.

40. The stakes are serious. First, for the self-understanding of the Catholic Church. Then, for the ecumenical incidence: other churches

and ecclesial communities that are not in communion with Rome will never accept an ecclesiology that prefers the bond of jurisdiction to the relationship of ecclesiality. We need to know if we are determined to commit irrevocably and irreversibly to the ecumenical movement (see for example the encyclical *Ut Unum Sint*, no. 99a).

41. Ratzinger, *Le nouveau peuple de Dieu*, 117.

42. Ibid., 114; see also the previous page: in this picture, "the pope's primacy cannot be understood on the model of the absolute monarchy, as if the bishop of Rome was the absolute monarch of a supernatural 'church' with a central structure. It rather means that, within the network of churches that are in communion with each other and from which the only Church of God is constituted, there is an obligatory fixed point, the *sedes romana*, on which the unity of faith and the *communio* must be oriented."

43. See the introduction to the Apostolic Constitution *Pastor Bonus*, no. 8; see also *CD* 9.

44. See W. Stoffers, "Bischofssynode," in Campenhausen, Riedel-Spangenberger, and Sebott, *Lexikon für Kirchen- und Staatskirchenrecht*, 1:282–84; A. Viana, "Sínodo de obispos," in Otaduy, Viana, and Sedano, *Diccionario general de derecho canónico*, 345–50. See our also our recent study: A. Borras, "Trois expressions de la synodalité depuis Vatican II," *Ephemerides Theologicae Lovanienses* 90 (2014): 643–66, esp. 658–62.

45. The Code deals in fact with the college of bishops in the section on the supreme authority of the Church, after the first chapter on the Roman pontiff and the college of bishops (canons 330–41) and, by John Paul II's express wish (see *Communicationes* 14 [1981]: 180), before the third and fourth chapters, respectively on the college of cardinals (can. 349–59) and the Roman curia (can. 360–61).

46. J.-M. R. Tillard, *L'Église locale. Ecclésiologie de communion et catholicité* (Paris: Cerf, 1995), 480.

47. John Paul II, Discourse to the Council of the General Secretariat of the Synod of Bishops, April 30, 1983 (https://w2.vatican.va/content/john-paul-ii/en/speeches/1983/april/documents/hf_jp-ii_spe_19830430_sinodo-vescovi.html). The exaltation of collegiality in this discourse is of the order of the *affectus collegialis* and not of the collegial acts. "Episcopal collegiality" is considered "the particular responsibility of the bishops around the bishop of Rome." The concept is taken in the broad sense and not in the strict sense (*LG* 22b; can. 337; see can. 333, §2).

48. Ibid.

49. In time, the Dombes Group had expressed the hope of a "rebirth of synodal activity at all levels of church life" and, particularly, of the attribution of "more deliberative competencies" to the synod of bishops,

here referred to as the "three-year Roman synod": *Il ministero di comunione nella chiesa universale*, September 5, 1985, no. 146.

50. For example, the decision to admit to presbyteral ordination married men, the so-called *viri probati*.

51. See Y. Congar, "Struttura o regime conciliare della chiesa," *Concilium* 7 (1983): 15–26.

52. Pope Francis, *L'Église que j'espère. Entretiens avec le Père Spadaro sj* (Paris: Flammarion, 2013), 75.

53. See A. Borras, "*Votum tantum consultivum*. Les limites ecclésiologiques d'une formule canonique," *Didaskalia* 45 (2015): 145–62.

54. F. Coccopalmerio, *De paroecia* (Rome: Pontificia Università Gregoriana, 1991), 172–74. See also his study: "La 'consultività' del Consiglio pastorale parrocchiale e del Consiglio per gli affari economici della parrocchia," *Quaderni di Diritto ecclesiale* 1 (1988): 60–65.

55. Worth noting is the distinction, equally present in secular law, between opinion and vote. An opinion is the advisory opinion given in response to a question, while a vote is issued spontaneously. The ecclesial community and the faithful who compose it have the right to votes as to a common conduct to be adopted or a path to take together. Pastoral authority must listen to these votes.

56. The Code of Canon Law states that when a superior needs the opinion of a group of people (*coetus*) or a college (*collegium*), he has to convene and consult it in accordance with the law (can, 127, §1 and can. 166–73 and the statutes of the group in question). In this hypothesis, for the consultation act to be valid, the superior should seek the opinion of all (can. 127, §1).

57. In this regard, we would like to quote the Congregation for the Clergy "Circular Letter to the Presidents of Episcopal Conferences Regarding the Priests, Council *Presbyteri Sacra*," (*AAS* 62 (1970): 459–65; English trans. in *The Pope Speaks* 15 (1970): 157–62), which, on the advisory character of the presbyteral council, offered a description valid for other synodal bodies: "[The presbyteral council] is called consultative because it does not have a deliberative vote." And continues, "Therefore, it is not competent to make decisions which bind the bishop, unless the universal law of the Church provides otherwise or the bishop in individual cases gives a deliberative vote to the council" (9). In 1997, the instruction on diocesan synods explained their advisory nature in the sense that the bishop is free to accept, or not, the recommendations made to him: "However, this does not imply that such a 'votum' is of little importance or merely an 'external' consultation involving someone with no responsibility for the final outcome of the Synod." (I, 2). Finally, the 2004 Directory *Apostolorum Successores*, regarding the bishop, free to

accept, or not, the views expressed by members of the synod, states, "On the other hand, the Bishop will not dissociate himself from opinions and votes expressed by a large majority except for grave doctrinal, disciplinary or liturgical reasons. If necessary, the Bishop should explain from the outset that the Synod can never set itself in opposition to the Bishop by claiming to 'represent' the People of God" (171).

11

THE RENEWAL OF SYNODAL LIFE IN LOCAL CHURCHES

Gilles Routhier

The renewal of local churches surely overrides the renewal of their synodal life. On the one hand, this renewal must rest on a solid foundation, which can only be the proclamation of the gospel, which is the *raison d'être* of the local churches.[1] True, this *raison d'être* of local churches can be reformulated, saying that it should appear as a sign of the offering of eschatological gifts in a particular history, or that it is called upon to offer a precursory sign of the kingdom, being themselves a concrete proclamation of the gospel. The people of God gathered in the assembly by the word in a given place, in the Holy Spirit and under the guidance of the ministry, for the praise of God, is called to be a sign of unity and reconciliation. However, it is called to be the sign of the gospel in a concrete world, with those cultural features within which it is inscribed. This fact requires a discernment about the ways in which this proclamation will be made. It is then that the synodal life takes place.

The synodal renewal of local churches is therefore in the service of this purpose, and if it were to be guided by another goal it would be pointless to work for it. Synodal renewal falls in the order of means, and not a goal to be pursued. The synodal renewal that we propose must allow two things: (1) the emergence and expression of a Church of people who participate in a conscious and active way in the life of the Church, particularly in its government; (2) the discernment of what must become, be, and achieve a Church in a given situation, and perform a constant revision of the evangelical life of a local Church.

Moreover, we must point out that the renewal of the synodal life of a local Church life can be based on different approaches. In this context, the Church cannot "impose a rigid uniformity" (*SC* 37). In this area, as in the liturgical sphere, the Church is called to cultivate and develop the qualities and gifts of different peoples. The diversity of the forms of expression of the synodality must lead us to distinguish, on the one hand, the principle or the synodal system, or the synodal nature of the Church, and, on the other, its concrete institutional forms.[2]

Finally, it is important not to reduce synodality to the organization of institutional figures. Synodality involves equally procedures and processes, practices and attitudes; in other words, a spirit. It is important to keep these four elements together and not to overlook them. In short, we must keep in mind these four levels if we want to cultivate the synodal life of a local Church.

In the following pages, we will consider each of these elements, which so far, we have only mentioned as an introduction.

The Proclamation of the Gospel as the Goal of the Synodal Life of a Local Church

We must be very clear about the purpose pursued by the renewal of the synodal life, if we do not want to find ourselves engaged in the false debate that has been dealt with regarding the episcopal collegiality, when some have suspected that the claim of collegiality was reduced to a power struggle. We must therefore connect the synodal life with the proclamation of the gospel, because the former should favor the latter. In fact, the gospel must be proclaimed and understood within a given human space: to meet the particular challenges of people living in a place, and to be proclaimed in an environment with a culture of its own. The gospel is not a timeless discourse; and, if it is universal, it is not so in the sense that it presents itself as a "master key" discourse, suspended in imponderability, crossing all cultures and eras.

That is why the announcement of the gospel is based on a preliminary reading of the signs of the times, or on a reading of the situation of the recipients, as did the Council fathers, and as Pope Francis demands us to do. At Vatican II, the Council fathers in fact pledged to "recognize and understand" (*GS* 4) the world in which they lived and of which they sought to share the joys and hopes, the sadness and anguish (*GS* 1), to know the aspirations (*GS* 4, 8, and 9), needs (*GS* 11), and the deepest questions (*GS* 3, 4, 9, and 10). They hoped to bring the gospel to the world and, in so doing, to respond to "Man's calling" (*GS* 11).

> To carry out such a task, the Church has always had the duty of scrutinizing the signs of the times and of interpreting them in the light of the Gospel. Thus, in language intelligible to each generation, she can respond to the perennial questions which men ask about this present life and the life to come, and about the relationship of the one to the other. We must therefore recognize and understand the world in which we live, its explanations, its longings, and its often dramatic characteristics. (*GS* 4)

Following the systematics of *Gaudium et Spes*, the proclamation of the gospel represents an answer, since "people are waiting for an answer to these questions." (*GS* 11). This corresponds perfectly in fact to the teaching of Vatican II on the ministry of bishops: "The bishops should present Christian doctrine in a manner adapted to the needs of the times, that is to say, in a manner that will respond to the difficulties and questions by which people are especially burdened and troubled" (*Christus Dominus* 13).

It is by way of reconciliation that they have sought to understand this world, its expectations, its needs, its inspirations, its anxieties, its sorrows, its hopes, and joys. In a word, with the Council, the Church has gathered—to borrow the Paul VI's expression—to understand these questions of the world and to reread the gospel. In a conciliar fashion, the Church scrutinized the signs of the times and interpreted them in the light of the gospel.

The same path, which consists in interpreting the signs of the times and in scrutinizing the world in which the gospel must be announced, is resumed by Pope Francis in the second chapter of the apostolic exhortation *Evangelii Gaudium*.[3] The moment in which he undertakes this reading of the signs of the times, Francis recognizes that "it is not the task of the pope to offer a detailed and complete analysis of contemporary reality." Therefore, he exhorts "all the communities to an 'ever-watchful scrutiny of the signs of the times'" (*EG* 51). After articulating his thought, the pope recalls what he had said earlier: "As I mentioned above, I have not sought to offer a complete diagnosis, but I invite communities to complete and enrich these perspectives on the basis of their awareness of the challenges facing them and their neighbours" (*EG* 108).

This is exactly a way to promote the synodal life in local churches: to authorize and invite community members to read the signs of the times. This reading directly concerns the evangelizing action, as the pope recalls in the first few lines of this second chapter: "Before taking up some basic questions related to the work of evangelization, it may be helpful to mention briefly the context in which we all have to live and work" (*EG* 50).

To put it in Pope Francis's terms, the synodal life of a local Church is the implementation of a community process of discerning the context in which it is called to proclaim the gospel and missionary conversion that the announcement in this context demands. The pope will return often on this in his apostolic exhortation, always connecting this discernment realized in synodal form to the missionary activity of the Church, thus always joining the synodal life to that which is its purpose: the proclamation of the gospel. In this sense, he invites all the baptized, the churches and the communities, to discern the paths to take. After recalling that "all of us are called to take part in this new missionary 'going forth,'" Francis concludes by saying, "Each Christian and every community must discern the path that the Lord points out, but all of us are asked to obey his call to go forth from our own comfort zone in order to reach all the "peripheries" in need of the light of the Gospel" (*EG* 20). Later, he will add, "To make this missionary impulse ever more focused, generous and fruitful, I encourage each particular Church to undertake a resolute process of discernment, purification and reform" (*EG* 30). Continuing in the same direction, and evoking a path of synodal inspiration that allows the people of God to march together, he recalls that in the realization of this missionary turn, "the important thing is to not walk alone, but to rely on each other as brothers and sisters, and especially under the leadership of the bishops, in a wise and realistic pastoral discernment" (*EG* 33). This discernment realized in a synodal form, therefore, has to do with the reading of the signs of the times and the particular challenges that the proclamation of the gospel involves in a given human space, as well as the identification of the ways that this proclamation of the Gospel will take, and the revision of pastoral practices and the ecclesial structures that it will require. In a word, it is a revision of the evangelical life by a local Church that allows, on the one hand, to focus on the challenges that the proclamation of the gospel implies in each situation, and, on the other, to undertake a review of the ecclesial structures and practices, so that they manifest the heart of the gospel in a more transparent way and become truly at the service of the happiness of men, women, and children of a local Church.

The Emergence of a Church of Active Subjects

Synodal life presupposes an adequate understanding of the Church and the role of ministries in the Church. In fact, synodality cannot exist unless the Church is conceived as the people of God and if we do not take as a starting point the fact that the entire local Church is the subject of the proclamation of the gospel. If we do not have the deep conviction that the people of God are the subject of the Church's missionary activity and that evangelization is based on all the baptized who are responsible and protagonists of it, then synodal life does not manifest itself. Synodal life thus relies on ecclesiological basics and presupposes a theology of the local Church.

> In virtue of their baptism, all the members of the People of God have become missionary disciples (cf. Matt 28:19). All the baptized, whatever their position in the Church or their level of instruction in the faith, are agents of evangelization, and it would be insufficient to envisage a plan of evangelization to be carried out by professionals while the rest of the faithful would simply be passive recipients. The new evangelization calls for personal involvement on the part of each of the baptized. (*EG* 120)

The revival of the synodal life of a local Church leads to overthrowing the dequalifying process or exclusion of laypeople by integrating them as protagonists of Church life, especially in the field of the decisions regarding the guidelines taken by a local Church. It allows not only proposing a model of Church more in line with the nature of the Church herself, in which every baptized person is actively involved in ecclesial life and is responsible for proclaiming the Gospel, but also to favoring an ecclesial experience that develops an awareness of what the Church is. It thus enables Christians to develop a proper representation of what the Church is, according to the adage, "The Church is represented on the basis of how it is experienced."[4] In other words, if synodal life requires an understanding of the Church as people of God, it can also be said that it favors the emergence of a Church subject and a Church of subjects. It becomes a learning place for the active participation of all.

Such learning can naturally develop at the diocesan level, but it seems more appropriate to implement learning at an infradiocesan level, especially at the level of parishes or pastoral gatherings.

Synodal Regime of the Church and Institutional Figures That Encourage Synodality

We find it very important to distinguish between synodality understood as principle, that is, the Church's synodal regime, and the institutional figures that favor the realization of this principle. Synodality is a quality of the Church that derives from its very nature. In terms of the *munus regendi*, it expresses a particular type of relationship between people (a right), which promotes the participation of all, the structured and organic cooperation of all (or of the "many"), under the presidency of the bishop (or of the "one"), to a common action: the profession of the same faith. In other words, it actualizes the communion between the members of the people of God who constitute a local Church, a communion that takes the form of collaboration to a common action. It is, in the sphere of the *munus regendi*, analogous to everyone's participation in the celebration of the Eucharist, presided by the bishop of a Church. By virtue of the synodal principle, no one acts on one's own: everyone must instead act in solidarity. That is how each one becomes present to the action of the other, or is included in the word of the one who presides. By rooting synodality in the Church's nature, we distance ourselves from a purely functional or administrative approach to synodality and ecclesial government. This is not about paying homage to contemporary culture or administrative efficiency. Synodality is linked to the very nature of the Church.

On the other hand, if we do not want synodality to be reduced to a vague principle, or abstract magnitude, it needs concrete historical forms and a coherent legal expression. The synodal principle is expressed concretely in reality or in synodal practice. A concrete expression of a communion among members of a local Church, it needs institutional structures, frameworks, or forms that can actualize it; practices and specific procedures to implement it; and attitudes that support it. It is important to distinguish these diverse levels very well, just as it is important to work concretely on the development of procedures for the exercise of synodality. We are convinced that, to some extent, the *deficit* of synodal life in the local churches is linked to a lack of institutional creativity and an overly theoretical approach to this problem, since the studies are particularly interested in repeating the same discourse on the synodal principle instead of striving to examine *how* it can be realized in practice through institutional figures culturally fitting, appropriate and efficient practices, and attitudes worth cultivating.

SOME SUITABLE INSTITUTIONAL FORMS

To implement its constitutive synodal regime, the Church has valorized through the centuries various institutional forms. The two main ones are assemblies and councils that represent the basic forms of synodal life. These two fundamental forms, however, have been variously implemented in time and space. This diversity is evident when examining its different forms in the East and the West. Despite the centralizing tendencies at work in the history of the Church, this has always made available—to varying degrees—a home suited to the specific customs of certain places. On this point, we can say that the Vatican II reversed a secular centralizing trend, recognizing the Eastern churches' own rights. However, even if Vatican II admits some openness in the adaptation of liturgical forms and the recognition of a diversity of forms of Church life according to the cultures and inclinations of the various nations,[5] it still does not take sufficient account of the fact that the Church, which is now part of the various cultures of the world, can hardly actualize the synodal principle in the same way all over the world. The institutional forms, not only in the context of the *munus sanctificandi* and the *munus docendi,* are not universal and, therefore, are not present always and in all places. Aware of this diversity, the Council fathers, during the discussion on the revision on the revision of the Code of Canon Law in the first ordinary assembly of the Synod of Bishops in 1967, had the following questions:

> III.—One Code for the whole Church? Or two, or more: one for the Latin Church and others for the Eastern Church? Diverging views, defended with equal ardor, concluded that the proposition of a single Code is not mature enough....IV.—The principle of subsidiarity is welcomed by all...that the Code be one for the Latin Church, but allowing or even requiring special statutes according to the multiple situations of time and places.[6]

In the present situation, the only Codex of the Latin Church is valid for the churches of Africa, Asia, North America, Europe, and Latin America. All these human spaces are not homogeneous from the standpoint of the norms of deliberation and decision-making. The present question is therefore the plausibility of an appropriate institutional form for the concrete realization of synodality in different cultural spaces. The current *Code* makes frequent use of framework laws, as is the case especially in the chapter on diocesan synods. This means—if we really want to revive the synodal practice—that we must encourage the bishops' conferences to reflect on concrete forms and institutional measures that would be able to favor it in a sociocultural space, and to explicitly propose the use of these forms on one's territory. The responsibility to create, in reference to the two historical forms that are the assemblies and councils, sound institutional forms in a given cultural space, should be the in the hands of the episcopal conferences.

In this regard, it is interesting to reread the passage of the *Presbyterorum Ordinis* that prescribes the establishment of a council of the *presbyterium*: "There should be—in a manner suited to today's conditions and necessities, and with a structure and norms to be determined by law—a body or senate of priests representing all the priests." (*PO* 7). The need to adapt to current conditions and needs, as set out in no. 40,[7] is clearly stated here. And the same goes when the conciliar texts deal with pastoral councils, enumerating the following:

> Among the collaborators of the bishop in the government of the diocese are numbered those presbyters who constitute his senate, or council, such as the cathedral chapter, the board of consultors or other committees according to the circumstances or nature of various localities (*secundum diversorum locorum circumstantias vel indolem*). These institutions, especially the cathedral chapters, should be reorganized wherever necessary in keeping with present day needs (*necessitatibus odiernis aptatae*). (*CD* 27)

The same injunction to adaptation is formulated in the paragraph that deals with a rebirth and a reinvigoration of synods and particular councils (*CD* 37). Work in the direction of this adaptation has been realized in the years after the Council.[8] Further, local statutes and diocesan laws regulating the diocesan synod celebration have allowed the introduction of certain adjustments. However, even though the Code does not in reality provide a framework law on presbyteral and pastoral councils, we must note that we have not yet reached the end of this necessary adaptation to present conditions and needs, beyond all cultural areas in which the Catholic Church is by now a part. Therefore, the revival of synodality requires revised institutional forms.

PROCEDURES THAT ALLOW INFORMATION, EXCHANGE OF IDEAS, AND DECISION-MAKING

The simple arrangement of institutional forms does not guarantee synodal practice. These forms are nothing more than places for discussion, confrontation of points of view, maturation of ideas, and dialogue. They must be inhabited. The actualization of synodality therefore requires procedures and decision-making and must be based on appropriate processes: procedures that promote more complete dissemination of information; consultation procedures that allow the expression of points of view; procedures of studies conducive to the maturation of ideas; exchange and deliberation procedures leading to decision-making; feedback procedures to allow the understanding of the directions taken; and so on. The procedures call for meetings, exchanges, and dialogue, establishing networks and typical relationships among people. Here too, there are characteristic customs of the various cultural places in which the Catholic Church is inscribed. Theologians, jurists, specialists in the sciences of organization and management sciences, and anthropologists should, in every major cultural place, be able to work together to propose a set of procedures that could inspire local churches, procedures that could revive diocesan and infradiocesan synodality (parochial or regional).

ON PRACTICES

As we have seen, the goal of synodality is the proclamation of the gospel. It initiates a particular kind of relationship: the collaboration and participation of all to a common work, and the interdependence between the ministry and all the baptized. Synodality is realized through the exchange and the communion, under the guidance of the Spirit, in the framework of an assembly or council. It is supported by procedures and framed by shared information, communication, and decision-making processes. These processes, in turn, are linked to practices, particularly the practice of dialogue. Following Vatican II, this dialogue must take place between the bishop and his priests. It must be focused on pastoral care, because—as it is stated—the dialogue will lead to identifying "which forms make apostolic activity more fruitful" (*AA* 25).[9] An institutional form proves to be immediately necessary: the constitution of a council (see *CD* 28). We can clearly see the close connection between practice (dialogue), an institutional body (council), and a goal (more fruitful apostolic activity).

Vatican II, therefore, presents practices, especially those of dialogue, and at the same time initiates the promotion of institutional forms, to give a framework and a statute for these practices. A closer examination of the decree *Presbyterorum Ordinis* is proof of this: the bishops "gladly listen [*audient*] to their priests, indeed consult them [*consultant*] and engage in dialogue with them [*cum eis colloquantur*] in those matters which concern the necessities of pastoral work and welfare of the diocese." Immediately after, because this is not just a pious promise whose implementation is left to someone's good will, the text adds, "In order to put this into effect, there should be—in a manner suited to today's conditions and necessities, and with a structure and norms to be determined by law—a body or senate of priests representing all the priests. This representative body by its advice will be able to give the bishop effective assistance in the administration of the diocese." (*PO* 7). In this way, institutional practices and forms are necessary for the realization of synodality.

It will be noted in this passage that the word *dialogue* (*dialogus*) does not appear, even if there is a related concept (*colloquium*). In the texts of Vatican II, three actions specifically describe what dialogue is, which in this way is modulated based on these three actions: to express one's opinion, to listen, and to counsel. The duty to listen appears for the first time in no. 27 of *Lumen Gentium*, dedicated to the function of episcopal government. Listening realizes its reciprocity in the laity's duty to express their feelings regarding the good of the Church (*LG* 37).[10] As for the decree

Christus Dominus, it orders bishops to listen to their priests in order to advance to a shared pastoral mission in the diocese. Continuing the investigation in the texts of Vatican II would have showed us that this duty extends to other spheres associated with the *munus regendi*. Thus, priests should be willing to listen to the laity, to consider fraternally their desires, to acknowledge their experience and their expertise in the various fields of human activity, so that they can read the signs of the times (*PO* 9); and parish priests are called upon to take advice from their "vicar" (*CD* 30) since the duty to listen falls on the Roman dicasteries (*CD* 10) as well: "Finally, the fathers of the council think it would be most advantageous if these same departments would listen more attentively to laymen who are outstanding for their virtue, knowledge, and experience. In such a way, they will have an appropriate share in Church affairs."

All these paragraphs are interesting because they contribute, on the one hand, to building the interpretation and interdependence between the ministry of the one and the participation of the many in the field of the *munus regendi*: through dialogue, "the many" become present to the action and word of the "one." On the other hand, they point to the purpose of such a dialogue: the pastoral action that we traced back to its core, the proclamation of the gospel.

The dialogue that structures liturgical action (*synáxis*)[11] and, even more fundamentally, the relationship between God and humanity in the act of revelation,[12] thus becomes the basis of the Church's relationship[13] with the world, with separated Christians and non-Christians,[14] along with nonbelievers and people of good will,[15] and with culture. This concept is used to describe the relationships that will be found in the reconciled world.[16] It is not surprising that in turn it structures the *synodos* of the *ecclesia*, which is called to be the sacrament of unity of mankind and reconciliation in the world, and that it is at the center of the practice and the synodal reality of the Church. If the Church, "by virtue of her mission," wants to present herself

> as a sign of that brotherhood which allows honest dialogue and gives it vigor,...such a mission requires in the first place that we foster within the Church herself

> mutual esteem, reverence and harmony, through the full recognition of lawful diversity. Thus all those who compose the one People of God, both pastors and the general faithful, can engage in dialogue with ever abounding fruitfulness. (*GS* 92)

The purpose assigned to dialogue is the search for truth, as stated in the declaration *Dignitatis Humanae* 3. Its importance stems from its relation to the aim pursued and the result it brings, that is, to build "communion between persons" (*GS* 23) and build the Church: for this reason, the Council urges the laity,[17] the seminarians,[18] and young adults[19] to form themselves in dialogue.

On Attitudes

Synodality however, cannot be reduced to a formal mechanism, as if the arrangement of institutional forms, the activation of procedures, and the resulting practices were sufficient to inspire life. Synodality calls for specific attitudes and proceeds from a disposition. Bernard Franck has described the "synodal spirit" as follows:

> Mutual listening, exchange and communication, sharing and solidarity, the desire to reach consensus, or a common conviction. It takes the will to collaborate and to cooperate, to accept and to welcome, to give and to receive. This supposes relationships marked by respect, charity, humility, and poverty. This is the synodal spirit.[20]

In short, these institutional forms, these procedures and practices are at the service of the particular relationship between the faithful, which can be described as support to the concepts of collaboration, cooperation,[21] and solidarity. These concepts are used to indicate that no one can act in isolation in the Church, but others are also present to her action, being all included in the mission that is that of the whole Church. Ultimately, synodality is a path of communion.

Conclusion

In its intention and purpose, in the means and procedures it puts into operation place, in the specific relationships it establishes between people and in its spiritual nature, synodality is nothing other than the manifestation of communion at the level of the *munus regendi*. If understood in this way, we can say that its forms of expression and actualization become places of manifestation of the *ecclesia* as a gathering of people in different situations and with different roles, and as communion in sharing and listening to the word of God. It is in this sense that synodality, as we have seen, is a "constitutive reality of the Church," or that it is "a constitutive element of the Church," and expresses "its very nature as a communion of saints." Synodal life, which actualizes this constitutive principle through the practice of sharing and relationship, expresses the attitude of the reconciled human being, that is, what is accomplished by God's salvific work.

NOTES

1. See *Evangelii Nuntiandi* 14: "The task of evangelizing all people constitutes the essential mission of the Church....Evangelizing is in fact the grace and vocation proper to the Church, her deepest identity. She exists in order to evangelize."

2. On this point, see Y. Congar, "Struttura o regime conciliare della chiesa," *Concilium* 7 (1983): 15–26; "Conclusion," in *Le Concile et les Conciles. Contribution à l'histoire de la vie conciliaire de l'Église* (Paris: Cerf, 1960), esp. 308–10; "Remarques sur le concile comme assemblée et sur la conciliarité foncière de l'Église," *Le concile au jour le jour. Deuxième session* (Paris: Cerf, 1964), 39, in which he underlines that "the conciliar principle is essentially related to the nature of the church." See also H. M. Legrand, who talks about a "synodal dimension of the Church" and "the essential conciliarity of the Church" pointing out that conciliarity-synodality "is essential to the church" (H. Legrand, "Synode et conseils de l'Après-concile. Quelques enjeux ecclésiologiques," *Nouvelle revue théologique* [98, no. 3 {1976}: 193–216]), and that it "depends on the fundamental order of the church" (Legrand, "Grâce et institution dans l'Église. Les fondements théologiques du droit canonique," in *L'Église: institution et foi*, ed. J.-L. Monneron, M. Saudreau, G. Defois [Brussels: Publications des facultés universitaires Saint-Louis, 1979], 139–72, at

164). See also J. Neumann, *Synodales Prinzip. Der größere Spielraum im Kirchenrecht* (Freiburg: Herder, 1973), 9: later, this author emphasizes that "only this form [synodal] corresponds to the church's self-understanding as supported again by Vatican II, and as founded in the New Testament and the original tradition of the Church" (ibid., 92). Many theologians and canonists recognize that conciliarity and synodality belong to the nature of the church. These, however, have found different expressions throughout history. See M. Dortel Claudot, "L'évêque et la synodalité dans le nouveau Code de droit canonique," *Nouvelle revue théologique* 106 (1984): 641–57. For his part, B. Franck speaks of synodality as a "constitutive reality of the church": see B. Franck, "Les expériences synodales après Vatican II," *Communio* 3, no. 3 (1978): 64. This judgment is shared by other Christian traditions; as such, it recalls the Ecumenical Council of Churches, which notes that conciliarity-synodality "is a constant structure of the church, a dimension which belongs to its nature" and also "conciliarity belongs necessarily to the life of the Church" (see the final report "The Importance of the Conciliar Process in the Ancient Church for the Ecumenical Movement" in *Councils and the Ecumenical Movement* [World Council of Churches Studies 5] [Geneva: WCC, 1968], 10). In terms of Waldensian theology, we mention this statement by P. Ricca, according to which "all organized expressions of Christianity realize some form of conciliarity: Christianity in all, or almost all, its versions appear to be constitutionally conciliar" (P. Ricca, "Il concilio ecumenico: assemblea di vescovi, o di chiese, o di tutta la comunità dei fedeli?" *Concilium* 7 [1983]: 141–50). From an Orthodox perspective, we have A. Scrima, who observes that "for the East 'conciliarity' is present with the church: it arises, so to speak, with its cultic foundations. One is almost tempted to see a tautology in it: the Church is conciliar because Church, because it is a living communion in Christ" (A. Scrima, "Semplici riflessioni di un ortodosso sulla Costituzione," in *La Chiesa dal Vaticano II*, ed. G. Baraúna [Florence: Vallecchi, 1965], 1188–1202). Of the same opinion is G. Larentzakis, who, borrowing S. Harkianakis's statement, writes, "The Church without synodality is a contradiction in terms, since etymology accords to *ekklesia*, 'synod,' and 'council,' almost the same root." (G. Larentzakis, "Die dogmatische Begründung der Synodalität und der Gremialität," in *Konziliarität und Kollegialität als Strukturprinzipien der Kirche* [Innsbruck: Tyrolia Verlag, 1975], 64). On the contrary, W. Aymans claims that "the synods of the Orthodox Church have a constitutive meaning for the organization of the Church, while in Latin constitutional law they a more organizational character." (W. Aymans, "Konzil-Bleibendes und Veränderliches im kirchlichen Synodalwesen," in *Synodale Strukturen der Kirche. Entwicklung und Probleme*, ed.

W. Brandmüller [Donauwörth: Ludwig Auer, 1977], 188). Elsewhere, he observes, "If consequently synodal nature cannot be understood as constituting the Church, it is not excluded that the synods constitute the organs of ordinary Church guidance." ("Synodalität—ordentliche oder außerordentliche Leitungsform in der Kirche," *L'Année canonique* I [1992]: 33, an out-of-series supplement that gathers the Acts of the VII International Congress of Canon Law: *La synodalité. La participation au gouvernement dans l'Église*).

3. It has been observed that the structure of *Evangelii Gaudium* follows the "see-judge-act" method: the first two chapters are dedicated to "see," the third to "judge," the fourth to "act." See S. Lanza, "La teologia pastorale secondo la scuola lateranense," in *La teologia pastorale oggi* (Rome: Lateran University Press, 2010), 45–48. See also G. Whelan, "*Evangelii gaudium* come 'teologia contestuale': aiutare la Chiesa ad 'alzarsi al livello dei suoi tempi'," in *Evangelii gaudium: il testo ci interroga. Chiavi di lettura, testimonianze e prospettive*, ed. H. M. Yáñez (Rome: Gregorian Biblical Press, 2014), 23–38.

4. "As a person experiences the Church, so he will come to think of the Church": P. W. Collins, "The Diocesan Synod. An Assembly of the People of God" *The Jurist* 33 (1973): 402.

5. In addition to the openings in *Sacrosanctum Concilium*, which have been reinforced during the postcommunist period, it is essential to read no. 19 of the decree *Ad Gentes*: "In such new churches,…the Faith is taught by an adequate catechesis; it is celebrated in a liturgy in harmony with the genius of the people, and by suitable canonical legislation, it is introduced into upright institutions and local customs."

6. "Le débat sur la révision du Code de droit canonique," *La Documentation catholique* LXIV 1505 (1967): 1971.

7. Note 41 states, "The Cathedral Chapter is already found in established law, as the 'enate and assembly' of the bishop (*Code of Canon Law*, c. 391), or if there is not one, an assembly of diocesan consultors (see *Code of Canon Law*, cc. 423–428). It is our desire to give recognition to such institutions so that modern circumstances and necessities might better be provided for."

8. See esp. Congregation for the Clergy, circular letter *Presbyteri Sacra* of April 11, 1970, in *AAS* 62 (1970): 459–65 (in *EV* 3 [Bologna: EDB, 1977], 1456ff.), and the circular letter *Omnes Christifideles* of January 25, 1973 (in *EV* 4 [Bologna: EDB, 1978], 1196ff.).

9. See also *AA* 10 and *AG* 20 on relations between priests and laity.

10. This right and duty of all the faithful to share their opinion is restated in can. 212, §2 of the 1983 Code.

11. See *SC* 33.

12. See *DV* 2, 3, 4, 5.
13. See *GS* 3, 40; *PO* 12; *CD* 13.
14. See *GS* 92; *AG* 16, 34, 41; *NA* 2, 3, 4; *GE* 11.
15. See *AA* 14.
16. See *GS* 56, 68, 90, 92.
17. See *AA* 29 and 31.
18. See *OT* 19.
19. See *GE* 1, 8.
20. Franck, "Les expériences synodales après Vatican II," 77.
21. The term often reappears to describe the relations between the bishop and the priests: it is said, "And let the bishop regard his priests as his co-workers and as sons and friends" (*LG* 28), as they are the "prudent cooperators of the episcopal order" (*CD* 28). *CD* 27 also mentions them first "among the collaborators of the bishop in the government of the diocese." The same term *cooperation* also defines the ties between the priests themselves and the laity's participation in the apostolate of the pastors (*LG* 33).

12

FROM MEDELLÍN TO APARECIDA

The "Lesson" of a Regional Experience in Searching for Forms and Styles of Effective Collegiality

Silvia Scatena

A Unique Collegial Tool

This contribution will be strictly historical, and will be developed starting from the study of the peculiar reception of Vatican II in Latin America and the unique collegial path of the churches of that continent. The hope is that a brief overview of the five general conferences of the Latin American Bishops can offer to those who have other tools some useful ideas in the search for forms of effective collegiality and in the prospect of building a communion of regional churches.[1]

An overview on this path must necessarily begin recalling the creation of CELAM, the Episcopal Council of Latin America and the Caribbean, in 1955, on the initiative of the Holy See, which understood the potential of continental Catholicism in the new international scenario of the post–Second World War period.[2]

Created with the aim of instilling a new spirit in Latin American Catholicism, traditionally lacking in resources, structures, and personnel; and in view of a Latin-Americanization of the bishops' conferences, not immune to the mobilization instances of the last phase of Pius XII's pontificate; CELAM, on the other hand, recorded an autonomous growth in a rather dialectical process, not without tension with the Holy See.[3] Generally viewed with indifference by the majority of the bishops of the continent, the birth of this body—and in particular of its permanent general secretariat, modeled on that of the CNBB, the National Bishops' Conference of Brazil—institutionalized the continuity of the discontinuous and fragmentary activity of the Latin American episcopate, making it possible for an accumulative and organic experience to remain a unique phenomenon, later imitated by other continental episcopal organizations, but never actually reproduced.[4]

The body and soul of the new organization was in particular a small group of bishops who had the experience of the JOC, the Jeunesse Ouvrière Chrétienne (in English: Young Christian Workers): a "school" that had facilitated the maturation of a more continental vision of social and pastoral problems, the creation of new ties and solidarity, and the collaboration with a specialized Franco-Belgian staff who greatly contributed to the launching of new and creative pastoral practices.[5] Thanks to the efforts of this small group, CELAM soon became a particularly dynamic body, not only limited to coordinating existing pastoral strategies, but also promoting a series of initiatives involving a growing number of bishops. The beginning of a practice of relationship and collaborative work thus gave to the peripheral Latin American episcopate an instrument that at the Second Vatican Council would become a unique heritage and that from Vatican II would receive, as is well known, new life and new consciousness.[6]

A Pentecostal Experience

Even for CELAM, the experience of the Council was obviously of paramount importance and, during the presidency of Manuel Larraín, it would not be incorrect to speak of a true "conciliar refoundation" of the council of delegates of the twenty-two national conferences, starting with the new awareness of their own ecclesial significance conveyed by the new theological horizons disclosed by Vatican II and the conciliar reflection on episcopal collegiality. It was in this context that, in the summer of 1965, the idea of a second general conference of the Latin American bishops took shape to bring about the actualization of the conciliar gains.[7]

If CELAM was therefore a unique "creature," even more so would it be for the instrument of the "General Conference": a bishops' meeting to which the conferences—a change with respect to the continental meeting in Rio de Janeiro in 1955—would send a number of representatives proportional to their number (thus compensating for the obvious disproportion that at general CELAM assemblies would have seen the participation, in addition to the presidency and the *mesa directiva*, of only one delegate member for each conference, with a somewhat striking lack of representation as in the case of Brazil).[8]

The assembly of Medellín was an expression of the "collegial church" that, in 1990, Émile Poulat placed at the intersecting point of the downward trend of a plurisecular "colonial Church" and of a rising "popular Church," characterized by the opening of an endless dialectic between repression and protest. Medellín (Colombia) in 1968 represented, from many points of view, an innovative, original, and unprecedented experience in the history of subsequent general conferences of Latin American bishops.[9] In a nutshell, we believe that three elements essentially help to understand the specificity of this experience: three elements whose combination, never again reproposed, helps to grasp the singular *dýnamis* of that assembly, at the origin of a widespread reading of Medellín as "palpable outpouring of the Spirit of Pentecost," as the Argentine Eduardo Francisco Pirono put it a few years later.[10]

A "SENCILLO EJERCICIO COLLEGIAL"

Medellín was the landmark of a long preparation that had its "engine" in the collegial exercise systematically promoted by the first postconciliar CELAM to transpose the major guidelines of Vatican II in the life of the particular churches in Latin America. The unique synodal experience lived in Medellín—the first official meeting after the Council where a small fraction of non-Christian bishops had voice and vote in deliberations—cannot be understood apart from the implementation of that group of bishops converted to team work by Larraín, the president of CELAM from 1963 until his accidental death in 1966.[11] The special form of "extended" collegiality, expressed at the 1968 conference, finds in other words its background in the "collegial training ground" promoted by this team of bishops; a "training ground" that, thanks to the involvement of priests, religious, and laypeople, is soon projected beyond the perimeter of a strictly episcopal collegiality, seeking its meaning and its significance in the ability to listen and interpret the ferment and demands of change of extended ecclesial environments. It seems essential in this regard that the intention of this group to be an echo chamber for thoughts, practices, and awareness that were maturing in significant sectors of the continental Church in the wake of the Conciliar renewal. A little over a year before Medellín, in May 1967, at a meeting organized by the Secretary Marcos Gregorio McGrath for an assessment of the path undertaken by CELAM in the postconciliar period, that intention was clearly spelled out in a document that highlighted how CELAM would really express the fundamental sacramental aspect of the episcopal collegiality to the extent that collegial form and prophetic function—"that listens, interprets and proclaims"—were integrated and sustained, since the former became a condition of the exercise of the latter, and the second gave meaning and significance to the former, lest the essence of CELAM be forever lost.

THE ROLE OF THE LITURGY

The liturgical group of the Institute of Pastoral Liturgy in Medellín managed to make of the development of the daily liturgy a truly "integral and integrating" moment of the assembly, an assembly that, precisely in liturgical celebrations and daily prayers, identified the true "spiritual essence" of the conference. Thought and prepared for the assembly works—as "one element in service to the Latin American reality"—the liturgical plan of the assembly played, in many ways, a structuring role, becoming a privileged space of reflection on the needs and responsibilities of one's ministry and contributing to unite the more characteristic options of the conference in the form and with the peculiar stamp with which they have been expressed.

THE *MECÁNICA DE TRABAJO*

The third decisive element to understand the peculiar importance of that synodal experience is finally represented by the *mecánica de trabajo*, which helped all the assembly participants to work together, in a climate of great freedom: bishops, religious, laypeople, men, women, representatives of other Christian churches. This climate, characterized by a certain "constructive disorganization," gradually in many cases made available a more continental vision of the problems, and was felt the extent to which the conciliar transformation had taken hold of the collective consciousness.

Medellín is the only conference whose final document, with the unexpected permission of Paul VI, was immediately disclosed before the Roman scrutiny in accordance with regulations and practice.[12] It immediately received a consensus and an extraordinary gravitational force, more for what it suggested or encouraged than for what it stated. In the following years the instance of poverty was translated into pastoral styles, priorities, and practices reproposed by an episcopal magisterium that, on the eve of the Puebla Conference (Mexico), would count more than five thousand documents.[13]

Even in the case of Medellín, then, as often happens for those events that end up having a strong symbolic and historical value, there was a gap between what the assembly was and what it became when the overall background changed in which its outcomes are located. The changes on the broader international stage and the related political developments in the Latin American region exacerbated in fact the internal polarization of continental Catholicism, radicalizing the processes, realignments, ruptures, and crises that marked all ecclesial spheres the 1968 movements, which was the beginning of a second postconciliar period. It is in this broader context that Medellín soon took on the meaning of a "watershed moment," fueling hopes or crystallizing fears. Not all bishops felt sufficiently committed to its conclusions and different conferences, as CELAM emphasized,[14] confining themselves to merely repeat the conference guidelines, without adjusting them to the concrete realities of their respective countries. Among the most noteworthy results of the 1968 Assembly is undoubtedly an unprecedented awareness of the ecclesial unity that transcends national horizons; however, this did not eliminate the burden of profound stratification and historical differences, as well as the keeping of daily practices in significantly different church models. The years between the conferences coincide with a phase of intense and rapid changes, which do not take place everywhere in the same ways and with the same intensity, and in many cases create strong resistance.

The Course Change of 1972

Such resistance on the ground would find new resonances in the overall evolution of the directions of the Roman curia and, then, of the new pontificate. This new context did not fail to reflect, rather noticeably, on the course of CELAM in the seventies. In particular, the doubling of members, with the arrival of the presidents of the national conferences as established by the new statutes (finally approved in November 1969), on the one hand gave CELAM greater institutional weight; but on the other, it started a rapid downsizing of the influence of the group of bishops who organized the 1968 conference. This scaling down was even more substantial after the unexpected election of Alfonso López Trujillo to the Secretariat in October 1972 and a further amendment of the statutes, two years later, allowing the young Colombian bishop to ferry CELAM to Puebla, significantly altering its objectives and functions.[15]

The secretary and later president of CELAM from March 1979, the Colombian prelate became the principal director of a sharp change in direction of the Latin American Council of Bishops—a change that began with the systematic replacement of departmental staff, and soon focused even on matters related to interpretation, in the attempt to provide an official interpretation of the conference in the face of the spread of radical or "abusive" readings of its final document, sensitive to Marxist influence. The events related to the interpretations of Medellín and the same evolution of CELAM in the seventies and eighties thus became increasingly intertwined, as is well known, with the debate on liberation theology, in whose genesis the role of local actors appears to be no less important than the overall guidelines of John Paul II's pontificate.[16]

Ten years after the 1968 assembly, the CELAM preparing the Puebla conference was therefore very different from the episcopal team created by Larraín, and the Church that met in Puebla in January 1979 was more than ever experiencing profound internal tensions that the *Documento de consulta* further contributed to accentuate.[17] Expected by some as an opportunity to defuse dangerous political deviations, and feared by others as a final act of an attack on the ecclesial process that began at Medellín, Puebla therefore was not able to overcome its internal divisions, though it still highlighted the lasting richness of theological and pastoral ferments crossing the Latin American Church. It thus marked the beginning of an ecclesial season characterized by a further exacerbation of the controversy concerning liberation Christianity, an exacerbation of which CELAM—with the election to the chairmanship of Secretary General López Trujillo—became a significant protagonist. The turnover at the helm of the episcopate's continental body thus marked the official start of an ecclesial period whose history is well known, from John Paul II's visit to the Nicaragua of the Sandinista regime in 1983, after his visits to Brazil and Argentina in 1980 and in 1982, to the well-known instruction from the Congregation for the Doctrine of the Faith in 1984: a season marked by a new policy of episcopal appointments, canonical visits to theological faculties and seminaries, and the parsimonious bestowal of *imprimaturs* for the publications of books, and frequent self-censorship.[18] The end of experiences, such as the *Nordeste* regional seminar (Brazil) to name just one, or the normalization of an organization such as CLAR, the Latin American Confederation of Religious men and women, drastically changed the landscape in which CELAM now moved, a CELAM that, in synergy with other actors, seemed to gradually undo the potentials of what had been its most original and fruitful "creature"—the general conference—the "victim" of a history that it had helped to create.[19] Between Puebla and the fourth General Conference of the Continental Church celebrated in Santo Domingo (Dominican Republic) in 1992, the intention to correct or scale down the achievements of Medellín increasingly played out as a questioning of the authority and magisterial value of the conclusions of the general conference as such—a questioning against which, on the eve of Santo Domingo assembly, Angel Antón reacted, in a rare in-depth analysis of the theological and legal *status* of this atypical document.[20]

Antón's hope for a clarification of the magisterial value of the general conference documents, one that would go beyond a purely formalistic approach and be accompanied by a further insight into their theological status, remained, as we know, unfulfilled. What happened in Santo Domingo is in this sense emblematic. One of the three presidents of the conference, Secretary of State Angelo Sodano, and the Chilean Cardinal Jorge Medina Estévez, the assembly secretary, worked to prevent any final document from appearing and sent to Rome only a few proposals that needed to be further examined and published afterward, according to the practice of the Roman synods. A similar approach was taken by the five members of the drafting committee, previously appointed and not elected. By the explicit will of the assembly and by the vote of the various bishops, only Dom Luciano Mendes de Almeida was added to the drafting committee.[21]

The context was by then that of the Special Assembly for America of the Synod of Bishops of 1997, which seemed also to close the "anomalous" chapter of the general conferences: an impression that is only reinforced by paragraphs 5 and 12 of the 1998 *motu proprio* on the episcopal conferences, and then the next directory *Apostolorum Successores* of 2004—which ignore, in fact, the very reality of supranational bodies of the episcopate.[22] The concern to dilute the historical value of Medellín in the *continuum* of a continental collegial path that went from the Plenary Council of 1899 to the Special Assembly for America in our view played a significant role in this process. It is significant that in an intervention at the conference organized by CAL, the Pontifical Commission for Latin America, for the centenary of the Plenary Council of 1899, Germán Doig Klinge concluded that none of the four general conferences of the Latin American Bishops met the formal recognition standards expected for conciliar decrees and for those of episcopal conferences recognized as "authentic magisterium."[23] Kling, then vicar-general of the *Sodalicio de vida cristiana*, and former lay consultant at Santo Domingo and auditor at the Special Assembly for America in 1997, was responding to López Trujillo's request to clarify the authority and value of the conclusions of the four conferences in the light of the criteria of *Apostolos Suos.*

The Surprise of Aparecida

Thus the option for an advisory body attached to the office of the pope through the continental synods went hand in hand with the definitive failure of episcopal leadership, although the conference had an extraordinary ability to speak to the local and universal church, despite the fragility and canonical uncertainty of its instrument. In this context must be placed the convening, and then the actual celebration, of Aparecida (Brazil), though it was a conference that did not fail to fend off the skepticism of some and the fears of others, mainly because of the fact, not taken for granted, that it was "offered" and held in Latin America. The delay of its official announcement by the Holy See in October 2005—four years after President Óscar Rodriguez Maradiaga's proposal of a fifth general conference to celebrate the jubilee of the Latin American Episcopal Council at the 2001 CELAM assembly—was proof of the difficulties encountered on its path, as well as the resistance of those who now considered closed this unique collegial experience.[24] Sodano had explicitly said no to a fifth conference; CELAM's *mesa directiva* referred the matter then to John Paul II, who then asked for a consultation both with the twenty-nine Latin American cardinals (seventeen of whom spoke in favor of the conference and twelve for a synod in Rome) and at the twenty-two episcopal conferences (only one spoke in favor).[25] Originally conceived for 2005, at that time only the definition of the theme and the choice of date and venue were decided at a papal hearing, on the fringes of the synod of bishops, granted to CELAM's president, Francisco Javier Errázuriz Ossa, and three other Latin American cardinals (Hummes, Bergoglio, and the Colombian Rubiano Sáenz). On that occasion, they expressed to Benedict XVI their desire not to hold the conference in Rome, as previously proposed by the Holy See, given John Paul II's poor health.[26]

This was perhaps the first "surprise" of Aparecida: CELAM knew how to "insist" on not breaking a line of continuity with the unique collegial history of the Latin American church. All this was while CELAM sought the involvement of twenty-two national conferences, associating their chairmen with CELAM's leadership in making decisions related to the launch of the conference; this was a way to strengthen the position of the body in Bogotá (Colombia) in opposition to those who he had worked against its convocation and intended to condition and control its preparation.

A second surprise was therefore the climate of dialogue in which the conference took place and on which few would have bet, considering the overall ecclesial situation and the signs to the contrary in the months before its celebration. Those who did not expect anything and who feared until the very last that the assembly could convey parallel or antagonistic demands recognized unanimously that there was an unexpected freedom of speech at Aparecida: a freedom that was used and allowed often conflicting ecclesiastical positions to express themselves and discuss. As with the "heterogony of ends," the episode of the notification on the works of Fr. Jon Sobrino, SJ, in February 2007, and the strong reaction it provoked in large ecclesial spheres on the continent, seemed to have played positively in this regard, communicating a desire for greater conciliation.[27] In this sense should probably be read CELAM's decision to hold a small private meeting between five bishops of CELAM and five liberation theologians in Bogotá at the end of March 2007,[28] as well as the last-minute acceptance of a substantial presence in Aparecida of a group of Amerindian theologians[29] as external collaborators available for those bishops who needed assistance. This presence, though not official, was clearly recognized even in the final document.[30]

In a constant alternation between fears and hopes, possibilities and frustrations, and with the result of a long and heterogeneous final text that both pleased and dissatisfied almost all, therefore, Aparecida represented, first of all, the confirmation of a common path, giving once again to the bishops of the continent the unique opportunity of a meeting and a long-standing confrontation on the spot.[31] It was a text of compromise, in which the recognition of the peculiarities of the path of the Latin American church of the last fifty years, and therefore of some of the fundamental decisions of the previous conferences beginning from the preferential option for the poor, was in our opinion the gateway for the best content.

The more relaxed atmosphere, even more surprising for those who participated in Aparecida with the still-lingering memory of Santo Domingo, did not, however, eliminate the limits of the preparation and composition of the assembly, as well as, obviously, the tensions among its various natures. Something about these limits should be said; in what follows we will mention two.

THE IRRELEVANCE OF CELAM'S PREPARATORY WORK

Just as in the case of the Puebla *Documento de consulta*, the long *Documento de participación* prepared by CELAM[32] was overwhelmed by criticism, primarily from the same CNBB.[33] The first aspects to be criticized were its abandonment of the inductive method of "seeing-judging-acting," dear to the theological tradition of the continent, and a certain distancing from some great ecclesiological axes and fundamental insights of Vatican II. Even the following *Documento de síntesis* was able to actually take into account the ongoing debate and contributions received from the various local churches, and only to a small extent.[34] Hence the decision to start in a sense from scratch, taking the time for a broad and free initial discussion, which was strongly supported by the drafting committee and chaired by Bergoglio, not without a certain tension with the Assembly Presidency.[35] This choice in itself was undoubtedly fruitful, but in the small amount of time available ended up reserving special powers to the editors, subtracting in many ways the text from the control of the assembly. The moment of "seeing" came, in other words, too late.[36]

COMPOSITION OF THE ASSEMBLY AND INSUFFICIENCY OF REPRESENTATION

With its more than 160 bishops; some eighty other guests, including priests, religious, and laypeople; fifteen experts; and eight observers; for a total of 266 participants—as representatives of a continental Catholicism that in 2007 exceeded 42 percent of the world total—the last general conference of the Latin American episcopate has certainly been confirmed as a collegial opportunity without equal in all other continents.[37]

Of the 162 official members of the assembly, only 58 percent were elected delegates of the episcopal conferences:[38] a group of just under one hundred bishops, whose weight was massively counterbalanced by the presence in Aparecida of all Latin American cardinals—apart from Medina Estévez—three nuncios, members with the right to speak and vote, a large group of cardinals and prelates of the curia appointed by Benedict XVI, along with the presidents of the bishops' conferences of the United States, Canada, Spain, and Portugal. The pope's ability to directly appoint a certain number of members de jure helped to ensure a greater curial attendance, or to remedy the missed election of the bishop of an important see like that of Montevideo (Uruguay): sixteen members were appointed by the pope, like at Medellín, but the criteria of choices were different (Paul VI "recovered," for example, Samuel Ruiz García, who was not elected by the Mexican episcopate).[39]

A similar approach was adopted to choose the official experts at the conference and the few delegates of the lay movements, where clearly the new movements were favored. Only the insistence of the CNBB, on the eve of the opening of the assembly, obtained the addition of a representative of the Christian base communities in Brazil, chosen by the National Council of the Laity (CNLB), and the same chairman of the CNLB.[40] These last-minute corrective measures, however, did not substantially change the overall insufficient representation of large and significant ecclesial sectors.[41]

Numbers aside, it was also felt that thirty years of episcopal appointments and creations of cardinals had almost wiped out the episcopal leadership, composed of many Latin American archbishops of diverse theological and political leanings in the sixties and seventies. Aparecida was in this sense also the mirror of a reality of the Church: a Church that, with the disappearance of the protagonists of the past ecclesial season, found a new leadership with difficulty. On the other hand, for some bishops, in cases of recognized leadership in their respective countries, Aparecida allowed them to raise their profiles, to forge or strengthen relationships and partnerships, and in general, for those who had come to the conference without a precise agenda, it was one of the first and decisive experiences of continental collegiality, which left much more than just one document.

This was certainly the case of Bergoglio, whose participation in the conference clearly marked his path, as, in hindsight, it has been clearly observed: before his total identification with the major aspects of the conference, behind what Pablo Dabezies of Amerindia has defined as his "fanaticism por Aparecida,"[42] there was undoubtedly the strong and rare experience of a collegial experience,[43] despite the shortcomings already mentioned, the regulatory constraints, and certain unobtrusive interventions of the last hour (for example, cuts to the paragraphs in the final text on the Christian base communities after the Holy See examined the document).[44]

Some Concluding Remarks and Some Hopes Moving Forward

At the end of this overview, I will attempt to outline some concluding reflections and some aspirations, in the hope that they can be of some use to a more prospective and appropriate enunciation of some of the issues.

1. As in the case of the exercise of primacy, the whole course of CELAM seems to show that the implementation of a collegial body of the episcopate depends, in the end, on the self-awareness of its function, responsibilities, and ecclesiological significance—and therefore, in the end, on the self-awareness of the men who animate it. Even without drastic interventions or statutory changes, the same structure can be functional in terms of intentionality, objectives, and even very different ecclesiologies, which can evolve, change, or be transformed with the rotation of its protagonists, in turn connected to the changing of the overall "landscape" in which they operate.
2. The moment of greater "strength" of CELAM—that is, the greater impact on the concrete life of the Latin

American churches and greater capacity to express a new model of local responsibility at the heart of the universal church—was perhaps that of its more fragile institutional features. Initially regarded with indifference, then with growing suspicion by some "unenthusiastic" local bishops due to the invasive activism of a structure that had its only office in Bogotá, the first postconciliar CELAM had to cope with the ongoing questioning of its powers in reference to the preparation of the general conference by the Pontifical Commission for Latin America and, above all, of some national conferences (in 1968, the Colombian bishops planned a preparatory "counterdocument"). CELAM's standard of the preparation for general conferences was included in the statutes only in 1969. The institutional consolidation of this organization with the introduction of the presidents of the national conferences in 1972 seems to usher instead in many ways a time of growing dependence on the comprehensive guidelines of the new pontificate.

3. To emphasize this does not obviously mean to underestimate the importance of statutory and legal arrangements, much less the urgency to rectify as soon as possible the silence of *Apostolos Suos* on this intermediate level of episcopal collegiality, specifying its canonical status and theological significance in the wake of *LG* 23, which, regarding the gatherings of episcopal conferences, explicitly evokes the model of the "ancient patriarchal churches" to which it invites one to look, with a view to understanding the Church as a communion of churches. It means instead to emphasize the strong link between the need to strengthen the current supranational structures of episcopal cooperation to support an awareness of regional churches as subjects of law and initiative within the whole Church, and the urgency of addressing the issue of a crisis of the *episkopē*, too often humiliated by an interpretation of the episcopal role as a reiteration of the Roman magisterium.

4. In the specific case of the continental conferences of the Latin American episcopate—proposed and organized by CELAM, but convened by the Holy See and characterized by nonbinding conclusions—it would be crucial to remedy to the fundamental paradox represented by the fact that the episcopal assemblies that had the greatest impact in the concrete life of the churches of the continent (and for which, above all, CELAM is known, as evidenced by the frequent terminological confusion when it is referred to as "conference" and not as "council") are the more undefined ones in legal terms. It seems therefore no longer possible to further postpone a clarification of the canonical status of these assemblies, adapted to their theological *status* rooted in the principle of episcopal collegiality at the service of communion and catholicity and to the reception that they had in the churches of Latin America and beyond.
5. It is also desirable that the fruitfulness of this unique collegial experience of continental episcopal assemblies celebrated on site may convey a renewed reflection and also a rethinking of the formula and manner of celebration of special synods for continents, on the model and type of involvement in the synodal process of other continental episcopal bodies (the Symposium of Episcopal Conferences of Africa and Madagascar, the Federation of Asian Bishops' Conference, the Federation of Catholic Bishops Conferences of Oceania, the Council of the Episcopal Conferences of Europe). In any case, continental synods should always be celebrated locally and not in Rome.
6. To give the conferences and regional structures of the episcopate the legal possibility of exercising an effective collegiality corresponding to their theological dignity is an unavoidable step with obvious ecumenical implications. It may, however, remain irrelevant if not accompanied by a contextual reconsideration of the criteria and methods for the selection of bishops and

return to the practice of local churches having a say in the choice of their pastors.

7. The reason for the extraordinary consensus that solidified around the conclusions of Medellín lies in the fact that the conference was perceived as "a fact of the whole Church," which in its preparation and to some extent in its celebration involved all the people of God. The full participation of the representatives of the various ecclesial members in the elaboration of texts in the committees, and the small proportion of priests and religious who, for the first time at an official meeting, had voice and vote in the final deliberations, not only represented a form of tribute to the new ecclesiology of the people of God, but also the outline of an "enlarged" collegiality open to a synodality in which all the baptized are involved in the responsibilities for the life and mission of the Church. We should develop, in the wake of Francis's speech of October 17, 2015,[45] a notion of collegiality structurally integrated with forms of effective synodal participation of the rich diversity of the ecclesial body to the process of common discernment of the signs of the times and the search for ecclesial and pastoral responses starting with the realities and possibilities of the different local and regional churches.
8. Looking ahead, the peculiar collegial "form" of the Latin American Church—the "form" that in May 2004 John Paul II allowed to continue after three years of confusion—should actually be able to express itself through assembly regulations that may provide a different proportion of delegates elected by the assemblies and members appointed by the Holy See and greater, effective secular and ecumenical participation (where representatives of the other churches do not have the status of mere "observers"). The latter would be essential to give credibility and more concrete expression to the image of a Church "going forth" in which the role of the laity, their organizations and their participation in the nonordained ministries, has become increasingly more crucial in the life of the community. In the event

of a future General Conference of the episcopate, each of the national conferences could include, for example, the participation of at least two laypeople, a man and a woman, with right to voice and vote, thus numerically and qualitatively expanding the quota of Christians who are not bishops and who at Medellín had the status of members and not just guests. CELAM could in this sense apply pressure on the Holy See to implement significant regulatory changes, thus opening the way for a first overcoming of evident imbalances in the participation of the various components of the people of God to the various occasions in which decisions are at stake concerning the future of the churches and communities. An exemplary experience in this direction would be a valuable and powerful contribution with a view to overcoming the connection between the episcopal office and synodality, historically affirmed in increasingly exclusive terms, and a more adequate institutional translation of the ecclesiology of the Council.

NOTES

1. For a quick outline of this topic, see my article: "La 'chiesa collegiale' latinoamericana: un rapido percorso attraverso le cinque conferenze generali dell'episcopato continentale," in *Chiesa e teologia in America Latina*, ed. S. Scatena, L. C. Susin, and S. Gallazzi, intro. by Armido Rizzi (Padua: EMP, 2013), 29–50. More recently: J. J. Legorreta Zepeda, *Cambio e identidad de la Iglesia en América Latina. Itinerario de la eclesiología de comunión de Medellín a Aparecida* (Mexico: Universidad Iberoamericana, 2015).

2. See M. Mugnaini, "Santa Sede, America Latina e politica internazionale: alcune considerazioni sul periodo bipolare," in *L'America Latina fra Pio XII e Paolo VI. Il cardinale Casaroli e le politiche vaticane in una chiesa che cambia*, ed. A. Melloni and S. Scatena (Bologna: Il Mulino, 2006), 1–27.

3. In this sense, see the brief but effective contribution of F. Houtart, "CELAM. The Forgetting of Origins," in *Church and Politics in Latin America*, ed. D. Keogh (London: Macmillan, 1990), 65–81.

4. See A. Methol Ferré, "Del Vaticano II a Medellín," in *CELAM, Elementos para su historia. 1955–1980* (Bogotá: Consejo Episcopal Latinoamericano, 1982), 89–99. On the CNBB, see volume edited by the National Institute of Pastoral Care: *Presença pública da Igreja no Brasil (1952–2002). Jubileu de ouro da CNBB* (São Paulo: Paulinas, 2003). See also L. Fürer, "Le conferenze episcopali nei loro rapporti reciproci," in *Natura e futuro delle Conferenze episcopali. Atti del colloquio internazionale di Salamanca (3–8 gennaio 1988)*, ed. H. Legrand, J. Manzanares, and A. García y García (Bologna: EDB, 1988), 167–94; M. Wijlens, "Cooperation of Bishops on Supranational or Continental Level: A New Institution on the Intermediate Level?" in *Synod and Synodality: Theology, History, Canon Law and Ecumenism in New Contact; International Colloquium Bruges 2003*, ed. A. Melloni and S. Scatena (Munster: Lit Verlag, 2005), 33–60; Wijlens, "Exercising Collegiality in a Supra-national or Continental Institution Such as the FABC, CCEE, and ComECE," *The Jurist* 64 (2004): 168–204; "Between Local and Universal Structures for Episcopal Leadership," in *Religious Leadership and Christian Identity*, ed. D. Nauer, R. Nauta, and H. Witte (Munster: Lit Verlag, 2004), 28–38; H. Legrand, "Iglesia(s) local(es), Iglesias regionales o 'particulares', Iglesia católica. Dossier de hechos y reflexión sistemática," in *Iglesia universal, Iglesias particulares*, ed. J. C. Scannone and C. M. Galli (Buenos Aires: San Pablo, 2000), 81–162.

5. See A. M. Bidegain, "La Organización de Movimientos de Juventud de Acción Católica en América Latina. Los casos de los obreros y universitarios en Brasil y en Colombia" (PhD diss., Leuven, 1979), and A. J. Soneira, "La Juventud Obrera Católica en Argentina (y notas comparativas con desarrollo en Brasil y México)" in *Innovaciones y tensiones en los procesos socio-eclesiales. De la Acción católica a las Comunidades eclesiales de base*, ed. A. Puente Lutteroth (Cuernavaca: Universidad Autónoma del Estado de Morelos–Consejo Nacional de Ciencia y Tecnología, 2002), 29–55. See also A. Brighenti, "Raíces de la epistemología y del método de la teología latinoamericana," *Medellín* 78 (1994): 207–54.

6. On this point, we refer to the first chapter of S. Scatena, *In populo pauperum. La chiesa latinoamericana dal concilio a Medellín (1962–1968)* (Bologna: il Mulino, 2007).

7. Ibid., and J. O. Beozzo, "Das Zweite Vatikanische Konzil (1962–1965) und die Kirche in Latinamerika—Vatican II and the Church in Latin America," in *Transkontinentale Beziehungen in der Geschichte des Außereuropäische Christentums—Transcontinental Links in the History of Non-Western Christianity*, ed. K. Koschorke (Wiesbaden: Harrassowitz, 2002), 219–42. By the same author, see also "Medellín. Inspiration et racines," in *Volti di fine concilio. Studi di storia e teologia sulla conclusione*

del Vaticano II, ed. J. Doré and A. Melloni (Bologna: il Mulino, 2000), 361–93.

8. See B. Restrepo, *El CELAM. Apuntes para una crónica de sus 25 años* (Bogotá: Consejo Episcopal Latinoamericano, 1982), and J. Hortal, "Risposta alla relazione di Fürer," in Legrand, Manzanares, and García y García, *Natura e futuro delle Conferenze episcopali*, 189–98.

9. See É. Poulat, "The Path of Latin American Catholicism," in Keogh, *Church and Politics in Latin America*, 3–24. For a review of the literature, we refer to our "Per una storicizzazione di Medellín. Prime ipotesi e problemi aperti," in Melloni and Scatena, *Synod and Synodality*, 647–62.

10. See E. F. Pironio, "Nello spirito di Medellín," in *Medellín. Testi integrali delle conclusioni della seconda Conferenza generale dell'episcopato latinoamericano* (Rome: ASAL, 1974), 9–21. On the following three points, we refer to our *In populo pauperum*; on the liturgy at Medellín, see also a previous, more specific contribution: S. Scatena, "'Sapere ascoltare e sapere essere': la liturgia alla conferenza di Medellín," *Cristianesimo nella storia* 28 (2007): 175–216.

11. See R. Rojas, *Manuel Larraín Errázuriz. El legado de un precursor. Escritos completos y testimonios* (Santiago: Universidad Católica del Maule, 2008).

12. See J. Mejía, "Crónica de la vida de la Iglesia. El pequeño Concilio de Medellín–II," *Criterio* (September 26, 1968): 686–89.

13. See P. Vanzan, "Per una lettura 'contestualizzata' dell'Enchiridion: le coordinate storico-pastorali della vicenda ecclesiale latinoamericana," in *Enchiridion. Documenti della Chiesa latinoamericana*, ed. P. Vanzan, F. Grasselli et al. (Bologna: EMI, 1995), 7–36. Although not exhaustive, the best collection of episcopal documents for the decade between Medellín and Puebla is J. Marins, *Praxis de los Padres de América Latina. Documentos de las Conferencias Episcopales de Medellín a Puebla (1968–1978)* (Bogotá: Ediciones Paulinas, 1978). For this decade, see also the documentation in E. Dussel, *De Medellín a Puebla. Una década de sangre y esperanza. 1968/1979* (México/DF: Edicol–Centro de Estudios Ecuménicos, 1979).

14. See the *Balance* of the Presidency of CELAM elaborated in view of the extraordinary meeting of May 27–31, 1969, which we deal with in our *In populo pauperum*, 514ff.

15. See L. F. Escalante, *El Consejo Episcopal Latinoamericano (C.E.L.A.M.) y sus Estatutos* (Madrid: Cofas, 2001). On the election of López Trujillo to the General Secretariat and the change in the direction of CELAM, see, in the absence of rigorous historical reconstructions, Houtart, "CELAM: The Forgetting of Origins"; C. Antoine, "Pentecôte

en Amérique Latine. De Medellín à Puebla," in *Les rendez-vous de Saint-Domingue. Les enjeux d'un anniversaire (1492–1992)*, ed. I. Berten and R. Luneau (Paris: Centurion, 1991), 99–139; J. Comblin, "Medellín et les combats de l'Église en Amérique Latine," in *Le retour des certitudes. Événements et orthodoxie depuis Vatican II*, ed. P. Ladrière and R. Luneau (Paris: Centurion, 1987), 34–53; Comblin, "Medellín: Vinte anos depois. Balanço temático," *Revista eclesiástica brasileira* 48/192 (1988): 806–29; J. O. Beozzo, *A Igreja do Brasil. De João XXIII a João Paulo II* (Petrópolis: Vozes, 1994), 207ff.

16. For a rapid summary we refer to R. Gibellini, *Il dibattito sulla teologia della liberazione* (Brescia: Queriniana, 1990[2]); L. Ceci, "Liberazione e teologia (1973–1992)" in *Storia ed esperienza religiosa. Studi per Rocco Cerrato*, ed. A. Botti (Urbino: Quattro venti, 2005), 269–82; G. Miccoli, *In difesa della fede. La Chiesa di Giovanni Paolo II e Benedetto XVI* (Milan: Rizzoli, 2007), 31–70; S. Scatena, *La teologia della liberazione in America Latina* (Rome: Carocci, 2008).

17. See Dussel, "De Medellín a Puebla," and *Celam-Puebla 79: ¿desilusión o esperanza?*, ed. I. Méndez Torres (Mexico City: Editorial Diana, 1980).

18. See J. O. Beozzo, "La reprise en main d'une Église: le Brésil," in Berten and Luneau, *Les rendez-vous de Saint-Domingue*, 178–206.

19. On the Nordeste regional seminar, see E. Pinheiro, "Dom Helder Camara como arcebispo de Olin—da e Recife (1964–1985)," in *Helder, o Dom. Uma vida que marcou os rumos da Igreja no Brasil*, ed. Z. Rocha (Rio di Janeiro: Vozes, 2000), 67–87, and N. Darwin De Andrade Cabral, *Onde está o povo, aí está a Igreja? História e memória do Seminário Regional do Nordeste II, do Instituto de Teologia de Recife e do Departamento de Pesquisa e Assessoria* (Recife: FASA, 2008). On the CLAR, see J. Kiesler, *Signs and Instruments of Liberation: The Confederation of Latin American Religious (CLAR) and a Contextual Theology of Religious Life from 1966 until 1991* (Kampen: Kok, 1996), 254ff.

20. See A. Antón, "Santo Domingo: IV Conferencia General del Episcopado Latinoamericano. Su sta- tus teológico y el valor magisterial de su documento conclusivo," *Gregorianum* 73, no. 3 (1992): 437–67. This contribution was later referred to by J. J. Legorreta Zepeda, "Las conferencias episcopales en el debate teológico postconciliar," *Revista iberoamericana de teología* VII/13 (2011): 31–55.

21. See V. Codina and J. Sobrino, *Santo Domingo '92: crónica testimonial y análisis contextual* (Santander: Sal Terrae, 1993), and J. O. Beozzo, "Dom Luciano. Compaixão e Misericórdia, Inteligência e Lucidez," in *Deus é Bom—Homenagem a Dom Luciano*, ed. M. H. Arrochellas (São

Paulo: Paulinas, 2008[2]), 199–209. A few references are also in C. Mendes, *Dom Luciano, o Irmão do Outro* (São Paulo: Paulinas, 2007).

22. See A. Melloni, "Per il papa esiste una sola America," *Limes* 4 (2003): 179–86, and the previously mentioned contributions by Myriam Wijlens.

23. See A. López Trujillo, "A los treinta años de la Conferencia de Medellín. Consideraciones particulares" in *L'Osservatore Romano* (Spanish ed.) of January 22, 1999, and G. Doig Klinge, "Las Conferencias Generales del Episcopado Latinoamericano: Rio de Janeiro, Medellín, Puebla y Santo Domingo," in *Los últimos cien años de la evangelización en América Latina. Centenario del Concilio Plenario de América Latina*, ed. L. Ferroggiaro and V. M. Ochoa Cadavid (Vatican City: Libreria Editrice Vaticana, 2000), 373–404. See also C. Calderón, "Cómo leer los documentos del episcopado latinoamericano," *Anuario de historia de la Iglesia* 12 (2003): 338–41.

24. See in particular V. M. Fernández, *Aparecida. Guía para leer el documento y crónica diaria* (Buenos Aires: San Pablo, 2007), 10–13.

25. See F. J. Errázuriz, OSSA, "La Preparación de la V Conferencia General del Episcopado latinoamericano y del Caribe," *L'Osservatore Romano* (Spanish ed.) February 23, 2007 and March 2, 2007.

26. See Fernández, *Aparecida*. We also refer to our contribution at www.statusecclesiae.net and titled *La conferenza di Aparecida. Dietro il testo un cambiamento di clima?* written immediately after the conference, and based on the testimonies and documentation of several participants in the meeting and from the daily information provided by various sites, particularly that of CELAM (www.celam.org), but also www.amerindiaenlared.org, www.aica.org, http://observatorioeclesial.org.mx/boletin-alas, etc.

27. On the episode of the Notification and Explanatory Note and its texts, we refer to *Il Regno—Documenti* (7/2007): 225–32; and, by way of example, the dossier on Jon Sobrino in *Concilium* (3/2007): 171–82.

28. These were, in particular, Óscar Rodríguez Maradiaga, Andrés Stanovnik, Mario Cargnella, Santiago Silva, José Luiz Lacunza, and Pablo Bonavía, Gustavo Gutiérrez, Maria Clara Bingemer, Carlos Mesters, and José Oscar Beozzo. We thank Oscar Beozzo for sharing his notes with us.

29. For a presentation of this group, see www.amerindiaenlared.org/quienessomos.

30. See, among others, P. Suess, "V Conferencia del CELAM, 2007. Amerindia en Aparecida: participación de los teólogos de la liberación," in *Construyendo puentes entre teologías y culturas. Memoria de un itinerario colectivo*, ed. R. Hermano and P. Bonavía (San José: Editorial DEI, 2012), 241–47.

31. In addition to the aforementioned volume by Víctor Manuel Fernández, *Aparecida*, among the now abundant literature worth mentioning are the following: M.C. Bingemer, "La V Conferenza dell'episcopato latinoamericano. La sfida della fede e il lavoro dell'ermeneutica," *Concilium* (4/2007): 159–72; J. B. Libânio, "Conférence d'Aparecida. Cinquième conférence de l'épiscopat latino-américain et des Caraïbes" *Études* 407/11 (2007): 498–509; the collective volume edited by Amerindia, *V Conferência de Aparecida. Renacer de uma esperança* (Montevideo: Amerindia; São Paulo: Paulinas, 2007); A. Brighenti, *Para entender Aparecida. El pretexto, el contexto y el texto* (Mexico City: Dabar, 2008).

32. See CELAM, *Hacia la V Celam. Discípulos y misioneros de Jesucristo, para que nuestros pueblos en Él tengan vida. "Yo soy el camino, la verdad y la vida" (Jn. 14, 6), Documento de participación* (Bogotá: CELAM, 2005).

33. See the *Síntese das contribuições da Igreja no Brasil à Conferência de Aparecida* of November 2006. The critical bibliography with respect to the *Documento de participación* is too abundant to be exhaustively listed here. We limit ourselves to mentioning some contributions by P. Trigo and V. Codina, "Elementos teológico-pastorales que no pueden estar ausentes en la V Conferencia," *Revista latinoamericana de teología* 23 (2006): 286–97; A. Brighenti, "El Documento de participación de la V Conferência," *Pasos* 123 (2006): 95–118; L. D. Valentini, "Expectativas da Quinta Conferencia," *Perspectiva teológica* 34, no. 1 (2007): 4–18; and the collective volume by several Amerindia theologians, *Aportes para Aparecida* (Montevideo: Amerindia, 2006).

34. See the *Documento de síntesis: CELAM, Síntesis de los aportes recibidos para la V Conferencia General del Episcopado Latinoamericano* (Bogotá: CELAM, 2007).

35. See the recent L. D. Valentini, "Los 'Buenos Aires' de Aparecida," in *Aparecida. Por un nuevo tiempo de alegría y esperanza en la vida ecclesial*, ed. E. Robles (Barcelona: Herder, 2014), 217–19.

36. On this point, see, among others, L. D. Valentini, "Aparecida: valores e limites," and A. Brighenti, "Crônica do desenrolar da V Conferência," both in Amerindia, *V Conferência de Aparecida*, 9–21 and 25–33.

37. For the official list of participants, see the special issue of *L'Osservatore Romano* (March 31, 2007): I–III.

38. See the regulation of the conference, submitted by CELAM (esp. art. 2).

39. See our *In populo pauperum*, 347.

40. See J. O. Beozzo, "El proceso participativo del Fórum brasileño," in Robles, *Aparecida. Por un nuevo tiempo de alegría y esperanza*, 29–36.

41. See the letters of J. O. Beozzo (whom we thank for sharing them) to Cardinal Francisco Javier Errázuriz Ossa and Geraldo Majella Agnello,

Conference Presidents along with Cardinal Re, respectively, of June 29 and 19, 2006. In the letter to Cardinal Errázuriz it was asked, inter alia, to restore the electoral eligibility of the working committees by the assembly: "The Rules of Procedure of the V Conference states that it is within the competence of the Presidency of the Conference, in collegiate form, 1.4: *to establish and integrate the commissions they deem necessary and to monitor their proper functioning.* At the council, after Cardinal Achille Liénart had requested the interruption of the first session to allow the bishops to consult with each other, the commissions were constituted based on the election of their sixteen members by the conciliar assembly; the pope then appointed eight other members. It can be said that the council, in the form in which it unfolded, began from there with this sovereign gesture of the assembly which had profound repercussions on the next course of events. In Medellín and Puebla all the commissions were elected. In Santo Domingo, however, there was a deadlock, as there were already ready and closed lists; nonetheless, the assembly voted, which led, for example, to the election of Dom Luciano Mendes de Almeida for the drafting committee. It would be a gesture of deep respect for the assembly, thus reviving the great synodal and collegial tradition restored by Vatican II, if all commissions were elected by the Aparecida assembly. The regulation leaves the matter open and in the hands of the presidency, without determining the way in which the commissions are constituted. The fact that the assembly, with an act of free choice, can have its own working bodies, creates a climate of trust and co-responsibility and brings a breath of fresh air for subsequent works."

42. We refer, among others, in this regard to the editorial published in *Concilium* (5/2009): 13–18 (issue edited by S. Scatena, J. Sobrino, L.C. Susin, and titled "Padri della chiesa in America latina"). In a more general sense, see in particular some considerations of H. Legrand, "Il primato romano, la comunione tra le chiese e la comunione tra i vescovi," *Concilium* (5/2013): 90–109.

43. In Amerindia, ed., *Observatorio Eclesial, ¿Una nueva época? Elementos sobre la actual coyuntura ecclesial* (Montevideo: Amerindia, 2013), 21.

44. See J. O. Beozzo, "Il primo papa latino-americano," in *In Argentina per conoscere Papa Bergoglio*, ed. F. Strazzari (Bologna: EDB, 2013), 5–27. But on Bergoglio's experience at Aparecida, see in particular the *crónica diaria* by Victor Manuel Fernández in *Aparecida*.

45. For a synoptic table, see R. Muñoz, "As mudanças no Documento de Aparecida," in Amerindia, *V Conferência de Aparecida*, 277–95.

IV

THE REFORMS OF THE UNIVERSAL CHURCH AND THE PARTICULAR CHURCHES

13

PRIMACY AND EPISCOPAL COLLEGIALITY

Problems and Perspectives

Severino Dianich

Introduction

If the purpose of any reform, according to Pope Francis, is to make ecclesiastical institutions "more missionary" (*EG* 32), the problem of episcopal collegiality must also be framed by looking at the present world situation and following the intent of making the Church institutions increasingly able to relate to and communicate with the different contemporary cultures.[1]

The First Vatican Council had intended to respond to the urgent needs of the Church in a society in which the secularization processes appeared, to the more widespread Catholic consciousness, overwhelming. Pius IX became its spokesman in the bull of indiction of the Council, complaining that "not only our most holy religion, but also human society is so miserable and distressed."[2] As part of the *societas christiana*, dominant in the Catholic consciousness, only the pope's authority could act as a bulwark against what was considered the huge drift of the contemporary world. In 1856 Alexis de Tocqueville wrote that "the pope is driven more by the faithful to become an absolute ruler of the Church, rather they are impelled by him to submit to his rule."[3]

To this we should add the politics of the nineteenth century states, which tended to subordinate ecclesiastical institutions to their power. The nationalist wave, which among the Orthodox ushered in the birth of autocephalous churches, also constituted for the Catholic Church the risk of the emergence of national churches, whereby only the strengthening of papal primacy could continue to assure the authentic catholicity of the church.

Changes occurred in the meantime in society's culture and structure that pushed the Church in the opposite direction: the emergence, after the Second World War, of a mature secularism and the democratic government system, save the case of persistent dictatorships; in line with the growing pluralism of contemporary society, the strong sense, though sometimes exasperated, of individual liberties, of particular local identities with their different cultures; and the recognition, which occurred later with Vatican II, of the value of religious freedom. In the consciousness of the faithful, the need for everyone to participate in what is of interest and, therefore, the need for restoring synodal practices at all levels, has grown to the point of moving beyond the concentration of authority in the figure of the pope and in the institutions of the Holy See for a more robust exercise of episcopal collegiality.

A reform in this direction can immediately take its steps by means of special adjustments to the present legislation. But the consideration of the issues on a purely theological level needs to expand into wider horizons. The dynamics of reform cannot be set in motion without the participation of different actors and cannot but lead to their necessary succession. The first subject is the people of God, with the demands that emerge from ordinary ecclesial life, in view of a renewed promotion of evangelization in the contemporary world. An additional subject is represented by the theologians who, by their own methods, elaborate ideas and put forward proposals, which are also able to advance boldly forward, without fear of brushing against utopia. This is precisely the level on which our contribution moves. A third protagonist is represented by the canonists, without whose essential creation and proposal of new regulations *de jure condendo*, to submit to legislators, institutional reform would not be possible. The decisive final instance is, of course, that of the *suprema potestas* of the pope and the College of Bishops, appointed by God's will to the government of the Church.

The consideration of these four main factors will have to be considered when assessing this contribution. The theologian's task is to reflect on the imperatives of Scripture and tradition, starting with the needs of the people of God, regarding God's mission in the contemporary world. It is not the task of the theologian, but of the canonist, to formulate new norms in their own form. Even less so—as anybody with a sound mind would confirm—is it the task of the theologian to decide anything. This condition reduces, on the one hand, the role of theological reflection, while, on the other, it amplifies it, as it allows to delineate future paths, even daring and very advanced ones.

In this perspective, it seems difficult to outline properly the problems of a reform of ecclesiastical institutions without going the root of the problem through a critical investigation of the same basic system of the Code of Canon Law. Suffice to recall here that its editors in the introduction explicitly stated that they intended to exclude from the Code "norms on the external relations of the Church."[4] This results in an introverted regulatory system, a symptom of which is already the lexicon used, typical of a self-referential ecclesiastical language and extemporaneous with respect to the legal culture more prevalent today, to the point of not hesitating to use the term *subjects*, which civil ordinances, since the US Constitution of 1787, have banned as undermining the dignity of the human person. Therefore, there is a fundamental problem that needs to be addressed, which precedes that of episcopal collegiality: the reorientation of the Church toward the real purpose of its existence, the evangelization of the contemporary world.

The Unfinished Theology of Vatican II

One of the most important positions of Vatican II is the statement *LG* 21, with its solemn though not definitive tone, of the sacramental foundation of the episcopal ministry. This ends, once and for all, the dispute over the foundation of the episcopal ministry, which is thus recognized as an institution of divine right.

This leads to the overcoming of an exclusively judicial view of this ministry in which the bishop could be defined only on the basis of the *missio canonica* received by the pope and regardless of any collegial implication of his ministry.[5] The structure of the College of Bishops, however—despite the fact that *LG* 23 states that by "governing well their own church," the bishops " are effectively contributing to the welfare of the whole Mystical Body"—is still formed starting from the person of the bishop, each with his own sacramental charism, and not from the relationships that bind the churches and their pastors to each other. It has been observed that this could have happened because the constitution on the Church is still marked by the fact that its wording was developed as part of a more permanent universalist ecclesiology.[6]

From a more purely theological point of view, we can observe that the subject is developed from a single aspect of the sacrament, that is, from the transcendent value of the *actio Dei* at work in it, and not from the sacramental celebration, which is *actio ecclesiae*. If a Christian is a bishop for the sacrament received, by virtue of an *actio Dei*, his ministry cannot be confined within the *missio canonica* given to him by the pope: he is destined by divine right to the universal Church. The subject of the sacramental celebration (*actio ecclesiae*) of his ordination, however, is the liturgical action of a particular church, since the universal Church cannot be the empirically and visibly agent of the subject, since it has no *place* to celebrate and can operate only from within the action of a community *here and now* determined. Similarly, the only place in which the bishop may exercise his sacramental ministry will still be only a community *here and now* determined. There are no sacramental actions if not in interpersonal proximity: the position of a sacramental act is inconceivable at a distance—no sacramental absolution can be given by phone, nor the eucharistic communion delivered in a postal package.

The *munus docendi* and the *munus regendi*, from a judicial point of view, will be exercised by the bishop, collegially, even in relation to the universal church, but, if his *triplex munus* is sacramentally founded, it is very difficult to think of its realization independently from the exercise of liturgical preaching and the pastoral guidance of the faithful in a particular church. No one preaches if not to specific recipients who are given the opportunity to listen; no one can give the eucharistic unless men and women are present in the flesh; and there are no pastors without the responsibility of a flock. While it is true that today the episcopal college includes also bishops without their own *munus* in a local church, this is an anomaly created by anomalous situations, as that of bishops ordained during the schism, welcomed back into the episcopal body, or that of the bishops *in partibus infidelium,* who were deprived of their churches with the advance of Islam in Northern Africa.[7] Nor should anyone be in the position to imagine a College of Bishops composed of titular bishops, destined to govern the universal Church, regardless of "habitual and daily care" of souls (*LG* 27) in the particular churches.

Lumen Gentium 25–27 dedicated ample space to the description of the ministry and life of the bishop, and could not do it without referring to the experience lived in the local church. For the Council, the bishops "lead new disciples to Christ" (*LG* 25), "by the ministry of the word they communicate God's power to those who believe unto salvation (168) and through the sacraments... they sanctify the faithful" (*LG* 26), "as vicars and ambassadors of Christ, govern the particular churches entrusted to them by their counsel, exhortations, example, and even by their authority and sacred power" (*LG* 27). All this is possible only thanks to the daily presence of the bishop among his faithful. It is only in this integral view of the episcopal ministry that *Sacrosanctum Concilium* could have been able to argue that

> the pre-eminent manifestation of the Church consists in the full active participation of all God's holy people in these liturgical celebrations, especially in the same eucharist, in a single prayer, at one altar, at which there presides the bishop surrounded by his college of priests and by his ministers. (*SC* 41)

If, therefore, for the council the "pre-eminent manifestation of the Church" (*praecipua manifestatio ecclesiae*) is given in the celebration of the sacraments around the bishop, we must also assume that no manifestation of the universal Church, much less episcopal collegiality, can deviate from the reality of the particular church. It all comes from the fact that the sacramental order in its transcendence belongs to the universal Church, but not to the point of making in fact possible, or even conceivable (except for the hypothesis that in the world there is only one and small ecclesial community), a eucharistic celebration that has as its celebrant subject the universal Church. The Mass celebrated by the pope in St. Peter's Square is the Eucharist of the Roman Church, which welcomes in its celebration the faithful pilgrims from all over the world who have come to Rome to venerate the tombs of the apostles: the universal Church, even in this case, has no other place to celebrate the sacraments that is not a local church.

This character of proximity and locality of the sacramental economy is deduced immediately from a simple anthropological analysis of the very structure of the sacramental sign. But we could also advance to our purpose the axiom, "Never without the other," which Michel de Certeau proposed as a hermeneutical key for every protagonism of the Church:

> Every form of authority in Christian society, is marked by the absence of what it is based upon. Whether it is the Scriptures, traditions, council, pope, or anything else, what *allows it to be* is that which it *lacks*. Each authority *manifests* what *it is not*. Hence, the impossibility for each to be the whole, the "center," or the one. Only an irreducible *plurality* of authorities can indicate the relationship that each of them has with what it postulates as "Christian." As authorities, neither the pope nor the Scriptures, nor any other tradition, are enough; the others are lacking.[8]

He, therefore, concludes that "every Christian, every community and all Christianity" in the end is called "to be a *sign of what one lacks*."[9] Applying these acute observations to our problem, we must say that the authority of the College of Bishops over the universal Church is unthinkable without the authority of the bishops over their particular churches, as the figure of the pastor-bishop of a particular church is inconceivable without considering his collegial ministry in the universal Church. By virtue of the sacrament, which belongs to the universal Church, the bishop, when exercising his ministry in its particular dimension, should always be "a sign of what he lacks," that is, of his service to the universal Church. Similarly, the episcopal college must be a "sign and instrument" of that which, when operating at the service of the universal Church, "it lacks," that is, the ministry of each bishop in his particular church. Not for nothing did the tradition describe the ecumenical council as an entity *ecclesiam universalem repraesentans*: the College of Bishops gathered in council exercises its *suprema potestas* over the universal Church, establishing itself as the sign and instrument of the particular *potestas* of the individual bishops in their particular churches.

In conclusion, starting with the sacramental character of the episcopal ordination, what takes shape is the figure of a pastor-bishop of a particular church, who *also has* a universal ministry, and not of a bishop who has a universal ministry and *can also* be a pastor of a particular church. The conciliar determination of the episcopate as a sacrament must, therefore, be brought beyond the consideration of the transcendent character of the sacrament to the level of its exercise in the proximity of the shepherd to his flock.

The Regulations of the Holy See after the Council

More than of the absence of application tools of the principle of collegiality in the legislative acts of the Holy See after the Council, we must speak of a gradual rise of defense walls, for fear that its implementation could compromise the papal primacy.[10] Already during the Council Paul VI established a synod of bishops with purely advisory powers to stymie the debate on the possible creation of a permanent collegial body, thus conditioning the same dictate of *Christus Dominus*.

The new Code of Canon Law (1983) legislates on the exercise of the *suprema potestas* of the episcopal college without connecting it to the ministry of the bishops in the particular churches, deriving from it the right of all the bishops ordained, including titular bishops, to participate in ecumenical councils, and excluding any others from among the faithful.[11] For the preparatory commission of Vatican I, however, as the titular bishops are devoid of the power of jurisdiction over a particular flock, it was unclear if they were "successors of the apostles in the full sense," and therefore, if they had the right to participate in it.[12] The present Code, opting for the power of orders instead of that of jurisdiction, seems to reintroduce, in fact, in reverse, the old distinction between order and jurisdiction, which the Council had intended to abandon.[13] Consistently, can. 446, even to particular councils, compared to *CD* 36 (which remained rather laconic in this regard), is imposed the condition of the *recognitio* of the Apostolic See, despite the fact that the great tradition of the Church gave them also a doctrinal authority for the universal Church.[14] Canon 455 on the authority of a conference of bishops, quoting *CD* 38.4, limits it to these cases only " where universal law has prescribed it or a special mandate of the Apostolic See has established it either *motu proprio* or at the request of the conference itself" (§1). Otherwise, their decrees "do not obtain binding force unless they have been legitimately promulgated after having been reviewed by the Apostolic See (*nisi ab Apostolica Sede recognita*)" (§2).

It will be *Communionis Notio*, the letter of the Congregation for the Doctrine of the Faith in 1992, that tries to offer theological support to this legal norm, arguing that the universal Church is "a reality ontologically and temporally prior to every individual particular church." The wording of *Communionis Notio* is all played on the intricate, not to say ambiguous, use of the image of the living universal Church on earth, with its institutions and its specific structure, and the image of the "Church-mystery" living in the eternal plan of the Father. This thesis was immediately widely and authoritatively contested and, as the same author, Cardinal Ratzinger, acknowledged, there was "a storm of criticism over it from which it could hardly recover."[15]

Nevertheless, six years later, the *motu proprio* of Pope John Paul II *Apostolos Suos*, legislating on episcopal conferences, affirmed in no. 12 that the episcopal college "as an essential element of the universal Church, it is a reality which precedes the office of being the head of a particular Church." If it is so, we must ask whether it is still possible to say that a council is ecumenical when it is *universalem ecclesiam repraesentans* in the sense in which *LG* 23 stated that the bishops "with the Pope represent the entire Church [*totam ecclesiam repraesentant*]." In reality, no one ever imagined a council to represent the universal church, regardless of whether the individual bishops represent individual local churches. Among other things, to imagine an episcopal college "a reality which precedes the office of being the head of a particular Church" is impossible at least for the pope, who is part of it and is its head only because he is the bishop of a local church.

Supported by a previous statement by John Paul II, for which the episcopal college is one "indivisible theological subject,"[16] *Apostolos Suos*—adding at no. 12, "And this is the express will of the Lord"—excludes the possibility of a partial exercise of the collegial *potestas* over the churches of a given territory. A footnote cites *LG* 22, where the idea of the indivisibility of the college is stated and reaffirmed regarding the college's relationship with its head, not in reference to any particular implementation of the collegiality that would remain, albeit always in union with the pope. Therefore, *Apostolos Suos* 20 declared that the bishops, even if they wanted, "whether individually or united in Conference, cannot autonomously limit their own sacred power in favour of the Episcopal Conference." It is an interesting fact that in no. 17, the document is concerned to state that titular bishops hold the right to vote with deliberative power only if it is granted to them, "in order that a possible majority of the latter may not condition the pastoral government of the diocesan Bishops"—a concern that, to be honest, should have not gone missing in the Code regulation regarding ecumenical councils.

The conclusion to be drawn is that in the current legislatio,n the *potestas* of the episcopal college remains viable only as an exercise of "supreme and full power over the whole Church" (*Nota explicativa praevia* 3) and therefore only in ecumenical councils. The synod of bishops is not an expression of the college's *potestas*, as it has no jurisdictional powers. All the other collegial expressions of the episcopate, excluding a few specific cases contemplated by common law, have no decisional power except through the *recognitio* of the Holy See, according to an explanatory note of the Pontifical Council for the legislative texts.[17] It is instead

> a typical act of the power of governance with which the act of the conference is completely revised and eventually changes are made to it as well. This is an additional

control and protection intervention, typical of the supreme authority.[18]

The critical observations made to this legislative process, after the Council, do not refer, of course, to its legitimacy; the entire Western Church recognizes in it the authority of the pope's *suprema potestas*. This does not mean, however, that the documents have the same value on the doctrinal level: John Paul II, in apostolic exhortation *Pastores Gregis*, clarified that if this "collegial nature of the apostolic ministry is willed by Christ himself....the various ways in which affective collegiality comes to be realized in effective collegiality belong to the human order" (*PG* 8). The theological arguments, therefore, put forward in the legislation motivation, can and must be compared with the conciliar theology of the episcopate, distinguishing between what it is deduced, in effect, at the regulatory level and what can be consistently inferred in a perspective open toward the needs of the future.

The Consequences on the Future of the Ecumenical Council

After Vatican II no one could repeat what was said after the first Vatican Council, that is, that when the pope's infallibility was defined, it would be no longer necessary to convene an ecumenical council: the conciliar dimension of the Church is its essential structure. The Code, however, by creating the structure of a council of bishops convened only based on the sacrament received, did not provide the council with the quality of being adequately representative of all the churches. The ability of the council to be representative today is in question, because currently, of 5020 bishops, 2432, almost half, are titular bishops or emeriti.[19] Now, if the College of Bishops, "insofar as it is composed of many, expresses the variety and universality of the People of God, but insofar as it is assembled under one head, it expresses the unity of the flock of Christ" (*LG* 22), and if the bishops "with the Pope represent the entire Church "(*LG* 23), it is still necessary that the composition of the college corresponds to its nature to be "representative of the universal church."

The formula, in truth, became suspicious after the decree *Haec Sancta* of the Council of Constance[20] and its resuming by the dissident bishops who remained in Basel, after the pope had moved the council to Ferrara in 1437.[21] Yet, despite all this, in Ferrara the fathers of the *legitima continuatio* of Basel declared without any problem to be an assembly "representing the universal church."[22] At Trent, the formula was not used, but when it was discussed at the beginning of the council, it was decided to do without it in order to avoid the Protestants' scorn, as they were only a scattered group of bishops, fewer than forty. However, Francisco Pacheco would argue that the sense of the *repraesentatio* of the Church belongs to the ancient tradition, starting from Acts 15:28, and Girolamo Seripando, even though he thought it was inappropriate to use it, judged it dogmatically correct. If in the end it was not adopted, it was only because very few fathers were interested in using it.[23]

The problem of representation is, however, also a possible solution to the difficulty that the growing number of bishops is posing to the convening and functioning of a future ecumenical council. In reality, the number of bishops never should be considered a problem. Only a misleading image of the bishop as a high-ranking dignitary of the Catholic Church can create instinctive fears that a numerical growth will degrade his role and dignity; of course, the instinct of faith desires that churches multiply more and more on the earth and therefore, thus increasing the number of bishops. This is a fantasy of faith, not a cause for concern. The prospect, rarely envisioned by theologians and canonists, that one day there will be seven thousand, ten thousand, fifteen thousand bishops, creates the problem of the concrete possibility of summoning and running an ecumenical council. Modern communication technologies could perhaps provide everyone with the right to speak and the possibility of listening, advance proposals and counterproposals, discussions and common decisions, but the ecumenical council cannot be reduced to a videoconference meeting of a board of directors. The council, in fact, has a sacramental value: it is a sign and instrument of the communion of bishops and churches, it is choral invocation of the Spirit and the solemn liturgy of the

Church. We, therefore, need to develop a *theology* of representation, not a *jurisprudence*, which, however, already exists—a theology that does not distort the sacramental nature of the episcopate and allows the convening of a council of representatives.[24]

The hypothesis of such a council would have not have disturbed anyone in the ancient Church, because the ministry was not thought of in separate categories of order and jurisdiction. This was even so in the second millennium, before Vatican II, because the jurisdictional conception of the episcopate would have made it entirely obvious. However, in the past, the problem of a possible impracticality to celebrate a council because of a too-large number of bishops had never appeared on the horizon, whereas today, with the successful departure from the long season of a juridical conception of the episcopate, the problem seems to emerge in a new form. If the jurisdiction, considered in itself, is exercised by proxy, the same cannot be said for the sacramental *triplex munus*, in its entirety, and thus the council is not a purely juridical act. To summon, then, at the council some, and not all, seems an unacceptable limitation.[25]

The problem is to consider jurisdiction as an act within the sacramental substance of the episcopal ministry. A system of pure and simple delegation, created in any electoral assembly with a majority and a minority, as it is the case today for the Synod of Bishops, would give the council the appearance of a purely judicial body, unlike what would happen to the Eastern Church, where patriarchs or metropolitans would represent episcopal bodies already united by the election and ordination within them of their members, as well as by a regular collegial exercise of ministry in all their churches. Only a vital bond, within every particular *coetus* (assembly, grouping) of bishops, who should be represented by one of them at the council, based on the interlacing of election and ordination celebrated among them, would be able to confer the value of a lived sacramentality on the relationship between the represented and representatives. This is, in fact, a feature of the Eastern system, where bishops are elected by the patriarchal synod, ordained by the patriarch, and destined to a church belonging to the same patriarchy. This does not occur in the West, where the bishop is elected and appointed by the pope and can be ordained by anyone and be sent anywhere, in any local church. Consider the importance the genealogy of churches and bishops had in the determination of the valid apostolic succession of bishops in the first centuries. Only in this way would representation assume an iconic-sacramental quality, as befits the nature of an ecumenical council, and it would not be a purely juridical entity operating in a bureaucratic system of delegation.

Toward New Forms of Collegiality

Pope Francis acknowledged that the "papacy and the central structures of the universal Church also need to hear the call to pastoral conversion" (*EG* 32) and he has done that by complaining that the hope of a concrete realization of the sense of collegiality "has not been fully realized," believing that "excessive centralization, rather than proving helpful, complicates the Church's life and her missionary outreach." In this regard, he hopes that it will be "a juridical status of episcopal conferences which would see them as subjects of specific attributions, including genuine doctrinal authority," recalling the reference of Vatican II to the ancient patriarchal churches, of which the episcopal conferences should constitute a similar instrument (*EG* 26 and 32).

In the Western system, what makes the idea of partial forms, on a local basis, of the exercise of the real bishops' *potestas* on a particular group of churches extemporaneous, in a certain sense, is the present form of an episcopal college radically homogeneous in its interior, made up of bishops, all of whom are dependent only on the Holy See, without the mediation, still typical in the Church, of the institutions of the metropolitan and patriarchate, with their unitary episcopal bodies, endowed with a collegial juridical structure for the pastoral governance of their local churches. A gradual exercise of the episcopal *potestas* belongs to the great tradition of the Church, which starts from the pastoral guidance of each bishop in his particular church, and rises to the government of a group of local churches, jointly exercised under the guidance of a *protos*, to finally reach, the exercise of its *suprema potestas, cum Petro et sub Petro*, on the universal Church. Not for nothing was the practice of particular councils the original form, prior to the practice of the ecumenical councils, of the collegial exercise of the episcopal ministry. The same Council of Trent considered anomalous the figure of a bishop dependent only on the pope, since it required him, where possible, to choose a metropolitan on whom to depend, at least to participate in provincial councils.[26] Finally, it was precisely to remedy the ensuing isolation of the bishops, each responsible in an isolated manner of the guidance of his church, that episcopal conferences were created.

Looking at the different situation of the Christian East, *LG* 23 considered the "several groups, organically united" of various churches as a fact that occurred throughout history "by divine providence," and alluded to the patriarchal churches as "parent-stocks of the Faith," which the missionary work "have begotten others as daughter churches." *Orientalium Ecclesiarum* hoped that "new patriarchates should be erected where there is need" (*OE* 11), which is enough, in addition to their persistence in the Eastern law, to ensure that the overcoming of the prohibitions of intermediate collegial instances, created by *Apostolos Suos*, poses no problem of a dogmatic nature.

The synod of bishops will certainly not be an antidote to that "excessive centralization" of the Church government lamented by Pope Francis; on the contrary, precisely its concrete experience is proving the great difficulty of reaching a common decision on so many problems that, from one part of the world to the other, are presented in such a diverse way. The national episcopal conferences, as they have originated, and as they are currently regulated, reveal a very weak theological structure, because they do not have at their base, like the patriarchates, episcopal bodies unified by a sacramental genealogy and internal relationships of interdependence. We should also reflect on the fact that their national character does not always reflect the ethnic and cultural unity of the people, thus creating a relationship with the states that is exposed to ambiguity, to the point of risking the involvement of the conferences of bishops in the crisis processes of the states themselves—not at all rare today—for the emergence of new aspirations for independence of earlier ethnic identities absorbed by national states. The Eastern system, however, is not exactly reproducible for the universal Church because, even though it is able to offer some interesting suggestions, the groups of churches are determined by their unique liturgical traditions and not by the church's need to fit into cultural and social forms of the population of the territory in which it is engaged in missionary work. This can be clearly seen in today's widespread diaspora of these churches that find themselves in some parts of the world surviving like islands in contexts totally different from their traditions and, moreover, with more than one in the same territory: in the Middle East, for example with just over three million Catholics, there are seven different patriarchates present. The episcopal conferences, in this respect, have the advantage of adhering to the territory and integrating themselves into the social and political situation of the population.

The arrangement of the Eastern tradition, however, offers the richness of a theology of the church founded on a sacramental system that is not mortified by the historical distinction between *potestas ordinis* and *potestas iurisdictionis*, which has characterized instead Western theology. A significant sign of this is the combining of the procedures for sacramental ordination and the settlement of the bishop as president of his church, which characterizes the appointment of bishops. The Council traces the picture beginning with the definition of the Eastern patriarch: "The bishop to whom belongs jurisdiction over all bishops, not excepting metropolitans, clergy and people of his own territory or rite, in accordance with canon law and without prejudice to the primacy of the Roman Pontiff" (*OE* 7). It preserves, however, immediately its mystical character, when, assuming the grace of the sacrament underpinning the pastor's paternity in the church is at work, it affirms that he "is set over his patriarchate as father and head" (*OE* 9). The patriarchal synod is "the highest authority for all business of the patriarchate, including the right of establishing new eparchies and of nominating bishops of their rite within the territorial bounds of the patriarchate, without prejudice to the inalienable right of the Roman Pontiff to intervene in individual cases" (*OE* 9). Implicit in all this, even because it is never questioned, is the sacramental character of the episcopate, to the point that can. 78, §1 of the Code of Canons of the Eastern Churches establishes that the patriarch "cannot constitute a vicar for the whole patriarchal Church, nor can he delegate his power," which thus appears determined by the *potestas ordinis*, as the jurisdiction is always delegable. This is also revealed by the norm according to which the power of nominating bishops lies with the synod, while the patriarch is responsible for the ordination and enthroning.[27] It is no surprise, therefore, that in the liturgy, after the pope and before the local bishop, the patriarch is commemorated by name. The difference with the president of a bishops' conference is, therefore, radical, given the statutory irrelevance of the former, who is simply the chairman, holds office for a brief time, and does not have any authority over other bishops. But, going deeper to the bottom of things, the bishops cannot acknowledge, in any way, in the whole of the churches and their pastors that make up the conference, the sacramental body from which their election originated and in which was celebrated their sacramental ordination, as is the patriarchate for the Eastern bishops, in which is made their appointment, ordination and, of course, the enthronement at a local church of the same patriarchate.

To restore the traditional practice of the exercise of episcopal collegiality in the Western system, not only as an expression of "concern for all the churches," but as a true and proper exercise of episcopal *potestas*, we should finally see its overcoming in canonical law, not only in theological texts, but also in the distinction between order and jurisdiction. Its logical consequence is the pope's taking upon himself the appointment of bishops. This implies, in principle, that the newly elected can then be ordained by anyone and sent to any local church in the world. This creates an episcopal college in which the jurisdictional relationships remain loosened from the sacramental fabric, which a real integration of appointment, *missio canonica*, and ordination within a given episcopal entit, would be able to generate and consolidate. This would ensure the overcoming of some forms of ecclesiastical practices that risk transforming, in the eyes of the people of God, the bishop, sent by the pope and coming from who knows where, into an outsider, while allowing the same bishop to overcome the risk of focusing, in his pastoral role, more on Rome than on the needs of his people.

This does not mean that the Eastern system is not concerned with making sure that everything happens and remains in communion with the pope of Rome.[28] However, the fact that, in the Eastern churches, bishops are appointed by the patriarchal synod and ordained by the patriarch or metropolitan allows each particular body of churches, with their bishops, to become a unique organism of both a sacramental and legal nature. It appears to be consistent then that, unlike what happens to episcopal conferences, the decisions of patriarchal synods have no need to be submitted to the *recognitio* of the Holy See.

In conclusion, in the Catholic Church today we are still in the presence of two systems consistent with two profoundly different theologies of the episcopate.[29] And the comparison between the two systems reveals the inconsistencies of the Western one with the doctrine of Vatican II on the sacramental nature of the episcopate. Anyone can see that the overcoming of this situation would further favor a rapprochement with the Orthodox Church.

An Episcopal Ministry for Different Peoples and Cultures

In the wide and profound reflection, as well as in the debates, stirred positively in the Catholic Church during the Council, the awareness that the episcopate had a vital need to regenerate itself over time developed in a lively manner, seeking an ever-greater adherence to the life and history of the churches in their differences across various territories, integrating more and better with the different peoples, their traditions, their culture, and their social and political problems.

The possibility and opportunity was not ignored, then, of the creation of bodies of particular churches and episcopal colleges with an exercise of their *potestas* in intermediate form between that of the individual bishop and the *suprema potestas* of the pope and the college on the universal Church. Joseph Ratzinger, one of the conciliar experts, argued that the right to determine the liturgical legislation, the election and deposition of bishops, and other similar disciplinary functions were not part of the primacy, but of those patriarchal tasks that, especially after the separation from Rome of the great patriarchal churches, played a role in determining even those of the papal primacy. For the problems that had emerged, he saw the solution precisely in the creation of particular episcopal classes that he called *patriarchale Räume*, so as not to reproduce, in every detail, the systems of the patriarchates.[30] Among theologians, the idea did not fall on deaf ears. Later, Yves Congar observed the incongruity of the model of a *Western* church that goes from Rome to Japan, and advanced the hypothesis of the possibility of creating patriarchies of Africa, of Latin America, and the Indies.[31] Walter Bühlmann, in a book that at the time had great resonance, proposed a kind of new pentarchy on a continental basis, as he believed, with good reason, that the marked cultural unity of the five continents were relevant in determining the life of local churches.[32] The experiences of the Latin American bishops, from Puebla to Medellín to Aparecida, as those of the bishops of Asia and Africa, would have quite a few things to teach.[33] It is also interesting to note that already before the First Vatican Council, while discussing the codification of canon law, three hypotheses were advanced: that of a single Code, which in the end prevailed, but also that of two, or several different codes.[34]

The fundamental criterion of the eventual creation of intermediate episcopal colleges, unlike the Eastern system that prefers the continuity of the different liturgical traditions, wherever an ecclesial community is to be found, should be that of the adherence of the ecclesiastical structures to cultural traditions and life situations of the territories on which a certain number of churches are to be found. This would also result in a criterion of belonging of the faithful to this or that group of churches not based on family tradition or personal choice, but on the territory in which they live and where they are called to fulfill their mission as Christians. The constitution of territorial episcopal colleges, possible at distinct levels and with different dimensions, would not only be an opportunity to implement the "concern for all the churches," but rather the place of a real exercise of the episcopal *potestas* on a certain group of churches. Their fundamental amalgam should remain the sacramental root constituted by the communion of bishops appointed and ordained within their group, however always in communion and with the consent of the pope, but so that the self-regeneration of every episcopal *coetus* makes their ministry internally homogeneous and more responsive to the *sensus fidei* and the context of their people.

A system of this kind, moreover, would allow the creation of plausible forms of representation in the composition of the ecumenical councils, to ensure the survival of the conciliar practice, otherwise jeopardized by the growing number of bishops. The determination of the representatives would start from the reality of the local episcopal colleges, as they are unified by the transmission of the sacrament. It would therefore be able to make a decisive contribution to the character of the council, as the voice of all the particular churches. This is a fact that has already proved to be a key factor in the dynamics of Vatican II, through the common proposals of episcopal conferences.[35] The auxiliary and emeriti bishops, for their links with the local church, would naturally fall in the processes of representation of each particular episcopal college. Titular bishops at the service of the Holy See, on the other hand, could not be represented from within a particular episcopal college, because in reality they represent the pope. The pope carries out his ministry of primacy in the council for the Lord's will, already and only because he is the successor of Peter. It would be, to say the least, improper to broaden his decision-making capacity at the time of voting. It would be reasonable, however, that titular bishops serving the Holy See would send their representatives to the council, to advance the requests of the individual sectors in which they serve for the good of the universal Church.

Conclusions

Pope Francis, hoping for a "pastoral conversion" of the papacy and central structures of the universal Church (*EG* 32), quotes John Paul II: "All renewal in the Church must have mission as its goal if it is not to fall prey to a kind of ecclesial introversion."[36] For any reform project one can imagine, it is vital not to lose sight of the necessity of the whole Church to come out of its centuries-long introversion.[37] Further, the Code of 1917, regarding the bishops' commitment to evangelize the "non-Catholics" (!) of their territory, invited the bishops to consider them "entrusted to them in the Lord" and reserved the "whole care of the missions" in "non-Christian countries," exclusively to the Holy See (can. 1350). After quoting Vatican II on evangelization as a "fundamental duty of the people of God" (can. 781), the current Code dedicates to missionary activity a meager twelve canons and confirms the principle that "the Roman Pontiff and the college of bishops have the supreme direction and coordination of endeavors and actions which belong to missionary work and missionary cooperation" (can. 782, §1), leaving to the bishops, with respect to this commitment, only a "special solicitude" (can. 782, §2). And still now, after forty years since *La France pays de mission?* of the Abbés Daniel and Godin,[38] the Code persists in the idea that "the specifically missionary action" applies only to the territories in which the Church "has not yet taken root" (can. 786), as if the evangelization of non-Christians is not an urgent task today even in the countries of ancient Christian tradition.

The Council, on the other hand, in *AG* 20 had stated that the church should "realize that it has been sent to those also who are living in the same territory with it, and who do not yet believe in Christ." It was followed immediately by the concern "that episcopal conferences should form a common line of action" in certain regions and adopt, where there are "groups of men are to be found who are kept away from embracing the Catholic Faith because they cannot adapt themselves to the peculiar form which the church has taken in there," those "special measures" needed in appropriate circumstances. Thus *AG* 22, stating that it is "be hoped that episcopal conferences within the limits of each major socio-cultural territory will so coordinate their efforts that they may be able to pursue this proposal of adaptation with one mind and with a common plan," reunited the discourse on evangelization to a form of collegiality to be exercised at the local level.

The churches of countries of ancient Christian tradition today seem incapable of adequately addressing the new situation that has arisen with the increasingly massive presence in their territories of non-Christians and Christians who have abandoned the faith. But surprisingly, even the churches founded by European and American missionaries on other continents are afflicted, in many cases, by an impressive lack of missionary initiative, almost as if local churches did not have the duty to evangelize their people and had to wait for the Holy See to send missionaries to their peoples. Therefore, it will not be the persistence of the current centralism of the government of the universal Church to unlock the situation. Only local bishops can foster the renewal of evangelization in their territories, by engaging with the culture, language, costumes, and sociopolitical situation in which their peoples live. From the very beginning, from the different versions with which Paul and the apostles translated the gospel message in the various situations in which they found themselves, there is a fundamental lesson to learn. It is clear for all to see that the evangelization of Europe is different from that in Africa, or New Zealand, or China. Moreover, as soon as we are fully engaged with the creation of new churches, with a broader communication of the faith and, hopefully, with more extensive practice of adult baptism, we will touch firsthand how every new church that is built among a people changes the face of the universal Church, for already every new believer who enters a church changes its entire face—by bringing their unique life experience.

Only a Christian tradition that originally developed within the great Hellenistic *ecumene*, where Greek was spoken everywhere and identical temples, baths, and theaters were built in the Pontus and Iberian regions, and in Britain, could have created the idea of a church that could speak one language and have one single order—an idea that at the end of the millennium could not avoid colliding dramatically with the differences between the East and the West. Today the coexistence, on the one hand, of the phenomenon of globalization, and, on the other, of the preservation of the singular identities of people and social groups, is urging the Church to reinvent the forms of her mission, to be up to the task of bringing the human person, in its singularity, to communion with God and of being, at the same time, at the service of the unity of mankind, in the different regions of the world.

NOTES

1. Y. M. Congar, *Vraie et fausse réforme de l'Église* (Paris: Cerf, 1968), 511: "Today's reform arises from apostolic concerns and from the desire for an effective witness that priests and laity ask for." Translated as *True and False Reform* (Collegeville, MN: The Liturgical Press, 2011), 337.

2. Pius IX, Bull *Aeterni Patris* (*EE* 2, 795).

3. K. Schatz, *Il primato del papa. La sua storia dalle origini ai nostri giorni* (Brescia: Queriniana, 1996), 199–210; J.-M. R. Tillard, *L'évêque de Rome* (Paris: Cerf, 1982), 32ff.

4. *Code of Canon Law*, preface: http://www.vatican.va/archive/eng1104/_index.htm.

5. On the question in its historical course, see L. Villemin, *Pouvoir d'ordre et pouvoir de juridiction. Histoire théologique de leur distinction*, afterword by di Hervé Legrand (Paris: Cerf, 2003); A. Dusini, "Il decreto dogmatico sul sacramento dell'ordine sacro promulgato nella sessione XXIII del concilio di Trento," in *Il concilio di Trento e la riforma tridentina. Atti del convegno storico internazionale. Trento, 2–6 settembre 1963* (Rome: Herder, 1965), 2:577–613; S. Dianich, "La teologia del presbiterato al concilio di Trento," *La scuola cattolica* 99 (1971): 331–58, and Dianich, *Teologia del ministero ordinato* (Cinisello Balsamo: Edizioni Paoline, 1993[3]), 52–69. Regarding the consequences on the papacy's theology of passing from a jurisdictional to a sacramental structure, see S. Dianich, *Per una teologia del papato* (Cinisello Balsamo: San Paolo, 2010), 81–118.

6. S. Noceti, "Commento al capitolo III di Lumen gentium," in *Commentario ai documenti del Vaticano II*, vol. 2, *Lumen Gentium*, ed. S. Noceti and R. Repole (Bologna: EDB, 2015), 220.

7. It is significant that *Pastores Gregis*, the apostolic exhortation of John Paul II (2003), felt the need to justify the existence of titular bishops in no. 8. He does so by leaning on the *motu proprio* of 1998 *Apostolos Suos*, which in no. 12 states, "The College of Bishops…is a reality which precedes the office of being the head of a particular Church," and which in turn justifies this statement (see n55) since "there are many Bishops who are not heads of particular Churches, although they perform tasks proper to Bishops."

8. M. De Certeau, *La faiblesse de croire* (Paris: Seuil, 1987), 215.

9. Ibid.

10. See the detailed analysis of Hervé Legrand: "La collegialità dal Vaticano II in poi," in *Primato e collegialità. "Partecipi della sollecitudine per tutte le Chiese,"* ed. R. La Delfa (Rome: Città Nuova, 2008), esp. 106–12.

11. The composition of the council according to the current Code of Canon Law is an absolute novelty in the history of the Church: in fact, still according to can. 223, §1 of the1917 Code, abbots and *praelati nullius*, the abbot primate, the abbots-presidents of monastic congregations, and the general superiors of the exempt clerical congregations participated in Vatican II.

12. U. Betti, *La Costituzione dommatica Pastor aeternus del Concilio Vaticano I* (Rome: Pontificio Ateneo Antonianum, 1961), 10n19.

13. E. Corecco and L. Gerosa, *Il diritto della Chiesa* (Milan: Jaca Book, 1995), 177. The authors lament that the most important novelty of Vatican II, that is, "the unified concept of *sacra potestas*, has not been incorporated in the new Code."

14. It was only after the Council of Trent that the *recognitio* of the Holy See was imposed on particular councils: see Sixtus V, apostolic constitution *Immensa Aeterni Dei*, of January 22, 1588, in *Bullarium Romanum*, ed. Taurinense, VIII (1863), coll. 985–88.

15. Joseph Ratzinger, "The Ecclesiology of the Constitution on the Church, Vatican II, 'Lumen Gentium'": http://www.ewtn.com/library/curia/cdfeccl.htm.

16. John Paul II, Christmas greetings to the members of the Roman curia and prelature (December 20, 1990): https://w2.vatican.va/content/john-paul-ii/it/speeches/1990/december/documents/hf-jp-ii_spe_19901220_curia.html.

17. The juridical nature and extension of the *recognitio* of the Holy See (April 28, 2006): http://www.vatican.va/roman_curia/pontifical_councils/intrptxt/documents/rc_pc_intrptxt_doc_20060428_recognitio_it.html.

18. Nonetheless, the above Note states that the documents of the conferences of bishops "remain, however, also because of their binding force, of the same authority that issues them."

19. *Annuario Pontificio 2015* (Vatican City: Libreria Editrice Vaticana, 2015), 1140.

20. Council of Constance, Session 5, April 6, 1415 (*COD* 409).

21. H 1309; Y. M. Congar, *L'Église. De saint Augustin à l'époque modern* (Paris: Cerf, 1970), 327ff.

22. Council of Basel-Ferrara-Florence, Session 2 (*COD* 514).

23. M. Cassese, "Girolamo Seripando, il concilio di Trento e la riforma della Chiesa," in *Geronimo Seripando e la Chiesa del suo tempo nel V centenario della nascita*, ed. A. Cestaro (Rome: Edizioni di storia e letteratura, 1997), 194. See also H. J. Sieben, *Vom Apostelkonzil zum ersten Vatikanum. Studien zur Geschichte der Konzilsidee* (Paderborn: Schöningh, 1996), 446–48.

24. On the category and practice of representation, see the classic study by Hasso Hofmann, *Rappresentanza-Rappresentazione. Parola e concetto dall'Antichità all'Ottocento* (Milan: Giuffrè, 2007).

25. This is already the case when the right to become a conciliar father is not recognized for Orthodox bishops, Old Catholics, and Lefebvrians, despite recognizing the validity of their ordinations.

26. Council of Trent, Session 24, *Decretum de Reformatione*, can. 2 (*COD* 761).

27. See the Code of Canons of the Eastern Churches can. 86, §1.

28. The pope is required to be informed "as soon as possible" of the creation of a new patriarch, who will have to obtain the *litterae communionis*, and the appointment of bishops is based on a list of candidates

that was first approved by the Holy See; see the Code of Canons of the Eastern Churches, can. 110, §3; 76, §§1 e 2; 183, §2; 184.

29. Congar, *L'Église. De saint Augustin à l'époque moderne*, 101ff.: "The Ecclesiology of the Latin church followed the path that we already know: the development of papal authority, juristification, clericalization, a challenge to secular power which brought the church to see itself as a power....The structures of horizontal or conciliar catholicity will be overshadowed by the structures of vertical Catholicism and centralization..., a development that would not have happened if the Latin West had maintained a truly active communion with the East and Rome had not been so closely tied to specifically Latin concepts."

30. T. Weiler, *Volk Gottes—Leib Christi. Die Ekklesiologie Joseph Ratzingers und ihr Einfluss auf das Zweite Vatikanische Konzil* (Mainz: Grünewald, 1997), 240; H. J. Pottmeyer, "Primato-collegialità episcopale nella ecclesiologia eucaristica di Joseph Ratzinger," in La Delfa, *Primato e collegialità*, 71–90.

31. Y. M. Congar, *Église et papauté. Regards historiques* (Paris: Cerf, 1994), 29ff.

32. W. Bühlmann, *La terza Chiesa alle porte. Un'analisi del presente e del futuro ecclesiale* (Alba: Edizioni Paoline, 1975). Translated as *The Coming of the Third Church: An Analysis of the Present and Future of the Church* (Maryknoll, NY: Orbis, 1977).

33. On some of these institutions and the canonical limits in which they are subscribed, see M. Wijlens, "Exercising Collegiality in a Supranational or Continental Institution Such as the FABC, CCEE, and ComECE," *The Jurist* 64 (2004): 168–204.

34. C. Fantappiè, *Storia del diritto canonico e delle istituzioni della Chiesa* (Bologna: il Mulino, 2011), 256ff.

35. That all this has proved to be decisive in the tradition is proved by the councils prior to Trent: at Constance and Basel, for example, they would vote according to "nations"—not in the sense of modern nationalism but of guilds, which were characteristic of medieval society (K. Schatz, *Storia dei concili. La Chiesa nei suoi punti focali* [Bologna: EDB, 1999], 127ff.).

36. John Paul II, apostolic exhortation *Ecclesia in Oceania*, November 22, 2001, no. 19: http://w2.vatican.va/content/john-paul-ii/en/apost_exhortations/documents/hf_jp-ii_exh_20011122_ecclesia-in-oceania.html; Pope Francis, Ceremony Commemorating the 50th Anniversary of the Institution of the Synod of Bishops, October 17, 2015: http://w2.vatican.va/content/francesco/en/speeches/2015/october/documents/papa-francesco_20151017_50-anniversario-sinodo.html.

37. In 1987, I published this short essay: *Chiesa estroversa. Una ricerca sulla svolta dell'ecclesiologia contemporanea* (Cinisello Balsamo: Edizioni Paoline, 1987).

38. H. Godin and Y. Daniel, *La France pays de mission?* (Lyon: L'Abeille, 1943).

14

TOWARD AN *ORDO COMMUNIONIS PRIMATUS* (ORDER OF COMMUNION OF PRIMACY) AS DIACONAL PRIMACY*

Salvador Pié-Ninot

The papacy, "the most famous Western institution" (Arnold J. Toynbee), in its historical and institutional expression exceeds the theological essence of the Petrine ministry. Indeed, the Petrine ministry in its history has seen very remarkable developments in relation to its establishment in the New Testament and with its concrete realization in the various historical and ecclesial contexts, and it will only be at the end of the nineteenth century, with Vatican I (1870), that such developments gained dogmatic force with the definitions of the primacy of jurisdiction and infallibility *ex cathedra* of the pope. Conversely, freed from past forms, which crystallized in a very visible way in the division of Christians (in the

---

* See my synthesis and relative bibliography: S. Pié-Ninot, "¿Hacia un *ordo communionis primatus*?," *Gregorianum* 89 (2008): 5–26; "La dimensión jerárquica del ministerio petrino," in *El ser sacerdotal*, ed. G. Urribari (Madrid: San Pablo–Universidad Pontificia Comillas, 2010), 201–20; and *Eclesiología* (Salamanca: Sígueme, 2015³), 513–48.

year 1054, with the Eastern Churches, and in the sixteenth century, with the Reformation), the Petrine ministry, from the Second Vatican Council, in the context of an ecclesiology of communion, has been vigorously relaunched by the encyclical *Ut Unum Sint,* 1995. This papal document represents the most challenging and consequential in the ecclesiological and ecumenical context of the postconciliar period, beginning with Pope John Paul II's invitation to all "pastors and theologians of our Churches" to establish a "a patient and fraternal dialogue" in order to "find a way of exercising the primacy which, while in no way renouncing what is essential to its mission, is nonetheless open to a new situation," so that "this ministry may accomplish a service of love recognized by all concerned"(*UUS* 95).[1]

More recently, Pope Francis has raised this issue, emphasizing a more intraecclesial perspective, in his apostolic exhortation, *Evangelii Gaudium,* as a "a pastoral conversion" of the papacy in the section dedicated to "an ecclesial renewal which cannot be deferred" (*EG* 27–33), with these clear words:

> Since I am called to put into practice what I ask of others, I too must think about a conversion of the papacy. It is my duty, as the Bishop of Rome, to be open to suggestions which can help make the exercise of my ministry more faithful to the meaning which Jesus Christ wished to give it and to the present needs of evangelization. Pope John Paul II asked for help in finding "a way of exercising the primacy which, while in no way renouncing what is essential to its mission, is nonetheless open to a new situation". We have made little progress in this regard. The papacy and the central structures of the universal Church also need to hear the call to pastoral conversion. (*EG* 32)

In fact, the significant difficulty created by the recognition of the Petrine ministry by the other Christian Churches is well known, as Paul VI recalled (in his address to the members of the Secretariat for the Unity of Christians [April 28, 1967]) stating that "the Pope, as we well know, is undoubtedly the greatest obstacle on the path of ecumenism" and for this reason he implored forgiveness at the Ecumenical Council of Churches (see *UUS* 88). Aware of this reality, *Ut Unum Sint* locates the basis of its invitation to revise the exercise of this ministry in the Scriptures and in the common tradition, since "for a whole millennium Christians were united in 'a brotherly fraternal communion of faith and sacramental life.... If disagreements in belief and discipline arose among them, the Roman See acted by common consent as moderator'" (*UUS* 95, citing here *UR* 14).[2]

The Innovations Introduced by the Second Vatican Council and *Ut Unum Sint* on the Petrine Ministry Regarding the First Vatican Council

At the beginning of chapter 3 of *Lumen Gentium*, the two papal dogmas defined by the First Vatican Council (*LG* 18) are clearly ratified, but it should be noted that such ratification involves a series of developments and nuances proper to the sacramental and communional context of Vatican II. Thus, in *LG* 22 and 25, more directly referring to the dogmatic constitution *Pastor Aeternus*, the acts of Vatican I are quoted with various explanations that highlight the openness of both papal dogmas to the recognition of the proper power of bishops. In this sense, Vatican II performs a new hermeneutics, not previously performed in any ecclesial document, such as citing a precedent council with clarifications that come from its proceedings. All this is a clear sign of the historical difficulty of the first reception of Vatican I (worth noting here is that its complete proceedings were not published until more than fifty years later). Within this framework, here are the subtle "novelties" that Vatican II made to the two dogmas on the pope as defined by Vatican I, and their references in *UUS*:

1. First, in *LG* 18 and 23, Vatican II answers a key question: What is the meaning of the primatial ministry of the pope in the Church? And the answer can be formulated as follows: *the pope, as Peter's successor, is*

the "perpetual and visible foundation of unity" (Vatican I–II), which has the ministry, responsibility, and last word for the whole Church to be "united in one faith and one communion" (Vatican I–II). Peter's successor, then, takes on the role that Jesus assigned to Peter: that of being the foundation of faith (see Matt 16:18) and confirming believers (*confirma fratres tuos*: Luke 22:32), guiding them as a shepherd (see John 21:15–17). This is, therefore, the Catholic Church's self-understanding of the role of the Petrine ministry, even though its concrete form of exercising such ministry has undergone many changes in its long history. In addition, Vatican II complements this purpose of the pope's ministry with that of the bishops, affirming the importance—*cum et sub Petro*: *LG* 23—of "episcopal collegiality" in full responsibility for the whole Church (*LG* 22–23).[3] In *UUS* 88.94–95, these conciliar statements are resumed in a beautiful synthesis.

2. Second, it is worth bearing in mind a "novelty," strangely little observed by commentators, in this case due to an absence, since in the eight times that Vatican II uses the word *primacy* referred to the pope, it never adds the adjectival phrase *of jurisdiction* proper to Vatican I (*LG* 13, 18, 22(2x),45; *OE* 3, 7; *AG* 22). The same occurs thirty years after Vatican II with *UUS* 88, 89, 94, 95(3x). What is visible here is the will to interpret the primacy of the pope in the Church not in a political-civil way, which could be justified by the word *jurisdiction*, but in the form of the apostolic-sacramental ministry that the pope exercises as Bishop of Rome.
3. It is telling that in the first and last conciliar use of the word *primacy*, a reference to Ignatius of Antioch is made when it comes to the "the primacy of the Chair of Peter, which presides over the whole assembly of charity" (*LG* 13, *AG* 22; see *LG* 23). Thus, the primacy is situated in the sphere of the community of love that is the Church, since this is equivalent to Ignatius's *agápē*.[4]

4. The primacy associated with "the Chair of Peter" (*LG* 13 and *AG* 22) appears eight times referring to the "Roman See," seven of which are in an ecumenical context (*UR* 13(3x), 14(2x), 19; and *OE* 24; the remaining is *OT* 16). In this way, a process is delineated that goes from "the Primacy of the Church of Rome to that of its bishop," and for this reason *UUS* will privilege the use of the papal title "Bishop of Rome" (twenty-two times).[5]
5. The recovery of the title "Vicar of Christ" appears, also applied to the bishops (*LG* 27; see 20, 21), initially used by Cyprian (third century), followed by the Latin tradition (Ambrosiater, fourth century, Pope Hormisdas to the bishops of Spain, sixth century; Catulfo and Amalar of Metz, ninth century; and the abbot of Saint Germain-des-Près, tenth century; Thomas Aquinas; etc.); starting from Innocent III, thirteenth century, it was reserved for the pope and is consecrated at the Council of Lyons II (1274). *UUS* 95 will resume this qualification—unfortunately little used in the post-conciliar period—giving it to all the bishops as well.
6. In introducing the articulation between the power of the bishops and that of the pope, *LG* removed the complex qualification given by Vatican I to the papal authority as "ordinary and immediate"—adjectives only remembered in a magisterially minor document of Vatican II like *CD* 2. Instead, it subtly states that "this power, which they personally exercise in Christ's name, is proper, ordinary and immediate, although its exercise is ultimately regulated by the supreme authority of the Church, and can be circumscribed by certain limits, for the advantage of the Church or of the faithful" (*LG* 27).
7. In dealing with "such definitions of the Roman Pontiff are therefore irreformable of themselves (*ex sese*), not because of the consent of the Church" (a clear reference to Vatican I: see *DH* 3074), it is significantly added that this is because "they are pronounced with the assistance of the Holy Spirit" (*LG* 25).

8. For the first time in a Council it is stated that the authoritative word of the Church, which is the magisterium, "is not above the word of God, but serves it, teaching only what has been handed on, listening to it devoutly, guarding it scrupulously and explaining it faithfully" (*DV* 10). And in this context, it is noted that in addition to the infallible, solemn, and "extraordinary" magisterium of the pope defined by Vatican I, there is the "ordinary" magisterium, which is present only according to the use made of these three criteria: "the character of the documents, from his frequent repetition of the same doctrine, or from his manner of speaking" (*LG* 25).
9. And finally, the universal Church is innovatively described as a "body of churches" (*corpus ecclesiarum*) articulated "from" and "in" (*ex quibus et in quibus*) particular-local churches (*LG* 23) including the church of Rome, whose mission is, according to the beautiful Ignatian expression, to "preside over the whole assembly of charity" (*LG* 13,23; *AG* 22), which is how the whole Church is described.[6]

All these subtle "novelties" of Vatican II are grounded in the new understanding of the whole Church "like a sacrament" (*LG* 1; ten times during the Council), based particularly on the patristic tradition (Cyprian, Augustine, etc.), and specifically on the episcopate as "the fullness of the sacrament of Orders" (*LG* 21), as attested in the episcopal ordination rituals of the first millennium (see the reference in *LG* 21n19). This meant that Pope Paul VI in 1965 dispensed with the papal tiara, and resumed the episcopal miter, and subsequently this change was made visible in the papal coat of arms of Benedict XVI in 2005, and that of Pope Francis in 2013.

Another crucial element is the specification provided by *LG* 27, when it states,

> This power, which they personally exercise in Christ's name, is proper, ordinary and immediate, although its exercise is ultimately regulated by the supreme authority of the Church, and can be circumscribed by certain limits, for the advantage of the Church or of the faithful.

Indeed, this text emphasizes that that there is no talk of two concurrent powers, that of the pope and that of the bishops, but that each has a distinct role, since the bishop's own authority is that of the "habitual and daily care of their sheep," which however is "ultimately regulated" by the "supreme authority"—that is, the pope and the Episcopal College with him—"for the advantage of the Church or of the faithful." The relevant meaning of such a formulation is well described by the chief editor of *LG*, Gérard Philips, as follows:

> The term "ultimately" [*ultimatum*] is meant to express that Rome is not continually intervening in the administration of the other dioceses; the central authority distributes tasks and exercises the appeal function in the last instance to protect the bishops and their diocesans.[7]

Unfortunately, this distinction has often been forgotten in the postconciliar period, and has not been included in the Code of Canon Law, since more importance was given to the Preliminary Explanatory Note (*Nota explicativa praevia*)—more interpretive than constitutive at a conciliar level, with a strong primatial connotation—which stresses, at nos. 3 and 4, that the pope can act "according to his own discretion" (*propria discretio*) and "at will" (*ad placitum*). Not without theological finesse Joseph Ratzinger commented,

> It cannot be argued that both formulations are infelicitous!...and that the exercise of this power (of the Pope) resides simply in "his own discretion" and "at will" has not been stated so far in any ecclesiastical document. In fact, the Explanatory Note also adjusted the two formulations, adding the expression "taking account of the Church's welfare."[8]

In the context of the expression *ultimately*, various authors, both ecclesiologists and canonists—the latter dealing with the papal *recognitio* and *reservation*—stress that such a formula characterizes the way of the Petrine ministry is exercised. In effect, the expression *ultimately* typifies an exercise of primacy and infallible teaching particularly in cases of necessity and emergency, in limited and conflicting cases, or in exceptional situations requiring extraordinary measures—an exercise of the primacy that can be exercised when the competent body fails in its function or, in extreme cases, when there is negligence or need.[9]

This expression "ultimately regulated" helps to better define the "ordinary" power of the diocesan bishop and that of the pope, since the use of the same word for both can create confusion, and this was the reason for its omission regarding the pope in *LG*, even though it appears in a less significant—as mentioned earlier—magisterial document like *CD* 2. To clarify this difference, it is useful to recall the distinction present in the Joint Declaration of the German Bishops of 1875 in response to Otto von Bismarck on the First Vatican Council where the papal functions are distinguished as follows: (1) "In this position, the pope must see to it that each bishop fulfills his duty to the entire extent of his charge"; (2) in extraordinary circumstances, that is, "if a bishop is prevented from that, or if some type of need should be felt, the pope has the right and the duty, not by his rank as bishop of the diocese, but that of pope, to order everything which is necessary for the administration of the diocese" (*DH* 3113).[10] A paradigmatic example of the latter is expressed in the definition that the same Vatican I gives for situations in which the pope can exercise an infallible magisterium, where the "extraordinary" character is confirmed.

On the other hand, the Code of Canon Law resumes with some surprise the term *jurisdiction*, going beyond Vatican II, by asserting that "the power of governance, which exists in the Church by divine institution and is also called the power of jurisdiction" (can. 129, §1) where it essentially repeats the wording of the previous 1917 Code (can. 196), which showed the equivalence between the two. Angel Antón rightly and acutely observed,

> We are disappointed to see that the new *Codex iuris canonici* did not go deeper into the ecclesiological and canonical significance of the distinction introduced by Vatican II between *munus* and *potestas* regarding the subjects of ecclesiastical ministry, but decided rather to use again the term *potestas jurisdictionis*, from which the Council had moved away, being fully aware of the

> negative effects of the net distinction (in some authors ending up in *separation*) between the *potestas jurisdictionis* and the *potestas ordinis* had had on the evolution of the ecclesiological ideas. Even more lamentable than the use of the term *potestas jurisdictionis* was the decision to separate in the new *Codex iuris canonici* concerning the power of jurisdiction (*munus regendi*) from that concerning *munus docendi* and *sanctificandi*. This decision was equivalent to going back to pre-conciliar positions.[11]

Along this line of understanding, Walter Kasper aptly commented,

> The last Council did not reach a satisfactory synthesis or concrete solutions (regarding primacy); rather than the culmination of an evolution, Vatican II is the starting point of a new historical configuration of the primacy for the third millennium....This task requires, without further delay, the framing of Peter's ministry in a context that is not only ecclesiological, but also christological and theological, as well as a new interpretation, theological and practical, in light of the totality of the Gospel. Indeed, although the Church's doctrine of primacy can be accurately understood as a historical interpretation of the New Testament, its fault is that all its forms of thought and expression are not coined according to the biblical authority of the disciple, apostle, and pastor, but according to the "secular" model of *suprema auctoritas*.[12]

Some Perspectives

TOWARD A BETTER UNDERSTANDING OF PAPAL JURISDICTION?[13]

But going deeper, why does Vatican II dispense with the specific qualification *jurisdiction*—as well as the subsequent papal magisterium—especially in the passages quoting the text of Vatican I on the primacy? This omission is highly significant, albeit little noticed by ecclesiologists and canonists.[14] The reason for such an absence is based on the vision of Vatican II concerning the sacramentality of the Church and the episcopate, and above all the "sacramental power" in which the sacramental origin is the cause and the jurisdiction is situated at the level of its condition (see *LG* 22). Thus, the unitary vision of such sacramental power comes into view, in which "jurisdiction" is not another power but the condition that makes possible the execution of this sacramental power, which is the fruit of ordination.[15]

In this context, the pope's "jurisdiction" appears as a second dimension—which does not mean secondary—as a condition of possibility regarding the primary sacramental power that is constitutive, as shown by the virtually common theological belief that the ordinations of the non-Catholic Orthodox churches are considered valid. With the primacy of "jurisdiction," Vatican I basically wanted to remember that the pope has the "full and supreme power" and this was done on the basis of the notion, common at that time, of the double power (ordination/jurisdiction) in the Church.[16] When such a clear distinction, from a better historical knowledge, disappears, focusing on a single "sacramental power," it is no longer necessary to speak of the primacy "of jurisdiction" of the pope, just as Vatican II did, and it is advisable to continue in this way, as *UUS* exemplarily attests, which also omits this adjectival phrase.

In short, the ecclesial faith defined by Vatican I on the primacy "of jurisdiction"—the *res significata* (meaning) of this definition—affirms the full capacity and necessary authority of the pope that is needed for the truly decisive, binding, and "ultimate" fulfillment of the sacramental ministry bestowed upon him as Bishop of Rome, and therefore as the "primate" of the whole Church (cf. *LG* 22, 23, 25, 27). In this sense, the specific mission of the Petrine ministry has its formal reason in "the unity of faith and communion of the whole Church" (Vat. I: Proem: *DH* 3051; Vat. II: *LG* 18, and *UUS* 88), and in this line, the Congregation for the Doctrine of the Faith, "The Primacy of the Successor of Peter in the Mystery of the Church" (1998), and *UUS*, formulate with clarity the character of the jurisdiction, compared to its formal reason as faith and communion, recalling that it is a matter—as literally stated—of performing "acts of ecclesiastical governance necessary or suited to promoting and defending the unity of faith and communion" (no. 10).

On this question, in 2001 then Cardinal Ratzinger offered an illuminating reflection, which, starting with the title given to Pope Paul VI by Patriarch Athenagoras I of "first in honor" (*primus inter pares*) and of the "one who presides in charity," said to the Orthodox Metropolitan Damaskinos,

> I believe that we could correctly define "jurisdiction over the whole Church" on that basis: the "honor" of the first is not, indeed, to be understood in the sense of the honor accorded by worldly protocol; honor in the Church is service, obedience to Christ. Then again, *agape* is not just a feeling entailing no obligations, still less a form of social organization, but it is in the final analysis a eucharistic concept....If the Church in the very depth of her being coincides with the Eucharist, then the presidency of love carries with it a responsibility for unity, which has a significance within the Church yet...the pope is not an absolute monarch whose will is law, but quite the opposite—he always has to try to resist arbitrary self-will and to call the Church back to the standard of obedience; therefore, however, he must himself be first in obedience....A patristic interpretation of the primacy is in any case encouraged by the First Vatican Council itself, when it says that the constant practice of the Church stands for the teaching proclaimed there, as do ecumenical councils, especially those in which the East and West met together in unity of faith and love; here Vatican I refers to the Fourth Council of Constantinople.[17]

TOWARD AN *ORDO COMMUNIONIS PRIMATUS* AS DIACONAL PRIMACY

As an expression of the "pastoral conversion" of the papacy (*EG* 32), we should bear in mind the conciliar preference for the formulation of the hierarchy as *ministry* and *diakonia*, beautifully drawn in *LG* 24 ("a true service, which in sacred literature is significantly called 'diakonia' or ministry"), which is reflected in Gregory the Great's use of the papal title "servant of the servants of God" (*servus servorum Dei*), inspired by the Rule of St. Benedict (no. 64, 8) and that St. Bernard will convert in the papal motto "You preside over the Church to serve" (*praesis ut prosis*).[18] A papal title and motto that rightly qualifies the Petrine ministry is *diaconal primacy* at the service of "the unity of faith and communion," that is, with the mission of the *confirma fratres tuos* of Luke 22:32!

It is in this context that an *ordo communionis primatus* as diaconal primacy could be articulated, based on the "relation of reciprocity between the Roman Pontiff and the Bishops" (*PG* 56). If we examine the Code of Canon Law, it is established that it only regulates the hierarchical communion (*communio hierarchica*) of the bishops with respect to primacy (canons 336 and 375). On the other hand, however, a new perspective appears in the postsynodal exhortation *Pastores Gregis* of 2003, formulated as a "*relation of reciprocity* between the Roman Pontiff and the Bishops," the result of the principle of the ecclesial communion in which the Petrine ministry has the primacy. The text in question (*PG* 56) states,

> The reality of communion, which is the basis of all intraecclesial relationships and which was also emphasized in the Synod discussions, is a relation of reciprocity between the Roman Pontiff and the Bishops.... Consequently, in the communion of the Church, just as the Bishop is never alone but always related to the College and its Head and sustained by them, so also the Roman Pontiff is never alone but is always related to the Bishops and sustained by them. This is yet another reason why the exercise of the supreme power of the Roman Pontiff does not destroy, but affirms, strengthens and vindicates the ordinary, proper and immediate power of each Bishop in his particular Church.[19]

In this context, the most recent reflections of Pope Francis in the above-cited *Evangelii Gaudium*, on the relationship between the pope and the episcopate, should be integrated when he lucidly states,

> Nor do I believe that the papal magisterium should be expected to offer a definitive or complete word on every question which affects the Church and the world. It is not advisable for the Pope to take the place of local Bishops in the discernment of every issue which arises in their territory. In this sense, I am conscious of the need to promote a sound "decentralization." (no. 16)

To this is added the recognition of the local church as "primary subject of evangelization" (*EG* 30), where the irreplaceable role of the bishop has a particular responsibility to "encourage and develop the means of participation proposed in the Code of Canon Law, and other forms of pastoral dialogue" (*EG* 31). In turn, Francis acknowledges the importance of the Episcopal Conferences with this analysis:

> The Second Vatican Council stated that, like the ancient patriarchal Churches, episcopal conferences are in a position "to contribute in many and fruitful ways to the concrete realization of the collegial spirit." Yet this desire has not been fully realized, since a juridical status of episcopal conferences which would see them as subjects of specific attributions, including genuine doctrinal authority, has not yet been sufficiently elaborated. Excessive centralization, rather than proving helpful, complicates the Church's life and her missionary outreach. (*EG* 32)[20]

To conclude, a possible *ordo communionis primatus as diaconal primacy* of the Petrine ministry could be proposed in two forms of its exercise:[21]

a) The diaconal primacy of the Petrine ministry *in its "habitual and daily" exercise in the Church*, where the usual procedures of the relationship of the primate with the diocesan churches and their bishops are more "formally" needed. In fact, it would be desirable if the relation of reciprocity were made explicit, both for the bishops and for the Petrine ministry in the context of its decisive primacy for "communion," actualizing the very significant *visita ad limina,* as well as the two collegiate institutions of Vatican II: the episcopal conferences—further strengthening the regional bodies—and the *synod of bishops*—expanding its propositional force –as well as purifying the classic *"services" proper to the Apostolic See* (for example: by reducing their scope and coordinating them formally with the episcopal conferences endowed with new powers; reviewing how to promote to the episcopate; reducing the weight of diplomatic representatives for the benefit of the local episcopate). In this way, we could respond to Pope Francis's double call for "decentralization" (*EG* 16, 32).

b) The diaconal primacy of the Petrine ministry *in its "extraordinary and ultimate" exercise in the Church,* where it is stated "formally" that the primate acts in the presence of major causes (*causae maiores*) and special and extraordinary situations, whether of necessity, emergency, or urgency, by virtue of his personal, unique, definitive, and nontransferable responsibility, as primate in the Church that "ultimately regulates" always "for the advantage of the Church or of the faithful "(*LG* 27), keeping as its goal "the unity of faith and communion" (Vatican I, Vatican II, *Ut Unum Sint*), of which he must give an account only to God.[22]

To better clarify this extraordinary exercise it would be necessary to examine in greater depths the "major causes [*causae maiores*]," already cited by Innocent I (in 402) and formulated by Gregory VII's *Dictatus Papae* 21 (in 1075), as exclusive competence of the Roman See.[23] St. Thomas Aquinas himself will approve this formulation by founding the authority of the pope precisely in the fact that "he addresses the major and most difficult issues."[24] In this context it must be remembered that "the mission of Peter's Successor for the whole Church entails the right to perform acts of ecclesiastical governance necessary or suited to promoting and defending the unity of faith and communion."[25]

In this line we find the reference of Vatican I to the extraordinary magisterium of the pope with its definitions:

> When the Roman Pontiff speaks *ex cathedra*, that is, when, in the exercise of his office as shepherd and teacher of all Christians, in virtue of his supreme apostolic authority, he defines a doctrine concerning faith or morals to be held by the whole Church, he possesses, by the divine assistance promised to him in blessed Peter, that infallibility which the divine Redeemer willed his Church to enjoy in defining doctrine concerning faith or morals. Therefore, such definitions of the Roman Pontiff are of themselves, and not by the consent of the Church, irreformable of themselves, not because of the consent of the Church...[since] they are pronounced with the assistance of the Holy Spirit. (*DH* 3074, *LG* 25)

Bearing in mind, moreover, that

> undeniably the serious discussions that gave rise to the definition of Vatican I allow us to perceive better the distinction between the "sense of the Church" (*sensus Ecclesiae*), an organ of the tradition that the pope can never do without, and the "consent of the Church" (*consensus Ecclesiae*), which is not necessary.[26]

In this way, this *ordo communionis primatus* as diaconal primacy could make possible a better ecclesial vision of the proper character of the Petrine ministry and of the significance of the primacy of the Bishop of Rome for the whole Church, in the two forms of its diaconal primacy. And this without changing one iota while reaffirming the unique and nontransferable responsibility in the entire Church of the Bishop of Rome as the *perpetual and visible principle and foundation of unity*, which, when manifested as diaconal primacy within the ecclesial communion generates the "relation of reciprocity" (*PG* 36) with the bishops. And in this way, and "in no way renouncing what is essential to its mission," it might be possible—with due respect for a better opinion (*salvo meliori iudicio*!)—to approach the "new situation" of the papacy, espoused by *UUS* 95 and seen as "pastoral conversion" of the primacy (*EG* 32), within the fervent desire of Pope Francis to enable "an ecclesial renewal which cannot be deferred" (*EG* 27).

NOTES

1. Among the vast new general bibliography, see these already classic ones: J.-M. R. Tillard, *El obispo de Roma* (Santander: Sal Terrae, 1986) and K. Schatz, *El primado del Papa. Su historia desde los orígenes hasta nuestros días* (Santander: Sal Terrae, 1996); the following encyclopedias: P. Levillain, ed., *The Papacy: An Encyclopedia* (New York: Routledge, 2002); W. Kasper, ed., *Diccionario enciclopédico de los Papas y del Papado* (Barcelona: Herder, 2003); articles of the *LThK*[3] 1993–2001; and W. Klausnitzer, *Der Primat des Bischofs von Rom. Entwick—lung—Dogma—Ökumenische Zukunft* (Freiburg: Herder, 2004); the entries: G. Alberigo and S. Dianich, "Papa," in *Nuevo Diccionario de Teología*, ed. G. Barbaglio and S. Dianich (Madrid: Cristiandad, 1982), 1271–96 (originally published as "Papa," in G. Barbaglio and S. Dianich, eds., *Nuovo dizionario di teologia* [Cinisello Balsamo: Edizioni Paoline, 1988[5]], 1096–1121); S. Pié-Ninot, "Ministerio Petrino," in *Diccionario de Teología Fundamental*, ed. R. Latourelle, R. Fisichella, and S. Pié-Ninot (Madrid: Ediciones Paulinas, 1992, 2010[3]), 959–64; H. Legrand, "Pape," in *Dictionnaire critique de théologie*, ed. J.-Y. Lacoste (Paris: Presses universitaires de France, 1998, 2013[3]), 1018–21; and D. Valentini, "Primato romano," in *Dizionario di ecclesiologia*, ed. G. Calabrese, P. Goyret, and O. F. Piazza (Rome: Città Nuova, 2010), 1128–50.

2. For the ecumenical reception of *Ut Unum Sint*, see among others the assessment drawn up by the Pontifical Council for the Unity of Christians, "Le Ministère pétrinien," *Service d'information* 109 (2002): 22–47; the complete documentation by G. Cereti, *La Chiese cristiane di fronte al Papato: Il ministero petrino del vescovo di Roma nei documenti del dialogo ecumenico* (Bologna: EDB, 2006); the overview by J. F. Puglisi, ed., *How Can the Petrine Ministry Be a Service to the Unity of the Universal Church?* (Grand Rapids, MI: Eerdmans, 2010); and the synthesis by W. Kasper, "El ministerio petrino en el diálogo ecuménico," in *Iglesia Católica. Esencia, realidad, mission* (Salamanca: Sígueme, 2013), 391–397. See also W. Kasper, ed., *The Petrine Ministry—Catholics and Orthodox in Dialogue* (Mahwah, NJ: Paulist Press, 2006).

3. See among others, the synthesis by J.-M. R. Tillard, "The Mission of the Bishop of Rome: What Is Essential, What Is Expected?," *One in Christ* 34 (1998): 198–211, and the historical-theological assessment

by W. Henn, *The Honor of My Brothers: A Brief History of Relationship between the Pope and the Bishops* (New York: Crossroad, 2000).

4. Ignatius of Antioch, *To the Trallians* XIII, 1; *Rom* IX, 3; *Fil* XI, 2, and *Smir* XII, 1. Thus, in Ignace d'Antioche, *Lettres*, ed. P.-Th. Camelot (Paris: Cerf, 1969[4]), 107, which is the choice of Vatican II.

5. See *UUS* 4(3x); 24; 52; 55; 62; 88(3x); 89; 90; 92; 94(2x); 95(4x); 97(2x); 99, and on the Apostolic See/church of Rome, *UUS* 50; 52; 64; 95; 97(2x); 102.

6. See our analysis: "*Ecclesia ed Ecclesiae*," *Gregorianum* 83 (2002): 761–66.

7. G. Philips, *La Iglesia y su misterio en el Concilio Vaticano II* (Barcelona: Herder, 1968), 1:436. Even before the Second Vatican Council, G. Thils wished this to be "the coexistence of the pontifical jurisdiction and the jurisdiction of bishops....This is what mostly was missing at the First Vatican Council I, and it is perhaps here that the Second Vatican Council will be able to render a valid service to ecclesiology"; in "*Potestas ordinaria*," in *L'Épiscopat et l'Église universelle*, ed. Y. M. Congar and B. D. Dupuy (Paris: Cerf, 1962), 689–707.

8. J. Ratzinger, "La colegialidad episcopal," in *La Iglesia del Vaticano II*, ed. G. Baraúna (Barcelona, 1966), 773; see J. Grootaers and G. Thils, *Primauté et collégialité. Le dosssier de Gérard Philips sur la Nota Explicativa Praevia* (Leuven: Leuven University Press, 1986), 39 and 43ff.

9. That is how W. Onclin and K. Mörsdorf agree; see W. Onclin, "Le pouvoir de l'évêque et le principe de la collégialité," and K. Mörsdorf, "L'autonomia della Chiesa locale," both in *La Chiesa dopo il Concilio. Atti del Congresso internazionale di diritto canonico, Roma, 14–19 gennaio 1970* (Milan: Giuffrè, 1972), 135–61 (esp. 155) and 163–86 (esp. 178). On the qualification of emergency situations and necessity, see "Notfällen, Grenz- und Klonfliktfällen" in J. Werbick, *Kirche. Ein ekklesiologischer Entwurf für Studium und Praxis* (Basel: Herder, 1994), 383; *Ausnahmenfall, außerordentliche Maßnahme* (extreme situations, conflicting cases), in K. Mörsdorf, "In Artikel CD 8," *LThK*[2] 2 (1966): 158–60; and as *letze Instanz* (last instance), in P. Hünermann, "LG 27," in *Herders Theologischer Kommentar zum Zweiten Vatikanischen Konzil*, ed. P. Hünermann and B.J. Hilberath (Frieburg: Herder, 2004), 2:448. For its part, the Code of Canon Law, though not citing *LG* 27, contemplates canonical figures similar to the "papal reserve" and *recognitio*: see can. 446; 455, §2; 456.

10. See O. Rousseau, "La vrai valeur de l'Épiscopat dans l'Église d'après importants documents de 1875," in Congar and Dupuy, *L'Épiscopat et l'Église universelle*, 709–36; K. Schatz, *Vaticanum I 1869–1870* (Paderborn: Schöningh, 1994), 3:92–99.

11. A. Antón, "Eclesiología postconciliar: esperanzas, resultados y perspectivas para el futuro," in *Vaticano II: balance y perspectivas*, ed. R. Latourelle (Salamanca: Sígueme, 1989), 275–94, at 291. Translated in Renè Latourelle, *Vatican II Assessment and Perspectives Twenty-Five Years After (1962–1987)*, vol.1 (Mahwah, NJ: Paulist Press, 1988), 430–31.

12. W. Kasper, "Ciò che permane e ciò che muta nel ministero petrino," *Concilium* (8/1975): 43–58, esp. 55.

13. See H. J. Pottmeyer, *Towards a Papacy in Communion: Perspectives from Vatican Councils I and II* (New York: Crossroad, 1998), 51–75; K. Schatz, "Die Debatten um den Jurisdiktionsprimat auf dem Ersten Vatikanum," in *Communio—Ideal oder Zerrbild von Kommunikation*, ed. B. J. Hilberath (Freiburg: Herder, 1999), 39–53; Schatz, *El primado del papa*, 212–26; as well as S. Dianich, *Per una teologia del papato* (Cinisello Balsamo: San Paolo, 2010), 81–95.

14. Among the few who refer to this absence, see K. Mörsdorf, "Das oberste Hirtenamt des Papstes," in *Études de droit et d'histoire. Mélanges Mgr H. Wagnon* (Louvain la Neuve: Faculté internationale de droit canonique, 1976), 321–37; R. Minnerath, *Le Pape, Évêque universel ou premier des évêques?* (Paris: Beauchesne, 1978), 117–19; K. Walf, "Lacunes et ambiguïtés dans l'ecclésiologie de Vatican II," in *Les Églises après Vatican II. Dynamisme et prospective. Actes du colloque international de Bologne, 1980*, ed. G. Alberigo (Paris: Beauchesne, 1981), 207–21, at 213.

15. See L. Villemin, *Pouvoir d'ordre et pouvoir de juridiction. Histoire théologique de leur distinction*, afterword by Hervé Legrand (Paris: Cerf, 2003), and the sacramental rereading by A. Carrasco, "La recepción del Primado de jurisdicción papal a partir del Concilio Vaticano II y de *Ut unum sint*," *Diálogo ecuménico* 42 (2007): 7–39.

16. See in this sense, P. Rodríguez, "Naturaleza y finalidad del primado del Papa: el Vaticano I a la luz del Vaticano II," in *El primado del sucesor de Pedro en el misterio de la Iglesia. Consideraciones y comentarios*, ed. Congregación Para La Doctrina De La Fe (Madrid: Palabra, 2003), 103–39 (at 123n54), where for this type of understanding the reference is to *Declaration II* of the Anglo–Catholic International Commission, nos. 16ff.

17. Translated by Stephan Otto Horn and Vincenz Pfnür as *Pilgrim Fellowship of Faith* (San Francisco: Ignatius Press, 2005),234–35. In this sense, see also his acute reflection before Vatican II, when he pointed out the two mistakes in the understanding of primacy: to see it purely as an honor and not as an apostolic ministry, or to interpret it in a "civilist societal" manner and not in the sense that it entails only "spiritual and juridical power that goes with the responsibility for the word and for communion." See the entry "Primat," in *LThK*[2] 8 (1963): 761–63.

18. Bernard of Clairvaux, *De consideratione ad Eugenium papam* III, 1, 2. See Y. M. Congar, "La hiérarchie comme service," and, "Quelques expressions traditionnelles du service chrétien," both in Congar and Dupuy, *L'Épiscopat et l'Église universelle*, 67–99 and 101–32.

19. In comments to the published *Pastores Gregis*, no mention is made of this expression; see A. Cattaneo, ed., *L'esercizio dell'autorità nella Chiesa. Riflessioni a partire dall'esortazione apostolica "Pastores gregis"* (Venice: Marcianum Press, 2005); "Vescovi servitori del Vangelo per la speranza del mondo," the same topic to which is dedicated the periodical *Lateranum* 71 (2005): 219–683; G. Bausenhart, *Pastores gregis* (2003), in *Herders Theologischer Kommentar zum Zweiten Vatikanischen Konzil* (Freiburg: Herder, 2005), 3:299–301. It should be remembered that Cardinal Bergoglio, archbishop of Buenos Aires, was the speaker for the Synod of Bishops to which this apostolic exhortation corresponds.

20. See the lucid reflections on Pope Francis by S. Madrigal, "El Papa en la Iglesia. Dimensión doctrinal," in *El Papado en la Iglesia y en el mundo de hoy*, ed. D. Tolsada (Madrid: Boadilla del Monte-PPC, 2014), 112–44, esp. 141–44.

21. For some distinction of its forms of exercise, see also G. Colombo, "Tesi per la revisione dell'esercizio del ministero petrino" *Teologia* 21 (1996): 322–39; J. M. Rovira Belloso, *Vaticano II: un concilio para el tercer milenio* (Madrid: BAC, 1997), 117–23; S. Madrigal, "*Praesis ut prosis.* Consideraciones en torno a la *Ut unum sint*," *Miscellanea Comillas* 55 (1997): 391–403; M. J. Buckley, *Papal Primacy and the Episcopate: Towards a Relational Understanding* (New York: Crossroad, 1998), 62–74; A. Acerbi, "Per una nuova forma del ministero petrino," in *Il ministero del Papa. In prospettiva ecumenica. Atti del Colloquio: Milano, 16–18 aprile 1998* (Milan: Vita e Pensiero, 1999), 303–38; C. Schickendantz, *¿Adónde va el papado? Reinterpretación teológica y reestructuración práctica* (Buenos Aires: Agape, 2001); Klausnitzer, *Der Primat des Bischofs von Rom*, 508–19; P. A. Sequeri, "Ministero petrino, ministero ecclesiale," *Teologia* 32 (2005): 117–23; L. Villemin, "Le ministère de Pierre," *Cahiers Évangile* 165 (2013): 50–57; H. Legrand, "Réformer la papauté pour servir l'unité entre les Églises," *Nouvelle revue théologique* 136 (2014): 565–76; see our *Eclesiología*, 529–41.

22. Charles Journet notes that in the face of a pope acting *in destructionem ecclesiae* the only remedy would be prayer; in *L'Église du Verbe incarné*, vol. 1, *La hiérarchie apostolique* (Paris: Desclée de Brouwer, 1955), 547–50. Karl Rahner observes that we must trust in the assistance of the Holy Spirit in the pope's decisions, because otherwise the charismatic and prophetic force of the Church would make possible an "open opposition" (Gal 2:11), in "In Artikel LG 22" in *Lexikon für Theologie und*

Kirche. Das Zweite Vatikanische Konzil. Dokumente und Kommentare, vol. 1 (Freiburg: Herder, 1966), 227. Joseph Ratzinger recalls that the Council of Constance was an example of the limitation that can be found in the legal formulas that prohibit "appeals" against the acts of the pope, although certain situations of necessity or urgency may be "morally" obliging, bearing in mind that the decree *Haec Sancta* by that council was a measure in an "emergency" situation, in "*Nota Explicativa Praevia*," in *Lexikon für Theologie und Kirche. Das Zweite Vatikanische Konzil*, 356ff.

23. Text in Schatz, *El Prado*, 249; in fact, both in the West as in the East, one was aware that the *causae maiores* had to be sanctioned in Rome, according to Y. M. Congar, *L'ecclésiologie du haut Moyen-Âge. De Saint Grégoire le Grand à la désunion entre Byzance et Rome* (Paris: Cerf, 1968), 229 and 358ff. Giuseppe Alberigo, referring to the twentieth century, emphasizes that "the limitless expansion of the *causae maiores* imposed on the papacy the burden of a number of decisions far superior to the personal forces of a pope. What followed was an ever-increasing disarray in decision-making—and non-executive—areas no longer covered by the pope, but by the curia or individual collaborators." In P. Prodi, ed., *Forme storiche di governo nella Chiesa universale. Giornata di studio in occasione dell'ultima lezione del prof. Giuseppe Alberigo* (Bologna: Clueb, 2003), 207–25, at 222.

24. *Summa theologiae* II–II, q. 1, a. 10. See S.-T. Bonino, "La place du pape dans l'Église selon s. Thomas d'Aquin," *Revue thomiste* 86 (1996): 392–422.

25. According to the 1998 Considerations of the Congregation for the Doctrine of the Faith, *The Primacy of the Successor of Peter in the Mystery of the Church* 13.

26. This is how the great specialist of Vatican I clarified this question: R. Aubert, "La eclesiología en el concilio Vaticano I" in *El concilio y los concilios. Aportación a la historia de la vida conciliar de la Iglesia*, ed. B. Botte, H. Marot, P. Camelot, et al. (Madrid: Paulinas, 1962), 289–331, at 328.

15

REFORM AND RENEWAL

Implementing Vatican II

Myriam Wijlens

On December 1, 1962, the bishop of Bruges, Joseph DeSmedt, appealed to the Second Vatican Council to terminate the triumphalist, clerical, and juridical appearance of the Church.[1] His address soon summarized what the Council had achieved: it moved away from a juridical to a more theological and spiritual—yes, "pastoral"—way of thinking. Many experienced this as a great liberation. Canon law was looked upon with great suspicion and associated with impeding and obstructing rather than supporting reform and renewal of the Church. It is, therefore, a bit of a surprise, albeit a pleasant one, when fifty years after the closing of the Council a canon lawyer is invited to participate in a conference on "Reform(s) of and within the Church."[2] Indeed in recent times, there seems to be a change: those who are eager to continue the renewal and reform of the Church have begun to see that a lasting reform and a permanent renewal must find its way into the institutions and structures. A community that desires to live in agreement with the doctrine it holds benefits from structures that support, promote, and protect this doctrine. Reform(s) of and within the Church, without a consideration for the structures, might not be lasting and successful in the long run.

Hence, Pope John XXIII had the right intuition when in 1959

he not only announced the convocation of what would be Vatican II, but said in the same address that with the Council a necessary aggiornamento of the 1917 Code had to occur[3] and the law for the Eastern Churches had to be completed.[4] Established in 1963, the Pontificia Commissio Codici Iuris Canonici Recognoscendo—the Pontifical Commission for the Revision of the (Latin) Code of Canon Law—decided to begin its work only as the Council was coming to a close.[5] Pope Paul VI, who was a canon lawyer himself and had seen the tensions that had occurred between minority and majority groups at the Council, went a step further: on November 20, 1965, he stressed to the Commission that the work to be done was not merely a revision of existing laws—as had been the case when the 1917 Code was drafted—

> but rather it was also and especially a matter of reforming the norms to accommodate them to a new mentality [*novus habitus mentis*] and new needs even if the old law was to supply the foundation for the work of revision. Careful attention was to be paid to all the decrees and acts of the Second Vatican Council since they contain the main lines of legislative renewal either because norms were issued which directly affected new institutes and ecclesiastical discipline, or because it was necessary that the doctrinal riches of the Council, which contributed so much to pastoral life, have their consequences and necessary impact on canonical legislation.[6]

On several other occasions, he pointed out that a true reform was necessary and that this reform required a *novus habitus mentis*.[7] Indeed, the internal disposition of the one who drafts, interprets, or applies the law is of decisive relevance. To do so with an old mentality will not bring about the desired reform. It is necessary to attend to hermeneutical dispositions and decisions of legislators and those who apply the law.

This study will offer some reflections about the legislative process, to shed light on what it takes to reform the current institutions. The intention is to create an awareness for the kind of help drafters of legislation need from historians, theologians, and particularly ecclesiologists. Furthermore, the study hopes to invite theologians to go beyond their theoretical reflections and investigate how their conclusions could be implemented in the life of the Church. The relationship between the local and universal Church as well as between the primacy and collegiality will serve as a kind of illustration for the theoretical reflections.

Even if a revision of the legislation of the Church were to be announced in the near future, it cannot to be expected that it will be completed in a short time. Does that mean that nothing can be done but to sit and wait? Two things can be done: first, the road can be paved by academic projects of theologians and canon lawyers who propose drafts—albeit unsolicited—for potential future legislation. The drafts could be discussed in the academic realm. Such a practice is common in states or other bodies that have laws. One outcome of the conference on "Reform(s) to and within the Church" could be to set up such a project.[8] The project could begin immediately, but it would only bear fruit in the long term. Much quicker results can be obtained through an increased awareness of what happens in the application of the law, that is, when life and law meet. Both the description of the situation in which the law is to be applied as well as the interpretation of the law are governed by doctrinal presuppositions and perspectives. Identifying them, determining whether they are the only and best ones, and eventually changing them, could lead and contribute to a transformation of the community. Ultimately it could lead to a request to adapt the norms to the new situation. To phrase it more academically, through an increased awareness of hermeneutical options leading to conscious theological decisions that reflect and support the belief of the community, it is possible already to enter the process of renewal while the current norms are still in force. Hence, when those who apply the law take on the *novus habitus mentis*, a transformation of the community will occur, resulting in a different way of interacting that then will lead to new norms.[9] New wine in old wineskins will cause the wineskins to burst. The action will urge a reform of the law, and then once again the adage *ius sequitur vitam* will become true.[10] The process implies that law is seen again as an ordinance of reason (*lex est ordinatio rationis*, Thomas Aquinas). It would finally depart from the notion that interpretation is a mere searching for the will of the legislator (*lex est voluntas legislatoris*, Francis Suarez), which was common from the post-Tridentine era at least until Vatican II. It also implies that legal development is acknowledged as a process independent from the one who enacts the law.[11]

This study offers some reflections on the legislative process and on the application of the law. They are applicable to all areas of canon law and to all levels of laws, whether universal or particular. At the same time, there must be a caution: limited space only allows for raising an awareness of the issues. No definite answers can be offered.

Legislating after Vatican II: Then and Now

Imagine sitting in an office in the Vatican on December 9, 1965. The Council fathers just went out the door full of energy and ideas to bring the results of the Council to their local churches. They have been transformed by their experiences and, therefore, affirmed with an overwhelming majority the documents of the Council. There is a new energy, there is a sense of hope for the Church and for the world. Left behind is a relatively small group of canon lawyers who have been appointed to draft norms to assist the community in receiving the Council. The Church should be transformed by the Council and the canonical norms are to facilitate, and in a way, enforce this process. (An aside: the bishops and many theologians might not have seen it this way, as they associated law with impeding and obstructing reform.) Some members of the small group had been involved in the Council as advisors to bishops or commissions. Others had seen the Council from a distance. Some were excited by the Council and had begun to take on that new attitude of mind; others watched it with great skepticism and had, for example, been wholeheartedly involved in drafting the *Nota explicative brevia* to *Lumen Gentium*.[12]

The task ahead of the group was difficult and above all totally new. They could not draw from the experience of the 1917 Code, as that Code had only been a reordering of already existing laws at the request of the fathers at Vatican I. Until then, only unofficial collections of laws had existed. The purpose of the legislation issued in 1917 had neither been a modernization nor a revision of existing laws, let alone the implementation of a specific theology. All the Council fathers had wanted was a clarification of what was binding, because there were so many different laws whose authority was unclear as such or in relation to each other.[13]

The first decision to be made for the 1917 Code concerned the format. Modern states had constitutions or codes. This had seemed to be a good instrument for the Church, because it fitted with its self-understanding as a *societas perfecta*. In fact, the promulgation of a Code forcefully demonstrated the Church's autonomy to the outside world.[14] In 1965 the question of format reappeared: Would a Code for the "universal" Church be a good instrument for the postconciliar norms? What ecclesiological understanding of the Church is portrayed with a Code? Moreover, the task as given was to work on a Code only for the Latin Church, but was that in line with the Council? What about the Eastern churches and what about the unity of and legitimate diversity in the Church? Was thinking in categories such as "universal" and "local" correct, or was there a need to consider a threefold structure: local, particular, and universal, thus acknowledging the patriarchal structure as well? How was the internal structure of the Latin Church to be understood now that the existence of episcopal conferences was officially acknowledged, even though the Council had deliberately decided not to clarify its theological foundation?

The Commission had to attend to other questions as well: Who would be involved in the legislative process and who would promulgate the law? These were truly ecclesiological questions that needed to consider the heritage of Vatican I, which was, however, complemented by Vatican II's newly affirmed doctrine on collegiality of the bishops. In 1917 the pope alone was considered competent, not only to promulgate the law for the universal Latin Church, but possibly more important—certainly from an ecclesiological perspective—was the fact that "with that single legislative act he 'made it all his own,' and swept aside all previous canonical enactments."[15] The dogma of primacy of jurisdiction enforced the idea that the pope—and the pope alone—had indeed that power. Furthermore, through the papal action of promulgating and abrogating laws, the dogma on the primacy of jurisdiction found not only a maximalist application, but the action also communicated strongly and visibly the conformity of such an interpretation of the dogma with Vatican I.[16] With the abrogation of the existing particular laws and customs, an implicit theological statement was made about the authority of diocesan bishops, the relevance of the local Church—including diocesan synods, which had often been instrumental in issuing legislation—about the authority of metropolitan structures including provincial and plenary councils, and so on. In 1917 this action was most likely seen as a strong expression of the unity of the Church. Considering today's ecclesiology, the action would be seen as a disrespect for local synodal institutions and enactments and as an understanding of unity that favors uniformity over diversity in unity. Yet, there was more to it: the decision to have one Code in combination with the then newly developed sophisticated method of conceptual juridical abstraction implied that the norms are completely set apart from the concrete social situations, which in life are the mainspring of law itself.[17] This decision has been a challenge for the Church up until today as it touches on unity and diversity as well as on the relevance of context that gives rise to an institution and thus indicates also why it might be changed as circumstances change.

Vatican II complemented the doctrine of Vatican I with the doctrine of collegiality of the bishops who exercise a solicitude for the whole Church (*LG* 22 and *CD* 6). Furthermore, Vatican II complemented the focus on the universal Church as expressed by Vatican I by affirming that the local Church is fully Church (*LG* 26). Vatican II affirmed that the local and the universal cannot be thought of independently from each other and sought to express this with the terminology of *in quibus et ex quibus* (*LG* 23). In addition, it is relevant that the Council affirmed not only that the pope is Vicar of Christ, but that the diocesan bishop is also vicar of Christ for the diocese entrusted to his care (*LG* 27). Hence, the decision about which authority is competent to legislate on what issues was to be discussed not only then, but also now and in the future. Furthermore, the relationship between universal and particular law, and with it the requirement that particular law must remain within the framework of universal law (c. 135, §2 *CIC*), must be studied in light of what lies behind the phrase *in quibus et ex quibus*. Such a discussion must attend to the tension between an unavoidable generality of universal norms—as they cannot consider the specificities of a given situation—and more particular law structures that can recognize specific and local circumstances, traditions and conditions, but must see to it that the local is not closed in but remains open to the universal (*LG* 13). Such reflections entail sophisticated theological consideration even when it is often referred to with the simple term *decentralization*.

The Commission did address some of these questions when the project of a *Lex Ecclesiae Fundamentalis* (*LEF*) was considered. The *LEF* was a proposal to have one fundamental law for both the Latin Church and Eastern churches together, and separate Codes for the Latin and Eastern churches as well. This originated from a discussion in Vatican II on whether there should be a separate Decree on the Eastern Churches or if the Dogmatic Constitution on the Church could treat the whole Church and then see as well to the peculiarities of the Eastern and the Latin church(es). For pragmatic reasons, the decision was made to have a separate Decree. Yet, it was above all the experience of unity amid diversity that made the Council fathers seek to investigate whether this could find expression in the legal structure of the Church as well. Considering the legitimate diversity and legal autonomy granted to the Eastern churches, it was clear that one Code common to all could not be issued. Envisioned was a Code that would contain the constitution of the Church (*ius constitutivum Ecclesiae*). It would be accompanied by a Code for the Latin Church and one for the Eastern churches. This instrument enabled them to merely live beside each other, while at the same time honoring legitimate diversity. The *LEF* idea lasted as late as May 1981. To the end, the cardinals and bishops on the Commission supported it, but Pope John Paul II stopped it for reasons still unknown.[18]

Even though the project was terminated, important questions remained for the future: How do we see the communion among the Latin Church and the current twenty-three churches *sui iuris*?[19] How can unity and diversity find adequate expression, particularly in the structure of the Church? What does the legislative power and authority of a diocesan bishop mean? What does the rightful autonomy of a Church *sui iuris* imply for its legislative competence and how is it best expressed? These questions took on urgency, since different churches *sui iuris* increasingly lived side by side in the same territory.

In the Latin Church, there was an increased need to clarify with a certain freshness not only the theological status of (national) episcopal conferences, a topic that has caused many discussions over the past fifty years, but also of continental structures that have emerged since the Second World War. If the Church has moved from being a European Church to a world Church (K. Rahner), there might be a need to clarify the ecclesiological status of these continental structures and with it the possibility of legislative and teaching authority.[20]

A third area concerns the relationship between the primacy and collegiality in the act of promulgating the two Codes: were these mere pontifical acts? They were, but more can be said. The Commission for the Revision of the Latin Code drafted ten principles to govern the project.[21] Pope Paul VI submitted them to the first Synod of Bishops ever held in 1967 and they were approved. This could be seen as an expression of collegiality of bishops or of solicitude of bishops for all churches and for the universal Church. Furthermore, drafts of the Code were submitted to episcopal conferences around the world for comments. I am not aware whether there was ever a discussion to have an additional session of the Council, or if anyone contemplated submitting the final draft to another synod of bishops, which could have been done. The fact stands that Pope John Paul II promulgated the 1983 Code by himself. While doing so he evaluated the involvement of the Synod of Bishops in 1967 and the submission of the draft to episcopal conferences for comments as expressions of true collegiality.[22] One may ask whether what was done was indeed a true expression of collegiality or a rather minimal understanding and expression of what the doctrine entails. In any case, the doctrine would have allowed and possibly asked for a more intense expression and involvement of all bishops or certainly of the diocesan bishops. A synod could have been such a modality, especially because historically, synods were legislative instruments.

The drafting of the Eastern Code was also governed by principles that, however, had been written by the Pontifical Oriental Institute and were approved by the Plenaria of the PCCIORR in March 1974. Thus, there was no formal consultation of the bishops of the Eastern churches. In 1990 Pope John Paul II promulgated the Code for the Eastern Churches, again by himself. It had been explicitly suggested that he do so together with the respective patriarchs, but the pope decided otherwise. Remarkably, the forewords to the respective Codes do not even mention the *LEF*!

The reflections so far illustrate that there are ecclesiological options and therefore decisions that must be made regarding (a) who is competent to legislate, (b) on what issue, and (c) for which community is that legislation binding. It seems that the decisions made are of imminent relevance for the implementation of the Council as it touches so deeply on many of the ecclesiological questions that the Council addressed.

Drafting: The Identification of Doctrine

The process of legislating involves two major decisions: First, one must be made about the content, that is, the doctrine that is being fostered and protected by way of structures. The second consists of determining a modality. Both processes bear some challenges.

Due to the nature of Vatican II, the identification of doctrine is a rather complex task. Three major points may be mentioned: renewal through juxtaposition, the so-called seminal locutions, and the hermeneutical lenses of reform.

Vatican II oftentimes renewed by way of juxtaposition: a new understanding is introduced, while preserving the former well-known doctrine. It is a mistake to believe, therefore, that two different doctrines simply stand side by side. Herman Josef Pottmeyer has explained that such an understanding of renewal of juxtaposition is incorrect: when the old is complemented by the new, the old is automatically transformed because it is to be understood within the new context. Thus, the road is paved for further development, which should lead to a new synthesis. Pottmeyer acknowledges that the Council itself did not complete this renewal process with a synthesis, but left this task to the postconciliar Church.[23] One could say this belongs to the reception process of Vatican II. Whereas such a process can be easily accepted for a Council, it causes major problems for the legislator who must identify the doctrine that needs protection and promotion by way of institutions at a given point in time. Indeed, that point in time was soon after the closing of the Council and possibly before the reception process could really begin. Hence, when the drafters of the law had to make decisions, they were faced with documents that contain juxtapositions. It was unavoidable that decisions would lean in one direction or the other.

Regarding the 1983 Code, we must recall that most decisions were made in the 1970s when academic discussions about the interpretation of the Council—and thus about the juxtapositions—were only beginning. The conciliar acts were not yet available, as they appeared only between 1970 and 1999! Moreover, the 1983 Code was promulgated two years before the Extraordinary Synod of Bishops commemorating the twentieth anniversary of Vatican II, and it was there that the issue of juxtapositions and related hermeneutics was openly acknowledged and discussed.[24]

With regard to the juxtapositions a second remark is fitting: from a methodological and theological perspective, it would be incorrect to expect a doctrinal decision from the legislator regarding a development of a new syntheses surpassing the juxtapositions. This task belongs to the teaching office of the Church, while acknowledging the *sensus fidei* as well as the reflections by theologians. Indeed, the legislator must resist the temptation to act as teaching authority.

Furthermore, the legislator was confronted with discussions in which some saw the Council as completed at its closing—thus restricting the Council to documents it produced—whereas others saw it as the beginning of a process because reception would be part of the Council. The legislator could not close these discussions, but had to attend to three dimensions: (a) provide institutions that protect and promote the doctrine that has been identified as in need of a support by way of structures; (b) these structures must enable the community not only to receive the doctrine as it is known and understood at the time of promulgation; but (c) they must also allow for development in the understanding of the doctrine—including new results in handling the juxtapositions on their way to a new synthesis—which would then have an impact on the application of the norms.

Pope John Paul II was acutely aware of the old and new (*vetera et nova*) in the Council as he promulgated the 1983 Code. He stated explicitly that the newness of the Council was to be the newness of the Code. He even mentioned four aspects that characterize the true and genuine image of the Church:

- the doctrine in which the Church is presented as the people of God (cf. *Lumen Gentium* 2), and authority as a service (cf. ibid., 3);
- the doctrine in which the Church is seen as a "communion," which, therefore, determines the relations that should exist between the particular Churches and the universal Church, and between collegiality and the primacy;
- the doctrine according to which all the members of the people of God, in the way suited to each of them, participate in the threefold office of Christ: priestly, prophetic, and kingly. With this teaching, there is also linked that which concerns the duties and rights of the faithful, and particularly of the laity; and finally,
- the Church's commitment to ecumenism.[25]

These points are not just relevant for the legislation in the universal Church, but also for other levels. Furthermore, they are relevant for the interpretation and application of the law, as they are to function as hermeneutical criteria.

Vatican II held another challenge for the drafters of the law: the Council contains so-called seminal locutions. They are ideas that the Council accepted but left to the postconciliar Church to understand more deeply. At times the Council deliberately avoided fixating a notion, at other times it did so implicitly. Among these are, for example, collegiality, *coetus/collegium episcoporum, communio hierarchica, ecclesia, communitas ecclesiales, communio (plena), subsistit in,* and *sensus fidelium,* to mention a few. Remarkably, some of these terms can be found in the Code of Canon Law. Some canonists would have preferred clearly defined terms and see this as a weakness.[26] Others see it as opening the possibility of continuous development in doctrinal insights in interpretation and application.[27]

In conclusion, the juxtapositions and the seminal locutions both require a sensitivity for hermeneutical options and decisions. It has an impact on legislation as well as on interpretation and application of the law.

What does all of this imply? The legislation currently in force should be evaluated in light of the fifty-year reception process. The legislation should not be evaluated in light of the knowledge about the Council when the norms were promulgated, but they must be seen in light of today's knowledge of the Council. In doing so, one admits there is a continuation in understanding the Council and allows for a development in the legal structures as well. The research might lead to proposals for a reform of the law.

Drafting: Determining the Modality

Once the content that should govern the institution has been determined, the legislator must find a fitting modality. It implies taking into consideration the people for whom the law is issued, the circumstances and culture in which they live, the means available to implement the structure (e.g., personnel and financial recourses), and so on. These aspects refer to context, inculturation, relevance of local Church, and all that comes with it.

Choosing a modality also implies asking the important theological—yes again ecclesiological—question: What is being legislated and on at what level? Is it necessary to issue laws that bind the faithful throughout the universal Church or could it be left to the diocesan bishop or the episcopal conference to determine whether and how something can be best organized and realized by way of particular laws? The issue of context and inculturation is of imminent relevance here. Currently the legal system acknowledges a legislative power for the diocesan bishop. It results from the understanding that he is vicar of Christ in his diocese and has all the power necessary to govern his diocese unless it is reserved to a higher authority. Episcopal conferences work much more based on what might be called a concession system: unless the power to legislate (and teach) has been granted to them either by law or by special concession, they cannot act.[28] It implies an understanding that the episcopal conference is acting as a part of the college and that it cannot act for the college as such. The particular is seen from the perspective of the universal. Quite different would be a system in which the episcopal conference is seen as a cooperation of diocesan bishops within a given territory on matters that surpass their local Church. The former could be seen as a top-down understanding of cooperation of bishops, the latter as a bottom up. It would be necessary to reflect this in light of a concession—a reservation system of power. Indeed, the ecclesiology behind the cooperation and the consequences for the legislative (and teaching) authority must be seriously addressed. Hence, determining the modality implies ecclesiological decisions.

Deciding on a modality also requires determining whether something is for liceity or validity, whether the system operates primarily based on permissions or prohibitions, and so on. Finally, the legal system must leave space for development and adaptation to specific circumstances, as no legal system can possibly provide for every conceivable situation. Laws, therefore, have so-called discretionary clauses such as "if opportune," "in case of necessity," and "for a grave reason." Once they are part of the laws, these clauses must be considered in the application of the law. For that the internal disposition and the hermeneutical perspective will be decisive again.

Differentiation between Doctrinal Content and Modality

It is important to differentiate between determining the doctrine that governs the law and the modality. First, it allows for handling with greater ease unity in diversity—and thus also for subsidiarity and decentralization—for respecting culture, inculturation, the availability of resources, the civil law in which context the Church has to operate, for a differentiation between what is considered to be *ius divinum* and the expression—or if you like "translation"—of it in ecclesiastical structures.[29] Second, it allows for a careful analysis and appropriate response when the norms are not received or fall into disuse or cannot respond adequately to changed needs and circumstances: when the cause of the non-reception lies with the doctrine, the teaching office, while respecting the *sensus fidei*, needs to respond, but when the modality is not appropriate (any longer) the legislator must provide for another modality. A community is a living entity and thus new challenges will occur which might stipulate new norms.[30]

Finally, the differentiation allows for a consideration of ecclesiological criteria that surpass specific topics and could function as hermeneutical lenses. Indeed, the four aspects that pope John Paul II mentioned while promulgating the Code of Canon Law can be taken as such hermeneutical lenses: the understanding of the Church as people of God and hierarchical authority as service, as well as the commitment to ecumenism, could also function as hermeneutical perspectives in deciding which modality would promote these aspects.[31]

The considerations offered reveal that the legislative process is heavily determined by ecclesiological and hermeneutical decisions. It would be a wonderful outcome of this conference when historians of Vatican II, systematic theologians, ecclesiologists, and canon lawyers would dare together to write drafts for potential future legislation to assist the Church in receiving the Council in our time. Indeed, it is a long-term project. So, what can be done in the meantime? A greater appreciation for what happens and what is possible in the application of the current norms is indispensable.

Application of Law

It is necessary to distinguish the interpretation from the application of law. Interpretation is the scholarly act of understanding the law. It is often performed in commentaries and articles. In the application, an encounter of law and life occurs. The application of the norms begins, therefore, with the formulation of the situation in which the law is to be applied. This formulation is governed by theological premises.[32] Reflections about the premises occur rather seldom and therefore there is little awareness to which extent they determine the ultimate response to the situation. The reflections offered above about the juxtapositions could lead to a reconsideration of the formulation of the question and thus to a different application of the law. Indeed, the conscious awareness and use of theological premises that govern a situation can postulate a change leading to a transformation of the community and thus contribute to a reform of the community. Two examples can illustrate what is meant. A diocesan bishop asks, Does the law oblige me to ever consult any layperson for any decision? The answer is no. The finance council, although obligatory, does not have to be composed of laity and the diocesan pastoral council is as such not an obligatory institution. There is also no legal obligation to consult with laity before any teaching authority is exercised. Quite different is the response when the theological premises change. Now the diocesan bishop states, I was ordained for service to the people of God in the diocese of XX. It is my primary task to help them to encounter Christ and obtain salvation. The Lord has promised that the Holy Spirit works in each member of my diocese and in the community as such. How can I decide what to do if I do not need their needs, belief, and possibilities available to live in agreement with their belief? What vehicle do I have to assist me? He will install the diocesan pastoral council as it provides a structure for the diocese and him to engage in dialogue. He will convoke it regularly and will put items on the agenda that are of relevance to the life of the diocese. His eagerness to consult will be an appeal to the faithful to take seriously their responsibility that originates from baptism and confirmation. Hence, the "success" also depends on the willingness of the laity to take their responsibility seriously. Ultimately the whole community will be transformed as it will change decision makers and receivers into a community. The ecclesiology of people of God and hierarchical authority as service has an impact on the application of the law. It leads to another question, and the answer transforms the community, even though the law itself has not changed. Indeed, even if it is not obligatory to consult the faithful, it is also not forbidden. A bishop who acts like this will influence the parish priests, who will begin to act differently with regard to the parish councils. Moreover, it is likely that such a bishop will bring the concerns from his diocese—or at least bring them differently—to the episcopal conference or a synod of bishops. It must be admitted as well that even if the law would oblige the bishop to install a diocesan pastoral council, nothing would come out of it if he would not believe in the theological relevance of such an institution, as he would hardly convoke it and would not put issues on the agenda of relevance.[33]

The example can be transferred to the pope. Vatican II affirmed the doctrine of collegiality of bishops and placed the doctrine of the primacy in the context of collegiality. At the same time, the Council decided to have the chapter on the hierarchy preceded by a chapter on the people of God, but it did not draw consequences from this change for the third chapter. Although this all led to a new understanding of the cooperation of the pope and college of bishops with regard to exercising their teaching authority (*LG* ch. 3), it was juxtaposed with an understanding that all participate in the *munus propheticum* (*LG* 12, ch. 2). The legislator only "received" the understanding expressed in chapter 3 of *LG*. The institution of the Synod of Bishops was to give expression to this. The legislator did not provide for a structure expressing *LG* 12 in combination with the doctrine of chapter 3. There is no provision for ascertaining the *sensus fidei*. There is only a norm determining that the faithful may express their needs and desires to the pastors, and to make their opinion known to the pastors and other faithful (c. 212 *CIC*). There is no norm determining that the pastors are to listen. While thinking and above all acting based on a theology of the people of God and hierarchical authority as service, Pope Francis "transformed" the Church in that he urged every diocesan bishop—not only those who were to attend the Synod on the Family in 2014 and 2015—to engage with the faithful in dialogue about their concerns, needs, and belief, and to bring this to the Church universal. With his action Pope Francis overcame the juxtaposition and placed the doctrine of collegiality of bishops in the framework of people of God. The vehicle for it is synodality.[34] The law did not change, but the action by the pope—which was not against the law but beyond the law and yet rooted in the solid doctrine of Vatican II—transformed the community. It will not be possible to return to the status ante quo. Rather, the law might have to be adapted according to the principle *ius sequitur vitam*.

Conclusion

Reflections about a continuous renewal and reform belong not only to the realm of theology, but also to the area of canon law. Within the realm of canon law, renewal and reform can take place by issuing new legislation and through the application of the norms. Whereas the former is a long-term project, the latter can begin immediately. In either case, developing a strong awareness of ecclesiological and hermeneutical presuppositions, options, and decisions could assist the Church in the process of renewal, leading to a transformation of the Church. There will be no reform, though, without a true *novus habitus mentis*.

NOTES

1. AS I/IV, 142–43.

2. Conference held at *La Civiltà Cattolica* in Rome, September 28–October 2, 2015.

3. John XXIII, papal allocution "Questa festiva," *AAS* 51(1959): 65–69. English translation in *The Pope Speaks* 4 (1959): 398–401, at 400–401. In the act of promulgating the 1983 Code of Canon Law, Pope John Paul II speaks of an "intuition" of Pope John XXIII when he announced the revision of the Code together with the convocation of the Council. Pope John Paul II writes furthermore, "I must recognize that this Code derives from one and the same intention, the renewal of Christian living. From such an intention, in fact, the entire work of the council drew its norms and its direction." He then explains that the Code is "a translation from conciliar doctrine and ecclesiology into canonical language," by which the conciliar image of the church remains the point of reference. John Paul II, apostolic constitution *Sacrae Disciplinae Leges*, *AAS* 75 (1983): VII–XIV. English translation: *Code of Canon Law: Latin-English Edition, New English Translation*, (Washington, DC: Canon Law Society of America, 1998), xxvii–xxxii, at xviii and xxx.

4. As early as the eighteenth century, collections of canons for the Eastern churches had been assembled informally. During Vatican I, the Eastern Catholic patriarchs and bishops expressed the need for a body of laws that would govern all Eastern Catholic churches. After the 1917 Code had been promulgated for the Latin Church, the wish was expressed again at meetings of the Congregation for the Eastern Churches. Although a Commission for the Eastern Codification was composed and ultimately even a draft for a *Codex Iuris Canonici Orientalis* was completed by 1948, nevertheless, due to an urgent need, some parts were promulgated in 1949, whereas others never made it. Pope John XXIII referred to this when he said that final parts were to be promulgated. For a detailed description of the process, see "Preface to the Latin Edition" of the *Code of Canons of the Eastern Churches: Latin-English Edition, New English Translation* (Washington, DC: Canon Law Society of America, 2001), xxix–xli.

5. Only in 1972 Pope Paul VI established the Pontifical Commission for the Revision of the Code of Eastern Canon Law (PCCICOR).

6. "Preface to the Latin Edition" of the *Code of Canon Law* of 1983, xxxv–xxxvi.

7. For example, Pope Paul VI used the expression *novus habitus mentis* on December 14, 1973, when he addressed students at a course on the Renewal in Canon Law and spoke of "the germane force and significance of the revised canon law which, in accord with the new attitude of mind introduced by the said Vatican Council, contributes very much to the pastoral care and new needs of the people of God" (*Canon Law Digest* vol. 8: 100–101). In an address to the Roman Rota on February 4, 1977, he said, "Let these principles be kept before your eyes in the execution of the office entrusted to you to the extent that from them a new attitude of mind may be brought about" (ibid., 111). For further reflection on this see also Ladislas Örsy, *Theology and Canon Law: New Horizons for Legislation and Interpretation* (Collegeville, MN: Liturgical Press, 1992).

8. The international research group Peter and Paul Seminar (=PPS), which is composed of systematic theologians and canon lawyers, investigates which existing institutions can and must be reformed in light of Vatican II and the unity of the Church. The group was established by Ladislas Örsy, SJ, in 1998. PPS takes its inspiration from the Groupe des Dombes's publication "Pour la conversion des Églises." Current members of PPS are, e.g., Catherine Clifford, James Coriden, Peter DeMey, Eugene Duffy, Joseph Famerée, Thomas Green, Astrid Kaptijn, Gilles Routhier, Laurent Villemin, and Myriam Wijlens. After focusing on the "collegiality of bishops" (Georgetown University, Washington, DC, 2004), the group concentrated on "leadership in the local church" (St. Paul University, Ottawa, 2008). When, in 2008, these two projects were completed and the group concluded that it was possible to offer concrete suggestions for change, it became clear that the ecclesial situation—the mental disposition of those in leadership—at the time was not ripe for any such proposal. In fact, any proposal to change anything might have led to more restrictive norms than those that are in place. As a result, the PPS studied the process of conversion of a community as prerequisite for a reform (University of Erfurt, 2010). Examples of questions that were addressed include the following: What does it take for a community to enter a process of conversion that leads to reform? How does it take place and how does the community handle opposition to reform? It was followed by a case study, "Liturgy as Litmus Test of Reform in Ecclesiology" (Louvain, 2012, and Baltimore, 2013). The contributions are published in issues of *The Jurist* of 2004, 2008, 2009, and 2011 as well as in *Questions liturgiques* 2013

and 2014. See also https://www.uni-erfurt.de/en/canon-law/peter-and-paul-seminar/ (accessed September 20, 2015).

9. A caution: first, my proposal is not a call for disobedience to the law, but rather an appeal to use the space allowed by the theology governing the law. Second, my proposal does not affect procedural law, penal law, or other areas that could touch on the protection of rights of persons.

10. The current attempts to reform the Roman curia as well the penal law of the Latin Church shows how difficult and in a way how slowly such a reform progresses. Objections to a reform show how important it is to "bring everyone concerned on board" and not just impose a reform. Moreover, proposed new norms must possible to implement, which implies the necessity of consultation. Otherwise, there is a risk of nonreception or even of bishops invoking their *ius remonstrandi*!

11. A legal system must provide for stability and for adaptation. See Ladislas Örsy, "Das Spannungsverhältnis zwischen Beständigkeit und Entwicklung im kanonischen Recht," *De processibus matrimonialibus* 8 (2001): 299–312. Regarding the interpretation of canon law, the influence of the principle *lex est ordinatio voluntatis legislatoris* (Francisco Suarez, 1564–1617) can still be felt. The purpose lies in the will of the legislator. In this understanding, the *mens legislatoris* has relevance as long as the law is binding. Development only takes place through authentic interpretations. Vgl. Rosalio J. Castillo Lara, "Die authentische Auslegung des kanonischen Rechtes im Rahmen der Tätigkeit der päpstlichen Kommission für die authentische Interpretation des ius canonicum," *Österreichisches Archiv für Kirchenrecht* 32 (1987): 209–28.

Quite different is the school of thought that returns to Aquinas's understanding, *lex est ordinatio rationis*. It sees laws as autonomous once they are promulgated. The *mens legislatoris* has only historical relevance, and the interpretation occurs not *ex tunc*, but *ex nunc*: "Der Geist eines kanonischen Gesetzes erschließt sich nicht immer und notwendigerweise als Geist der Gesetzgebung von damals, sondern er erfährt seine aktuelle Interpretation im Lichte des Verständnishorizontes der Kirche von heute." Winfried Schulz, " 'Der Geist des Konzils' als Interpretationsmaxime der kanonischen Rechtsordnung? Zur Auslegung der kodikarischen Interpretationsregeln," *Apollinaris* 55 (1982): 449–60, at 459. See also Helmuth Pree, *Die evolutive Interpretation der Rechtsnorm im kanonischen Recht*, Linzer Universitätsschriften Monographien, vol. 6 (Wien: Springer, 1980) and Hugo Schwendenwein, "Der 'Geist der Gesetzgebung' als dynamischer Interpretationsfaktor," *Revue du Droit Canonique* 22 (1972): 315–32.

12. Inasmuch as there are studies about bishops who participated in the Council and the theological advisors they had, it would be worthwhile to study the canon lawyers who were official members of the different commissions. For example, see the study on the archive and work of the Belgian canon lawyer Willy Onclin: Constance van de Wiel, *Repertorium van de documenten in het archief Monseigneur Willy Onclin. Tweede Vaticaans Concilie en Pauselijke Commissie voor de herziening van het Wetboek van Canoniek Recht,* Novum Commentarium Lovaniense in Codicem Iuris Canonici (Leuven: Peeters, 1998).

13. Pietro Cardinal Gasparri (1852–1934), who led the commission, went through all existing norms, including those of councils and synods and all legal provisions issued for example for the missionary countries and determined carefully which one had what kind of authority. It was indeed a major hermeneutical act, but it was not a modernization. The structure of the Code was governed by Roman law institutions of persons, things, and actions. The footnotes added to the 1917 Code indicate the origin of the norms. These sources, except those already contained in the liturgical books, the *Corpus*, or the Tridentine Decrees are published in Pietro Gasparri and Iustiniani Serédi, eds., *Codex iuris canonici fontes,* 9 vols. (Rome: Typis Poliglottis Vaticanis, 1926–1939).

14. At that time the adage *ubi societas iubi ius* was often invoked to explain why the Church has laws.

15. James A. Coriden, *An Introduction to Canon Law* (Mahwah, NJ: Paulist Press, 2004), 27.

16. It would be worthwhile to study the perception of these actions from an ecumenical perspective. For example, the Group of Farfa Sabina, *Communion of Churches and Petrine Ministry: Lutheran-Catholic Convergences* (Grand Rapids, MI: Eerdmans, 2015). The study reveals what can be achieved when documents are read with an awareness of hermeneutics.

17. "In March 1904, Pius X set in motion the 'truly difficult task' (*arduum sane manus*) of 'collecting the laws of the universal church, in a clear and concise order, and adapting them to the conditions of our time.'...All previous collections of canons had been in the form of collections of documents: the original words, pastoral situation, date, and issuing authority were retained. The canonical rule remained in its historical context. 'Codification' is an exercise in conceptual juridical abstraction. It strives to reduces the rule to terse and abstract formulations and arrange them in a carefully constructed system. It is strong on clarity, brevity, consistency, and order, but the rules are entirely set apart from the social and historical context that gave rise to them" (Coriden, *An Introduction to Canon Law,* 27–28). The method of juridical abstraction, the so-called *Begriffsjurisprudenz,* was very well developed in German legal philosophy

at the beginning of the twentieth century. See also Stephan Kuttner, "Il Codice di diritto canonico nella storia" in *Commemorazione del cinquantesimo anniversario della promulgazione del Codex iuris canonici, celebrata alla augusta presenza del Santo padre Paolo VI il 27 maggio 1967* (Rome), 17–39; also in *L'attività della Santa Sede in 1967* (Rome, 1968): 1620–34.

18. For a description of the development of the *LEF*, see Daniel Canalor Palanca, *La ley Fondamental de la Iglesi. Historia y análisis de un proyecto legislative* (Pamplona: EUNSA, 1991), and Thomas J. Green, "*Lex Fundamentalis*: The Law Within," *CLSA Proceedings* 67 (2005): 21–76.

19. Vatican II used the expression "particular church" for both the diocese and for the patriarchal churches (Cf. *LG* 23). The 1983 *CIC* uses "particular churches" in its heading "particular churches and their groupings" and thus refers mainly to dioceses (cf. c. 368). While drafting the Code for the Eastern Churches, a reflection about terminology started again. The new term is *ecclesia sui iuris*. The CCEO determines "a community of the Christian faithful, which is joined together by a hierarchy according to the norm of law and which is expressly or tacitly recognized as sui iuris, is called in this Code a Church sui iuris." Cf. Ivan Zuzek, "Le 'ecclesia sui iuris' nella revisione del diritto canonico," in *Vaticano II: Bilancio e prospettive venticinque anni dopo (1962–1987)*, ed. René Latourelle (Assisi: Gregorian University Press, 1987), 2:869–82.

20. Pope Francis referred to teaching statements by some of the continental structures in his 2013 apostolic exhortation *Evangelium Gaudium*, thus recognizing that these bodies have theological relevance. Hence, their legislative and the teaching authority needs to be clarified. For example, see Myriam Wijlens, "Exercising Collegiality in a Supranational or Continental Institution such as the FABC, CCEE and ComECE," *The Jurist* 64 (2004): 168–204.

21. Cf. Thomas J. Green, "The Latin and Eastern Codes: Guiding Principles," *The Jurist* 62 (2002): 235–79. It should be noted that the introductions to the respective Codes themselves only provide summaries of the principles.

22. See John Paul II, *Sacrae Disciplinae Leges*, xxviii.

23. Hermann Josef Pottmeyer, "Vor einer neuen Phase der Rezeption des Vaticanum II: Zwanzig Jahre Hermeneutik des Konzils," in *Die Rezeption des Zweiten Vatikanischen Konzils*, ed. Hermann Josef Pottmeyer, Giuseppe Alberigo, and Jean Pierre Josua (Düsseldorf: Patmos, 1986), 47–65, at 59.

24. Cf. Walter Kasper, ed., *Zukunft aus der Kraft des Konzils. Die außerordentliche Bischofssynode, 85. Die Dokumente mit einem Kommentar von Walter Kasper* (Freiburg: Herder, 1986).

25. John Paul II, *Sacrae Disciplinae Leges*, xxx.

26. During the drafting of the 1983 Code the suggestion was made to provide definitions in the Code. The proposal was rejected, stating that a legal text is not a textbook for educational purposes! Indeed, it would have blocked any legal development. "Consulto omissae sunt definitiones, quippe quod Codex non est manuale scholasticum et in iure definitiones ipsae periculosae sunt" *Communicationes* 16 (1984): 38.

27. Reflections on such processes become fascinating and challenging once one realizes that neither the doctrine itself nor the situation in which the doctrine must permeate the whole body are static entities.

28. Cf. John Paul II, *motu proprio Apostolos Suos, AAS* 90 (1998): 641–58.

29. For a reflection about *ius divinum* and its "translation" in canonical norms, see Helmuth Pree, "*Ius divinum* between Normative Text, Normative Content, and Material Value Structure," *The Jurist* 56 (1996): 41–67.

30. The situation in which the Church must live her faith has dramatically changed, not only after the closing of the Council, but also after the promulgation of both Codes. Today there are issues that did not even exist fifty years ago and need a response both doctrinally and on the level of canonical institutions, such as an increasing theological knowledge of laity, the decline in priestly ordinations, the abuse scandal and the cover-up by bishops, and the accountability in finances. For reflections on areas in need of reform, see John A. Alesandro, "The Code: 25 Years Reflection on the Past and Looking to the Future," *CLSA Proceedings* 69 (2007): 11–69, and Francis G. Morrisey, "Twenty-Five Years of the 1983 Code: Reflections on the Past; Thoughts on the Future," *CLSA Proceedings* 70 (2008): 1–27.

31. For further elaborations, see Myriam Wijlens, "'That All May be One...' (John 17:21): The Lord's Prayer in the Work of Canon Lawyers; A Mere Option?" *The Jurist* 65 (2005): 181–204.

32. Myriam Wijlens, "'The Newness of the Council Constitutes the Newness of the Code' (John Paul II): The Role of Vatican II in the Application of the Law," *CLSA Proceedings* 70 (2008): 285–302.

33. Cf. Myriam Wijlens, "The Doctrine of the People of God and Hierarchical Authority as Service in Latin Church Legislation on the Local Church," *The Jurist* 68 (2008): 328–49.

34. This is quite evident from Pope Francis's discourse on the Commemoration of the Fiftieth Anniversary of the Institution of the Synod of Bishops, October 17, 2015, https://w2.vatican.va/content/francesco/it/speeches/2015/october/documents/papa-francesco_20151017_50-anniversario-sinodo.html.

16

FOR A REFORM OF THE CENTRAL GOVERNMENT OF A *COLLEGIAL* AND *SYNODAL* CHURCH FIFTY YEARS AFTER VATICAN II

Massimo Faggioli

Status Quaestionis

The issue of the Roman curia has become more urgent than ever, in light not only of the scandals and indignities of these last few years, but also for theological reasons.[1] On the one hand, there have always been theological reasons for criticizing the very existence of the curia, given the theologically questionable foundations for its existence and power. We lack a plausible "theology of the Curia,"[2] and at the same time the anticuria literature is one of the most resilient literary genres in the Church and beyond (Dan Brown comes to mind here as the most recent and popular example). On the other hand, the Roman curia seems to be a separate body from the theology of the Church, and especially from the ecclesiology that comes to us from the Second Vatican Council.

There is an undeniable resilience in the institution that we call "the Roman curia," an institution at the same time inseparable from the person of the pope and potentially antagonist of the pope. The curia has gone through and survived every reform of the central government of the Catholic Church since the Catholic Church gave itself a central government: just to limit ourselves to the modern era, the loss of the Papal States in 1870; and finally, the reforms during the twentieth century—Pius X's *Sapienti Consilio* (1908), Paul VI's *Regimini Ecclesiae Universae* (1967), and John Paul II's *Pastor Bonus* (1988).

Vatican II plays a role in this issue as both an ecclesiological breakthrough and a missed opportunity. The proposals for a reform of the curia made in conciliar speeches did not have a systematic form, and they never became operational plans, except for the idea of a *Consilium episcoporum centrale* in Rome *above* the curia (proposals of Cardinal Alfrink and Maximos IV Saigh versus Cardinal Marella's proposal of a cooptation of some bishops in the curia).[3] The pope never lost control of the issue, and the idea of such a "central board" *above* the Roman curia was buried on September 15, 1965, when the pope published the *motu proprio Apostolica Sollicitudo* that created the Bishops' Synod.[4] Moreover, Paul VI failed to account for Cardinal Döpfner's proposal for a reform of the college of cardinals in the shape of a *Senatus Romani Pontificis*, a collegial body to assist the pope that would set aside the historical role played by the Roman curia. The pope chose rather to create a *Synodus Episcoporum*, a purely consultative body subject to the pope as well as to the Roman curia.

Nevertheless, from a theological point of view, at Vatican II the ground shifted significantly. In the debate of November 1963 and in the *motu proprio Pastorale Munus* (November 30, 1963), the new guiding principle was to restore to bishops the powers of office that Rome had appropriated in the previous centuries. That principle entailed other changes brought by Vatican II, such as the episcopal conferences and their role in the liturgical reform, which had a deep impact (even unconsciously or indirectly) on the perception of the theological legitimacy of the Roman curia in the eyes of the rest of the Church.

Paul VI's reform of the curia of 1967 was meant to be a reform according to Vatican II, but it can be said that it reflects more

Montini's experience in the Roman curia under Pius XII than the ecclesiology of the Council. In Paul VI's *Regimini Ecclesiae Universae*, the strengthening of the role of the Secretary of State was a corollary of stronger papal power: "The Secretary of State became almost a prime minister, but at the same time also the head of cabinet in a presidential republic."[5] Paul VI shaped the Roman curia vertically, placing the Secretariat of State at the pinnacle of curial authority, paralleling the pope's own leadership in directing the reception of Vatican II.[6] The curia became more international and less Italian. Under Paul VI and John Paul II, Roman curia and papal power became bigger, dominant, and at odds with the authority of the Bishops' Conferences and the Bishops' Synod.

The guiding principles stated in John Paul II's *Pastor Bonus* (1988) were, allegedly, an idea of the Church as a communion, the pastoral nature of episcopal ministry, episcopal collegiality between the bishops and the pope, and the vicarial nature of the Roman curia in relation to the pope.[7] But *Pastor Bonus* applied Vatican II nominalistically more than substantially. The 1988 reform simplified the structure of the dicasteries, reducing their number (nine congregations, twelve councils, three offices) and creating a system at least formally of equals. The structure of the curia, however, did not change fundamentally—and the CDF was also formally given (even before *Pastor Bonus*) a renewed pivotal role. With *Pastor Bonus* "the Curia stays closely connected to the papal primacy."[8]

Under Benedict XVI the close connection between papal primacy and Roman curia breaks down: the person of the pope clearly tries to liberate himself from the association with the curia, but the price of this liberation is a central government of the Church without visible and accountable leadership. The curia appears to be a player potentially independent from the pope—that is, operating with an agenda that is not the pope's and therefore not coherent, not visible, and not accountable. The events afflicting the pontificate of Benedict XVI until his resignation showed urgent need not to govern *through* the curia, but to govern *the* curia—even before reforming it. But the issue of reform is more urgent than before.

Theoretical Points

At fifty years from Vatican II, an honest look at the issue of the Roman curia and its reform cannot avoid identifying the key problems affecting the central government of the Church—knowing that the alleged corruption, uselessness, merciless, and aloofness of the Roman curia from the real world constitute one of most effective *topoi* in literature, theological and not.

The question to be asked today is, "What is the curia?" On a more practical level, the first subquestion is whether the future reforms of the curia are to be inspired by the theological and ecclesiological reflection developed at Vatican II and in the post–Vatican II period, or whether they are to be inspired by a criterion that is legal-rational, related to the need of effectiveness and efficacy. It seems to me that the reforms of the post–Vatican II period tried to respond to the call for a more legal-rational system while not considering the ecclesiological side of the issue. The reforms of the post–Vatican II period avoided especially the conciliar call to a more collegial Church (not only in terms of "episcopal collegiality" as it is framed by chapter 3 of *Lumen Gentium*, but also in terms of "synodality") and the renewed emphasis on the local Church vis-à-vis a universalist mindset.

VATICAN II AND FUTURE REFORMS

The first theoretical point concerns the relationship between Vatican II—clearly a "reform council"[9]—and the reform of the Roman curia. If the reform of the curia is to receive in some way the theological legacy of Vatican II and of the post–Vatican II debate, it seems to me that there are three issues to be considered:

1. When it comes to the issue of Church reform, there is a gap between what Vatican II said (in the debates in the aula and in the proposal made in conciliar commissions) and what Vatican II and Paul VI decided (especially what the popes of the post–Vatican II period decided about the curia). In particular, it is known that the commission *de episcopis* of Vatican II was about to

propose (in 1963–1964) a reform of the curia with the creation of a *synodos endemousa* (a permanent, standing synod of bishops in which the activity and business of the patriarchate of Constantinople was decided)[10] and a reform of the procedure for bishops' appointments, both of which were rejected by the Roman curia (through the leadership of Vatican II) and never became a subject for public discussion. It is worth reconsidering those proposals in light of the history of Church institutions in these last fifty years, but also in the long-term historical perspective.

2. A second question regards the gap between what Vatican II said (the Catholic theological and ecclesiological reflection at the time of the Council) and what was already necessary back then. It is about acknowledging the shortcomings of the ecclesiology of Vatican II, its silences and omissions, and the need to go beyond the letter of Vatican II. In this sense, the most visible issue concerns the role of women and lay faithful in the Church and in Church government and administration, but also the shortcomings of the theology of episcopal collegiality.
3. A third question is about the kind of implementation of Vatican II by the papacy. It seems to me that until Francis the reforms of the Roman curia were not conciliar, in the sense that they did not consider (except for the *language*, though in a nominalistic way) the ecclesiology of Vatican II. The issue is now about what kind of relationship (explicitly or implicitly) this reform wants to have with Vatican II. Pope Francis has so far implemented reforms that restore the spirit of Vatican II in these new institutions (the Bishops' Synod as a real moment of debate; the consistory of cardinals as representative of all the Catholic world, not just of those traditional cardinal sees; the wish for a stronger role for Bishops' Conferences). It remains to be seen if a "restorative" approach is adequate and sufficient, or if the reform of the Roman curia needs a restructuring more radical of those of 1908, 1967, and 1988.

Despite all the good-faith attempts to update the system in these last fifty years, the now-existing Roman curia has more to do with the Roman curia between the Council of Trent, Vatican I, and the period leading up to Vatican II than with the ecclesiology of Vatican II. What today must follow Vatican II—the most consequential Council in modern Church history after the Council of Trent—is a reform no less radical than Pope Sixtus V's establishment of the modern Roman curia in 1588. The global and pastoral turn of the Catholic Church at Vatican II needs a radical rethinking of Church government.

THEOLOGICAL-CANONICAL DEVELOPMENTS AND CURIA REFORMS

In these last fifty years, the ecclesiology of Vatican II has developed in the sense of a Catholic Church that is collegial, synodal, ecumenical, local and global, personal and not only territorial. But these changes in ecclesiology are in dialogue with a few *facts* in the life of the Church that are dramatically different from the Church of the time of Vatican II—just fifty years ago. In other words, there has been a clear disconnect—if not a contradiction—between the developments in ecclesiology and the practices of the central government of the Church.

COLLEGIAL CHURCH

Episcopal collegiality at Vatican II means that the papacy and the college of bishops need to work collegially to develop reflections necessary for the government of the Church. On the other hand, collegiality is typical of a "guild," of a separate group. Therefore, collegiality must be integrated with synodality. Moreover, Vatican II did not articulate properly the relationship between *collegio episcoporum* and *communio ecclesiarum*.[11] The incompleteness of Vatican II about collegiality and synodality has been made worse by postconciliar practices. The college of bishops has been largely seen as the rubber stamp of papal primacy. Episcopal collegiality has meant (until Francis) something "affective" without being "effective."[12] The Roman curia has proven a liability for the authority of papal primacy because of the link between the primacy and the identification of the curia as part of the primacy. One concrete issue here is the "spoils system"—a practice in which the pope after the conclave gives jobs to his supporters. Overall it is telling the fact that if the curia was created to strengthen the power of the pope, in recent times the curia in its actual state has in fact damaged the authority of the pope in the global Church.

SYNODAL CHURCH

In the Church, there are some issues that deserve to be matter of a larger process of reflection and discernment, not just limited to the pope and the bishops, but involving the clergy and the laity (meaning also women). The nonepiscopal component of the Catholic Church (clergy, religious orders, laity) have received fewer and fewer opportunities to express themselves on some pressing issues thought out and decided in the Vatican. The Roman Catholic Church today is expected to be less clerical with more lay faithful and women in leadership positions; the disconnect between some magisterial pronouncements and large portions of the world Church is also a fruit of a lack of synodality in the Church.

ECUMENICAL CHURCH

The Roman Catholic Church is a Church whose decisions and acts have an impact not only on Catholics but on Christianity worldwide. At the same time the Catholic Church receives input from world Christianity. So far, the ecumenical relations of the Catholic Church have been still largely handled by the papacy and the CDF, with the Pontifical Council for Promoting Christian Unity having only limited access to the process of decision-making in the Vatican in terms of doctrinal policy. In this sense, the simple addition of a dicastery in charge of the ecumenical issue on the structure of the Roman curia has been strikingly incomplete.

LOCAL AND GLOBAL

The Catholic Church is not supposed to be global in the sense of the "franchising," that is, an expansion of the Church of Rome, but a global Church *ex*, from local churches—where Rome is at the service of the local churches. But the relations between the center and the periphery are still marked by the assumption of a top-down model of administration. The global nature of the Church is made more visible by the fact that membership in the Roman Catholic Church today is much more global: less European, more Latin American, African, and Asian. The principle of "subsidiarity," whose origin is in Catholic social doctrine, could be of use here once it receives proper ecclesiological articulation.

PERSONAL AND NOT ONLY TERRITORIAL

The Roman Catholic Church today is less based in the structures of Church government (dioceses), less institutional and territorial, and it relies more on movements, groups, and associations that have a varied relationship with the institution and its local and central government, also due to an increased mobility of the faithful. The sympathy of the post–Vatican II papacy toward the new forms of Christian life in "movements" and associations has been translated only in a limited way in the central government of the Church, limiting also the transparency and accountability of some of these new ecclesial bodies (e.g., Legionaries of Christ).

MISSIONARY CHURCH AND INSTITUTIONAL STATUS QUO

The very idea of government has changed in these last fifty years. What is the role of Church government in a Church more missionary than established? The Roman Catholic Church today is aware of the necessity of looking forward instead of preserving the institutional status quo. The central government of the Church should be the agent of more missionary and less established Catholicism.

EPISCOPALISM AND CLERICAL CHURCH

This question regards the chances of overcoming a Church government system that is based on the episcopacy and on the clergy, in light of the baptismal ecclesiology of Vatican II. The power of governance has been kept strictly in the hands of ordained members of the Church. Episcopacy has remained the requirement for leading whatever office of the curia, and this violates the very meaning of episcopacy as pastoral ministry.

Last but not least, we cannot forget here that in these last fifteen years especially, our ecclesial consciousness has been touched also by the shock of the *moral crisis* brought about by the *sex abuse scandal* in local Churches and in religious orders. All this has altered the perception of the Catholic Church worldwide, and particularly in the secularized Western world, in terms of the credibility and authenticity of Catholic Christians and of their leaders specifically. This tells us that the reform of the curia must be part of a reform that responds to the questions asked of the Church in terms of its ability to adhere to the gospel more than to the instinct of self-preservation. This has deep theological consequences that must inform any and every project of institutional reform. The concept cannot be only a streamlining of bureaucratic methods in light of a necessarily healthy "ecclesial cybernetics,"[13] but must be a radical call to conversion of the structures.

Proposals

These reflections are just a preliminary attempt to tackle the issue of the reform of the Roman curia. They have no aspirations to be complete and definitive, but on the contrary, they need to be complemented with other contributions. Regarding the choice to renew/reform old institutions or create new ones, this chapter argues in favor of a two-step approach, in keeping with an ecclesiology of institutional sobriety: a renewal of existing institutions in the short term, and a more radical step with the creation of new institutions in the middle and long term.

MIDTERM PERSPECTIVE: RENEWING ALREADY EXISTING INSTITUTIONS

The renewal of existing institutions in the short and midterm should have in mind a more *inclusive and responsive* representation of the global Catholic Church in terms of local Churches. The spirit of this first step is a renewal of this institution following the *intention of the reform proposals put forward at Vatican II and in the early postconciliar period.*

THE ROMAN CURIA TODAY

It seems urgent to restore a *term limit* for all curia officials, with as few exceptions as possible. The general principle should be that priests and bishops serve in the curia knowing that they will go back to their local churches or communities or to another ministry (Pope Francis is already doing this and it must be strengthened). The curia is (also) a *career system* that needs serious change. Moreover, a substantial move toward appointing more men and women (religious and lay) is urgent and expected by the whole Church. These cannot be "token" appointments—appointments of members of minority groups as purely symbolic and instrumental to the status quo. It is necessary to send signals in terms of a *decentralization*—at least going back, in the midterm perspective, to the early postconciliar balance between national Bishops' Conferences and Roman curia (the recent case of the new translation in English of the Missal being the most serious example of the recentralization).

THE CURIA AND THE BISHOPS' SYNOD

The issues here are the Synod's role vis-à-vis the papacy (deliberative or consultative vote), its composition (who are the members), and the frequency of its meetings. About the issue of the deliberative versus consultative vote, I would argue that it is not advisable to pursue the "constitutionalization" of the papacy through a parliament-like Synod: the relationship between decision-making procedures in the Church and what Niklas Luhmann called *"legitimation by procedure" is a delicate one.*[14] But it appears to be necessary first of all to limit effectively the influence of the Roman curia on the Synod (thus changing the provision of Paul VI, *Apostolica Sollicitudo* of September 15, 1965, nn. V–VI). That can be done through a stronger *separation between the Synod's leadership and the Roman curia,* and a composition of the General Secretariat of the Synod and of the *Council of the General Secretariat more representative of the global Church*—in the sense of also lay members and women. Another problem is the fact that the Council of the General Secretariat is elected by the old Synod to be active until (in order to prepare the next Synod) and at the next Synod.[15] Another crucial change in the midterm would be the change to a Synod that gathers *more frequently*, possibly every year in the fall (September–October). The agenda of the Synod should not remain entirely in the hands of the pope, but instead should reflect the *needs of the global Church in a missionary perspective*. Issues that are now in the hands of the Roman curia should increasingly become part of the purview of the Bishops' Synod and of the bishops' conferences.

THE CURIA AND THE BISHOPS' CONFERENCES

These issues are related to their relationship to the Roman curia in terms of the representation of the voices of the bishops. It is important to give the Bishops' Conferences power to interact with the Roman curia—*not for diocesan bishops individually*, but collegially as a conference (national or continental). The manifest humiliation of the prerogatives of the Bishops' Conferences (such as in the recent case of the new English translation of the Missal) must become a thing of the past.

THE CURIA AND THE CONSISTORY

These issues are the role of the consistory vis-à-vis the papacy, its composition (who are the members), and the frequency of its meetings. In the midterm, it seems possible to leave the consistory as a tool of the papacy to gauge reactions from the cardinals (many of them being the electoral college of the pope) about particular issues of his choosing, but also on issues brought up by the cardinals. It is important that the consistory gathers *at least once a year*.

THE CURIA AND THE DIOCESAN SYNODS AND PARTICULAR COUNCILS

Diocesan synods and particular councils must be part of a new consideration of the relationship between center and periphery for a reform of the Roman curia. It is advisable to *jump-start the synodal life of the local Churches* with some provision requiring the celebration of diocesan synods and particular councils at least every ten years (see Code of Canon Law 1917).

The role of *Vatican diplomacy and the nuncios* for their work at the service of the local Churches is as well in need of a new appraisal considering the ecclesiology of Vatican II. In particular, *the procedures for the bishops' appointments must be changed—at least initially from a symbolic point of view*, in the sense of more participation of the local Churches (clergy, lay, and women) bound to receive a new bishop. This would be in line both with the ancient tradition, with some proposals drafted at Vatican II, and with a correct ecclesiology of the local Church. The role of Vatican diplomacy should be maintained, being one of the distinctive elements of the activity of the Catholic Church as a service to the world and to the world Church.

LONG-TERM PERSPECTIVE: CREATING NEW INSTITUTIONS (FOUND IN THE TRADITION)

There are two issues especially that a series of reforms in the long-term must address, *from an ecclesiological point of view*:

1. the turn from a Church that is not collegial (even if it says so) to a Church that is synodal, articulating the relationship between episcopal collegiality (pope and bishops) and synodality of the Church (the entire Church).
2. the turn from a curia as part of the monarchic-absolutist papacy, to a curia that serves the whole Church, accountable and responsive to the global Church and not only to the pope—according to a model that is evangelical and not merely constitutional (such as a "constitutionalization of the papacy" through the creation of elected, representative bodies with a deliberative vote).

Here are some major points for our consideration.

WHAT TO DO WITH THE EXISTING CURIA

During the last century, the usual way to streamline the business of the Roman curia has been to merge competencies of different dicasteries, and add new dicasteries over the existing structure built in 1588. The Roman curia that exists today is the fruit of a historical process of addition of institutions—congregations, tribunals, offices, secretariats/councils—built to deal with Church government, according to a mixed criterion—"geography, issues, and constituencies."[16] Here it is useful to bring up some examples that show contradictions between this mixed criterion and ecclesiology.

About *geography*, the concept of a *Congregation de Propaganda Fide* needs serious rethinking, given the missionary state of the Church in its entirety. The *Congregation for Oriental Churches* mixes geography, issues, and constituencies. Overall, the renewed awareness of the Church that it is all a "missionary church" on one side and the new face of "Catholic globalization" must lead to reconsidering the use of the geographical criterion in a much more limited way.

About *issues*, the role of the *CDF* needs serious rethinking in terms of its universal role, especially in light of the "competition" with other voices in the Church that are more qualified ecclesiologically and better positioned (that is, at the local level) to proceed in case of controversial teachings and opinions. The standing of the International Theological Commission must be an integral part of this rethinking. Secondly, *evangelization* needs to inspire the ethos of the whole curia, and not be limited to a particular dicastery ad hoc.

About *constituencies*, considering the changes in Church membership in these last fifty years, a rethinking of the relationship between the *Congregation for Institutes of Consecrated Life and Societies of Apostolic* and the *Pontifical Council for the Laity* is in order. This change would take stock of the end of the *duo genera Christianorum*, repair Vatican II's forgetfulness about the religious orders, and better integrate the new forms of communal life in the Catholic Church (new movements, associations, and communities).

Moreover, there is an issue of balance between the universal and local level that must be addressed by the reform of the curia. The issue of *decentralization* (see Francis, *Evangelii Gaudium*) must be dealt with in the sense of giving back to the bishops and the mid-level ecclesial bodies the faculties they used to have, without multiplying offices—starting with the doctrinal assessments.

Decentralization could mean also giving the global Church a say on the "ethos of government" by the Roman curia. The role of the *Secretariat of State* as supercongregation with power of oversight over the rest of the curia must be seen in synopsis with the need of a new body called to act together with the pope and to oversee and direct the curia (see *infra*).

The need for a more synodal form of the Roman curia calls for a new balance between *residential and nonresidential members* of curia dicasteries (and the issue of the proliferation of "titular bishops"). A more general issue is the relationship between *the curia and the pope, and the curia and the college of cardinals, the curia and the bishops*: these actors in the government of the Church share areas of power and influence that seem more "politically" intertwined than ecclesiology would allow.

More specifically, the reform must address the issue of the use of *legislative power of the dicasteries* (*diritto d'ordinanza*). More generally, there is an overarching issue of the whole structure of the Roman curia in light of the reform. The late sixteenth century is the age of the shift from the consistory (frequent meetings of cardinals with the pope) to the special congregations (dicasteries) for the government of the Church (but also of temporal affairs of the Church as a kingdom). The issue is about the possible coexistence between the congregations and something like the early modern consistory.[17] In this sense it seems necessary to restore a *mechanism of control of the bureaucracy that is above the curia*.

ABOVE THE CURIA

A primary goal is to distinguish more carefully between the curia and the papal primacy—in a way similar to what the creation of the institution of the conclave did in the second half of the eleventh century in order to separate the papacy from the aristocracy of Rome and its interests in occupying the throne of Peter.[18] It seems necessary to redefine the relationship between the ministry of the pope and the power and faculties of the Roman curia in the sense of a stronger system of control of the administrative and executive (not legislative) nature of the curia.

This is, in my view, the key element for the future reform of the curia: a new role for the Bishops' Synod and the creation of the central board. I suggest it is advisable to build a *system of oversight and direction of the Roman curia* giving some of this power of oversight to the *Bishops' Synod* and to a *Consilium episcoporum centrale* (this was one of the names in the proposals made at Vatican II. Other names are possible, such as *Senatus communionis*).[19]

The *Synod* should become the time and place for a synodal reflection in the Church with the pope about issues concerning the whole Church and requiring collective discernment. The curia should be mostly on the receiving end of the synodal process: not without participating in it in some way, but without the presumption of preparing and steering the discussion and its results. The results of the synodal reflection serve as a general orientation for the decision-making process (legislative moment).

The composition of the *oversight authority like the Consilium or Senatus communionis* should not be made of bishops only. Different options are available. The key issue here is to have oversight that makes communication between representatives of the world Church and this body possible on the one hand, and that keeps a line of communication open between the pope and this body. In the actual form, the C9 (created by Francis on April 13, 2013) carries a few risks. The centralization of authority on the person of the pope is far from over. The geographical origins of the cardinals (one member for each "continent"—difficult as the geographical idea of a "continent" is for Catholic ecclesiology), is an update of Vatican II's push for an internationalization of the curia.[20] The C9 has the positive effect of bypassing the curia (symbolically and not), but the C9 is governed by the pope, who uses his own discretion to choose its members and to set its agenda and meetings. This institution in its current form is thus left for Francis's successor to decide—that is, to keep it or not. Instead, the institution of the C9 should be solidified. What must be retained in this model is the return to the early modern consistorial system in an updated form, where the Roman curia is subject to the oversight of representatives of the local churches who gather periodically, several times a year. There are several options for the membership of this *Consilium* or *Senatus communionis*: cardinals, bishops, and lay members together with the Secretary of State or other possible models. Another item is their term, fixed or *ad nutum*.

THE CURIA AND THE REST

The reform of the curia cannot be isolated from a more general reform in the Church—in its institutions as well. An open question is the future of the general (ecumenical) Council: its membership, its role vis-à-vis local, national, and continental conciliar-synodal events.[21]

More urgent (at least ecclesiologically) is the issue of the relations between the reform of the curia and other ecclesiastical reforms needed at the local level, in the sense of a rejuvenation of the role of the mid-level ecclesiastical institution (that in the last two centuries took the form of national bishops' conferences).[22] There is little doubt that a rebalancing of the middle level of the Catholic institutions is more and more urgent. One possible solution is the revival of the patriarchates.[23] Another solution (not necessarily in contradiction with the renewal of patriarchates) is a new role for metropolitan archbishops.

Conclusion

This chapter offers a few preliminary ideas about a possible path of institutional reform of the Roman curia, in light of the ecclesiology of Vatican II and of the developments of the post–Vatican II period, with a combined short-midterm and long-term approach. In Church history synodality is not less relevant than episcopal collegiality. The reform of the curia cannot stop at updating the central government of the Church with more episcopal collegiality, or a redistribution of faculties among dicasteries, or the injection of some lay and women curia officials.

Real reform needs steps toward a curia that reflects (1) a *synodal Church* in the context of a truly *global Catholicism*; (2) a curia whose structure is an *expression of a theology* more than a system of Church bureaucracy made of stratified layers of different administrative cultures—premodern, early modern, modern constitutional; (3) a curia whose activity is monitored and inspired by *frequent celebrations of the Bishops' Synod and by the oversight of a "central board"* governing the global Church with the pope whose primacy does not cover the authority of the curia.

NOTES

1. See also Massimo Faggioli, "The Roman Curia at and after Vatican II: Legal-Rational or Theological Reform?" *Theological Studies* 76, no. 3 (September, 2015): 550–71; *Il vescovo e il concilio. Modello episcopale e aggiornamento al Vaticano II* (Bologna: Il Mulino, 2015).

2. Quite interestingly, Pope Francis, in his unforgiving speech to the Roman curia of December 22, 2014, tried to frame the Roman curia as a as "a small-scale model of the Church": http://w2.vatican.va/content/francesco/en/speeches/2014/december/documents/papa-francesco_20141222_curia-romana.html.

3. See John R. Quinn, *Ever Ancient, Ever New: Structures of Communion in the Church* (Mahwah, NJ: Paulist Press, 2013), 29–30.

4. See Massimo Faggioli, *Il vescovo e il concilio: Modello episcopale e aggiornamento al Vaticano II* (Bologna: Il Mulino, 2005), 389–438; Antonino Indelicato, *Il Sinodo dei Vescovi: La collegialità sospesa 1965–1985* (Bologna: Il Mulino, 2008), 33–63.

5. Andrea Riccardi, *Il potere del papa da Pio XII a Giovanni Paolo II* (Rome: Laterza, 1993), 292.

6. See Andrea Riccardi, "L'evoluzione della Segreteria di Stato dopo il 1870," in *Les Secretaires d'Etat du Saint-Siege, XIX–XX siècles*, Melanges de l'École Française de Rome 116, no. 1 (2004): 33–44.

7. See Jean Beyer, "Le linee fondamentali della Costituzione Apostolica '*Pastor Bonus*,'" in *La Curia Romana nella Cost. Ap. "Pastor Bonus,"* ed. Pier Antonio Bonnet and Carlo Gullo (Vatican City: Libreria Editrice Vaticana, 1990), 17–43.

8. Gian Piero Milano, "Riforma della Curia e collegialità episcopale dal Vaticano II alla *Pastor Bonus*," in *Scritti in memoria di Pietro Gismondi*, vol. 2/1 (Milan: Giuffrè, 1990), 673–752, at 725.

9. See John W. O'Malley, *What Happened at Vatican II* (Cambridge MA: Harvard University Press, 2008).

10. See Joseph Hajjar, *Le synode permanent dans l'Église byzantine des origines au XIe siècle* (Rome: Pont. Inst. Orientalium Studiorum, 1962).

11. See Hervé Legrand, "Les *évêques*, les *Églises locales et l'Église entière*. Evolutions institutionnelles depuis Vatican II et chantiers actuels de recherche," *Revue de Sciences Philosophiques et Théologiques* 85 (2001): 461–509.

12. About this distinction, see Joseph A. Komonchak, "The Roman Working Paper on Episcopal Conferences," in *Episcopal Conferences: Historical, Canonical and Theological Studies*, ed. Thomas J. Reese (Washington, DC: Georgetown University Press, 1989), 177–204. On April 1, 2014, in a message to Cardinal Lorenzo Baldisseri, secretary general of

the Synod of Bishops, Pope Francis spoke of the synod as an institution in terms of "affective and effective collegiality," adding a significant "effective" to the more typical (in the post–Vatican II period) "affective." See *Bollettino: Sala stampa della Santa Sede*, April 8, 2014.

13. See Patrick Granfield, *Ecclesial Cybernetics: A Study of Democracy in the Church* (New York: Macmillan, 1973).

14. See Günther Wassilowsky, "La verità ai voti?" in *Il Regno—attualità* 7 (2015): 486–92.

15. "§ 1. At the end of each ordinary general synodal assembly, the Ordinary Council of the General Secretariat is formed. § 2. The Council is comprised of 15 Members; 12 of whom are elected from the Synod, taking into account the representation of Bishops scattered throughout the world, and 3 designated by the Roman Pontiff."

16. See Thomas Reese, *Inside the Vatican: The Politics and Organization of the Catholic Church* (Cambridge, MA: Harvard University Press, 1996), 281.

17. See Maria Teresa Fattori, *Clemente VIII e il Sacro Collegio, 1592–1605. Meccanismi istituzionali e accentramento di governo* (Stuttgart: Hiersemann, 2004).

18. See Agostino Paravicini Bagliani, *Morte e elezione del papa. Norme, riti, conflitti. Il Medioevo* (Rome: Viella, 2013), 22.

19. See Alberto Melloni, "Senatus Communionis," *Concilium*, November 2013.

20. See Galavotti, "Sulle riforme della Curia Romana nel novecento."

21. See Severino Dianich, *La chiesa cattolica verso la sua riforma* (Brescia: Queriniana, 2014), 121–34.

22. See Pope Francis, apostolic exhortation *Evangelii Gaudium* (November 24, 2013), 32.

23. See Quinn, *Ever Ancient, Ever New*, 21–27.

17

THE EPISCOPAL CONFERENCES

"This Desire Has Not Been Fully Realized" (*EG* 32)

Carlos Schickendantz

The following reflections on the episcopal conferences fall within the context of the present considerations on the reform of the Church. Hence, the contribution provides, on the one hand, an update on the *status quaestionis,* and on the other, some ideas that may help to identify recommendations for potential future steps. The text includes four main points. The first proposes a review of some of the key moments in the historical development of the episcopal conferences, particularly in recent decades. The second, more importantly, attempts to describe the new situation in which we find ourselves with the teachings and actions of Pope Francis, which, no doubt, offer a new ecclesial context on the subject. Third, in our contribution we refer to the many questions at stake and pending issues by considering the *motu proprio Apostolos Suos* of 1998. Finally, we identify the main questions to be developed for further progress of the theological status of the episcopal conferences while making some recommendations. We will focus primarily on the theological issues, even though in this area the joint work between theologians and canonists is even more necessary.

As Cardinal Walter Kasper stated in his ecclesiology of 2011, "Unfortunately, the development of collegial/synodal structures was only hesitatingly followed up after the Council."[1] This general statement finds particular application in what has happened with the episcopal conferences in recent decades. The theme is relevant because, even though it is about a narrow topic—the episcopal conferences, their nature, and their responsibilities—it reflects fundamental discussions and, to a significant extent, the basic orientations that have directed the ecclesiology in these postconciliar years.

Key Moments in the Development of Episcopal Conferences

The comprehensive treatment of the subject requires attention to different moments that help shape the situation we have inherited.

First, a consideration of the *historical origins* of the episcopal conferences. The causes that give rise to these forms of episcopal collaboration are multiple and complex. They emerged in the nineteenth century not as the result of a mere process of decentralization, in explicit communion with Rome, in line with the emergence of national feelings but distinct from them, but as a response to specific common pastoral issues, influenced by the processes of separation of Church and state and in the presence, too, of bellicose strategies of the secularist state of the mid-nineteenth century. They represented complementary instances to regional and provincial councils that were easier to convene and assemble, but without the same legal authority. They were not conceived as an alternative to them, albeit they clearly coincided with a decline of these councils. There is no doubt on the attribution to them of the eminently pragmatic functions of consultation, mutual assistance, and coordination of efforts.[2]

A second significant moment is represented by what happened at Vatican II, particularly in *Christus Dominus* (no. 38) and *Lumen*

Gentium (no. 23). Both texts are fundamental because they offer the theological framework from which specific themes in the postconciliar period developed. Some of the doctrinal points that emerged are the following: the recognition of "divine providence" as the cause of this ecclesiological development,[3] the analogy (*simili ratione*) between conferences and Eastern patriarchates (*LG* 23d), between *coetus episcoporum* and *coetus ecclesiarum*, as well as the similarity with synods and provincial councils (*CD* 36), the legislative power conferred on the conferences (*CD* 38.4), as well as the recommendation on the dissemination of this institution "born out of canon law"[4] to the whole Catholic Church in the world (*CD* 37).

Despite these concrete developments at the Council, we must not forget the coincidence of the incipient or only initial developments regarding the episcopal conferences added to the general limitations of the ecclesiology of Vatican II and already studied in the specialized literature—coexistence of two ecclesiologies, the local church in a predominantly universalist vision, and so on. Two examples may suffice here, one referring to *Lumen Gentium*, the other to *Christus Dominus*.

Commenting on *LG* 23, Peter Hünermann wrote in his important commentary,

> When episcopal conferences are considered merely as an expression of *collegialis affectus*, we refuse to see in them an expression of collegiality—of course, limited and temporal—and we show here and in the immediate post-conciliar discussion the difficulty to situate in a wider context the thought of collegiality of service in the Church.[5]

Even *Christus Dominus*, which only recommends (but not orders) the institution of episcopal conferences, has its limits. In 2014, Massimo Faggioli wrote,

> In the end, it showed more interest in the tutelage of diocesan autonomy than in the necessity of uniformity among bishops from the same country. *Christus Dominus* remains very ambiguous and vague about the legislative

> powers of episcopal conferences, limiting their decisions to a minimum and rejecting the proposal to ascribe to conferences and their decisions some measure of collegiality. *Christus Dominus* offered a framework law for conferences but left their future to their statutes and to the reform of the *Codex Iuris Canonici* that was then beginning.[6]

Several authors point out a "trend reversal" in the postconciliar period: from a more strongly recognized authority of the conferences, ascribing to them wide powers in the legislative, administrative, and judicial fields, to many practical obstacles and doctrinal restraints.[7]

As part of the first phase, we find two of Paul VI's *motu proprio*: *Sacram Liturgiam* (1964) and *Ecclesiae Sanctae* (1966), which instituted the conferences—as a "new" (de jure, not de facto) legal entity—that Vatican II had only recommended. The 1969 Synod of Bishops, which, according to the then Special Secretary, Angel Antón, "did not bring new elements in the doctrinal field," meant a "new impulse" for practical implementations of collegiality. Without explicitly affirming the idea of episcopal conferences as "intermediate instances between the Holy See and the diocesan bishop," this understanding found favorable starting points.[8]

The analysis of what the 1983 Code of Canon Law establishes for episcopal conferences is very complex. If positive steps are evident, such as the recognition of the conferences as a permanent institution with certain stable structures and legal status, as well as an extensive list of responsibilities assigned to them at the legislative and administrative level and in collaboration with other ecclesial governing bodies, we must recognize, on the other hand, a lack of progress or, even more, a growing trend—very visible in those years—contrary to any consideration of them as intermediate entity, in particular arguing that they endanger the autonomy of diocesan bishops. Regarding the treatment of conferences in canons 447–59, a very different style from the texts of the previous period is also evident to Faggioli: the codification process marked the "first step" of a progressive reduction of legislative powers. In his view, it was the "first reaction" to the positive postconciliar trend aimed at giving greater powers to conferences.[9]

The most important teaching of the Extraordinary Synod of 1985 states that the "the ecclesiology of communion is a central and fundamental idea in the documents of the council" (II. C 1). As Pottmeyer notes, if we take into account the ecclesiologies not adequately mediated present in the conciliar texts, this statement is an important step in the interpretation of the Council.[10] A second valuable statement is that the "ecclesiology of communion provides the sacramental foundation of collegiality" (II. C 4). Therefore, an important link between ecclesiology of communion and the principle of collegiality is affirmed. Although it mentions partial realizations of *collegiality* ("diverse partial realizations authentically sign and instrument of the collegial spirit": II. C 4), the use of the word to indicate the episcopal conferences is avoided. In addition, it says, incomprehensibly, that like other ecclesial actualizations, such as the synod of bishops, "they cannot be directly deduced from the theological principle of collegiality; but they are regulated by ecclesial law" (II. 4 C). This may explain, on the one hand, the existence of negative opinions over the outcome of the Synod, and, on the other, on the other, the fact that various authors resort to the texts of Walter Kasper, special secretary of that extraordinary assembly, to find a more favorable interpretation. The German theologian clearly states, for example, that episcopal conferences are "are *de jure ecclesiastico*, but *cum fundamento in iure divino*."[11] However, the doubts of various members of the Roman curia and of some circles of theologians and canonists regarding the activity of the episcopal conferences that emerged in many interventions in the general debate and in the various linguistic *circuli minors* cannot be ignored.[12]

The synod celebrated twenty years after the closing of Vatican II had great impact on this topic because of its recommendation:

> Since the episcopal conferences are so useful, indeed necessary, in the present-day pastoral work of the Church, it is hoped that the study of their theological "status" and above all the problem of their doctrinal authority might be made explicit in a deeper and more extensive way, keeping in mind what is written in the Conciliar Decree "Christus Dominus" n. 38 and in the Code of Canon Law can. 447 and 753. (II. C 8)

Two negative moments in the further development of the matter should be recorded. The first refers to a text of 1984 of the International Theological Commission: "Select Themes of Ecclesiology." It is stated that, in relation to episcopal conferences, one can only speak of collegiality in an "analogical, *theologically improper*" sense.[13] The second one, even more important, is the *Instrumentum Laboris* of 1988, which, as acknowledged by the same authors who belonged mainly to the Congregation of Bishops, received "rather critical" evaluations, suggesting the drafting of a second, "completely new" *Instrumerntum Laboris*.[14] We will return to this text later, when commenting on the *motu proprio Apostolos Suos* of 1998.

The "trend reversal" mentioned earlier has found its most visible expression in the radical change of opinion of two important figures of the postconciliar period: Cardinal Jérôme Hamer—Secretary of the Congregation for the Doctrine of the Faith between 1973 and 1984 and prefect of the Congregation for Institutes of Consecrated Life at the time of the publication of *Instrumentum Laboris*, 1988[15]—and, above all, then Cardinal Joseph Ratzinger.[16] It can be said that the position Ratzinger took during the Council—expressed with great clarity in the texts of 1963 and 1965[17]—which he abandoned in the eighties, without explanation, is the same one taken by a large number of theologians and canonists who have spoken, for example, at the Congress of Salamanca of 1988 and in other important publications, in this regard.

How Can the Current Situation Be Characterized?

The first factor to consider is the reflection contained in the pastoral exhortation *Evangelii Gaudium* of 2013. After speaking of the "conversion of the papacy" and after the reference to the pastoral conversion that must affect also the "central structures of the universal Church," it states,

> The Second Vatican Council stated that, like the ancient patriarchal Churches, episcopal conferences are in a

> position "to contribute in many and fruitful ways to the concrete realization of the collegial spirit." Yet this desire has not been fully realized, since a juridical status of episcopal conferences which would see them as subjects of specific attributions, including genuine doctrinal authority, has not yet been sufficiently elaborated. Excessive centralization, rather than proving helpful, complicates the Church's life and her missionary outreach. (*EG* 32)

The text expresses, above all, dissatisfaction with the results obtained during the postconciliar period. The mere remark in the papal text is already very relevant. Let us highlight some points.

a. *EG* questions the outcome of the process that has had its last expression in the *motu proprio* of 1998. While the "has not been fully" or "not yet been sufficiently" add nuance to the judgment, the statement is significant, even more so compared with the position of Ratzinger/Benedict XVI.
b. Everything indicates are that with these expressions—"status," "subjects of specific attributions," "doctrinal authority"—the pope is considering new steps, precisely in matters already posed in the postconciliar process: theological nature and legal *status*, with special emphasis on its *mandatum docendi*.
c. The reference to the "missionary outreach"—central throughout the document—is important because it places the issue within the context of the catholicity of the Church and in the process of inculturation of Christianity in the different regional and cultural contexts. We will return to this aspect because, beyond the apostolic exhortation, it substantially characterizes the situation of Francis's pontificate.
d. The explicit mention of the conciliar expression *simili ratione* (*LG* 23), which establishes an obvious analogy between the "patriarchal Churches" and the "episcopal conferences," is not without significance based on postconciliar debates. What it establishes here is a "certain

> equation between the terms of the binomial *coetus ecclesiarum–coetus episcoporum*, so that the Council passes naturally from one to the other because they are two terms that recall one another."[18] The episcopal conference would thus appear initially, at the same time, as a *coetus episcoporum* and a *coetus ecclesiarum*. There is here a significant theological element.

A second important fact is given by the multiple citations made of texts of episcopal conferences, both in *Evangelii Gaudium* and *Laudato Si'*. The first cites texts of the episcopates of Brazil, Congo, United States (twice), India, the Philippines, and France (twice). Worth noting is that the pope uses not only the texts of the conferences emanating from their plenary assemblies, but also those of the permanent committee (Congo) and of two episcopal committees (*Conseil Famille et Société* and *Commission sociale* of the Conférence des Évêques de France). In addition to these are the two quotations from the *Puebla Document* and the eleven quotations from the *Aparecida Document*, therefore of the General Conferences of the Bishops of Latin America and Caribbean of 1979 and 2007.

Laudato Si' shows a similar pattern. Expressly cited texts include those of the bishops of South Africa, the Philippines, Bolivia (twice), Germany (twice), Argentina (twice), United States, Canada, Japan, Brazil, Dominican Republic, Paraguay, New Zealand, Portugal, Mexico, and Australia, thus encompassing all continents. Even in this case, it cites texts not only of plenary assemblies of bishops, but of specific commissions as well.[19] In addition, it also refers to a colloquium promoted by the Federation of Asian Bishops' Conferences, and a citation of the *Aparecida Document* (the fifth General Conference of the Bishops of Latin America and the Caribbean).

To the question of the theological statute and the magisterial authority of the episcopal conferences, it seems therefore that Francis is weighing in, or at least is offering his contribution to the matter, by way of facts.

Francis's speech of October 2015 on the occasion of the fiftieth anniversary of the institution of the Synod of Bishops requires special consideration for the whole theme of this volume. In particular, it is worth stressing his use of the technical expression "intermediate types of *collegiality*" when referring to episcopal conferences, which was deliberately avoided throughout the previous process.[20]

An important element of the new context is the *Catholic—less Eurocentric—and missionary spirit*, which, on the one hand, represents the guiding lines of Francis's pontificate expressed in many teachings, gestures, and decisions and, on the other, a qualitative leap compared to the pontificate of Benedict XVI. Both aspects are important when reflecting on the theological status of episcopal conferences. In this regard, the repeated references to episcopal conferences in the conciliar decree *Ad Gentes* have been significant, particularly in a very important passage, from a hermeneutical point of view, in the process of re-reading the word of God in a new cultural context (*AG* 22).[21]

Another relevant factor of the new situation lies in the permanence, at the highest level of government of the Curia, of one of the skeptical positions on the theological nature of the conferences. This opinion was expressed for the first time in the famous interview of 1985 by Vittorio Messori to then Cardinal Ratzinger: "We must not forget that the episcopal conferences have no theological basis, they do not belong to the structure of the Church, as willed by Christ, that cannot be eliminated; they have only a practical, concrete function."[22] Therefore, the expression of Cardinal G. Müller in an interview published in March 2015, which states that the episcopal conferences are a "practical organization" in a context already known that indeed fails to recognize their theological significance, is not new.[23] The novelty is that now it seems to represent a theological and pastoral sensitivity different from that of the Bishop of Rome (see *EG* 32). Will the Congregation for the Doctrine of the Faith undertake initiatives to confront the task that *EG* 32 claims?

A sixth factor can also be mentioned here. The specialized theological literature seems to have diminished considerably after the publication and comments to *Apostolos Suos* (1998). Although it is not always possible to distinguish them, I am not referring here to the very large number of those that directly addresses the issue of the reform of the papacy, but to the more specific one about episcopal conferences. The works published by H. Müller and H. Pottmeyer, T. Reese, and the proceedings of the Colloquium of Salamanca—which saw sixty-five participants from sixteen nationalities—edited by H. Legrand, J. Manzanares, and A. García y Garcìa and translated into several languages, represent probably the most extensive and relevant work on the topic. They identify the major theological and canonical arguments. To a great extent, they also reflect a broad consensus on key issues of the dispute.[24]

Subsequently, contributions have been rather sporadic, and I dare say, have not added significant new input, even though they often contain useful assessments of the process experienced in these years. In some recent ecclesiologies, the issue is ignored or barely mentioned.[25] Nevertheless, there are some publications that keep the subject at hand alive in the first decade of the twenty-first century.[26] Perhaps this bibliographic situation is one more expression of the crisis of synodal and conciliar activity at the different levels of the Church, including the synod of bishops, as Massimo Faggioli notes in his recent contribution.[27]

In this sense, it is true that the issue of the episcopal conferences can be considered a "test case" of collegiality and synodality in the Church, which is reflected in a series of documents issued in the last decades. While addressing various issues, these have a common guiding line: a renewed *attempt to centralize* the Church, devaluate the particular churches and the coresponsibility of all believers among the people of God.

The issue of episcopal conferences is, then, closely linked to the general development of the ecclesial experience in recent decades. The *theological presuppositions* that constitute the core of the nature of conferences and their consequent legal *status* have been theoretically and practically devalued: (a) the communion of churches, (b) the collegiality of bishops, (c) the autonomy of regional and particular churches to carry out their processes of inculturation, (d) in general, the synodal experience and coresponsibility of the believers at all levels of the life of the Church.

From this perspective, stagnation or dissatisfaction—which even *EG* detects—concerns issues and developments that go beyond episcopal conferences. This is just one particular point in a broader, more closely linked, and articulated agenda.

The *Motu Proprio Apostolos Suos* (1998): Pending Issues

It is not my purpose to offer a general presentation of the various aspects contained in the papal document of 1998, which include several theological works cited here, but above all to highlight important arguments to bring to light the inadequacies that *EG* 32 pointed out. It is very significant that already in 1999, Walter Kasper himself described this *motu proprio* as "at best a partial result."[28]

It is not necessary to recall here the long history that elapsed until the appearance of this document. Requested by the Synod of 1985, it had an important moment in the publication of the *Instrumentum Laboris* (1988). As the responses to the *Instrumentum* were rather critical, the suggestion was made to draft, as already mentioned, a second and "completely new" *Instrumentum Laboris*.[29] The new text, published more than a decade later, has a more limited scope than the previous one. The fact that it is a *motu proprio* undoubtedly places it in a more disciplinary context. In this sense, the "complementary norms," included at the end, are particularly relevant. In addition, unlike the *Instrumentum Laboris*, the 1998 text declined definition of the theological foundation. The very brevity of the document shows that the legislator did not want to address the issue in all its amplitude.[30] However, careful reading makes it possible to see the choices behind several of its formulations.[31]

A *mandatum docendi* in *Apostolos Suos* (*AS*)? To a significant extent, all the theological reflection in the text is intended to provide a basis for the "complementary rules" offered at the end of the document. To the question of whether bishops' conferences can issue a doctrinal declaration, the answer is yes. This answer, together with the conditions established for such teaching to be legitimate and to obliging the faithful from a region to adhere to them with *obsequium religiosum*, "is significantly new."[32] The required conditions are the following: (a) it must be issued by a plenary meeting, not by conference committees; (b) it must be unanimously approved; (c) if approved by two-thirds of the members but not unanimity, it cannot be published without review (*recognitio*) of the Apostolic See.[33]

Hence, it has been possible to say, as did the current Prelate Auditor of the Roman Rota, Alejandro W. Bunge, that the clearest result brought by *AS*, at least from a legislative point of view, was to elucidate on the magisterial capacity of episcopal conferences. If authors debated on this issue for a long time, with strongly opposing positions, now the pope seems to have settled the canonical discussion, stating, with no room for doubt, that the magisterial authority of the conferences can properly provide an authentic magisterium in precise circumstances and in the manner specified in the new norms. This presupposes, as Bunge argued, a clear improvement over the *Instrumentum Laboris* of 1988, which affirmed that the episcopal conferences, as such, did not enjoy *munus magisterii*.[34]

But a closer look seems to lead to a different conclusion. What is the source of the authority of doctrinal statements according to the *motu proprio*? The document requires either unanimity or Rome's *recognitio* on a text approved by the two-thirds of the members of the conference. As Francis A. Sullivan clearly points out, these conditions "imply a theory."[35] They presuppose that doctrinal authority resides properly only on two levels: at the universal level, of the pope and of the college of bishops and, at the local level, of the diocesan bishop. As Sullivan notes, there is no historical precedent for the requirement that a conciliar decree must have unanimous support to be approved and published on behalf of a council. The councils have always sought moral unanimity, but unanimity was never a requirement. This means that the document clearly implies that the authority of the conference comes from that provided by each individual bishop.[36] This position is consistent with the idea of the then Cardinal Ratzinger that a conference of bishops as such does not have a *mandatum docendi*; such a mandate would belong only to each individual bishop and to the college of bishops with the pope.

In short, as Ladislas M. Örsy puts it, to the "central question" about the "direct source of authority" according to *AS*, the answer is, in the document, that the "source of full jurisdiction [*Vollmacht*] is the pope." One could also point to the individual bishop, or the authority of the Apostolic See, through the *recognitio*. There is, therefore, no room for an intermediate body with its own authority. It is true that in John Paul II's *motu proprio* there is no explicit statement denying that the episcopal conferences have a *mandatum docendi*, but the solution adopted implies, strictly speaking, that authority rests only with the individual bishop and the college of bishops with the pope—or unanimity, or two-thirds with Rome's *recognitio*. The activity of the conference would be endorsed by the sum of the action of each of its members. "In my opinion, it is Ratzinger's perspective that prevailed," said Sullivan.[37]

On the contrary, the theologians and canonists who participated in the colloquium at Salamanca unanimously recognized episcopal conferences as intermediate bodies of an authoritative magisterium. Its magisterial role cannot be interpreted merely as the simultaneous action of its individual members. This is also the opinion of A. Dulles, L. Örsy, and H. Pottmeyer, among others.[38] W. Kasper is also in this line of thought.[39]

Sullivan's conclusion also leads to another important finding by *AS*. It implies that there is *a fundamental theological difference between episcopal conferences and the ancient regional councils*.[40] It establishes a "clear dividing line" between the two.[41] On the contrary, the recognition of that analogy would have led to a different stance. *AS* attributes the binding efficacy of the decisions of the episcopal conference to its own creation by the Holy See and to the delegation that the latter confers on it on certain matters. Hence the pertinent remark of the canonist A. Bunge: one could ask whether this same argumentation, to support the power to make binding decisions of episcopal conferences, should be applied to other meetings of bishops such as particular councils. If this were so, it would be very difficult to explain how this power was granted to the particular councils of the first centuries of the Church, at a time when there was no effective exercise of the primacy of Peter as we know today, and Peter's successor did not know of these councils until after they were long concluded and implemented. Therefore, one might ask whether *other foundations*, which were given for the exercise of the power with which particular councils made binding decisions since the early days of the Church, would be applicable also to episcopal conferences as well, which would be more comprehensive and definitive compared to what is stated in *AS*.[42]

Even if we still take into account that bishops always act as members of the episcopal college, we carefully avoid applying the adjective *collegial* to any action of several bishops on behalf of their respective churches, as already observed in previous documents. The *motu proprio* does not call these acts "collegial," not even in an improper manner, as did the text of the International Theological Commission (1984), nor does it qualify them for analogical collegiality; it only considers them as manifestations of the collegial spirit or *affectus collegialis*, which is proper to all episcopal action.[43]

As noted earlier, many have pointed out that there is no historical precedent for the requirement that a conciliar decree must have complete unanimity to be approved and published on behalf of the Council. "No document of the Second Vatican Council would have reached the standard required by this apostolic letter," recalls J. Komonchak.[44] A total unanimity is not only difficult to achieve in large groups, argues Örsy, but is also "not desirable," given the enrichment that a legitimate plurality means.[45]

Because one of the fair objections to the required unanimity is that this procedure may impede the work of conferences, it would be useful, in addition to the theoretical discussion of these ideas, to have a clear and informed picture of what has happened in these years for the documents of episcopal conferences around the world: how many needed the Holy See's *recognitio* for lack of unanimity required by *AS*?

I think that Sullivan's opinion that "Ratzinger's perspective is the one that prevailed" is correct.[46] Nevertheless, I think that there is a point to be made: in the texts of the Synod of 1985 and the document *Apostolos Suos*, his extreme positions did not materialize fully and explicitly. I call extreme the following ideas: (a) episcopal conferences have "no theological basis";[47] (b) their authority is the sum of the authority of the individuals who take part in it; (c) the notion of collegiality does not apply to episcopal conferences if not, and at best, "improperly"; (d) episcopal conferences have *nomandatum docendi*;[48] (e) therefore, any analogy between episcopal conferences and the regional synodal and conciliar experiences of antiquity is excluded. Hence, according to Ratzinger, in no way can one speak of an "intermediate instance,"[49] as Pope Francis and many theologians now do,[50] or of a "triadic structural form," or "triadic ecclesial structure" as several authors do.[51]

Theological Arguments to Be Developed and Some Recommendations

To address a further development on the subject, as required by *Evangelii Gaudium*, the *theological arguments* are already well identified. All of them are subject to detailed consideration in this volume:

a. The *Communio ecclesiarum*.[52]
b. The *coetus episcoporum*: the dynamic character of collegiality,[53] "partial and analogical."[54] The synodal aspect.[55] Starting from an analogic concept of collegiality that admits diverse forms of realization.
c. The analogy with the particular councils:[56] the triadic structural form.
d. The catholicity of the Church, inculturation, mission. These are based on historical, geographical, and cultural foundations. An instrument of the *traditio* and the *receptio*. Guarantors of unity in diversity.[57]

We must trust in the *via facti*. Since the way of the facts for the existence and development of episcopal conferences has been so important, *before* the theological and juridical formulation, the praxis that is visible in the current course of action of the Bishop of Rome is particularly important. Two arguments, at least, would support this conviction: (a) episcopal conferences originated thanks to the personal initiative of certain bishops in new cultural, political, and ecclesial situations in the nineteenth century; only much later was a theological reflection and canonical regulation elaborated; (b) bishops themselves "discovered" episcopal collegiality during the Council; they experienced it before they could formulate it.

In this sense, we might ask what further concrete steps could be recommended. (a) Should we encourage the continuation of the course of events along Francis's line and hope that this process, as it has happened in the past, will help to create a more favorable scenario for a serene and profound approach to these issues? (b) Or, on the contrary, suggest that a new process take place, as requested by the 1985 Synod, which culminated in the unsatisfactory 1998 text? (c) A path at an intermediate level of the Church, which at first would not formally involve the pope and the bishops, could encourage an international and interdisciplinary study group that, within a given period, proposes the draft of a new project more in line with the ecclesiology that we share today, qualitatively more collegial and synodal.

It is necessary to carry out *interdisciplinary research on the concrete experiences* of the episcopal conferences in the various regions. Even in this area of study a valid criterion is to pay attention to what is happening. We must listen to the people involved: in this case, first, the bishops themselves. The information gathered will be essential for further steps. This was the recommendation of Antonio Acerbi at the symposium of Salamanca:

> Episcopal Conferences represent a novelty and the balance with existing powers must be sought empirically. It might be useful to study the concrete behavior of the episcopates and the Holy See in order to see what areas they have considered that the conference could and should look in, or not, and to know what the individual bishops and the Holy See have considered to accept or not. In this way it would be possible to draw the boundaries of responsibility that would represent a *consensus* among the various instances of authority.[58]

A comparative study of the statutes of episcopal conferences also seems appropriate, as already said, along with, in particular, a study of the *recognitio* of the decisions of the conferences.

Another good recommendation seems to be to not undermine difficulties and the *diversity of opinions*. When we recall the initial steps taken at Vatican II, or review the reflections made by the language groups at the Synod of Bishops of 1985, or even at the Symposium of Salamanca (1988)—which brought together theologians with mostly similar views—we sense a number of issues still in need of clarification, as well as the perplexities and existing fears.[59] Similarly, it would not be prudent to underestimate the tremendous challenge of articulating an ever wider and boundless plurality. Nor should we disregard the tendency to build "national churches," which emphasize the importance of a renewed service of unity on the part of the Church of Rome.

NOTES

1. See W. Kasper, *Katholische Kirche. Wesen—Wirklichkeit—Sendung* (Freiburg: Herder, 2011), 385. Translated as *The Catholic Church: Nature, Reality, and Mission* (London: Bloomsbury/T & T Clark, 2015), 271.

2. See G. Feliciani, *Le conferenze episcopali* (Bologna: il Mulino, 1974), 15–349.

3. See K. Rahner, "Dogmatische Konstitution über die Kirche. Kommentar zum Drittes Kapitel, Artikel 18–27," in *Lexikon für Theologie und Kirche. Das Zweite Vatikanische Konzil. Dokumente und Kommentare,* vol. 1, (Freiburg: Herder, 1966), 211–46, at 232: "It is to be noted that though only formulated as a historical observation, the first sentence of the section involves an important principle, since the historical findings are regarded as marking a special divine providence. It affects particularly the Latin or Western branch of the Catholic Church because this has in fact been practically identified with the Church as a whole. Major Churches with their own discipline, their own liturgy and their own spiritual and theological heritage could also be formed in the future, by 'divine providence', say in Africa, Asia or South America." English translation by Herbert Vorglimler, *Commentary on the Documents of Vatican II,* vol. 1 (New York: Herder and Herder, 1962), 207.

4. M. Faggioli, *Il vescovo e il concilio. Modello episcopale e aggiornamento al Vaticano II* (Bologna: il Mulino, 2005), 444. It is important to note the role given to conferences already in the field of liturgy, in *Sacrosanctum Concilium* and in the *motu proprio Sacram Liturgiam* of January 1964. See M. Bonet, "Las conferencias episcopales," in *Concilium* (8/1965): 50–57, here 51; R. Sobanski, "La teología y el estatuto jurídico de las conferencias episcopales en el Concilio Vaticano II," in *Naturaleza y futuro de las conferencias episcopales,* ed. H. Legrand, J. Manzanares, and A. García y García (Salamanca: Sígueme, 1988), 99–129, at 122ff. (translated as *The Nature and Future of Episcopal Conferences* [Washington, DC: Catholic University of American Press, 1988]; Faggioli, *Il vescovo e il concilio,* 287, 315, 366, 437.

5. P. Hünermann, "Theologischer Kommentar zur dogmatischen Konstitution über die Kirche *Lumen gentium,*" in *Herders Theologischer Kommentar zum Zweiten Vatikanischen Konzil,* ed. P. Hünermann and B.-J. Hilberath (Freiburg: Herder, 2004), 2:263–582, at 432. See Sobanski,

"La teología y el estatuto jurídico de las conferencias episcopales," 105–9 and 126ff.

6. English trans: Massimo Faggioli, *A Council for the Global Church: Receiving Vatican II in History* (Minneapolis: Fortress, 2015), 210.

7. See Faggioli, *Il vescovo e il concilio*, 457; Antón, *Conferencias episcopales*, 140 and passim.

8. See Antón, *Conferencias episcopales*, 117–137.

9. Faggioli, "The Role of Episcopal Conferences," 216; see Antón, *Conferencias episcopales*, 142–56.

10. See H. J. Pottmeyer, "Der theologische Status der Bischofskonferenz. Positionen, Klärungen und Prinzipien," in *Die Bischofskonferenz. Theologischer und juridischer Status*, ed. H. Müller and H. J. Pottmeyer (Dusseldorf: Patmos, 1989), 44–87, at 64.

11. See W. Kasper, "Der theologische Status der Bischofskonferenzen," *Theologische Quartalschrift* 167 (1987): 1–6, at 3.

12. See Antón, *Conferencias episcopales*, 197–99.

13. International Theological Commission, "Select Themes of Ecclesiology, on the Occasion of the Twentieth Anniversary of the Closing of the Second Vatican Council" (1984), no. 5.3: http://www.vatican.va/roman_curia/congregations/cfaith/cti_documents/rc_cti_1984_ecclesiologia_en.html.

14. See A. Antón, "La carta apostólica MP 'Apostolos suos' de Juan Pablo II," *Gregorianum* 80, no. 2 (1999): 263–97. For the text of the 1988 preparatory draft, see Congregation for Bishops, Draft Statement on Episcopal Conferences, in *Origins* 17 (1988): 731–37.

15. See J. Hamer, "Les conférences épiscopales, exercice de la collégialité," in *Nouvelle revue théologique* 95 (1963): 966–69; "La responsabilité collégiale de chaque évêque," *Nouvelle revue théologique* 105 (1983): 641–54.

16. See W. Kasper, "Nochmals: Der theologische Status der Bischofskonferenzen," *Theologische Quartalschrift* 168 (1988): 237–40, at 237; Pottmeyer, "Der theologische Status," 47–60. Kasper attributes the change to Henri de Lubac's influence.

17. J. Ratzinger, "Konkrete Formen bischöflicher Kollegialität [Papst, Patriarch, Bischof]," in *Gesammelte Schriften*, vol. 7, *Zur Lehre des Zweiten Vatikanischen Konzils. Formulierung, Vermittlung, Deutung*, ed. Gerhard L. Müller (Freiburg: Herder, 2012), 1:348–57; "Le implicazioni pastorali della dottrina della collegialità dei vescovi," in *Concilium* (1/1965): 44–73, esp. 71ff.

18. Antón, *Conferencias episcopales*, 112.

19. The Social Affairs Committee of the German Bishops' Conference, the Social Affairs Committee of the Canadian Bishops' Confer-

ence, the Argentine Bishops' Pastoral Social Commission, the bishops of Patagonia-Comahue (Argentina), and the Episcopal Commission for Social Pastoral Care of the Mexican episcopal conference.

20. Pope Francis, Ceremony Commemorating the 50th Anniversary of the Institution of the Synod of Bishops, October 17, 2015: http://w2.vatican.va/content/francesco/en/speeches/2015/october/documents/papa-francesco_20151017_50-anniversario-sinodo.html.

21. Also, *AG* 16; 18; 20; 26; 29; 31–33; 38.

22. J. Ratzinger and V. Messori, *Informe sobre la fe* (Madrid: BAC, 1985), 68. Originally published as *Rapporto sulla fede. Vittorio Messori a colloquio con il cardinale Joseph Ratzinger* (Cinisello Balsamo: Edizioni Paoline, 1985), 60. Translated as *The Ratzinger Report* (San Francisco: Ignatius Press, 1985), 59–61.

23. At the interviewer's question, "Could the episcopal conferences have major say in these matters?" The prefect of the Congregation for the Doctrine of the Faith replied, "We need to distinguish two levels: dogmatic and concrete organization. Jesus instituted the apostles with Peter as a principle of unity of the faith of the Church and of its sacramental communion. It is an institution of divine right. Beyond that, we have canonical structures that evolve according to the circumstances. The episcopal conferences are an expression of the collegiality of bishops at the level of a country, a culture or a language, but it is a practical organization. The Catholic Church exists as a universal Church, in the communion of all the bishops in union with and under the aegis of the pope. And it also exists in local churches. But the local church is not the church of France or Germany: it is the church of Paris, of Toulouse....They are the dioceses! The idea of a national church would be entirely heretical. Autonomy in faith is impossible! Jesus Christ is the Savior of all, he unifies all men." See http://www.la-croix.com/Religion/Actualite/Cardinal-Gerhard-Ludwig-Mueller-La-mission-%20du-pape-est-d-unifier-le-monde-2015-03-29-1296678.

24. See Legrand, Manzanares, and García y García, *Naturaleza y futuro de las conferencias episcopales*; Müller and Pottmeyer, *Die Bischofskonferenz*; T. J. Reese, ed., *Episcopal Conferences: Historical, Canonical and Theological Studies* (Washington, DC: Georgetown University Press, 1989). Interestingly, A. Antón has observed that, up to his contribution in 1988, in the postconciliar period the theme of episcopal conferences has been more emphasized in canon law than in theology. See "Estatuto de las conferencias episcopales," in Legrand, Manzanares, and García y García, *Naturaleza y futuro de las conferencias*, 233–268, at 233.

25. See R. R. Gaillardetz, *Ecclesiology for a Global Church: A People Called and Sent* (Maryknoll, NY: Orbis, 2008); R. P. McBrien, *The*

Church: The Evolution of Catholicism (New York: HarperOne, 2008), 310ff. and 316; Kasper, *Katholische Kirche*, 385; N. Ormerod, *Re-visioning the Church: An Experiment in Systematic Historical Ecclesiology* (Minneapolis: Fortress Press, 2014); R. R. Gaillardetz and E. Hahnenberg, eds., *A Church with Open Doors: Catholic Ecclesiology for the Third Millennium* (Collegeville, MN: Liturgical Press, 2015).

26. See M. Faggioli, "Institutions of Episcopal Collegiality-Synodality after Vatican II: The Decree *Christus Dominus* and the Agenda for Collegiality-Synodality in the 21st Century," *The Jurist* 64 (2004): 224–46; T. Green, "The Legislative Competency of the Episcopal Conference: Present Situation and Future Possibilities in Light of Eastern Synodal Experience," *The Jurist* 64 (2004): 284–331; P. de Mey, "Is 'Affective' Collegiality Sufficient? A Plea for a More 'Effective' Collegiality of Bishops in the Roman Catholic Church and Its Ecumenical Implications," in *Friendship as an Ecumenical Value*, ed. A. Arjakovsky and M. Tardivo (Lviv: Ukrainian Catholic University Press, 2006), 132–53; F. Sullivan, "Developments in Teaching Authority since Vatican II," *Theological Studies* 73 (2012): 570–89, esp. 571–77; M. Faggioli, "The Regulation of Episcopal Conferences since Vatican II," *The Japan Mission Journal* 68, no. 2 (2014): 82–96; H. Legrand, "Enjeux ecclésiologiques des réformes institutionnelles du pape François," in *Le grand tournant. L'an I de la révolution du pape François*, ed. M. Dubos (Paris: Cerf, 2014), 185–210, esp. 204–7; S. Dianich, *La chiesa cattolica verso la sua riforma* (Brescia: Queriniana, 2014), 121ff.

27. See Faggioli, "The Role of Episcopal Conferences," 226.

28. W. Kasper, "Zur Theologie und Praxis des bischöflichen Amtes," in *Gesammelte Schriften*, vol. 12, *Die Kirche und ihre Ämter. Schriften zur Ekklesiologie II* (Freiburg: Herder, 2009), 482–96, at 492.

29. See Antón, "La carta apostólica MP 'Apostolos suos,'" 264.

30. See B. Malvaux, "Un débat toujours actuel: le statut théologique des conférences des évêques," *Nouvelle revue théologique* 123 (2001): 238–53, at 250.

31. Antón, "La carta apostólica MP 'Apostolos suos,'" 272.

32. F. Sullivan, "The Teaching Authority of Episcopal Conferences," *Theological Studies* 63 (2002): 472–93, at 485.

33. For decisions that have binding force of law (*CD* 38,4), the *recognitio* is explicitly extended to "doctrinal declarations." See Faggioli, "The Role of Episcopal Conferences," 223. This was exactly the personal position of G. Ghirlanda, "De episcoporum conferentia deque exercitio potestatis magisterii," *Periodica* 76 (1987): 573–603, esp. 589–99. Regarding can. 753, there are different interpretations, as A. Dulles points out, and whose opinion is in favor: "It is therefore difficult to deny that

can. 753 accords some doctrinal power to episcopal conferences" (A. Dulles, "Doctrinal Authority of Episcopal Conferences," in Reese, *Episcopal Conferences*, 207–31, at 215). See H. Schmitz, "Die Lehrautorität der Bischofskonferenz gemäß c. 753 CIC," in Müller and Pottmeyer, *Die Bischofskonferenz*, 196–235; J. Manzanares, "La autoridad doctrinal de las conferencias episcopales," in Legrand, Manzanares, and García y García, *Naturaleza y futuro de las conferencias*, 289–321, at 306ff.

34. A. Bunge, "Comentarios sobre el motu proprio *Apostolos Suos*," 1–11, at 9: http://www.mercaba.org/Codigo/Organiza/comentarios_sobre_el_motu_propri.htm. In fact, the Congregation for Bishops, Draft Statement on Episcopal Conferences, 735, said, "The episcopal conference, however, is not a doctrinal instance: it is not able to establish content in matters of doctrine and morals." See J. Komonchak, "The Roman Working Paper on Episcopal Conferences," in Reese, *Episcopal Conferences*, 177–204.

35. Sullivan, "The Teaching Authority," 487. This is also Antón's prudent opinion: although the text does not deal with the theme of the theological foundation, a careful reading leaves a glimpse of the views behind the various formulations (Antón, "La carta apostólica MP 'Apostolos suos,'" 272).

36. Sullivan, "The Teaching Authority," 486. See J. Famerée, "Au fondement des conférences épiscopales: la *communio Ecclesiarum*," *Revue théologique de Louvain* 23 (1992): 343–54.

37. Sullivan, "The Teaching Authority," 491. Sullivan himself ("Developments in Teaching Authority," 572) recalls the personal position expressed by Cardinal Ratzinger during a meeting between some members of the USCCB and the Congregation for the Doctrine of the Faith, held in 1983. At the opening of the meeting, Ratzinger stated, "A conference of bishops as such does not have a *mandatum docendi*. This belongs only to individual bishops or to the college of bishops in union with the pope."

38. See "Autoridad magisterial de las conferencias episcopales," in Legrand, Manzanares, and García y García, *Naturaleza y futuro de las conferencias*, 329–34; Dulles, "Doctrinal Authority," 217, 224, 226; L. Örsy, "Reflections on the Teaching Authority of the Episcopal Conferences," in Reese, *Episcopal Conferences*, 233–52, at 251; H. Pottmeyer, "Das Lehramt der Bischofskonferenz," in Müller and Pottmeyer, *Die Bischofskonferenz*, 116–33. In particular, A. Dulles's text concludes with a series of interesting, concrete guidelines on the matter.

39. "It would be wrong, however, to consider the morally concordant teaching expressed by an episcopal conference as a mere addition and sum of the full magisterial power of the individual bishops": Kasper, "Der

theologische Status der Bischofskonferenzen," 5; see also *Nochmals: Der theologische Status*, 239.

40. See Sullivan, "Developments in Teaching Authority," 574. *Apostolos Suos* does not cite the text of *LG* 23 that highlights the relationship between both ecclesial experiences: "In like manner [*simili ratione*] the Episcopal bodies of today are in a position to render a manifold and fruitful assistance, so that this collegiate feeling may be put into practical application."

41. See L. Örsy, "Die Bischofskonferenzen und die Macht des Geistes," *Stimmen der Zeit* 218 (2000): 3–17, at 7.

42. Bunge, "Comentarios sobre el motu proprio *Apostolos Suos*," 8. Another question about *Apostolos Suos*: Who has the authority to set up conferences? *Apostolos Suos* 13 and the Code of Canon Law 449, §1, appear to differ from *CD* 38, 3 and from the 1966 *motu proprio Ecclesiae Sanctae* 41. Is there an important change here? See A. Acerbi, "Respuesta a la conferencia de P. Krämer," in Legrand, Manzanares, García y García, *Naturaleza y futuro de las conferencias*, 183–90, at 183ff.

43. See Bunge, "Comentarios sobre el *motu proprio*," 7; Örsy, "Die Bischofskonferenzen," 7. On the other hand, *Apostolos Suos* 4 and 15 cites the decree *Christus Dominus* on the usefulness of episcopal conferences (37), but does not mention the statement that bishops "exercise their pastoral office in harmony and closeness with other bishops" (*munus suum pastorale coniunctim exercent*). See Faggioli, "The Role of Episcopal Conferences," 223. Already the Code of Canon Law (can. 447) states that bishops in the episcopal conference exercise united "certain pastoral functions [*munera quaedam pastoralia*]," while *Christus Dominus* used the expression *munus suum pastorale*. As Antón observes, unlike Ghirlanda, the intention is to reduce the field of expertise of conferences, emphasizing its advisory nature: see Antón, *Conferencias episcopales*, 146; Ghirlanda, *De episcoporum conferentia*, 583ff.

44. J. Komonchak, "On the Authority of the Bishops' Conferences," *America* 6 (1998): 7–10, at 10.

45. See Örsy, *Die Bischofskonferenzen*, 8.

46. Sullivan, "The Teaching Authority," 491. See above, n37.

47. Also in the postsynodal exhortation *Pastores Gregis* of 2003 there is some "theological foundation": "Since membership in Episcopal Conferences is limited to Bishops and all those equivalent in law to Diocesan Bishops, even if not possessing the episcopal character, the immediate *theological foundation* of Episcopal Conferences, unlike that of Particular Councils, is the collegial dimension of responsibility for episcopal governance. Only indirectly is it communion between the Churches" (emphasis added).

48. This is also Félix A. Pastor's interpretation. *Apostolos Suos* would have assumed an intermediate position: it does not deny the possibility of a magisterial *munus*, but it requires some sine qua non conditions to exercise it. See F. A. Pastor, "Authenticum episcoporum magisterium. Las conferencias de obispos y el ejercicio de la 'potestas docendi,'" *Periodica de re canonica* 89 (2000): 79–119, at 117.

49. J. Ratzinger, "Presentazione," in *L'Osservatore Romano* of July 24, 1998, 1 and 6, here 6 col. 1, cit. in Antón, "La carta apostólica MP 'Apostolos suos,'" 285.

50. See Pope Francis, Ceremony Commemorating the 50th Anniversary; G. Greshake, "'Zwischeninstanzen' zwischen Papst und Ortbischöfen," in Müller and Pottmeyer, *Die Bischofskonferenz*, 88–115.

51. "The renewal and further development of the triadic structural form is an essential condition for the Church to recover its original configuration as a community of churches": H. Pottmeyer, *Die Rolle des Papsttums im Dritten Jahrtausend* (Freiburg: Herder, 1999²), 144. See P. Leisching, "Le conferenze episcopali," *Concilium* (4/1990): 99–108, at 99ff.; H. Müller, "La conferencia episcopal y el obispo diocesano," in Legrand, Manzanares, and García y García, *Naturaleza y futuro de las conferencias*, 139–61, at 144.

52. In addition to the contributions of Legrand, Antón, Pottmeyer, Mazanares, Fameree, etc., see J.-M. R. Tillard, "Respuesta a la conferencia de A. Antón," in Legrand, Manzanares, and García y García, *Naturaleza y futuro de las conferencias*, 269–78; J. Provost, "Episcopal Conferences as an Expression of the Communion of Churches," in Reese, *Episcopal Conferences*, 267–89.

53. See the contributions by Antón, Kasper, and others. As Pottmeyer observes, the ontological-sacramental or theological-systematic use and the juridical-canonical level must not be confused: *Der theologische Status*, 72–78.

54. Dulles, "Doctrinal Authority," 217. To the repeated argument that the episcopal conferences endanger the authority of the diocesan bishop, it must be said that this authority, being ordinary, self-evident, and immediate, does not imply that it can be realized without limits, as for example with the reservation of certain powers to the supreme authority of the Church. This limit is a legal consequence that inevitably derives from the consideration of the Church as communio, from the collegiality of the episcopate, and from the very nature of its ministry. See Müller, "La conferencia episcopal y el obispo diocesano," 152ff.

55. See the documents of the USCCB (*The Challenge of Peace*, 1983, for example), where the reflection of a regional church is expressed in its various representations.

56. In addition to the previous, see also B. Daley, "Bishops' Gatherings in the Early Church," in Reese, *Episcopal Conferences*, 25–58; Dulles, "Doctrinal Authority," 215ff.; Y. M. Congar, *Conversazioni d'autunno* (Brescia: Queriniana, 1988), 18ff.

57. See Tillard, "Respuesta a la conferencia de A. Antón," 272ff.; Greshake, "'Zwischeninstanzen,'" 114: G. Colombo, "Respuesta a la conferencia de R. Sobanski," in Legrand, Manzanares, and García y García, *Naturaleza y futuro de las conferencias*, 131–35, at 134.

58. Acerbi, "Respuesta a la conferencia de P. Krämer," 190.

59. See Legrand, Manzanares, and García y García, *Naturaleza y futuro de las conferencias*, 225–29, 279–87, 329–34.

V

CHRISTIAN UNITY AND THE REFORM OF THE CHURCH

18

EXCHANGE OF GIFTS

Reception of the Fruits of Dialogue and the Reform of the Church

William Henn, OFM Cap

In the introduction to his collection of essays published in 2004 under the title *That They May All Be One: The Call to Unity Today*, Cardinal Kasper wrote several pages that might be considered a brief assessment of the ecumenical situation at that time. He wrote that "the very shape of the future Church depends to a significant degree on the ecumenical endeavor aimed at visible unity among divided churches, and that there is no realistic alternative to ecumenism." Nevertheless, he added, "the fact that ecumenism is facing a critical moment cannot be denied"; many believe that "traditional differences are irrelevant for the majority of people today."[1]

Kasper's assessment was not totally negative. He notes that, during the second half of the twentieth century,

> not only were many misunderstandings overcome, but a certain degree of convergence and consensus was attained in questions of faith which had been clearly divisive in the past. After centuries of drifting apart and a lack of mutual understanding, divided Christians

> today no longer see each other as hostile adversaries but as friendly brothers and sisters. The atmosphere between the churches has profoundly changed. Despite the many encouraging results achieved so far, however, there is one point on which no major progress has yet been accomplished: the question of ecclesiology.[2]

Kasper finds it helpful to view the current ecumenical situation as a transition stage or an interim period.

> We will have to fill the interim stage what we have reached (of a real if not complete church *communio*) with real life. The "ecumenism of love" and the "ecumenism of truth," which both naturally remain very important, must be complemented by an "ecumenism of life." We have to apply all that we have achieved to the way we actually live. The churches did not diverge only through discussion, they diverged through alienation, i.e. the way they lived. Therefore they have to come closer to each other again in their lives; they must get accustomed to each other, pray together, work together and live together, bearing the pain of incomplete *communio* and of not yet being able to share Eucharistic communion around the Lord's table. Thus this ecumenism of life is not to be understood in a static way; it is a process of healing and growing.[3]

That may serve as a short account of the *status quaestionis* of ecumenism in the words of one whose involvement in Catholic ecumenical efforts has made him an exceptionally authoritative source. His assessment was made before Jorge Maria Bergoglio was elected to the papacy in 2013. A week after that election, in a meeting with representatives of churches and ecclesial communities, the new pope said,

> Let us ask the Father of mercies to enable us to live fully the faith graciously bestowed on us on the day of our Baptism and to bear witness to it freely, joyfully and courageously. This will be the best service we can offer

> to the cause of Christian unity, a service of hope for a world still torn by divisions, conflicts and rivalries. The more we are faithful to his will in our thoughts, words and actions, the more we will progress, really and substantially, towards unity. For my part, I wish to assure you that, in continuity with my predecessors, it is my firm intention to pursue the path of ecumenical dialogue.[4]

The following pages will, first, offer several main theoretical points regarding the prospects for ecumenical progress in light of some of Pope Francis's teachings. His Argentinian theology of the people, his call for reform, his interest in the hierarchy of truths, and his emphasis upon reception all open some paths to pursue in Catholic ecumenical efforts during the coming years. A second section will offer some practical recommendations in light of these theoretical reflections.

Major Theoretical Points

ECUMENICAL IMPLICATIONS OF POPE FRANCIS'S "THEOLOGY OF THE PEOPLE"

In an interview six months after his election as Bishop of Rome, Pope Francis was asked about his understanding of the Church, to which he replied,

> The image of the church I like is that of the holy, faithful people of God. This is the definition I often use, and then there is that image from the Second Vatican Council's "Dogmatic Constitution on the Church" (No. 12). Belonging to a people has a strong theological value. In the history of salvation, God has saved a people. There is no full identity without belonging to a people. No one is saved alone, as an isolated individual, but God attracts us looking at the complex web of relationships that take place in the human community. God enters into this

> dynamic, this participation in the web of human relationships.[5]

In chapter four of *Evangelii Gaudium*, Pope Francis addresses what is required for there to occur "progress in building a people in peace, justice and fraternity" (*EG* 221). Within the "constant tensions present in every social reality," four principles are necessary if individuals are to become fashioned into a people.

First, one must give priority to time over space. Francis writes, "This principle enables us to work slowly but surely, without being obsessed with immediate results. It helps us patiently to endure difficult and adverse situations, or inevitable changes in our plans. It invites us to accept the tension between fullness and limitation, and to give a priority to time."[6]

Second, one must give priority to unity over conflict. Francis teaches,

> Unity is greater than conflict. Solidarity, in its deepest and most challenging sense, thus becomes a way of making history in a life setting where conflicts, tensions and oppositions can achieve a diversified and life-giving unity. This is not to opt for a kind of syncretism, or for the absorption of one into the other, but rather for a resolution which takes place on a higher plane and preserves what is valid and useful on both sides.[7]

Third, priority must be given to realities over ideas: "Realities are greater than ideas," writes the Holy Father. "This principle has to do with incarnation of the Word and its being put into practice: 'By this you know the Spirit of God: every spirit that confesses that Jesus Christ has come in the flesh is from God' (1 John 4:2). The principle of reality, of a word already made flesh and constantly striving to take flesh anew, is essential to evangelization."[8]

Finally, the global should be given priority over the local. Pope Francis writes,

> The whole is greater than the part, but it is also greater than the sum of its parts. There is no need, then, to be overly obsessed with limited and particular questions.

> We constantly have to broaden our horizons and see the greater good which will benefit us all. But this has to be done without evasion or uprooting. We need to sink our roots deeper into the fertile soil and history of our native place, which is a gift of God.[9]

These priorities of the pope's theology of the people seem very relevant to Catholic commitment to Christian unity in the years ahead. They are reflected in several of Pope Francis's comments in ecumenical settings. Regarding the priority given to time, during his meeting with Patriarch Bartholomew in Jerusalem to commemorate the fiftieth anniversary of the encounter between Patriarch Athenagoras and Pope Paul VI in 1964, Francis said,

> We know that much distance still needs to be travelled before we attain that fullness of communion which can also be expressed by sharing the same Eucharistic meal, something we ardently desire; yet our disagreements must not frighten us and paralyze our progress. We need to believe that, just as the stone before the tomb was cast aside, so too every obstacle to our full communion will also be removed. This will be a grace of resurrection, of which we can have a foretaste even today.[10]

The priority of unity over conflict finds a lovely expression in the then Cardinal Bergoglio's discussion of the tensions in the Middle East with his friend Rabbi Abraham Skorka. He noted that always concentrating upon points of conflict and upon differences puts obstacles in the path of genuine encounter with others: "One need not emphasize the error of the other person, since each of us has errors too; we have all made mistakes. Harmony among persons and peoples comes about seeking other paths."[11] While these words were spoken regarding peace between peoples and nations, something similar can be said regarding ecumenism. Shortly after these comments about the nations, Bergoglio adds,

> There is a sentence from the Lutheran theologian Oscar Cullman which explains how to arrive at unity among the various Christian confessions. For Cullman, the

> aim is not that all, right from the start, affirm the same thing, but rather that they walk together in reconciled diversity. The solution of religious conflict between the many Christian confessions is to walk side by side, to do things together, to pray together. We are asked not to throw stones, but to continue to walk side by side. This is the right way to proceed in resolving conflicts, drawing on the potential of all, without rejecting the various traditions or falling into syncretism. Each rooted in its own identity, in a spirit of reconciliation, seeking unity in truth.[12]

The third priority of the "theology of the people" is that of reality over idea, and here too one can see its influence on the ecumenism of Pope Francis. Because of the prevailing attitudes of that time in his country, Catholics tended to consider Protestants in a very derogative way. These words follow:

> But I remember one time I was with my grandmother, a great woman, and two women from the Salvation Army had just passed by. I was about five or six years old, and I asked her if they were nuns, because they were wearing that little hat that they used to wear. She responded to me: "No, they are Protestants, but they are good." That was the wisdom of the true religion. They were good women who did good things.[13]

This story reflects his grasp of the reality that that many, many Christians who are not Catholic are committed and practicing believers. Francis does not limit Catholics to recognizing the holiness of other Christians but also invites them to recognize the orthodoxy of their faith on most of the central doctrines of Christianity. He believes that, while doctrinal agreement may not be yet sufficient for the sharing of the Eucharist, it is sufficient for the sharing of many things, including the mission of the new evangelization (see *EG* 246).

The fourth priority of the theology of the people is to privilege the whole over the part. One of the first great Catholic books on ecumenism—Yves Congar's *Divided Christendom*, published in

French in 1937—had as one of its most important contributions a chapter on the catholicity of the Church. The fact that God's will for the unity of the Church includes as an essential quality the Church's catholicity means that unity should never be understood as uniformity, in which all Christians are the same. This would have to be applicable also to groups of Christians, who form a particular people on the basis not only of their culture and language, but also their religious practices and traditions and the particular preferences that their family of Churches holds dear. This is what Pope Francis meant when he wrote in *Evangelii Gaudium* of the precious and abundant gifts of the Holy Spirit that are present in the various Christian communities even now in their divided state and that need to be treasured (246). There remain contradictions on questions like the number of the sacraments, who can be ordained, and various moral issues that need to be addressed and resolved. But resolving such issues should not result in all groups of Christians being identical. Here is where the geometrical image of the polyhedron comes in. Cardinal Kasper describes this in a very helpful way:

> [Francis's] model of unity is not that of a sphere "where every point is equidistant from the center, and there are no differences between them. Instead it is the polyhedron [that is, a three-dimensional body with many angles and surfaces], which reflects the convergence of all its parts, each of which preserves its distinctiveness" and seeks "to gather in the polyhedron the best of each" (EG 236)....[This model] makes possible a unity that preserves the distinctiveness of the different churches without, however, obscuring the identity of the whole. This image enables a mutual, ecumenical process of learning and a complementary relationship that is mutually enriching (EG 246). That is harmony, as created by the Spirit of God.[14]

The brief clarification by the Congregation for the Doctrine of the Faith about the nature of the Church as communion—*Communionis Notio* of 1992—concluded by saying that the divisions between Christian communities today not only damage in some way those churches who do not share that fullness of the means of salvation that is available within the Catholic Church, but also they damage the Catholic Church herself, in that, without these others, the Catholic Church cannot achieve that fullness of catholicity that God wills for her.[15] Pope Francis's priority of the whole over the part seems to open a door toward that unity of Christians that will also benefit the Catholic Church, helping her to be even more Catholic than she already is.

These four priorities (1) of taking the time necessary for building community rather than trying to rush to results; (2) of privileging peace, unity, and understanding over conflict; (3) of giving more importance to persons and situations as they really are rather than to theories or ideas; and (4) of aiming at including the whole and not just any particular part of the community or of any problem or question go a long way in explaining the fresh style that Francis has brought to his exercise of the papal ministry and that has captured the imagination of so many people around the world. These priorities help explain why he has celebrated the feast of the Lord's Supper on Holy Thursday by washing the feet of prisoners, or made his first visit outside of Rome to comfort refugees who had miraculously made the passage to the island of Lampedusa and to pray for and honor those many who were not so fortunate and who died, shipwrecked in the Mediterranean Sea. It helps explain his style of speaking, which uses simple language addressed to the heart of everyone instead of elevated phrases that, while valuable to some, leave many others feeling uninspired. These priorities show why he gives so much respect to the popular piety of the people (cf. *EG* 237) and reaches out to all those on the periphery, especially the poor and the marginalized.

Perhaps one of the most striking ecumenical gestures in recent times by the Bishop of Rome was John Paul II's humble and generous offer to dialogue with the theologians and leaders of Christian communities not in full communion with the Catholic Church about the way that he could change the manner of exercising his ministry to be more acceptable to the other churches. In his encyclical letter on ecumenism, John Paul wrote,

> This is an immense task which we cannot refuse and which I cannot carry out by myself. Could not the real

> but imperfect communion existing between us persuade Church leaders and their theologians to engage with me in a patient and fraternal dialogue on this subject, a dialogue in which, leaving useless controversies behind, we could listen to one another, keeping before us only the will of Christ for his Church and allowing ourselves to be deeply moved by his plea "that they may all be one… so that the world may believe that you have sent me?" (John 17:21)[16]

The distinction that John Paul makes here between "what is essential" to the primacy and "a way of exercising" it leads one to surmise that in Pope Francis one can see a genuinely new way of exercising the primacy. This is not to say that his way is "better" than that of his predecessors. Nevertheless, his way of ministering seems to be profoundly rooted in the Argentinian "theology of the people" described above and it has resonated very positively not only with Christians who are not Catholics and even with non-Christians and unbelievers. At the Tenth General Assembly of the World Council of Churches held in Busan, South Korea, in late October and early November of 2013, several speakers at the plenary sessions added spontaneous comments in praise of Francis. Something about his style of exercising a ministry of primacy has resonated very positively with other Christians.

REFORM AND CHRISTIAN UNITY

Any attempt to bring about serious reform, especially if it involves historic and institutional changes, in bound to make some feel uncomfortable. One could rightly fear that attempts to alter some aspects of ecclesial life in a substantial way might, albeit unintentionally, introduce some changes that might risk losing what is essential and what must remain perennial within the life of the Church.

Nevertheless, it may be even more dangerous to have an exaggerated fear of reform and change. One of the most important passages of *Lumen Gentium* points out that the Church is "at once holy and always in need of purification" (*sancta simul et semper purificanda*; *LG* 8). The relation between reform and renewal, on the one hand, and progress toward unity among Christians, on the other, is explicitly underlined in several paragraphs of *Unitatis Redintegratio*:

> In ecumenical work, Catholics must assuredly be concerned for their separated brethren, praying for them, keeping them informed about the Church and making the first approaches toward them. But their primary duty is to make a careful and honest appraisal of whatever needs to be renewed and done in the Catholic household itself, in order that its life may bear witness more clearly and faithfully to the teachings and institutions which have been handed down from Christ through the apostles, (4)

Or again,

> Every renewal of the Church essentially consists in an increase of fidelity to her own calling. Undoubtedly this explains the dynamism of the movement toward unity. Christ summons the Church, as she goes her pilgrim way, to that continual reformation of which she always has need, insofar as she is an institution of men here on earth. Consequently, if, in various times and circumstances, there have been deficiencies in moral conduct or in Church discipline, or even in the way that Church teaching has been formulated – to be carefully distinguished from the deposit of faith itself—these should be set right at the opportune moment and in the proper way. Church renewal therefore has notable ecumenical importance. (6)

These conciliar teachings suggest not only that reform and renewal must go on continually in life of the Christian community, but also that they are essential to the path toward unity. Many historians would concur that at least some divisions in the Church were caused precisely because of the lack of reform.[17] Yves Congar produced one of the classic studies of the history of reform in his book *True and False Reform in the Church*, in which he demonstrates that the entire history of the Church can be characterized by a series of reforms.[18] This should help to assuage the fears of those who may worry about any major reforms that Pope Francis might promote. But perhaps more important, Congar provided several criteria to distinguish what makes for a true reform. A true reform seeks to promote charity and pastoral well-being rather than simply being the result of systematic or deductive theorizing. It seeks above all to foster communion, especially by trying to overcome currently opposed points of view that are not sufficiently expressive of the fullness of the Catholic tradition. A true reform is characterized by patience and avoids being hasty to arrive at an immediate solution of problems. It should employ "good sense" in seeking to apply traditional principles to the realities of the current situation.

Such principles seem to be helpfully present in one of the paragraphs of *Evangelii Gaudium* that deals explicitly with renewal and reform.

> In her ongoing discernment, the Church can also come to see that certain customs not directly connected to the heart of the Gospel, even some which have deep historical roots, are no longer properly understood and appreciated. Some of these customs may be beautiful, but they no longer serve as means of communicating the Gospel. We should not be afraid to re-examine them. At the same time, the Church has rules or precepts which may no longer have the same usefulness for directing and shaping people's lives. St. Thomas Aquinas pointed out that the precepts which Christ and the apostles gave to the people of God "are very few" (*S.Th.* I–II, q. 107, a. 4). Citing St. Augustine, he noted that the precepts subsequently enjoined by the Church should be insisted upon with moderation "so as not to burden the lives of the faithful" and make our religion a form of servitude, whereas "God's mercy has willed that we should be free" (Ibid.). This warning, issued many centuries ago, is most timely today. It ought to be one of the criteria to be taken into account in considering a reform of

> the Church and her preaching which would enable it to reach everyone. (43)

This quotation not only reflects much of that "good sense" that Congar underlined as essential to a true reform of the Church but also calls on two of the greatest doctors of the Church in support of discernment about what needs to be required for continuity with the tradition. For unity, it is important not to require more than what is necessary (cf. Acts 15:28; *Ut Unum Sint* 78). It further suggests that the most important criterion for reform is the gospel. This focus on what is essential invites a few comments about another major point—the hierarchy of truths.

THE HIERARCHY OF TRUTHS

One of the refreshing aspects *Evangelii Gaudium* is its retrieval of what was once considered by many to be among the most important teachings of Vatican II, that is, *Unitatis Redintegratio*'s paragraph about the hierarchy of truths. The first reference to this teaching appears rather early in *Evangelii Gaudium*:

> All revealed truths derive from the same divine source and are to be believed with the same faith, yet some of them are more important for giving direct expression to the heart of the Gospel. In this basic core, what shines forth is the beauty of the saving love of God made manifest in Jesus Christ who died and rose from the dead. In this sense, the Second Vatican Council explained, "in Catholic doctrine there exists an order or 'hierarchy' of truths, since they vary in their relation to the foundation of the Christian faith" (Decree on Ecumenism, *Unitatis redintegratio* 11). This holds true as much for the dogmas of faith as for the whole corpus of the Church's teaching, including her moral teaching. (36)

The words about deriving "from the same divine source" and being believed "with the same faith" call to mind the encyclical *Mortalium Animos* of 1928, which Pope Pius XI issued in response to the founding of the Faith and Order Movement the previous year.[19] Faith and Order was established precisely to seek doctrinal unity by means of theological dialogue between representatives of Christian communities divided from one another. In this context, Pius XI felt it advisable to teach that unity in faith could not be based upon a list of fundamental articles that were sufficient, leaving other, less fundamental articles optional. His point was that any official teaching must ultimately derive from divine revelation. The gift of faith embraces such truths based on God's authority. Not to accept some doctrines would amount to refusing to accept the authority of God. Christians are not free therefore, based on their own authority, to select some but not all.

Can such a rejection of unity based on fundamental articles be reconciled with Vatican II's teaching about the hierarchy of truths? First, *Mortalium Animos* considers all doctrines equal based on their relation to the authority of revelation. It does not consider and therefore cannot be interpreted as rejecting the possibility that, when considered from the point of view of their content and not their authority (the *fides quae* and not the *fides qua*), some doctrines are more central to the gospel than others. Indeed, the vision of revelation presented in Vatican II's Dogmatic Constitution *Dei Verbum* is very much focused on a few central or foundational truths.[20]

> It pleased God, in his goodness and wisdom, to reveal himself and to make known the mystery of his will (cf. Eph 1:9). His will was that men should have access to the Father, through Christ, the Word made flesh, in the Holy Spirit, and thus become sharers in the divine nature (cf. Eph 2:18; 2 Pet 1:4). By this revelation, then, the invisible God (cf. Col 1:15; 1 Tim 1:17), from the fullness of his love, addresses men as his friends (cf. Exod 33:11; John 15:14–15), and moves among them (cf. Bar 3:38), in order to invite and receive them into his own company.... The most intimate truth which this revelation gives us about God and the salvation of man shines forth in Christ, who is himself the mediator and the sum total of Revelation. (2)

This description suggests that to acknowledge an order or hierarchy of truths based on their relation to the foundation of Christian faith is not to reject the authority of God who reveals, but quite the opposite. It is to accept the divine authority of revelation since revelation itself proves to have a center. Not to acknowledge that center would be not to accept the authority of revelation. In fact, presuming that all doctrines are equally important for the unity of Christians in faith would be a lack of full respect for the authority of God. It is revelation itself that shows revealed truth to have a center.

For the hierarchy of truths be of greater effect in promoting Christian unity, two steps need to be taken. First, the errors that came to light from attempts to base unity on a selection of fundamental articles, some of which were pointed out in *Mortalium Animos*, need to be avoided. What are such errors? I would list the following. First, it would be a mistake to overlook the fact that all normative Christian teaching must be rooted in revelation and, therefore, ultimately in the authority of God. To affirm that all doctrines are not equally important is precisely to accept God's authority. It is God who so reveals himself. Second, it would be a mistake to overlook the organic unity of revelation. The teaching about the hierarchy of truths is not about denying any revealed truth but helps, instead, to explain why, at any given point in time, the Christian community can arrive at a deeper understanding of revelation than was possible at another point in time. Even within a fully united church, one culturally conditioned community may have insights that have not yet been unveiled to another differently conditioned community. When communities have been divided from one another and antagonistic toward one another for generations, the likelihood of such differences is magnified. The mystery of God, the *prima veritas* according to St. Thomas Aquinas, is sublimely simple and any other aspect of revelation is related to this simple core. Hopefully, by focusing on this core, all can gradually advance to a common grasp also of less central aspects of revealed truth. Third, to base unity on a list of fundamental articles could suggest that the faith of the people of God can be adequately summed up in a list of propositions, overlooking the fact that communion in faith is communion in life. Unity of faith is based on how believers worship and live. Lists of doctrines are never a sufficient measure of unity in faith. Fourth, some theories concerning fundamental articles tended to call for a return to an earlier stage in the life of the Church, such as the first four centuries, before some later doctrinal decisions were taken. This cast doubt on the value of development of doctrine under the guidance of Holy Spirit and the ministry of official teachers, and showed insufficient appreciation for the fact that the Christian community can grow in its comprehension of revelation over the course of time. These errors can and must be avoided. Perhaps the greatest difficulty in making effective and practical use of the doctrine of the hierarchy of truths would not be theological but rather pastoral. Pastors would need to try to protect the faithful from falling into one or another of the previously mentioned misinterpretations or errors associated with the proposal of unifying around a selected list of fundamental articles.

Second, there is need to introduce greater historical sensitivity into the understanding of how the people of God comes to and maintains unity in faith. In the aftermath of the infallibility debate, the Congregation of the Doctrine of the Faith issued a clarification entitled *Mysterium Ecclesiae* in 1973, which might serve as a kind of *magna charta* for developing a "hermeneutics of dogma," something that was treated in much greater detail by the International Theological Commission in its study "The Interpretation of Dogmas" of 1989.[21] The historical circumstances surrounding the definitions of Nicaea or Chalcedon are quite different than those surrounding the definitions of the immaculate conception and the assumption of the Blessed Virgin Mary. In overly simplified terms one might say that Nicaea and Chalcedon intended to avoid the division of the Church over essential trinitarian and christological doctrine. They were necessary to preserve unity in faith. The later Marian dogmas of 1854 and of 1950 did not have the same context or motivation. It was not necessary to define them to preserve the unity of the Church in faith. St. Thomas Aquinas's treatise on faith in the *Summa Theologiae* could provide very authoritative support for arguing that the unity of the Church in faith over the course of time, which is subject to the various conditions of the many subjects who make up the Christian community, can be explained by distinguishing between explicit faith and implicit faith and by recognizing the different capacity for explicit faith between those who have had the privilege of advanced study and those who have not. A historically sensitive understanding of the

Church's unity in faith might be expressed in the following principles. The objective source of unity in faith is divine revelation. The subjective source of such unity is the common acceptance of this revelation under the inspiration of the Holy. Revelation is received in faith by human beings who are subject to the contingencies of time and space, of history and culture. This historical contingency inevitably and necessarily leads to a certain degree of pluriformity in the expression of the faith.[22] One could reasonably expect that such pluriformity would be diachronic, in that even a great doctor of the Church who lived in an earlier age may not have explicitly professed a doctrine that even a simple believer of a later age may profess. One could also reasonably expect this pluriformity to be synchronic, in that in any given age the paths that Christians travel in contemplating revealed truth will lead to some legitimate differences because of their various linguistic and cultural contexts. Differences would especially be likely between members of ecclesial communities that have been separated from one another for many generations. The Church as a whole, under the guidance of its official teachers, is an adequate subject both to discern both the order that exists among Christian doctrines and the relevance of that order for the unity of the Church in faith.[23]

This section can conclude simply by quoting a second text from *Evangelii Gaudium*, this time from one of its paragraphs devoted explicitly to ecumenical dialogue.

> If we concentrate on the convictions we share, and if we keep in mind the principle of the hierarchy of truths, we will be able to progress decidedly towards common expressions of proclamation, service and witness. The immense numbers of people who have not received the Gospel of Jesus Christ cannot leave us indifferent. Consequently, commitment to a unity which helps them to accept Jesus Christ can no longer be a matter of mere diplomacy or forced compliance, but rather an indispensable path to evangelization. Signs of division between Christians in countries ravaged by violence add further causes of conflict on the part of those who should instead be a leaven of peace. How many important things unite us! (246)

RECEPTIVE ECUMENISM

"Reception" seems to have been explored in relation to ecumenism in two distinctive ways, which are not mutually exclusive. First, the explosion of bilateral dialogues after Vatican II occasioned reflection about what the churches should do with the results of these conversations.[24] Already in 1985, Cardinal Willebrands discussed the relation between reception of the results of ecumenical dialogue and progress toward Christian unity. He wrote,

> "Reception" is a word and, indeed, a concept that has assumed a new meaning and a new urgency in the ecumenical movement. The word has its origin in the field of jurisprudence. In theology it is now used to designate the acceptance of a doctrinal statement or a council decision by a local church or by the universal church. But in the ecumenical movement reception now has a new meaning, especially as regards the results of a dialogue between two churches. In the narrower sense it refers to the formal decision of the competent church authorities, though in the wider sense it embraces all the phases and aspects of the process by means of which a Church adopts the results of such a dialogue.[25]

Thomas Rausch added,

> While the classical concept emerged in a church which understood itself as a communion of churches, it was nonetheless a united church. In the ecumenical context, however, a new element appears; for now what is involved is a process of reception between churches separated from one another by differences of history, doctrine and structure. In the absence of communion between the churches, the process of reception is complicated considerably; as Anton Houtepen observes, "more theological consensus is needed to restore unity than to preserve unity."[26]

John Paul II dedicated two paragraphs of his encyclical *Ut Unum Sint* to the "reception of the results already achieved," noting that "while dialogue continues on new subjects or develops at deeper levels, a new task lies before us: that of receiving the results already achieved. These cannot remain the statements of bilateral commissions but must become a common heritage" (80). His encyclical can provide a positive example of promoting reception of these results in that it quotes from or refers to a considerable number of them. Thus, he has made part of his own magisterium some of the results of dialogue and, as such, they will remain before the eyes of Catholics who read his teaching. Another outstanding form of the reception has been the *Joint Declaration on the Doctrine of Justification* between the Lutheran World Federation and the Roman Catholic Church. This agreement, endorsed officially by high authorities of both traditions, was based upon a harvesting of many previous results of bilateral dialogue between Lutherans and Catholics. Other Reformation communities have considered or have actually associated themselves with this joint declaration on a fundamental point of conflict in the sixteenth century.

But a second form of reception also emerged from reflection on the results of dialogue. One of the forums on bilateral dialogues regularly organized by the Faith and Order Commission published three reports, entitled respectively "Aspects of Reception," "Authority within the Process of Reception," and "Opportunities and Difficulties within the Present Situation of Reception."[27] One of its statements suggests that reception is about more than simply receiving "texts":

> Ecumenical reception is the comprehensive process by which churches make their own the whole range of results of their encounters with each other. It is thus far more than the official response to the results of dialogues, although such responses are essential. Reception is an integral part of the movement toward that full communion which is realized when "all the churches are able to recognize in one another the one, holy, catholic and apostolic Church in its fullness." (Canberra statement on *The Unity of the Church as Koinonia: Gift and Calling*)[28]

Here the meaning of reception is obviously broadened. The texts serve to acknowledge one another. Günther Gassmann, once director of Faith and Order, wrote that the reception of mere texts is but "the tip of the iceberg."[29] Here we are already moving toward another idea expressed by John Paul II in *Ut Unum Sint*, that ecumenical dialogue entails an "exchange of gifts." He writes,

> Dialogue is an indispensable step along the path towards human self-realization, the self-realization both of each individual and of every human community. Although the concept of "dialogue" might appear to give priority to the cognitive dimension (*dia-logos*), all dialogue implies a global, existential dimension. It involves the human subject in his or her entirety; dialogue between communities involves in a particular way the subjectivity of each.... Dialogue is not simply and exchange of ideas. In some way it is always an "exchange of gifts." (*Ut Unum Sint* 28)[30]

John Paul develops his teaching on the gifts given to believers that are meant to be shared in his apostolic letter summing up the experience of the Great Jubilee 2000, especially when he writes of a "spirituality of communion."

> A spirituality of communion indicates above all the heart's contemplation of the mystery of the Trinity dwelling in us, and whose light we must also be able to see shining on the face of the brothers and sisters around us. A spirituality of communion also means an ability to think of our brothers and sisters in faith within the profound unity of the Mystical Body, and therefore as "those who are a part of me." This makes us able to share their joys and sufferings, to sense their desires and attend to their needs, to offer them deep and genuine friendship. A spirituality of communion implies also the ability to see what is positive in others, to welcome it and prize it as a gift from God: not only as a gift for the brother or sister who has received it directly, but also as a "gift for me." (*Novo Millennio Ineunte* 43)

Since then, a further development of the notion of ecumenism as an "exchange of gifts" has emerged in the "receptive ecumenism" conceived and promoted by Dr. Paul Murray of the University of Durham in England.[31] This receptive ecumenism has spawned three international conferences so far, as well as local and international projects. It has been given a succinct and excellent description by Myriam Wijlens, who dates its origin to 2006. She writes,

> What is Receptive Ecumenism? Receptive Ecumenism is about showing "wounded hands," recognizing deficiencies and acknowledging areas for growth within one's own tradition leading to a willingness to ask what can and must be learned, with dynamic integrity, from the dialogue partner. It is a receptive *ecclesial* learning and receiving in humility in order to grow and be enriched oneself. It is an ecumenical learning that implies enrichment rather than diminishment of identity. Engaging in Receptive Ecumenism thus requires a programmatic shift from asking: What do our dialogue partners need to learn from us?, to asking What do *we* need to learn and *what* can we learn from our dialogue partners?[32]

This latest approach to ecumenism is very nicely expressed by Pope Francis:

> If we really believe in the abundantly free working of the Holy Spirit, we can learn so much from one another! It is not just about being better informed about others, but rather about reaping what the Spirit has sown in them, which is also meant to be a gift for us.... Through an exchange of gifts, the Spirit can lead us ever more fully into truth and goodness. (*Evangelii Gaudium* 246)

Thus, the theology of the people, reform, the hierarchy of truths, and reception are four theoretical principles relating to the thought of Pope Francis that have profound implications for possible action on behalf of ecumenism by the Catholic Church in the years ahead. What practical recommendations might these four principles suggest?

Practical Recommendations

FOR MEDIUM-TERM REFORMS

1. Given Cardinal Kasper's assessment that the principal ecumenical problem about which no significant progress has been made concerns ecclesiology, it is of great importance for the Pontifical Council for the Promotion of Christian Unity (hereafter PCPCU) to devise a thorough process for the reception of the Faith and Order convergence text *The Church: Towards a Common Vision* (2013). It has been called an "extraordinary ecumenical achievement" and compared to the famous Lima text *Baptism, Eucharist and Ministry* of 1982. The text could be distributed without great cost through the Internet to all the Bishops' Conferences and even to all the diocesan ecumenical officers throughout the Catholic Church for their consideration and response. It would be a tragic to miss this opportunity for ecumenical reception of a convergence on what has been such an essential ecumenical issue; it deserves to be distributed and reflected upon as widely as possible.
2. The tenth general assembly of the World Council of Churches established as its guiding theme for the coming years "The Pilgrimage towards Justice and Peace." This theme is intended also to include common reflection upon and action in the protection of the environment. Given Pope Francis's encyclical *Laudato Si'* on the environment and the initiatives of the Ecumenical Patriarch Bartholomew in this area, could not the PCPCU, together with other appropriate dicasteries of the curia, explore ways to join in this work of the WCC and to encourage knowledge and participation in it at local levels?
3. The year 2017 will mark the five-hundredth anniversary of the Protestant Reformation. Might not a joint teaching by the Holy Father and the leaders of the Lutheran World Federation reflect on the event, point out that it was not intended to lead to permanent

divisions within the Church and, without overlooking developments that are regrettable, acknowledge the positive aspects of the Reformation and of its response in the so-called Counter Reformation? This could be done also at national or local levels. Also, the leaders of other Reformation communities might be invited to join in making such a declaration.

4. Several bilateral dialogues—such as the Methodist–Roman Catholic conversations—have explicitly taken up the method of looking at dialogue as an "exchange of gifts" and even proposed what gifts the churches involved might offer to one another. These lists of gifts should be made more widely known. Local projects of receptive ecumenism—such as that in the North of England—can also be encouraged.[33] The PCPCU could encourage the members that it nominates to serve in the various dialogues to make use of the method of receptive ecumenism.
5. The International Theological Commission might be invited to dedicate a new project to the hermeneutics of doctrine, especially focused upon exploring the harmony between the rejection of "fundamental articles" by *Mortalium Animos*, the proposal of a hierarchy of truths by Vatican II, and the historically conditioned nature of the development of doctrine in *Mysterium Ecclesiae* and in "The Interpretation of Dogma." The purpose would be to describe more adequately the "unity in faith" that is the aim of ecumenical dialogue. In this regard, the importance for unity of the practice of the faith could also be explored. Whether and to what extent could the ecumenism of the martyrs, whose practice is beyond question, be extended to those committed Christians of communities not yet in full communion with the Catholic Church?
6. The challenge to which efforts for a "new evangelization" attempt to respond is a challenge shared by all the currently divided churches. The Pontifical Council for the New Evangelization might be encouraged to

devise ecumenical proposals for collaboration in the new evangelization.

7. Synod of Bishops dedicated to ecumenism could explore the various aspects of efforts to reestablish unity and would, by its very happening, be an aid in making Catholics and other Christians more aware of the necessity of overcoming divisions and of seeking full visible unity.

FOR LONG-TERM REFORMS

1. The most important long-term reform for ecumenical progress is to continue with the new style of exercising the ministry of primacy as begun by Pope Francis and to move ahead carefully with his efforts at decentralization, such as giving greater voice to particular churches and episcopal conferences and reforming the Roman curia. As recent popes have acknowledged, the exercise of the primacy and the centralization of the Catholic Church have played a significant role in the reluctance of other Christian communities to seek full communion with the Bishop of Rome.
2. Given the power of the liturgy in the ongoing formation of the people of God, and given the fact that interest in and enthusiasm for overcoming Christian divisions seems to have weakened, a study might be made of ways that the liturgy might more effectively raise the awareness of the faithful about Christ's will for the unity of his Church and the serious obligation of believers to work for that unity. Could slight additions to the anaphoras begging God for the grace to overcome divisions be judiciously added?
3. The ecumenical situation varies from country to country and from culture to culture. One of the reasons underlying the establishment of Bishops' Conferences is precisely to proclaim the gospel considering the culture that their people share. Each Bishops' Conference could be encouraged to devise ecumenical catechesis

and activities suitable to its cultural and ecclesial circumstances.

4. Given that baptism is incorporation into the Body of Christ and the foundation for a believer's participation in the public worship of the Church—a point made in Pius XII's *Mediator Dei* and a principal source of ecumenical inspiration for Cardinal Bea, the first president of the PCPCU—the possibility of eucharistic sharing with practicing baptized Christians might be further explored.[34]
5. As baptism initiates one into the prophetic, priestly, and royal people of God, this ecclesiological theme could be given greater prominence in ecumenical dialogue and relations, complementing the emphasis given in recent decades to the ecclesiology of communion. The emphasis upon the triad prophet, priest, and king has been associated with John Calvin and thus might well appeal to the many Christians whose communities trace their roots to his theology. But this theme also played a key role in the ecclesiological doctrine of Vatican II. Moreover, this approach would allow for greater attention to the relation of the common priesthood to the ordained priesthood, as well as reflection on the role of the layperson in the Church and the gift of the *sensus fidei*. Perhaps this is an area in which the Catholic Church might "receive" the gifts of other Christian communities and learn from them.
6. After the example of John Paul II in *Ut Unum Sint*, official Catholic teachings might continue to refer to or, when appropriate, quote the results of ecumenical dialogue. This would be an excellent form of the reception of the dialogues. One could explore whether this could be done only at the universal level by the Holy Father and in synods or whether it might be possible also at the level of episcopal conferences and even by local bishops.
7. The formation of the clergy is essential for the wider reception of the results of ecumenical dialogue and the "exchange of gifts" among Christian communities. The

formation of the Latin rite clergy seems to be quite lacking regarding facilitating familiarity with Eastern theology, liturgy, and spirituality. Probably the same could be said regarding familiarity with the various families owing their roots to the Reformation. Sustained effort should be made to insure an adequate ecumenical component be present in priestly formation and that Catholic clergy are not ignorant of the gifts the Holy Spirit has bestowed upon the other communities.

Conclusion

Given the fact that Pope Francis chose his name after St. Francis of Assisi, perhaps a good way to conclude these reflections would be to refer to a well-known story of the conversion of the *poverello* as narrated in St. Bonaventure's *Legenda Maior*. Francis was praying in the church of San Damiano, which was somewhat abandoned and in need of repair. Bonaventure writes,

> Then, all of a sudden, he heard a voice coming from the cross and telling him three times, "Francis, go and repair my house. You see it is all falling down." Francis was alone in the church and he was terrified at the sound of the voice, but the power of its message penetrated his heart and he went into an ecstasy. Eventually, he came back to himself and prepared to obey the command he had received. He was quite willing to devote himself entirely to repairing the ruined church of San Damiano, although the message really referred to the universal Church which Christ "won for himself at the price of his own blood" (Acts 20:28), as the Holy Spirit afterwards made him realize and he himself explained to the friars.[35]

The voice from the crucifix saying, "Repair my house" can today be seen as a wonderfully appropriate encouragement for involvement in the work of Christian unity. Within the context of the vocation of St. Francis of Assisi, it reflects the very same notion expressed in Jesus' prayer and will the night before his passion: "that all may be one, so that the world will believe" (John 17:21).

NOTES

1. All three quotations are from W. Kasper, *That They All May Be One* (London: Burns & Oates, 2004), 1.

2. Ibid., 2. This comment was made several years before a major convergence document entitled *The Church: Towards a Common Vision* was approved by the Faith and Order Commission of the World Council of Churches and published in 2013. The text can be found in several languages at the following website: https://www.oikoumene.org/en/resources/documents/commissions/faith-and-order/i-unity-the-church-and-its-mission/the-church-towards-a-common-vision.

3. Ibid., 72.

4. Available at http://w2.vatican.va/content/francesco/en/speeches/2013/march/documents/papa-francesco_20130320_delegati-fraterni.html.

5. Antonio Spadaro, SJ, "A Big Heart Open to God: The Exclusive Interview with Pope Francis," *America*, September 20, 2013, available at http://americamagazine.org/pope-interview.

6. *EG* 223; paragraphs 222–25 are entitled "Time Is Greater Than Space."

7. *EG* 228; paragraphs 226–30 are entitled "Unity Prevails over Conflict."

8. *EG* 233; paragraphs 231–33 are entitled "Realities Are More Important Than Ideas."

9. *EG* 235; paragraphs 234–37 are entitled "The Whole Is Greater Than the Part."

10. Quoted by Walter Kasper in his *Pope Francis' Revolution of Tenderness and Love* (Mahwah, NJ: Paulist Press, 2015), 60.

11. Jorge Bergoglio and Abraham Skorka, *Il cielo e la terra* (Rome: Mondadori, 2013), 191, also 192–93.

12. Ibid., 194–95. On this point, see also Kasper, *Pope Francis' Revolution of Tenderness and Love*, 55.

13. *Il cielo e la terra*, 73. The English version is taken from Hector Scerri, "The Ecumenical Commitment of Pope Francis," *Roczniki Teologii Ekumenisznej* 5 (60) (2013): 25–42, at 26.

14. Kasper, *Pope Francis' Revolution of Tenderness and Love*, 57.

15. Paragraph 17 admits that the lack of unity hinders the Catholic Church from attaining "the complete fulfilment of its universality in history"; available at http://www.vatican.va/roman_curia/congregations/cfaith/documents/rc_con_cfaith_doc_28051992_communionis-notio_en.html.

16. John Paul II, *Ut Unum Sint*, paragraphs 95–96.

17. See, for example, the opening chapter of Owen Chadwick's *The Reformation* (New York: Penguin, 1964), 11–39, which bears the title "The Cry for Reformation." But see also *Reassessing Reform: A Historical Investigation into Church Renewal*, ed. Christopher M. Bellitto and David Zachariah Flanagin (Washington, DC: Catholic University of America Press, 2012), which includes well-documented essays demonstrating that various reforms had taken place in the several centuries prior to the Protestant Reformation.

18. Y. Congar, *Vrai et fausse réforme dans l'Église*, Unam Sanctam 20 (Paris: Cerf, 1950).

19. The text can be consulted at the following website: https://w2.vatican.va/content/pius-xi/it/encyclicals/documents/hf_p-xi_enc_19280106_mortalium-animos.html.

20. See the fine doctoral study on the foundations of Christian faith by Henk Witte, *"Alnaargelang hun band met het fundament van het christelijk geloof verschillend is." Wording en werwerking van de uitspraak over di 'hiërarchie; van waarheden van Vaticanum II* (Tillburg: Tillburg University Press, 1986).

21. *Mysterium Ecclesiae* can be found at http://www.vatican.va/roman_curia/congregations/cfaith/documents/rc_con_cfaith_doc_19730705_mysterium-ecclesiae_en.html and "The Interpretation of Dogma" can be found at http://www.vatican.va/roman_curia/congregations/cfaith/cti_documents/rc_cti_1989_interpretazione-dogmi_en.html.

22. See the text on "The Unity of Faith and Theological Pluralism" by the International Theological Commission in 1972, available at http://www.vatican.va/roman_curia/congregations/cfaith/cti_documents/rc_cti_1972_fede-pluralismo_en.html. The first thesis of this document states, "Unity and plurality in the expression of the Faith have their ultimate basis in the very mystery of Christ that, while being at the same time a mystery of universal fulfillment and reconciliation (Eph 2:11–22), goes beyond the possibilities of expression of any given age and thus eludes exhaustive systematization (Eph 3:8–10)." Its fourth thesis adds, "The truth of the Faith is bound up with its onward movement through history, from Abraham on to Christ, and from Christ to the parousia. Consequently, orthodoxy is not consent to a system but a sharing in the

onward movement of the Faith and so, in the Church's own selfhood that subsists, identical, through all time, and is the true subject of the Credo."

23. These principles form the conclusion of W. Henn, "The Hierarchy of Truths and Christian Unity," *Ephemerides Theologicae Lovanienses* 66 (1990): 111–42.

24. A survey of the literature on this topic up until 1996 can be found in W. Henn, "The Reception of Ecumenical Documents," in *Reception and Communion among Churches*, ed. H. Legrand, J. Manzanares, and A. García y García (Washington, DC: Catholic University of America Press, 1997), 362–95, a volume that also appeared as *The Jurist* 57 (1997).

25. Johannes Cardinal Willebrands, "The Ecumenical Dialogue and its Reception," *One in Christ* 21 (1985): 220.

26. Thomas Rausch, "Reception Past and Present," *Theological Studies* 47 (1986): 500.

27. See the "Faith and Order Paper 168," in *Sixth Forum on Bilateral Dialogues*, ed. Günther Gassmann (Geneva: WCC Publications, 1995), 5–21.

28. Ibid., 5.

29. "Es ist ein Mangel vieler Dialogtexte, daβ sie selbst nicht deutlich genug auf diesen breiten Dialogprozeβ hinweisen, dessen 'Spitze des Eisberges' sie sind. Die Dialogue *und* ihre Ergebnesse, und nicht bloβ Texte, sind zu rezipieren." In Gassmann, "Die Rezeption der Dialogue," *Ökumenische Rundschau* 33 (1984): 362.

30. This text includes a footnote to *Lumen Gentium* 13, which speaks of the sharing of gifts within the Catholic Church: "In virtue of this catholicity each part contributes its own gifts to the other parts and to the whole Church, so that the whole and each of the parts are strengthened by the common sharing of all things and by the common effort to attain to fullness in unity." By adding this reference to his comment on and ecumenical exchange of gifts, John Paul is applying what *Lumen Gentium* says here about that catholicity that is internal to the life of the Catholic Church to relations between currently divided Christian communities.

31. See Paul D. Murray, "Receptive Ecumenism and Catholic Learning: Establishing the Agenda," *International Journal for the Study of the Christian Church* 7 (2007): 279–301.

32. From Myriam Wijlens, "Future Paths for the Ecumenical Movement: Canonical Considerations, Challenges and Contributions," *CLSA Proceedings* 76 (2014): 13–41, at 30, who refers in this passage to Paul D. Murray, "Receptive Ecumenism and Ecclesial Learning: Receiving our Gifts for our Needs," *Louvain Studies* 33 (2008): 30–45, at 33.

33. For some projects devoted to receptive ecumenism at the local and at the universal levels, see Wijlens, "Future Paths for the Ecumenical Movement," 31–37.

34. See Cardinal Bea's essay "The Catholic Attitude toward the Problem," in his *The Unity of Christians* (New York: Herder, 1963), 19–37, at 30–34, where he quotes Pius XII's *Mediator Dei* on one of the effects of baptism being that the baptized become "by a common title members of Christ the Priest" (quoting the encyclical from *Acta Apostolicae Sedis* 39 [1947]: 555. Obviously neither Pius XII in his encyclical nor Cardinal Bea in his essay were addressing the question of eucharistic sharing. Bea notes that, in the canon law then in vigor, various situations could block the rights and duties that baptism imparted. This essay by Bea first appeared as "Il cattolico di fronte al problema dell'unione dei cristiani" in the first volume of *La civiltà cattolica* for the year 1961 at pages 113–29.

35. St. Bonaventure, "Major Life of St. Francis," in *St. Francis of Assisi: Writings and Early Biographies; English Omnibus of the Sources for the Life of St. Francis,* ed. Marion A. Habigs (Chicago: Franciscan Herald Press, 1973), 640.

19

AN EXCHANGE OF GIFTS

The Catholic Church and the Eastern Churches—The Strategic Significance of the *Ravenna Document*

Piero Coda

Introduction: Two Possible Paths

We begin with two quotations from Pope Francis taken from statements he made on ecumenism and, in particular, on the perspective of dialogue between the Catholic Church and the Orthodox Church.[1] The first is from *Evangelii Gaudium* (246):

> How many important things unite us! If we really believe in the abundantly free working of the Holy Spirit, we can learn so much from one another! It is not just about being better informed about others, but rather about reaping what the Spirit has sown in them, which is also meant to be a gift for us. To give but one example, in the dialogue with our Orthodox brothers and sisters, we Catholics have the opportunity to learn more about the meaning of episcopal collegiality and

> their experience of synodality. Through an exchange of gifts, the Spirit can lead us ever more fully into truth and goodness.[2]

The second quotation is from the interview given by Pope Francis to Antonio Spadaro on August 19, 2013, which appeared in *La Civiltà Cattolica*:

> In ecumenical relations it is important not only to know each other better, but also to recognize what the Spirit has sown in the other as a gift for us. I want to continue the discussion that was begun in 2007 by the joint [Catholic–Orthodox] commission on how to exercise the Petrine primacy, which led to the signing of the Ravenna Document. We must continue on this path.[3]

Two clear directions can be derived from these statements that express Francis's *mens* regarding the close link between the spiritual and institutional reform in the Catholic Church and the ecumenical perspective of the path toward full and visible unity, particularly with the Orthodox Church. This is not only a demanding and costly imperative—on both sides—but above all a positive chance for the missionary conversion of the Church in the urgent and demanding *kairos* of our time.

The first direction touches on the conscience and the approach to the ecumenical commitment: it is to "gather what the Spirit sowed" in the experience and tradition of our sister churches "as a gift to us."[4] This is the evangelic perspective that we are asked to adopt, with clear implications in terms of historical hermeneutics, theological discernment, and pastoral practice.

The second direction identifies the path to take in the theme of the relationship between synodality and primacy, from the promising beginning offered to the Catholic-Orthodox dialogue in the *Ravenna Document* written by the Joint International Commission for Theological Dialogue between the Catholic Church and the Orthodox Church, on October 13, 2007, and titled, "Ecclesiological and Canonical Consequences of the Sacramental Nature of the Church: Ecclesial Communion, Conciliarity and Authority."[5] Both Pope Francis and Patriarch Bartholomew have pointed out the meaning and value of this document in the two joint statements of Jerusalem (May 25, 2014) and Istanbul (November 30, 2014): "This is no mere theoretical exercise, but an exercise in truth and love that demands an ever-deeper knowledge of each other's traditions in order to understand them and to learn from them," not to "reach a compromise," but in view of

> deepening one's grasp of the whole truth that Christ has given to his Church, a truth that we never cease to understand better as we follow the Holy Spirit's promptings. Hence, we affirm together that our faithfulness to the Lord demands fraternal encounter and true dialogue. Such a common pursuit does not lead us away from the truth; rather, through an exchange of gifts, through the guidance of the Holy Spirit, it will lead us into all truth (cf. John 16:13).[6]

Having been called to be part of the joint Catholic-Orthodox Theological Commission since the fall of 2005, when it resumed its work after the interruption following the misunderstandings on the thorny issue of the so-called uniatism,[7] it seems to me worthwhile to offer some food for thought in the perspective described above, in accordance, therefore, with Pope Francis's *mens*, in three brief points: the strategic significance of the *Ravenna Document*; the current situation of the work of the Joint Theological Commission in developing this document; and the theological issues and the perspectives that we consider to be the most important, even crucial, in view of the effective continuation of the path.

The Strategic Significance of the *Ravenna Document*

Concerning the fundamental content of the *Ravenna Document* (*DR*), worth recalling here briefly is the following. In October 2007 in Ravenna, the Joint Commission approved a document on the "Ecclesiological and Canonical Consequences of the Sacramental Nature of the Church," fully explored in the previous documents,[8] and focusing especially on the relationship between "Ecclesial Communion, Conciliarity and Authority."

The close connection between the Church's sacramental nature—by virtue of baptism and the Eucharist and in reference to the exchange, through them, of the very life of the most Holy Trinity to humanity redeemed in Christ—and her synodal form is explicated in the questions to which the document intends to give an initial response. This is in interdependence with a diversified exercise, at its various operating levels, of the primacy, and that is, in our view, of crucial importance. Here are the questions:

> Since the Eucharist, in the light of the Trinitarian mystery, constitutes the criterion of ecclesial life as a whole, how do institutional structures visibly reflect the mystery of this *koinonia*? Since the one and holy Church is realised both in each local Church celebrating the Eucharist and at the same time in the *koinonia* of all the Churches, how does the life of the Churches manifest this sacramental structure? (*DR* 3)

In the first part, the document recalls the foundations of both the authority inherent in the ecclesial institution per se, and the synodality (or conciliarity; see *DR* 5) that flows from the mystery of the Church as communion (see *DR* 4).

The authority (*exousia*) in the Church "has as its goal the gathering of the whole of humankind into Jesus Christ," and—as it is stated (*DR* 13)—belongs to Jesus Christ, her only head, and through his Spirit is made part of the whole Church, his body. In particular, the specific authority linked with the grace received in episcopal ordination is destined for the *diakonía* (service) of the community. It is founded upon the word of God, received in the living tradition in the Church from the apostles, whose living center is the celebration of the Eucharist. The Church's authority, therefore, is linked to the apostolic succession, and its exercise is regulated by the canons and statutes of the Church, and is regulated by the supreme criterion of reciprocity, since it stems from the sacramental nature of the Church shaped by the life and grace of the Triune God:

> The authority of which we are speaking, since it expresses divine authority, cannot subsist in the Church except in the love between the one who exercises it and those subject to it.[...]the evangelical identification between authority and service constitutes a fundamental norm for the Church. (*DR* 14; see also 12–16)

Synodality, on the other hand, invests all members of the Church, by virtue of baptism. As it involves the responsibility of each baptized regarding the faith proclaimed, celebrated, and experienced, it invests in a peculiar way the episcopal ministry:

> In proclaiming the Church's faith and in clarifying the norms of Christian conduct, the bishops have a specific task by divine institution. As successors of the Apostles, the bishops are responsible for communion in the apostolic faith and for fidelity to the demands of a life in keeping with the Gospel.[9]

The document also states,

> Conciliarity reflects the Trinitarian mystery and finds therein its ultimate foundation. The three persons of the Holy Trinity are "enumerated," as St Basil the Great says (*On the Holy Spirit*, 45), without the designation as "second" or "third" person implying any diminution or subordination. Similarly, there also exists an order (*taxis*) among local Churches, which however does not imply inequality in their ecclesial nature. (*DR* 5)

In the second part, the *Ravenna Document* outlines the theme of the threefold implementation of synodality, which must be present at the three levels of ecclesial communion: local, regional, and universal.[10] The fundamental idea that is developed is that the Church's synodality not only does not exclude the authority in the diverse and qualified form of the exercise of the primacy, but rather requires it as its internal condition and peculiar guarantee.[11] In this sense, the reference to the Apostolic Canon 34 is crucial for the development of the document (*DR* 24):

> A canon accepted in the East as in the West, expresses the relationship between the local Churches of a region: "The bishops of each province (*ethnos*) must recognize the one who is first (*protos*) amongst them, and consider him to be their head (*kephale*), and not do anything important without his consent (*gnome*); each bishop may only do what concerns his own diocese (*paroikia*) and its dependent territories. But the first (*protos*) cannot do anything without the consent of all. For in this way concord (*homonoia*) will prevail, and God will be praised through the Lord in the Holy Spirit" (Apostolic Canon 34).

The first level in which the interdependence between primacy and synodality is expressed is the local diocese entrusted to the bishop and his presbyters. Synodality, as required by the communal nature of the Church, in fact, concerns all members of the community in unity with the bishop, who is the first (*protos*) and the head (*kefale*) of the local church (*DR* 20). The episcopal ministry does not, therefore, exclude synodality; rather, it presupposes and promotes it. Thus, "All charisms and ministries in the Church converge in unity under the ministry of the bishop, who serves the communion of the local Church" (*DR* 21).

The second level is the regional one of group of local churches with their bishops who recognize their *protos*—similarly to what happens at the level of the local church and in diversified form at various levels of synergy between local churches—in the figure of the metropolitan or patriarch. The communion of local churches finds expression in the regional synods and councils, and specifically in the communion of their bishops, manifested sacramentally at the time of their ordination (see *DR* 22–26). Each bishop, in fact, is "responsible for the whole Church together with all his colleagues in one and the same apostolic mission." (*DR* 27).

The third level of implementation of synodality is the universal one. The document states that "each local Church is in communion not only with neighbouring Churches, but with the totality of the local Churches" (*DR* 32). In the universal synodality, exercised in particular form in ecumenical councils, can be recognized the primary and active role of the bishop of Rome. The ecumenical council is not an institution whose frequency can be regulated by canons, but is rather an event, a *kairos* inspired by the Spirit in the life and mission of the holy Church (cf. *DR* 33, 35, 39). The Church of Rome, as the Church "presiding in love"—in the words of Saint Ignatius of Antioch[12]—in fact occupies the first place in the *taxis* (ancient order), being the Bishop of Rome, the *protos* among the patriarchs.

In summary,

> Primacy and conciliarity are mutually interdependent. That is why primacy at the different levels of the life of the Church, local, regional and universal, must always be considered in the context of conciliarity, and conciliarity likewise in the context of primacy. (*DR* 43)

As is clear from what has been briefly stated here, it is the first time that in a joint document Catholics and Orthodox articulate the question of primacy at the level of the universal Church in the spirit of Apostolic Canon 34. However, this does not imply the reaching of an agreement on the tenor of historical testimonies and the theological interpretations concerning the prerogatives of the Bishop of Rome as *protos* at the universal level and the form of exercise of this *diakonía*. And, in fact, differences exist and persist in understanding regarding the manner in which it is to be exercised and—in essence—its scriptural and theological foundations (cf. *DR* 41–43). In any case, it reaffirms with conviction that

> we, the members of the Joint International Commission for the Theological Dialogue between the Roman Catholic Church and the Orthodox Church, are convinced that the above statement on ecclesial communion, conciliarity and authority represents positive and significant progress in our dialogue, and that it provides a firm basis for future discussion of the question of primacy at the universal level in the Church. (*DR* 46)

In conclusion, the *Ravenna Document* outlines a task: in view of reaching a consensus, it "remains for the question of the role of the bishop of Rome in the communion of all the Churches to be studied in greater depth" (*DR* 45). The questions that have been proposed and still to be addressed are timely and precise:

> What is the specific function of the bishop of the "first see" in an ecclesiology of *koinonia* and in view of what we have said on conciliarity and authority in the present text? How should the teaching of the first and second Vatican councils on the universal primacy be understood and lived in the light of the ecclesial practice of the first millennium? These are crucial questions for our dialogue and for our hopes of restoring full communion between us. (*DR* 45)

The Current State of the Theological Dialogue

As is well known, the *Ravenna Document* was not signed by the Moscow patriarchate's delegation, which abandoned the work at the defining and ratifying session, due—as officially announced—to an ongoing dispute at that time between the ecumenical patriarchate of Constantinople and the patriarchate of Moscow.

The Moscow patriarchate's delegation participated in the Commission's subsequent sessions (Vienna, September 20–27, 2010; Amman, September 15–23, 2014), as well as in the interim working sessions of the Commission's coordination and drafting committee. But the *Ravenna Document*, not having been formally signed by this relevant expression of the Orthodox church, has in fact rendered precarious and uncertain the continuation of the works, which, on the Orthodox side, could not rest on a substantially shared base. In addition, the subsequent and formal official position of the Moscow patriarchate on the *Ravenna Document*, taken in the document promulgated by the session of the Holy Synod of the Russian Orthodox Church on December 25–26, 2013, outlined in two fundamental points the basic critique of the consensus position reached in Ravenna: (a) the fact that, at a universal level "the functions of the primus on various levels are not identical and cannot be transferred from one level to another" (no. 3); (b) the fact that, at the universal level, "primacy is determined in conformity with the tradition of sacred diptychs and represents *primacy in honour*" especially as the "order in diptychs has been changing in history" (no. 2).[13]

This position, while making it difficult to continue the dialogue in the direction outlined in Ravenna, also explains the reason why the post-Ravenna course was unfortunate and ultimately hindered. This is so much so that we have not been able to produce to an additional document by now following the three steps that, at least at first, seemed to emerge from the *Ravenna Document*: (1) first, the relationship between primacy and synodality in the first millennium; (2) then, in the second millennium—addressing the difficult ecclesiological issue of the Constitution *Pastor Aeternus* of Vatican I; and (3) finally, coming to the proposal to open a new situation in the light of Vatican II, the results achieved in the subsequent theological dialogue, and a sincere and vulnerable openness to what the Spirit says to the churches today (see Rev 2:7).

At this time, the only way out that appears and is perhaps the only feasible way to reopen the dialogue is to present the ecclesiological experience of the first millennium, despite its variety and conflictuality, as a common heritage of the Catholic Church and the Orthodox Church and as an effective and resolute source of inspiration in the quest for reconciliation of the churches at the beginning of the third millennium.[14] This is based on the fact that throughout the first millennium the churches of the East and West were united in preserving and transmitting the apostolic faith, maintaining the apostolic succession of bishops, and developing structures of synodality inseparably linked, at the various levels of its expression, to the exercise of the primacy.

Although the unity between the churches of the East and the West has experienced harsh difficulties in the first millennium, the bishops of the East and the West were aware of belonging to one church and one episcopate. The first millennium, therefore, does not represent so much a definitive model, but offers some fixed points gained and shared at the theological and canonical level, which have their measure and their normative point of reference in the gospel of Jesus and in the vital and doctrinal experience of the one Church, expressed at the highest level in ecumenical councils. We must restart from here, open to the newness of the

Spirit, in the logic of the path "into all the truth" (John 16:13) reaffirmed with sincerity and determination in the Joint Declaration of Pope Francis and Patriarch Bartholomew in Istanbul in November of 2014.

In any case, the objective difficulty in the mutual understanding between the Catholic Church and the Orthodox Church in reading and recognizing the "gifts of the Spirit" of which both traditions are bearers, with the commitment to free them from their exclusivism and to positively share their specific riches, making them mutually fruitful, is further complicated and, in many ways, accentuated, by the differences in theological sensitivity and ecclesial and cultural strategy between the patriarchate of Constantinople and that of Moscow. The former is definitely geared to continue in the line drawn in Ravenna, recognizing the specific gift represented by the ministry of the Bishop of Rome in interdependence with the principle of synodality , especially thanks to the recognition given to the theological magisterium by the metropolitan of Pergamon, Johannis Zizioulas,[15] according to the logic advocated by John Paul II in *Ut Unum Sint* (see 88 and 95) and continued by Pope Francis. The latter, however, the patriarchate of Moscow—based on its own theological reading—accentuates the situation of independence of the two ecclesial traditions.

In this case, the fatal risk is not so much of a prolonged impasse, but settling for a compromise solution such as a *gentleman's agreement,* in which the drive initiated by the balanced approach—provisional, no doubt, and entirely in the making—of the *Ravenna Document* would in fact come to a dead end. We must be aware of what is really at stake in the institutional relations between the Church of Rome and the churches of Constantinople and Moscow, which certainly intend to optimize their relations with the Church of Rome, but in a context where it can be tempting to not go too far into the central ecclesiological question that remains open.

Theological Issues and Perspectives

We come now to the last question that we intended to propose in this reflection: What are the real issues that still need resolution, and what shared perspectives of commitment can there be?

From the experience we have gained in person, in these ten years, it seems safe to say that the issues that are to be addressed at the theological level and ecclesial practice—setting aside, in a sincere spirit of permanent conversion, the improper but often still decisive influence of simple ecclesiastical policy strategies—do not concern, as it should be clear by now, the *depositum fidei* and the *traditio vivens ecclesiae*, in the legitimate plurality of its authentic forms, but *the experience and the intelligence of access to them and their concrete embodiment*, which must be enriched with each other to open *from and in this reciprocity in the Spirit to a new situation of reconciliation and mission*. In particular, I think it is necessary to focus on two points to promote this operation, with a realistic expectation of success.

The first is to become aware of the diversified and complementary process through which the lived interpretation of the scriptural canon, and the dogmatic canon linked to it, in which the "sister churches" recognize their unity, has expressed a distinct *Wirkungsgeschichte*. By virtue of this, in the logic of the inculturation of faith, the peculiar ecclesial expressions that have developed over the centuries—at the theological and institutional levels—need now to be reconciled and reconfigured in the logic of unity in diversity, under the action of the Spirit and listening to the signs of the times.[16]

Suffice it to think, in fact, of the central theme of the dispute, that is, the Roman conception of the primacy at the universal level. The primacy developed from a specific reading of the Scriptures and was articulated from peculiar historical and cultural situations, and must now be refined from what is contingent and even distorted, and linked in interdependence with the synodal principle embodied—even here not without unilateral temptations—by the Eastern churches, starting from a more rich and balanced perception and translation of eucharistic ecclesiology and the trinitarian *communio*. It is worth noting what the *Ravenna Document* says in this regard at nos. 29, 30, and 31:

> In subsequent centuries, both in the East and in the West, certain new configurations of communion between local Churches have developed. New patriarchates and autocephalous Churches have been founded in the Christian

> East, and in the Latin Church there has recently emerged a particular pattern of grouping of bishops, the Episcopal Conferences. These are not, from an ecclesiological standpoint, merely administrative subdivisions: they express the spirit of communion in the Church, while at the same time respecting the diversity of human cultures.
>
> In fact, regional synodality, whatever its contours and canonical regulation, demonstrates that the Church of God is not a communion of persons or local Churches cut off from their human roots. Because it is the community of salvation and because this salvation is "the restoration of creation" (cf. St. Irenaeus, *Adv. Haer.*, 1, 36, 1), it embraces the human person in everything which binds him or her to human reality as created by God. The Church is not just a collection of individuals; it is made up of communities with different cultures, histories and social structures.
>
> In the grouping of local Churches at the regional level, catholicity appears in its true light. It is the expression of the presence of salvation not in an undifferentiated universe but in humankind as God created it and comes to save it. In the mystery of salvation, human nature is at the same time both assumed in its fullness and cured of what sin has infused into it by way of self-sufficiency, pride, distrust of others, aggressiveness, jealousy, envy, falsehood and hatred. Ecclesial *koinonia* is the gift by which all humankind is joined together, in the Spirit of the risen Lord. This unity, created by the Spirit, far from lapsing into uniformity, calls for and thus preserves—and, in a certain way, enhances—diversity and particularity.

The second point: a very important element to emerge from the *Ravenna Document* is the subject of the peculiarity of authority (*exousia*) in its meaning and exercise in the Church, as it is read and exercised since its original and permanent christological and pneumatological configuration. This itself invests the entire ecclesial community as the Body of Christ and the people of God who lives and proclaims the gospel in a human and cultural place. This point has only marginally, in our view, has been brought to light and not developed at all.[17] We have the impression that—looking at the demanding contemporary context—reducing too soon the question of authority in the Church to the problem of the relationship between primacy and synodality, interpreting it according to a logic that ultimately invests only or mainly the episcopate, risks becoming a matter of institutional engineering without effective consequences (that is without real and fruitful reception) in the consciousness of the people of God and, therefore, with no actual incidence on its evangelizing mission.

What we must urgently and thoroughly focus on is the awareness—inherent per se in Christian faith and discipleship—that the risen *Kyrios*, and he alone, is the basic principle and the dynamic form of the ecclesial identity and mission. This means at least two things: namely, on the one hand, that it is Christ, crucified and risen, who conforms to himself each and all together the members of people of God, in the immediacy of the action of the Holy Spirit; and, on the other, that the sacraments, the charisms and ministries, are the mean and not the end to the achievement of salvation and mission that it brings about, and are the fruit and at the service of this Christ-shaping action of the Holy Spirit.

This has relevant consequences in understanding the meaning and the management of the episcopal ministry, as it is designated to express and ensure the apostolicity and unity of the ecclesial event.[18] In fact, by definition and by vocation, it must understand and exercise itself as *competent and responsible guarantee of the presence and action of the Risen Christ, in the outpouring of his Spirit, in relation to the life and mission of the Church*. It is in this perspective that the *Ravenna Document*—by its explicit intention—should be read. As such, the episcopal ministry is therefore called upon to serve, in the exercise of its specific authority in the form of communion, the presence and efficacious action of the *exousia* of the Risen Christ *in the multiple and converging plurality of his manifestations*. This implies and requires a demanding and rigorous theological reinterpretation of the meaning and resulting form of exercise of its specific authority—at its various levels and in its various explanations—in the life of the Church.

In other words, it seems crucial to place the meaning and the exercise of synodality in its interdependence with primacy in the context of the historical exercise of *communio* as a reality that qualifies the historical experience of the entire people of God, while keeping adequately distinct the level of the *res*, signified and realized by the ecclesial event, and the level of the *sacramentum* (in the ecclesiological sense of the term) that favors and promotes it at all levels, in the life and mission of the Church.

Because it is in fact the entirety of the people of God, in the multiplicity, variety, and richness of charisms and ministries, as Vatican II taught us, that is called to offer its irreplaceable and creative contribution to the discernment of "what the Spirit is saying to the churches" (Rev 2:7). The synodal structure and dynamics, in other words, are the living and necessary context within which, and in favor of which, the charism/episcopal ministry in relation to the charism/specific ministry of the Bishop of Rome find its appropriate place of development and its proper form of exercise, as both are called, in their interdependence, to embody the *seal of apostolicity and unity* (in the light and power of the *exousia* of the Risen Christ) on the decisions and guiding principles that promote and guide the path of the people of God in history.

As Pope Francis exhorts with wisdom and foresight, here too the essential thing is to "generate new processes" (cf. *EG* 223). And this is true both at summit and at the grassroots, in official relations between the Church of Rome and the Orthodox Church, as well as in the beginning and maturation of an authentic, rich, and effective synodal practice at the level of local churches—diocesan and regional.

NOTES

1. We use here, for convenience, the synthetic and ecclesiologically inaccurate expression of "Catholic Church" and "Orthodox Church," while aware that the first term presupposes the intrinsic distinction and articulation—in the lexicon of Catholic ecclesiology—between the universal church and local church, while the latter expresses the *koinonia* of the whole (*pleroma*) of the churches that recognize themselves in the tradition that understands itself to be Orthodox.

2. A clarification is necessary here, in relation to these words of Pope Francis, regarding the references he made to "episcopal collegiality" and "synodality." In reality, the pontiff distinguishes the two concepts and the

respective prospects of dialogue that, in relation to them, can be further promoted between the Catholic Church and the Orthodox Church. In the first case, regarding episcopal collegiality, Bergoglio emphasizes—on the part of the Catholic Church— "the opportunity to learn more about the meaning," evidently referring to the need for an in-depth analysis of what Vatican II defines as *ordinis Episcopal indoles et ratio* (see *LG* 22) in dialogue, in fact, with the ecclesiological tradition of the Christian East. In the second case, regarding synodality, it is "to learn more…about their experience of synodality," where the reference is, in fact, to the experience of synodal practice, in the deep and organic theological sense of the concept, that has been preserved and developed by the Eastern Churches. The reference to episcopal collegiality and synodality, therefore, implies the awareness of the distinction between the two concepts and the prospect of further investigation that allows and promotes a better understanding and practical articulation of the two.

3. Interview published in *La Civiltà Cattolica* 2013 /III: 449–77, at 466.

4. It seems worthy of the utmost interest what St. John Paul II proposed as an innovative and enlightening key to the interpretation of the history of the one and only Church of Christ through the tragic experience of the divisions that plagued her visible body over the centuries: "Yes, indeed, we can truly ask ourselves: *Why did the Holy Spirit permit all these divisions?* In general, the causes and historical development of these divisions are well known. It is legitimate, however, to wonder if there is perhaps a *metahistorical reason as well*. There are two possible answers to this question. The more *negative* one would see in these divisions the bitter fruit of sins committed by Christians. The more positive answer is inspired by trust in the One who is capable of bringing forth good even from evil, from human weakness. Could it not be that these divisions have also been *a path continually leading the Church to discover the untold wealth contained in Christ's Gospel and in the redemption accomplished by Christ?* Perhaps all this wealth would not have come to light otherwise.…It is necessary for *humanity to achieve unity through plurality, to learn to come together in the one Church, even while presenting a plurality of ways of thinking and acting, of cultures and civilizations*. Wouldn't such a way of looking at things be, in a certain sense, more consonant with the wisdom of God, with His goodness and providence?" (*Crossing the Threshold of Hope* [New York: Knopf, 2005], 167). The same reflection reappears in the encyclical *Ut Unum Sint* of May 25, 1995: "Since God in his infinite mercy can always bring good even out of situations which are an offence to his plan, we can discover that the Spirit has allowed conflicts to serve in some circumstances to make explicit certain aspects

of the Christian vocation, as happens in the lives of the Saints. In spite of fragmentation, which is an evil from which we need to be healed, there has resulted a kind of rich bestowal of grace which is meant to embellish the *koinonia*. God's grace will be with all those who, following the example of the Saints, commit themselves to meeting its demands" (85).

5. The document is the result of the works of the tenth plenary session of the Commission (Ravenna, October 8–14, 2007). The original text in English can be consulted on the Holy See website: http://www.vatican.va/roman_curia/pontifical_councils/chrstuni/ch_orthodox_docs/rc_pc_chrstuni_doc_20071013_documento-ravenna_en.html (translations of the document, by the Pontifical Council for the Promotion of the Unity of Christians, are available in Italian, French, and German; see *Il Regno—Documenti* 21/2007: 708–14). Francis also reiterated in the address to the Ecumenical Delegation of the Patriarchate of Constantinople on June 27, 2015 that "the careful examination of how in the Church the principle of synodality and the service of the one who presides are articulated, will make a significant contribution to the progress of relations between our Churches."

6. Common Declaration of Pope Father Francis and the Ecumenical Patriarch Bartholomew I, Jerusalem, May 25, 2014, no. 4. The importance of this latter statement must not be underestimated ("Such a common pursuit does not lead us away from the truth; rather, through an exchange of gifts, through the guidance of the Holy Spirit, it will lead us into all truth [cf. John 16:13]"). In fact, it is decisively binding on both sides of the dialogue, and particularly on the Catholic side, taking into account a certain suspension, bordering on suspicion, with which up until now the *Ravenna Document* has been viewed in some environments, as it expresses an attitude decidedly open and promising, in keeping with the magisterial and pastoral style of Pope Francis. Such a precise theological statement, which in itself implies an equally precise direction of engagement, stresses, among other things, the need to live with awareness, openness, and acceptance of the risk that always involves listening to the Holy Spirit to be faithful to the gospel of Jesus, the specific "between" (*zwischen*) that intrinsically connotes the life and mission of the Church. This is the "between" in which every now and then, in faithfulness to the revelation, the plan of God is enfleshed in Christ in history; and, in correlation to this, the "between" that unfolds itself in the space opened by Christ's passover in the relationship of those who converse in the exercise of that communal discernment in the Spirit of Christ in which the language and the salvific and cultural meaning of revelation is actualized.

7. On the resuming of the works of the Joint Theological Commission, see D. Salachas, "Riconfermata la volontà della Chiesa Cattolica e della Chiesa Ortodossa di proseguire il dialogo teologico," *Studi ecumenici* 25 (2007): 101–21.

8. See the Munich Document, "The Mystery of the Church and of the Eucharist in the Light of the Mystery of the Most Holy Trinity," July 6, 1982; the Bari Document, "Faith, Sacraments and Unity of the Church," of June 16, 1987; the New Valamo Document, "The Sacrament of Order in the Sacramental Structure of the Church, with Particular Reference to the Importance of the Apostolic Succession for the Sanctification and Unity of the People of God," of June 26, 1988; the Balamand Document, "Uniatism, Method of Union of the Past, and the Present Search for Full Communion," of June 23, 1993; and finally, the Communiqué from the Eighth Plenary Session of the Joint International Commission for the Theological Dialogue between the Roman Catholic Church and the Orthodox Church, Baltimore, July 9–19, 2000, declaring the stall at which the path was at that time. For a general presentation of the direction, method, and spirit of this dialogue, see the essay of the late E. F. Fortino, "Impostazione del dialogo teologico tra la Chiesa cattolica e la Chiesa ortodossa," in *Divinarum rerum notitia. La teologia tra filosofia e storia. Studi in onore del Cardinale Walter Kasper*, ed. A. Russo and G. Coffele (Rome: Studium, 2001), 449–76.

9. The Valamo Document, no. 40 is cited here.

10. It is worth pointing out that Pope Francis in his important speech for the ceremony commemorating the fiftieth anniversary of the institution of the Synod of Bishops on October 17, 2015, after remarking that it "is precisely this path of *synodality* which God expects of the Church of the third millennium," "he presents the three levels of exercise of synodality: what is "had in the particular Churches", "that of the Ecclesiastical Provinces and Ecclesiastical Regions, Particular Councils and, in a special way, Conferences of Bishops" and "that of the universal Church," in the end underlining that " I am persuaded that in a synodal Church, greater light can be shed on the exercise of the Petrine primacy."

11. See the brilliant and exhaustive presentation by F. Bouwen, "Ravenne 2007. Xe Session plénière de la Commission mixte internationale pour le dialogue théologique entre l'Église catholique et l'Église orthodoxe," *Proche-Orient Chrétien* 58 (2008): 59–78.

12. Ignatius of Antioch, *Letter to the Romans*, prologue.

13. Position of the Moscow Patriarchate on the Problem of Primacy in the Universal Church (Minutes, no. 157): https://mospat.ru/en/2013/12/26/news96344/.

It should be noted that Bursa's Metropolitan Elpidophoros reacted vividly to the position of the Moscow Patriarchate with the article *Primus sine paribus*, to which replied in turn Metropolitan Hilarion of Volokolamsk, president of the Moscow's patriarchate External Relations Department and member of the Joint Theological Commission, representing the same patriarchate in the *lectio magistralis* pronounced at the award ceremony for doctor of divinity at St. Vladimir's Orthodox Theological Seminary in New York on December 8, 2014 (Primacy and Synodality: http://mospat.ru/en/2014/11/09/news111091).

14. As is well known, the shared reference to the theological doctrine and the ecclesial practice of the first millennium is a fundamental point of the dialogue between the Catholic Church and the Orthodox Church. During his visit to the Fanar for the Feast of St. Andrew on November 30, 2014, Pope Francis reiterated that, with the decree *Unitatis Redintegratio* of Vatican II, "the Catholic Church acknowledges that Orthodox churches 'possess true sacraments, above all—by apostolic succession—the priesthood and the Eucharist, whereby they are still joined to us in closest intimacy' (no. 15). The Decree goes on to state that in order to guard faithfully the fullness of the Christian tradition and to bring to fulfilment the reconciliation of Eastern and Western Christians, it is of the greatest importance to preserve and support the rich patrimony of the Eastern Churches. This regards not only their liturgical and spiritual traditions, but also their canonical disciplines, sanctioned as they are by the Fathers and by Councils, which regulate the lives of these Churches (cf. 15–16). I believe that it is important to reaffirm respect for this principle as an essential condition, accepted by both, for the restoration of full communion, which does not signify the submission of one to the other, or assimilation. Rather, it means welcoming all the gifts that God has given to each, thus demonstrating to the entire world the great mystery of salvation accomplished by Christ the Lord through the Holy Spirit. I want to assure each one of you here that, to reach the desired goal of full unity, the Catholic Church does not intend to impose any conditions except that of the shared profession of faith. Further, I would add that we are ready to seek together, in light of Scriptural teaching and the experience of the first millennium, the ways in which we can guarantee the needed unity of the Church in the present circumstances. The one thing that the Catholic Church desires, and that I seek as Bishop of Rome, 'the Church which presides in charity', is communion with the Orthodox Churches. Such communion will always be the fruit of that love which 'has been poured into our hearts through the Holy Spirit who has been given to us' (cf. Rom 5:5), a fraternal love which expresses the spiritual and transcendent bond which unites us as disciples of the Lord."

15. His ecclesiological view is well known and is widely acknowledged in the *Ravenna Document*, being that the Metropolitan Zizioulas was the copresident of the Joint Theological Commission. Without mentioning the classical essays that best exemplify Zizioulas's prolific career (*Hē Henotēs Tēs Ekklēsias En Tē Theia Eucharistia Kai T Episkopō Kata Tous Treis Prōtous Aiōnas* [En Athinais 1965]: doctoral thesis published in French as *L'Eucharistie L'évêque et l' Eglise durant les trois premier siècles* [Paris: Desclée, 1994]; *L'Être ecclésial* [Geneva: Labor et Fides, 1981]; *Communion & Otherness: Further Studies in Personhood and the Church* [London: T & T Clark, 2007]; *The One and the Many: Studies on God, Man, the Church, and the World Today* [Alhambra, CA: Sebastian Press, 2010]), a reference should be made to his intervention at the symposium organized by the Centro Pro Unione of Rome (December 4–6, 1997) on the theme, "The Petrine Ministry and Authority in the Church: 'Toward a Fraternal and Patient Dialogue'"; see J. Zizioulas, "The Primacy in the Church," *Il Regno—Attualità* (2/1998): 5–9 ; and, more recently, on the meaning of the trinitarian foundation of this vision, the inaugural lecture he delivered on the occasion of the conferral of the honorary doctorate by the Theological Faculty of Northern Italy (January 24, 2015) entitled, "The Holy Trinity and the Human Person" (see: http://scindeks-clanci.ceon.rs/data/pdf/1450-9148/2016/1450-91481610009Z.pdf). On his thought, see P. McPartlan, *The Eucharist Makes the Church: Henri de Lubac and John Zizioulas in Dialogue* (Edinburgh: T&T Clark, 1993), and, by the same author, one of the Catholic members of the Joint Theological Commission, *A Service of Love: Papal Primacy, the Eucharist & Church Unity* (Washington, DC: The Catholic University of America Press, 2013).

16. In this regard, worth mentioning here is the *lectio magistralis* held by the Ecumenical Patriarch Bartholomew on the conferral of the honorary doctorate in "Culture of Unity" at the Istituto Universitario Sophia di Loppiano (Florence), on October 26, 2015 (forthcoming).

17. For a synthetic overview, see "Authority," in *Dizionario del Cristianesimo*, ed. P. Coda and G. Filoramo (Turin: UTET, 2006), 1:92–106.

18. I have developed some elements in this regard in "Erneuerung des synodalen Bewusstseins im Volk Gottes," *Theologische Quartalschrift* 192, no. 2 (2012): 103–20.

20

EXCHANGE OF GIFTS

The Catholic Church and the Eastern Churches—For a Differentiated Consensus

Joseph Famerée, SCI

In the perspective of reforming the Catholic Church, we would like to ask ourselves what Christians gifts—spirituality, theology, ecclesiology—the Catholic Church (Latin) could or should receive from the Eastern churches (particularly from the Byzantine Orthodox churches).[1] This exchange between churches has always existed to a certain extent, but has taken on a stronger and qualitative meaning since the beginning of the ecumenical movement. Recently, this ecumenical dimension has been formalized under the expression "receptive ecumenism."[2] This is therefore the perspective in which we would like to identify certain possible contributions of the Eastern churches to the Latin Catholic Church, to promote the necessary reforms of the latter.

The Latin Catholic Church is present today in many cultural areas: the Northwest, Latin America, Africa, Asia, and so on. The question is not, therefore, for the Latin Church to literally copy certain aspects of the Eastern Church's way of being Christian. The question is how the Latin Church could or should be challenged and inspired by that way of being Christian, even though it is necessarily limited and culturally situated. It is clear to us that even the Latin Catholic Church has gifts to offer to the Eastern churches, but this is not the point on which we would like to focus our attention. In other words, what we intend to expose is based on the Gospel recommendation of fraternal correction (see Matt 18:15–18): to be more authentically Christian, every Christian must feel and integrate the legitimate criticisms or proposals for conversion of his or her "fellow" Christian. What is true of every Christian individually considered, is the same for every Christian Church.

At first, we will therefore, point out some fundamental (spiritual, theological) aspects of the Eastern Christian way of thinking that could inspire the Latin Catholic Church, so that it is more fully faithful to Christ. Then, we will consider the more institutional aspects of the Eastern way of being Church and working as a Church that could be indicative and inspiring for certain institutional reforms of the Catholic Church.

Theological and Anthropological Aspects

FOR A DIFFERENTIATED CONSENSUS WITH THE CHRISTIAN EAST

First, the very existence of Eastern churches is already a global demand for a permanent and healthy conversion for the Latin Catholic Church. The churches of the Greek-Byzantine[3] tradition are a first and original inculturation of Christianity, before the same Latin inculturation.[4] These Eastern churches represent for the Latin Church an authentic form of Christianity, but different. Thus, they constitute a permanent and indisputable otherness for the Latin Church. This alterity is beneficial, as it always reminds the Latin Church of the fact that is not alone, that it cannot withdraw into itself, into its "Latinity" or "Westernism," albeit today it is already diversified (Northwest, Latin America, Africa, Asia). "Out of" herself, but also in her (Roman) Catholic communion (with the Eastern Catholic churches), there is therefore a radical alterity, another original way ("matrix") of being a Christian that requires a radical respect and thus constitutes a promise of richer and more complete Catholicism, not only for universal Christianity, but also for the Latin Catholic Church herself.

In this sense, the existence of the Eastern churches is itself a global and continuous invitation to a profound conversion of the Latin Church, a conversion of perspective and mental attitude (theological, spiritual, ethical); a conversion that drives the Latin Church to accept the difference in and out of itself more radically. The Latin Church has always known a certain diversity (Augustine, Thomas Aquinas, Bonaventure, Duns Scotus, etc.); however, it is still not accustomed to living a permanent and tense diversity within itself. Rather, it has a recurring tendency to a certain uniformity and univocity of language, especially in the expression of its ecclesial magisterium. The differentiated consensus is not yet sufficiently transposed and anchored in its theological thinking and in its ecclesial life, or in the way of conceiving and living communion with another Church.

The differentiated consensus, as acknowledged, officially received its right of citizenship in the Latin Catholic Church with the signing of a Lutheran-Catholic agreement, the Joint Declaration on the Doctrine of Justification, on October 31, 1999.[5] However, prior to its being discussed from a theological and ecumenical perspective, the differentiated consensus had already been practiced by the Latin Church with the Christian East. The Council of Florence (1439–1445) was a prime example: in the solemn bull on union with the Greeks of July 6, 1439, *Laetentur Caeli*, the council fathers acknowledged the legitimacy of the difference of language and conceptuality between Greeks and Latins. They declared an equivalence ("tendential") between the Latin formulation of the Creed—"who proceeds from the Father and the Son [*ex Patre Filioque*]"—and the Greek patristic formulation (*ex Patre per Filium*), or between the Greek notion of *causa* and the Latin one of *principium*, with regard to the procession of the Holy Spirit.[6] The council fathers in Florence also accepted a diversity of liturgical practices between East and West, with the use of unleavened or leavened bread for the eucharistic celebration.[7] All this was in a way an *ante litteram* differentiated consensus.

More recently, the same Second Vatican Council solemnly recognized a legitimate diversity of forms of spiritual life and discipline, liturgical rites, and even theological elaborations of the revealed truth (see *Unitatis Redintegratio* 4), particularly in the churches of the East (see *UR* 14–18).

Even more recently, the *ante litteram* differentiated consensus has been in fact practiced by the Catholic Church in its christological dialogues with the Assyrian Orthodox Church and the Oriental Orthodox churches (Coptic, Syriac, Armenian, etc.). Consider the example of the Common Christological Declaration of November 11, 1994, between the Catholic Church and the Assyrian Church of the East, signed by Pope John Paul II and the Catholicos Mar Dinkha IV.[8] The text affirms the legitimacy and the accuracy of the different expressions preferred by both traditions in liturgical life and piety of devotion for the Virgin Mary: "Mother of Christ our God and Savior" for the Assyrian Church, "Mother of God "or "Mother of Christ " for the Catholic Church, based on the confession of the same faith in the Son of God who became man so that men can become sons and daughters of God through his grace. In 2001, the *Guidelines for Admission to the Eucharist between the Chaldean Church (Catholic) and the Assyrian Church of the East,* elaborated by the Pontifical Council for the Promotion of Christian Unity,[9] also recognized the validity of the anaphora of Addai and Mari, one of the three traditional anaphoras of the Assyrian Church of the East, which does not formally contain the "narrative" of the eucharistic institution, whereas the words of the eucharistic institution are an indispensable part of the Eucharistic Prayer for the Catholic Church. Here too, therefore, the Catholic Church has exercised de facto the differentiated consensus.

This way of thinking theologically and ecumenically should be extended and applied to all ecumenical dialogues of the Catholic Church, particularly with the Byzantine Orthodox Church. The actual reception in the reality of the Catholic Church (diocese, parish, Christian life) of the results of this dialogue with the Byzantine Church would be a welcoming of the alterity (of the Eastern churches) in the heart of the Catholic Church,[10] and thus contribute to thinking and experiencing (more) truly the Catholic Church in the way of unity in diversity. It would be an important contribution to a fundamental reform of the common thinking and traditional functioning of the Catholic Church.

Specifically, the differentiated consensus should also apply—and perhaps even before that—to the inner life of the Catholic Church: in its heart, a greater diversity of theological thought, liturgical rites, discipline, even ethical practice, especially in the magisterial discourses (of popes, bishops, etc.), should be acceptable without impeding the unity of the Catholic Church. On the contrary, this would favor a richer and more internal Catholic unity. It would therefore be a profound mental reform that would sustain and make possible, in a lasting way, other reforms, perhaps more superficial and fortuitous. As already mentioned, this would also be a very appropriate way—the only one, it seems to me—to be in communion with the Christian East, to create unity with it with legitimate differences, certainly a challenging task because it would mean accepting and "cultivating" diversity, the alterity of others, and, first and foremost, cultural diversity.

On this background of a fundamental cultural difference with the East, let us consider now the most accurate and detailed differences that may inspire conversions and reforms of the Latin Catholic Church.

INTERPELLATIONS OF THE EASTERN LITURGY, SPIRITUALITY, AND THEOLOGY

We will be brief here but also more concrete, before we get to the second part of this contribution, that is, to proposals for institutional reforms. In any case, we are convinced that the most fundamental and lasting reforms are spiritual (existential) and theological. Institutional reforms are indispensable for expressing and sustaining a profound theological and spiritual reform, but are contingent and always improvable. Institutional reforms never measure up to personal and ecclesial conversions, and are never a satisfactory "translation" of faith and theology. Institutions are necessary, but always imperfect. So, before we get to some institutional reforms inspired by the functioning of the Eastern churches, let us look at some aspects from the Eastern liturgy, spirituality, and theology.

It is not necessary, nor even possible, to describe here the key features of the Eastern liturgy. However, we would only like to recall that John Paul II's Apostolic Letter *Orientale Lumen*, in 1995, rightly considered the monastic liturgy and spirituality as the two "lungs" of the Christian East, and presented them wonderfully in terms of aptness and acumen.

What is worth emphasizing in the *Eastern liturgy* that could, in our opinion, bring about a useful "conversion" in the Western liturgical practice, already very simple and beautiful? The Eastern understanding of the liturgy is holistic. It is the celebration of the Orthodox faith, the faith of the ecumenical councils, and opens to the transcendent mystery of God as totally Other and to the mystical encounter with the One who became totally near to us in the Lord Jesus, through the creation of a spiritual environment that envelops and moves the whole man.

The Oriental symbolism is much (often too much) richer than that of the Western liturgy: primary or fundamental symbolism of life and light, liturgical poetry, theological lyricism, beauty of the songs, colors and paintings (frescoes, icons, etc.), architectural symbolism, gestures, and so on. Thus, the faithful are stimulated in all the dimensions of their being: senses, sensitivity, imagination, and not just rational intelligence. The whole body of the believer is integrated in the rites: numerous movements of the body (like signs of the cross and prostrations) and the senses in question—sight, hearing, smell (incense), touch (veneration of icons), and taste (not just communion with the consecrated bread and wine, but also the distribution of the *antíd ron*, a blessed bread at the end of the divine liturgy). All this bodily experience has as its purpose the liturgical contemplation of the splendor of the thrice-holy God, that is, to somehow make the invisible visible. This not only reconciles the heart and mind, but also the bodily senses—thus, the whole being. The numerous liturgical fasts need to be understood in the same way: they aim for a carnal or bodily lessening for a spiritual experience of the invisible. All this contrasts with a Western liturgy sometimes considered too intellectual and cerebral, even verbose: the word of God and its rational explanation through the human word occupies a large place, which is a good thing, but sometimes this verbal and rational commentary on the word of God takes too much space, to the point of even verbally commenting on the liturgical symbols. The Western liturgy could be inspired by the Eastern liturgy by being a little less prolix and intellectual, and more symbolic, holistic: it should not only develop rational or discursive intelligence, but also, and above all, the spiritual intelligence or intelligence of the heart of the liturgical celebration. It would be a useful and beneficial conversion or mental reform for the Catholic Church.

Similarly, the entire cosmos is involved in the Eastern rites, not only in the deaconal litanies that embrace the spiritual needs of the faithful present, as well as the suffering of mankind and the life of nature, but also and especially in the sacraments, where the kingdom of God takes possession of elements of creation, and more widely in the sacramentals, where the Church blesses natural elements. To this presence of the totality of the cosmos in the Eastern liturgy must be added the presence of the invisible heavenly world: the angels, the communion of saints and the dead (present through the frescoes and icons). It is already the ultimate, eschatological kingdom that is offered to contemplation in the holy mysteries. The new heaven and the new earth are already anticipated. The time of the liturgy or of prayer is thus an "internalized," eschatological time: another world is being already enjoyed. All of this, which is very important for man's communion with the entire present creation (visible and invisible), in expectation of the new creation, is less present, less pronounced in the Western liturgy.[11]

It would be possible for the Latin Catholic Church to find many benefits in Eastern spirituality as well. We list here only a few.

The intrinsic link between spirituality (especially monastic) and liturgy seems essential to us. A true Christian spirituality cannot be individualistic and subjectivist (purely emotional) nor can it be separated from the ecclesial life and all the criteria of discernment that it proposes. Spirituality must also be informed by the doctrinal (dogmatic) tradition of the Church to avoid arbitrariness and irrationality.

The "all-encompassing" or holistic character of Eastern spirituality has already been considered in connection with the liturgy. It is not just about interiority, the spirit, the heart, but also the body, which has now been called to transfiguration and deification. The spirituality of the human body extends even to matter as a whole. Matter itself has become theophoric in the incarnation of Christ and is in the process of pneumatization like the human body. Incarnation, resurrection, and eschatology structure this spirituality.

Another essential point in Eastern spirituality is its sense of the absolute transcendence of God, who can only be worshiped "in silence": God is inaccessible in his essence or in himself; God is beyond the capabilities of our intelligence, but, by grace, we can participate in his uncreated energies, which are the irradiation of his glory. This is spiritual and apophatic theology: what may not be said about God is truer that what *is* said.

In direct connection with spirituality, we can thus point out some aspects of Eastern theology that are likely to inspire Western theology.

We will not make use of negative theology, just mentioned, which favors the mystical experience and paradoxical, antinomic, and metaphorical theological discourse, that can overcome the binary logic and the law of excluded middle, as well as the uniqueness of the formulations. We prefer instead to emphasize the existential and spiritual understanding of theology in the East. The purpose of theology—in all its disciplines—is always the contemplation of the glory of God and the transfiguration or correlative deification of man. The way of doing theology is also existential and spiritual: an authentic theologian is a saint and mystic, speaks of what he lives and contemplates. "If you pray, you are a theologian" (Evagrius of Pontus). For the East, theology is not primarily an intellectual act, but a spiritual experience of God, as expressed to the extent possible. Theology is as authentic and profound as the theologian is holy, contemplating the glory of a God totally Other and loving his neighbor. Theology presupposes a true existential transformation of the theologian's participation in the divine life through mystical contemplation, thanks to the meditation of the Scriptures and celebration of the sacraments in the Church. If this charismatic vision of theology is not without ambiguity, nevertheless it still has the merit of inviting the theologian's personal unification, and the integration of spirituality (prayer) and theology. This existential unification of the theological act manifests also the profound unity of the various theological disciplines: liturgy, exegesis, Church history, dogmatics, moral and pastoral practices.

In the second part of this exposition, we would now like to develop an aspect of Eastern theology—the ecclesiology and its institutional implications—as a possible source of inspiration for reform in the Catholic Church.

Ecclesiological and Institutional Aspects

ECCLESIOLOGY

Even here it is neither possible nor necessary to present Orthodox ecclesiology on a long and wide scale. It is a eucharistic and episcopal ecclesiology of the local Church (diocesan) in communion with other local churches. The grouping of local (diocesan) churches at a regional level (often national) of an autocephalous Church (the Church of Greece, for example), or of a patriarchal Church (the Moscow patriarchate, for example) is consubstantial to the current Orthodox ecclesiology. These "regional" churches are at the same time independent (at the ecclesiastical level) and in communion with each another (primarily on the level of faith, the sacraments, the Eucharist). The entire Orthodox Church is conceived as a *communio ecclesiarum* (*regionalium*) in the image and likeness of the Holy Trinity. Thus, the Byzantine Orthodox Church is the communion of sixteen patriarchal, autocephalous. or autonomous, churches.

From an Eastern point of view, the Church is both hierarchical and synodal ("collegiate"); it is universal, but it is only fully realized in the eucharistic assembly, in which a group of simple sinners become fully people of God. The synodal life of the Church (the relations between the faithful and their bishop, between the bishops and their primates) is therefore a question of sacramental communion (eucharistic), before being a matter of authority and canonical rules.

We can only briefly say here that the local Church is the full manifestation in a particular place of the one, Catholic, and apostolic Church, which has its origin in the mystery of trinitarian communion. The Holy Spirit unites the baptized in one and the same body, that of Christ, through the proclamation of the gospel and the celebration of the sacraments (especially of the Eucharist), under the presidency of a pastoral bishop. However, a local Church cannot be a manifestation of Christ's Church in an isolated or "autarchic" (self-sufficient) way, but it can only be it by maintaining dynamic and active bonds of communion with other local churches, as they also, and each one of them, are the only Church of Christ.

This is the theoretical ecclesiology of the Orthodox Church (especially Byzantine). Nevertheless, we do not ignore the historical tendencies of the real Orthodoxy to accentuate the local and national characteristics, even the independence of each Church (local, regional), thus manifesting the autocephalous temptation of phyletism.

Remaining on the theoretical basis of fundamental ecclesiology, before considering the institutional expressions of this, we would like to examine whether the Catholic Church fully receives this ecclesiology of *communio ecclesiarum* (*localium, regionalium*).

On the theoretical level, we find in the Second Vatican Council several important elements for a foundation of such ecclesiology, which later became the ecclesiology more or less common of the Catholic Church.[12] Thus, in 1990, the mixed working group between the Catholic Church and the World Council of Churches published a document entitled *The Local and Universal Church*.[13] In 2007, it was the Joint International Commission for Theological Dialogue between the Catholic Church and the Orthodox Church (Byzantine) that published a joint agreement, the so-called *Ravenna Document*: "Ecclesiological and Canonical Consequences of the Sacramental Nature of the Church Ecclesial Communion, Conciliarity and Authority," where representatives of both churches came to express a common ecclesiology.[14]

However, we believe that certain aspects of the official Catholic ecclesiology—from Vatican II onward—still present points of resistance to a full reception of the ecclesiology of *communio ecclesiarum* and should be reformed (rethought). We are thinking first of a *close correlation between bishops and diocesan local churches*. The Second Vatican Council did not think and express enough this close bond between a bishop and a concrete local Church. According to its teaching, one can become a member of the episcopal college by virtue of sacramental ordination and hierarchical communion with the head of the college and with its members, but still be detached from every local (concrete) Church.[15] Nevertheless, according to the rich theology of the local Church, which is also present in the conciliar teaching, and, therefore, of the necessary pastoral relationship between a bishop and the local Church entrusted to him (and vice versa), an "absolute" episcopal ordination is quite problematic: episcopal ordination is inseparable from the pastoral office of a real local Church. We are not referring here to the bishops of the dioceses who have resigned from the responsibility of their dioceses for reasons of age or health. We are thinking rather of the ordination of "titular" bishops, for the title only (of a local Church that has since disappeared), without the attribution of a real local Church: priests created cardinals and obliged by canon law to be ordained bishops, apostolic nuncios, presidents and secretaries of Roman dicasteries—without ever being previously bishops of a diocese, and so forth. If we consider the present number of these bishops *ad titulum*,[16] we can only claim a gradual correction of this serious theological distortion of ecclesial practice, which disconnects sacramental ordination and the presidency of a local Church. In the particular case of auxiliary bishops, who are actually in the service of a diocese, rather than giving them the title of a diocese that no longer exists as such, it would be more appropriate and more true to reconnect them to the diocese that they are called to serve in communion with the ordinary of the place.

On the basis of a plenary theology of the local Church (diocesan, episcopal), it would also be necessary to think more in the Catholic Church of a group of local churches as *autonomous regional churches* in the sense of a more intensive "horizontal" communion, beyond a binary and "vertical" relationship between each bishop taken individually and the pope. Even at the level of the *universal Church, as a communion of churches,* one can only think of and exercise the singular ministry of the Bishop of the local Church of Rome in the actual synodality or collegiality with the other bishops.[17] We will now consider these two elements from the point of view of possible institutional reforms in the Catholic Church.

INSTITUTIONAL EXPRESSIONS OF ECCLESIAL COMMUNION

For the Orthodox Church, synodality or a synodal organization are an essential institutional expression of ecclesial communion at all its levels (local, regional, universal),[18] even though, in the reality of ecclesial life, they do not always work properly. Let us consider here the regional and the universal levels. At the *regional level*, each head of an autocephalous or patriarchal Church is surrounded by a holy synod to govern that Church together, in reciprocity between the primate (*prôtos*) and his synod.[19] For more basic guiding principles, a regional council may be convened. At the *universal level*, the decision-making body is the council of the entire Orthodox Church, still called Pan-Orthodox. The Ecumenical Patriarch, *primus inter pares*, even if he has only a role of initiative—the breadth of which does not make unanimity in Orthodoxy—must exercise it in communion with his holy synod of Constantinople, but also with all the other Orthodox churches. Without this consent, he cannot speak in the name of the entire Orthodoxy.

In the Catholic Church, at the *regional level*, episcopal conferences must be conceived as the usual ministerial expression of a regional communion of local diocesan churches, where the bishop of each represents and connects one Church with the other local churches. To this end, they are an expression—partial, but real—of episcopal collegiality.[20] Thus, episcopal conferences are called to enjoy a genuine autonomy in the ecclesial communion. It is not only legitimate, but necessary for a true and genuine catholicity of the Catholic Church, as well as for its ecumenical credibility toward other Christian churches. For the sake of the necessary inculturation of the gospel, should episcopal conferences not become initiative centers in ecclesial life? For this purpose, should the scope of their competence not be extended widely, so that their decisions, apart from those directly affecting the common good of the universal Church, no longer need the confirmation of the Apostolic See?[21]

On a *universal level*, the extraordinary way of teaching and governing the entire Catholic Church is the general council, chaired by the Bishop of Rome. The ordinary way of this teaching and government, as far as he is concerned, should take on a permanent synodal form, in the likeness of the holy synod of every Eastern patriarchy. This way the Bishop of Rome would be well assisted by a number of residential bishops representing the regional churches of the entire Catholic Church, for a certain period of time. According to Maximos IV Saigh, Patriarch of Antioch and

All the East, and Alexandria and Jerusalem of the Melkite Greek Catholic Church, at the Second Vatican Council, in his speech of November 6, 1963, this "*sacred college* of the universal Church" would consist of residential and apostolic patriarchs, archbishop cardinals or residential bishops, and bishops chosen in the episcopal conferences of each country. Some members of this sacred college would take turns to be next to the pope, who always keeps the last word. This permanent supreme council (or synod) of the universal Church, presided over by the pope, would work in a deliberative manner, since the Roman dicasteries would defer to this executive and decisive center, open to the entire world.[22] From a purely theological point of view, this "holy synod" should ideally seek unanimity, or at least as wide a consensus as possible in the Holy Spirit. The pope would retain freedom of initiative in line with the recommendation of the ancient Apostolic Canon 34 concerning regional synodality: the synod does nothing without the agreement of the first, and the first will do nothing without the consent of the synod, so that harmony reign and God be glorified, in the Father, Son, and Holy Spirit. The universal decisions taken by this permanent synod for the pope should be rather rare. The most important ones would require the convening of a general council; all other provisions, without requiring a universal vision, would be regulated by special councils or episcopal conferences at the continental, regional, or national level.[23]

Such a "Copernican revolution" in the way of governing the Catholic Church can only be progressive and gradual, given the heavy monarchical tendencies inherent in the Catholic tradition.

Conclusion

From a perspective of reform of the Catholic Church, we have tried to identify some gifts that the Church could receive from the dialogue with the Orthodox Church (Byzantine in particular), and some suggestions, or efforts to conversion and reform. We have distinguished fundamental conversions or reforms from those that are more institutional and contingent.

The *fundamental reforms* concern the Catholic way of thinking, of doing theology. They are mental and spiritual reforms-conversions, therefore, existential. These are the most profound and difficult. The greatest mental conversion proposed here is to learn to think in terms of differentiated consensus to escape the binary logic of the excluded middle, and the univocity of language, to understand and accept that the same fundamental faith can be expressed in different ways, with different inflections, without breaking the unity of faith and the basic consensus. From this idea of unity in diversity, many divisions within the Catholic Church, but also between her and the other Christian churches, could be overcome, without, however, eliminating completely the tensions.

Institutional reforms inspired by the East—it should not be surprising—concern a greater synodality in the Catholic Church, above all at the regional and universal levels. At the regional level, episcopal conferences should enjoy greater autonomy in decision-making and wider powers. A more adequate inculturation of the gospel and a richer catholicity of the Catholic Church are at stake here. At the universal level, a permanent synod of residential bishops (regularly renewed) for the pope would make decisions more consistent with the catholicity of the entire Catholic Church.

NOTES

1. What we say about Orthodox churches is also, to a great extent, true for Eastern Catholic churches.

2. P. D. Murray, ed., *Receptive Ecumenism and the Call to Catholic Learning: Exploring a Way for Contemporary Ecumenism* (New York: Oxford University Press, 2008).

3. This is also true, *mutatis mutandis*, for Eastern Orthodox churches: Syrian, Coptic (Ethiopian), and Armenian.

4. The disappearance of this "matricial" form of Christianity (Greek-Byzantine, Syriac, Coptic) in the Near or Middle East would be, for the sake of its antiquity and originality, a considerable impoverishment for universal Christianity and its catholicity.

5. See J. Gros, H. Meyer, and W. G. Rusch, eds., *Growth in Agreement II: Reports and Agreed Statements of Ecumenical Conversations on a World Level, 1982–1998*, Faith and Order Paper 187, (Geneva: WCC Publications, 2000), 566–82.

6. "Declarantes, quod id, quod sancti Doctores et Patres dicunt, ex Patre per Filium procedere Spiritum Sanctum, ad hanc intelligentiam tendit, ut per hoc significetur, Filium quoque esse secundum Graecos quidem causam, secundum Latinos vero principium subsistentiae Spiritus Sancti, sicut et Patrem" (*DH* 1301).

7. *DH* 1303.

8. Gros, Meyer, and Rusch, *Growth in Agreement II*, 711ff.

9. J. Gros, T. F. Best, and L. F. Fuchs, eds., *Growth in Agreement III: International Dialogue Texts and Agreed Statements, 1998–2005*, Faith and Order Paper 204 (Geneva: WCC Publications, 2007), 197–205.

10. On the levels of an effective reception of an ecclesial teaching, see G. Routhier, *La réception d'un concile* (Paris: Cerf, 1993).

11. In the Catholic Church, we are moving more in this direction thanks to Pope Francis's encyclical, *Laudato Si'* (May 24, 2015) and the World Day of Prayer for the Integrity of Creation, established by the pope for September 1 of each year. This initiative is linked in fact to a Byzantine Orthodox tradition that has been in effect since 1989.

12. See *SC* 41; *LG* 23 and 26; *CD* 11.

13. Gros, Best, and Fuchs, *Growth in Agreement III*, 862–75.

14. The original English text is available on the Holy See website: http://www.vatican.va/roman_curia/pontifical_councils/chrstuni/ch_orthodox_docs/rc_pc_chrstuni_doc_20071013_documento-ravenna_en.html.

15. See *LG* 22: the presidency of a local Church is not mentioned.

16. According to the Pontifical Directory of 2013, 47.7 percent of Catholic bishops (of whom 26.1 percent are emeriti) were not in charge of any dioceses.

17. See J. Famerée, "What Might Catholicism Learn from Orthodoxy in Relation to Collegiality," in Murray, *Receptive Ecumenism and the Call to Catholic Learning*, 211–25.

18. See the *Ravenna Document*, second part (nos. 17–44): "The Threefold Actualization of Conciliarity and Authority."

19. In line with Apostolic Canon 34 (see pp. 437–39).

20. H. LeGrand, J. Manzanares, and A. García y García, eds., *Les conférences épiscopales. Théologie, statut canonique, avenir* (Paris: Cerf, 1988); J. Famerée, "Au fondement des conférences épiscopales: la *communio Ecclesiarum*," *Revue théologique de Louvain* 23 (1992): 343–54.

21. Without prior Roman recognition, their decisions would be communicated to the other local churches (the closest ones first), and particularly

to that of Rome, for reception and conformation of communion, or even fraternal correction if necessary.

22. See *Acta Synodalia* II/4, 516–19; G. Alberigo, ed., *Storia del concilio Vaticano II*, vol. 3, *Il concilio adulto*, Italian text ed. by Alberto Melloni (Bologna: il Mulino, 1998), 141ff.

23. According to the decisions of the Council of Sardica (343), the pope would retain his traditional role as an arbitrator in cases of "local" ecclesiastical conflicts that cannot be resolved locally.

21

LEARNING FROM A HALF-CENTURY OF DIALOGUE WITH THE REFORMATION CHURCHES FOR THE REFORM OF THE CATHOLIC CHURCH TODAY

Peter de Mey

Prelude: Pope Francis and Gustave Thils: The Expectations for Church Reform during the Second Vatican Council and Their Hoped-for Realization Fifty Years Later

I am personally very pleased that the organizers of this conference have not forgotten to pay specific attention to the link between ecumenism and reform of and within the Church. Pope Francis must have been aware of the same link, when dedicating the first of many references to the documents of the Second Vatican Council in *Evangelii Gaudium* to *UR* 6: "Every renewal of the Church essentially consists in an increase of fidelity to her own calling.... Christ summons the Church as she goes her pilgrim way...to that continual reformation of which she always has need, in so far as she is a human institution here on earth."[1] Exactly fifty years earlier, the Louvain theologian and member of the Secretariat for Christian Unity Gustave Thils had argued in the revised edition of his *Histoire doctrinale du mouvement œcuménique* that the ecumenical task of Catholic theologians consists in the first instance in "cleaning out their own house," so that it is not only "open" for everyone, but "inhabitable" by all.[2]

In my chapter, however, I will not focus on the first generation of members and collaborators of the Secretariat for Christian Unity, who sometimes already had views on the reform of the curia that remain helpful for Pope Francis today,[3] but I will rather reflect on the current obstacles in ecumenical relations between the Catholic Church and the mainstream Reformation churches and will ask whether in a number of issues the Catholic point of view is not in need of reform as well: does it make sense to keep complaining about the fundamentally divergent understanding of Church or model of unity? Do we fully live out the real but partial communion already existing between churches recognizing each other's baptism? Are the impediments for the restoration of the eucharistic communion as formulated in *Unitatis Redintegratio* still in place? Do we have to stick forever with the current ban on discussing the ordination of women in our ecumenical dialogues? In a postlude, I will ponder what lessons can be learnt for the unity of the churches from the way how Catholics and Protestants are preparing the commemoration of the Reformation in 2017.

Does It Make Sense to Keep Complaining about the Fundamentally Divergent Understanding of Church or Model of Unity?

While assessing the definitive version of *Unitatis Redintegratio*, it was not clear to the Lutheran observer and professor for dogmatic theology and ecumenism at the University of Heidelberg, Edmund Schlink, what the model of unity defended by the Catholic Church was. In his commentary, Schlink argued that "the goal of Christian unity depends very much upon the depth of the renewal of the Roman Church and how inclusive her understanding of catholicity will be in the future." In his opinion three viewpoints could be discerned among Catholics:

a. Those who are convinced that the Roman Church in her present form is a renewed and fully Catholic church will interpret the call to reunion to mean a return to the Roman Church.
b. But suppose the Roman Church looks upon this Decree on Ecumenism as a mere beginning. The renewal of the church is still to come. Thus, the call to reunion is not the result of the Roman renewal, but a call to all Christians to have a change of heart, to engage in dialogue, to talk with the separated brethren. It is not a call to "return," but to "reconciliation." If we understand the call to reunion in this way, then there is room for a discovery of each other's spiritual heritage, for a rapprochement, for cooperation whose end cannot be determined now and whose road cannot be charted in advance. It will be a way toward reunion that will be charted by the Holy Spirit. It is true that also in this interpretation of the Decree on Ecumenism it is assumed that the dogma of the Roman Church and the claim of papal primacy remain unchanged. But this fact does not exclude the possibility of a new interpretation or a different expression of the dogmas of the church and of their relation to reunion.
c. But there are also theologians and laypeople within the Roman Catholic Church who are less definite in their understanding of future Christian unity than the Decree on Ecumenism and the Constitution on the Church are. They are completely open on the question of the way this goal may be reached and even concerning the goal itself. They are open to the Holy Spirit, who cannot be put into the straitjacket of canon

> law. This avoidance of a dogmatically and canonically fixed conception of unity opens in the widest and most immediate sense a way for mutual giving and taking. It establishes a communion that essentially is a yearning for the realization of unity in confession, in the sacraments, and in the understanding of the ministerial office in the church. It is a communion between separated Christians that prays for a God-pleasing order by which this yearning for unity might be satisfied.[4]

Several decades later, when reflecting on the question why the landmark of the *Joint Declaration on the Doctrine of Justification* (1999) apparently did not lead to greater visible unity between Catholics and Lutherans, many ecumenists point to the existence of a "fundamental divergence" (*Grunddifferenz*) between, on one hand, the Catholic and Orthodox conception both of Church and of unity, and on the other the Protestant one. I could have referred to Lutheran theologians reflecting on this theme,[5] but because this book wants to promote reform in and of our own Catholic Church, I prefer to listen carefully to the viewpoint defended by the current president of the Pontifical Council for Promoting Christian Unity, Cardinal Koch. I will pay substantial attention to the plenary address the cardinal pronounced for the first time during the biennial *plenaria* of the Pontifical Council for Promoting Christian Unity in November 2010, and also to his stance in the current debate in Germany whether a common declaration between Lutherans and Catholics on "Church, Eucharist and Ministry" would make sense.[6]

In the second section of his *prolusio*, entitled "Ecclesiology as the Central Question in Ecumenism," Cardinal Koch contrasts Protestant and Catholic ecclesiology in a subsection with the meaningful title "The One and Only Church of Jesus Christ and the Pluralism of Churches."[7] Clearly in his opinion, the one Church of Jesus subsists in the Catholic Church, whereas *extra muros* one encounters the pluralism of churches.[8] The Protestant ecclesiology centering around the local Church is contrasted to a Church model that does not only consider the proclamation of the word and the right administration of baptism and Holy Supper in the local community as indispensable, but the sacramental nature of priestly and episcopal ordination as well.[9] This is Koch's version of the *Grunddifferenz* as far as the understanding of Church is concerned:

> There emerges the difficult ecumenical question of how to relate Catholic ecclesiology with its dialectic between the plurality of the local churches and the unity of the universal Church, and Protestant ecclesiology which sees the concrete community as the most authentic realization of the Church, and how it may be possible to arrive at a substantial consensus on the issue.[10]

Apparently, the ones who are to modify their ecclesiology are the Protestants. The choice for them is whether to remain "in continuity with or break from tradition."[11] Cardinal Koch invites them, in this period of preparation for the five-hundredth anniversary of the start of the Reformation, "to define themselves" and "to decide whether they see themselves as a 'reform and renewal of the universal Church'" or as a "new Christian and ecclesiological paradigm" characterized by "an enduring fundamental difference."[12]

For Cardinal Koch, the second *Grunddifferenz* consists in a different model of unity, as he explains in the third section of his *Prolusio*, dealing with "The Contentious Goal of Ecumenism." In his opinion, "The various churches and ecclesial communities have not yet been able to reach a consensus on the goal of the ecumenical movement itself, which indeed has become even more obscure itself."[13] He again contrasts the Protestant model of ecclesial communion, which "is a matter of pulpit and altar communion between churches with remaining different confessional traditions," with the Catholic model of unity, for whom "the goal of ecumenism is visible unity in the communion of faith, sacraments and ecclesial ministry."[14] In a more recent lecture, he makes it clear that ecumenical progress can only be made if the churches of the Reformation are willing to embrace the sacramental ecclesiology that the Catholic Church rediscovered at Vatican II by rereading the Church fathers.[15] He invites both churches to reflect together on the foundational elements of a patristic ecclesiology: "The canon of the Holy Scripture, the *regula fidei*, the basic structure of the Eucharist and the apostolic succession of bishops."[16]

Cardinal Koch is convinced that "the main point on the current and future task list, especially in the conversation with the ecclesial communities issuing from the Reformation, is the ecumenical clarification of the understanding of Church and unity."[17] While I fully agree that this conversation remains absolutely necessary based on both articles, one is left with the impression that the desired result of this endeavor can only be the acceptance of the Catholic position by the Protestants. Is it not also necessary for Catholics to be willing to learn from the Protestant model of unity?[18] Instead of making our profiles look artificially stronger, we could honestly make a SWOT-analysis of each other's confessions and formulate reform proposals in response to this analysis.[19]

In Cardinal Koch's articles, one will look in vain for a reflection on the appropriate hermeneutical method to achieve unity, or for a strong plea in favor of the method of the differentiated consensus, which has been developed within Lutheran-Roman Catholic regional and international dialogues, reaching its culmination in the *Joint Declaration on Justification* (1999).[20] This would have been welcome, though, in view of the strong critique on consensus ecumenism uttered by many Protestant defenders of the hermeneutical ideal of "reconciled diversity."[21] Therefore, I close this section of my chapter by giving the final word to an astute defender of the model of the differentiated consensus, Hervé Legrand:

> One has every reason to think that this new model represents a very significant step forward for bilateral dialogues which will in future be increasingly led to this method of expressing the same faith with differing emphases, differing conceptual frameworks, differing thought forms.[22]

In his opinion, "the bilateral dialogues remain absolutely necessary, but their future depends on a clear emphasis upon the method of differentiated consensus."[23]

Do We Fully Live Out the Real but Partial Communion Already Existing between Churches Recognizing Each Other's Baptism?

When looking back, in *Harvesting the Fruits,* to the consensus on baptism and Eucharist reached in the bilateral dialogues of the Catholic Church with Lutherans, Reformed, Anglicans, and Methodists, Cardinal Kasper believed that "a considerable consensus on baptism and a growing consensus on the Eucharist are emerging."[24] The most important challenge for the churches, Kasper says, is to make it better visible that "through our common baptism we live already today in a real—albeit not full—ecclesial communion as our common baptism is the basis of the growing communion between us."[25] One of the documents he quotes in order to make this more concrete is the 2007 *Growing Together in Unity and Mission* (2007), written by a special commission of bishops, the International Anglican-Roman Catholic Commission for Unity and Mission (IARCCUM).[26]

I only recall a few of the practical examples and suggestions made in part 2 of this document regarding four fields of action: "Visible expressions of our shared faith," "Joint study of our faith," "Co-operation in ministry," and "Shared witness in the world." As for the liturgical life of the Church, the suggestion is made "to pray for the local bishop of the other church as well as for their own bishop." (103) In the next section, the bishops are encouraged to take care of a more profound reception of ecumenical documents. Section 3 contains a few remarkable suggestions in view of "co-operation in ministry," especially when it pertains to bishops. Next to the plea to organize "jointly sponsored workshops for newly ordained bishops"[27] (112) "consideration should be given to the association of Anglican bishops with Roman Catholic bishops in their *ad limina* visits to Rome" (111). Suggestions regarding a fourth area, that of developing common efforts to engage with the world, are, among others, to develop "joint Anglican/Roman Catholic church schools, shared teacher training programs and contemporary religious education curricula for use in our schools" (122). *Growing Together in Unity and Mission* remains one of the most powerful attempts in the recent history of the ecumenical movement to translate more theoretical ecumenical statements into joint ecumenical practice. I believe we can and ought to develop more common initiatives as churches, as it seems to me that also in the current refugee crisis in Europe, solidarity is still very much being organized on a denominational basis.[28]

Despite the initiatives taken by previous popes in the domain of New Evangelization and despite the growing attention for adult initiation in the Christian faith, many Catholic parishes in Western Europe have lost their attractiveness. Maybe, in an exercise of receptive ecumenism, Catholics could learn from the Anglican-Methodist initiative Fresh Expressions of Church, a missionary movement that is trying to reach out to people who do not identify themselves as Christians.[29]

The Growing Frustration in the Protestant World about the Conditions for the Restoration of the Eucharistic Communion Posed by the Catholic Church

Eucharistic communion is still, and luckily so, presented in many dialogue statements as the goal of the ecumenical endeavors. To mention an example from the Methodist-Roman Catholic dialogue:

> By baptism, and the faith in Christ which it signifies, Catholics and Methodists already enjoy a certain measure of ecclesial communion. The purpose of the dialogue between us is to increase and deepen our relationship until we reach sufficient agreement in the Christian truth that our common baptism can without equivocation be

> completed in our mutual participation in the Meal to which the one Lord invites us and all his followers.[30]

Catholics participating in the dialogues feel obliged not to hide the teaching expressed in a concessive clause of *Unitatis Redintegratio* 22. Even if the Council could mention several praiseworthy characteristics of the Protestant understanding of the Eucharist, it believed, however, it was unable to acknowledge "the authentic and full reality of the eucharistic mystery," "especially because the sacrament of orders is lacking" (*praesertim propter sacramenti ordinis defectum*). To find out how to interpret the precise meaning of the word *defectum*, it is absolutely necessary to take into account the official *relatio*, which states that they "had to point to an essential deficiency (*deficientiam essentialem*) in the celebration of the Eucharist with the communities in the West."[31] Unfortunately, at the time of the Council many translations had already started to translate *defectum* as "absence." This has continued today. On the website of the Vatican, all translations of the answer to question 5 in the 2007 document of the Congregation for the Doctrine of the Faith, *Responses to Some Questions Regarding Certain Aspects of the Doctrine on the Church*, claim to remain faithful to the teaching of *UR* but speak about "the absence of the sacramental priesthood."[32] Yet, in 2004, The US Lutheran-Roman Catholic dialogue had unambiguously stated the following in its important statement on ecclesiology, *The Church as Koinonia of Salvation*:

> Ecumenical understanding would be furthered if in official Roman Catholic documents Vatican II's reference to *defectus* in the sacrament of Order among "ecclesial communities" were translated by such words as "defect" or "deficiency." Translations of *defectus* as "lack" misleadingly imply the simple absence of the reality of ordination. Translation as "defect" or "deficiency" would be consistent with the sort of real but imperfect recognition of ministries proposed above."[33]

Ecumenically committed Catholics and Protestants also ask themselves whether the teaching on the *defectus ordinis* would have to be repeated in the same terms today, considering the convergences reached between them regarding both the topics of Eucharist and ministry.[34]

Must We Forever Observe the Current Ban on Discussing the Ordination of Women in Our Ecumenical Dialogues?

In their ecumenical contacts with Reformed, Lutherans, Methodists, and Anglicans, Catholic ecumenists are used to encountering, collaborating, and celebrating with women priests and bishops. Because of my focus on the dialogue with these churches, allow me to also dedicate a small section on a topic that, until now, has never appeared on the agenda of official ecumenical dialogues. To my surprise, already in his first apostolic exhortation, Pope Francis felt obliged to repeat the teaching on ordination of women of Pope John Paul II. I found it strange, however, that a delicate discussion of this issue among theologians, and especially ecumenists, was immediately banned as well: "The reservation of the priesthood to males, as a sign of Christ the Spouse who gives himself in the Eucharist, is not a question open for discussion, but it can prove especially divisive if sacramental power is too closely identified with power in general" (106). At the same time, Pope Francis invites pastors and theologians "to recognize more fully what this entails with regard to the possible role of women in decision-making in different areas of the Church's life." One wonders whether the influence of Cardinal Kasper on the current pope has played a role in his decision. His recent monograph on the Church also contains a paragraph dealing with this topic:

> The Catholic Church is not at liberty to decide arbitrarily about its order, and, as there is no indication of women's ordination in Jesus's own teachings or in Holy Scripture or in Tradition, the Church does not consider itself authorized to ordain women priests or bishops. By now, this has been clearly stated by high-ranking ecclesiastical decisions. Concerning their level of authority,

> these decisions are so decisively authoritative that I can hardly envisage a change in the Church's teaching. They are of a binding and final character.[35]

To recall an earlier proposal by a theologian also contributing to this book, the door "should be kept open for responsible discussion."[36]

Postlude: The Commemoration of 2017 as an Opportunity for Catholics to Learn Lessons from the Reformation for Church Reform Today

Teaching in a faculty that was among the first to condemn Luther's theology in 1519, I ask myself, at the end of this reflection on our ecumenical relations with the churches originating in the Reformation, what chances might the jubilee year 2017 offer for ecumenical learning and receptive ecumenism?

The Catholic Church and the Lutheran World Federation did not wait long to publish a common statement on their intended "common commemoration of the Reformation in 2017." Its main title, *From Conflict to Communion*, indicates both that there is already a long history of mutual dialogue to overcome the conflict, but also the hope that this process will turn into full communion in the future.[37] This easily readable document aims especially at informing a broad readership on the results of recent historical studies on Luther as well as on the major themes of his theology. It is clear for both dialogue partners that "his intention was to reform, not to divide, the church"[38] and that "Luther had no intention of establishing a new church, but was part of a broad and many-faceted desire for reform."[39] The "five ecumenical imperatives" at the end of the document are addressed to Catholics and Lutherans:

- Catholics and Lutherans should always begin from the perspective of unity, and not from the point of view of division, to strengthen what is held in common, even though the differences are more easily seen and experienced.

- Lutherans and Catholics must let themselves be transformed continuously by the encounter with the other and by the mutual witness of faith.
- Catholics and Lutherans should recommit themselves to seek visible unity, to elaborate together what this means in concrete steps, and to strive repeatedly toward this goal.
- Lutherans and Catholics should jointly rediscover the power of the gospel of Jesus Christ for our time.
- Catholics and Lutherans should witness together to the mercy of God in proclamation in service to the world.[40]

Partially in response to the *Grundlagentext* of the Protestant Church in Germany, *Rechtfertigung und Freiheit: 500 Jahre Reformation 2017*, which enjoyed bad press in ecumenical circles for its limited attentiveness for the ecumenical dimensions of the jubilee,[41] the Ecumenical Study Group of Protestant and Catholic Theologians published the statement *Reformation 1517–2017: Ökumenische Perspektiven*.[42] The ecumenical intention is already visible in an introductory note on terminology, in which it is recalled that luckily nowadays one usually speaks about "Catholic Reform" instead of "Counter-Reformation."[43] This ecumenical intention is pursued in the section on "Systematic Perspectives." The document clearly states that a "consideration of the Reformation in ecumenical responsibility will start out from the Reformer's intention, which was not to leave the Christian Church, but to renew it in the spirit of the Gospel."[44] Both churches have to renew themselves continuously in order to be more faithful to the attributes of unity, holiness, catholicity, and apostolicity.[45] In referring to *LG* 8 and *UR* 6, the document makes it clear that "Christ's call to 'continual reformation' is not restricted to denominational limits."[46] The section ends with a reminder that, in the central paragraph of the *Joint Declaration on the Doctrine of Justification*, both churches have embraced the typically Protestant "*particulae exclusivae*, which describe the event of justification: *solus* Christus, *solo* verbo, *sola* gratia, *sola* fide."[47]

The last section of the document focuses on "Ecumenical Challenges," but also contains important pages narrating what Catholics have already received from the Reformation in the renewal of their own ecclesiology at Vatican II and which Roman Catholic insights have been appreciated in Protestant churches.[48] The document ends with a renewed invitation to address common challenges in society today "jointly" and to continue the ecumenical dialogues. One does not hide that in both churches questions are raised about the future of consensus ecumenism, but one also feels comforted by the *Harvesting the Fruits* project of Cardinal Kasper, and even makes constructive proposals about the future of the dialogue.[49]

LIST OF PROPOSALS

1. When speaking about the Catholic understanding of the Church and of unity, we should not be afraid of acknowledging the diversity of opinions that Edmund Schlink already found existing among Catholics after the Council.
2. Catholics and Protestants should remain focused on the understanding of Church and of Church unity in their ecumenical conversations.
3. For Catholics, receptive ecumenism also implies the willingness to learn from others, including the Protestant view on Church and their model of unity.
4. Catholic ecumenists should continue to apply the method of the differentiated consensus in the bilateral ecumenical dialogues they are engaged in and not be satisfied with reconciled diversity.
5. Far too often, common witness remains a dead letter in the Catholic Church. The IARCCUM initiative deserves to be multiplied to other dialogues to promote a better reception of the dialogue results into concrete practice.
6. Especially in Western Europe, the Catholic Church could and should learn from initiatives like Fresh Expressions of Church, to give greater attention to the missionary dimension of Church.
7. If one wants to remain faithful to the intention of the Council fathers, it is urgent that the translation of

defectus ordinis as "absence" in all relevant documents on the Vatican website be revised.

8. After all the efforts toward convergence in the past few decades, it seems increasingly unbearable that Protestant and Catholic Christians cannot celebrate the Eucharist together.
9. Delicate discussions on the topic of ordination of women should be possible in the *hortus conclusus* of private theological conferences or in the safe atmosphere of an ecumenical dialogue.
10. The commemoration of the five-hundredth anniversary of the Reformation ought to be an excellent occasion for Catholics and Protestants for mutual learning and reform, and for a renewed commitment to ecumenical dialogue and common witness.

NOTES

1. Pope Francis, apostolic exhortation *Evangelii Gaudium* (Rome, 2013), 26. Cf. http://w2.vatican.va/content/francesco/en/apost_exhortations/documents/papa-francesco_esortazione-ap_20131124_evangelii-gaudium.html.

2. Gustave Thils, *Histoire doctrinale du mouvement oecuménique*, Bibliotheca Ephemeridum Theologicarum Lovaniensium, 8 (Louvain: Warny, 1963[2]), 290: "Certains théologiens catholiques…ont donc constaté que leur tâche œcuménique consiste avant tout à 'balayer leur propre demeure'.…Dans quel sens? On peut y répondre en deux mots: pour que la 'maison de tous' soit, non seulement 'ouverte' à tous, mais 'habitable' par tous. En d'autres termes, pour que *tous* les chrétiens puissent y trouver et y épanouir *toutes* les formes légitimes de piété, de spiritualité, d'existence ecclésiale, et ne soient pas astreints à accepter *une* forme déterminée, fût-elle meilleure, pour être véritablement catholiques."

3. Ibid., 267–68: "Certes, il est des organes ecclésiastiques qui s'imposent de droit divin: tel le corps épiscopal uni et dirigé par le Souverain Pontife. Mais que de diversité possible dans leur condition concrète! On peut imaginer le Pape entouré d'une curie très nombreuse, les évêques étant amenés à se préoccuper seulement de leurs églises particulières. On peut imaginer le Pape, entouré d'une curie restreinte et d'ordre administratif, conseillé par une commission épiscopale siégeant à Rome à intervalles réguliers, et suscitant des conférences épiscopales

régionales, pour le grand bien de l'œuvre pastorale à réaliser par chaque évêque dans son église particulière. Tout cela—qui est 'accidentel'—peut changer considérablement la 'physionomie' concrète de l'Eglise." Cf. Peter De Mey, "Gustave Thils and Ecumenism at Vatican Council II," in *The Belgian Contribution to the Second Vatican Council*, ed. Doris Donnelly et al., Bibliotheca Ephemeridum Theologicarum Lovaniensium, 216 (Leuven: Peeters, 2008), 389–413.

4. Edmund Schlink, "The Decree on Ecumenism" in *Dialogue on the Way: Protestants Report from Rome on the Vatican Council*, ed. George A. Lindbeck (Minneapolis: Augsburg Publishing House, 1965), 186–230, esp. 206–8.

5. See for example *Grundkonsens, Grunddifferenz: Studie des Strassburger Instituts für ökumenische Forschung. Ergebnisse und Dokumente*, ed. André Birmelé and Harding Mayer (Frankfurt: Lembeck, 1992).

6. Kurt Kardinal Koch, "Progress in the Ecumenical Journey: The State of Ecumenism Today; *Prolusio* to the Plenary of the Pontifical Council for Promoting Christian Unity, November 15, 2010," *Information Service* 135 (2010/3–4), 75–93, and "Auf dem Weg zur Kirchengemeinschaft. Welche Chance hat eine gemeinsame Erklärung zu Kirche, Eucharistie und Amt?" *Catholica* 69 (2015): 77–94. For other voices in the same debate, see Dorothea Sattler, "Auf dem Weg zu einer 'Gemeinsamen Erklärung zum Herrenmahl'? Eine offene Frage im Für und Wider" and Friederike Nüssel, "Ist eine 'Gemeinsame Erklärung zum Herrenmahl' möglich und sinnvoll? Überlegungen aus evangelischer Sicht," *Ökumenische Rundschau* 61 (2012): 411–28 and 429–39.

7. Koch, "Progress in the Ecumenical Journey," 78. His 2015 article also starts with a phenomenological approach that, in light of the "current Pentecostalizing of Christianity," reconfirms Przywara's thesis of the Protestant "pluriversum." Cf. Koch, "Auf dem Weg zur Kirchengemeinschaft," 77–79.

8. In his more recent article one encounters, however, a more nuanced analysis of the *subsistit*. Cf. Koch, "Progress in the Ecumenical Journey," 84: "Mit der Basalformel des 'subsistit' wollte das Konzil genauer zwei Überzeugungen zusammenhalten und miteinander versöhnen: Es wollte auf der einen Seite den traditionellen Anspruch bestätigen und erneuern, dass die eine Kirche Jesu Christi in der katholischen Kirche unverlierbar existiert. Das Konzil wollte auf der anderen Seite aber auch Raum schaffen für die Anerkennung von Elementen der wahren Kirche Jesu Christi auch in anderen Kirchen und kirchlichen Gemeinschaften, und zwar in der Überzeugung, dass außerhalb der katholischen Kirche 'kein kirchliches Vakuum' besteht, wie der heilige Papst Johannes Paul II. Festgehalten hat."

9. For Catholics, "the invitation" to the eucharistic table "is conveyed by a minister whose ordination and mission are founded in Christ, and is therefore itself a sacrament," and she "considers and recognizes the apostolic ministry as a third criteria for the Church" (ibid., 81). Cf. Koch, "Auf dem Weg zur Kirchengemeinschaft," 85: "Für die katholische Ekklesiologie sind somit das Bischofsamt in apostolischer Sukzession und die Gültigkeit der Eucharistie die entscheidenden Kriterien für die Verwendung der Bezeichnung 'Kirche' für die von der katholischen Kirche getrennten Gemeinschaften."

10. Koch, "Progress in the Ecumenical Journey," 81. Cf. "Auf dem Weg zur Kirchengemeinschaft," 86: "Man kann über die Tatsache eines recht unterschiedlichen Kirchenverständnisses in den verschiedenen Kirchen und kirchlichen Gemeinschaften nicht hinwegsehen" and 89, which literally repeats the difficult question raised earlier on in his *Prolusio*: "wie sich das katholische Kirchenverständnis mit der ihm eigene Verschränkung von Vielheit der Ortskirchen und Einheit der Universalkirche und das evangelische Kirchenverständnis, das in der konkreten Gemeinde die primäre Realisierungsgestalt von Kirche erblickt, zueinander verhalten und wie eine ökumenisch tragfähige Verständigung darüber möglich sein kann. Entschwerend kommt hinzu, dass zwischen beiden Kirchen die sakramentale Dimension von Kirche außerst kontrovers gesehen wird." This is not to deny that the same contrast occurred already in *Harvesting the Fruits: Basic Aspects of Christian Faith in Ecumenical Dialogue* (New York: Continuum, 2009), Cardinal Kasper's farewell present as president of the Pontifical Council for Promoting Christian Unity. Cf. ibid., 153 (§ 78): "Notwithstanding all the important and welcome achievements, a full breakthrough in ecclesiological questions is still to come. Behind the many still unresolved individual questions can be identified one fundamental problem and one fundamental divergence in the understanding of the Church. This becomes clear when we not only ask: **What** is the Church? But also: **Where** is the Church and where is she realised in her fullness? While Protestants answer this question with the response that the Church is realised in communities in which the Word of God is correctly preached and the sacraments are duly administered (*Confessio Augustana* 8), Catholics answer that the Church of Christ subsists in (*subsistit in*) the Catholic Church, i.e., the Church is concretely, fully, permanently and effectively realised in communion with the successor of Peter and the bishops in communion with him (LG 8; UR 4)."

11. Koch, "Progress in the Ecumenical Journey," 80. He also is aware, however, of the sharp contrast between the Orthodox churches—with their strong focus on the nation—and the Catholic Church—with its focus on the universal dimension of the Church, and he cannot but

conclude "dass sich zwei verschiedene Ekklesiologien unausgeglichen gegenüber stehen." Compare "Auf dem Weg zur Kirchengemeinschaft," 89, and "Progress in the Ecumenical Journey," 79–80.

12. Koch, "Progress in the Ecumenical Journey," 82.

13. Ibid.

14. Ibid. Compare "Auf dem Weg zur Kirchengemeinschaft," 92–93.

15. See also De Mey, "The Sacramental Nature and Mission of the Church in *Lumen Gentium*," *International Journal for the Study of the Christian Church* 14 (2014): 348–61.

16. Koch, "Auf dem Weg zur Kirchengemeinschaft," 92: "Kanon der Heiligen Schrift, Glaubensregel, Grundform des eucharistischen Gottesdienstes und apostolische Sukzession im Bischofsamt sind die vier Grundgegebenheiten der frühen Kirche, die man nicht voneinander isolieren darf, die vielmehr engstens zusammengehören. Von daher stellt sich die Frage, ob eine gemeinsame Rückbesinnung auf die patristische Grundstruktur der Kirche, die allen historischen Kirchenspaltungen voraus liegt und die Gestalte der noch ungeteilten Kirche repräsentiert, ein Orientierungspunkt sein könnte, von dem her ein tragfähiger Konsens bei der Frage nach dem Wesen und der Sendung der Kirche gefunden werden könnte. Denn ohne Berücksichtigung dieses ekklesiologischen Gesamtzusammenhangs lässt sich wohl keine gemeinsame Erklärung zu Kirche, Eucharistie und Amt formulieren."

17. Ibid., 93: "dann kann diese Diagnose nur bedeuten, dass die ökumenische Klärung des Kirchen—und Einheitsverständnisses als Haupttagesordnungspunkt auf der gegenwärtigen und künftigen ökumenischen Traktandenliste vor allem im Gespräch mit den aus der Reformation hervorgegangenen kirchlichen Gemeinschaften stehen muss. Eine solche Klärung dürfte der wichtigste Schritt auf dem Weg zur Kirchengemeinschaft und—im Sinne einer In Via Erklärung—zu einem neuen Konsens über Kirche, Eucharistie und Amt sein."

18. For a synthesis based on two decades of research on this theme, see Wolfgang Thönissen, "Eucharistie und Communio der Kirche(n): Ist Kirchengemeinschaft ökumenisch heute möglich?" *Catholica* 69 (2015): 14–36.

19. Cf. Thomas Söding, "Reformation auf dem Prüfstand: Die ökumenische Debatte vor 2017—aus katholischer Sicht" *Catholica* 69 (2015): 1–13, at 3: "2017 bietet die Chance, statt einer 'Ökumene der Profile' eine Ökumene der Stärken zu etablieren.... Was ansteht, ist eine Reflexion darüber, was vom eigenen konfessionellen Standpunkt aus als Stärke und Schwäche der eigenen wie der anderen Konfession angesehen werden kann und welche Reformimpulse daraus abgeleitet werden können."

20. Cf. John A. Radano, *Lutheran and Catholic Reconciliation on Justification: A Chronology of the Holy See's Contributions, 1961–1999, to a New Relationship between Lutherans and Catholics and to Steps Leading to the Joint Declaration on the Doctrine of Justification* (Grand Rapids: Eerdmans, 2009). The World Methodist Council associated itself with the *Joint Declaration* in 2007; a similar move is currently being prepared within the World Communion of Reformed Churches.

21. Cf. Ulrich Körtner, *Wohin steuert die Ökumene? Vom Konsens- zum Differenzmodell* (Göttingen: Vandenhoeck & Ruprecht, 2005).

22. Hervé Legrand, "Receptive Ecumenism and the Future of Ecumenical Dialogues—Privileging Differentiated Consensus and Drawing its Institutional Consequences," in *Receptive Ecumenism and the Call to Catholic Learning: Exploring a Way for Contemporary Ecumenism*, ed. Paul D. Murray (Oxford: Oxford University Press, 2008), 385–98, at 386.

23. Ibid., 388.

24. Walter Kasper, *Harvesting the Fruits: Basic Aspects of Christian Faith in Ecumenical Dialogue* (New York: Continuum, 2009), 190 (§ 97).

25. Ibid., 190 (§ 97).

26. International Anglican-Roman Catholic Commission for Unity and Mission, *Growing Together in Unity and Mission: Building on 40 Years of Anglican-Roman Catholic Dialogue* (London: SPCK, 2007). Cf. De Mey, "Keeping Mission and Unity Together: Impulses from Roman Catholic Ecclesiology and from Multilateral and Bilateral Dialogue Processes" *Internationale Kirchliche Zeitschrift* 103 (2012): 64–89, esp. 75–80. In this article, I also pay attention to a visionary document from the US Orthodox-Roman Catholic Theological Consultation: *Steps Towards a Reunited Church: A Sketch of an Orthodox-Catholic Vision for the Future* (2010), equally suggesting practical steps. Cf. http://www.scoba.us/articles/towards-a-unified-church.html and pp. 86–88 of the article mentioned above. The Reformed-Roman Catholic international dialogue for its part has an equally strong interest in the effects of our ecumenical cooperation in view of creating a more just and peaceful world, as can be derived from the titles of several final reports: *The Presence of Christ in the Church and in the World* (1977), *The Church as Community of Common Witness to the Kingdom of God* (2005) and the report that is currently being drafted under the title *Justification and Sacramentality: The Christian Community as an Agent for Justice*.

27. Maybe such a joint formation for new bishops could also profit from the latest book by Paul Avis: *Becoming a Bishop: A Theological Handbook of Episcopal Ministry* (London: Bloomsbury T&T Clark, 2015).

28. Cf. *Reformation 1517–2017: Ökumenische Perspektiven. Für den Ökumenischen Arbeitskreis evangelische rund katholischer Theologen*

herausgegeben von Dorothea Sattler und Volker Leppin, Dialog der Kirchen, 16 (Freiburg: Herder / Göttingen: Vandenhoeck & Ruprecht, 2014), 109: "It is an open question whether the professionally managed social work of Diakonie and Caritas should strive towards stronger cooperation at the institutional level in order to ease the burdens and increase efficiency. Diversity could indeed prove to be a source of enrichment in this field."

29. See http://www.freshexpressions.org.uk/. This is not to deny that there are also exist strong criticism on this movement. See Andrew Davison and Alison Milbank, *For the Parish: A Critique of Fresh Expressions* (London: SCM Press, 2010).

30. International Commission for Dialogue between the Roman Catholic Church and the World Methodist Council, *The Word of Life* (1996), 10. Cf. *Harvesting the Fruits*, 168.

31. *Acta Synodalia* III/2, 344 (part of the "Relatio circa rationem qua schema elaboratum est"): "Quia plures Patres aliquam mentionem facere volunt de Eucharistia, novum incisum compositum est in quo, post deficientiam essentialem in Eucharistiae celebratione apud Communitates occidentiales enuntiatam, indicatur voluntas earum significandi plenam cum Christo communionem nec non annuntiandi mortem Domini donec veniat. Quae elementa positiva ut fundamentum dialogi inservire possunt."

32. See http://www.vatican.va/roman_curia/congregations/cfaith/documents/rc_con_cfaith_doc_20070629_responsa-quaestiones_en.html.

33. Lutheran-Roman Catholic Dialogue in the United States, *The Church as Koinonia of Salvation: Its Structures and Ministries* (Washington, DC: USCCB, 2005), 108. I appreciate that the same recommendation has recently been repeated by Cardinal Koch. Cf. "Auf dem Weg zur Kirchengemeinschaft," 85n21: "Bei einer adäquateren Übersetzung ist freilich nicht vom 'Fehlen des Weihesakramentes,' sondern von einem 'Mangel' die Rede."

34. *Reformation 1517–2017: Ökumenische Perspektiven*, 110: "After all the efforts towards convergence in the past few decades, it seems increasingly unbearable that Protestant and Catholic Christians cannot celebrate the Eucharist together."

35. Walter Cardinal Kasper, *The Catholic Church: Nature, Reality and Mission* (London: Bloomsbury T&T Clark, 2015), 237–38.

36. Hermann Josef Pottmeyer, "Refining the Question about Women's Ordination," *America*, October 26, 1996, 16–18, esp. 18. Professor Pottmeyer was hoping that the pope would invite "everyone to prayer and dialogue and that he was summoning a council to make a final decision."

37. Lutheran-Roman Catholic Commission on Unity, *From Conflict to Communion: Lutheran-Catholic Common Commemoration of the Reformation in 2017* (Leipzig: Evangelische Verlagsanstalt / Paderborn: Bonifatius, 2013). See also Thomas Söding, "Reformation auf dem Prüfstand," 4–7 and Volker Leppin, "2017—ökumenische Chance oder Desaster? Zu Dokumenten kirchlicher und ökumenischer Gremien im Vorfeld des Reformationsjubiläums," *Catholica* 69 (2015): 112–27, esp. 122–23.

38. Ibid., 20 (§ 29).

39. Ibid., 30 (§ 59).

40. Ibid., 87–89 (§§ 238–45). Marc Lienhard, "Luther 'notre maître commun'? Regards sur le document *Du conflit à la communion* (2013)," *Istina* 58 (2013): 245–61, esp. 261, would have appreciated if the document after commenting on the appropriate methodology would have encouraged Lutherans and Catholics to engage in a common reading of Luther's writings.

41. *Rechtfertigung und Freiheit: 500 Jahre Reformation 2017. Ein Grundlagentext des Rates der Evangelischen Kirche in Deutschland*, EKD, (Gütersloh: Gütersloher Verlagshaus, 2015[4]). The document is built around four classical and one new "sola": "solus Christus, sola gratia, solo verbo, sola scriptura, sola fide," and each time there is ample attention for "innerkirchliche" and "gesellschaftliche Herausforderungen." The ecumenical dimension is not entirely absent, since the document ends with the hope of being able to celebrate the anniversary together with the Roman Catholic Church and the Orthodox Church. A new introduction to the 4th edition explains that this document is more oriented toward an intra-Protestant readership and, therefore, presupposes important ecumenical documents such as the *Joint Declaration on the Doctrine of Justification* without mentioning them. For further analysis of this document, see Söding, "Reformation auf dem Prüfstand," 8–12; Leppin, "2017—ökumenische Chance oder Disaster?" 118–22.

42. *Reformation 1517–2017: Ökumenische Perspektiven*. The book contains both the German and English version of the agreed statement. Cf. Söding, "Reformation auf dem Prüfstand," 12–13 and Leppin, "2017—ökumenische Chance oder Disaster?" 124–27.

43. *Reformation 1517–2017: Ökumenische Perspektiven*, 77.

44. Ibid., 93.

45. Ibid., 95: "Therefore all actions for the renewal of the Church are reformatory, in which the unity, holiness, catholicity and apostolicity of the Church have a shaping influence and are given new radiance."

46. Ibid., 96.

47. Ibid., 98: "Today, there is agreement between Catholics and Protestants with regard to the positive expression of these *particulae exclusivae*

and their soteriological meaning: 'By grace alone, in faith in Christ's saving work and not because of any merit on our part, we are accepted by God and receive the Holy Spirit, who renews our hearts with equipping and calling us to good works' (JDDJ, § 15)."

48. Ibid., 103–7. For the Catholic learning process reference is made to the Council's teaching on the threefold mission of Christ, the priority of the word of God, and the attention for the liturgy of the word. Protestant churches have, among others, "come to a new appreciation of the lifelong commitment expressed by ordination" (ibid., 106).

49. Ibid., 110: "Nowadays ecumenical hermeneutics question whether the search for convergence should be limited to achieving agreement on the semantic content of church doctrines, or whether the respective doctrines should not be understood more pragmatically, that is to say, in the context of church practice.... The very question of the possibilities for a common celebration of the Eucharist by Protestant and Catholic Christians sets the ecumenical task of reviewing the normativity of the present ecumenical practice. Ecumenism is not merely concerned with texts, but also with present-day practice."

22

PENTECOSTALS AND CATHOLICS

Toward an "Exchange of Gifts" for a Renewed Proclamation of the Gospel

Jorge A. Scampini, OP

The choice of this topic may at first seem reductive. Perhaps it would have been more appropriate to opt for a broader spectrum of churches, such as the "free churches" in general, so that my presentation would be more clearly complementary to those that precede it in this volume. But the need to narrow the topic has led me to focus on the Pentecostals and, among them, the commonly called "classical" Pentecostals, that is, those groups that were influenced by the so-called holiness movements that lived the *revival* experience in the first decades of the twentieth century. To confirm this choice, it seems to me that David Martin's thesis is valid: it is possible to establish a structural analogy between Methodism and the Pentecostal movement—if the former corresponds to the second Protestant wave, and the latter to the third. However, both have broken with the traditional unity of people and religion, church and state, local community and local church, creating spaces of social freedom.[1] Both have presented challenges not only to established Protestant churches but also to the Catholic Church in historically Catholic countries, challenges that in part still await a satisfactory response. In addition, in a broader historical context, the Pentecostal movement represents in some respects the last expression of the radical Reformation since, according to its vision, personal faith precedes all sacramental action, leaving aside a "mediating" Church of grace and its institutions, while emphasizing a Church of the "covenant" or "alliance," founded on the commitment and free adherence of each believer. In this view, to belong means to belong "actively." Finally, from a Latin American perspective, it is a way of making present one of the greatest challenges that the Catholic Church must face.

Thinking from here of some aspects of a renewal and reform of the Catholic Church leads us to focus our attention more on the ecclesial "experience" rather than on the "institutional"; on what happens at the local level, in terms of "emergent" and in some respects "peripheral" realities;[2] and finally, on the relationship between renewal, reform, and "conversion," both personal and ecclesial (see *UUS* 16 and 82).

A Vision of Ecumenism and Some Reasons for Facing a Challenge

We must recognize that understanding the ecumenical dialogue as an "exchange of gifts" (*UUS* 28), and trying to draw the consequences of it in view of a renewal and reform of the Catholic Church (see *UR* 4 and 6), presents a great challenge when starting from the relations between the Catholic Church and the more evangelical currents of Protestantism and, above all, the Pentecostal movement. This movement still presents serious difficulties for the Catholic Church in many contexts. However, there are signs indicating that there have been changes in the last decades on both sides and that, consequently, there is the possibility of opening new relationships between them.

Indeed, at the beginning of our century, much of the Pentecostal movement has entered a state of relative stability, offering the first attempts at the theological elaboration of its own identity,[3] which has benefited, among others, the Catholic-Pentecostal theological dialogue.[4] It should also be pointed out that that same dialogue has provoked and encouraged a reflection on the side of the Pentecostal interlocutors that has led them to a more solid theological foundation of their positions.[5] In addition, it should be acknowledged that, as a contribution to the growth of people, and beyond the evident limits usually pointed out (excessively individualistic piety, little interest in social commitment, etc.),[6] in Pentecostal communities, its members develop, more experientially than technically, organizational skills as well as aptitude for group management and missionary discipleship, along with well-defined ethical conduct. These have been extensively analyzed by the social sciences, but there is still need of a theological reflection that, transcending the sociocultural phenomenon,[7] is capable of capturing the Christian and ecclesial elements at play.

In this context, where the positive signs are evident, reaching the aforementioned "exchange of gifts," actively involving the Catholic Church, still has a long way to go, which at first sight is not easy. There are sufficient reasons for this:

a) The asymmetry between the two traditions, both in the realm of lived ecclesiology and in terms of theological formulation, "disorients" the Catholic Church by requiring her to engage in dialogue from a position different from that in other dialogues. For this reason, these attempts have been called "improbable conversations" or "an exercise on the frontiers of ecumenism."[8] However, it is fair to acknowledge that another more radical question arises here: how to integrate in theological dialogues not only the ecclesiology formulated by each interlocutor, which at times is lacking, but the Church itself as it is *really* experienced. Or, in other words, how to keep in the dialogues the distance between the "ideal" and the "real."
b) The still-virulently anti-Catholic proselytism, in many places, produces a constant recruitment of members from the Catholic Church (who, without adequate pastoral responses, experiences a certain state

of vulnerability), and does not go beyond defining the "aggressors" except with sociological parameters describing them as "sectarian" groups.

c) It is difficult, when engaging in bilateral talks, to do so with figures representative of a movement as vast as it is complex,[9] which some prefer to call in the plural "Pentecostalisms," and this makes us think that we are facing a task that, if not impossible, is unlikely to be viable and effective.

Without wanting to detract from these reasons, four others lead us to not dismiss the attempt:

a) The Pentecostal movement, as a true "sign of the times," is the most dynamic and vital current of contemporary Christianity, mobilized by the explicit announcement of Jesus Christ,[10] and, together with Catholicism, represents the only two Christian presences on a global scale.

b) Apparently, the Pentecostal movement has managed to respond to several challenges of our time: while historical expressions of Christianity fail to bring new life to many of its institutional organizations, these groups, relativizing the institutional aspects, have vitally rediscovered the central role of the Holy Spirit; when the historical churches are struggling with the loss of members and the problem of those who belong but do "not believe," Pentecostals, by giving priority to personal faith, affirm that personal conversion to Christ is required explicitly and continuously throughout the entire life of the Christian. While it is not always clear how to give adequate responses to the spiritual pursuits in our contemporary world, Pentecostals emphasize prayer and its power—this is, I believe, the greatest challenge for churches, even more so than secularism, because they have been outshined in what should be "the specialty of the house"; and finally, without too much mediation, they have rediscovered spiritual charisms and gifts as a reality, effective and necessary in the life of each believer and the local congregations.

c) This means that the Catholic Church must take on the challenge that in many contexts, such as the Latin American one, is represented by confrontation with the action of other Christians, apparently more effective than she in proclaiming the gospel, and who have been able to touch on aspects of the people, leading many who have moved away from the visible communion of the Catholic Church to experience a deeper communion with Jesus Christ and a real change of life. This so-called theology of the people is an invitation to think where and how this people is today; and for the Catholic Church, accustomed to seeing society from its own point of view, judging it and wanting to provide guidance, it means facing the challenge of seeing itself from society's point of view and the changes experienced in it.

d) Finally, starting from the Catholic principles of ecumenism, the recognition of "elements of holiness and truth" (*LG* 15; *UR* 3) present in Pentecostal groups requires recognizing the ecclesiological consequences, since these elements, however scattered they may seem, are proper to the Church of Christ and impel "the Catholic unity of the Church" (*LG* 8).

Therefore, given these reasons, if the Catholic Church does not attempt to engage with Pentecostal groups, she would be expressing her own ecumenical commitment in a limited way, and, moreover, she would be unable to discover which elements of the Church of Christ are more tangible and at times more effective in the Pentecostal movement, urging her on the path of her own renewal and reform.[11]

Francis's Reasons for a Reform of the Church

I have the impression that some of the reasons I have just listed are related to intuitions present in Pope Francis's speeches and action.

a) The first of these is the need for a reform of the Church, called to be "go forth" and be more mission oriented (see *EG* 27). In Francis's thought, this requires conversion at different levels of the Church, so the place of local churches (see *EG* 30), and in these of the parishes (see *EG* 28), is irreplaceable and requires a renewal of the evangelizing spirit—which motivates and accompanies any structural reforms—of each and every one (see *EG* 120).
b) The second intuition, in my opinion, is one that has led Francis in the first years of his pontificate to repeated "private" meetings with evangelicals and Pentecostals, usually outside of protocol and the "controlled" agenda of ecumenical relations.[12] These gestures keep a certain continuity with what he already did as archbishop of Buenos Aires and with the place that he gave to "spiritual ecumenism" in his relations with those Christians with whom it is not yet possible to establish other forms of dialogue.[13] We must recognize that these gestures from Francis have not been without a "certain profit," favoring in many evangelicals and Pentecostals a change of attitude toward the Catholic Church and the papacy, which may mark the beginning of a new relationship. Obviously, they are not taking steps toward a recognition of the ministry of Peter, as we Catholics recognize, but, putting aside their historically critical attitude, they begin to recognize in him a spiritual leadership, capable of proclaiming the values of the gospel on behalf of all Christians.

If we consider these two intuitions of Francis, two great areas from which to think of an "exchange of gifts" in view of a renewal and reform of the Catholic Church can be outlined in relation to the evangelical-Pentecostal world: (1) a spiritual renewal as fruit of the encounter with Christ and the welcoming of the gifts of the Spirit; and (2) a renewed missionary impulse as a result of a full experience of Christian discipleship. Undoubtedly, these two areas invite us to consider, as the third and last step, the Church that emerges and benefits from them.

A Spiritual Experience That Becomes "Encounter"

What is most characteristic of the Pentecostal movement is undoubtedly the experience of conversion and baptism in the Spirit. It is shared today by more than 300 million charismatics in different churches, including the Catholic Church. They call to mind that, in the experience of the Christian, not everything can be reduced to the rational practice of faith, an inculturation probably necessary in a world marked by rationality, secularism, and economic efficiency, but one that cannot become a unique model, as there are other cultural needs, manifested in what has been called the *Global South*.[14]

From that experience of conversion, Pentecostals are motivated to preach the gospel in its integrity. Some summarize this in a scheme that contemplates four essential elements—the so-called *foursquare gospel*—which is a kind of simple creed: Jesus saves; Jesus baptizes in the Holy Spirit, giving power for missionary work and testimony; Jesus heals; and Jesus Christ will return. It is, therefore, a type of religiosity that emphasizes the experience of Christ under several aspects: the personal encounter with the Savior; the manifestation of his Spirit and the sending forth that springs from it; the soteriological dimension; and the eschatological openness. All this, especially the healing dimension, exerts an enormous power of attraction, especially to the simplest people, even more so when they experience their limits (disease, poverty, anonymity in large urban areas, social and cultural marginalization, etc.) and cannot find a satisfying answer. On the other hand, the experience of the encounter with Christ is part of the beginning of the itinerary of all Christian life. We may recall the words of Benedict XVI in *Deus Caritas Est* 1: "Being Christian is not the result of an ethical choice or a lofty idea, but the encounter with an event, a person, which gives life a new horizon and a decisive direction." It is an invitation to keep in mind the centrality of Christ in the Church's proclamation and the total relying of the Church on Christ. The crucial question that arises is this: What are the features under which Christ is present? And, therefore, what features should embody the community that announces him?

I think that, in the attempt to answer these questions, considering what is manifested in the Pentecostal phenomenon, it is possible to follow the sequence noted by O. González de Cardedal:

> First we must discern, welcome and be enlightened by the revelation of God in Christ (christophany), then be healed, transformed and deified by him (cristotherapy). From there we are given the necessary ability to discover the meaning, the foundation, and the truth of Christ (Christology).[15]

a) The first experience of Christ, that which leads to conversion, is undoubtedly that of Christ announced, proclaimed, and therefore revealed in his word (*christophany*). The centrality of the word in the Pentecostal announcement is clear. Hence, if the manifestation of Christ in it is full, it is not only the revelation of God, but the revelation to each human being of their own dignity and vocation. This revelation comes to meet us in the journey of our own life, following the paths of human successes and frustrations, since Christ has shared our destiny to the end, experiencing humanity to the extremes of humiliation and suffering as well as of power and glorification. This *christophany* is characterized by a peculiar feature: the Christ who is announced and revealed, is the one that heals and saves. This corresponds to the psychological structure of the act of faith: what is proposed to our faith is ultimately the promise of eternal life. It is a proposition that meets the opening of heart of the human being, in need of light, and where the movement of grace is accompanied by external signs and motives. In the Pentecostal experience, these signs are certainly not the sacraments but the manifestations of the Spirit, among them the "experience" of physical or spiritual healing, which introduces the second moment.

b) *Christotherapy* is the experience of care, service, healing, and solicitude. It is Christ who heals the ailments that afflict those who seek comfort, and who becomes an immediate and perceptible experience of longed-for eternal salvation. Sometimes, we judge too harshly the motivations that lead some to approach the Lord for the immediate interest of healing or a solution to a problem. Sociology and psychology of religion have pointed out the parallels between the experience of Pentecostal worship, some manifestations of popular Catholic piety, and other non-Christian cults. However, it cannot be ignored that this is an unavoidable human experience, the same experience that helped Scholastics understand the sacraments as medicine for the wounds of sin.[16] This therapeutic dimension of Christ cannot be relativized, nor can it be avoided, and, as a result, we cannot avoid the kind of Christian community that stems from it. In this sense, I think of the image that Francis many times has evoked of the Church as "field hospital," where urgency demands that we go out to meet the wounded (see *EG* 89). It is a matter of life and death and immediate response is required. In the often-ambiguous situations in today's world, the first manifestation of Christ, his first announcement, should be accompanied by the perception, in faith, of his curing, healing, restorative power, because he came so that we may have life and have it in abundance (John 10:10). But it is also true that this immediate response may be transitory in its urgency, and it is necessary to take further steps for the fullest reception of the totality of the mystery of Christ, on a path of discipleship—which leads to the third moment.

c) The last moment, that of *Christology*, is the moment of the word, meaning, and reason. Jesus does not articulate realities without accompanying them with a word that makes their meaning clear; he does not deliver speeches unaccompanied by signs. John affirms that Jesus is the Word, eternal life, that he lives in communion with the Father and the Spirit (John 14:12–26). Those who believe in him participate in that life that, being God's own, is not under the power of death. The

> incarnate *Lógos* is the one, who in the flesh and in the path of his life, brings about the unveiling-revelation of God. By walking with man and sharing the drama of our history, he is the *lógos* of human existence. This is the ultimate foundation of Christology, as a reflection of man on Jesus, the Son of God. The fact that God has assumed our humanity to express himself in it establishes the possibility and confidence that our reason can express God, not understanding God as a concept, as an idea, but as founding and illuminating sense. To remember and love him, to conform and adapt to him, Christ has given us his Spirit, realizing and bringing to the full his truth in history (see John 16:13). Christ is the Truth (John 14:6), not a truth articulated as a proposition, but a Person given as life.

The steps we have outlined question the way in which we often make Christ present and the temptation to reduce him to a discourse. Christology and all the discussions about Christ, even that of magisterial teaching, make sense and are possible because of the previous moments of *christophany* and *christotherapy* and should express them in some way. How, then, can our words become capable of expressing, communicating, and animating a Life, by offering to every human being the fundamental and illuminating sense of Christ?

A Discipleship That Drives Mission

In Pentecostal groups, each member, integrated by his or her faith and public profession that Jesus Christ is the only Savior and Lord, has a deep-rooted awareness of being chosen and of being part of a priestly and prophetic people. Baptism in the Spirit has been intimately linked to testimony (see Acts 1:8). Originally, Pentecostalism was conceived as a movement of revival and renewal, challenging and energizing the churches to regain their "apostolic" authority and calling them to bear witness to the ends of the earth, due in part to their eschatological orientation.[17] Consequently, each member of a Pentecostal community is—and indeed feels—

active and committed to missionary work. Each one is called to announce Christ. This announcement does not only take place inside the assembly, but also creates open, public spaces (streets and squares), generating a capillary presence of missionaries, which explains rapid Pentecostal growth. The main purpose of this mission has undoubtedly been "evangelism" and the expansion of the church, but the "ministry of mercy" is also increasingly present through numerous and varied initiatives. According to Francis's expression, we could say that is a true community "going forth." And, in fact, if one considers the areas of greatest development and the profile of those attracted to its message, Pentecostalism has been able to go to meet the social, cultural, and existential peripheries. At least we perceive this in Latin American countries. All are empowered to proclaim the wonders of God, according to their own abilities and despite their own broken stories in need of healing.

It is in the development of the mission that the greatest challenges are presented to the Catholic Church and where perhaps she still has something to learn, since the impression is that Pentecostal groups have "succeeded in transmitting their conception of faith in a 'simple,' 'good,' 'true,' and 'beautiful' way. The Catholic Church should make people understand the faith in the same way. Everything depends on a 'convinced and convincing communication of faith.'"[18]

In certain areas, seeing this embodied today in the figure of Francis, it is said that this is the time of the Church in Latin America. She still presents the features of a Church "going forth," and this has been reaffirmed by the bishops at the Aparecida conference. They have reminded us that we are all missionary disciples and have been summoned to the mission. The persistence of a certain vigor can be real in comparison with older Christianity. But this should not hide the fact that in the current Church in Latin America there are lights and shadows, successes and defeats, the potential of evangelical life, and a certain disorientation. To illustrate this point, I would like to recall the testimony of a bishop in his attempt to meet the challenges posed by reality:

> In the last few years we have witnessed a gradual erosion of the Church in Latin America (*ad intra* and *ad extra*).

Increasingly, our Church devotes more time to fewer people and with less success. And the present problem is not of validity of faith, but of relevance (social) of faith (and of the Church). While we believe that the problem of the late twentieth century in Latin America was not of "religious demand," but of "ecclesial offer," we see an increasingly different panorama at the beginning of this century; people demand less for God and of the Church, and the new generations no longer grow, as before, with that popular Catholic piety, which was almost connatural to Latin American identity.... Therefore, we cannot continue with the same pastoral methods of a society that no longer exists; we cannot continue with anachronistic ecclesial forms that no longer say anything to the parishioners; we cannot maintain visions and discourses that are not inculturated, which no longer correspond to the subject of our evangelization. And even less can we plan a continental mission without knowing exactly what are the new religious and social sentiments of Latin Americans. If we continue to do the same for years and keep not getting the positive results we expect, then we must change what we are doing. But if we change our actions, and we still have bad results, then we must change our view of ourselves and of reality; otherwise we will continue increasing our ecclesial myopia of social reality and of the Latin American parishioners, until it provokes a social entropy of the Church.

...After 500 years of Catholic religious monopoly we find ourselves without arguments and without creativity in front of a Latin American society that no longer considers the Catholic Church at the center of its institutionality and development, and where the Catholic Church is no longer the only (or necessarily the most appealing) one in the Latin American religious spectrum. In conclusion, if after the Conference of Aparecida we continue to think that our Catholic Church is going strong (and that everything bad comes from outside) and that we only need some pastoral recommendations and some cosmetic changes in the way to

> reach our parishioners, we will have wasted a wonderful opportunity to analyze and consider critically the great challenges of the Latin American Church in the coming years.[19]

This testimony invites us to discover what role the Church must play in the case of the changes it perceives, which require, first, the recognition of reality as it is, and, according to how things are, taking initiatives with the future in mind, which implies rethinking the ecclesial profile and the changes to be made in view of a new pastoral model. We should not be afraid to recognize that "the last important ecclesial events on the continent have been 'events' but not 'projects.'"[20] The celebrations of the five-hundredth anniversary of the discovery of America, the Year 2000 Jubilee, the Conference of Aparecida, have not always been followed by concrete steps and have not been given due relevance in the life of the diocesan churches. A further sign this of the distance that often exists between words and reality.

To discover some paths to help rethink the ecclesial profile, it is not enough to consider the experience of Christian life in the Pentecostal groups (in the Catholic Church this is already experienced in the Charismatic Renewal), nor assume the traits that characterize the way they announce the gospel. It is necessary to take a step further, trying to scrutinize the features that emerge in their way of being Church.

The "Emergence" of a New Way of Being Church

Beyond its experiential component and awareness that it has of its own identity, the Pentecostal movement represents, for its way of realizing the Church, the last manifestation of the "radical Reformation." The fact that personal faith precedes all sacramental action, leaving behind a "mediating" Church of grace, has led to emphasis on a Church that is constituted from the commitment and free adherence of every believer. In this way, a new way of being Church has emerged in many traditionally Catholic places, characterized by an extreme congregational vision that becomes manifest in great fragmentation.

For Pentecostals, historically, the concept of Church has not been central.[21] This is explained by the successive stages of development of the movement. Only in recent years have there been more elaborate versions of ecclesiology, with different emphases.[22] However, it is possible to identify some elements that have always been present and that have not developed uniformly.

The universal Church is invisible, while the reality of the local congregation captures attention; to refer to it, the Pentecostals usually use the word *assembly*. In its constitution, the ideal is to recreate the first Christian community (see Acts 2), especially in their gifts and charisms. As we well know, this ideal has had special resonance in successive reform movements of the Church, especially in the medieval monastic life and mendicant orders.[23] In addition, the Church understands itself as the people of God won by the blood of Christ and regenerated by the Holy Spirit (2 Pet 2:9–10). On that foundation, the Church is conceived as the Body of Christ, where the institutional organization is not as important as the awareness of having been gained by Christ and the preaching of the word. Within the "assembly," leadership and ministries are lived or recognized as charismatic. The features of this "assembly" can be synthesized in four elements, none of which are absent in the Catholic Church's view of herself, even though she integrates them into another context (and this may be one of the reasons why the Church has not been always able to reinforce them):

a) The role of the common priesthood of the faithful, or better still of the "prophetism" of all the faithful is emphasized not on the basis the sacrament of baptism but starting from the new birth in the Spirit and the experience of conversion.[24] The community is thus based on personal experience, provoking immediate existential response. This response manifests itself in active participation in worship, through "audible" signs that arouse a lively and celebratory community, but also lead almost immediately to the proclamation of the gospel. According to the model of the apostolic community of Acts, the experience of the Spirit is inconceivable without mission and announcement.

b) The experience of community lived by those who join a Pentecostal assembly is that of an evangelical community that welcomes, accompanies, stimulates, and goes out to meet the situations of anonymity, marginalization, and loneliness experienced in the big cities. This type of community has, for its dimension, but not only, managed to accomplish what remains a challenge in many Catholic parishes.[25] These communities soon discover personal "charisms," which not only allows individuals to find their own place, but also to put themselves at the service of the mission from their own reality. There is, therefore, no leadership that is not conveyed by a personal charism.[26]

c) Under an apparent uniformity, which leads to ignoring how often there are numerous autochthonous Pentecostal centers,[27] progressive diversification processes of the Pentecostal movement have been developed over the course of generations, depending on the different contexts in which it settled. This is not something planned or calculated; nor have all these processes been without difficulty. Even the internal splits that constantly lead to successive divisions are seen as opportunities for the proclamation of the full gospel elsewhere and the integration of new members. It is a sign of recognition of diversity—we prefer not to add here the adjective *legitimate*—in the incarnation of the gospel, and something that can only take place when there is room for the free action of the Spirit, even if there is a risk of human tensions that can lead to new divisions and the need for discernment.

d) The last element to point out is the adult "continuous" formation, which has its center of gravity in the word of God, thus emphasizing the centrality of Christ, and that can keep believers on the path of their Christian lives so they can bear witness to evangelical values. This centrality of Christ may explain why Pentecostals are less prone to syncretism than certain expressions of popular Catholic piety. This "continuous" formation, which is limited in many respects and fails to go beyond a literal reading of the biblical text, continues to question the limits also present in many Catholic education proposals of mass training, or at least their implementation and real repercussions, as well as the fears aroused in some hierarchical instances before the implementation of certain training programs, which, with so many limitations, have tried to meet the peculiarities of a specific people, their customs, their real abilities.

Obviously, I am not adding anything new, but there are four elements, repeatedly recognized at the level of magisterial and pastoral texts—with many attempts at implementation and mixed results—that highlight aspects of the daily life of the Church, at the local level, which in some cases may require structural reforms and always require a renewal:

a) From the recognition of the dignity of each baptized, and relying more on the *sensus fidei* of the people of God, stems the need to develop greater coresponsibility in Christian communities, excluding all kinds of clericalism and elitism, which allows to enhance the missionary role of each member. In fact, there are many local churches that are still far behind regarding what is indicated in the current ecclesial regulation.
b) Based on what has been said above, it is possible to develop communities in which the gospel is alive, and at the same time are able to create deep bonds of belonging, learning to discover and promote the gifts of nature and grace of each one. This would lead to rethinking, on the one hand, the structure of the parish as a community of small communities;[28] and on the other, the way in which vocations are discerned and promoted, particularly when it comes to candidates for the ordained ministries, which is connected necessarily with how the training process is conceived, which

should prevent divisions in and among people, and their communities of origin.

c) The local churches should experience greater openness to the motions of the Spirit, as true subjects, that make them capable of assuming the values of every local reality, without fear of diversity, but as true manifestations of the richness of the catholicity of the Church, leaving room for trial-and-error approaches to solving problems. Otherwise, the risk is to go back to "business as usual," which is always less.

d) Finally, creating spaces for real accompaniment and formation that consider the reality of the recipients, where it is necessary to consider not only the contents of faith, but also the pedagogical mediations, allow living that same faith as a real and continuous encounter with the Lord, and to experiencing the gospel as good news.

Each of these aspects indicates ways to go forward for a renewal of the local churches.[29]

Conclusion

If it is a question of renewing the pastoral plan and structures of the Church, favoring its missionary spirit, this is only possible thanks to a permanent conversion. This requires a fresh look of the Church—particularly the local church—at herself, and, consequently, the need to introduce the changes that this look requires. To do this, it is necessary to take on certain challenges, which should be shouldered by the whole Church and by all in the Church, taking into account different *dimensions* of ecclesial life, different *actors* who must each play their own role, and *basic criteria* that establish and indicate the way for moving forward.

a) First, we must consider all *the dimensions* of religious and ecclesial experience, according to the different recipients: the personal religious experience, the community experience, and a balanced and appropriate training schedule.

b) Second, *the actors* of evangelization must necessarily be diversified and include parishes that are truly renewed and diversified in ministerial roles, as true "communities of communities"; apostolic movements, not as monads rotating in their own orbits, seeking their own adepts, but as true charismatic gifts in the service of each local church; and popular piety, recognized as a value and starting point of the Christian experience, but requiring a growth in faith and in the itinerary of Christian life, and not as a static reality, at times ambiguous and not always free of syncretism.

c) Finally, the implementation of *criteria* are required: a Church that truly understands and lives as people of God, always on the road, in view of its eschatological fulfillment, in the freedom of the Spirit, and at the same time, as a communion of people, charisms, and ministries, and of local churches in the universal Church; a comprehensive pastoral care that does not neglect the personal in view of the social and does not retreat in the safe environment of an individualistic spirituality, ignoring the demands of the social and communal needs; and being able to point out the daily life of God, allowing us to live each day more fully a Christian life in its dimensions of testimony, celebration, and service.

If the proclamation of the gospel seeks to have every listener of the word meet Jesus Christ and to have faith in him, there is no discipleship without personal encounter. From there, the Christian life should be conceived as a spiritual dynamism that enables living that discipleship as a journey in which permanent conversion and call to holiness are constitutive, together with the deployment of a real missionary commitment. It is therefore vital to rethink the Church from the reality of baptism, discipleship, and the role of the Holy Spirit.

NOTES

1. See D. Martin, *Tongues of Fire: The Explosion of Protestantism in Latin America* (Oxford: Blackwell, 1990), 31.

2. This could be linked to Yves Congar's vision of the "starting point" of renewal movements: see Y. M. Congar, *Vraie et fausse réforme dans l'Église* (Paris: Cerf, 1968²), 251.

3. See C. A. Stephenson, "Pentecôtisme, théologie universitaire et œcuménisme: une introduction interprétative," *Istina* 57 (2012): 357–74.

4. See the Pontifical Council for the Promotion of Christian Unity to consult the final texts of each of the six phases of this dialogue carried out from 1972 to 2006: http://www.vatican.va/roman_curia/pontifical_councils/chrstuni/sub-index/index_pentecostals.htm.

5. See C. M. Robeck Jr., "The Achievements of the Pentecostal-Catholic International Dialogue," in *Celebrating a Century of Ecumenism. Exploring the Achievements of International Dialogue*, ed. J. A. Radano (Geneva: WCC Publications, 2012), 163–94.

6. This criticism can be relativized, if we think of the growing political commitment of Pentecostals, for example in Brazil, or the aid program of the Assemblies of God in the United States for the poor children of Latin America: see D. Petersen, *Not by Might, Nor by Power: A Pentecostal Theology of Social Concern in Latin America* (Oxford: Regnum, 1996).

7. K. Koch, preface, in *Movimientos Evangélicos—Iglesias Pentecostales—Movimientos Carismáticos. Nuevos Movimientos Religiosos como desafío para la Iglesia Católica. Resumen sistemático de los resultados de la Conferencia Internacional (Roma, 9 al 11 de abril de 2013)*, by V. Feneberg and J. Müller (Bonn: Conferencia Episcopal Alemana–Pontificio Consejo para la Promoción de la Unidad de los Cristianos, 2015), 5ff.

8. See K. McDonnell, "Improbable Conversations: The International Classical Pentecostal–Roman Catholic Dialogue," *Pneuma* 17 (1995): 163–74; V.-M. Kärkkäinen, "An Exercise of the Frontiers of Ecumenism: Almost Thirty Years of Roman Catholic–Pentecostal Dialogue," *Exchange* 29 (2000): 136–71.

9. Only some of the Pentecostal churches form the Pentecostal World Fellowship, which could be similar to Christian World Communions.

10. According to the Pew Forum's 2011 report, about half of all Christians in the world are Catholic, 12 percent Orthodox, and 37 percent "Protestants in the broad sense." The same study shows that there are about 279 million Pentecostal Christians and 305 million Charismatic Christians, and Pentecostals and charismatics together reach 27 percent of all Christians in the world, and more than 8 percent of the world's population. There are about 285 million Evangelicals, which means that together, the Evangelicals and Pentecostals are about 400 million. The number of "historical Protestants" (Lutherans, Reformed, Methodists,

etc.) and Anglicans continues to decline. The Pentecostals, for their part, represent two-thirds of Christianity in developing countries.

11. Probably the most realistic and ecclesiologically founded reading attempt in a diocesan church is that of Chosica (Peru); see N. Strotmann and J. L. Pérez Guadalupe, *La Iglesia después de Aparecida. Cifras y proyecciones* (Chosica: Instituto de Teología Pastoral "Fray Martín," 2008).

12. This has not gone unnoticed: see A. Nucci, "Francis, Ecumenism, and the Common Witness to Christ," *The Catholic World Report* (www.catholicworldreport.com/Item/3350/francis_ecumenism_and_the_common_witness_o_christ.aspx); A. Gagliarducci, "Evangelizing Evangelicals—Why Pope Francis Loves to Meet with Charismatic Movements," *Catholic News Agency* (www.catholicnewsagency.com/news/evangelizing-evangelicals-why-pope-francis-loves-to-meet-with-charismatic-movements-66914/); F. Rosica, "New Directions in Ecumenical and Interfaith Relations in the Mind & Heart of Pope Francis: Address to the USCCB Committee for Ecumenical and Interreligious Affairs," *Vatican Insider Documents* (http://www.lastampa.it/2015/02/23/vaticaninsider/eng/documents/new-directions-in-ecumenical-interfaith-relations-in-the-mind-heart-of-pope-francis-tOCFDZuNrn9CijIpMBHn7J/pagina.html).

13. As Francis himself recalled: see Private Visit of The Holy Father to Caserta, for a Meeting with the Evangelical Pastor Giovanni Traettino, Address of Pope Francis, Pentecostal Church of Reconciliation, Caserta, Monday, July 28, 2014 (http://w2.vatican.va/content/francesco/en/speeches/2014/july/documents/papa-francesco_20140728_caserta-pastore-traettino.html).

14. See Feneberg and Müller, *Movimientos Evangélicos—Iglesias Pentecostales—Movimientos Caris- máticos*, 29.

15. O. González de Cardedal, *Cristología* (Madrid: BAC, 2001), 571.

16. An idea developed by Hugh of St. Victor: "Ergo sacramenta Christi arma sunt? Non solum arma, sed et medicamenta. Quomodo? Medicamenta sunt, quia sanant infirmos; arma, quia protegunt sanos" (*De sacramentis christianae fidei*, in PL 176, 33D); and that the great medieval authors will follow: see Bonaventure, *IV Sent.*, dist. 2, a. 1, q. 3; Alexander of Hales, *IV Sent.*, Introitus, 11ff.; Thomas Aquinas, *IV Sent.*, dist. 2, q. 1, a. 2c.

17. See W. Ma, "The Theological Motivations for Pentecostal Mission," in *Mission Spirituality and Authentic Discipleship*, ed. W. Ma and K. R. Ross (Oxford: Regnum, 2013), 220–34.

18. Feneberg and Müller, *Movimientos Evangélicos—Iglesias Pentecostales—Movimientos Carismáticos*, 31.

19. N. Strotmann and J. L. Pérez Guadalupe, "Introducción: ¿Y después de Aparecida, qué?" in *La Iglesia después de Aparecida*, 12.

20. See ibid., 15.

21. See P. D. Hocken, "Theology of the Church," in *Dictionary of Pentecostal and Charismatic Movements*, ed. S. M Burguess and G. B. McGee (Grand Rapids, MI: Zondervan, 1988), 211–18.

22. M. Volf, *After Our Likeness: The Church as the Image of the Trinity* (Grand Rapids, MI: Eerdmans, 1998); S. Chan, *Liturgical Theology: The Church as Worshipping Community* (Downers Grove, IL: InterVarsity Press, 2006); V.-M. Kärkkäinen, *An Introduction to Ecclesiology: Ecumenical, Historical and Global Perspectives* (Downers Grove, IL: InterVarsity, 2002) and "The Church as the Fellowship of Persons: An Emerging Pentecostal Ecclesiology of *Koinonia*," *PentecoStudies* 6 (2007): 1–15; M. W. Mittelstadt, *Reading Luke-Acts in the Pentecostal Tradition* (Cleveland: CPT Press, 2010); D. Morgan, *Priesthood, Prophethood and Spirit-Led Community: A Practical-Prophetic Pentecostal Ecclesiology* (Saarbrücken: Lambert Academic Publishing, 2010); J.C. Thomas, ed., *Toward a Pentecostal Ecclesiology: The Church and the Fivefold Gospel* (Cleveland: CPT Press, 2011).

23. See H.-M. Vicaire, *L'imitation des Apôtres* (Paris: Cerf, 1963); P. Neuner, "Reform als Wesenselement von Kirche," in *In Verantwortung für den Glauben. Beiträge zur Fundamentaltheologie und Ökumenik*, ed. P. Neuner and H. Wagner (Freiburg: Herder, 1992), 169–71.

24. D. J. Wilson, "Church Membership," in Burguess and McGee, *Dictionary of Pentecostal and Charismatic Movements*, 196ff.

25. Of course, not everything arises spontaneously from the congregation, and the role played by a strong pastoral leadership among Pentecostals cannot be denied; even though in some cases this is more of a cultural component, in continuity with the social and cultural reality of Latin American peoples, than of a new link to the Protestant ecclesiological tradition.

26. See R. H. Hughes, "Church Leadership," in Burguess and McGee, *Dictionary of Pentecostal and Charismatic Movements*, 195ff.

27. This is one of the conclusions of David Martin, who argues that the Pentecostal movement, regardless of its North American roots, originated in South America as a completely autochthonous religion, referring to the wide organizational independence and receptivity of traditional popular religiosity: see D. Martin, "The Evangelical Expansion South of the American Border," in *Secularization and Sectarianism. Essays in Honour of Bryan Wilson*, ed. E. Barker, J. A. Beckford, and K. Dobbelaere (Oxford: Clarendon Press, 1993), 108.

28. This raises the question of the role played by the grassroots communities, which are questioned in their concrete realization by hierarchical entities and that, in some respects, were at odds with the Pentecostal message, especially in relation to social and political commitment; see M. Bergunder, ed., *Movimiento pentecostal y comunidades de base en América Latina. La recepción de conceptos teológicos de liberación a través de la teología pentecostal* (Heidelberg: Universidad de Heidelberg, 2009). Today, however, it is an ecclesial reality that should be recovered and integrated into a new configuration of the Church: see Feneberg and Müller, *Movimientos Evangélicos—Iglesias Pentecostales—Movimientos Carismáticos*, 32.

29. This presentation could be complemented with M. Eckholt's vision: *Wie nehmen die Akteure innerhalb der katholischen Kirche das Phänomen der Neuen Religiösen Bewegungen wahr? (Schwerpunkt Lateinamerika)*: http://weltkirche.katholisch.de/Portals/0/Dokumente/DBK_NRB_Eckholt_Wie_nehmen_die_Akteure_Neue_Religioese_Bewegungen_wahr.pdf.

VI

REFLECTIONS FOR A MORE POOR, FRATERNAL, AND INCULTURATED CHURCH

23

INCARNATION, KENOSIS, INCULTURATION, AND POVERTY

Juan Carlos Scannone, SJ

The reform of the Church according to the gospel—which Pope Francis wants— is aimed at having the Church renounce her self-referentiality and kenotically step outside of herself for the mission entrusted to her by Christ. She is the people of God sent to all the peoples of the earth (*LG* 13), and to each single person within them, in dialogue with them, as stated in *Gaudium et Spes* (*GS* 40–45). The same Council, in *LG* (2–4) and *Ad Gentes* (*AG* 2–4), recognizes the roots of the Church in the trinitarian missions of the Son and the Spirit, in an "admirable exchange" of places with the incarnate Son, as a continuation of his incarnation, his *kĕnōsis* and salvific action, inspired, guided, and moved by the anointing of the Spirit. This incarnational and kenotic pouring out of oneself implies inculturation, poverty, and service to the poor.

Therefore, both inculturation and the poverty of the Church fit in a christological and pneumatological manner in the model of the incarnation, with its fulfillment in the paschal mystery (cross and resurrection) and Pentecost.[1] This is how John Paul II,[2] in using the neologism *inculturation*, explicitly evoked the analogy with the incarnation, and Benedict XVI affirmed at Aparecida that the preferential option for the poor is based on the christological faith in the poor Christ.[3] In turn, the Paraclete is the other "hand of the Father" both in the life of Jesus and in his Church, especially in the poor "of Spirit" (Ignacio Ellacuría).

Hence the title of this contribution, which intends to frame the treatment of the inculturation of the gospel and the poverty of the Church for the poor, on the kenotic model of the incarnation, as a way to follow Christ in the Spirit for the glory and service of the Father, to offer a contribution to Church reform. This is illuminated both by the very *fact* of the incarnation of the Son who assumes humanity (John 1:14) as by the *way* he assumes it, that is, kenotically (Phil 2:6–7) and in poverty (2 Cor 8, 9), since "God became poor" (*AD* 391).

After this brief introduction, we will first address the issue of inculturation, and second, poverty and the poor, since the re-*form* of the Church must prolong the *forma Christi* according to the kenotic and paschal model of the incarnation.

The Inculturation of the Gospel

Already the theology of the people[4] and the *Puebla Document* (*DP* 1979) stressed the incarnation of faith in culture and cultures—according to Paul VI's apostolic exhortation *Evangelii Nuntiandi* (*EN*, 1975)—and recognized it in Latin America.

Later, John Paul II, in order to define it, used the aforementioned neologism *inculturation*, which, as mentioned earlier, evokes the analogy with the incarnation, which is explicitly dealt with later by the Conference of Santo Domingo (*DSD*, 1992) and other documents. But Francis took another step further when he talked about "evangelization *as* inculturation" (*Evangelii Gaudium*: *EG* 122, emphasis mine).

According to my interpretation, in the binomial "evangelization of culture" and "inculturation of the Gospel," which seemed to be *only* two sides of the same coin, Pope Francis privileges, with this formulation, inculturation, which thus appears clearly as the explicit purpose of the mission of the Church. Thus, he even states that it "is imperative to evangelize cultures in order *to* inculturate the Gospel" (*EG* 69, emphasis mine).

This is fully in line with what he says about the "beauty of her varied face" (*EG* 116)—*culturally* varied—of the Church, and the "multifaceted and inviting harmony" (*EG* 117), as it is in line with the importance that he gives to the local churches that, according to John Paul II, are the agents of inculturation.

When Bergoglio was rector of the faculty of philosophy and theology of San Miguel in Argentina, he organized an International Congress (1985) on the aforementioned binomial, which was also the title of the meeting. Then, in his inaugural address, he emphasized the theological and pastoral importance of the inculturation of the gospel, quoted Father Pedro Arrupe—a forerunner in the use of the neologism (at the Synod of 1974)—and evoked the practice of many venerable Jesuits such as Matteo Ricci, Roberto De Nobili, and José de Acosta.[5] At that Congress, one of the topics discussed was the insufficient inculturation of the liturgy, for example, in Africa. Now, in *Evangelii Gaudium* it appears clearly that, even though the gospel has been inculturated from the beginning in Western cultures, starting with the Greek and the Latin, it transcends them all and is called to incarnate in them all (*EG* 118).

Here the model of the polyhedron (*EG* 236) is applied as symbol of unity in and of differences, according to a genuinely trinitarian ecclesiology, in which the protagonism of the Holy Spirit (*EG* 116, 117) is recognized in a kind of communitarian circumsession of communities and people. The pope rejects the model of the sphere, "where every point is equidistant from the center, and there are no differences between them" (*EG* 236); and replaces it with the "polyhedron, which reflects the convergence of all its parts, each of which preserves its distinctiveness" (ibid.). That image serves him well not only to consider every people in the world and the interrelationship among them, but also the intercultural character of the people of God, thanks to the inculturation of the gospel in each of their respective cultures, and the communion between them in the plural unity of the Church.

All this is confirmed by the transposition that Francis makes of culture, of the Thomist theme of grace that presupposes nature. Thus, immediately after recalling that the "human person is always situated in a culture (*GS* 36)," he adds, "Grace supposes culture, and God's gift becomes flesh in the culture of those who receive it" (*EG* 115), thus extending the analogy with the incarnation and underlying the importance of inculturation.

I will not uncover here all the theological and pastoral wealth that these expressions imply. I will only briefly mention the concept implied here and its dogmatic foundation. Regarding the first, John Paul II's encyclical *Redemptoris Missio* (*RM*) states, "Through inculturation the Church makes the Gospel incarnate in different cultures and at the same time introduces peoples, together with their cultures, into her own community. She transmits to them her own values, at the same time taking the good elements that already exist in them and renewing them from within" (*RM* 52). But in this admirable exchange not only are cultures transformed, and refined according to their own characteristics, but the Church is transformed as well as it becomes "a more intelligible sign of what she is, and a more effective instrument of mission" and "is enriched with forms of expression and values in the various sectors of Christian life," which are then listed (ibid.).

Francis's application of the model of the incarnation to the relationship between grace and culture (*EG* 115)—as theology does with the binomial "grace/nature"—in union without confusion nor division, presupposes that somehow cultures have a *theological* value when they are assumed by the gospel, which is inculturated in them, just as inculturation is an *essentially* constitutive moment of evangelization. Thus, the pope's phrase above is more clearly understood: "evangelization as inculturation" (*EG* 122) without reducing the former to the latter.

On the other hand, a summary of its foundation is found in the General Conference of Santo Domingo, when, before applying the problem of "inculturated evangelization" to Latin America, it explains it "in light of the three great mysteries of salvation" (*DSD* 230), Christmas, Easter, and Pentecost. In fact, the first evokes the dynamism of the incarnation in that of inculturation; the second the death of cultures to their antivalues and their transformation, which perfects and elevates them from within in their values and symbols; and the third manifests the unity of universal communion in the plural distinction of the faithful people of God in the peoples, according to an image—as I explained in the introduction—of trinitarian communion.[6]

According to the same General Conference of 1992, the evangelization of culture penetrates it "to its dynamic nucleus" (*DSD* 229), which we may interpret, with Paul Ricoeur,[7] as its ethical-mythical core, that is—according to Ricoeur—*ethical* because it implies values, and *mythical* because it is expressed in symbols and symbolic narratives. And, from this center, it tends to expand at all levels of life and coexistence of a people, according to Thomas S. Eliot, to all the "lifestyle of a people"—or, as expressed by *EG*, "It has to do with the lifestyle of a given society, the specific way in which its members relate to one another, to other creatures and to God. Understood in this way, culture embraces the totality of a people's life" (*EG* 115).

Worth noting is that *EG* 115, following the *Puebla Document* (*DP*) 386, reinterprets the texts of *GS* 53a and *GS* 53b, which illustrate the humanistic concept of culture, starting from paragraph *GS* 53c, which addresses its "historical and social aspect" and its "sociological and ethnological sense"—which today we would call "cultural anthropology"—thus reinterpreting and enriching the former with a historical and social humanism.

In fact, the editing of no. 386 of the *Puebla Document* (of which one of the main leaders was one of the most important theologians of the people: Lucio Gera)[8] shows how this conciliar document was read by that Episcopal Conference in a Latin American perspective, since in the Puebla text there are the words "in a people" in the nonverbatim citation of no. 53a and b of the conciliar constitution, which are not in that text. Thus, the more humanistic conciliar meaning of culture of both the first few paragraphs is developed, to which the council then connects the historical and social dimensions, addressed by the constitution only in the third paragraph (no. 53c). Therefore, Puebla rereads 53a and 53b from the perspective of 53c and therefore changes the angle of approach to its understanding of culture. At a meeting of the professors of the faculty of philosophy and theology of San Miguel with those of the faculty of theology of the Catholic University of Argentina, immediately after Puebla, we asked Gera if the editors were aware of this shift in perspective, and he said no. That is, it was a spontaneous act and not a pondered reflection, probably due to the new hermeneutical place from which the text was interpreted (Latin

America), a change of point of view that was also not perceived as such by the bishops, as there were no objections.

The understanding that Pope Francis has of the Church and its mission (mentioned earlier); the importance that he gives to the cultures of peoples in relation to their promotion, humanization, and evangelization; and the discernment he is able to make of the signs of the times, for example, about the current relevance of the evangelization of Asia, create a sense of expectation from his pontificate and suggest, especially to the particular churches, a special emphasis on encouraging and accompanying the inculturation of faith in different peoples, as well as in the late modern and postmodern culture. It seems to us that, despite the theoretical directives of the last popes, from Paul VI to Francis, so far in that regard the Roman Congregations have been rather reticent, and local dioceses too fearful.

Of course, according to *Redemptor Missio*, the "process of the Church's insertion into peoples' cultures is a lengthy one" because "inculturation is a slow journey," typical of a "mature faith"; and this "process needs to take place gradually, in such a way that it really is an expression of the community's Christian experience" and it "must involve the whole people of God, and not just a few experts, since the people reflect the authentic *sensus fidei* which must never be lost sight." Therefore, "it must be an expression of the community's life, one which must mature within the community itself, and not be exclusively the result of erudite research" (*RM* 52–54).

These approaches coincide with Pope Francis's fundamental ideas, that is, his appreciation for the *sense of faith* of the faithful believers, especially the poor (*EG* 198) and, also, with the preeminence given to time over space, that is, when "initiating processes rather than possessing spaces" (*EG* 223). But often this maturation has already been accomplished "in the various sectors of Christian life, such as evangelization, worship, theology and charitable works" (*RM* 52), "in the field of liturgical expression, [92] and in the areas of catechesis, theological formulation, secondary ecclesial structures, and ministries" (*EN* 63), and so on. And yet, the pastors in question or the Vatican authorities are not always sufficiently aware of this, to explicitly recognize it both theoretically and in practical realizations, in the pastoral structures and norms of canon law. All are steps that should be taken through decentralization in favor of local churches and their respective episcopal conferences, and through listening, "with one ear to the Gospel and with the other, to the people of God" as the martyr bishop of La Rioja (Argentina), Enrique Angelelli (see *EG* 154) would say.

The encyclical *Redemptor Missio* provides two criteria for the discernment of a correct inculturation: (1) "compatibility with the gospel" (*RM* 54), which had previously been defined as "harmony with the objective requirements of the faith itself" (*RM* 53); and (2) "communion with the universal Church" (*RM* 54), which does not mean uniformity but unity, so that

> particular churches of the same region should work in communion with each other and with the whole Church, convinced that only through attention both to the universal Church and to the particular churches will they be capable of translating the treasure of faith into a legitimate variety of expressions. (*RM* 53)

We should remember that when Francis affirms the principle that the whole is greater than the parts and "greater than the sum of its parts," it is within the vital tension between the global and the local (see *EG* 234), which also applies to the Church and is best understood with the polyhedron model. In our view, this also refers to the fertile polarizing contrast between inculturation and interculturality in theology and pastoral mission of the Church today, both being two signs of times. The pope himself encourages us in the direction of inculturation, when he writes,

> This is always a slow process and at times we can be overly fearful. But if we allow doubts and fears to dampen our courage, instead of being creative we will remain comfortable and make no progress whatsoever. In this case we will not take an active part in historical processes, but become mere onlookers as the Church gradually stagnates. (*EG* 129)

A Poor Church for the Poor

Although the explicit wording of the preferential option for the poor was made at Puebla, not only had it already been expressed at Medellín, but implicitly it has always accompanied the history of the Church, from the poor Jesus who opted preferentially for the poor, as the prophets themselves had already done.[9] That is why I mentioned earlier the words of Benedict XVI at Aparecida, quoting St. Paul: "The preferential option for the poor is implicit in the Christological faith in the God who became poor for us, so as to enrich us with his poverty (see 2 Cor 8, 9)." Already, John Paul II, after quoting Matthew 25:35–37, had affirmed, "This Gospel text is not a simple invitation to charity: it is a page of Christology which sheds a ray of light on the mystery of Christ" (*Novo Millennio Ineunte* 49). And for this very reason it is a criterion for the Church, because by "these words, no less than by the orthodoxy of her doctrine, the Church measures her fidelity as the Bride of Christ" (*NMI* 49).

Furthermore, this page reveals the face of God himself, who gives "his first mercy" (*EG* 198, quoting John Paul II's homily at Santo Domingo, October 11, 1984) to the poor, so that God's unconditional love, unmerited and free, embraces *universally* all, because it begins from the *last*—the poor and excluded—those who will then be first.[10]

Pope Francis goes even further, not only *epistemologically* (with all the theoretical and practical consequences) when he teaches that for "the Church, the option for the poor is primarily a theological category rather than a cultural, sociological, political or philosophical one" (*EG* 198),[11] but also *ecclesiologically* and *pastorally* when he repeats what he had already said at the beginning of his pontificate (ibid.). "This is what I want, a poor church for the poor," a phrase in which the two terms mutually reinforce each other, and with which he implicitly gives the reason for the choice of his name: Francis. Already John XXIII, before the Council, in his radio message of September 11, 1962, had said, "The Church presents itself as it is and how it wants to be, as the Church for everyone, especially as the Church for the poor." Francis—as Pedro Trigo observes—has added that the Church "especially of the poor," had to be itself poor; and that for both popes, that yearning "should be understood as a plan, as a vital orientation and as a program," even if it "can be interpreted in various ways."[12] I will return to these later.

In this second part, I will describe my interpretation of that desire, repeatedly mentioned by Francis, dealing first with the poor Church, and then, with the Church for the poor, even if both approaches are intertwined and fertilize each other. For this reason, it is impossible to separate them in a clear-cut way, but, at most, examine them separately in each of the two sections of this part of my contribution.

Both are framed within the model of the incarnation until Easter (the dispossession of the cross, the joy of the resurrection according to the beatitude of the poor, the gifts of the Spirit in the poor of and with the Spirit). The dynamism of the incarnation implies that the *theological* option for the poor seeks to mediate itself in the "cultural, sociological, political, philosophical" dimensions (*EG* 198), making them first pass through the paschal discernment.

A CHURCH THAT IS POOR IN ITS BEING AND APPEARANCE

Pope John XXIII's proposal was reiterated, almost at the end of the first session of the Council, on December 7, 1962, by Cardinal Giacomo Lercaro, archbishop of Bologna, who proposed a "Church above all of the poor" and "that is to say, essentially, the Church of the poor" *as* "the great theme of the Council" and "the main reason even for the unity of Christians," focusing on "the mystery of Christ in the poor." Unfortunately, despite the enormous favorable impact it achieved then, it remained a secondary concern of the Council fathers. Later, the historian of the Council, Giuseppe Alberigo, would go so far as to say that "the main omission [of Vatican II] was the commitment to the poor, as John XXIII had requested, and the poverty of the Church."[13]

However, such initiatives were not in vain, because a group of fathers continued to work along that line, meeting at the Belgian College in Rome, where important contributions came that were then collected in *Gaudium et Spes*; Cardinal Lercaro, at the request of Paul VI, gave his contribution for a new encyclical, *Populorum Progressio* (*PP*, 1967) no less; and, near the end of the last session of the Council, on November 16, 1965, a group of about forty fathers (who then were late joined by another five hundred bishops from different continents) led by Dom Hélder Câmara, bishop of Olinda and Recife, made public the so-called *Pact of the Catacombs*.[14] This document remains valid today and can still inspire the reforms that Pope Francis wishes for. Therefore, I will try here to summarize its main points.

It is a personal and public commitment, which was to be made known in the fathers' respective dioceses. All proposals are framed within the *general rule* of living "in accordance with the common average level of our people" (Proposal 1) and are often accompanied by biblical citations to support each proposal. They took also into account the *appearance* of wealth (not only its reality), both in clothing and the use of expensive materials as signs of authority (Proposal 2) and the use of honorary titles, in speech or in writing (Proposal 5). Two paragraphs refer to movable or immovable *properties*, real estate, and bank accounts in their own name, for which it is recommended to put them under the name of the diocese or other social or charitable works (Proposal 3), to be managed, where possible, by commissions of laypeople (Proposal 4). Several other commitments talk about *social relations* with the rich and powerful (Proposals 6 and 7), with the poor and workers (Proposal 8) and the employees themselves (Proposal 12), giving priority only to the needy and those who dedicate their time to them, without affecting others. Regarding relations with *nonpersonal entities*, they propose to

a) "transform our work of welfare into in social works based on charity and justice," thus not merely welfare (Proposal 9);
b) "do everything possible so that those responsible for our *governments* and our *public services* establish and enforce the laws, social structures, and institutions, that are necessary for justice, equality, and the integral, harmonious development of the whole person and of all persons" to establish "a new social order" (Proposal 10);

c) implement *episcopal collegiality* "in jointly serving the two-thirds of humanity" both investing in poor nations, and trying to "request jointly, at the level of international organisms, the adoption of economic and cultural structures which, instead of producing poor nations in an ever richer world, make it possible for the poor majorities to free themselves from their wretchedness" (Proposal 11).

Although many of these concrete proposals are still valid for the reform of the Church today, the most essential element for this is the *spirit of evangelical dispossession* that permeates them and the attitude of *authority as service* that transpires from them. Any canonical rules or recommendations can reinforce this dynamism, but only the Spirit of God is able to transform hearts and habits, and thus renew structures.

In his treatise *De Consideratione,* St. Bernard contrasts Pope Eugenius III—a Cistercian monk like him—with his going "forth adorned with gold and surrounded by colorful array," to the appearance of St. Peter and St. Paul, thus refuting the objections of the palace environment in which he lived. Knowing well the fallacious criticisms of those whom he will then compare to wolves and scorpions, he writes to him saying,

> You see the entire zeal of the Church burn solely to protect its dignity. Everything is given to honor, little or nothing to sanctity. If, when circumstances require, you should try to act a little more humbly and to present yourself as more approachable, they say, "Heaven forbid! It is not fitting; it does not suit the times; it is unbecoming to your majesty; remember the position you hold."[15]

Bernard will then return to the example of St. Peter, "who is known never to have gone in procession adorned with either jewels or silk, covered with gold, carried on a white horse, attended by a knight or surrounded by clamoring servants....In this finery, you are the successor not of Peter, but of Constantine."[16]

Nonetheless, the saint concedes to the future blessed pope a certain conformity to the spirit of the times, adding, "I suggest that things must be allowed for the time being, but are not to be assumed as a right."[17] In our view, the reasons given by Bernard for refusing to place in such pomp the signs of reverence for authority and dignity remain valid. But, according to contemporary sensitivity, and what our times now require, from the Church is expected evangelical simplicity and pastoral charity, for it is the authority and dignity of the pastoral charity received as a gift from God who is love.

A CHURCH OF AND FOR THE POOR

A CHURCH "OF" THE POOR

According to Trigo, there are at least three possible interpretations for that expression used by Pope John XXIII and Cardinal Lercaro: (1) if, without being poor, the Church has the poor as the preferred recipients of her action; (2) if the poor feel "at home" in the Church; or (3) if, moreover, the poor are the active and privileged subjects of her life and mission,[18] that is, they are the heart, as it were, of the Church. The first interpretation must be excluded if we consider Francis's wish for a *poor* church, not only *for* the poor. The second, thank God, is already occurring, at least in most of the local and regional churches of the world: the Church is here a space that the poor can consider their own, along with those who are not poor. But we lack a true *spiritual, pastoral, and structural conversion* to the poor Christ and the poor, to implement the third one. One way to accomplish this is to take seriously—as Church as communion in the Spirit, an evangelizing community and institution—what the pope tells us in *EG*, immediately after expressing his wish:

> They [the poor] have much to teach us. Not only do they share in the *sensus fidei*, but in their difficulties they know the suffering Christ. We need to let ourselves be evangelized by them. The new evangelization is an invitation to acknowledge the saving power at work in their lives and to put them at the centre of the Church's pilgrim way. We are called to find Christ in them, to lend our voice to their causes, but also to be their friends, to

> listen to them, to speak for them and to embrace the mysterious wisdom which God wishes to share with us through them. (*EG* 198)

Worth noting here is the convergence with Trigo's third interpretation, indicating the poor as *subjects* of teaching, evangelization, and wisdom, and inviting us to "put them at the center of the Church's pilgrim way," in addition to "feel[ing] at home" (*EG* 198, 199, citing *NMI* 303).

AN ESSENTIAL DIMENSION OF EVANGELIZATION

The question of the option for the poor according to the gospel is intimately connected, from a theological, pastoral, and historical perspective, to the relationship between evangelization, on the one hand, and, on the other, justice in the world, liberation, development, and human promotion. The Synod of Bishops of 1971 taught that the fight for justice is *constitutive* of evangelization as mission of the Church. At that time, it was discussed whether it is an *essential* constitution or only an *integral* one, because if it is essential, without it there is *no* true evangelization. In *Evangelii Nuntiandi* Paul VI, even though he affirms the strong anthropological, theological, and eminently evangelical ties between both spheres (*EN* 21), does not define the question. But John Paul II, in his first encyclical *Redemptor Hominis* (*RH*) states,

> Inspired by eschatological faith, the Church considers an *essential, unbreakably united element of her mission* this solicitude for man, for his humanity, for the future of men on earth and therefore also for the course set for the whole of development and progress. (*RH* 15, emphasis added)

Thus, he provides the christological foundation: "She finds the principle of this solicitude in Jesus Christ himself, as the Gospels witness" (ibid.). Later he will use twice the adjective "essential" in *Centesimus Annus* (*CA* 5), referring to the social doctrine of the Church. Therefore, Francis makes Benedict XVI's words his own: "the service of charity is also a constituent element of the

Church's mission and an indispensable expression of her very being" (*EG* 179, citing the introduction to the *motu proprio Intima Ecclesiae Natura*); it includes charity in the "macro-relationships (social, economic and political ones)" (*EG* 205, citing *Caritas in Veritate* 2).

Without an integral element, for example, an eye, a leg, a hand, or all, I am still myself, because they are not essential, even though they are still very important to me; however, without my soul or my body I would not be myself. The same is true of evangelization: if it only encompasses the merely religious and cultic, without the social element, there is *no* evangelization, even if that element is not *the most* essential part of it.

The novelty of Pope Francis with respect to the earlier mentioned magisterium of his two predecessors—in my opinion, a novelty inspired by the Latin American reflection—probably lies in the fact that he talks very *matter of factly*, even if he does so *as pastor*, as Juan-Yves Calvez said about the pastoral work of the US bishops on the economy, who were concrete but *open* to changing their judgment and choice on debatable issues.[19] That same spirit moves Francis when he says,

> The Church's teachings concerning contingent situations are subject to new and further developments and can be open to discussion, yet we cannot help but be concrete—without presuming to enter into details—lest the great social principles remain mere generalities which challenge no one.... The Church's pastors, taking into account the contributions of the different sciences, have the right to offer opinions on all that affects people's lives....It is no longer possible to claim that religion should be restricted to the private sphere and that it exists only to prepare souls for heaven. We know that God wants his children to be happy in this world too. (*EG* 182)

Thus, it is a matter of drawing "practical conclusions, so that they 'will have greater impact on the complexities of current situations'" (ibid., citing the *Compendium of the Social Doctrine of the*

Church 9). From this position, the pope emphasizes the *public* character of religion—and not only Christian—stating,

> No one can demand that religion should be relegated to the inner sanctum of personal life, without influence on societal and national life, without concern for the soundness of civil institutions, without a right to offer an opinion on events affecting society. (*EG* 183)

Then Francis recalls the words of his predecessor, in *Deus Caritas Est,* when he states that justice is the main task of politics, but that "cannot and must not remain on the sidelines in the fight for justice" (28–30). However, "neither the Pope nor the Church have a monopoly on the interpretation of social realities or the proposal of solutions to contemporary problems" (*EG* 184). That is why Francis repeats the wise words of Paul VI, when he asserted in his letter *Octogesima Adveniens,* 4: "It is difficult for us to utter a unified message and to put forward a solution which has universal validity" because it "is up to the Christian communities to analyze with objectivity the situation which is proper to their own country" (*EG* 184). In fact, "It is not advisable for the Pope to take the place of local Bishops in the discernment of every issue which arises in their territory. In this sense, I am conscious of the need to promote a sound 'decentralization'" (16).

CHURCH "FOR" THE POOR AND SOCIAL INCLUSION

Chapter 4 of Francis's apostolic exhortation is like the positive side of the current crisis, because—as it says—today it is not just about exploitation, but *exclusion* of the "leftovers,"[20] of the "society's most neglected members" (*EG* 186): people, nations, and even continents. And their cries reach our Father in heaven (*EG* 187). The answer should range from "small daily acts of solidarity" to "working to eliminate the structural causes of poverty" (*EG* 188; see also 202), which is not only "loving attentiveness" (*EG* 199) but also political will (*EG* 205). Structures facilitate or hinder personal acts and cultural behaviors, and are the result of them as well.[21] In our present case, "a society becomes alienated when its forms of social organization, production and consumption make it more difficult to offer the gift of self and to establish solidarity between people" (*EG* 196, citing *Centesimus Annus* 41).

But it is not enough to change structures without culture. Therefore, solidarity, as a virtue of both people and cultures requires the following:

> The creation of a new mindset that thinks in terms of community and the priority of the life of all over the appropriation of goods by a few (*EG* 188).
>
> These convictions and habits of solidarity, when they are put into practice, open the way to other structural transformations and make them possible. Changing structures without generating new convictions and attitudes will only ensure that those same structures will become, sooner or later, corrupt, oppressive and ineffectual (*EG* 189).
>
> "A new political and economic mindset" (*EG* 205), contrary to "an individualistic, indifferent and self-centered mentality" (*EG* 208), allows for more humane structures. And these, in turn, confirm and facilitate "a way of living and thinking which is more humane, noble and fruitful, and which will bring dignity to their presence on this earth" (*EG* 208).
>
> Both the culture of solidarity with the poor and the structures that express and facilitate it have their solid foundation, above all in the example of the Lord: "Jesus taught us this way of looking at others by his words and his actions. So why cloud something so clear?" (*EG* 194). And the Scriptures and the fathers teach it, with a message "so clear and direct, so simple and eloquent, that no ecclesial interpretation has the right to relativize it" (*EG* 194).

Revelation and the tradition are the foundation of the social doctrine of the Church, particularly concerned with modern issues from Leo XIII onward. In fact, it recognizes

> the social function of property and the universal destination of goods are realities which come before private

> property. The private ownership of goods is justified by the need to protect and increase them, so that they can better serve the common good; for this reason, solidarity must be lived as the decision to restore to the poor what belongs to them. (*EG* 189)

These principles do not apply only to the poor in a specific society, but also to the poor people in the global world, since the Church also recognizes "the rights of peoples" (*EG* 190, citing the *Compendium of the Social Doctrine of the Church* 157). Thus, "with due respect for the autonomy and culture of every nation, we must never forget that the planet belongs to all mankind," and that "the mere fact that some people are born in places with fewer resources or less development does not justify the fact that they are living with less dignity" (*EG* 190).

In the next paragraph Francis refers to "the difficulties and sorrows of the Brazilian people, especially of those living in the barrios and the countryside—landless, homeless, lacking food and health care" (*EG* 191) and, later, "the option for those who are least, those whom society discards" (*EG* 195) as a sign of the gospel that must never be missing, faithful to the Pauline criterion to "not forget the poor" (*EG* 195). But that option ought to emerge from the depths of the heart, one moved by grace, since "the duty of hearing the cry of the poor when we are deeply moved by the suffering of others" (*EG* 193). Here the model of the incarnation ("we incarnate," *EG* 193) emerges again, brought to its logical conclusion of mercy in the most personal and intimate feelings.

However, the option for and with the poor is neither a pauperist ideology nor "unruly activism," but "loving attentiveness" that considers the other "in a certain sense as one with ourselves" (*EG* 199).[22] Therefore, this "entails appreciating the poor in their goodness, in their experience of life, in their culture, and in their ways of living the faith. True love is always contemplative" (*EG* 199).

POPULAR MOVEMENTS: A NEW SIGN OF THE TIMES[23]

The pope not only emphasizes the dignity of the poor, but knows how to read the signs of the times represented by the popular movements; he encourages and supports them as a way to implement the option for and with the poor, as they are "active collective subjects" (*EG* 122). When he received these groups on October 28, 2014, he confirmed and encouraged them by saying,

> You want to be protagonists. You get organized, study, work, issue demands and, above all, practice that very special solidarity that exists among those who suffer.... Solidarity...means fighting against the structural causes of poverty and inequality; of the lack of work, land and housing; and of the denial of social and labour rights. It means confronting the destructive effects of the empire of money: forced dislocation, painful emigration, human trafficking, drugs, war, violence.[24]

It is not only the suffering of the poor—the crucified of history—but also the glimpses of Easter that are *already* evident in their protagonism, their creativity, their active struggle for justice without violence and against the idolatry of money and, especially, in solidarity, because this means "thinking and acting in terms of community. It means that the lives of all take priority over the appropriation of goods by a few....Solidarity, understood in its deepest sense, is a way of making history, and this is what the popular movements are doing" (ibid.).

Trigo already said this when speaking about the culture of the neighborhoods where signs of life and unexpected human and Christian values shine and become tangible in contexts where only signs of death would be expected. In this way are manifested the novelty in history,[25] and "a way of making history," as referred to in the same text, by Francis.

Such solidarity, which creates history, is made possible when "*land, housing, and work*" are safeguarded as "sacred rights." That is how Francis praises farmers (in this same address) because they are "caring for the land, for cultivating it and for doing so in community" and recalls that "a house to be a home, it requires a community dimension, and this is the neighborhood...and it is precisely in the neighborhood where the great family of humanity begins to be built, starting from the most immediate instance, from living together with one's neighbors." Then he mentions that "settlements are blessed with a rich popular culture where public areas are not just transit corridors but an extension of the home, a place where bonds can be forged with neighbors," and says,

> So many of you who are excluded workers, the discards of this system, have been inventing your own work with materials that seemed to be devoid of further productive value....But with the craftsmanship God gave you, with your inventiveness, your solidarity, your community work, your popular economy, you have managed to succeed, you are succeeding....And let me tell you, besides work, this is poetry. I thank you.[26]

Moreover, this very meeting, supported and accompanied by the pope and the Church, is itself a sign of the times, an indicator of novelty, even of an alternative globalization. This is what Francis finds:

> I know that you are persons of different religions, trades, ideas, cultures, countries, continents. Here and now you are practicing the culture of encounter, so different from the xenophobia, discrimination and intolerance which we witness so often. Among the excluded, one finds an encounter of cultures where the aggregate does not wipe out the particularities. That is why I like the image of the polyhedron, a geometric figure with many different facets. The polyhedron reflects the confluence of all the partialities that in it keep their originality. Nothing is dissolved, nothing is destroyed, nothing is dominated, everything is integrated. Nowadays you too are looking for that synthesis between the local and the global.

In short, the recognition and support of organizations, struggles, and solidarity of the poor are part of Francis's wish for a poor Church for the poor. Just as he envisions for the poor—at a specifically Christian level—a key role in the new evangelization, he also expects them to show a historical protagonism in the creation of a more just, more fraternal, and more humane humanity in an alternative globalization. As for the question that each of the poor and the lesser ones pose, "What can I do?" the pope replies,

> [You] can do a lot....You, the lowly, the exploited, the poor and underprivileged, can do, and are doing, a lot. I would even say that the future of humanity is in great measure in your own hands, through your ability to organize and carry out creative alternatives, through your daily efforts to ensure the three "Ls"—do you agree?—(labor, lodging, land) and through your proactive participation in the great processes of change on the national, regional and global levels. Don't lose heart! (Second World Meeting of Popular Movements, July 9, 2015)

POPE FRANCIS'S NOES[27]

Francis's ability to "be practical, without overdoing" is even more incisive when he prophetically criticizes today's society, to the point that some have labeled him a Marxist and communist, although on this point he is simply continuing the traditional doctrine of the Church, especially of recent pontiffs. To be brief, I would like to recall his repeated noes regarding the social order, as Víctor Codina sums them up, and then discuss some of them. And today, after the encyclical *Laudato Si'* (*LS*), we must add his ecological "no!" in defense not only of nature, but of an integral ecology, which explicitly takes the poor into account.

> Let us say NO to an economy of exclusion and inequality, to an economy that kills, an economy without a human face; NO to an unjust social and economic system that crystallizes in unjust social structures; NO to a globalization of indifference; NO to the idolatry of money, or money that rules instead of serving; NO to inequality that breeds violence (may no one hide behind God to justify violence); NO to insensitivity that anesthetizes us to the suffering of others; NO to the arms race and the war industry; NO to trafficking of human beings; NO to any form of provoked death.[28]

Many of these challenges are condensed in the phrase "Inequity is the root of social ills" (*EG* 202), which in some languages, such as

English or German, was mistranslated as "inequality is the root…," while in Spanish the two terms are not equivalent, because *inequity* (*inequidad*) necessarily implies injustice in inequality, and injustice affects the poor more than poverty itself.

This same context has been misunderstood, as if the pope refuses free enterprise and the market economy. What he criticizes instead is "the *absolute* autonomy of markets and financial speculation" (*EG* 202, emphasis added).[29] He had earlier alluded to the "ideologies which defend the absolute autonomy of the marketplace and financial speculation" (*EG* 56), since these are *ideologies* that mask power relations, that is, the hegemony of capital over labor, already rejected by John Paul II in *Laborem Exercens* 13, and defined by him in his visit to Havana "capitalist neoliberalism." The market therefore, as a valid economic tool, is transformed into an end and, instead of being ethically, socially, and politically regulated in view of the common good, becomes *self-regulating*, thus opposing the approach advocated by John Paul II in *Centesimus Annus* 42,[30] so that all confidence is placed in "sacralized workings of the prevailing economic system" (*EG* 54). Even worse, what proliferates is the hegemony of finance over production, that is, over productive capital and labor.

Worth noting are the qualifying adjectives *absolute* and *sacralized*, since here lies the core of the pope's criticism. The same is said when he rejects not money as a means, but the "idolatry of money," "its dominion over ourselves and our societies," the "dictatorship of an impersonal economy lacking a truly human purpose," the creation of "new idols. The worship of the ancient golden calf" (*EG* 55), "the interests of a deified market, which become the only rule" (*EG* 56), thus uncover the anthropological and moral crisis underlying the current "worldwide crisis affecting finance and the economy" (*EG* 55). This same crisis corroborates what the pope has criticized, which already Pius XI and Paul VI had called "international imperialism of money,"[31] and that now, rather than improving, has worsened *culturally* through consumerism (see *EG* 60) and the "globalization of indifference" (*EG* 54). To this we should add the "debt and the accumulation of interest" that hinder the development of poor countries and "widespread corruption and self-serving tax evasion, which have taken on worldwide dimensions" (*EG* 56).

It is this system *currently and truly* in force, and not an economic theory, that Francis is referring to when he states that "such an economy kills" (*EG* 53) or "the socioeconomic system is unjust at its root" (*EG* 59). Further, Francis has referred to the "trickle-down theories," which have been heavily criticized, as "opinion, which has never been confirmed by the facts" (*EG* 54), providing examples to the contrary. I will not get into that discussion, as this case could fit within those expected when pastors speak of contingent things. What seems certain is that, although the situation of the poor has improved in some regions,[32] nevertheless (1) the gap between rich and poor and between rich and poor nations has increased, thus increasing "inequity… the root of all social ills" (*EG* 202)[33]; (2) the idols that the pope condemned are now materializing; and (3) in reality this economy ends up *excluding*, creating *leftovers and waste* and *killing*, both within the same poor countries and in the many migrants, displaced persons, and refugees. It is not the market economy as such, but an unbridled market that claims to be self-regulating, a hegemony—indeed political—of finance over production, of economic power over civil society and states, and the rule of private interests of the increasingly few over the common good of humanity as a whole and on nature.

*"CALLED TO CARE FOR THE VULNERABLE OF THE EARTH" (*EG *209)*

Under the concept of fragility, Pope Francis connects the poor, including the new forms of poverty, and "creation as a whole" (*EG* 215), now threatened both by the ruling technocratic model (see *LS* 101–14) and the alliance between the economy and technology (*LS* 53), which is imposed on the culture, politics, and economy. Almost every section of the new encyclical shows or presupposes a close relationship between the poor and nature, social ecology and ecology strictly speaking,[34] thus forming a very clear profile of an "integral ecology" (*LS* 137) that challenges not only the poor Church for the poor, but all humanity.

The Holy Father delves deep into the roots of that challenge, that is, all the way to the dominant cultural *model*. To this, and to the logic of instrumental reason (*LS* 108, 196, 210, 219) we must oppose—establishing a different understanding of nature, man, and their interrelation—a new "model" and another "mindset" (*LS* 196): that of gratitude, generosity, solidarity, and fraternity, which involves, on the one hand, changes "in lifestyles, models of production and consumption, and the established structures of power which today govern societies" (*LS* 5, citing *CA* 38) and, on the other, a new ethics, culture, and spirituality, with its own values, motivations, passion, and mysticism, that not only convince the mind, but deeply move the heart to convert and act.[35] All this is intimately connected with the "revolution of tenderness" which, somehow, the popular movements live and feel, and to whom Francis said,

> We are moved because "we have seen and heard" not a cold statistic but the pain of a suffering humanity, our own pain, our own flesh. This is something quite different than abstract theorizing or eloquent indignation. It moves us; it makes us attentive to others in an effort to move forward together. That emotion which turns into community action is not something which can be understood by reason alone: it has a surplus of meaning which only peoples understand, and it gives a special feel to genuine popular movements.[36]

In that same address at Santa Cruz de la Sierra, referring to the many forms of exclusion and injustice, Francis said that "an invisible thread" joins them because they "are part of a system which has become global," and which "has imposed the mentality of profit at any price, with no concern for social exclusion or the destruction of nature" (ibid.). Such statements recall what was said in *Laudato Si'* on the model that must change, as well as the mindset. Precisely the popular movements are already living that new mindset and are spreading the seeds of a new model.

To establish it requires a truly integral *ecological conversion* (*LS* 5, 217, etc.) not only individual but of a *community* (*LS* 219), toward the poor and the fragile nature, driven by the aforementioned mysticism. Its signs are peace and harmony with oneself, with others, with nature, and with God (*LS* 225–226). Such a conversion, which includes an effective option for the poor, moves us to become aware and to pay the current social and "ecological debt" (*LS* 51).

However, this is not only a question of *mere* needs and tasks for the future, because the emergence of a new cultural model and the beginning of a new mindset are already occurring in civil society and social movements. This is how we experience *realities* of the "quality of human life" (*LS* 147), of creativity and beauty, which imply *real possibilities* for better social and ecological cohabitation in a wider, even global, context. The pope does not hesitate to point them out, especially when it comes to the ecology of everyday life (see *LS* 147–55) and local examples (see *LS* 179, 232).

Such seeds of the future often arise among the poor (cf. *LS* 148, 149), among whom more easily are created "experience[s] of communal salvation" (*LS* 149). In fact, from "those seeds of hope patiently sown in the forgotten fringes of our planet, from those seedlings of a tenderness which struggles to grow amid the shadows of exclusion, great trees will spring up, great groves of hope to give oxygen to our world."[37] Those seeds show that another world is possible; for the believer they are signs of the renewing and reforming presence of the Spirit of Love.

FINAL REFLECTION OF PART 2: PARADOXICAL TENSION BETWEEN A *POOR* CHURCH AND A CHURCH *FOR* THE POOR

The pope's wish for a poor Church for the poor stems in fact from the intersection between the gospel read *sine glossa* and the current situation of a vast majority of the poor and excluded and the "common home" threatened in a globalized world. In that desire and pastoral and theological option there is in fact a "polarized tension," in some paradoxical and dialectical way, between wanting to be, on the one hand, a "*poor* Church" and on the other, to be "*for* the poor." In fact, to question and reverse the *structural* causes of an unjust poverty are needed both the moral, but also political *power*, in the noblest sense of the word, finalized for the common good—and the *goods* of this world, to help the poor in cases of urgency, and normally to promote and accompany their self-development, and to exercise their *advocacy* against the powerful of this world, moving these to a conversion to the poor, or at least a just understanding of their own long-term interests, which include the well-being of the poor today.

For those who are familiar with Ignatian spirituality, it would be a life-giving tension similar to that of those trying to live *subjectively* the third degree of humility in the total and radical imitation of the poor and humiliated Christ, in the *objective* use of the things of this world (even material goods, fame, and power) just *as much* as they are ordered to the greater glory and service of God, and, in our case, the greater good of the poor. All this seems to correspond to a *kenotic* and paschal ecclesiology, but realistic according to the model of the incarnation, which presupposes creation culminating in the resurrection.

I think that from this tension several traits and signs emerge. First of all is the spirit of the Beatitudes and the opening—"poor in spirit"—to God, which also includes the attitude of mercy and tenderness toward the poor as friends, the promotion of their dignity and their being subjects of history, culture, wisdom, spirituality, *sensus fidei* and, even more, of evangelization and historical praxis, the experience of profound solidarity with them, and the placing at their service of the goods and the potentials (of the Church), along with an inner disposition of simplicity and humility, which corresponds to a simple lifestyle (in the spirit of the *Pact of the Catacombs*). Both this practice of compassion and tenderness and the true signs of humility are criteria of discernment that prevent an ideological option for the poor, making it instead authentically evangelical.

Conclusion

The two points discussed in both sections of my contribution—inculturation and poverty—characterize not only the pastoral strategy, but also the theology of Pope Francis who, without being a theologian by training, continues to advance, compared with the previous magisterium, both issues on a theoretical level as well. As far as inculturation is concerned, its advancement is, in our view, brought about in his notion of evangelization *as* inculturation and the latter as *goal* of the evangelization of cultures. Such a notion is founded on the fact that grace presupposes culture (human and of every people) in its incarnated form, and is embedded in the understanding of the multifaceted face of the people of God and of the interculturality among peoples, based on the model of the polyhedron, in which find room both communion and the circumsession of irreconcilable differences.

As for the option for the poor, Francis understands it as a *theological* category—not just a philosophical, sociological, or political one—and not merely as a pastoral option, as it is *theological*, that is, of Christ as "merciful face of the Father"[38] and, therefore, of the preferential love of God for the poor, in the communion of the Spirit of love between them and for all, especially the most vulnerable, poor, and excluded, without forgetting our "Sister Mother Earth."

That is why the re-*form* of the Church, according to its trinitarian, incarnating, kenotic, and paschal con-*formation*, fundamentally requires both the inculturation of the gospel and the preferential option for the poor and the vulnerable, to reach the inculturation of the gospel itself in the culture of the poor.

NOTES

1. See my article: "L'inculturazione nell'*Evangelii Gaudium*: chiavi di lettura," in *Evangelii Gaudium: il testo ci interroga. Chiavi di lettura, testimonianze e prospettive*, ed. H. M. Yáñez (Rome: Gregorian and Biblical Press, 2014), 159–70.

2. See John Paul II, apostolic exhortation *Catechesi tradendae*, of October 16, 1979, no. 53; the pope himself had already used this neologism in his address to the Pontifical Biblical Commission (April 26, 1979) https://w2.vatican.va/content/john-paul-ii/en/speeches/1979/april/documents/hf_jp-ii_spe_19790426_pont-com-biblica.html.

3. See Benedict XVI, Discourse at the Fifth General Conference of the Bishops of Latin American and the Caribbean, May 13, 2007: (https://w2.vatican.va/content/benedict-xvi/en/speeches/2007/may/documents/hf_ben-xvi_spe_20070513_conference-aparecida.html).

4. On the theology of the people, see J. C. Scannone, "La teología argentina del pueblo," *Gregorianum* 96 (2015): 9–24; S. Politi, *Teología del pueblo. Una propuesta argentina a la teología latinoamericana 1967–1975* (Buenos Aires: Guadalupe, 1992); M. González, *Reflexión teológica en Argentina (1962–2010). Aportes para un mapa de sus relaciones y desafíos hacia el futuro* (Buenos Aires: Docencia, 2010). On the relation between the theology of the people and Francis, see our work: J. C. Scannone, *Le*

pape du peuple. Bergoglio raconté par son confrère théologien, jésuite et argentin. Entretiens avec Bernadette Sauvaget (Paris: Cerf, 2015), "Papa Francesco e la teologia del popolo," *La Civiltà Cattolica* (2014/I): 571–90, and "El papa Francisco, ¿teólogo del pueblo?" *Criterio* 2414 (2015): 44–47.

5. See J. M. Bergoglio, "Discurso inaugural," in *Evangelización de la cultura e inculturación del Evangelio* (Buenos Aires: Guadalupe, 1986), 15–19.

6. See my study: "La inculturación en el documento de Santo Domingo," *Stromata* 49 (1993): 29–53.

7. See P. Ricœur, "Civilisation universelle et cultures nationales," in *Histoire et vérité* (Paris: Seuil, 1964³), 286–300. Translated as *History and Truth* (Evanston, IL: Northwestern University Press, 2007).

8. See J. C. Scannone, "Lucio Gera: un teologo 'dal' popolo," *La Civiltà Cattolica* (2015/I): 539–52.

9. See Congregation for the Doctrine of Faith, Instruction *Libertatis Conscientia*, March 22, 1986, nos. 66ff. (EV 10, 119–239, at 195ff.).

10. See J. C. Scannone, "'Aus der Peripherie heraus kann man die Wirklichkeit besser erfassen'. Die Armen und die Gesellschaft in *Evangelii Gaudium*," in *Eine arme Kirche für die Armen. Theologische Bedeutung und praktische Konsequenzen*, ed. J. Gallegos Sánchez and M. Luber (Regensburg: Pustet, 2015). The whole book clarifies our theme; among others, we have taken special note of the work of Francisco de Aquino Júnior and Dirk Ansorge.

11. In his article, "Diez claves de la exhortación *Evangelii Gaudium*," in *Francisco: la alegría que brota del pueblo. Una reflexión compartida de Evangelii Gaudium*, ed. J. Benedetti et al. (Buenos Aires: Santa María, 2015), 139, Carlos María Galli links this paragraph to what was said at the Argentine episcopal conference in his *Líneas Pastorales para una Nueva Evangelización* (Buenos Aires: CEA, 1990), 32: "Before being a sociological, economic or ideological reality, the poor is primarily a theological reality."

12. See P. Trigo, "Una Iglesia pobre para los pobres. ¿Adónde nos lleva el sueño del papa Francisco?" *Revista Latinoamericana de Teología* 30 (2013): 247–62.

13. See P. Corbelli, "La 'Iglesia de los pobres' en el Concilio Vaticano II," *Revista Umbrales* (2010–2011): http://umbrales.edu.uy/articulos/pobres.php.

14. For the text of the *Pact of the Catacombs*, see X. Pikaza and J. Antunes da Silva, eds., *Una Iglesia pobre y al servicio de los pobres. Pacto de las Catacumbas* (Estella: Verbo Divino, 2015), but esp. C. M. Galli, "Los pobres en el corazón de Dios y del Pueblo de Dios. Del 'Pacto de las Catacumbas' a la *Evangelii gaudium* de Francisco," 259–96; see also

A. Zanotelli, *Soldi e Vangelo* (Bologna: EMI, 2013). English translation at http://religionnews.com/2015/11/03/the-catacombs-pact-emerges-after-50-years-and-pope-francis-gives-it-new-life/.

15. See Bernard of Clairvaux, *Cinco libros sobre la Consideración*, IV, 2, 5, in *Obras completas* II (Madrid: BAC, 1955), 638. Translated by John D. Anderson and Elizabeth T. Kennan as Bernard of Clairvaux, *Five Books on Consideration: Advice to a Pope* (Kalamazoo, MI: Cistercian Publications, 1976), 115.

16. Ibid., IV, 3, 6. English ed., 117.

17. Ibid.

18. See Trigo, "Una Iglesia pobre para los pobres." Uruguayan theologian Pablo Bonnavía also distinguishes a Church *for*, *with*, and *of* the poor, and in the third of these reflections he writes "what the poor do *in* and *for* the church" as "subjects of ecclesial configuration": see P. Bonnavía, "*Iglesia pobre, para los pobres y de los pobres*," in www.amerindiaenlared.org/biblioteca/7681/iglesia-pobre-para-los-pobres-y-de-los-pobres.

19. See United States Catholic Conference, *Economic Justice for All: Pastoral Letter on Catholic Social Teaching on the U.S. Economy* (Washington, DC: U.S. Catholic Conference, 1986).

20. The *Aparecida Document* 65 already stated that the "excluded are not simply 'exploited' but 'surplus' and 'disposable,'" on the initiative of the then Cardinal Bergoglio. English trans. at http://www.aecrc.org/documents/Aparecida-Concluding%20Document.pdf.

21. See John Paul II, encyclical letter *Sollicitudo Rei Socialis*, December 30, 1987, no. 36, which cites the apostolic exhortation *Reconciliatio et Paenitentia* (December 2, 1984), no. 16.

22. Citing here Thomas Aquinas, *Summa Theologiae* I–II, q. 27, a. 2.

23. On these movements, see J. C. Scannone, "El comunitarismo como alternativa viable," in *El futuro de la reflexión teológica en América Latina*, ed. L. Mendes de Almeida et al. (Bogotá: CELAM, 1996), 195–241. On Francis's meetings with the movements, see, for example, M. Czerny and P. Foglizzo, *The Strength of the Excluded: World Meeting of Popular Movements at the Vatican*, posted on January 29, 2015, http://www.thinkingfaith.org/articles/strength-excluded-world-meeting-popular-movements-vatican.

24. Francis, Address to the Participants in the World Meeting of Popular Movements, October 28, 2014: https://w2.vatican.va/content/francesco/en/speeches/2014/october/documents/papa-francesco_20141028_incontro-mondiale-movimenti-popolari.html

25. On the culture of the neighborhood, see P. Trigo, *La cultura del barrio* (Caracas: Universidad Católica Andrés Bello/Fundación Centro Gumilla, 2004); *Relaciones humanizadoras. Un imaginario alternativo*

(Santiago, Chile: Universidad Alberto Hurtado, 2013); on the concept of novelty in history, see *Creación e historia en el proceso de liberación* (Madrid: Paulinas, 1988).

26. Later in Bolivia, Francis will say, "You are social poets: creators of work, builders of housing, producers of food." See Second World Meeting of Popular Movements, July 9, 2015: http://w2.vatican.va/content/francesco/en/speeches/2015/july/documents/papa-francesco_20150709_bolivia-movimenti-popolari.html.

27. This is the title of an article by Víctor Codina, published in *Religión Digital*: http://amerindiaenlared.org/noticia/413/los-no-del-papa-francisco/.

28. See ibid.

29. On economic aspects in *Evangelii Gaudium*, see D. Alonso-Las Heras, "Evangelizzazione ed economia: denuncia e proposta," in Yáñez, *Evangelii Gaudium: il testo ci interroga*, 221–34; R. González Fabre, "Significados económicos en la *Evangelii Gaudium*," in Benedetti et al., *Francisco: la alegría que brota del pueblo*, 287–332.

30. Of the encyclical for the centenary of *Rerum Novarum*, see also no. 19; see also my article: "Economía de mercado y doctrina social de la Iglesia. Aporte teológico desde y para América Latina," *Medelllín* 85 (1996): 57–87.

31. Pius XI, encyclical letter *Quadragesimo anno*, May 15, 1931, no. 109; Paul VI, encyclical letter *Populorum Progressio*, March 26, 1967, no. 26.

32. See M. Novak, "A proposito di etica e capitalismo. *Evangelii Gaudium* secondo me," *I Martedí* 324 (2014): 30–35.

33. See T. Piketty, *Le capital au XXIe siècle* (Paris: Seuil, 2013). Translated by Arthur Goldhammer as *Capital in the Twenty-First Century* (Cambridge, MA: The Belknap Press of Harvard University Press, 2014).

34. Without any claim of exhaustiveness, see *LS* 6; 16; 20–22; 25; 29; 48; 64; 91; 108; 122; 137; 139; 141; 175; 190; 196; 198; 201; 214; 224; 232; 241; 243.

35. *LS* 216 speaks of a "spirituality," to "motivate us to a more passionate concern for the protection of our world," (see also *LS* 233). Ecological conversion—as well as the option for the poor—presupposes, then, an *affective* conversion such as the one theorized by Bernard Lonergan: see F. E. Crowe, ed., *A Third Collection: Papers by Bernard J. F. Lonergan, SJ*, (Mahwah, NJ: Paulist Press, 1985).

36. Pope Francis, Second World Meeting of Popular Movements.

37. See ibid.

38. See Francis, bull *Misericordiae Vultus*, April 11, 2015, no. 1.

24

"SO THAT BY HIS POVERTY YOU MIGHT BECOME RICH" (2 COR 8:9)

Diego Fares, SJ

The quotation from Paul—"though he was rich, yet for your sakes he became poor, so that by his poverty you might become rich" (2 Cor 8:9)[1]—is central to Francis's thought, his lifestyle, his gestures, and his way of governing. Paul draws inspiration from an attitude of solidarity—the churches of Macedonia have organized a collection to help the Corinthian church—to show that the essence of Christianity lies there. Paul points out that it was a grace given to them from the Lord: in fact, in the great test of affliction "their abundant joy and their extreme poverty have overflowed in a wealth of generosity on their part" (2 Cor 8:2). He points out that those brothers, "begging us earnestly," (8:4) "gave themselves first to the Lord and, by the will of God, to us" (8:5).

Bergoglio has always before his eyes the path of lowering himself, which the Lord has chosen to save us. We can discern it immediately in that phrase that came from his heart when he recounted his election as supreme pontiff: "How I would like a poor church for the poor." In *Evangelii Gaudium* Francis develops the theme:

> This is why I want a Church which is poor and for the poor. They have much to teach us. Not only do they share in the *sensus fidei*, but in their difficulties they know the suffering Christ. We need to let ourselves be evangelized by them. The new evangelization is an invitation to acknowledge the saving power at work in their lives and to put them at the centre of the Church's pilgrim way. We are called to find Christ in them, to lend our voice to their causes, but also to be their friends, to listen to them, to speak for them and to embrace the mysterious wisdom which God wishes to share with us through them. (*EG* 198)

In the previous chapter in this volume, Juan Carlos Scannone shows that in this desire of the pope there is a vital direction, a program that can be interpreted in various ways.[2] In dialogue with Scannone's text, we will focus on the light that the phrases of Paul and of the Holy Father shed on the topic of Church reform.

We do not consider poverty something that can be defined sociologically or by the cliché that it is "common knowledge," but we consider it in the mystery of its inner dynamism:[3] to become poor, for the Lord, is not a state or a condition that one reaches, but "his way," which impresses on all his actions the dynamism of those who lower themselves to raise others, those who by their poverty we become rich.

The stamp of poverty, which from the first moment of his papacy Francis has impressed on the life of the Church, has its own christological foundation in this way of being of the Lord.

The Value of Poverty in Jesuit Spirituality

As a Jesuit, Bergoglio has always seen and preached what St. Ignatius teaches: that poverty is a "wall" and the "mother" of consecrated life [4] (and of the life of the whole Church). It is a wall because it protects against the attacks of the devil, and a mother because it allows the Lord to act fruitfully in the littleness of his servants. To the professed of the Company, St. Ignatius asks that they promise to "do nothing to alter what in the Constitutions regards poverty, except to make it, rather, somewhat stricter" (Constitutions 553). The possibilities for the Jesuits to "reform" their own lives or the Society should increasingly shift toward greater poverty and to "abasement in all things with Christ."[5]

Faced with the choice of poverty and humiliation where an "equal glory of God" could be given—that is, where no duty is at stake—St. Ignatius cites the reason to "more closely resemble Christ": that is, choice is made out of free love conforming to the One who freely assumed our human condition.

From this spirituality of the *Exercises* comes Bergoglio's practical proposals, which follow the spirit of the XXXII General Congregation of the Jesuits regarding the issue of "walking patiently with the poor, learning from them." Pope Francis does not fail to insist that it is not only for justice and mercy that we must help the poor, but above all because we recognize their dignity and want to receive what they have to give and to teach us (*EG* 198). In fact, as the Chilean Jesuit St. Albert Hurtado said, "The sense of the poor is the essence of Christianity."[6]

Temptations against Poverty

In Ignatian discernment, poverty and humiliation are the key for spiritual things to "materialize."[7] This discernment is the instrument of Pope Francis's spiritual government and, in this regard, one of his writings, from when he was provincial of the Argentine Jesuits, can come to our aid.

Poverty, writes Bergoglio, saves us from "these desperate attitudes [that] follow the same steps of the anti-kingdom: they begin little inclined to poverty, go on to become vanity, and end up imbued with pride."[8] Poverty protects us from temptations of wealth, which can express themselves through temporal categories.

Compared to the future, temptation is a "wealth made of futurable things" and goes against that poverty that "puts hope in God alone." The futurable things give rise to a kind of sociology of possible futures from which the present of the Church becomes a battlefield around "disputed issues" which constitute a kind of wealth of what is negative, of complaint, and protest. Francis describes all this as a kind of Gnosticism, an enlightened and elitist Christianity that does not participate in the patient walk of the faithful people of God.

Compared to the past, the temptation is the richness of preserving what is already acquired, in which we place our security. It is the Pelagian proposal, as the pope refers to it, to restore past forms that today do not possess a culturally significant capacity.

Compared to the present (even the other two temptations are enacted in the present, but this one is more concrete today) the temptation is functionalist wealth: wealth of documents and plans; wealth of efficient management of things, goods, and money. It is a kind of "theology of prosperity" in the organization of pastoral work, as the pope said in Brazil.[9]

The Dynamics of Becoming Poor as a Synthesis of the Logic of Love

From the Lord's part, becoming poor to enrich us with his poverty is not a result—as the phrase "he became poor" might suggest—but the dynamism of his own daily way of loving us. The reason and desire—so we "might become rich"—gives a dynamic character to "becoming poor." Whenever the Lord wants to "gives and shares with the beloved what he possesses, or something of that which he has or is able to give" (*Sp. Ex.* 231), as St. Ignatius says in the *Contemplation to Attain the Love of God*, he does so in a way that follows the path of "lowering and emptying oneself." We see it throughout Jesus' life, but especially in his way of meeting the community as a poor nobody, with the appearance of an ordinary man, who asks for shelter in Emmaus and "something to eat" on the lake shore. In Jesus' "becoming poor" there is no measure except to give everything up to his life on the cross, to remain under the form of a renewed poverty in every Eucharist and tireless forgiveness of our sins, as the pope says.

We are even more surprised by the third element of Paul's phrase: the fact that he makes us rich "with *that* poverty."[10] Let us distinguish which poverty to which he alludes in this phrase: not any poverty, but the one with the dynamism that adapts to make the other rich. The richness of Christ, therefore, is not given to us and communicated as if it were a thing, but as a dynamism we can associate with, to enter and participate in. The Lord's commandment, "Love one another as I have loved you," can be read in this light: "Become poor to make others rich as I do." The example of the poor widow who gave the two small coins—all she had to live on that day—is not merely an edifying example. In the small daily gestures practiced by the little ones of the faithful people of God, the Lord can already see in action this dynamism of his love, and therefore rejoices in the fact that "the kingdom of God was revealed to little ones," as he said several times in the Gospels.

Thus, the step forward that Francis will take—or has already taken—in the direction of a so-called reform of the Church, can only go in the direction of "making us rich by his poverty."

Are we not intrigued by the indescribable joy that Pope Francis's small gestures of dispossession create in almost all of us? (*almost* all because there is always a Judas who complains bitterly when he sees someone breaking the jar of precious perfume). People realize that these are not gestures of personal asceticism, but gestures that enrich the people of God, embodied in each of those before whom the pope stoops to wash their feet, for example, or with whom he spends time by telephoning them. Every day the pope enriches the Church with his lowering gestures for love, which are increasingly becoming "bare," so to speak, and do not end up in the newspapers, as when he gave up the papal red slippers or chose to reside in the provisional lodgings at Casa Santa Marta. One must learn how to read them in small details: the way, for example, to ask for prayers for himself after the first Mass in Cuba: "Please"—and he dropped his arms—"*like a beggar* I ask that you pray for me." His requests to reporters incline the same way: "Please interpret it accurately, keeping in mind the context." Francis "impoverishes" a papal language that, by being infallible in every sentence, had become understandable only to specialists, to enter dialogue with people, confident in the fact that those who have good will "save the proposition of the neighbor," as recommended by St. Ignatius. Behind the blunt "I get this pope," said by ordinary people, is hidden the experience of having "become rich."

A perfect example is one of the interpretations that the Holy Father gave to this verse of Paul, in his message for Lent 2014, where he found that in that phrase there is God's style and logic, Jesus' way of loving us with "his 'poverty which is rich' and 'his splendor which is poor,'" which is "like a child who feels loved." Pope Francis said, "It is striking that the Apostle states that we were set free, not by Christ's riches but by his poverty. Yet Saint Paul is aware of the 'the unsearchable riches of Christ' (Eph 3:8), that he is 'heir of all things' (Heb 1:2)." And he went on, saying,

> This is no mere play on words or a catch phrase. Rather, *it sums up God's logic, the logic of love, the logic of the incarnation and the cross*. God did not let our salvation drop down from heaven, like someone who gives alms from their abundance out of a sense of altruism and piety. Christ's love is different! When Jesus stepped into the waters of the Jordan and was baptized by John the Baptist, he did so not because he was in need of repentance, or conversion; he did it *to be among people* who need forgiveness, among us sinners, and to take upon himself the burden of our sins.[11]

Through the dynamics of becoming poor, the Lord reforms (makes new) the way to love: in this style of his is synthesized the logic of love. Thus, the pope's interpretation brings us to the theme of "being amongst the people" as the concrete place where this logic becomes understandable and practicable, rather than just a pious recommendation.

Impoverishing Our Way of Living

The relational and inclusive character of evangelical poverty reforms our way of living: it leads us to be, as one among others, among the faithful people of God.

"Be in the midst of people" is another recurring expression of Francis. He said that for him to stay at Santa Marta was a matter of psychological health, because in the rooms of the Vatican Palace, which are like an "inverted funnel," he could not get into a spontaneous relationship with the people. Some interpret it as a somewhat extravagant and certainly transient choice. However, the faithful people of God of the ecclesial fold and even those of "other sheep folds" love this personal contact with the pope and seek it as if they had deeply desired it.

The Holy Father said to a group of new bishops,

> Now allow me to speak to you openly on several themes that are close to my heart. I feel the need to remind the Pastors of the Church of the inalienable bond between the steadfast presence of the Bishop and the growth of the flock. Every authentic reform of the Church of Christ begins with presence, that never-failing presence of Christ, but also from that of the Pastor who governs in the name of Christ. And this is not a pious recommendation. When the Pastor is remiss or unavailable, pastoral care and the salvation of souls are at stake (*De reformatione* Decree of the Council of Trent, IX). This was rightly said by the Council of Trent.[12]

The manner of being that Francis aims is "situated"—among people and "in human form" (Phil 2:7)—and involves the three "movements" that he always performs: to lower himself (bowing his head to receive the blessing), to go forth (toward the peripheries to include all), and from there, preach *a word* that focuses on Christ. These are pastoral gestures, not of a prince, and even less so of an official.

What do we want to show with this? That knowing how to position oneself transcends any structure, though some are more helpful than others. To position oneself is a *relational attitude* and it matters that the place and the approach, chosen carefully in every "situation," in fact, reveal the underlying attitude.

Therefore, the sequence of the Pauline message interpreted by Francis is this: no one can make another rich for love without becoming poor for love, and one cannot become poor lovingly except *amid the people* one loves, in the midst of the family, one's country, in the midst of the Church. Without this communal belonging, there is no evangelical poverty, but misery, exclusion. Even the most sublime asceticism, if practiced without reference to the social and communal dimension, becomes something "strange," as the gift of tongues of which Paul said were destined to remain incomprehensible if there was no one to translate them, and benefited only one, while the gifts of the Spirit are always for the common good.

The Lord's "being among people," therefore, is not a "expedient." It is not a "useful" good, but an "honest" one. It is the concrete way for the Word to be "incarnate," not only in a human nature, but in the culture of a people. Here we find the theological foundation of why the incarnation did not occur in an abstract nature, but in the culture of a concrete people. As *Evangelii Gaudium* states, "The human person is always situated in a culture: 'nature and culture are intimately linked (GS 53)' (*EG* 115). Just as the incarnation cannot "occur" in the abstract, but by enriching others in their concrete culture, in the same way the cultures that have been enriched with the gift of the gospel, thanks to all those who have become impoverished and inculturated in them, are transformed in sources of grace for themselves and for the other cultures to which they open. This is the wealth of the faithful people of God, its popular piety that has "received" the richness of the inculturated gospel and that in turn, by entering this dynamism, enriches and evangelizes itself in its children (*EG* 122, *DA* 264).

From "becoming poor to enrich with this poverty," seen as the very gospel, from its dynamic of inculturation, will flow the reflections on the reform of the Church, which will have to be "reform of the Churches," impoverishing abstract structures and strengthening those of each diocese and concrete parish. The "presence" of which the pope spoke about to the bishops is an *inculturated* presence and is translated for every pastor—priest, bishop, or pope—in his indissoluble bond with his flock, dodging the temptation of abstract ministries, of bishops without a people.[13]

Impoverishing the Receptacle

Since what make us rich is the Lord's "poverty," the gospel that he sends us to proclaim, the sacraments he left to us, and ecclesial government and management structures must share this style and this way of being of the Lord. They do not have to acquire the character of "riches" whose integrity, for example, must be preserved through an excessive concern to avoid a formal contamination. When the

Lord says that what defiles man does not come from outside but from within his heart and declares all foods to be whole, this "outside" and this "food" are not just things or a spatially defined place, but they speak of the dynamism of the Spirit that enters every life that approaches him, as the pope says, and gradually transforms it from within. The Spirit also disrupts traditions (e.g., circumcision) and the temporal order of events, as when Cornelius and his family receive the Spirit and then are baptized.

The receptacle of mercy, as the pope said recently, is sin. Yes, the receptacle of God's infinite mercy is poverty, the fragility of the clay pot, the illness of the sick, and the sin of sinners. The Lord has loved us as sinners.

And this sentence should not be read only in reference to the past. Speaking to the religious in Korea, Francis said,

> Through the evangelical counsel of poverty you are able to recognize God's mercy not only as a source of strength, but also as a treasure. It seems contradictory, but being poor means finding a treasure. Even when we are weary, we can offer him our hearts burdened by sin and weakness; at those times when we feel most helpless, we can reach out to Christ, "who made himself poor in order that we might become rich" (cf. 2 Cor 8:9). This fundamental need of ours to be forgiven and healed is itself a form of poverty which we must never lose sight of, no matter how many advances we make in virtue. It should also find concrete expression in your lifestyle, both as individuals and as communities.[14]

This dynamic of becoming poor to receive and to give cannot stop at packaged products,[15] namely those that the church administers, as if to say, The Lord's love is infinite, but I cannot give it to you except in this perfect mold in which it has been entrusted to me. The Lord has not given himself to us in any "perfect mold," but in his broken body and in his shed blood. Prefiguring that, Mary broke the jar of perfume and the fragrance spread throughout the whole house.

To carry one's most valuable good in "clay pots"; to turn water into wine using as container the basins used to wash dirty objects;

to say gently, "Neither do I condemn you" to the sinner caught in the act; to transform a circumstance of unjust division of family property, as the eldest son claimed, in a case of returning from death to life: herein lies the essence of Christianity. And it is urgent to escape forever the trap of the "perfect mold" by grace. The Sower sows in all types of soil; he does not remove the weeds; he goes in search of the lost sheep; he reclines at table with sinners; he heals on the sabbath; he goes out to hire workers until the eleventh hour, and invites everyone he meets on the road to his party.

To become poor—to the point of becoming sin—to give oneself is not an exception to the rule that may sometimes, only sometimes, occur, but rather it is the specific way to give oneself to save us—in the poverty of the flesh for the poverty of the flesh—that the Lord continuously does.

Impoverishing the Attitudes

In an informal interview, in which Pope Francis commented on some questions that had been submitted to him for a journalistic report, Fr. Antonio Spadaro made reference to one of them, asking Francis about the "orientation" he wanted to give to the Church. We were impressed by how the pope touched on this theme and he paused by putting a lot of emphasis in what he said, so much so that we still remember his words:

> There is nothing to re-orient. It is all about understanding where is the center,[16] to center on Christ. Anything that is not centered on Christ is *disorientation*. If we focus on Christ, the Holy Spirit leads the Church as He wants. And this is indeed what He does. The Church is fine. In the Church there is so much holiness! So many holy people....

He said this to us Jesuits at the two Masses he celebrated at the Church of the Gesù: "And if the God of surprises is not at the center, the Society becomes disorientated." The image that the Holy Father has in mind is that of Ignatius's first companions, Xavier and Faber:

> Faber experiences the desire to "allow Christ to occupy the centre of his heart" (*Memoriale*, 68). It is only possible to go to the limits of the world if we are centred in God! And Faber travelled without pause to the geographic frontiers, so much so that it was said of him: "it seems he was born not to stay put anywhere" (mi, *Epistolae* i, 362). Faber was consumed by the intense desire to communicate the Lord. If we do not have his same desire, then we need to pause in prayer, and, with silent fervour, ask the Lord, through the intercession of our brother Peter, to return and attract us: that fascination with the Lord that led Peter to such apostolic "folly."[17]

Thus, the abasement of oneself in the image of the Lord, who "emptied himself" of his divine status, does not exactly translate into a poverty of things, as in a poverty of oneself.[18] This means—adds Francis—"to not be centered on themselves, but to be centered on Christ," and this means "to be a person of incomplete thought, of open thought: because he thinks always looking to the horizon which is the ever greater glory of God, who ceaselessly surprises us. And this is the restlessness of our inner abyss. This holy and beautiful restlessness!"[19]

This incomplete thought speaks to us of an "incomplete form"—"there is no accomplished glory in this world," said the *gaucho priest* Jose Gabriel Brochero, who, stricken with leprosy wanted to die on the back of a mule—and, therefore, of an "incomplete reform." This incomplete form should not be interpreted with functionalist categories, as if improvising is better than planning. Incomplete thought is such *toward the horizon*, toward the ever-greater God, not in front of the immediate action in which it is defined and put into practice by mercy. Paradoxically, when our thinking impoverishes intellectual pretension—the desire to dominate ideal forms—opening to the God who will always be greater than anything one can think of, and then focusing on the concrete action of mercy that is in plain sight and can be achieved here and now, that same thought becomes extraordinarily creative and is capable of expressing real works of art, as we see in the institutions founded by the saints.

The Reform of Attitudes

Someone said that since man is a creature of habit, all in all, the saints are nothing more than people accustomed to doing good. In the life of the Spirit, reforms always take place in the free sphere of virtues and attitudes chosen freely and repeatedly. Therefore, Pope Francis insists that reform is first and foremost a "reform of attitudes" of a "Church who is Mother and Pastor."[20] When becoming poor is cultivated to receive grace, to enrich others, be among the people, and becomes a habitual, connatural attitude, we are not talking of accidental things, but of virtuous attitudes.

Let us reflect on one of Pope Francis's other favorite texts: chapter 2 of Paul's Letter to the Philippians. When Paul tells us, "Let the same mind be in you that was in Christ Jesus," he is referring to a very precise feeling, that of one

> who, though he was in the form of God,
> did not regard equality with God
> as something to be exploited,
> but emptied himself,
> taking the form of a slave,
> being born in human likeness.
> And being found in human form... (Phil 2:6–8)

It is this lowering movement made by the Lord to make the Father in turn enhance and attract all men to his love.

By reading this passage, if we focus on the word *form* and reading every word, so to speak, according to its "definition," it causes translations such as the Jerusalem Bible to include an infinite number of footnotes to say that "form" should not be understood as if Christ got rid of his nature. But if we look at Christ's feeling, the dynamics of his love, which is what Paul wants to express, everything is easier and is perfectly clear that the "something to be exploited" of Philippians 2:6 is an image that gives precision to that of "he became poor, so that by his poverty you might become rich" of Paul's Second Letter to the Corinthians. The dynamism of the "something to be exploited" is very expressive: it shows how wealth is achieved and maintained in a world where there is so much iniquity.

In the interpersonal language of love it is clear that those who, in the context of a relationship—friendship, couple, family, or social—"become impoverished" of something that they possessed as "their own," and who avoid turning into "something to be exploited," are enriched in sharing it with others. Love reveals that there is nothing that is not in common.

There occurs the fundamental reform of the human heart: in the experience of the joy of being poor, replacing the act of jealously guarding things with the one of giving or emptying oneself, as did the Christians of the churches of Macedonia.

The movement of Church reform, therefore, must strive to turn into a habitual reality this sentiment of spiritual poverty of Christ Jesus, who lowered himself to put himself in the hands of the Father and in ours, thus generating the movement of attraction of all the scattered children of God.

The Reform of Practices

The reform of attitudes, which summarize what we are by character, what has been given to us by grace, and the practice of a way of life chosen and cultivated in our lifetime, finds its source in the *Spiritual Exercises,* which aim at a reform of life that focuses us more and more on Christ.

It can be useful, since the word *reform* is historically characterized by the Protestant Reformation and the Catholic Counter Reformation, to go back briefly to the St. Ignatius's time and watch his companion St. Peter Faber with the eyes of a contemporary Jesuit, Michel de Certeau. De Certeau makes us contemplate Faber on a "shifting border,"[21] that of cities such as Mainz, Cologne, Speyer, and Worms, where in the years 1540–1542 Protestantism was gaining ground, but failed. He writes, "On this shifting border a daily drama takes place in which Favre is both actor and witness; every abandonment and every return is important. What is the process of these abandonments? How can one work to help these returns?" This is the point of view from which Faber considers the Protestant problem (or we could say of anyone who leaves the church). "When the heart stops being truly Catholic, the conduct quickly does the same, and soon after is the turn of thoughts: this is the process." Favre's discernment is mystical before being moral or theological (or sociological).

Three years later, Favre will propose to Diego Laínez a method of behaving with the separated brethren to bring them back to the Catholic faith. It is a method that follows the reverse path (compared to that of defection) and Favre expresses a suggestive thought: "Their evil does not lie in the first place or primarily in their intelligence, *but in the feet and hands of the soul and body*. It is necessary to start with those and then come to what may awaken good feelings, and finally arrive, soon after, to the righteousness of faith."[22]

Faber recounts in his *Memoriale* (218), "Then I noted and began to realize how those who abandon the Church begin by becoming more and more lukewarm in the performance of the works and practices which correspond to the graces and different gifts of God."[23]

Favre notes what happens in the hearts of those who leave the Church and aims at the heart to bring about its return. He does not linger on the effects of the moral disputes and theological justifications. He identifies the source of the problem in the "way they squander the gifts infused by the Spirit," in not recognizing as a gift of the Spirit the concrete blessings that each has received, which have been given to us to be put into practice.

This link between "the practices and works" and the Spirit is remarkable. Recognizing that we prayed with pleasure or performed a work of mercy with joy is a true grace of the Spirit; it is the basis of the Catholic experience of faith. Therefore, the people who to this day "perform works of mercy" in our charitable works, easily then acquire a taste for practices that the Church recommends and proposes, and they believe without difficulty the most difficult questions of faith. Pope Francis follows the same method when speaking of a new humanism consisting of "practicing the works of mercy and living the beatitudes." From this practice, from these "feet and hands of the soul and body" (works of spiritual and corporal mercy), then the reform of other aspects of the life of the church life emerges as well.

The key to Favre's vision, which de Certeau defines as mystical, lies in "recognizing that what is practiced is the *grace of the Spirit*." This is opposed to the idealistic thought that the Spirit gives ideal gifts, of which no one is ever worthy, and what in fact each practices is a kind of diluted version, moved more by one's own defects than by the Spirit. Those who practice little, feel that what they do is little, more sin or omission than merit. Those who focus on fulfillment think that all the credit is theirs. Grace is thought as in need of a "perfect mold" in which it must be poured. And all the theological discussion revolves around this ideal mold, while the love of God is poured into our hearts when we do what is good. The practices and concrete works that a Christian accomplishes are the grace of the Spirit. The fruits of the practices overflow from the "clay pot" through which they are accomplished.

The practices that the pope recommends and of which he himself gives an example go in this direction; they are easy to accomplish and bring immediate joy to the people: carry along a pocket-sized Gospel book, to pray for him and wish him well, visit the prisoners, greet friends, and so on.

To Become Poor as a Dynamic of Inculturation

The dynamic of becoming poor so that the Lord's poverty may enriches others is the very essence of what we call inculturation. "Inculturation" is not an expedient to let a gospel already given be accepted and understood; rather, the gospel itself is the inculturated word that continues to inculturate itself. What is specific of every culture, as Benedict XVI said at Aparecida, is to be "open, or better still, they are seeking an encounter with other cultures."[24] "Grace supposes culture, and God's gift becomes flesh in the culture of those who receive it." (*EG* 115). And cultures are the heart of every people.

In his 2015 speech to the religious movements, the pope gave us a very nice example of this lowering of oneself to enrich the other. Appealing to the hearts of his listeners, at one point he urged them, "Let us always have at heart the Virgin Mary," described as "a homeless mother," and added, "I pray that Our Lady of Mount Carmel, patroness of Bolivia, will allow this meeting of ours to be a leaven of change."[25] After that emotional moment, he concluded, "Apparently these priests talk a lot, don't they?" This ability to relativize himself and his speech, looking from the possible perspective of the less touched listener, reveals a pastoral desire. While delivering the most valuable message—the Virgin—he makes a step back culturally: he is no longer "the pope," but "a priest who talks too much," so that "his" Madonna can remain with the listeners.

A speech is "pastoral" when it inculturates to evangelize by using the cultural mediations of the other, when it is lowered so that the other, from his or her cultural space, chooses what to do of what is offered to him or her, and, as it were, "evangelize oneself." Or, better, so that the Spirit comes into direct contact with that person or group or people, without the preacher's culture becoming an obstacle, not because it is bad but because different. It is Paul's "become all things to all people." An example can be seen in the "concealment" of the pope's catechesis, to make room for the Virgin.

Horizon, Place of Action, and a Sense of Time in the Question of Reform

To conclude, we present some theoretical reflections of Bergoglio that can help us tune into his way of thinking. We use as a source a draft of the doctoral dissertation he was working on before he became bishop and that he would have titled *Cultural Mediation in Romano Guardini*.[26] Bergoglio described in it the categories of focus (or horizon), place, and time that he himself used as provincial in the opening of the XV Provincial Congregation of the Jesuits in Argentina (August 8, 1978).[27] These are the categories at stake when we talk about reform: the vast horizon to which incomplete thought opens; the concrete place from which one acts and where prudent decisions can be made; the sense of time; and so on.

Bergoglio was astonished by Romano Guardini's ability to "preach the *kerygma* by summoning Europe." He thought that this was because Guardini "chose cultural mediations well" and therefore wondered, "What awareness has Guardini of focus, place, and time?"

Of Guardini's focus, or horizon, what impressed Bergoglio was the sapiential aspect, "its structuring starting from the end as if it withdrew, pulled by the transcendent" (Augustine). The sapiential outlook placed on the end allows to "solve opposites at a higher level, without dissolving them. And not only in theory, but in time." The privileged expression of this area in Guardini is the work of art that becomes impoverished and "inserts the transcendent in the immanent, imitating reality in an understandable way for us."

Of place, which is "place from which to act," Bergoglio was struck by the prudent political character. "The place of action is defined from the concrete realization, the one which best allows (on the ground of the concrete 'possible') to reach the transcendent end." Here the work of art reappears. Bergoglio said,

> When the work of art is such, its realization has shaped something transcendent in a certain place, and that experience of something beautiful creates an appropriate horizon for understanding what is happening in the transmission of faith (which explains why we have the parables).

This "realization" and letting itself "be contained by what is small" of the place of action, is also a form of poverty.

As for time, Bergoglio's attention went to its special relationship with the will, in what it has of freedom, when its object is presented to it by Wisdom (not as a lesser will, dependent on impulses). Because introducing a sense of time into action requires not only conscience, but, above all, strength, fidelity, constancy. That is, time is structured according to the quality of its attachment to the good. The more universal it is, the better. The more the attachment is strong, stable, and durable, the better.

Thus Bergoglio concluded,

> The focus-place-time relationship is structural: they do not exist without each other. There is no place from which to act that does not have a horizon, by which the will infuses a sense of time in the action. There are no horizons that are not concretely at stake in the place of action in which we are tempted and in which God reveals himself.

First, let us emphasize this last consideration. While the "upward" relationship, so to speak, is commonly accepted, which recognizes the dependence of the place of action on a paradigm (horizon), it is not common to say that "there are no horizons (nor true paradigms)" without being "concretely at stake in the place of action in which we are tempted (abasement) and in which God reveals himself (incarnation)."

His advice comes to mind, to "always attack a 'no man's land' with one small step further." We could say that the contrast is between structures that create life (combining horizons, place of action, and sense of time), and no man's lands (of abstract paradigms, possession of spaces, and erratic or circular times), between the pastors of the people and abstract characters.

The other point to note is to "see the transcendent in the immanent." Bergoglio does not expect "perfect forms" (or rich) to "sow" the seed of the gospel. He trusts in his strength and in sowing in any soil, in life as it comes to him, where we are "tempted" and where God becomes incarnate.

Finally, his conception of time is a "non-theoretical" variable but of "practical love," where what matters is fortitude, perseverance, and loyalty.

From all this we can think that Francis will be (and is already) at work on reform in the concrete place of the action given to him, as situations will present to him;[28] that his horizon is not an ideal paradigm, but that of an already incarnate Christ, in whom it is a matter to be "centered" more and more. This was the meaning of his assertion that there is no need to "re-orient the Church," but rather to consider carefully where the Center is, to center on Christ so that the Spirit will lead the Church as he pleases; and that the sense of time that Francis wants to infuse in the reforms is that of "irreversible steps forward." Whether the steps that the Lord will grant him to take will be many or few, the desire is for them to be irreversible.

Wisdom is not a "meta-science," it is not the theory of a theory, but is tied to reality, incarnate, so to speak, to provide humble service to help solve real opposites on a higher level. Here, reform can be understood as creating horizons where "opposites are solved on a higher level," where the Spirit can harmonize differences, where structures do not imprison life. That is Wisdom and not theological ideology. This bond of Wisdom with concrete opposites is important because these vary according to time, place, and people, like St. Ignatius used to say. They vary in every culture. And the same goes in every horizon where "conflicts" emerge that seem to paralyze the action of the Spirit. At times, they are theoretical—ideological attitudes—but there are also practical ones, and here the time factor comes into play (what to do before or when to do or say something). And we can also add the conflicts concerning manners, style, literary genres. The reform, which aims to the end—the salvation of souls—is making its way amid all these conflicts and solves them at a higher level: that of "becoming poor like Christ so that by his poverty we may become rich."

NOTES

1. "Γινώσκετε γὰρ τὴν χάριν τοῦ Κυρίου ἡμῶν Ἰησοῦ Χριστοῦ, ὅτι δι᾽ ὑμᾶς ἐπτώχευσεν πλούσιος ὤν, ἵνα ὑμεῖς τῇ ἐκείνου πτωχείᾳ πλουτήσητε" (2 Cor 8:9).

2. See Scannone's chapter in this volume, 513–41, esp. 520–37.

3. See P. Gilbert, *Metafísica: La paciencia de ser* (Salamanca: Sígueme, 2008). Gilbert, following St. Thomas's *De veritate* 1, 1, says that the order of the transcendentals articulates "the kenotic movement of the *ens*," which determines itself as something (*res*) and becomes internal to *something other* (to the spirit, as a true-good-beautiful). We reflect on the Lord's poverty as "an act of becoming poor to enrich others," in harmony with the act through which each being comes to existence.

4. "In the consecrated life, poverty is both a 'wall' and a 'mother.' It is a 'wall' because it protects the consecrated life, a 'mother' because it helps it to grow and guides it along the right path." Address of Pope Francis at the Meeting with the Religious Communities of Korea at the Training Center "School of Love" in Kkottongnae, Saturday, August 16, 2014: http://w2.vatican.va/content/francesco/en/speeches/2014/august/documents/papa-francesco_20140816_corea-comunita-religiose.html.

5. Ignatius of Loyola, *Autograph Directories* of the Spiritual Exercises, 23.

6. See Fr. Alberto Hurtado's letter to Fr. Arturo Gaete (Santiago, Chile, January 1952), in *Cartas e informes del Padre Alberto Hurtado, SJ* (Santiago: Ediciones Universidad Católica de Chile, 2013), 315ff.

7. In the encyclical *Laudato Si'*, for example, when ecological issues susceptible to many opposing theoretical views are related to the life of the poor today, they acquire dramatic realism and urgency (see D. Fares, "Povertà e fragilità del Pianeta," *La Civiltà Cattolica* [2015/III]: 35–49).

8. J. M. Bergoglio, *Nel cuore di ogni padre. Alle radici della mia spiritualità* (Milan: Rizzoli, 2014), 111ff.

9. Pope Francis: Address to the Leadership of the Episcopal Conferences of Latin America during the General Coordination Meeting, Sumaré Study Center, Rio de Janeiro, Sunday, July 28, 2013: http://w2.vatican.va/content/francesco/en/speeches/2013/july/documents/papa-francesco_20130728_gmg-celam-rio.html.

10. The *eptócheusen* (he has become poor as a beggar) is like the *ekénōsen* (he has disavowed, abated, stripped himself) of Phil 2:7. Both have a permanent character in the "Word became flesh" of John 1. Christ, as he is still man and has our flesh (with its wounds), sits at the right of the Father as a poor beggar, "interceding" (begging) for us. His identification with the poor in history is real, not symbolic.

11. Pope Francis, Lenten Message, 2014, December 26, 2013: https://w2.vatican.va/content/francesco/en/messages/lent/documents/papa-francesco_20131226_messaggio-quaresima2014.html.

12. Address of Pope Francis to Bishops Appointed Over the Past Year, Clementine Hall, Thursday, September 18, 2014: http://w2.vatican.va/content/francesco/en/speeches/2014/september/documents/papa-francesco_20140918_nuovi-vescovi.html.

13. For this reason, he will give more authority to the bishops on issues such as those of declarations of nullity, thus diminishing administrative processes and the multiplying of interventions (see Pope Francis, *motu proprio Mitis et Misericors Iesu*, September 2015).

14. Pope Francis, Meeting with the Religious Communities of Korea, August 16, 2016: https://w2.vatican.va/content/francesco/en/speeches/2014/august/documents/papa-francesco_20140816_corea-comunita-religiose.html.

15. In dealing with the theme of grace, Cardinal Müller has highlighted the danger of limiting grace to a "created effect" and leaving aside "self-giving of God." The pneumatological foundation guarantees the primacy of God's self-giving and self-communication (*gratia increata*) with respect to the created effects of grace in man. From the ecclesial and sacramental point of view, grace takes place in the historical and eschatological space of God's kingdom that begins with the incarnation of God in his Son and by the sending of the Holy Spirit to the hearts of men (see Rom 5:5) (see G. L. Müller, *Dogmatica Cattolica* [Cinisello Balsamo: San Paolo, 1999], ch. 12, § III.12).

16. "Christ is at the centre, Christ is the centre. Christ is the centre of creation, Christ is the centre of his people and Christ is the centre of history....In him we are all one, one people, united with him and sharing a single journey, a single destiny. Only in him, in him as the centre, do we receive our identity as a people. Christ is *the centre of the history of humanity and also the centre of the history of every individual.* To him we can bring the joys and the hopes, the sorrows and troubles which are part of our lives. When Jesus is the centre, light shines even amid the darkest times of our lives; he gives us hope, as he does to the good thief in today's Gospel." (Holy Mass for the Conclusion of the Year of Faith on the Solemnity of Our Lord Jesus Christ, King of the Universe, Homily of Pope Francis, Saint Peter's Square, Sunday, November 24, 2013: https://w2.vatican.va/content/francesco/en/homilies/2013/documents/papa-francesco_20131124_conclusione-annus-fidei.html).

17. Holy Mass on the Liturgical Memorial of the Most Holy Name of Jesus, Homily of Pope Francis, Church of the Gesù, Rome, Friday, January 3, 2014: https://w2.vatican.va/content/francesco/en/homilies/2014/documents/papa-francesco_20140103_omelia-santissimo-nome-gesu.html.

18. "Our Jesuit coat of arms is a monogram bearing the acronym of '*Iesus Hominum Salvator*' (IHS)....And this brings us Jesuits and the whole Society to be 'off-centre', to stand before 'Christ ever greater', the '*Deus semper maior*', the '*intimior intimo meo*', who leads us continuously out of ourselves, leads us to a certain *kenosis*, 'to give up self love, self-seeking and self-interest'; (*EE*, 189)." Homily of Holy Father Francis on the Occasion of the Feast of Saint Ignatius, Church of the Gesù, Rome, Wednesday, July 31, 2013: http://w2.vatican.va/content/francesco/en/homilies/2013/documents/papa-francesco_20130731_omelia-sant-ignazio.html.

19. Ibid.

20. A. Spadaro, "Intervista a Papa Francesco," *La Civiltà Cattolica* [2013/III]: 462.

21. For the following, see P. Favre, *Mémorial*, trans. Michel de Certeau, SJ (Paris: Desclée de Brouwer, 1960), 70ff. For quotations from Favre's texts, see P. Favre, *Memorie spirituali* (Rome: La Civiltà Cattolica / Milan: Corriere della Sera, 2014). Translated by Edmond C. Murphy, SJ, as *The Spiritual Writings of Pierre Favre*, intr. by Edmond C. Murphy, SJ, and John W. Padberg, SJ (Saint Louis: The Institute of Jesuit Sources, 1996).

22. Ibid.

23. Ibid. English: *The Spiritual Writings of Pierre Favre*, 194.

24. Inaugural Session of the Fifth General Conference of the Bishops of Latin America and the Caribbean, Address of His Holiness Benedict XVI, Conference Hall, Shrine of Aparecida, Sunday, May 13, 2007:

http://w2.vatican.va/content/benedict-xvi/en/speeches/2007/may/documents/hf_ben-xvi_spe_20070513_conference-aparecida.html.

25. Second World Meeting of Popular Movements, Address of the Holy Father, Expo Feria Exhibition Centre, Santa Cruz de la Sierra (Bolivia), Thursday, July 9, 2015: http://w2.vatican.va/content/francesco/en/speeches/2015/july/documents/papa-francesco_20150709_bolivia-movimenti-popolari.html.

26. J. M. Bergoglio, *Personal Letter from Boppard*, August 20, 1986.

27. "The Jesuit thus has a focus, a horizon: the universality of his mission that as such draws individual elements into solidarity. He has a place from which he acts: that place defines him as a member of a body, and works, paradoxically, both centrifugally and centripetally (*communitas ad dispersionem*). He has a sense of time that energizes his activity. When the Jesuit has this focus, this place from which to act, this sense of history, then he is also allowing the initiating forces of the Society's Institute to pass through his heart. These forces give him a grounding, an identity, a sense of belonging." Jorge Mario Bergoglio, "Writings on Jesuit Spirituality," trans. and ed. by Philip Endean, SJ, *Studies in the Spirituality of Jesuits* 45, no. 3 (2013): 24.

28. At the question of journalist Juan de Lara, "What kind of reform do you have in mind, do you foresee the possibility of suppressing the IOR, the so-called Vatican Bank?" the pope replied, "The steps I have taken during these four and a half months come from two sources: the content of what had to be done, all of it, comes from the General Congregations of the Cardinals....the Commission of eight Cardinals...the maturing of the relationship between synodality and primacy....The second source has to do with present circumstances. I admit that it was no great effort for me, during the first month of the pontificate, to organize the Commission of the eight Cardinals, which is an initial step. The financial part I was planning to address next year, because it is not the most important thing that needed to be done. But the agenda changed on account of circumstances that you know about, that are in the public domain. Problems arose that had to be dealt with....That is to say, the economic problem was not on the agenda when it had to be addressed, but these things happen when you're in governance: you try to go in one direction, but then someone throws you a ball from another direction, and you have to bat it back. Isn't that the way it is? So, life is like that, but this too is part of the wonder of life." (Francis, Apostolic Journey to Rio De Janeiro, Press Conference during the Return Flight, Sunday July 28, 2013: https://w2.vatican.va/content/francesco/en/speeches/2013/july/documents/papa-francesco_20130728_gmg-conferenza-stampa.html).

25

REFORM AND INCULTURATION OF THE CHURCH IN EUROPE

Reevaluating an Announcement, Reconsidering a Model of Church, Facing a "Serious Case"

Serena Noceti

Yes, room for millions more I shall provide
Where, though not safe, men active-free abide.

(W. Goethe, *Faust* II, Act V)[1]

A Changed Context

"In these first two Christian millennia, countless peoples have received the grace of faith, brought it to flower in their daily lives and handed it on in the language of their own culture." (*EG* 116). Pope Francis's reflection on the challenges of inculturation assumes a peculiar sense in the European context, in comparison with the two-thousand-year history of a continent whose culture has developed in close connection with the Christian faith. Between the first and fifth centuries, Christianity articulated itself in a fruitful confrontation with the Hellenistic logos, developed in the Roman imperial society, assuming its organizational structure and assimilating in many respects its theological-political system, to unfold later in the Latin-Germanic and Slavic-Greek cultures. The political events and cultural evolution in the second millennium are also closely interrelated to ecclesial affairs and the understanding of Christian doctrine. These passages did not, however, take place without problematic aspects and configuring a model of Christianity that deeply linked faith and its ecclesial form to a sociopolitical structure and cultural vision of domination and power, and has been unable to deal adequately with alterity.[2] The history of the last century saw the emergence of deep contradictions, first in the massacre of a war fought among Christian nations between 1914 and 1918 (which led to the condemnation of war as a "useless slaughter" by Benedict XV), then in the tragedy of World War II and the *shô'âh*. Auschwitz remains an open question and a perpetual warning in the heart of the events of Christian Europe.

The reference to Christian identity has therefore marked for centuries all the expressions of family, social, and cultural life, from the political to the legal sphere, from religious meaning to philosophy. The symbolic structures and linguistic-conceptual codes that characterize European man's identity are still inspired by it today (consider the idea of person, of historical consciousness, of the value of individual freedom).[3] However, we should not underestimate the contradictions in the reception of the gospel in Europe and the limits of the historical models of "Christianities" that have arisen over the centuries.

In recent decades, the cultural scenario has been further transformed and there is an urgent need to (re)understand and proclaim the gospel of Jesus in a significant manner, in the face of new paradigms of the interpretation of humanity and social life, with those anthropological, soteriological, and social identification models that are widespread in this era of late modernity (or postmodernity). The factors at work in this complex transition that is changing the face of Europe are innumerable. To offer here a comprehensive review of them, as well as examine in depth the sociocultural changes that have taken place in the last decades, appears impossible: suffice here to mention the revolution of 1968, the fall of the communist regimes, the European Union project and its current crisis caused by monetary and financial policies, the armed conflict in the Balkans, the shift of the geopolitical balance, the recent economic crisis, the emergence of neoliberal models that deconstruct the European model of universal welfare, the growing phenomenon of migration, the growth—in the last decades—of a multicultural and multireligious society, and the surge of localist identity movements and xenophobic tendencies.[4]

From a socioreligious point of view, studies reveal profound change taking place, which invests both individual practices and self-awareness, and the forms of the presence of the churches in the public sphere.[5] In all European countries, albeit in different ways due to historical events and confessional forms, the decline of the *societas Christiana* is evident, along with the rapid and irreversible development of secularization processes.[6] The number of practitioners is in decline, while the number of those who claim to be Christian remains high; traditional practices are abandoned, even though there is still a connection with churches for life-passage rituals; religious behaviors are increasingly individualized and privatized, and ethical choices are decided autonomously and in personalized ways, regardless of one's denominational affiliations; the indifference for otherworldly matters goes hand in hand with the search for new forms of religion and the development of fundamentalisms and radical forms of belief. Religious institutions have lost their power to lead with a general code of meaning and to define recognized social customs; secularization combines an unprecedented set of religious systems in society (which claims its autonomy) with the recomposition of new forms of religious representation (personal).[7]

This complex process takes place in the context of a late modern *mens* and the horizon of a cultural, even more than economical, globalization.[8] The primacy of instrumental, scientific-technological reason; the exaltation of the individual subject and his or her freedom and independence; the disillusionment of the world; the end of metanarratives; the experience of permanent change; the widespread satisfaction of basic needs: these are only some of the prospective elements around which the question of human identity and the sense of reality is articulated today. Europe has become a multicultural and plurireligious society, in which, however, the contradiction between the proclaimed and announced principles as universal rights and their negation in practice increasingly appears.[9] If for centuries, Europe lived in a regime of Christianity, the migratory phenomenon—a true sign of the times for the European *Church*—and the spread of a secularized *mens* have interrupted this union (if not symbiosis) of Christianity and social belonging, and involve a redefinition of Christianity at the beginning of the twenty-first century, in line with convivial hospitality,[10] secularism, and dialogue in the plurality of languages.

Proclaiming the Gospel of Jesus in Europe Today

Therefore, the challenge of inculturation urges Europe, in view of a new understanding of the gospel and of the emerging of new historical models of Christians and churches, in the awareness that thinking of the relationship between the gospel and Europe involves seeing how a continent can find itself in a critical relationship with its roots and its future.[11] The acceptance of the gospel by European men and women involves re-exploring symbolic resources already delivered and known by many, critically revisiting the organizational structures and public presence of the Catholic Church, re-articulating a faith and doctrine that have been transmitted in Hellenistic-Latin inculturated form, rethinking the ritual forms and languages of the widespread religious experience received from past experience and considered inadequate today. This is in the acute awareness, on the one hand, that this cannot ignore tradition (it is a question of critically recovering a cultural heritage), and, on the other, that we live in a posttraditional society, in which the dynamics of the transmission of collective memory among generations has failed.[12]

In recent decades, there has been a strong investment by the Catholic hierarchy in the public sphere, driven by the desire to regain a visibility with which to offer a meaningful interpretation of the human and a clear statement of values considered "non-negotiable."[13] There have been countless stances of bishops or episcopal conferences, with interventions in the media, or through mediations that provide political influence on issues of social relevance: in past decades, issues dealing with bioethics and secularism; today, social moral issues (justice, individual rights, migration). This form of presence has always been coupled with the competent and widespread task of interpreting reality, condemnation, the active presence on the ground facing emerging forms of poverty carried out by Caritas and Catholic organizations operating in the line of promotion and cultural education, rights protection, social integration, effective assistance, and response to people's needs. They have conveyed an effective testimony to the core of the Christian faith and guaranteed the permanence in the public view of a Church capable of putting in practice evangelical charity and solidarity.

The commitment to collective action in the public sphere and the importance of strong condemnation of what prevents the path of full humanization, justice, and peace, are unlikely to be underestimated regarding the gospel proclamation,[14] but the strategies geared toward the recovery of a public prominence have proved fruitless in many aspects. As Church, it primarily means accepting the fact of being only one speaker among others in the public *agora*, accepting the logic of creating consensus in a democratic context, in the perspective of a secularism that has a public word to offer, but without imposition and pretense of privileged channels. It means becoming capable of rationally motivating the choices made for the good of all, the appeals to "values," and the demands for changes at the legislative level.[15] Even more deeply, what is felt is the urgency of an overall rethinking of the dynamics of gospel proclamation that is meaningful to European men and women, one that can regenerate the drained ecclesial body.[16]

The widespread demand for identity and fulfillment, as well as the perception of fragility and the search for greater security in times of crisis, suggest that the evangelical proposal be correlated with the "soteriological" patterns spread in the European cultural context, the gift of divine life in Christ in relation to the desires of salvation, to the subjects and contexts in which this salvation is sought and built. It is a matter of developing lines of thought on existence that can bring out, in accordance with biblical wisdom literature, the depth of "salvation" present in some spaces and forms of the human being, favoring their interpretation in the light of the christological event, deconstructing the claims of self-affirmation, to announce—even in an alternative key and critical instance—the horizons of the promise of the kingdom of God. In term of content, four points seem relevant today: the question about/on power and its limits, questions that economics and technology carry along with them today; the confrontation with alterity and the relationship with the other as space of humanization;[17] the narration of future visions related to the "social us," which allow and motivate a common path (at the European level and in different national or local contexts); the theme of justice and civil and social rights, on the basis of the recognition of each person's dignity, as belonging to the one human family, and the common responsibility for Mother Earth. As J. B. Metz writes, Christians must reaffirm "the unconditional recognition of a very specific authority: the authority of the those who suffer....It is on this basis that Christianity could and should come into play in the debate about a new morality, bringing its sensitivity to suffering and its vision of justice."[18]

A proclamation of faith with a strong christological focus, rooted in the person and story of Jesus of Nazareth, the Prophet of the kingdom and "defeated Messiah," can show what is the true fulfillment of the human being and together offer a critical breakdown of the models of individual realization (narcissistic, and of the neoliberal type) predominant today.

Such an inculturated hermeneutics of the gospel necessitates restructuring religious language (verbal and nonverbal), a greater space for the emotional, mystical, aesthetic dimension (for example, with a stronger appreciation of the artistic heritage, an expression of Christian faith over the centuries), and above all rethinking liturgical forms. These are all instances in which distance from the languages of contemporary communication seems most palpable.[19]

The Question about the Institutional Form of the Church and Its Necessary Reform

However, the discussion of the socioreligious transformations taking place in Europe shows that it is not enough to merely rethink the content and forms of communication of the faith, without questioning the collective subject "Church," the ability to correlate differently the necessary institutional dimension, and the choices of faith and of belonging of the individual. It is not only a matter of proposing the Christian faith in beliefs, expressions, and practices that are more most appropriate to contemporary feelings, and understanding through these languages forgotten or unedited features of the gospel. But what is at stake is the ability to share the faith and convey it to the new generations.[20] The inculturation of faith in Europe entails opening sites for ecclesial reform.

The reform processes of complex, heterogeneous institutions (such as the Catholic Church) always take place in the interaction of three interconnected levels: the maturation of the content of collective consciousness (and its categorization); the change in the form of social life and in relational dynamics; and the reform of participatory, decision-making, organizational structures. In fact, a given content of collective consciousness is conveyed and made true by a given relational form and from a given structure. Transmission and learning processes are undoubtedly fundamental, but intellectual formation is not enough: there must be change in relational dynamics and the institutionalization of these relationships, in the awareness that reforms always start from the interface of problems between beliefs and practices, and that only a transformation in terms of the level of the collective structure can adequately support a change in self-awareness.[21] The characteristic features of the current European culture and the explicit demands for reform that have emerged in recent years from the "base" bring out two points from which to think of a transformation of the *forma ecclesiae*: the model of parish and subjectivity of women.

For a Participatory and Responsible Ecclesial Form

The question about the processes of inculturation of the Church in Europe involves first the awareness of having to rethink the Tridentine parish model, which—even after Vatican II—is still there to qualify the collective consciousness (of the practitioners and of the public opinion) and represents the basic reference point. The ecclesial participation and the existential reference to the Christian experience (particularly in life passages), in fact, still happens for the most of the faithful in the parishes. On the other hand, parish life is at the crossroads of those spaces in which change must be developed for a posttraditional and secularized sociocultural context such as the European one: between the institutional moment (whose memory is kept in the generational cycles) and the free choice of the adult; between personal experience of faith and recognition of belonging to the community of believers, in its form of people.

The Tridentine model of the parish was functional to a defined, organic, stable social system,[22] whose pastoral proposal was articulated in the perspective of sacramentalization and care of souls, for those who—in a prevalent infant baptism regime and religious socialization in infancy—developed a traditional membership that guaranteed "social identity." It was a model conceived according to a "closed-system" logic to order and give (or maintain) meaning to the existent, with stable roles and functions, with a continuity in time that was ensured by the application of consolidated procedures and the transmission of a doctrine of established truth. This model of parish was structured in the context of a universalistic ecclesiology, based on the principle of delegated authority (with the parish priest at the center), and with substantially unidirectional communicative dynamics: from those who know to those who do not, from those who can to those who cannot, from clergy to laity, from adult to child.

The cultural and ecclesiological inadequacy of this *Church* model is evident. The contrast is in the first place with some of the features that characterize today's European culture: urbanization and diffusion of an urbanized *mens* (with the changing pace of life, ease of movement, pluralization and differentiation of spaces of existence, change in the form of social relations); the de facto cultural pluralism, recognized as a de jure value; mass education; the emergence of "second secularization" phenomena (Charles Taylor), with the idea of free choice on the part of the individual of forms of belief;[23] the assumption of a democratic-participatory *mens* and intolerance for any reduction to "subject";[24] the suspicion and distrust of institutions, especially those that claim to act as all-encompassing and absolute on the place of meaning; and the crisis of the principle of tradition.[25]

The distance from the ecclesiological vision of Vatican II is also evident. The founding principle of the Church is in evangelization and in eucharistic celebration in line with *participatio activa* (active participation); the recognized subjectivity of the laity is a key point for rethinking the ecclesial dynamics; all the baptized are called to be active in evangelization; the communal form implies multidirectional communicative dynamics, though with a specific role of ordained ministers in the authoritative interpretation of the gospel (cf. *LG* 12; *DV* 8). The Council's reception has evidently tackled the "parish" issue—at the level of practice, theology, and magisterial hermeneutics—but what is missing is a radical revision of the form: today we face, in the end, a "revised Tridentine model." The novelty represented by the lay movements is undoubtedly relevant, especially for the possibility of formation of the laity; for the relationships and active participation they sustain, we underestimate the fact that movements have largely helped to maintain a unidirectional form of communication (from the center to the periphery) and a precedence of a universalistic perspective at the expense of local churches.[26] In addition, in their profession of faith and in their form of belonging, they define themselves along homogeneous lines, thus losing sight of that dimension of the people that is heterogeneous and pluralistic in terms of culture, age, spirituality, and so on, that the Council provides in the second chapter of *Lumen Gentium*.

If the parish "model" is necessary and still significant for its ability to correlate—from its very origins—the triad "gospel, territory, eucharistic celebration," the Tridentine model must be overcome with determination and a new "form" of parish must be reformulated, as the fruit of an inculturation of Church in the forms of participation and organization of the European social bodies that in recent decades have changed.

In particular, the paths of reform should do the following:

1. Rethink the life of the parish in the horizon of the local Church, with the development of pastoral proposals that look to the city or to portions of territory larger than the parish, and are more responsive to the needs and social dynamics within the territory.
2. Recognize forms of belonging, beyond the primary criterion of the simple residential address, to open, in respect of the freedom of choice of the individual, to the idea of a "declaration of belonging" to a parish community, in which to live permanently in formation, dynamics of participation decision, ministry, and Eucharist.
3. Redefine the pastoral agenda with a priority given to adult education (biblical), not oriented to the practitioner, as in the Tridentine model, but to the adults who are capable of critically thinking and of explaining the reasons for their faith.[27]
4. Adjust to a presence and action of the parish on the ground that is informed and incisive, combining gospel, experience of charity, and visibility of an "alternative community," which is capable of proactively attesting the logic of participation and inclusion. The support for diaconal figures, little appreciated in the postconciliar period, is essential at this level.
5. Promote and secure multidirectional communication spaces for the parish to become a "hermeneutic community," able to read and understand the gospel in the today of history, thanks also to the contribution of speech, experience, and skills of the laity. A new image of the parish involves a complete rethinking of the priests' activities and forms of the ministry, as well as a radical revision of the initial and permanent formation of the clergy.

Women: An "Emergency Case" for the Inculturation of the Church in Europe

A second path for change may come from the recognition of women as subjects in their own right in the Church. This is certainly an "emergency case" for the reception of Vatican II ecclesiology and the future of the Church in Europe.[28] In little more than a century, women's living conditions of in the West have radically changed, with a process of emancipation and equality recognition in terms of civil rights, access to education, professions, and active politics, which has transformed the face of society, the relational dynamics between men and women, and the patterns of family life.[29] After centuries of marginalization, of underestimation on the anthropological level, subordination, and minority status, women have become aware of their dignity and their role. They are recognized as subjects in the public sphere,[30] beyond the confines of the home and family where they carried out their unique role throughout history. A "successful revolution," as Luce Irigaray called it,[31] which questions the Christian faith: many of the open questions of the cultural debate in Europe today are directly related to the feminine condition (the relationship between nature and culture; corporeality and life; freedom as self-determination; and the relationship between justice and rights) and the recognition of women's subjectivity is one of the most delicate challenges facing different religions and cultures.

The transformation that took place on the cultural, social, and political level also touched the Catholic Church profoundly. Vatican II even in this sense represents a watershed moment: the topic is addressed in some few, rapid passages in the conciliar documents, but the conditions for new spaces of presence and speech for women in the Church are emerging in the recovery of the subjectivity and ministry of the laity, in the opportunities for access to biblical and theological studies, in the different consideration of the Church-world relationship.[32] In the postconciliar period, the public and authoritative voice of women has risen, with the development of innumerable forms of concrete ministry, the maturation of a unique theological reflection, and a strong involvement in the life of the dioceses and lay movements.[33]

Fifty years after the conclusion of the Council, the "female question" is a key link for a renewed inculturation of the Catholic Church in Europe today, which remains a topic for certain aspects removed or underestimated; many men and women complain about the anachronism of ecclesial positions, the distance (not to say the contradiction) of the present model of Church from the inclusive logic of the gospel and the life of the first communities; as well as the delay, slowness, and resistance with which these issues are handled.

Anthropological questions and demands of ecclesial reform define the crossroads we are in today. The transformations that have taken place and the reflection of women have highlighted the androcentric perspective that has marked Western culture (philosophy and theology) and have questioned a widespread anthropological vision that—perhaps unconsciously—has thought the human (*ánthrōpos, homo*) from a universalized masculine and the feminine as a secondary act of specification of this "neutral (allegedly) human."[34] *Mulieris Dignitatem* represented a first significant approach to women's issues, with an anthropological reflection on the reciprocity of the sexes, but the document refers to the female Marian archetype of wife and mother, of which today we undoubtedly grasp the partiality and cultural debt.[35] The philosophy of difference[36] and the social sciences, with the analytical-critical use of gender categories (in the sense of cultural, linguistic, symbolic interpretation of the gender difference), while revealing the processes of building and maintaining the subordinating differences and secular stereotypes, call for the overcoming of the consideration of the "feminine" and "woman" in absolute terms and according to a perspective of an ahistorical "nature," as well as to think—in a correlative and contemporary way—the identity of "men and women."[37] In some contexts a new approach to feminine/feminist thought is emerging, more attentive to existential paths and the maternal theme; many young women consider concluded the phase of struggle for equality (or expansion) of their rights and strive to highlight what distinguishes men and women, based on style, priorities, sensitivity, and psychological characteristics. Theological reflection and magisterial hermeneutics have responded inadequately to this paradigm shift. The suspicion toward feminism, the preference for thinkers whose approach to the theory of difference is mainly essentialist, the absence of reflection on masculinity, the failure to require policies aimed at greater coresponsibility of fathers in family life and child care, are just as revealing elements of the distance and limited awareness (particularly of the hierarchy) of the profound transformations that have occurred.

The question then arises at the ecclesiological and ecclesial level. Those "mystical demarcation lines" between men and women—as Virginia Woolf called them—establishing our ecclesial identity have shifted and have been reshaped. We must become aware of what remains largely unstated: the Church, like all institutions, is sex-gender oriented and contributes (with its symbolic system, roles and functions, and practices) to maintaining the system of interpretation of sexual/gender difference and male-female relational models. A patriarchal vision marks a part of the clergy at the level of instinctive consciousness and manifests itself in language, in liturgical symbolism, and ecclesial life. Women are regulated under a chapter of an "obvious, loyal, helpful presence," even though sociological research is showing a growing distancing from the Church specifically of girls and mature women. The "glass ceiling," that is, the discrimination in the advancement of one's "career" seems unreachable: few women can participate in strategic decision-making processes and, in any case without a vote of deliberation; women's demand for greater space in the participation and decision-making bodies is too easily labeled as "claiming power"; the ministries truly exercised by women go rarely beyond the traditional fields of care and education.[38] The public word in proclaiming the gospel and service to the Christian community, as in the preservation of the apostolic faith, is conveyed only by men, since all three of the ranks of the ordained ministry are exercised only by men.

The eruption of the "forgotten partner" (Elisabeth Schüssler-Fiorenza) in society urges a rethinking of the entire ecclesial form (functions, relationships, roles), while providing new perspectives in understanding the gospel and the ecclesial tradition. To be a Church in Europe, starting from a gospel message more deeply understood through one of the languages of our time (*GS* 44), that is, thanks to the words of women's self-awareness, demands facing boldly the question of women's rights, that is, their "right to speak," the recognition of their role, and of adequate conditions so that this exercise of an authoritative, public word, relevant for the edification of the Church, is made possible.

If in the first postconciliar phase the attention was focused on the level of ecclesial transformations necessary for a stronger presence of women, and if from the nineties onward, the "feminine question" was addressed in anthropological terms (though isolating it from an overall rethinking of the thought of and on the *ánthrōpos*), today it seems necessary to correlate the two perspectives and broaden the question of how to be a "Church of women *and men*."

For a reform at this level, I suggest four possible steps:

1. A review of the studies of theological anthropology, with a reflection on the "repressed" theme (because identified with the human *tout court*) of masculinity;[39] without this step, reflection on women will remain partial, a secondary undertaking after a reflection on the human in itself, and changes at the level of mentality will remain limited.
2. The celebration of a "women's synod for women," at the level of local churches and the European Church, so that a free and frank dialogue, in the plurality of positions, would favor a clearer recognition of the challenges women face today in Europe and would also allow recognition—even as Church—of the unique contribution that women can offer.
3. The professional involvement of women in pastoral offices at the diocesan and national level.
4. Theological research on the ordination of women to the diaconate.[40] Vatican II outlines the rationale for ordained ministry—in varying degrees—to the preservation of the apostolic faith and service to the unity, holiness, and mission of the people of God, and recognizes the historicity of ministerial figures who embody this ministry (*iam ab antiquo* in *LG* 28). John Paul II's apostolic letter *Ordinatio Sacerdotalis* deals with the clerical ranks (episcopate and presbyterate) and refers to the *traditio* as the ultimate reason for reserving priestly and

episcopal ordination to men only; the diaconal ordination of women is not included, since, according to *LG* 29 the diaconate is a nonpriestly rank of the ordained ministry but, in the case of women's diaconate (even though references to ecclesial functions are not always clearly and unambiguously attested) we have evidence ranging from the New Testament to the seventh century. Throughout history, the theological reason of the ordained ministry has always been maintained, but the figures have changed; changes in the ministry never seem to have been clearly outlined from the beginning, but were required by the cultural and ecclesial transformations that the churches were facing. Thus, history confronts us with a Church that has had the opportunity to reshape the ordained ministerial *figures*, according to the Church's evolution and emerging needs, to remain in its foundational apostolicity in the evolution of cultures. In the horizon of the theology of ministry delivered in the third chapter of *Lumen Gentium*, thanks to a timely historical recognition of the liturgical, literary, and historical sources concerning the ministry of deaconesses, facing new demands of inculturation of the Christian faith and the Church, in my opinion it becomes possible and necessary to reopen the debate on women's diaconal ordination.

Conclusion: An Evocative Image

Acts 16 narrates the beginning of the evangelization of the European continent as a response to a need (the dream of the Macedonian), and starting with an announcement made in a place of religious experience outside traditional structures (where women prayed, along the river; Acts 16:13–15), thanks to the reception of a woman, Lydia. She is an evocative image for the European Church, to dynamically remember the original roots of an experience of faith and, at the same time, to address the challenges for a renewed proclamation of the gospel.

NOTES

1. English trans: J. F. L. Raschen, ed., *Goethe's Faust* (Ithaca, NY: The Thrift Press, 1949), 317.

2. After the discovery of the "new world," the pursuit of a cultural and economic system of domination; the interpretation of evangelization as an adherence to Western cultural models identified with Christianity; the justification of the destruction of cultures and peoples and slavery: these are all similar signs of this impasse. T. Todorov, *La conquista dell'America. Il problema dell'altro* (Turin: Einaudi, 1984). Translated as *The Conquest of America: The Question of the Other* (New York: Harper & Row, 1984).

3. See G. Reale, *Radici culturali e spirituali dell'Europa* (Milan: Raffaello Cortina, 2003); *Concilium* 2/2014, issue titled "Ripensare l'Europa," esp. the contributions by R. A. Siebenrock, "Europa: un tentativo di definizione" (ibid., 20–34) and A. Melloni, "Immagini dell'Europa e sfide dell'Europa per la Chiesa. Uno sguardo storico al cattolicesimo" (ibid., 35–47).

4. A. Cavalli and A. Martinelli, *La società europea* (Bologna: il Mulino, 2015); L. Sciolla, ed., *Processi e trasformazioni sociali. La società europea dagli anni Sessanta ad oggi* (Rome: Laterza, 2014); E. Morin and M. Ceruti, *La nostra Europa. Cosa possiamo sperare? Che cosa dobbiamo fare?* (Milan: Raffaello Cortina, 2013). The task becomes even more complex if one considers the significant differences between Northern Europe and Mediterranean Europe, between the West and the East. See P. Hünermann, ed., *Das Neue Europa. Herausforderungen für Kirche und Theologie* (Freiburg: Herder, 1993).

5. See H. McLeod and W. Ustorf, eds., *The Decline of Christendom in Western Europe, 1750–2000* (New York: Cambridge University Press, 2003); L. Kennis, J. Billiet, and P. Pasture, eds., *The Transformation of the Christian Churches in Western Europe, 1945–2000. La transformation des églises chrétiennes en Europe occidentale* (Leuven: Leuven University Press, 2010); K. Michalski, ed., *Condition of European Solidarity*, vol. 2, *Religion in the New Europe* (New York: CEU Press, 2006); A. Cortesi and A. Tarquini, eds., *Europa e Vangelo oggi. Una sfida per i cristiani* (Florence: Nerbini, 2005).

6. See J. Casanova, *Public Religions in the Modern World* (Chicago: University of Chicago Press, 1994); W. Gräb and L. Charbonnier, eds., *Secularization Theories, Religious Identity and Practical Theology: Developing International Practical Theology for 21st Century* (Berlin: LIT, 2009); M. Warner, J. Van Antwerpen, and G. Calhoun, eds., *Varieties of Secularism in a Secular Age* (Cambridge, MA: Harvard University Press, 2010).

7. G. Davie and D. Hervieu-Léger, eds., *Identités religieuses en Europe* (Paris: La Découverte, 1996), 16. Cf. P. Berger, G. Davie, and E. Fokas, eds., *Religious America, Secular Europe? A Theme and Variations* (Burlington, VT: Ashgate, 2008); G. Davie, *Europe—The Exceptional Case: Parameters of Faith in the Modern World* (London: Darton, Longman & Todd, 2002); T. Dienberg, T. Eggensperger, and U. Engel, eds., *Säkulare Frömmigkeit. Theologische Beiträge zu Säkularisierung und Individualisierung* (Münster: Aschendorff, 2013); *Himmelwärts und Weltgewandt Kirchen und Orden in (post-) säkularer Gesellschaft* (Münster: Aschendorff, 2014)

8. J. Eade, ed., *Living in the Global City: Globalization as Local Process* (London: Routledge, 1997); U. Beck, *Che cos'è la globalizzazione. Rischi e prospettive della società planetaria* (Rome: Carocci, 1999); U. Hannerz, *La diversità culturale* (Bologna: il Mulino, 2001); G. Heller, *Die Grenzen der Solidarität. Europa und die USA im Umgang mit Staat, Nation und Religion* (Berlin: Aufbau, 2002).

9. H. Vilaça, E. Pace, I. Furseth, and P. Pettersson, eds., *The Changing Soul of Europe: Religions and Migrations in Northern and Southern Europe* (Burlington, VT: Ashgate, 2014); M. Honecker, "Europäische Christentum im Horizont der Globalisierung," in *Christenheit—Europa 2000: die Zukunft Europas als Aufgabe und Herausforderung für Theologie und Kirchen*, ed. W. Fürst and M. Honecker (Baden-Baden: Nomos, 2001), 15–38.

10. C. Theobald, *Trasmettere un vangelo di libertà* (Bologna: EDB, 2010).

11. See C. M. Martini, *L'Europa, la fede, la Parola. Tre interviste sulla chiesa e il mondo* (Bologna: EDB, 2012); see also K. Gabriel, *Christentum zwischen Tradition und Postmoderne* (Freiburg: Herder, 1992).

12. D. Hervieu-Léger, *Religion as a Chain of Memory* (New Brunswick, NJ: Rutgers University Press, 2000); G. Davie, *Religion in Modern Europe: A Memory Mutates* (New York: Oxford University Press, 2000).

13. J. Ratzinger, *Chiesa, ecumenismo e politica. Nuovi saggi di ecclesiologia* (Cinisello Balsamo: Edizioni Paoline, 1987). Translated as *Church, Ecumenism, and Politics: New Endeavors in Ecclesiology* (San Francisco: Ignatius Press, 2008).

14. Worth recalling are the indications in the Ecumenical Charter, signed in Strasbourg in 2001 by the Conference of European Churches and the Council of European Episcopal Conferences, for an evangelical and responsible ecclesial presence in the process of European integration: reconciliation of peoples and cultures, opposition to forms of nationalism, safeguarding of creation, actively opposing economic systems that generate poverty, building relationships with Islam and Judaism, and protecting religious freedom. See T. Noble, I. Noble, M. E. Brinkman, and

J. Hilberath, eds., *Charting Churches in a Changing Europe: Charta Oecumenica and the Process of Ecumenical Encounter* (Amsterdam: Rodopi, 2006).

15. A. Cortesi and A. Tarquini, eds., *La laicità e le radici cristiane in Europa* (Florence: Nerbini, 2006); G. Preterossi, ed., *Le ragioni dei laici* (Bari: Laterza, 2005); P. Scoppola, *La nuova cristianità perduta* (Rome: Studium, 1985).

16. P. Grogan and K. Kim, eds., *The New Evangelization: Faith, People, Context and Practice* (New York: Bloomsbury-T&T Clark, 2015); L. Luzbetak, *The Church and Cultures: New Perspectives in Missiological Anthropology* (Maryknoll, NY: Orbis Books, 1988).

17. See J. Kristeva, *Stranieri a noi stessi. L'Europa, l'altro, l'identità* (Rome: Donzelli, 2014).

18. J. B. Metz, "La nuova Europa, sfida al cristianesimo e alla teologia," *Il Margine* 3 (1994): 16–23, at 19.

19. R. Jost, "Spiritualität in Europe in 21. Jahrhundert," in *Europa braucht Spiritualität*, ed. E. Möde (Freiburg: Herder, 2014), 59–71; H. Durel, ed., *Acculturation/Inculturation du christianisme en Europe* (Lyon: Université Jean Moulin, 1998); D. Bosch, *Believing in the Future: Toward a Missiology of Western Culture* (Leominster, UK: Gracewing, 1995).

20. M. E. Brinkman, "The Modern Inculturation Debate and the Catholicity of the Church," in Noble, et al., *Charting Churches in a Changing Europe*, 85–94.

21. N. Brunsson, *Reform and Routine: Organizational Change and Stability in the Modern World* (Oxford: Oxford University Press, 2009); M. Ferrante and S. Zan, *Il fenomeno organizzativo* (Rome: Carocci, 2007[11]), 214–50; J. G. March, *Explorations in Organizations* (Stanford, CA: Stanford University Press, 2008), 191–296; D. C. North, *Istituzioni, cambiamento istituzionale, evoluzione dell'economia* (Bologna: il Mulino, 2005). Originally published as *Institutions, Institutional Change, and Economic Performance* (Cambridge: Cambridge University Press, 1995). See S. Dianich, *La chiesa cattolica verso la sua riforma* (Brescia: Queriniana, 2014); G. Lafont, *La chiesa. Il travaglio delle riforme* (Cinisello Balsamo: San Paolo, 2012); F. X. Kaufmann, *Quale futuro per il cristianesimo?* (Brescia: Queriniana, 2002), originally published as *Wie überlebt das Christentum?* (Freiburg: Herder, 2000).

22. G. Ziviani, *Una chiesa di popolo. La parrocchia nel Vaticano II* (Bologna: EDB, 2011); L. Bressan, *La parrocchia oggi* (Bologna: EDB, 2004); V. Bo, S. Dianich and G. Cardaropoli, *Parrocchia e pastorale parrocchiale* (Bologna: EDB, 1986), 55–101. The Tridentine parish was articulated in relation to a social belonging defined by limited territorial boundaries, which saw a correlation of place of residence, work, and social life, with

limited relational networks and strong social class divisions—a social system with extremely slow and contained changes.

23. C. Taylor, *L'età secolare* (Milan: Feltrinelli, 2009); see also M. Gauchet, *La religione nella democrazia* (Bari: Dedalo, 2009).

24. F. Riva, *La democrazia che verrà* (Rome: Edizioni Lavoro, 2013).

25. See M. Bettini, *Contro le radici. Tradizione, identità, memoria* (Bologna: il Mulino, 2011); M. Augé, *Futuro* (Turin: Bollati Boringhieri, 2012); A. Schiavone, *Storia e destino* (Turin: Einaudi, 2007).

26. See M. Faggioli, *Breve storia dei movimenti cattolici* (Milan: Carocci, 2008). Translated by Demetrio S. Yocum as *Sorting Out Catholicism: A Brief History of the New Ecclesial Movements* (Collegeville, MN: Liturgical Press, 2014).

27. See E. Biemmi and A. Fossion, eds., *La conversion missionnaire de la catéchèse. Proposition de la foi et première annonce* (Brussels: Lumen Vitae, 2009); D. Villepelet, *Les défis de la transmission dans un monde complexe* (Paris: DDB, 2009); L. Bressan and A. Borras, eds., *Habiter notre temps en chrétiens. XXIVe Colloque européen des paroisses, Porto, 8–12 juillet 2007* (Brussels: Lumen Vitae, 2009).

28. "Serious Case" (*Ernstfall*) in the sense of "serious and difficult case," and at the same time in the sense of "essential element," of a perspective that allows verification of the real meaning of an event. See H. U. Von Balthasar, *Cordula ovverosia il caso serio*, Prefazione di Angelo Scola (Brescia: Queriniana, 2016^{7}).

29. G. Bock, *Le donne nella storia europea. Dal Medioevo ai nostri giorni* (Rome: Laterza, 2003); G. Duby and M. Perrot, eds., *Storia delle donne*, vol. 5, *Novecento* (Rome: Laterza, 2003^{4}); A. Touraine, *Il mondo è delle donne* (Milan: Il saggiatore, 2009).

30. European legislation, at a general level and in individual states, now envisions several rules for the protection of rights, and works for the promotion of equal opportunities and gender culture.

31. Particularly interesting is the rereading of this "successful revolution" to understand how the profound changes of society and institutions are taking place: women's more vocal public impact and certain nonviolent strategies of evolution of the public opinion; the deconstruction of an anthropological and religious imagination that justified exclusion, through the critical interpretation of sources; the empowerment and spreading of higher education; the progress in the goals to be achieved; the experiences in strategic sectors with strong symbolic value, which anticipate the desired end result.

32. M. Perroni, A. Melloni, and S. Noceti, eds., *Tantum aurora est. Donne e Concilio Vaticano II* (Munich: LIT, 2012); M. Eckholt, *Ohne die Frauen ist keine Kirche zu machen. Der Aufbruch des Konzils und die*

Zeichen der Zeit (Ostfildern: Matthias Grünewald, 2012). Important is also the contribution that comes from Catholic forms of association and the expansion of active women's religious life (between the nineteenth and twentieth centuries).

33. See the volumes published by Peteers of the European Society of Women in Theological Research.

34. See A. Cavarero and F. Restaino, *Le filosofie femministe. Due secoli di battaglie teoriche e pratiche* (Milan: Bruno Mondadori, 2002); H. Bussmann and R. Hof, eds., *Genus. Geschlechterforschung/Genderstudies in den Kultur- und Sozialwissenschaften* (Stuttgart: Kohlhammer, 2005); D. Fougeyrollas-Schwebel and C. Planté et al., *Le genre comme catégorie d'analyse. Sociologie, histoire, littérature* (Paris: L'Harmattan, 2003).

35. See C. Militello, "Sponsalità, verginità e maternità, coordinate ecclesiologiche della *Mulieris Dignitatem*," *Convivium Assisiense* 11 (2009): 51–60.

36. L. Irigaray, *Sessi e genealogie* (Milan: La tartaruga, 1989).

37. S. Noceti, "*Sex-gender system*? Una prospettiva," in *Avendo qualcosa da dire*, ed. M. Perroni and H. Legrand (Cinisello Balsamo: San Paolo, 2014); C. Simonelli, "Teologia, differenza e *gender*: un dibattito aperto," *Studia Patavina* 62 (2015): 73–88.

38. The ministries of lector and acolyte, which are primarily for the laity and grounded in baptism, could be conferred on women, but what Paul VI established in *Ministeria Quaedam* (1972) on the basis of the dual motivation of venerable tradition and pastoral opportunity, indisputably remains in force (despite some attempts).

39. S. Ciccone, *Essere uomini. Tra potere e libertà* (Turin: Rosenberg & Sellier, 2009).

40. P. Hünermann, ed., *Diakonat. Ein Amt für Frauen in der Kirche—ein frauengerechtes Amt?* (Ostfildern: Schwabenverlag, 1997); M. Scimmi, *Le antiche diaconesse nella storiografia del XX secolo* (Milan: Glossa, 2004); S. Noceti, "Donne e ministero: una questione scomoda. Orientamenti e prospettive interpretative nella riflessione teologica delle donne," in *Liturgia e ministeri ecclesiali*, ed. A. Calapaj Burlini (Rome: C.L.V.-Edizioni Liturgiche, 2008), 67–99. Cardinal Kasper suggested a diaconal ministry of women in the form of an "instituted" ministry. It seems to me that we need to go beyond this hypothesis, though it reflects what was certainly practiced in the Church of the early centuries (charitable activity, baptism, catechesis, with service exclusively aimed at women), in favor of a debate on an ordained ministry at the diaconal level.

26

ECCLESIAL REFORM AND INCULTURATION OF FAITH

The Latin American Ecclesial Configuration

Mario de França Miranda, SJ

An ecclesial reform requires a theological reflection to shed light and correct misinformation, voids, and false insights that correspond to current practices and structures in the Church. This, in fact, as a human community inserted in history, must end sooner or later with the assumption of a concrete configuration, appropriate to each age, to be truly understood as sacrament of salvation and thus accomplish its mission. Of course, the theological components of the Church and its sociocultural and historical characteristics are intimately connected. Faced with the sociocultural transformations taking place in society, our contribution aims to provide the basis for the urgency of changes in the current ecclesiastical configuration, so that the theological truth of the Church will shine in all its evidence for our contemporaries. It is a contribution to ecclesial reform in the sociocultural perspective of Latin America.

Our reflection will be divided into four stages: the sociocultural conditioning of knowledge, the ever-inculturated Christian faith, the relationship between inculturation of faith and ecclesial reform, and its realization in Latin America, especially starting from of the *Aparecida Document*.

Human Knowledge of the Truth

This introduction to our topic is crucial to open the possibility and respond to the need for an evolution in understanding and expressing the truth of God's revelation. We start from the classical definition of truth as the "correspondence of the intellect to reality," but we observe that this correspondence is not a conformity or adoption of things: it is first a correspondence between an operation (which presents things in a certain perspective) and what ensures the actual adherence of things to this perspective.[1] In this way, the known reality is an event in which subject and object are intertwined, in mutual conditioning: the object determines the subject and the latter in turn determines the object. Thus, the known reality is something we cannot find outside of this relationship (or this event), since it is exactly this the point where the subjective and objective prove to be identical.[2] Therefore, reality is presented with diverse ways of being, corresponding to the different modes of access to it. The modes of existence and those of access are two moments of the event put in close symmetry with each other: what the access is, that is, the mode of existence, and vice versa. After all, they are the two sides of a single process.[3]

There may be differences between the various modes of existence, but never between the way of existence and the object. Access modes represent the horizon of understanding within which the object is known, and in connection with which reality is manifested and is affirmed as truth. Therefore, the truth of Christian revelation can receive different expressions, all open to new insights due to the characteristics of human knowledge. Thus, the truth of faith can be revealed during history from the various perspectives of interpretation and from the various historical situations. In this way, we are already reaching the second theme of this reflection, that is, the incidence of the sociocultural context in the understanding and expression of Christian truth.

Christian Faith and Culture

Let us begin with a *fundamental* truth: there is revelation only when the self-communication of God is welcomed by man and thus reaches its goal. Therefore, acceptance in faith is an integral part of the understanding of the disclosed message, so that the free response of faith will be intrinsic to the content of what the word of God is for us. Considered as a strictly *God-directed* action, the salvific action of God cannot be "object of knowledge,"[4] it is not directly accessible to us, but is always mediated in its objectifications: expressions, symbols, and practices. Such objectifications resulting from the acceptance of faith constitute the anthropological basis of God's action in history. We know that, recently, it has had a significant impact on the approach to the Bible, Christology, Trinity, grace, and to the Church itself as a human community. In other words: the "theologal" (God's actualization) is accessible only in the "theological," which already contains the understanding and the corresponding expression of the human being.

However, worth noting is that there are no abstract human beings, as they are always inserted within a particular culture that enables them the opportunity to realize their own identity as "humans." Thus, in an anthropological perspective, we intend culture as that reality that constitutes the reference framework (worldview) and the related ethical practices (ethos) of a concrete social group, with the meanings, values, and patterns embedded in its daily life and assumed as a person's own expression. Therefore, human beings are such only within a culture that offers them the language, the vision of reality, and the patterns of behavior in coexistence with their fellow human beings, and the answers to their existential questions. We are always conditioned by the culture in which we are born, both in our way of thinking and in our actions.

By accepting God's salvific action in faith, human beings experience it, grasp it, express it, and transform it into action within the cultural horizon of their historical context. This is a general law of human knowledge, which is always a knowledge with an ever-present interpretation, because it is realized within a horizon or interpretive framework. In this way, the entire statement of a revealed truth, as a historical expression, cannot be final and definitive, even though it cannot be excluded from the ecclesial tradition as it correctly expressed the truth of faith in a specific era. And this is not only because it is a historical statement, but also because it is a culturally conditioned, since every culture presents assets and limits when compared with others.

What we have said earlier happened already in the person of Jesus Christ himself as eternal Word of God who, in the incarnation, assumed the human condition with its limits and characteristics. As Paul says, "For in him the whole fullness of deity dwells *bodily*" (Col 2:9). In other words, this fullness manifests itself within a sociocultural context, in this case the Semitic, which simultaneously allows and influences its expression.[5] The human substrate always present in the doctrinal expressions, in the ethical precepts, or legal structures, does not allow in Christianity any kind of supernaturalism that prevents the development in the understanding, expression, and lived experience of faith. The truth of faith is accessible to us only in the historical form in which it is presented. The latter is always limited, and may not coincide perfectly with the former, as Yves Congar acknowledged, even though it allows and seeks to advance the understanding of what it seeks to express, even if imperfectly.[6]

However, the *process of perception of the revealed truth* continues in history thanks to the new interpretive frameworks offered by new sociocultural contexts that will generate richer expressions and practices of Christian experience, discover new dimensions of truth until then only latent, and correct unilateral perceptions. But it may also limit or reduce the richness of divine truth, keeping it in inappropriate understandings and expressions, as the history of the Church attests. In addition to this, we must keep in mind the action of the *Holy Spirit* in the community of faith, which not only makes possible the access to the revealed truth (1 Cor 12:3), but also leads the disciples to a deeper perception of this truth (John 14:26; 16:13).

The elaboration of new expressions and practices of the Christian faith is not only possible, as we have just seen, but also *necessary*. The Second Vatican Council warned that the "split between the faith which many profess and their daily lives deserves to be counted among the more serious errors of our age" (*GS* 43). In fact, professed faith requires that the life of the Christian, in all its dimensions, be oriented and lived in the light of the gospel. However, historical and sociocultural transformations can become ineffective—antiquated or no longer understood—expressions and practices, making the experience of faith more difficult for later generations, because they reflect unknown contexts, unintelligible languages, and irrelevant practices. Hence, the recommendation of the Council itself for an appropriate language: "so that revealed truth can always be more deeply penetrated, better understood and set forth to greater advantage" (*GS* 44). In this sense, John Paul II's words pronounced on the occasion of the Pontifical Council for Culture on May 20, 1982, remain valid: "A faith that does not become culture is a faith which has not been fully received, not thoroughly thought through, not faithfully lived out."

Let me point out again that our theme is closely related to the complex issue of the transmission of faith in an era of the dizzying sociocultural transformations that we face today. In fact, the task of the Church is not to convey exactly to other generations doctrines and formulas, but to transmit the *salvific reality* itself of God's self-communication in Christ, *experienced* in the Spirit and in faith. Thus, the struggle for the inculturation of faith is the struggle for other generations also to have access to the salvific event in a language that, faithful to tradition, is meaningful and relevant to them.[7]

Inculturation of Faith and Ecclesial Reform

Having seen the importance of an inculturated faith for Christians, it remains for us to examine the challenges that such inculturation of faith represents for the Church in view of a future reform. Just as in revelation in general, we distinguish what constitutes God's action on the part of human beings in faith, which influences the divine initiative in its understanding, expression, and experience within a historical sociocultural context, the same happens with the determining and constitutive characteristics of what we mean by Church.[8] We can characterize it with images of the people of God, the Body of Christ, and the temple of the Holy Spirit, or affirm that the Church is a communion. Or indicate its fundamental elements, such as the proclamation of the word of God, the welcoming in faith, the profession of faith in Jesus Christ as the Son of God, the celebration of his salvation, especially in baptism and the Eucharist, the ordained ministry, and the community of the faithful. These characteristics, which Congar calls the "founding principles," come from God's first, free, creative initiative, and are not subject to reform.[9]

At the same time, there is no Church without the human response to faith.[10] The latter is a fundamental element of the ecclesial community as its foundation.[11] Where the gospel is not welcomed, the Church cannot arise in any way. To imagine the Church in God in a Platonic way without considering the real human community implies attributing characteristics to God that, being contingent, are authentic only because these contingent realities really exist. Only in this way can we say that God is the Creator, the Savior, and the ultimate origin of the Church.[12]

What we saw earlier regarding God's action as received in faith by the human being and, therefore, necessarily understood and expressed in a sociocultural context, also applies to the elements that constitute the Church. We cannot reach these elements unless through their historical actualizations, which do not manifest themselves in a pure state, but are already culturally conditioned. In fact, the divine is accessible only in the human, in the historical, and in the already inculturated: unconfused and undivided, as the Council of Chalcedon teaches us.

However, we must point out that the various ecclesial configurations throughout history have been created by the ecclesial awareness of the need to proclaim for society the salvation of Jesus Christ in a *meaningful* and *pertinent* way. In short, the various historical configurations show that the Church, moved by the Spirit, changes to continue to be a Church, to maintain its identity as a *sacrament of salvation* during historical transformations. In this sense, we can say that during history the Church *is self-institutionalized*, or that a certain ecclesiogenesis always accompanies it.[13] As a matter of fact, the Church must transmit to its contemporaries, in an accessible manner, what she believes and lives (*DV* 8). To identify specific modes of configuration as essential components would mean to absolutize what is historical and prevent new configurations, with serious negative consequences for the Church herself.[14]

Of course, new configurations create new insights on the essential constitutive elements of the Church, which, in turn, will give rise to a reaction, which will give rise to new configurations. Already in the New Testament we encounter differentiated forms of community, community life, and ecclesial structures influenced by the sociocultural context in which they were located.[15] In fact, the concrete way of organizing the community does not fall from the sky ready-made, but is naturally assumed by the Church from what it finds in the surrounding society, to respond to the challenges that gradually emerge. Thus, the enormous influx of new members transforms Christianity into a mass religion, the monoepiscopate is strengthened and the distinction between clergy and laity emerges. In the fourth century, the organized civil society with its *body* of officials influenced the hierarchical structure of the Church.[16] In the course of history, other determining sociocultural factors were the creation of the hierarchical stratification of medieval society, the question of investitures, the reaction to sovereign absolutism, and the creation of the Christian enclaves in the modern pluralistic society.[17] A significant example of the mutual interference between theology and historical context is the papacy, an institution that has different configurations throughout the history of the Church.[18] The same thing happens with the many concretizations of synodality in the first millennium of the Church,[19] which opens the possibility of new modes of implementation to our day, as it is already happening.[20]

The main agent of the inculturation of faith is the *local church*, which includes the diocese, regions of episcopal conferences, episcopal conferences, as well as the union of several episcopal conferences in the same sociocultural region. For the designation of the local church, we prefer the cultural context,[21] admitting that it does not solve the canonical or ecclesiological impasse.[22] The history of the Church presents examples of this primary or metropolitan Church that, in a synodal regime, regulated issues such as the ordination of bishops, the subdivisions in dioceses, the canonical and liturgical norms, and the discipline of the clergy and laity. Of course, the cultural context shaping a *peculiar configuration* of the local Church had immense importance.[23] Hence, today's need for greater *autonomy of the episcopal conferences*, much limited and diminished in recent years, to meet the expectations of the Second Vatican Council (*LG* 23, end of par.),[24] and to take seriously different regional characteristics. Therefore, *from the sociocultural point of view*, there is an *inevitable diversity* within the unity of the Church. History offers us different expressions in the dogmatic, liturgical, pastoral, and organizational fields.[25] Diverse cultural models imply different "forms of thought"[26] that allow for several different readings of the revealed data and corresponding ecclesial structures. The current theological reflection, mainly in India and Africa, could produce not only new insights and expressions of the revealed data, but also new moral practices.[27] We want to hope that the Church's magisterium will allow its pronouncements on this subject to become a reality, without the sanctioning interventions of these last years!

The Latin American Ecclesial Configuration

The reception of Vatican II in Latin America was fundamentally and originally concretized at the Second General Conference of Latin American Bishops held in Medellín (1968).[28] As in every reception, a review[29] was made of what had been received following the new context. Already in the *Message to the Peoples of Latin America* it was clear that the bishops assumed the Latin American realities, wanted to promote a more just society, encouraging full evangelization, and renewing ecclesial structures. They also praised popular piety and insisted on a poorer church. Medellín continued in the "pastoral" line of the Council and had decisive importance for subsequent years.[30] Understanding and living the Christian faith in the perspective of the poor will eventually give rise in this region to a liberal, yet diverse, theological reflection.[31]

The Episcopal Assembly of Puebla (1979) revived the basic orientation of Medellín, improving it with greater attention to the Latin American cultural element.[32] In Aparecida (2007) the *central point* of the document is a church completely centered on its mission (*AD* 11); this objective must permeate all "ecclesial structures and all pastoral plans" (*AD* 365). The document explicitly mentions "an ecclesial renewal that entails spiritual, pastoral, and also institutional reforms" (*AD* 367). The bishops involved expressly stated that it is urgent to give up "outdated structures that are no longer helpful for handing on the faith" (*AD* 365). However, in order to achieve this goal all "are called to assume an attitude of ongoing pastoral conversion, which entails listening attentively and discerning 'what the Spirit says to the churches' (Rev 2:29) through the signs of the times in which God is made manifest" (*AD* 366).

The Latin American ecclesial configuration, however, recognizing the rich cultural diversity of its various countries, can be summarized in three characteristics or, more appropriately, three options:

a) First, a church that emphasizes the experience of a personal encounter with Jesus Christ (*AD* 226), which implies also the embrace of his own mission (*AD* 129–148), thus eliminating any intimist religiosity, yet still emphasizing the mystical dimension of the Christian faith in reaction to the predominance of the doctrinal, moral, and legal aspects in the past. This option is reflected throughout the process of the formation of the faithful (*AD* 276–300). In this, we must recognize the great value of popular piety, a successful inculturation of faith in simple practices and expressions, which maintain the unity of religion and life and show a genuine relationship with God (*AD* 258–65).
b) The second characteristic concerns *the formation of the adult and active laity* in line with the Second Vatican Council, which states that they enjoy equal dignity (*AD* 184), are called to the mission "as an integral part of Christian identity" (*AD* 144), and should be considered true ecclesial and capable subjects and interlocutors between the Church and society (*AD* 497). Therefore, they "must play an active and creative role in the preparation and execution of pastoral projects" (*AD* 213), participating in the "discernment, decision-making, planning and execution" (*AD* 371). Faced

with the complexity of today's challenges, the Aparecida document called for new lay ministries (*AD* 202). Also, the chronic clergy shortage in the region enables a large participation of the laity in the Church's mission, through the creation and animation of smaller groups of young Christians.

c) The third feature is the option for the poor, always reaffirmed in previous assemblies, but solicited *more concretely* at Aparecida. This option cannot remain on a theoretical or emotional level, but must be translated into a real proximity to the poor, generating concrete options and deeds (*AD* 397). This preferential option "should permeate all our pastoral structures and priorities" (*AD* 396). And the reason is simple: in a continent where most of the population lives in poverty, only in this way can the Latin American Church be a "sacrament of love, solidarity, and justice within our peoples" (*AD* 396). It follows that "any evangelization process entails human promotion and authentic liberation" (*AD* 399). Of course, these options will require a new mentality both in the clergy and the laity, as well as in the ecclesial structures that support them.

As we can see, the *Aparecida Document* influenced Pope Francis's exhortation *Evangelii Gaudium*. This fact is important because the present pope takes on as the program for his pontificate an ecclesial configuration that has Latin American roots. Can we then say with Walter Kasper that "in the Church a South wind blows"?[33] Can general lines of this configuration be adopted by other regions? The reception of the option for the poor and the ecclesial base communities from other churches encourages in part a positive response. Yves Congar already recognized that the initiative of ecclesial renewal does not come from the center but from the periphery, not from the top but from the bottom.[34] In addition, because of the globalization phenomenon, current challenges in some ways damage all regions of the planet, and allow local solutions to be more universal. Without asking for an answer, this question remains open.

Conclusion

The goal of any Church reform has a *salvific trait*: bring its members to live in a more authentic way the Christian message and to proclaim it more effectively to society. This was the intention of John XXIII for the Second Vatican Council, better known as the "pastoral" character of that conciliar gathering.[35] This objective implies a new ecclesial awareness and a corresponding institutional reform, but subject to the conditions wisely described by Yves Congar.[36]

Of course, this is always an ongoing process, because cultures are not static realities but, more properly, processes that are constantly transforming. The catholicity of the Church is dynamic and its identity cannot be ignored by its history.

NOTES

1. J. Ladrière, "La verité et ses critères," *Revue Théologique de Louvain* 18 (1987): 152.

2. W. Schulz, *Philosophie in der veränderten Welt* (Pfulingen: Günther Neske, 1972), 841.

3. L. B. Puntel, "Wahrheit," in *Handbuch philosophischer Grundbegriffe*, ed. H. Krings, H. M. Baumgartner, and C. Wild, *Studienausgabe* 6 (Munich: Kösel, 1974), 1659ff.

4. O. H. Pesch, "Das Wort Gottes als objektives Prinzip der theologischen Erkenntnis," in *Handbuch der Fundamentaltheologie*, vol. 4, *Traktat theologische Erkenntnislehre*, ed. W. Kern, H. J. Pottmeyer, and M. Seckler (Tübingen: A. Francke Verlag, 2000^2), 41.

5. E. Schillebeeckx, *L'histoire des hommes, récit de Dieu* (Paris: Cerf, 1992), 163: "The human face of Jesus not only reveals the face of God in very clear contours, but at the same time veils the face (because it is a revelation of the inexpressible God through Jesus' real-human, historical, and thus contingent and limited expression)." Translated as *The Collected Works of Edward Schillebeeckx*, vol. 10, *Church: The Human Story of God* (London: Bloomsbury-T&T Clark, 2014), 99.

6. Y. M. Congar, *Vraie et fausse réforme dans l'Église* (Paris: Cerf, 1968^2), 166ff. Congar here quotes Saint Thomas Aquinas, who attributes to Isidore a famous phrase: "Perceptio divinae veritatis tendens in ipsam" (*Summa Theologiae* II–II, q. 1, a. 6, sed contra).

7. John Paul II, *Address to the Cardinals, to the Members of the Pontifical Family and to the Roman Curia*, December 21, 1984: "Such specific experiences concern: the word of God, which must be read and understood in the light of the facts that emerge from one's existential journey; liturgical prayer, which must draw from the culture in which the signs, gestures, and words used for adoration, worship, and celebration are inserted; theological reflection, which must be based on categories of thought typical of each culture. And finally, the same ecclesial communion that is rooted in the Eucharist, but which depends on its concrete unfolding from the historical-temporal constraints resulting from the insertion into the background of a certain country or a certain part of the world."

8. H. Legrand, "Le statut pluridisciplinaire de l'ecclésiologie," *Science et Esprit* 59 (2007): 333–49.

9. Congar, *Vraie et fausse réforme dans l'Église*, 100.

10. J.A. Komonchak, *Foundations in Ecclesiology* (Boston: Boston College, 1995), 151: "Against the holiest abstractions, it is necessary to insist that the Church is not the divine initiative itself, but the human social response to God's grace and word."

11. Thomas Aquinas, *Commentary on Epistle to the Colossians* I, 1, 5: "Fides est sicut fundamentum, ex cuius firmitate tota firmatur ecclesiae structura."

12. B. Lonergan, *Insight: A Study on Human Understanding* (London: Longman, Green, 1958), 661ff. See also J.A. Komonchak, "L'epistemologia della recezione," in *Recezione e comunione tra le Chiese. Atti del Colloquio Internazionale di Salamanca. 8–14 aprile 1996*, ed. H. Legrand, J. Manzanares, and A. García y García (Bologna: EDB, 1998), 210.

13. S. Dianich and S. Noceti, *Trattato sulla Chiesa* (Brescia: Queriniana, 2002), 445.

14. P. Hünermann, *Ekklesiologie im Präsens. Perspektiven* (Münster: Aschendorff, 1995), 23.

15. See J. Gnilka, "Strukturen der Kirche nach dem Neuen Testament," in *Die Kirche im Wandel der Gesellschaft*, ed. J. Schreiner (Würzburg: Echter, 1970), 30–40.

16. See A. Faivre, *Chrétiens et Églises. Des identités en construction* (Paris: Cerf, 2011), 27–78.

17. J. A. Komonchak, "Modernity and the Construction of Roman Catholicism," *Cristianesimo nella storia* 18 (1997): 343–85.

18. W. Klausnitzer, *Der Primat des Bischofs von Rom. Entwicklung—Dogma—Ökumenische Zukunft* (Freiburg: Herder, 2004); H. J. Pottmeyer, *Towards a Papacy in Communion: Perspectives from Vatican Councils I and II* (New York: Crossroad, 1998).

19. C. Gallagher, "Collegiality in the East and the West in the First Millennium: A Study Based on the Canonical Collections," *The Jurist* 64 (2004): 64–81.

20. M. Faggioli, "Institutions of Episcopal Collegiality-Synodality after Vatican II: The Decree *Christus Dominus* and the Agenda for Collegiality-Synodality in the 21st Century," *The Jurist* 64 (2004): 224–46; A. Join-Lambert, "Les processus synodaux depuis le Concile Vatican II. Une double expérience de l'Esprit Saint," *Cristianesimo nella storia* 32 (2011): 1137–78; A. Borras, "Trois expressions de la synodalité depuis Vatican II," *Ephemerides Theologicae Lovanienses* 90 (2014): 643–66.

21. See the discussion in H. Legrand, "La réalisation de l'Église en un lieu," in *Initiation à la pratique de la théologie*, vol. 3, *Dogmatique II*, ed. B. Lauret and F. Refoulé (Paris: Cerf, 1993), 151–59. On the same line, rejecting the expression "particular church," Dianich and Noceti, *Trattato sulla Chiesa*, 345ff., which also mentions also B. Lanne, J. Ratzinger, A. Amato, and J. A. Komonchak, as examples of scholars expressing the same opinion.

22. See H.-J. Pottmeyer, "Respuesta a la conferencia del prof. Angel Antón Gómez," in *Iglesias locales y catolicidad. Actas del Coloquio Internacional de Salamanca, 2–7 abril de 1991*, ed. H. Legrand, J. Manzanares, and A. García y García (Salamanca: Universidad Pontificia de Salamanca, 1992), 771–75.

23. G. Greshake, "'Zwischeninstanzen' zwischen Papst und Ortsbischöfen," in *Die Bischofskonferenz. Theologischer und juridischer Status*, ed. H. Müller and H. J. Pottmeyer (Düsseldorf: Patmos Verlag, 1989), 98ff.

24. H. Legrand, "Enjeux ecclésiologiques des réformes institutionnelles du pape François," in *Le grand tournant. L'an I de la révolution du pape François*, ed. M. Du-Bost (Paris: Cerf, 2014), 185–210, at 205ff.

25. Y. M. Congar, *Diversités et communion. Dossier historique et conclusion théologique* (Paris: Cerf, 1982).

26. See H. Legrand, "La légitimité d'une pluralité des 'formes de pensée' (*Denkformen*) en dogmatique catholique. Retour sur la thèse d'un précurseur: Otto Hermann Pesch," in *La responsabilité des théologiens. Mélanges offerts à Joseph Doré*, ed. F. Bousquet (Paris: Desclée, 2002), 685–704.

27. See, for example, B. Bujo, *Wider den Universalanspruch westlicher Moral. Grundlagen afrika- nischer Ethik* (Freiburg: Herder, 2000).

28. C. Schickendantz, "Único ejemplo de una recepción continental del Vaticano II," *Teología* 48 (2012): 52.

29. This reinterpretation originated in the new hermeneutic "locus" of "Latin America," which can also be a "locus theologicus, "as it enjoys a

universal reach. See "Autoridad teológica de los acontecimentos históricos. Perplejidades sobre un lugar teológico," *Teología* 50 (2014): 157–83, at 177.

30. Id., "Zeichen der Zeit heute aus lateinamerikanischer Perspektive," in *Das Zweite Vatikanische Konzil und die Zeichen der Zeit heute*, ed. P. Hünerman, in collaboration with Bernd Jochen Hilberath e Lieven Boeve (Freiburg: Herder, 2006), 179.

31. J. C. Scannone, "La teología argentina del Pueblo," *Gregorianum* 96 (2015): 14–17.

32. On this issue, Lucio Gera's contribution has been significant. See C. M. Galli, "Aproximación al "pensar" teológico de Lucio Gera," in *Escritos teológico-pastorales de Lucio Gera, II: De la Conferencia de Puebla a nuestros días (1982–2007)*, ed. V. R. Azcuy, C.M. Galli, and M. González (Buenos Aires: Agape, 2007).

33. W. Kasper, *Katholische Kirche. Wesen—Wirklichkeit—Sendung* (Freiburg: Herder, 2011), 50; translated as *The Catholic Church: Nature, Reality, and Mission* (London: Bloomsbury, 2015). C. M. Galli, "En la Iglesia sopla un Viento del Sur," *Teología* 49 (2012): 101–72.

34. Congar, *Vraie et fausse reforme dans l'Église*, 251.

35. G. Alberigo, "Réforme ou 'aggiornamento' de l'Église?" in *Communion et réunion. Mélanges Jean-Marie Roger Tillard*, ed. G. R. Evans and M. Gourgues (Leuven: Leuven University Press / Peeters, 1995), 323–32.

36. To give primacy to charity and the pastoral, to remain within "the communion of all," to be patient with the process, and to carry out renewal by a return to the principle of tradition. See *Vraie et fausse reforme dans l'Église*, 211–317.

27

INCULTURATION OF THE GOSPEL AND REFORM OF THE CHURCH IN AFRICA

Reflections on Authentic Catholicity in the Light of *Ad Gentes* 22

Léonard Santedi Kinkupu

Many observers of the life of the Church consider the Second Vatican Council as an event of grace that has breathed new life in the Church. Addressing Catholics gathered in Lourdes for the fiftieth anniversary of Vatican II, Pope Benedict XVI said that this Council was and remains an authentic sign of God for our time.

The reform of the Church proposed by Pope Francis is in the innovative spirit of Vatican II. On the occasion of this symposium on reform of and in the Church, I will propose to consider this reform in relation to the demands of the inculturation of the gospel. In fact, it will be a way for us to deal with the question of authentic catholicity in the light of the theology of inculturation as expressed in the decree *Ad Gentes*, particularly in section 22.

Therefore, I will begin by identifying the relevance of the decree *Ad Gentes* 22 in its relationship to the question of catholicity. I will then turn to the question of inculturation in relation to this decree. I will then emphasize the importance of the Pentecostal dimension of inculturation, and, finally, I conclude by opening the perspective of a historically and culturally open catholicity.

Relevance of the Decree *Ad Gentes*

One of the questions addressed by the Second Vatican Council is that of the particular churches, which is dealt with in the third chapter of the decree *Ad Gentes*, where it is seen in relation with the missionary activity of the Church. What then is the nature and purpose of missionary activity?

Without providing a synthetic theory, the Council offered various elements of response borrowed from different schools, which, however, seemed to be mutually exclusive. In fact, the decree *AG* uses all the traditional formulas: Christian witness, propagation of the faith, preaching, gathering of the people of God, implantation of the Church. Thus, it avoids taking a rigid and partial position.[1]

However, in Alfonso Ngindu Mushete's opinion, the central affirmation of Vatican II was that of a true and authentic catholicity of the Church.[2] The Council solemnly affirms that the Church is one and diverse—not diverse reluctantly and for lack of a better arrangement, but by the same requirement of its nature. The constitution *Lumen Gentium* reminds us that the Church of Jesus Christ is built from the community of many local churches. Let us quote the text of the Council (*LG* 13):

> Moreover, within the Church particular Churches hold a rightful place; these Churches retain their own traditions, without in any way opposing the primacy of the Chair of Peter, which presides over the whole assembly of charity (11*) and protects legitimate differences, while at the same time assuring that such differences do not hinder unity but rather contribute toward it. Between all the parts of the Church there remains a bond of close communion whereby they share spiritual riches, apostolic workers and temporal resources. For the members of the people of God are called to share these goods in common, and of each of the Churches

> the words of the Apostle hold good: "According to the gift that each has received, administer it to one another as good stewards of the manifold grace of God" (see 1 Peter 4:10).

As it can be seen from the central document on the Church, the Council affirms and emphasizes its essential perspective: that of the ecclesial peculiarities in the unity of faith. This perspective is of major interest not only to the churches of Africa, but also to those of the East and West. We shall return to this point. For the time being, let us remember that the decree *Ad Gentes* articulates in three points in a clear and implicit way the directives and perspectives to folllow for the realization of a truly local church.

1. *Ad Gentes* first indicates the conditions under which the constitution of a young Church is recognized:

> The work of planting the Church in a given human community reaches a certain goal when the congregation of the faithful already rooted in social life and somewhat conformed to the local culture, enjoys a certain firmness and stability. That is to say, it is already equipped with its own supple (perhaps still insufficient) of local priests, Religious, and lay men, and is endowed with these institutions and ministries which are necessary for leading and expanding the life of the people of God under the guidance of their own bishop. (19)

2. *Ad Gentes* then describes the missionary activity and recalls its primary objective: to respect in the young churches the diversity in the unity of the Church, by a constant concern for communion and rootedness (20; see also *LG* 13).

This is a recognized task for the Church, a requirement of her catholicity. Yves De Montcheuil wrote, "The Church is Catholic not only because it brings truth and salvation to all peoples and all ages, but because it requires the co-operation of all civilizations and all men to bring to light these riches of the repository entrusted to her and to build the eternal city of God."[3]

The magisterium of the Church, often uncompromising about the unity of faith, has never rejected diversity. The Second Vatican

Council accepted the value of human culture. The Church has indicated her place in the divine plan of the diversity of nations and cultures. The Church is not a monolithic society; rather, it is the people of God, made of a series of local churches that contribute to the wealth of the universal Church.

3. It is worth noting that the Council fathers realized that an incarnation of Christianity does not manifest itself profoundly and seriously unless it reaches the level of theological reflection. To be truly Catholic, theology must be affected by the particular cultural ways of thinking and feeling of the various peoples. The Council does not hesitate to speak of a theological response, of an in-depth analysis of sorts, of the data of Christian revelation. Let us cite again *Ad Gentes*:

> The seed which is the word of God, watered by divine dew, sprouts from the good ground and draws from thence its moisture, which it transforms and assimilates into itself, and finally bears much fruit. In harmony with the economy of the Incarnation, the young churches, rooted in Christ and built up on the foundation of the Apostles, take to themselves in a wonderful exchange all the riches of the nations which were given to Christ as an inheritance (cf. Psalm 2:8). They borrow from the customs and traditions of their people, from their wisdom and their learning, from their arts and disciplines, all those things which can contribute to the glory of their Creator, or enhance the grace of their Savior, or dispose Christian life the way it should be. (22)

Here we grasp all the importance that the Council gives to the rooting of the Church in one place. The Church is fundamentally local and this locality is not a threat to the unity of the Church, but on the contrary, it appears to be a source of enrichment for the whole Church. We shall return to this point. Let us add here that by this affirmation of the ecclesiological significance of place, we also discover the undeniable importance of the dialogue between faith and local culture. The dialogue between faith and culture is a source of fertility not only for the culture that opens to the faith but also for the faith itself. Thus, it is with good reason that Pope

John Paul II said, "A faith that does not become culture is a faith not fully accepted, not entirely thought out, not faithfully lived."[4] And that is not all. Let us also say that all the importance of *Ad Gentes* 22 for the theology of inculturation is here revealed. Let us look at this more closely.

Ad Gentes and the Prospect of Inculturation

First, let us affirm that the Second Vatican Council did not make use of the notion of inculturation. However, proponents of the theology of inculturation have always considered this passage of *Ad Gentes* 22, among many others, as a true leitmotif for the work of inculturation. For them, the profound incarnation of Christianity and the full inculturation of the Christian faith will be realized, at the level of doctrinal assimilation, through the most advanced internal theological development, which will produce and manifest characteristic contributions. *Ad Gentes* 22 is crystal clear about this. It says that to achieve this goal successfully each sociocultural entity must undertake a theological reflection that accounts for the philosophy and wisdom of its people. We cannot resist the temptation to quote at length from this fundamental text of Vatican II on inculturation:

> To achieve this goal, it is necessary that in each major socio-cultural area, such theological speculation should be encouraged, in the light of the universal Church's tradition, as may submit to a new scrutiny the words and deeds which God has revealed, and which have been set down in Sacred Scripture and explained by the Fathers and by the magisterium. Thus it will be more clearly seen in what ways faith may seek for understanding, with due regard for the philosophy and wisdom of these peoples; it will be seen in what ways their customs, views on life, and social order, can be reconciled with the manner of living taught by divine revelation. From here the way will be opened to a more profound

> adaptation in the whole area of Christian life. By this manner of acting, every appearance of syncretism and of false particularism will be excluded, and Christian life will be accommodated to the genius and the dispositions of each culture (6). Particular traditions, together with the peculiar patrimony of each family of nations, illumined by the light of the gospel, can then be taken up into Catholic unity. Finally, the young particular churches, adorned with their own traditions, will have their own place in the ecclesiastical communion, saving always the primacy of Peter's See, which presides over the entire assembly of charity. (*AG* 22)

Thus, inculturation appears to be closely linked to the plural destiny of catholicity. And diversity is thus perceived as constitutive of the catholicity of the one Church of Christ. Therefore, catholicity is unity in diversity. One of the missions of the whole Church is therefore to prevent the risk of syncretism and false particularism, to promote mutual and universal exchange and collaboration among local churches (*AG* 38). *AG* 22 expresses it in these terms: "By this manner of acting, every appearance of syncretism and of false particularism will be excluded, and Christian life will be accommodated to the genius and the dispositions of each culture."

This clear and precise position of Vatican II in *Ad Gentes* 22 prompted African Christians to pursue a Christian reflection to respond more adequately to the needs and requirements of Christian communities and of African society in general.

A solemn affirmation in favor of this statement of *Ad Gentes* 22 on inculturation remains the declaration of the bishops of Africa and Madagascar to the Synod of Bishops on Evangelization in 1974. The African prelates affirmed,

> Every activity in the process of building up our Churches must operate in constant reference to the life of our communities. Starting off from these communities, we must bring to our Catholic faith not only those cultural and artistic experiences which are part of our heritage...but also a theology which enables us to tackle the challenges

> arising out of our historical background and the ongoing evolution of our societies. Our theological thinking must remain faithful to the authentic tradition of the Church, and at the same time be attentive to the life of our communities, and respectful of our traditions and language, that is of our philosophy of life.[5]

As it can be seen, expanding on *AG* 22, the African prelates consider the theology of adaptation and implantation as completely outdated and opt for the theology of incarnation, or, better, of inculturation. According to them, a theology open to the fundamental aspirations of the African peoples will lead Christianity to become effectively embodied in the lives of the peoples of the black continent.[6] A fundamental aspect emphasized here is the recognition to the local hierarchy, and to the incarnate and living communities, for the capacity of a directive action for the deepening of the gospel and the achievement of the priority objectives. Communities are now the axis around which the "construction" of the churches in Africa is organized. This renews the mission and turns Africans into missionaries.[7]

The Council, taking into consideration the new state of consciousness of humanity, sees history as a true theological place. Clearly, for Vatican II, each culture is called to express the Christian message in the manner that best suits it, using its own concepts that enable it to render vivid and vivifying the mystery of Christ without breaking the communion. It is important to put in place a process of re-elaboration and reinterpretation based on the existential categories and requirements of each culture. In this sense, cultures must fulfill a hermeneutic function in relation to faith.[8]

AG 22 encourages the same attitude when it affirms that young churches must borrow from the customs and traditions of their peoples, from their wisdom, culture, arts, scientific knowledge, everything that can contribute to confessing glory of the Creator, to highlight the Savior's grace, and to order the Christian life as it should. It is therefore in the light of tradition that the churches can, through their specific tradition, subject to a new examination the word of God as it has been understood and interpreted by the Church for centuries.

Ad Gentes perceives and underlines the intrinsic link between the announcement of the gospel and the interpretation of the present condition of humanity. Thus, the whole is entrusted to the many historical and cultural contexts of the world and the interpretations that they require. In this relationship, what is at stake is not only identity and truth, if not the eschatological status of Christianity, but also revelation itself.[9]

As we can see, the Second Vatican Council opened the doors to a more dynamic conception of revelation. Revelation is not fixed in a text of the past, neither in a repository, nor in a ready-made meaning. If it is said to be closed in its constitutive and scriptural phase with the death of the last of the apostles, as self-communication of God in the history of salvation, it continues, and its actualization in the human consciousness is never completed.[10]

Therefore, let us affirm, at the risk of repeating ourselves, that the decree *Ad Gentes* 22 commits especially the young churches to a theological reflection which "in the light of the universal Church's tradition," submits "to a new scrutiny the words and deeds which God has revealed, and which have been set down in Sacred Scripture and explained by the Fathers and by the magisterium."

We are therefore called again to perform an interpretive task. In Paul Ricoeur's words, this demands that revelation be addressed more to the imagination of the believers[11] than to their passive and repetitive obedience to truths, to a creative imagination that is in constant renewal, under the action of the Spirit, and the understanding of this revelation, and the obedience due to it.

In this context, the hermeneutics of the revelation of the divine message, closely linked to the hermeneutic of human existence, is deeply embedded in the project of inculturation. It expresses the perpetual quest for modes of expression and thought from a particular milieu and according to the needs of this milieu. The hermeneutic effort translates in its own way the will to speak of God by assuming the challenges of transformation, intelligence, and emergence of new cultures.[12]

At this stage of our reflection on *Ad Gentes*, we want to offer some perspectives in relation to the task of inculturation facing new challenges in today's context.

The Pentecostal Perspective of Inculturation

We want to emphasize here the profound links of inculturation with the mystery of Pentecost: "Thanks to the outpouring and action of the Spirit, who draws gifts and talents into unity, all the peoples of the earth when they enter the Church live a new Pentecost, profess in their own tongue the one faith in Jesus, and proclaim the marvels that the Lord has done for them. The Spirit, who on the natural level is the true source of the wisdom of peoples, leads the Church with a supernatural light into knowledge of the whole truth."[13] This Pentecostal perspective of inculturation is a real challenge for churches in Africa. These are called to enrich the Church by welcoming the gospel. This is the requirement of creativity and inventiveness within each church. The churches of Africa cannot be duplicates or certified copies of the European churches. We know that Meinrad Pierre Hebga liked to say, "Young churches are born old." The churches of Africa are therefore called upon to define the authentic image of themselves. The ecclesial expression of faith in all its forms, doctrinal, liturgical, ethical, and so on, is always tending toward fullness.

It is in this eschatological perspective of God's self-revelation that we can justify the integration of preexisting religious elements into a culture that opens to Christianity. The Pentecostal dimension of inculturation is thus what obliges each religious community to take back, from its own linguistic registers, its own epistemological radars, the divine message received under pain of living in permanent linguistic nonsense (see *AG* 22).[14]

But that is not all. This Pentecostal perspective of inculturation has serious implications for both the churches of Africa and the universal Church. It means that the life and thought of the Church are no longer to be conceived in a monolithic way, but in terms of cultural diversity. This implies the practical assertion of cultural identities within the universal Church and the ability of these people to interpret and express Christianity differently in their lives. This also implies that the churches previously on the periphery are moving toward the center of the life and activity of the universal Church, so that the universality of the Church is expressed in terms of communion with the churches and collegial sharing of power rather than in terms of uniformity and conformity to a model pattern.

Oscar Bimwenyi Kweshi expresses this more vividly:

> The Black-African language, with its own internal grid, allows the "recipients" of the grove to capture, according to the sensitivity of their own antennas, what happens in its universe of meaning, which penetrates the space explored by their own radars. These radars perceive *man, God, the Word, life, death, etc.*, based on the preliminary meanings which these fundamental notions bear in their own horizon of meaning.[15]

These assertions lead us to support the possibility of a doctrinal inculturation, that is, to recognize that the definitions of faith of the Church cannot call for a uniform reception. If the same gospel could know different formulations according to whether it addressed to the Jewish or the Gentiles, even more so, the interpellation of a council can be expressed in various forms. The gospel needs a culture to express itself and there is no ideal or universal culture that can express it perfectly. If it is true that each culture limits the gospel, it must also be said that each culture reveals or sheds on one or other of its aspects.

In fact, inculturation as a mysterious and complex encounter between a culture and the gospel allows a culture to grasp it again and again. The fruits that emerge from this marriage between a land and the gospel of Christ confessed by a council testify to the diversity of stories, mentalities, and cultures.[16] These specific responses, sometimes confusing and unforeseen, allow the Church to be universal and fully Catholic. Thus, each culture enriches, through its creativity, the adornment of the bride. This is the image of authentic catholicity, which we can define, after Carlos Kalonji, as a historically and culturally open catholicity.

Perspectives of a Historically and Culturally Open Catholicity

Speaking of the relevance of a historically and culturally open catholicity, we will show here that this model of catholicity is consistent with our time, insofar as it enables the Church to make its universality more meaningful, faith to function in any culture, and any place to be recognized in its status as a responsible subject.[17]

History attests that the Christian Church has always been called to account for its way of bearing tradition. Even today her destiny depends on it. If the contexts of theological and dogmatic assertions are necessarily local and diverse, the whole problem is whether the Church is capable today of maintaining in harmony different readings and various implementations of the only Christian revelation. To this question, the answer, affirming the necessity of a historically and culturally open catholicity, is yes.

St. Augustine liked to say that the peoples "will not come by migrating from their own places but by believing in their own places."[18] It was his way of emphasizing the ecclesiological scope of the geographical, historical, cultural, and sociological roots of the local churches. In his perspective, confessing faith in one's land means remaining faithful to one's culture, history, immemorial traditions, and memory. It is also to structure the answers to be given to the Christian proposition based on the social, historical, and cultural factors specific to one's land, as assumed by the word of life and transformed by grace. Augustine thus opens the way to considering the future, historicity, and the variety of human mediation. Thus understood, Augustine's assertion unfolds the potentialities of catholicity understood as an articulation of unity and diversity expressed as appropriation and particularization of the revealed data according to the heritage, language, traditions, and customs of the various peoples (see *AG* 15, 22; *GS* 58, 62; *SC* 37–38). The first century of the Church attests to this appropriation and perspective of catholicity that we call "historically and culturally open catholicity."

The real issue of an option for a historically and culturally open catholicity is to show that we can and must finally emerge from this false dilemma: the uniformity of a single expression of the common profession of faith, or the fragmentation of faith. A historically and culturally open catholicity holds that not only has the Church always been plural in practice and on a doctrinal level, but that it must also be so in the contemporary epistemological context. Without supporting on the one hand, the totalitarianism of unity and, on the other, the Babel of dissemination, a historically and culturally open catholicity is communion in diversity.[19]

This catholicity is the expression of the tension between the identical word of God concerning all the believers and the weight of the historical and cultural reality of the Christian communities dispersed in the world. The word of God is current only in the diversity of its reception. At the very moment when it bears witness to the richness of plurality and diversity, the historically and culturally open catholicity affirms the shared responsibility in the witness of the Lordship of Christ.

Let us add that a historically and culturally open catholicity is relevant when one has a clear idea of tradition, that is, not as a simple organic development of what is in the beginning or as a continuous repetition of a dogmatic definition, but as a dialectical understanding of tradition. This, indeed, makes possible a vision of unity that incorporates tensions without bursting.

To understand tradition as the event of the communication of God in the incarnate Word to bring men back to him in the Holy Spirit is to grasp simultaneously that we cannot dissociate revelation from the experience of faith that welcomes and expresses it, a welcoming and expression that cannot be predetermined. Tradition is alive. It rejects the idea of a full development that the Church would have already achieved in time and space. Because it is alive, tradition cannot be reduced to an array of attitudes already experienced, to a jurisprudence that recovers, whatever happens, an earlier solution that makes law. It is not the weight of a past that hinders or weighs down, but the richness of an experience that allows audacity and creativity. Thus, tradition is expressed so well in the document of the International Theological Commission: "Tradition is therefore something living and vital, an ongoing process in which the unity of faith finds expression in the variety of languages and the diversity of cultures. It ceases to be Tradition if it fossilizes."[20]

Through its living character, tradition makes possible the continual process of interpretation of Christian salvation and allows it to intervene in ever-changing situations and cultures. Indeed, if the *éschaton* has truly entered history, the expression of the authentic evangelical meaning is constitutively linked to the context of those who express themselves. Because the context enters the grasp of revelation, a necessary correlation must be established between revelation and context, which keeps the interpretive field open. Indeed, no one can determine precisely the evangelical message if it puts in brackets the current situation of the believer and communities, in which human beings experience the meaning of life and has an interpretative status for the faith.

Thus, from the text of *Ad Gentes* 22, we see tradition as a transmission endowed with innovative power. Edward Schillebeeckx defines it as a transmission of meaning necessary to interpret the facts. For Claude Geffré, "the true tradition is not the mechanical transmission of doctrinal content in the sense of a chemically pure invariant. It is made of creative revisions of the original message."[21] Hence, there is an intimate connection between tradition and invention. Because, on the one hand, it is tradition that, by transmitting the past in the present, makes it possible to realize at the same time an advance in the future, which constitutes the proper feature of invention; and, on the other, invention acquires importance only if it can create a tradition, because only then does it gives rise to history.[22] But tradition as a constitutive reality of history is constitutive of a humanity in real development, of the *humanitas hominis*.[23]

It is therefore clear that the Pentecostal perspective of inculturation helps to answer one of the strong wishes expressed by the African churches for Vatican II: that the Church should recognize the quality of responsible subject to each history and culture, thus opening the era of responsibility and initiative to the local churches.

Let us add here that, according to Ignace Ndongala, the Latin Church with its dual structure (that is, articulated between papal primacy, on the one hand, and the dimension of episcopal collegiality, on the other) does not allow local churches to be realized as subjects of action and initiatives. This achievement requires intermediate structures. History has bequeathed to us the patriarchates and the churches *sui iuris*, but, for obvious reasons of ecumenism, Ndongala wonder whether it is better to opt for new structures to be created like the regional churches: a grouping of churches in a region on the basis of historical, cultural, and sociological affinities—and common problems and challenges.[24] In Ndongala's view, these developments find support in the history of ecclesial institutions of the first millennium, among theologians such as G. Greshake, H. J. Pottmeyer, H. Legrand, and influential confirmation in the words of the theologian Joseph Ratzinger, who in 1971 proposed patriarchates or great churches for the churches of Africa and Asia on the model of the Eastern Churches:

> The image of a centralized state offered by the Catholic Church right up to the Council does not stem only from the Petrine office but from its strict combination with the patriarchal function which continually increased in the course of history and which the Bishop of Rome assumed over the whole of Latin Christendom.... Therefore, it should be considered as a task for the future to clearly distinguish the authentic office of Peter's successor and the patriarchal function, and, where necessary, to create new patriarchates, which should no longer be considered incorporated in the Latin Church.

And he adds, even more specifically,

> Likewise, one could undoubtedly think also of a special form of reformed Christianity in the unity of the one Church. Finally, in the not too distant future, we should think about how to give to the churches of Asia and Africa, as well as those of the East, their own form as "patriarchates" or autonomous "great churches," or whatever these *ecclesiae* in the *Ecclesia* might be called in the future.[25]

Along these lines, let us consider this question of Y. Congar: "Is it possible, is it reasonable, is it realistic to imagine the structure of a reunited Church united in the form of a collegiality concretized in the collegiality of patriarchates: the five of the pentarchy; those of Moscow, Romania, Serbia, Africa, Latin America, India, and others?" Another approach to this issue is offered by the ecumenical dialogue as witnessed by the Dombes Group, which hopes that

> the present continental assemblies of bishops might receive, with a canonical recognition, a wide range of competencies in regard to the organization of the churches, the nomination of bishops, the liturgy, catechesis, etc. In this way continental 'great churches' would be established as renewal and adapted forms of the ancient patriarchates.[26]

This is what is apparent from Alphonse Borras's question:

> Why not conceive and establish an African Latin Patriarchate (for the continent of Africa and Madagascar), a Patriarchate of the Americas (or a Latin American patriarchate and a North American one), a Patriarchate of Asia (including Asia and Australia), a European Patriarchate (where the incumbent would be the bishop of Rome)?[27]

These considerations bring us to the wish of Pope Francis concerning the salutary decentralization of the structures of the Church. In the apostolic exhortation *Evangelium Gaudium*, he recalls that the Second Vatican Council affirmed that, in a manner analogous to the ancient patriarchal churches, episcopal conferences "are in a position 'to contribute in many and fruitful ways to the concrete realization of the collegial spirit.'" (*EG* 32). In his speech to the CELAM Coordinating Committee, the Episcopal Council of Latin America and the Caribbean, he said,

> The Church is an institution, but when she makes herself a "center," she becomes merely functional....She becomes increasingly self-referential and loses her need to be missionary....She stops being a bride and ends up being an administrator...[instead of] servant, more a facilitator of faith than an inspector of faith.[28]

According to Ignatius Ndongala, the pope wants more participatory and inclusive church structures that integrate subsidiarity at the level of dioceses and episcopal conferences. The culmination of his program is a more elaborate legal status for episcopal conferences whose doctrinal authority is to be restored as "concrete realization of the collegial spirit" (*EG* 32). A historically and culturally open catholicity falls into this perspective. Worth noting, after others, is that the renewal advocated by the pope is connected to the question of the autonomy of the local churches in the catholicity. One may then ask whether this salutary decentralization should not go beyond the episcopal conferences and touch on the structures of the Latin Catholic Church. Do the intensification and implementation of Francis's project not involve such a price?

Following Pope Francis, Ignatius Ndongala believes that posing the question of decentralization within the framework of the ecclesial structures, established once and for all *ne varietur* (irreformable), risk to drown the pope's innovative pastoral intuitions in the realm of pious aspirations. For him, therefore, the question that must be raised, in the wake of Pope Francis, is that of the present ecclesial configuration. Then, the task would be to distinguish again more clearly between the proper function of the successor of Peter and the patriarchal one, and, if necessary, to create new patriarchates detached from the Latin Church. For Ndongala it is therefore possible to go beyond the dual structure (papacy-collegiality of bishops) that strengthens the primacy and ensures both uniformity and centralization. Following Gisbert Greshake, he proposes, prior to the question of the doctrinal competence of the episcopal conferences and the reforms postulated by Pope Francis, to thematize the overcoming of the dual structure in favor of a triadic structure including the local church (with its bishop), the unity of regional churches (with their protos), and finally, the universal Church.[29]

In this regard, it is good to bear in mind the reassuring remarks made by Pope John Paul II to the bishops of Zaire on an *ad limina* visit: "In this field as in all other, the Holy See will not release you from any responsibility; it will invite you, however, to help you get to the bottom of your responsibilities. This journey necessarily involves cooperation, cohesion, and unity." It is to be hoped that the salutary decentralization advocated by the pontificate of Francis will inaugurate tomorrow a fruitful correlation between the *restauratio* and the *renovatio* for the catholicity of the one unique

Church of God and the emergence of true local churches in Africa. As such, it challenges the churches of Africa and the people of God who are staying there to be bold and creative in this duty of rethinking the objectives, structures, style, and evangelizing methods of their own communities (*EG* 33). The pope invites them to "apply the guidelines found in this document generously and courageously, without inhibitions or fear" (*EG* 33). In my humble opinion, only the courage of this application is likely to hasten the advent of the "one universal church of tomorrow," postulated by the African episcopate at Vatican II.

Conclusion

The Second Vatican Council, particularly through its Decree on the Missionary Activity of the Church, affirms the will of the people to build themselves up in the Church according to their own traditions and culture. *AG* 22 seems to us a text of great relevance that has raised the question of the unity and plurality of human thought in all its speculative generality—a problem more relevant than ever in the context of globalization and multiculturalism. This text proposes an approach to the universality of Christianity that integrates the local churches' own richness. It is with good reason that Geffré wrote on this subject,

> We are invited to seek the originality inherent in the Christian universal according to the analogy of faith. Unlike the imperialism of the abstract universal, the Christian universal is a universal of gift and mission. We must even speak of a Paschal universal: the Church puts to death its particularity to be reborn in and through this death, and she is universal insofar as she makes her own the universal cry of the oppressed with whom Christ identified himself. "I was hungry and I was thirsty…"[30]

AG 22 thus allows us to think of authentic catholicity as one that integrates and affirms the diversity and differences inherent in the historicity of human mediation, the diversity of historical situations, the variety of cultural localities, and the plurality of geographical determinations. It is therefore in and from each historical and cultural place that catholicity is realized and fully lived.

Ultimately, to speak of a historically and culturally open catholicity is primarily because the greater truth of God inevitably manifests itself in a diverse, plural way. This expression is therefore justified by the fact that this truth is grasped only by and in the diversity of places that necessarily condition the diversity of interpretations and therefore the variety of the formulations. This truth can even be unique and diverse: unique with diversity and diverse with unity. Thus, catholicity is one in its nature, but plural in its meaning.

To recognize the notion of a historically and culturally open catholicity means recognizing the quality of a responsible subject for each history and culture, and opening oneself positively to the evidence of an affirmation of the diversity of formulations of the truth of faith in the ethical, religious, theological, and doctrinal order. The originality, richness, and relevance of the paradigm of inculturation are discovered here as an intimate transformation of authentic cultural values through their integration into Christianity and, conversely, the rooting of Christianity in the various cultures. Inculturation thus understood is not merely orthodoxy; it is above all concrete life, open to the gospel and animated by it. It is in this sense a Christian orthopraxis. It enables us to make use of the engine of the creative genius of our cultures so that it is at the same time ferment of social transformation of humanity and a source of inspiration for the vitality of Christianity in the world today.

NOTES

1. A. N. Mushete, *Les thèmes majeurs de la théologie africaine* (Paris: L'Harmattan, 1989), 36.

2. Ibid.

3. Y. de Montcheuil, *Problèmes de vie spirituelle* (Paris: Éditions de l'Epi, 1947), 84ff.

4. John Paul II, Address of His Holiness John Paul II to the Plenary Assembly of the Pontifical Council for Culture, March 18, 1994.

5. Déclaration des Évêques d'Afrique et de Madagascar, in *L'Église de cinq continents. Bilan et perspectives de l'évangélisation. Principaux textes du Synode des évêques, Rome, septembre–octobre 1974,* Preface by Cardinal

François Marty (Paris: Centurion, 1975), 210. Translated by Aylward Shorter as *Toward a Theology of Inculturation* (Maryknoll, NY: Orbis Books, 1989), 212–13.

6. Ibid.

7. See I. Ndongala Maduku, *Pour des Églises régionales en Afrique*, Preface by Hervé Legrand (Paris: Karthala, 1999), 117.

8. See C. R. Kalonji Nkokesha, *Penser la Tradition avec Walter Kasper. Pertinence d'une catholicité historiquement et culturellement ouverte* (Leuven: Peeters, 2013), 39.

9. Ibid.

10. See C. Geffré, "Esquisse d'une théologie de la Révélation," in *La Révélation* (Brussels: Facultés Universitaires Saint Louis, 1984), 180.

11. P. Ricœur, "Herméneutique de l'idée de la Révélation," in *La Révélation*, 54.

12. J.-M. Éla, *Repenser la théologie africaine. Le Dieu qui libère* (Paris: Karthala, 2003).

13. John Paul II, apostolic exhortation *Ecclesia in Africa*, September 14, 1995, no. 61 (*EV* 14, 3108).

14. On this point, see my article: "Le paradigme de l'inculturation dans *Ecclesia in Africa*. Défis et perspectives," *Revue africaine de théologie* 29 (2005): 173–92.

15. O. Bimwenyi Kweshi, "Théandricité du langage théologique africain," in *Parole de Dieu et langages des hommes. La rencontre de Yaoundé, 24–28 septembre 1980* (Kinshasa: Association Œcuménique des Théologiens Africains [AOTA], 1980), 34ff.

16. See G. Routhier, *La réception d'un Concile* (Paris: Cerf, 1993).

17. Kalonji Nkokesha, *Penser la Tradition avec Walter Kasper*, 278.

18. Augustine, *Letter* 199, 12, 47, cit. by G. Alberigo in "Chrétienté et cultures dans l'histoire de l'Église," in *Église et histoire de l'Église en Afrique. Actes du colloque de Bologne, 22–25 octobre 1988*, ed. G. Ruggieri (Paris: Beauchesne, 1988), XI. English trans.: *The Works of Saint Augustine* (4th release), Electronic Edition, *Letters 156–210*, Volume II/3.

19. Kalonji Nkokesha, *Penser la Tradition avec Walter Kasper*, 278.

20. Commission Théologique Internationale, *La théologie aujourd'hui. Perspectives, principes et critères*, preface by Léonard Santedi (Kinshasa: Médiaspaul, 2013), n26. Translated as *Theology Today: Perspectives, Principles and Criteria*: http://www.vatican.va/roman_curia/congregations/cfaith/cti_documents/rc_cti_doc_20111129_teologia-oggi_en.html (accessed May 6, 2017).

21. C. Geffré, *Croire et interpréter. Le tournant herméneutique de la théologie* (Paris: Cerf, 2001), 41.

22. J. Ratzinger, *Les principes de la théologie catholique. Esquisse et matériaux* (Paris: Téqui, 2005), 93.

23. Ibid.

24. Ndongala, *Pour des Églises régionales en Afrique*, 266ff.

25. J. Ratzinger, *Le nouveau peuple de Dieu* (Paris: Aubier, 1971), 68ff.

26. Gruppo di Dombes, *Il ministero di comunione nella chiesa universale*, September 5, 1985, n. 144, in *Enchiridion Oecumenicum* 2 (Bologna: EDB, 1988), 1150. Translated as Catherine E. Clifford, ed., *For the Communion of the Churches: The Contribution of the Groupe Des Dombes* (Grand Rapids, MI: Eerdmans, 2010), 141.

27. A. Borras, "*Ut unum sint*. Une encyclique pour les chrétiens en voie de réconciliation," *Ephemerides Theologicae Lovanienses* 72 (1996): 349–70.

28. Pope Francis, Address to the Leadership of the Episcopal Conferences of Latin America during the General Coordination Meeting, July 28, 2013, no.2: https://w2.vatican.va/content/francesco/en/speeches/2013/july/documents/papa-francesco_20130728_gmg-celam-rio.html.

29. G. Greshake, "'Zwischeninstanzen' zwischen Papst und Ortsbischöfen. Notwendige Voraussetzung für die Verwirklichung der Kirche als 'communio ecclesiarum,'" in *Die Bischofskonferenz. Theologischer und juridischer Status*, ed. H. Müller and H. J. Pottmeyer (Düsseldorf: Patmos Verlag, 1989), 88–115; Ndongala, *Pour des Églises régionales en Afrique*.

30. C. Geffré, ed., *Théologie et choc des cultures. Colloque de l'Institut catholique de Paris* (Paris: Cerf, 1983), 12.

28

A TRIPTYCH ON INCULTURATION IN ASIA

José Mario C. Francisco, SJ

Inculturation in Asia and its relationship with the Church's constitutive aggiornamento—certainly a complex topic, with wide geographical scope and continuous historical development—are perhaps best addressed by considering the dynamics underlying these space-time dimensions. This contribution consists of a triptych of interconnected sections. The first of these outlines the theological foundations of inculturation in Asia based on representative documents, both ecclesial and theological, especially those of the Federation of the Episcopal Conference of Asia (FABC). The second focuses on cultural studies of the religious dynamics in Asian contexts. The third presents some key areas for deeper inculturation in those contexts, drawn from ideas and themes common to the first two sections.

Theological Foundations of Inculturation in Asia

This section does not intend to articulate a comprehensive theology of inculturation, but aims to outline fundamental theological points that underlie the practice of inculturation in Asia.[1]

Although not exclusive to Asia or isolated from other contexts, this brief presentation follows the line of the dynamics of religious traditions in Asian contexts.

INCULTURATION AS EVANGELIZATION

Inculturation involves nothing less than the preaching of the gospel of the kingdom of God addressed to and in a particular context in time and space, in this case Asia, and has to do with the proclamation of the God's historical revelation in Jesus Christ, his reception in faith, and his growth in the ecclesial and personal life of Christians. For this reason, "evangelization and inculturation are naturally and intimately related to each other."[2] "Inculturation" characterizes the process as well as the origin and the end of evangelization, which is "called to bring the power of the Gospel into the very heart of culture and cultures."[3] Hence,

> It is imperative to evangelize cultures in order to inculturate the Gospel. In countries of Catholic tradition, this means encouraging, fostering and reinforcing a richness which already exists. In countries of other religious traditions, or profoundly secularized countries, it will mean sparking new processes for evangelizing culture, even though these will demand long-term planning. (*EG* 69)

Therefore, inculturation cannot be considered secondary to evangelization in either priorities or over time. It is more than external changes of liturgical vestments and the appearance of garments, or updated ways of communicating the message of the gospel. Thus understood, inculturation includes what is defined as indigenization, acculturation, and contextualization.[4]

Moreover, since the Church gathers the disciples of Jesus sent to evangelize, to proclaim the kingdom of God to all people, inculturation cannot simply be a task of the Church *ad intra*. It involves the Church's nature, reality, and mission as bearer of evangelization, and touches on all ecclesial—and institutional and charismatic—dimensions, its inner life, and its mission *ad gentes*.

In particular, local churches in communion with the universal Church are the subject of inculturation through the whole process of evangelization. Under the guidance of the Spirit discovered through an ecclesial discernment, they are agents of evangelization from the initial proclamation of the gospel to its increasingly profound appropriation by Christian communities and individuals in particular contexts.

INCULTURATION AS CRITICAL DIALOGUE BETWEEN THE GOSPEL AND THE CONTEXT

Inculturation as evangelization in a given context recognizes the transcendent and historic character of both the gospel and its preachers, as well as the context of its proclamation. The inculturation process then necessarily becomes a dynamic and multidirectional relationship between gospel and context. It is not a deductive process from the gospel to the context, often expressed by some theologies of inculturation in terms of biblical and nonbiblical images such as the grain of wheat and chaff, seed and soil, and treasure and clay pots. Yet, the FABC's view of inculturation has matured from an earlier "one-way" vision (from faith to culture) to a dialogic understanding.[5] This understanding involves "a dialogical encounter process understood in its deepest meaning that comes from the salvific movement of the Triune God, because evangelization itself is above all a dialogue between the Gospel message and the given reality."[6]

The critical dialogue between the gospel and context is based on a theological understanding of both. On the one hand, the proclamation of the gospel presents itself in particular historical forms: "The gospel is always incarnate, incarnate in the reality of those who bring it to us, and incarnate in those who help us nurture the beginnings of the faith. Church is a complex of those cultural patterns in which the gospel has taken on flesh."[7] On the other, any concrete context, being created by the Father, redeemed by the Son, and sanctified by the Spirit, participates not only in what the Word has assumed through the incarnation, but also of what has been glorified by the resurrection. Thus, the context is never mere nature in opposition to grace.

As a result, the process of inculturation as a critical dialogue implies the recognition of God's presence and activity in the context, as well as questioning the historical forms through which the gospel is preached: "Inculturation is not a mere adaptation of a ready-made Christianity into a given situation, but rather a creative embodiment of the Word in the local church."[8] This ongoing dialogue is eschatological in character, for the infinite mystery of God's presence and of the pilgrim nature of the Church.

PRIMACY OF INCULTURATION OF THE CHRISTIAN FAITH AS PRACTICE

"Practice" refers to the total scope involved in inculturation and includes the different shades found in other expressions such as "experience" or "praxis." Since faith is the full and total response of the *ekklēsía* and its members to the revelation of God, Christian practice becomes then the privileged and integral field for inculturation: "The decisive new phenomenon for Christianity in Asia will be the emergence of genuine Christian communities in Asia—Asian in their way of thinking, praying, living, communicating their own Christ-experience to others."[9]

This field, in which "the question of the faith-and-culture integration is primarily encountered *concretely and pastorally*,"[10] is the totality of Christian life, as are the celebration of the sacraments, the various forms of worship, the moral decision and the behavior of individuals and communities, and the work aimed at integral human development. Although shaped by material and cultural resources, this integration is also shaped by human agents, through decisions and actions.

This encompassing sphere of the Christian practice expresses and nourishes the meaning embodied in the Christian faith through material signs and symbols and through human speech and action. Thus, we can say that all this is to constitute the living tradition of a local church, which, to articulate its meaning and significance, includes pastoral and theological reflection.

Inculturation therefore involves the practice of the Christian faith that truly proclaims the gospel in dialogue with a context as well as reflection on this practice. As such, inculturation as evangelization precedes any theology, which inevitably articulates the meaning of the Christian faith from and to a context, be it implicit or explicit. Each theology must, therefore, be measured by its faithful articulation of Christian practice in the context, its discovery of theological foundations, and its integration into the catholicity of the Christian faith.

Religious Dynamics in Asian Contexts

The inculturation of Christianity in Asia today must begin with the recognition of the growing geopolitical and demographic importance of the region and its constitution of numerous and diverse contexts, opposing resistance to essentialist definitions. Hence, Asia should be seen beyond a construction of historiography, or trivially reduced to what is not "Western."[11] In addition, the interwoven threads, formed by theological and cultural studies, come into play in describing its many contexts.

The first thread—the context as a "sign of the times"—comes from *GS* 4: "The Church has always had the duty of scrutinizing the signs of the times and of interpreting them in the light of the Gospel." And if Vatican II pointed to the context as a historic domain in which God speaks, it did not provide a more concrete description. This came with the second thread represented by studies that describes the context as cultural localization, already suggested in *Gaudium et Spes* (58ff.) and borrowed from the modern anthropological view of culture as "the total body of belief, behaviors, knowledge, sanctions, values and goals that mark the way of life of people."[12] This shift toward empirical and experiential evidence has nevertheless proved to be incomplete as cultures are not only dynamic and changeable, but they also show to be linked to power relations and social structures. This is how the third thread—the context as a social construction—has emerged, which is the focus of various forms of critique, including postcolonialism, feminism, and liberationism.[13] Finally, since no context is isolated and no consideration of it is totally inclusive or uniformly integrates its members, a fourth thread has been recognized—the context as intercultural dialogue: "There is a need to go beyond fragments towards a genuinely integrative theology, while avoiding the colonization of other disciplines."[14]

In line with the interconnected nature of the various Asian contexts, the task of inculturation must involve the dynamics of the religious traditions within them. Based on "family resemblance"[15] due to common geographies, linked ethnicities, and interacting stories, there are three social processes within this dynamic, but each one applies to different contexts in different degrees.

INTERACTION BETWEEN RELIGIOUS AND SOCIAL TRADITIONS

Asian contexts are characterized by numerous religious traditions in many and varied forms—ancient and new, as well as "large" and "small." In addition, these religious traditions interact with each other and with traditional local practices. For example, there are various forms of Buddhism, Islam, as well as Christianity in the Asian landscape that have interacted with ethical traditions such as Confucianism and Taoism, as well as with local practices such as shamanism and indigenous traditions.[16]

These religious traditions then go beyond what is commonly regarded as religion and world religion in the social sciences and theological discourses. These categories "do not adequately apply to non-Western religions, especially those religions that are not structured at all like Western religious organization with 'membership,' of individuals"[17] or characterized by articulated doctrinal and moral systems.[18]

Such inadequate views are reflected in Catholic official documents. Even the declaration *Nostra Aetate* (2–4) implicitly uses them to distinguish between different religions—the so-called traditional religions, those found in the most advanced civilization and the Abrahamic religions. In addition, Paul VI's *Evangelii Nuntiandi* 53 refers to the non-Abrahamic religions as "natural religious expressions," as opposed to Christianity—subtly implying a purely human origin. This exhortation not only distorts religious traditions in Asian contexts that do not conform to the dominant concepts of "religion" and "world religions," but does not pay enough attention to the presence of God in them.

THE LINK BETWEEN POLITICAL ORGANIZATION AND RELIGIOUS BODY

Asian contexts have been and continue to be deeply shaped by dominant religious traditions: Hinduism in India; Islam in West Asia, Pakistan, Indonesia, and Malaysia; Buddhism in Sri Lanka, Japan, Korea, Thailand, Myanmar, Cambodia, and Laos; Christianity in the Philippines and Timor.[19] Intimately linked to them, this dynamic often manifests itself in the social ethos of the people within each context and in the historical ties, if not the fusion, between the political and religious body, especially in the emergence of nationalism and nation-states.

The dominant social ethics in a context permeates many aspects of personal and social existence and makes the boundaries between religious and other social traditions porous. Thus "most Asian religions or religious traditions are, not unlike Christianity, ways of life, and in this sense they cannot be distinguished, much less separated, from culture."[20]

In addition, these dominant religious traditions have played a significant role in the historical formation of the nations in Asia—if understood as "imagined political communities"[21] or "nation-of-intent, i.e.—its own vision of what the national identity should be."[22] This link and the often-resulting combination of political and religious bodies generate a social logic that presupposes the unity of religious affiliation with other identities. For example, it is said that to be Thai is to be Buddhist.

This second dynamic then challenges modern discourses on secularism, and calls into question the differentiation of different social spheres from religion.[23] Religious practice in Asian contexts often occurs through socialization processes of traditional customs, rituals, and practices and not under the heading of autonomous personal choices, so strongly valued in Western societies.

If the secularization thesis

> no longer carries the conviction it once did, this is because the categories of 'politics' and "religion" turn out to implicate each other more profoundly than we

> thought, a discovery that has accompanied our growing understanding of the powers of the modern nation-state. The concept of the secular cannot do without the idea of religion.[24]

These dynamic processes in many Asian contexts frame the "complex or complicated religious-cultural identity" of individuals and communities:

> For in many parts of Asia, intimate and rather fluid encounters between different religious and cultural traditions have been going on for ages. In this kind of dynamic, there is a lot of mutual borrowing not only among religions but also among cultural traditions—or among religions within certain cultural matrices, given that "religion" never existed as a free-floating entity, apart from the particularities of culture and people—sometimes through not so nice avenues such as ideological rivalries, political and religious conquest, colonialism, and so forth.[25]

Indeed, beyond what has often been classified as religious conflict or religious violence in Asia, is a consequence of the fact that "various groups of people who belong to particular ethnic, religious, ethno-religious, and ethno-nationalist collective identities, castes, socioeconomic and political classes [tend] to renegotiate their position within a network of power relationships."[26]

RELIGIOUS PRACTICES "STRADDLING DIFFERENT REALITIES"

There are cultural studies that describe Asian contexts that are changing today, perhaps more in a state of unrest than most past and present societies, and in terms of a rapid, wide, and deep mobility, which produces new space-time configurations. Fueled by global movements of populations, resources, and information—though not entirely due to them—this configuration labeled "straddling" two realities is the movement of material and symbolic meanings from different spatial-temporal places, beyond the traditional boundaries of national states.[27]

It is no longer a movement in time and space imagined as a set of unidirectional linear paths, but as a set of circulating streams. Communities and individuals beyond and within nations inhabit "intermediate" situations marked by strong differences. Migrants move back and forth, and at the same time belong to their places of origin and those of destination. Communities live between subsistence agriculture and urban poverty, and the local population is connected through communication technologies to family members who moved to other parts of the globe. Traditional forms of power administration as monarchies and sultanates interact with constitutional governments of national states. In addition, these space-time configurations that are "straddling" or "in-between" affect all aspects of social and personal life in many Asian contexts and involve problems of transience and permanence, tradition and modernity, inclusion and exclusion.

Faced with the flaws of such mobility, Asia in the past was seen "a view of Asia as docile, nonagential site upon which technologies are mapped,"[28] but recent studies show "how the new media communications in the Asian context possess the potential both for democratizing processes as well as for maintaining the exclusion or marginalization of women, the elderly, and the poor."[29] Thus, negotiation becomes the constant imperative of the space-time configuration of today's world "straddling different realities."[30]

Religious practice in Asia has not been exempted in this regard. In Southeast Asia, as elsewhere, "every major historical transformation...has been attended by changes in religion."[31] The movements of entire populations have transformed religious practice at home and in host communities. Religious institutions and groups have created websites and social media accounts, but they are aware of the diminished ability to monitor and control religious practice where blogs can discuss religious issues, even subverting official voices. Spiritual accompaniment and forms of meditation are undertaken interactively through the internet worldwide.

Thus, "in this era of internationalization and cultural encounter no specific culture or religion, indeed no system of symbols, appears able comfortably to claim the exclusive grip it used to"[32]: contemporary mobility has strengthened, not weakened, the typical negotiations of socio-religious identity of communities and peoples in different Asian contexts.[33]

Critical Areas for Inculturation in Asia

Christianity suffers from the common stereotype of being foreign and in minority in the Asian context. Yet, its historical roots have produced generations of Asian Christians who have followed Jesus and made faster the growth of the religious tradition in this area.[34]

In such a situation, the FABC has exposed the task of evangelization in Asia through the iconic vocabulary of the threefold dialogue with cultures, religions, and people, especially the poor,[35] while adding the dialogue with creation. Moreover, this task is seen as involving both the announcement and the dialogue as "integral but dialectical and complementary dimensions of the Church's evangelizing mission."[36]

Thus, the Church in Asia has embarked on the mission of inculturation, understood as an integral part of evangelization, within various contexts characterized by negotiations between and with distinct religious and social traditions, in new space-time configurations. Several FABC offices have also formulated concrete directives corresponding to ministries in the Church.[37] Following the spirit of Vatican II, inculturation has taken place in some critical areas, but still needs to develop a greater breadth and depth. These critical areas show that the threefold dialogue cannot be done separately and requires a unified approach to inculturation.

LANGUAGE AND TRANSMISSION OF THE CHRISTIAN PRACTICE

The continued and profound inculturation is required in the language and in the spread of Christian practice. This language needs to be more rooted in the lingua franca of the life and stories of the people, and implies also the use of all the channels through which meaning is created and communicated, among others, material, verbal, corporeal, and symbolic channels—more than just the multitude of Asian indigenous languages; that is, it needs whatever supports the *ethos* of the people within a given context. Only inculturated Christian practice rooted in this communicative network can proclaim and express the Christian faith in this context, without the risks of distorting the faith itself.

Inculturation of Christian practice through language implies a dual course of action: "Inculturation consists not only in the expression of the Gospel and the Christian faith through the cultural medium, but includes, as well, experiencing, understanding, and appropriating the Gospel through the cultural resources of a people."[38] First, the Church is challenged to explore all these communicative resources in the various Asian contexts to inculturate its faith. Although these resources often carry traces of other religious and cultural traditions, the Church must remain open to these realities that are an integral part of the ethos of the people: for example, idiomatic expressions, gestures of reverence, ritual practices, and religious texts of other traditions, significant themes such as filial piety and the traditional ways of moral wisdom. The use that the Church makes of these resources is not mere syncretic juxtaposition, but is an integral part of the process of critical dialogue process between the gospel and the context.

Second, inculturation through language also requires translation of Christian discourses and practices of other contexts into the lingua franca of the people, including the magisterial sphere. This work not only includes textual translations, paraphrases, and summaries of fundamental texts, but also the interpretation of Christian practices from other contexts in the lingua franca of individual Asian contexts.

In both cases, this translation process is a multidirectional mediation involving the gospel and the context. As contemporary theory and practice point out, translation is more than finding words and equivalent expressions in different languages; rather, it is a mediation between the world of the original and the world of the new context—in this case, between the religious and spiritual world of Christianity as it is proclaimed and that of Asian contexts.[39] In this process of translation, both worlds should be respected, but neither should be considered immutable.

An inculturated Christian practice requires also a pastoral and theological reflection, as well as appropriate modes of transmission.

Reflection must, at least in part, be articulated in the languages of a particular context. Images and themes emerging from such a reflection form the basis of a more inculturated theology, which can then establish a more enriching dialogue with theologies of other contexts.

Ways of conveying Christian practice, considered under the rubric of catechesis, must not be based solely on appropriate methodologies, but also on inculturated methodologies. Religious practice in Asia is mainly transmitted through socialization and community formation, but traditional catechesis often focuses on instructions on Christian faith. More attention must be given to the role of stories, symbols, and rituals in the transmission of Christian practice in Asian contexts.

INVOLVEMENT IN THE PUBLIC SPHERE

Inculturation in terms of Church presence in the public sphere involves the Church's solidarity with the aspirations of the Asian peoples, especially the marginalized and the young (which represent a sizeable number), as well as the participation of the Church with the other social aggregations in seeking the common good. The Church's long tradition of social ministry in Asia is at the service of these affiliations, regardless of whether religious affiliation is an appropriate indication of this solidarity.

Thus, the mission of the Church in Asia has been referred to as mission *inter gentes*, not to deny the fundamental task of the mission *ad gentes*, but to emphasize "solidarity and harmony with the Asian peoples within their diverse and pluralistic *Sitz im Leben*" and to consider "the prior presence and activity of God in the world—in the great world religions, in the primal religions, and in the secular world."[40]

Efforts in social engagement are often silenced because of the minority status of the Church and its being foreign, which makes it reticent in the public sphere, particularly in those contexts where the political forces and other actors are indifferent, even hostile, to Christianity. Hence, in many cases, Christians are reduced to silence.

However, rather than focusing on their small numbers, Christian community and individuals could widen the wealth of the values of the kingdom beyond the boundaries of the Church and unite their voices along with those of many others who respond to the deepest aspirations of the people. This Christian commitment to promoting integral human spiritual development and meaning becomes more crucial in contemporary Asian contexts, when the dominant social forces, especially the economic and political neoliberalism, hinder social transformation.

Through them, the Church reinforces partnership with other associations—religious, civil, and governmental—forming wider social and religious movements. They could participate in shared work for the protection of the environment or in numerous civic and religious celebrations of the people, including those pilgrimages to holy places revered by the people of different religious traditions.[41]

Within this collaboration, which has been referred to as the dialogue of life or action rooted in "acting for justice and [in] participating in the transformation of the world,"[42] the Church is present not as the guide who owns ready-made answers, but as a fellow participant to the discernment of the often problematic common good—that is, as "a church in continuous, humble, and loving dialogue with the living traditions, the cultures, the religions—in brief, with all the life realities of life of the people."[43] In addition, as all the participants in this dialogue bring to the communal table their riches, the Church must learn to share its heritage in a language that others understand and in which they can identify. Her public voice should not seem authoritarian, selfish, and exclusive. Differences will arise, but partnership must always be clear in seeking what is good for the people.

THE CHURCH'S INTERNAL CULTURE

The inculturation of the Church's *corporate culture* does not call into question the hierarchical structures and the institutional offices of the same Church, but focuses on how individuals and groups relate, communicate, and collaborate with each other and with others in the public sphere, given its hierarchical and institutional nature. This area is crucial because it involves cultural problems of interpersonal relationship, government styles, and gender roles.[44]

The Church in Asia is therefore called upon to develop and cultivate an *ad intra* culture that promotes Christian principles of equal dignity, active participation, and interpersonal community, as well as the soundness of institutional practices, but always in dialogue with Asian ways of proceeding. These paths, among other things, show appreciation for the hospitality of the community, the harmony of personal relationships, and respect for authority. Although some of these values support the relationships based on the theological nature of the Church, others could reinforce what has been described as clerical culture within the Church, which diminishes the stature of the laity and women, and thus hinders the need for transparency and responsibility. As a result, the church in Asia is often seen as a highly differentiated and closed institution, rather than as a welcoming community: "As a social institution the Church is perceived as a foreign body in its colonial origins, while the other world religions are not"; not only that, but "the Church is even sometimes seen as an obstacle or a threat to national integration and to religious and cultural identity."[45]

In addition, the Church must seek to be inculturated in the networks of the world of contemporary connectivity that also reaches the most remote recesses in Asia. The community ties to the Church are primarily related to geography, that is, they are connected in terms of basic ecclesial communities, parishes, and dioceses. However, because of the unprecedented movements of populations through different forms of migration, new forms of connections and communities have emerged. Websites have become interactive and social media have become discussion groups, and religious practice is now facilitated by real-time digital communications. Spiritual accompaniment, the role of guiding meditation and contemplation, is now performed interactively in cyberspace. In addition, relatives and friends from various parts of the world can be virtually present and participate in prayer for a deceased loved one in another country. The church needs to further explore these new forms of technology as possible ways of building community and to extending her message.

The Church in Asia has started—but must continue—the mission of inculturation in these crucial areas. It must overcome internal and external obstacles, such as the identification of uniformity with Catholicism or mistrust between religious institutions and other groups. In addition, further efforts in these areas should be in line with ongoing reflections on ecclesiological and government structures within the Church, and can only be undertaken through the accompanying formation of all Christians, faithful and leaders alike, regarding the integral relationship between evangelization and inculturation.

Inculturation requires nothing less than what the FABC has defined as "a new way of being Church":

> A *communion of communities*...that faithfully and lovingly *bears witnesses* to the Risen Lord and reaches out to the people of other faiths and persuasions in a dialogue of life towards the integral liberation of all....It is the leaven of transformation in this world and serves as a *prophetic sign* daring to point beyond this world to the ineffable Kingdom that is yet fully to come.[46]

This could be the Asian translation of the New Evangelization that our last popes have required.

NOTES

1. It is said that the term *inculturation* was used for the first time in Paul VI's speech at the meeting of Asian bishops in Manila (Philippines) on November 28, 1970. See J. Kroeger, *Dialogue: Interpretative Key for the Life of the Church in Asia*, FABC Papers 130 (Hong Kong: Federation of Asian Bishops' Conferences, Hong Kong, 2010), 9.

2. John Paul II, apostolic exhortation *Ecclesia in Asia*, November 6, 1999, no. 21 (*EV* 18, 1205); T. Tosolini, ed., *Church and Culture: Selected Texts (1965–2009)* (Osaka: Asian Missionary Centre, 2010), 53.

3. John Paul II, apostolic exhortation *Catechesi Tradendae*, October 16, 1979, no. 53 (*EV* 6, 1253); Tosolini, *Church and Culture*, 22.

4. The documents of the magisterium and the authors of theological and cultural studies also use these terms, but *inculturation* is the most accepted and widely used expression; see, Kroeger, *Dialogue*, 9.

5. Ibid., 10ff.

6. *International Congress on Mission—Consensus Paper. Workshop II*, Manila, December 7, 1979, no. 7 (FAPA 1, 138ff.).

7. R. J. Schreiter, *Constructing Local Theologies* (Maryknoll, NY: Orbis Books, 1985), 21.

8. *International Congress on Mission - Consensus Paper. Workshop II*, n. 6 (FAPA 1, 138).

9. *Asian Colloquium on Ministries in the Church*, Hong Kong, March 5, 1977, n. 14.ii (FAPA 1, 70).

10. Kroeger, *Dialogue*, 8.

11. J. M. C. Francisco, "Introduction. Theological Ethics in Context," in *Transformative Theological Ethics: East Asian Contexts*, ed. A. M. Brazal et al. (Quezon City: Ateneo de Manila University Press, 2010), 1–6, at 2.

12. K. Tanner, *Theories of Culture: A New Agenda for Theology* (Minneapolis: Fortress Press, 1997), 27.

13. For example, C. E. Curran, M. A. Farley, and R. A. McCormick, eds., *Feminist Ethics and the Catholic Moral Tradition* (Mahwah, NJ: Paulist Press, 1996); B. Massingale, *Poverty and Racism: Overlapping Threats to the Common Good* (Washington, DC: Catholic Charities USA, 2008).

14. G. Newlands, *The Transformative Imagination: Rethinking Intercultural Theology* (Hampshire, UK: Ashgate, 2003), 3.

15. A. Ahmed, ed., *Wittgenstein's Philosophical Investigations: A Critical Guide* (New York: Cambridge University Press, 2010).

16. See F. Wilfred, ed., *The Oxford Handbook of Christianity in Asia* (Oxford: Oxford University Press, 2014).

17. M. B. McGuire, *Lived Religion: Faith and Practice in Everyday Life* (Oxford: Oxford University Press, 2008), 24.

18. T. Mazusawa, *The Invention of World Religions: Or, How European Universalism Was Preserved in the Language of Pluralism* (Chicago: University of Chicago Press, 2005).

19. "Religious Adherents in Asia by Country, Mid-2010—Statistics Table," in Wilfred, *The Oxford Handbook of Christianity in Asia*, 598–605.

20. P.C. Phan, ed., *Christianities in Asia* (Malden, MA: Wiley-Blackwell, 2006), 11.

21. B. Anderson, *Imagined Communities: Reflections on the Origin and Spread of Nationalism*, rev. ed. (Pasig City: Anvil, 1991), 6.

22. A. B. Shamsul, "Nations-of-intent in Malaysia," in *Shamsul A. B.: His Observations, Analyses & Thoughts*, ed. Anis Yusal Yusoff (Bangi: Institute of Ethnic Studies [KITA]/UKM, 2011), 31–50.

23. J. Casanova, *Public Religions in the Modern World* (Chicago: University of Chicago Press, 1994), 20–39.

24. T. Asad, *Genealogies of Religion: Discipline and Reasons of Power in Christianity and Islam* (Baltimore: Johns Hopkins University Press, 2003), 200.

25. A. B. Laksana, "Multiple Religious Belonging or Complex Identity? An Asian Way of Being Religious," in Wilfred, *The Oxford Handbook of Christianity in Asia*, 493–500, at 494.

26. J. L. Fernando, "The Role of Christianity in Peace and Conflict in Asia," in Wilfred, *The Oxford Handbook of Christianity in Asia*, 583–601, at 583.

27. J. M. C. Francisco, "Migration and New Cosmopolitanism in Asian Christianity," in Wilfred, *The Oxford Handbook of Christianity in Asia*, 575–92.

28. A. M. Brazal and K. Abraham, eds., *Feminist Cyberethics in Asia: Religious Discourses on Human Connectivity* (New York: Palgrave Macmillan, 2014), 1–12, at 2.

29. Ibid., 3.

30. *Negotiating Globalization in Asia* (Quezon City: Ateneo Center for Asian Studies, 2006).

31. P. Stange, "Religious Change in Contemporary Southeast Asia," in *The Cambridge History of Southeast Asia, II/2: From World War II to the Present*, ed. N. Tarling (New York: Cambridge University Press, 1999), 201–56, at 201.

32. Ibid., 253.

33. Francisco, "Migration and New Cosmopolitanism," 575–92.

34. J. Bautista and F. K. G. Lim, eds., *Christianity and the State in Asia: Complicity and Conflict* (London: Routledge, 2009), 1.

35. *Evangelization in Modern Day Asia*, Taipei, April 27, 1974, nos. 9–28 (FAPA 1, 14ff.).

36. FABC office of Theological Concerns, *Theses on Interreligious Dialogue, n. 6*; cf. J. Y. Tan, *Missio inter Gentes: Towards a New Paradigm in the Mission Theology of the Federation of Asian Bishops' Conferences*, FABC Papers 109 (Hong Kong: Federation of Asian Bishops' Conferences, 2004), 14.

37. F.-J. Eilers, ed., *For All the Peoples of Asia* (FAPA), vols. 2 and 3 (Quezon City: Claretian Publications, 1997 and 2002).

38. Theological Advisory Commission, *Theses on the Local Church*, FABC Papers 60 (Hong Kong: Federation of Asian Bishop's Conferences, 1990), 18.

39. J. M. C. Francisco, "Fidelity in Translating Religious Practice: Illustrations from Filipino Christianity," *Kritika Kultura. Online Journal* 21–22 (2013/2014); "Translating Vice into Filipino: Religious, Colonial and Nationalist Discourses on Sloth," in *Translation in Asia*, ed. R. Ricci and J. Van der Putten (Manchester, UK: St. Jerome Publishing, 2011), 104–18.

40. Tan, *Missio inter Gentes*, 83, 84.

41. Laksana, "Multiple Religious Belonging," 493–500.

42. *Evangelization in Modern Day Asia*, nos. 20–22 (FAPA 1, 15).

43. Ibid., no. 12 (FAPA 1, 14).

44. C. F. Keyes, L. Kandall, and H. Hardacre, eds., *Asian Visions of Authority* (Honolulu: University of Hawaii Press, 1994), 1–16.

45. *Church Issues in Asia in the Context of Evangelization, Dialogue and Proclamation*, no. 13 (FAPA 2, 195ff.).

46. *Journeying Together toward the Third Millennium*, nn. 8.1.1–4 (FAPA 1, 287ff.).

VII

SPIRIT AND SPIRITUALITY IN THE EVANGELICAL REFORM OF THE CHURCH

29

THE SPIRIT AND THE GOSPEL

Permanent Sources of Church Renewal

Mary Melone, SFA

Introduction

> The Holy Spirit is not a spirit of innovation, but of incessant renewal flowing from the original source, that is, from the gospel of Jesus Christ, because the task of the Holy Spirit is to continue to make Jesus Christ present in his novelty.[1]

In my opinion, these words of Cardinal Walter Kasper help clarify right away the perspective from which we should consider the relationship between Spirit, gospel, and Church renewal. This perspective basically consists of believing that the Holy Spirit is not so much a force of indeterminate, generic innovation, but rather of incessant, precise renewal. From the linguistic point of view, the difference is perhaps not so noticeable, but from a theological point of view it should not escape us, even because we usually link the Spirit to the idea of novelty.

For greater clarity, one might say that this question arises: *What novelty can we trace back to the Spirit?* One that consists of an *innovation*, that is, only in the change of structures, languages, behaviors, and so on, in dialogue with the signs of the times? Or one that, scrutinizing the signs of the times, tirelessly pushes toward *renewal*, that is, one that constantly returns to the generative point of the life of the Church, which is the gospel?

The alternative between *innovation* and *renewal* is therefore important insofar as it highlights the christological connotation of the action of the Holy Spirit: can its action, so radically marked by the need for the *beyond*, and therefore of liberty and novelty, make no reference to the gospel? Can the novelty, of which the Spirit is always the bearer as "maker of history," not refer to the gospel, that is, the Word made flesh in Christ Jesus? Certainly not. If it is considered not only in theoretical but also existential terms, what consequences does this observation, as simple and as obvious, produce in the context of ecclesial life?

These questions underlie this brief contribution, which will be structured as follows: first we will try to outline the ideas that seem essential to understand the Spirit-Church relationship, and then go on to consider more closely two constitutive dimensions of the action of this divine Person, namely the communal work created through charisms and ministries, and the guide to the understanding of "all" the truth.

The Spirit as Coinstituting Principle of the Church

The call to action of the Spirit in the Church always, and still today, is characterized by a strong ambiguity.

On the one hand, in fact, already in the fathers' minds, the link of the Church and this divine Person is clear and precise, which is clearly stated by the third article of the Nicene Creed when affirming that the profession of faith in the Spirit also involves the profession of faith in the action by which the Spirit unifies, sanctifies, catholicizes, and apostolicizes the Church. Some formulations of unsurpassed significance are in the writings of the fathers, such as Irenaeus of Lyon, such as, "Ubi enim ecclesia, ibi et Spiritus Dei, et ubi Spiritus Dei, illic ecclesia et omnis gratia."[2]

On the other hand, however, the fear that the reference to the third divine Person would pave the way to legitimizing fanaticism or challenging the institutional and hierarchical structure, as Joachim of Fiore seemed to do, for example, by claiming the advent of an exclusively spiritual age, has repeatedly fueled in the history of the Church the temptation to provide a "taming of the Spirit,"[3] so it would be available to the institution as much as possible, as its animating principle.

The enlivening work that the Spirit accomplishes in the ecclesial institution seems therefore to be simultaneously recognized as indispensable and constantly scaled down. This polarization essentially depends on the meaning that is attributed to the idea of *animation*, as it is precisely from the different way of interpreting this category that depends, in our view, the ambiguity of the reference to the Spirit.

In the postconciliar years, a theological position, very effective from an ecumenical point of view, gradually developed, that finds a privileged reference in the authority of Congar's reflection. This is the assertion of the Spirit as the *coinstituting* principle of the Church. The meaning of this perspective can be summed up in the belief that the Spirit "did not come simply to animate an institution that was already fully determined in all its structures, but that he is really the 'co-instituting principle.'"[4]

Even in this case—obviously—what is at stake is not just a question of terminological precision, leading to the formulation of a new title, but a precise ecclesiological perspective: in defining the Spirit as coinstituting principle the intent is to say that its work is neither functional nor secondary to Christ, but equally constitutive.

The consequences of this clear theological vision particularly invest the way of facing the question of the distinction between institutional structure and the charismatic reality of the Church, revealing the inadequacy of those reflections that insist on separating these two dimensions, simplistically reducing them to the historic will of Christ, on the one hand, and on the other to the animation of the Spirit, as if they were two separate works of their own. On the contrary, Christ and the Spirit—"Word and Spirit," as Congar would put it—reappear in both charisms and ministries and act "both within persons and in sacramental and legal structures."[5]

The fundamental gain of this approach can be identified in the nonresignation of the Christian conscience before the institution: the Christian, in other words, recognizes precisely in the institutional form not a dimension in contradiction with the freedom and novelty of the action of the Spirit, but an aspect of Church life through which the Spirit can accomplish its work of unification and sanctification.[6]

This last statement may seem, in some ways, a sophisticated expedient to elegantly overcome the contrast between the charismatic dimension and the institutional structure of the Church, which historically has been the cause of many tensions and divisions. The positive revaluation—better yet, the exaltation of the value of the institution in the name of the work that the Spirit accomplishes in it—would thus have the "merit" to finally put to rest the claims in favor of a Church "of the Spirit." to keep under control, so to speak, that call to freedom precisely advanced in the name of the power of the Spirit to bestow its gifts of grace to those whom it wants and how it wants, which generally goes beyond the institutional constraints.[7]

But, on a closer look, this position is not a mere expedient because, far from emphasizing institutional structures as such, it puts them under the total dependence on the action of the Spirit. Nothing that falls within the structure of the Church—that is, tradition, sacraments, apostolic ministry, magisterium, participating bodies, charisms—if it has the purpose of realizing communion, if it is at the service of unity, nothing of all this can in fact be considered irrespective of the work of Spirit,[8] that is, of the unifying and communal action that the Spirit accomplishes through the very institutional and charismatic element. Precisely by this action the Spirit is the coinstituting principle, as Congar explains: "It is the free power of Christ to build up the ecclesial body; and this power is the Spirit, with Jesus Christ as the criterion."[9]

After all, is this not what *Lumen Gentium* 8 suggests? Here, through the technical use of the verb *inservit* (to serve), is it not clear that it is not the Spirit to be thought of in function of the

Church, with the task of animating and unifying it, but, on the contrary, it is the ecclesial structure that has to be an instrument to serve the communal work of the Spirit? Let us read *LG* 8:

> As the assumed nature inseparably united to Him, serves the divine Word as a living organ of salvation, so, in a similar way, does the visible social structure of the Church serve the Spirit of Christ, who vivifies it, in the building up of the body.[10]

The true gain associated with the recognition of the coinstituting function of the Spirit seems to be emerging from these last notes: it is not, in fact, a naive and superficial attempt to bring a dignified balance between the two divine missions, so that it is not denied to the Spirit the role it deserves alongside Christ. The affirmation of an undeniable pneumatological dimension in the Church's structuring work, on the contrary, leads us to the understanding that reciprocity between Christ and his Church can be implemented only through the action of the Spirit, because only in the Spirit, the "intra-personal, the 'Immediacy' that makes room for the other,"[11] is possible the encounter between man and his risen Lord. Only in him the communion between God and man in the Church is possible. For this reason, the Spirit's coinstituting function appears at the same time as co-original, and permanent, with that of Christ.

The insistence on the role of the Spirit as an agent of the incessant formation of the Church is therefore fundamental to recognize that the tension toward reform is its essential dimension. In the Spirit, the Church lives precisely by constantly reforming itself, that is, in the commitment to constantly acquire its form, which gives it an identity to be itself, and this form depends on its relationship with Christ.

The task of the Spirit then is to return to the generative sources of ecclesial life, to highlight the generative force of the evangelical principles that are the foundation of very identity of the Church. Among them, the call to unity and service to the truth are particularly relevant.

The Spirit's Proper Work: Communion in the Church

Returning briefly to theological dimensions well known to all, it should be emphasized that, as the Nicene-Constantinopolitan symbol shows, the Spirit is *dominus et vivificans*, that is, has a privileged relationship with life, as the Greek term *zōopoión*, which can be rendered in English as "vivifier or life giver," better clarifies. This privileged relationship has been expressed in various ways throughout the history of the faith, in which the Spirit has been invoked as *Spiritus creator et sanctificator*. These are two closely related dimensions, because sanctification must be seen as the work of accomplishing Christ's redemption, and therefore as the re-creation that consists in the formation of a new man. Precisely in this way, the Spirit drives to the fullness both the single creature as the entire cosmos.

This powerful life-giving action of the Spirit is not, however, indeterminate, generic; on the contrary, it is well characterized and recognizable, because it brings the signs of communion. *Evangelii Gaudium* often recalls the communal work of the Spirit in the Church, emphasizing, as its distinctive characteristic, the ability to unite without unifying, so that the wealth of diversity creates "a multifaceted and inviting harmony" (*EG* 117).

With remarkable clarity, in this apostolic exhortation, Francis points to two basic criteria that guarantee the communion of the Church, which, at the same time, require the work of the Spirit: ecclesiality and reconciliation.

First, ecclesiality: if diversity is wealth, it is neither removed nor used to impose and rule over others. This point becomes particularly delicate regarding charisms, whose reason for being, as stated in the document, is solely to build up the Church. Therefore, charisms can be neither be a heritage of a group, or a pretext for affirming one spirituality at the expense of others. Charisms are gifts that renew and build, and as such are authentic only if they are ecclesial, that is, can integrate harmoniously into the life of the holy people of God for the good of all (see *EG* 130).

Second, *reconciliation*: differences between people and communities are no doubt riches for the Church, but they may cause difficulties and hardships. The action of the Spirit supports in this case the capacity for reconciliation of diversity (see *EG* 131).

Thus, the creative power of the Spirit, its being *life-giver*, manifests itself precisely in the fact that the Spirit connects and creates communion: from this perspective, some concrete choices should be made for the actual life of the Church. If, in fact, the Spirit constantly coestablishes the Church, and if the manner in which this coestablishment is realized is characterized by communality, then the institution is entirely in function of communion and has meaning only as it is intended for its realization, or, to use the more accurate words of Johannis Zizioulas, metropolitan of Pergamon, "the institution of universal unity cannot be self-sufficient or self-explanatory, or precedent to the communion event, but depends on it."[12]

Regarding this principle few, perhaps, would have something to say, but on its practical consequences we should reflect with courage: the communal perspective, in fact, demands that no ministry, no institution can exist without the relation between the guarantor of unity, that is, the ministry, and the subject of unity, that is, the community. Does it make sense, then, to have a bishop without a community? Or does it make sense to have an episcopal consecration, which is the ontologically constitutive act of the episcopate, that is not really in service of a community?[13] Where do titular bishops fit in this picture?

At the same time, what sense does the experience of an ecclesial community have if its normal pastoral practice tends to ignore the service of the unity exercised by the bishop? And what synodal methods can concretely translate and secure this necessary communal balance between "one and many"?

The Action of the Spirit between *Sensus Fidei* and Prophecy

Among the many ways in which we can approach the relationship between the gospel and the Spirit in the Church, we could privilege the one that focuses on the *hermeneutic function* of the Spirit of Truth, the one announced by Jesus in John 14:26: "But the

Advocate, the Holy Spirit, whom the Father will send in my name, will teach you everything, and remind you of all that I have said to you." This function can be understood as the work of *teaching by remembering* that the Spirit accomplishes in us. In this action, the evocation of the memory that the magisterium of the Spirit realizes in the heart of the believer forms itself as an interpretation, a deep understanding of the one truth that is the person and the word of Jesus Christ, the truth that in this way is actualized in the time of the Church.

This hermeneutic function is therefore decisive and warns the Church: its ability to speak and to announce the gospel, in fact, depends on its taking care of listening, that is, by its ability to let the Spirit arouse in it the memory that includes and actualizes. "In this sense, the Spirit makes the Church faithful: that is, it makes her the place of faith, the place where there is faith as the ability to listen to God and the place where there is faith as the ability to speak in the name of God."[14]

The Second Vatican Council strongly emphasized that the Holy Spirit has given to the people of God as a whole the gift of the *sensus fidei*, by virtue of which the people of God unfailingly adhere to the faith, penetrates it more deeply, and applies it to life (*LG* 12). The action of the Spirit, in this case, in its tension to preserve communion enables a specific function: the community, in fact, by creating that particular unity expressed in the *sentire cum ecclesia*, is enabled by the Spirit to discern the truth, to avoid error, to preserve the word of revelation.[15]

In the recent document of the International Theological Commission titled *The Sensus Fidei in the Life of the Church*, we find an important and articulate reflection on this theme. It is stated, among other things, that

> by the gift of the Holy Spirit, "the Spirit of truth who comes from the Father" and bears witness to the Son (John 15:26), all of the baptised participate in the prophetic office of Jesus Christ, "the faithful and true witness" (Rev 3:14). They are to bear witness to the gospel and to the apostolic faith in the Church and in the world. The Holy Spirit anoints them and equips them

> for that high calling, conferring on them a very personal and intimate knowledge of the faith of the Church.[16]

But what is particularly important is the articulation of the function of discernment of the truth with the communal dimension that the *sensus fidei* maintains and guarantees:

> On the one hand, the *sensus fidei* refers to the personal capacity of the believer, within the communion of the Church, to discern the truth of faith. On the other hand, the *sensus fidei* refers to a communal and ecclesial reality: the instinct of faith of the Church herself, by which she recognises her Lord and proclaims his word. The *sensus fidei* in this sense is reflected in the convergence of the baptised in a lived adhesion to a doctrine of faith or to an element of Christian *praxis*. This convergence (*consensus*) plays a vital role in the Church: the *consensus fidelium* is a sure criterion for determining whether a particular doctrine or practice belongs to the apostolic faith.[17]

Moreover, this document is in continuity with the statement made on several occasions by Pope Francis,[18] for example in *Evangelii Gaudium*, that he wanted to expound the potentialities contained in the gift of the *sensus fidei*, emphasizing the *connaturality* that, precisely because of this gift of the Spirit, is created between the reality of God and the community of believers:

> As part of his mysterious love for humanity, God furnishes the totality of the faithful with an instinct of faith—*sensus fidei*—which helps them to discern what is truly of God. The presence of the Spirit gives Christians a certain connaturality with divine realities, and a wisdom which enables them to grasp those realities intuitively, even when they lack the wherewithal to give them precise expression. (*EG* 119)

This gives rise to a significant question: if the people of God are not mistaken *in credendo*, is it not necessary to put in place methods that can really involve it in discernment? For example, what does the people of God, in their entirety, really say of the legitimacy of the rites that come to change the reality of the *actuosa participatio*? Does the *sentire cum ecclesia* not appeal to the activation of concrete approaches to synodality that will allow us to probe and preserve the unity of the truth in the Church?

This statement calls into question a further reflection, which has to do with formation to discernment, a formation that somehow must be assured to the community of believers. John Paul II, on March 25, 1993, had to say that the Roman pontiff, precisely because he was aware of the great responsibility that he faced in exercising his magisterium, "feels the need, one could even the duty, to explore the *sensus ecclesiae*, before defining a truth of faith."

To emphasize this "exploration," to remain in the pope's terminology, does it not necessarily involve an urgent investment in the formation of Christian communities in the spiritual dimension, which ensures the ability of discernment and intelligence?

The *sensus fidei* ultimately contains in its own way an appeal to ensure that ecclesial dimension of synodality that, viewed in the perspective of a path of the Church, leads to identifying an operational mode of community engagement. At the same time, however, the relationship between the *sensus fidei* and synodality recalls the fact that no reform can succeed if it falls out the path of communion, attracted by an idea that claims to become the governing principle of everything, that absolutizes its own point of view, thus losing solidarity with the whole Church. In other words, we cannot forget that the conditions of reform as an undertaking to ensure that Christian communities are genuinely educated in the freedom of Christianity.

This reference presupposes the recognition of the capacity for discernment of the whole people of God, an acknowledgment that arises, then, as one of the most urgent goals to attain. Such discernment, in fact, ensures the coresponsibility of the people of God in ordinary pastoral care, guarantees the quality of ecclesial communion precisely because it calls us all to assume the responsibility of one's believer's life, the responsibility to seek shared paths that can put together faith and the signs of the times.

From here emerges the importance of recognizing that Church reform, in the light of the relationship between the Spirit and the gospel, therefore, entails a serious commitment to formation:

> Evangelical docility that implies thinking, discerning, and taking responsibility. These three words spring from faith in the Holy Spirit, but they also signify an education, i.e., a formation of mind, a pedagogy of judgment, a training of the will, an apprenticeship in relationality.[19]

Conclusion

We can surely find many other perspectives on deepening the relationship between the Spirit and the gospel as inexhaustible sources of Church renewal. The attention placed on these two considerations, that is, the action of the Spirit in the service of communion, and the understanding of the truth, is necessary because it calls into question the essential dimensions of Church life. We cannot really think that the church is "going forth," that is, genuinely capable of proximity and attention, unless it is an educated to live in communion. We cannot think that the church is truly "going forth" if it is incapable of preserving plurality, welcoming diversity, and creating a space where the need of the other is authentic.

At the same time, a Church that strongly proclaims the *evangelii gaudium*, the joy of the gospel, cannot be deprived of *parrēsía*, because it cannot preach the gospel of freedom and truth it is a genuine place of reciprocity and of listening to all, where everyone can be engaged in a *liberating* communication.

The Church is "at the disposal" of the Spirit: to use a strong expression of Walter Kasper, what characterizes the action of the Spirit is the *inventiveness*, the irruption of novelty, since it is precisely the Spirit's nature to be ecstatic, leading out of all that appears as fixed and limited. Consequently, it is precisely of the Church, aware of its origin and nature, to venture courageously into the unpredictable, the new, in what is not programmable. The yes to the concrete Church implies the yes to an evolving Church.[20]

NOTES

1. W. Kasper, *Lo Spirito Santo dà la vita. Meditazione teologica sullo Spirito Santo* (Casale Monferrato: Piemme, 1989), 30.

2. "Where there is Church, there is also the Spirit of God; where there is the Spirit of God, there is the Church and all grace." Irenaeus of Lyons, *Adv. haer.* III, 24, 1.

3. W. Kasper and G. Sauter, *La Chiesa luogo dello Spirito. Linee di ecclesiologia pneumatologica*, ed. Andrea Milano (Brescia: Queriniana, 1980), 73.

4. Y. M. Congar, *Credo nello Spirito Santo, II: Lo Spirito come vita* (Brescia: Queriniana, 1982), 14ff. Translated as *I Believe in the Holy Spirit*, 2 vols. (New York: Seabury Press, 1983), 2:9.

5. Y. M. Congar, *La Parola e il Soffio* (Rome: Borla, 1985), 107.

6. A. Barruffo, "Lo Spirito Santo nella riflessione teologica sulle strutture della Chiesa," in *Verso una nuova età dello Spirito. Filosofia, teologia e movimenti*, ed. G. Colzani (Padua: EMP, 1997), 241–57, at 254: "Since its foundation to date, the Church maintains a fundamental structural continuity. Her institutional nature is not an accessory to a 'Church of the Spirit,' but is an indispensable dimension, so that the Spirit can manifest and produce its fruits."

7. See Congar, *La Parola e il Soffio*, 79–85.

8. See Barruffo, "Lo Spirito Santo nella riflessione teologica," 258ff.

9. Congar, *La Parola e il Soffio*, 103.

10. G. Cislaghi, *Per una ecclesiologia pneumatologica. Il Concilio Vaticano II e una proposta sistematica* (Milan: Glossa, 2004), 181: "What the Council suggests is the priority, transcendence, and freedom of the Holy Spirit on the Church, and, vice versa, the vital dependence of the ecclesial body on immanence of the Holy Spirit, and, therefore, the dutiful and persevering docility (a fruit of invocation and discernment) of all its members to the unifying movement aroused by the animation of the Spirit in all the spheres of their activity." In this same line are some notes of Ghislain Lafont, which to us seem very significant on how to connect the institution to the charismatic gift: see G. Lafont, *Imagining the Catholic Church: Structured Communion in the Spirit*, trans. John J. Burkhard (Collegeville, MN: Liturgical Press, 2000), 106: "In order to avoid thinking of charisms in this destructive way of inherent opposition to institutions, it is necessary to look deeper into reality of the 'influence of the Spirit.' The latter is found both in sacramental liturgy and in the search for holiness, in missionary initiatives, as well as in the institution of law and rights, in the confession of faith as well as in catechetical and theological research. Every initiative of the Spirit, i.e., *charism*, gives

rise to some *institution*, to some expression or organization in space and time, however tenuous, in the concrete life of the Church's communion. Moreover, the institution of a charism implies a certain *power* which is proportional to the goal pursued. All of the above is a retrieval of St. Paul's teaching on charisms: as soon as the Spirit imparts a gift, we can speak of an institution that is more or less permanent or more or less passing. Even the sacraments come from the influence of the Spirit and reciprocally give access to the Spirit."

11. N. Ciola, *Spirito, eschaton e storia* (Rome: Pontificia Università Lateranense, 1998), 9.

12. J. D. Zizioulas, "Cristologia, pneumatologia e istituzioni ecclesiali: un punto di vista ortodosso," in *L'ecclesiologia del Vaticano II: dinamismi e prospettive*, ed. G. Alberigo (Bologna: EDB, 1981), 121ff.

13. Ibid.

14. G. Lazzati, *Lo Spirito Santo nella vita della Chiesa* (Milan: Edizioni Corsia dei servi, 1964), 68.

15. Barruffo, "Lo Spirito Santo nella riflessione teologica," 269: "The truth of revelation lies in the living communion of the community, in the gift of the *sentire cum ecclesia*, by which the community of believers is made capable of discerning truth from error in matters concerning faith and Christian life, precisely because God's Spirit makes provision for it against any real deviation."

16. International Theological Commission, *The Sensus Fidei in the Life of the Church* (2014), no. 1.

17. Ibid., no. 3.

18. The document expressly mentions the first *Angelus* of Pope Francis: see ibid., no. 2.

19. Ghislain Lafont, *Imagining the Catholic Church*, 214.

20. See W. Kasper, "La Chiesa come sacramento dello Spirito," in Kasper and Sauter, *La Chiesa luogo dello Spirito*, 79.

30

THE GOSPEL, THE SPIRIT, AND ECCLESIAL REFORM IN THE LIGHT OF POPE FRANCIS'S THOUGHT

Archbishop Víctor Manuel Fernández

The purpose of this brief note is simply to integrate the ecclesiological aspects of the reform with some contributions specific to fundamental theology and spirituality. To do this, it seemed appropriate to dwell on five distinctive themes of Pope Francis's thought.

Self-Transcendence

Every time Francis speaks of purification, renewal, and transformation, he presupposes that this can only be done with renewed subjects, but he concludes with a basic, fundamental, radical attitude: self-transcendence.[1] Already in his writings and homilies preceding his pontificate, Cardinal Bergoglio often referred to two vices opposed to self-transcendence: "self-referentiality" and "isolated consciousness." Subjects entrapped in this dynamic are incapable of sustaining reform processes. We are then faced with a spiritual and anthropological substratum: the "coming out of oneself" that, applied to the ecclesial institution, constitutes an outgoing Church with all its structures engaged in this dynamism. We believe it is imperative to perceive this cornerstone of Francis's thought on reform. We need only to look at some of the passages in *Evangelii Gaudium* that speak of "absolute priority" (179) of the "going forth from ourselves," or of the vices opposite it. Here are some examples.

The current pope states that "to go out of ourselves and to join others is healthy for us. To be self-enclosed is to taste the bitter poison of immanence, and humanity will be worse for every selfish choice we make" (*EG* 87). He then mentions sadness of an "blunted conscience" that implies an inner life that is "caught up in its own interests and concerns" (2). He reminds that the "word of God constantly shows us how God challenges those who believe in him 'to go forth'" (20). He indicates that the joy of the gospel is the ever present "drive to go forth and give, to go out from ourselves, to keep pressing forward in our sowing of the good seed, remains ever present" (21). He shows that, thanks to the encounter with God's love, "we are liberated from our narrowness and self-absorption," and that "when we let God bring us beyond ourselves," precisely then "we find the source and inspiration of all our efforts at evangelization" (8). Referring to spiritual worldliness, he says that we "need to avoid it by making the Church constantly go out from herself" (97). From the point of view of the task of evangelization, he recognizes that "missionary outreach is *paradigmatic for all the Church's activity*" (15). For this reason, in a text explicitly referring to ecclesial reform, the pope states that "the renewal of structures demanded by pastoral conversion can only be understood in this light: as part of an effort to make them more mission-oriented, to make ordinary pastoral activity on every level more inclusive and open, to inspire in pastoral workers a constant desire to go forth" (27). The faithful Church of its own nature is therefore an ecstatic Church, in dialogue with the world, close to the weak, oriented toward the distant ones, decentralized in an evangelizing ecstasy.

Being a cornerstone of Francis's thought, we see it reappearing clearly in *Laudato Si'*: "We are always capable of going out of ourselves towards the other....Disinterested concern for others, and the rejection of every form of self-centeredness and self-absorption, are essential" (*LS* 208).

The Spirit and the Gospel

This going out of ourselves is not the result of a pure effort of human will; it is a supernatural dynamism brought by the Holy Spirit[2] in people and in the whole Church:

> At Pentecost, the Spirit made the apostles go forth from themselves. (*EG* 259)
>
> I once more invoke the Holy Spirit. I implore him to come and renew the Church, to stir and impel her to go forth boldly. (*EG* 261)

However, the reform movement designed to bring the Church out of itself is not only pneumatological, but also christological. For the Spirit guides into all the truth (John 16:13), and we know that in the fourth Gospel this "truth" is Christ himself. Therefore, the Spirit drives us forward, but not out of the mystery of the incarnation, but quite the opposite: by introducing us ever more fully into the mystery of Christ and his gospel. Therefore, the Spirit and the gospel are simultaneously the root that makes it possible for the Church to go forth in missionary reform.

If only we were to dwell on the action of the Spirit, it would encompass us all, to the point that even a Lefebvrian of good will, who lives in the grace of God, might be just following the Spirit's impulse. Although this may be true, because of the freedom of the Spirit, when we think of the Church that Jesus wants, we cannot forget that the freshness of the gospel has an *objective* sense as a *paradigmatic* source. For this reason, Francis says that when we return to this source everything is renewed, evangelization is always "new" (*EG* 11) and the "message is simplified" (*EG* 35).

This opening to the self-transcending dynamism of the Spirit must at the same time be a return to the objectivity of the gospel, which simplifies, brings to the essential, and makes it possible to purify and reform the obsolete structures. This aspect of "simplification" of the reform is developed in the section that Francis dedicates to the "hierarchy of truths" and virtues in *Evangelii Gaudium* 34–39. It is the hierarchy that refers to a fundamental core of the gospel, the *kērygma* (and charity *expressed in mercy*), distinct from secondary elements that end up overwhelming and burying the freshness of the Christian proposal.

Transcending a *Forma Mentis* (Way of Thinking)

Why is this important? Because if we do not understand this, introducing more participatory and decentralized structures will not be enough to produce a Church reform. Let us pause to reflect upon this risk.

The Church has always rejected fideism, and has supported the value of reason and the need for dialogue between faith and reason, which are not in contradiction. But what has happened in the last two decades is another story: *a* reason, a set of principles (nonnegotiable) that hold everything, is placed at the center of the Church, even though it is ultimately a *forma mentis*, more philosophical than theological, to which all else has to submit. The magisterium, revelation, everything that the pope or bishops propose, must all be subjugated to these fundamental principles. In other words, what for Luther was "justification by faith," today is a particular reason from which everything else must be judged.

In this sense, it is liberating that, in the context of a Church reform, the pope invites us not to put a philosophy or a rational scheme above revelation, and to return to the gospel. Thus, a passage in *Evangelii Gaudium* acquires a special significance: "When preaching is faithful to the Gospel, the centrality of certain truths is evident and it becomes clear that Christian morality is not a form of stoicism, or self-denial, or merely a practical philosophy or a catalogue of sins and faults." (*EG* 39). If not,

> the edifice of the Church's moral teaching risks becoming a house of cards, and this is our greatest risk. It would mean that it is not the Gospel which is being preached,

> but certain doctrinal or moral points based on specific ideological options. The message will run the risk of losing its freshness and will cease to have "the fragrance of the Gospel." (*EG* 39)

For the traditionalist sectors, we have a magisterium not at the service of revelation, but in the service of a philosophy, a way of exercising reason that it is judged by the magisterium itself. Hence, there seems to be a nonnegotiable reason that judges the gospel. This form of exercising reason controls us all, including the pope. Therefore, those who determine the correct interpretation of revelation and truth would be the ones who possess this *forma mentis*, this way of reasoning, this structure of rational principles.

Can any Christian doctrine be derived from some rational principles, or should it be interpreted from these? Perhaps even the resurrection of Jesus Christ, the initiative of his grace, the primacy of brotherly love, must be subordinated to these principles as to their source of meaning? This would be a sort of intellectual Pelagianism, because there is no longer the will that occupies the place of grace, but a certain reason occupying the place of the gospel. The Scriptures then are reduced to being only a source of accommodating quotations that serve only if they illustrate or confirm the nonnegotiable principles or the logic of *this* reason.

This explains the power of some ecclesiastics to come to terms with what the pope can or cannot say, and presenting themselves as guarantors of legitimacy and unity of faith. The *forma mentis* of which they consider themselves absolute guardians is a source of power that has sometimes been exerted in the Church in a heavy way, associated with a rigorous and capillary control mechanism.

Therefore, when we speak of a Church reform in which there is a greater participation of diocesan bishops, we must ask ourselves if many of them are not heirs of this *forma mentis* that seems to affect the understanding of revelation. In this regard, more than just a few believe, for example, that the conclusions of the Extraordinary Synod of Bishops of 2014 were not clearly placed on the renewal and evangelical line of Pope Francis, as expressed in *Evangelii Gaudium*. In these specific circumstances, ecclesial reform cannot be based solely on the principle of greater participation by the bishops, if at the same time no one listens to the pope's invitation to return to the simplicity of the gospel.

Aspects of the Return to the Gospel

What aspects can we highlight in Francis's proposal of returning to the gospel and its original freshness? We could mention several, but we will focus only on three.

a) *A law of freedom*: It is simply a matter of greater fidelity, which, as we have seen, means also simplifying, and this directly affects the moral doctrine of the Church as it supposes to not weigh useless burdens on the lives of the faithful and allow them to live the gospel as a law of freedom.[3] In this sense, it is crucial to cite from a text by St. Thomas Aquinas, as Francis aptly does:

> Saint Thomas Aquinas pointed out that the precepts which Christ and the apostles gave to the people of God "are very few." Citing Saint Augustine, he noted that the precepts subsequently enjoined by the Church should be insisted upon with moderation "so as not to burden the lives of the faithful" and make our religion a form of servitude, whereas "God's mercy has willed that we should be free." This warning, issued many centuries ago, is most timely today. It ought to be one of the criteria to be taken into account in considering a reform of the Church and her preaching which would enable it to reach everyone. (*EG* 43)

On the contrary, in the last decades, "precepts subsequently enjoined" seem to have become the domain of some sectors of the Church, through a moral doctrine or a legalism that seeks to scrutinize in detail all aspects of the lives of the faithful so that personal conscience and Christian freedom seem to turn into empty words.

In this sense, Francis's insistence on the Church as "people" of God, in whom the Spirit acts, spreading charisms and transmitting faith in uncontainable ways beyond the supervision of

Church ministers, is important. It should not be forgotten that the "Church, as the agent of evangelization, is more than an organic and hierarchical institution; she is first and foremost a people advancing on its pilgrim way towards God" (*EG* 111). Therefore, the pope exhorts audacity, trust, and patient mercy, so that the ministry of pastors does not restrain the wealth and creativity nor encroach on the *freedom* of the various members of the Church with their own charisms.

b) *Attention to the historical Jesus*: A return to the gospel in a genuine reform means also to retrieve the model of the historical Jesus[4] as an objective model:

> Jesus' whole life, his way of dealing with the poor, his actions, his integrity, his simple daily acts of generosity, and finally his complete self-giving, is precious and reveals the mystery of his divine life. Whenever we encounter this anew, we become convinced that it is exactly what others need. (*EG* 265)

Pope Francis's preaching reflects this appreciation and this recovery, this evangelical freshness that is felt in his gestures and in his style.

c) *Peter and the apostles*: In any case, it is true that returning to the gospel means also to recover the fundamental ecclesial structure of the Church proposed by it: Peter and the apostles. This way the Holy See's structures of service find their proper place. Why should these structures have more power than the various forms of collegiate ministry of the apostolic successors (synods, national and regional episcopal conferences)? It cannot be ignored that the management of the Church is changing and adapting in its secondary aspects, but these aspects must always be subordinate to its fundamental structure. This conviction does not seem to be in line with the fact that some say that "the safe compass" of the Church is a prefect at the head of one of the dicasteries of the Holy See, for example.

> But, beyond what is explicitly stated, there is an established practice that needs to be revised, because it runs the risk of being in contradiction with the fundamental structure of the Church that the gospel presents. In any case, it is necessary to give space to a synodality that leaves unconstrained the various charisms of the various members of the people of God in every local church, instead of granting excessive power to centralized structures.

Our Style and Our Spirit in the Proposal of a Reform

Finally, considering what has been said so far, I would like to mention our concern for the reform of the Church, because even our concern for reform needs an evangelical style and spirit.

First, it must be situated in the dynamics of self-transcendence and be truly oriented for the people. It concerns the people of God; therefore, even our attitude should be ecstatic. Our reform proposals are not based on an unruly complacency, but on a generous and flexible conviction, capable of letting itself be put into question by the specific needs of the people of God, by their culture and their way of living the faith.

It also implies humility, to endure derision and persecution, because for some sectors any reform is annoying, irritating. We refer not only to the more traditionalist sectors. Reforms may also be uncomfortable for moderate ecclesiatics who have already adapted to a pattern in which they move with a certain ease.

But it be must a humility open to the truth, which requires the recognition of other legitimate concerns, including those of the more conservative factions. In this line, I would like to recall a text by St. Thomas Aquinas (*ST* I–II, q.19, a.10). In it, he brings us the example of a judge who condemns a criminal because his function is to ensure the common good. Instead the mother of the criminal, for a natural maternal inclination, tries to save him. Both oppose the materiality of the fact, yet conform to the "formal motive" of God's will, because both "want what God wants them to want." This means that, even though there is conflict between them on the materiality of the facts, two people can be faithful to their own charism, for a particular purpose. Therefore, conflict in the Church should not always be considered bad, but sometimes these are the tensions that exist between honest and sincere people who respond to God's will by contributing to this world. The Spirit seeks and spreads communion, but this does not exclude a diversity that is sometimes painful and full of tensions, and in any case, is aimed at achieving higher syntheses.

Yves Congar said that it is useful to have tensions in the Church because of different orientations that are the origin of different approaches. In fact, "the manifestations of grace have often overcome the fossilized forms of the institution, [but] the life of the Church requires both forms."[5] In a famous text, Karl Rahner recalled that this was the cause of persecutions even among saints. He recalled the cases of people who led major renovations with distinctive styles, such as John of the Cross, Teresa of Avila, Johann Michael Sailer, John Henry Newman, and Mary Ward. And he concluded that these sufferings occurred from the beginning of the Church to our day, because "they are inevitable. They are part of that 'necessary' Passion that Christ continues to suffer in his members, in the Church, until the end. And he wanted his members to suffer with each other."[6]

We should not be alarmed then, that the dynamism of reform that God inspires is also a source of suffering, contradictions, and bitter moments. It is part of our commitment to the gospel, and is part of the Spirit.

NOTES

1. See C. Schickendantz, *Autotrascendencia radicalizada en extrema impotencia. La comprensión de la muerte en Karl Rahner* (Santiago: Universidad Católica de Chile, 1999). One can also refer to my book: *Salir de sí. Plenitud de conocimiento y de vida* (Córdoba, Argentina: Ediciones del Icala, 1991).

2. See V. M. Fernández, *Teología espiritual encarnada. Profundidad espiritual en acción* (Buenos Aires: San Pablo, 2004).

3. See S. Lyonnet, *El amor, plenitud de la ley* (Salamanca: Sígueme, 1981).

4. J. P. Meier, *A Marginal Jew: Rethinking the Historical Jesus*, 5 vols. (New York: Doubleday, 1991–2016); J. Caba, *De los evangelios al Jesús histórico. Introducción a la Cristología* (Madrid: BAC, 1971).

5. Y. M. Congar, *El Espíritu Santo* (Barcelona: Herder, 1983), 356ff. Translated as *I Believe in the Holy Spirit* (New York: Seabury Press, 1983). Originally published as *Je crois en l'Esprit Saint* (Paris: Cerf, 1979).

6. K. Rahner, *Das Dynamische in der Kirche* (Freiburg: Herder, 1958), 72. Translated by William Joseph O'Hara as *The Dynamic Element in the Church* (New York: Herder, 1964).

CONTRIBUTORS

Alphonse Borras is vicar-general of the diocese of Liege (Belgium) and professor of canon law at the Université Catholique de Louvain and at the Faculty of Canon Law of the Institut Catholique in Paris. He specializes in penal canon law, and is also interested in questions related to the particular church, the parish institution, and ministries. Among his many publications, he is best known for a treaty on excommunication and for a commentary on book 6 of the Code of Canon Law. He edited *Délibérer en Église* (Brussels: Lessius, 2010). Among his most recent works are his contributions in C. Theobald, ed., *Pourquoi l'Église?* (Paris: Bayard, 2014), and F. X. Amherdt, ed., *Vatican II: quel avenir? Évangile et culture, paroisses et ministères* (Fribourg: Fribourg Academic Press, 2016). Among his publications in Italian: *La parrocchia. Diritto canonico e prospettive pastorali* (Bologna: EDB, 1997); *Il diaconato, vittima della sua novità?* (Bologna: EDB, 2008); he also edited, together with Luca Bressan, *Abitare da cristiani il nostro tempo. Parrocchie d'Europa s'interrogano* (Bologna, EDB, 2009).

Piero Coda holds a doctorate in philosophy (University of Turin), and in theology (Pontifical Lateran University). He is a professor of theology and dean of the University Institute Sophia (Loppiano, Florence), and a member of the International Theological Commission and the Commission for Dialogue between the Church Catholic and the Orthodox Church, of the Pontifical Academy of Theology, the Italian Theological Association (of which he was president), the Committee of the Italian Bishops' Conference for higher studies in theology and religious studies, and consultant to the Pontifical Council for the Promotion of Christian Unity. Among his publications are *Evento pasquale. Trinità e storia* (Rome: Città Nuova, 1984); *Dio Uno e Trino* (Cinisello Balsamo: San Paolo, 1993, 2013); *L'agape come grazia e libertà* (Rome: Città nuova, 1994); *Teologia* (Rome: Città nuova, 1997, 2005); *Il Logos e il Nulla* (Rome: Città nuova, 2003, 2004); *La percezione della forma* (Rome: Città nuova, 2007); *Sul luogo della Trinità: rileggendo il "De Trinitate" di Agostino* (Rome: Città nuova, 2008); *Dalla Trinità. L'avvento di Dio tra storia e profezia* (Rome: Città nuova, 2011, 2012); *Contemplare e condividere la Luce di Dio. La* *missione della teologia in Tommaso d'Aquino* (Rome: Città nuova, 2014); *Il Concilio della Misericordia. Sui sentieri del Vaticano II* (Rome: Città nuova, 2015). With G. Filoramo he is coauthor of the two volumes of *Il cristianesimo: grande dizionario* (Turin: UTET, 2006).

Mario de França Miranda, SJ, received his doctorate in systematic theology at the Pontifical Gregorian University in Rome, with a thesis on the trinitarian theology of Karl Rahner. He is currently professor of theology at the Pontifical Catholic University of Rio de Janeiro (Brazil). A former member of the International Theological Commission and Consultant of CELAM and of the Brazilian Bishops' Conference, he was a member of the editorial board of the general conference of Santo Domingo and that of Aparecida. In 2015, he was the recipient of the "Ratzinger Award" of the Joseph Ratzinger-Benedict XVI Foundation in the Vatican. He specializes in theological anthropology, theology of religions, inculturation of faith, church, and society. Among his publications in the field of ecclesiology are: *A Igreja que somos nós* (São Paulo, 2013), *A Igreja numa sociedade fragmentada* (São Paulo: SP Ed. Loyola, 2006), and *Inculturazione della fede. Un approccio teologico* (Brescia: Queriniana, 2002). A more recent contribution is "A configuração eclesial latino-americana: ¿iniciativa do Espírito para a Igreja universal?" *Teologia* 117 (2015): 117–30.

Peter de Mey is professor of Catholic ecclesiology and ecumenism in the Department of Theology and Religious Studies of the Université catholique de Louvain (Belgium), and is a member of the Societas Oecumenica (European Society for Ecumenical Research), the Ecclesiological Investigations Network, the Peter and Paul Seminar, and the Vatican II Studies Group of the American Academy of Religion. He is chairman of the board of the National Commission for Belgian ecumenism and is among the presidents of the Commission for Dialogue with the United Protestant Church. In 2010, he was appointed by the Vatican as a member of the international theological dialogue between Catholics and Reformed Protestants. Among his publications are "Church Renewal and Reform in the Documents of Vatican II," *The Jurist* 71 (2011): 369–400; "The Arduous Journey from Exclusion to Communion: Overcoming Relationships of Distrust between Orthodox and Catholics," in *Ecclesiology and Exclusion: Boundaries of Being and Belonging in Postmodern Times*, ed. D. Doyle et al. (Maryknoll, NY: Orbis, 2012), 307–15; P. de Mey et al., eds., *Mission und Einheit. Gemeinsames Zeugnis getrennter Kirchen?—Mission and Unity. Common Witness of Separated Churches?* (Leipzig: Evangelische Verlagsanstalt, 2012).

Severino Dianich was born in 1934 in Fiume, Italy (now Rijeka, Croatia), and served as pastor of Caprona (Pisa) and then episcopal vicar of pastoral care for culture and university in the diocese of Pisa. He has been visiting professor at the Pontifical Gregorian University and the Theological Faculty of Sicily (Palermo), and is emeritus professor of ecclesiology at the Theological Faculty of Central Italy (Florence). A former member of the editorial board of the international journal of theology *Concilium*, he has also been a founding member and president of the Italian Theological Association. Among his publications are *La Chiesa in missione. Per una ecclesiologia dinamica* (Cinisello Balsamo, Paoline, 1987); *Una Chiesa dentro la storia* (Milan: Àncora, 2004); *Per una teologia del papato* (Cinisello Balsamo: San Paolo, 2010); *La Chiesa cattolica verso la sua riforma* (Brescia: Queriniana, 2015); *Diritto e teologia. Ecclesiologia e canonistica per una riforma della chiesa* (Bologna: EDB, 2015). With Carmelo Torcivia he has written *Forme del popolo di Dio tra comunità e fraternità* (Cinisello Balsamo: San Paolo, 2012).

Massimo Faggioli is full professor in the Department of Theology and Religious Studies of Villanova University. He is a contributor to several journals, including *Il Regno, Jesus, Commonweal,* and *La Croix International,* and is cochair of the Vatican II Studies Group of the American Academy of Religion. His major publications include *Il vescovo e il concilio. Modello episcopale e aggiornamento al Vaticano II* (Bologna: Il Mulino, 2005); *Breve storia dei movimenti cattolici* (Rome: Carocci, 2008) translated as *Sorting Out Catholicism: A Brief History of the New Ecclesial Movements* (Collegeville, MN: Liturgical Press, 2014); *Vatican II: The Battle for Meaning* (Mahwah, NJ: Paulist Press, 2012); *True Reform: Liturgy and Ecclesiology in Sacrosanctum Concilium* (Collegeville, MN: Liturgical Press, 2012); *Papa Francesco e la "chiesa-mondo"* (Rome: Armando, 2014) translated as *Pope Francis: Tradition in Transition* (Mahwah, NJ: Paulist Press, 2015); *A Council for the Global Church: Receiving Vatican II in History* (Minneapolis: Fortress, 2015).

Joseph Famerée, SCI, was born in 1955, and is a priest of the Sacred Heart of Jesus (Dehonians). Famerée is a professor of ecclesiology, ecumenism, and theology of the Eastern churches at the Université catholique de Louvain (Belgium), where, from 2012 to 2015, he was dean of the Faculty of Theology. He is also director of the Lumen Gentium Center of the same faculty. He is a member of the Académie internationale des sciences religieuses, of which he was president from 2011 to 2014, and the Group de Dombes. Among his most recent publications are B. Bourgine, J. Famerée, and P. Scolas, eds., *Intempestive éternité* (Louvain-la-Neuve: Academia-l'Harmattan, 2015); "Conciliarité et consensus—Συνοδικοντητα και Ὁμοφωνια," *Theologia* 86, no. 2 (2015): 7–194; J. Famerée, ed., *La situation critique de l'Église catholique. Analyses et perspectives* (Leuven: Peeters, 2015).

Diego Javier Fares, SJ, was born in Mendoza (Argentina) in 1955, and has been a member of the Society of Jesus since 1976 and an ordained priest since 1986. Fares received his doctorate in philosophy with a thesis entitled *Fenomenología de la Verdad en el pensamiento de Hans Urs von Balthasar*. He is full professor at the Faculty of Philosophy of the Universidad del Salvador (Área San Miguel), Buenos Aires (Argentina). For twenty years he worked at El Hogar de San José, providing service to the homeless and animating human development projects, aimed also at social reintegration. He currently lives in Rome and is part of the editorial staff of *La Civiltà Cattolica*. Among his most recent publications are *Papa Francesco è come un bambú. Alla radice della cultura dell'incontro* (Milan: Ancora, 2014); *Il profumo del pastore* (Milan: Ancora, 2015); *Aperti alle sfide* (Milan: Ancora, 2016).

Archbishop Víctor Manuel Fernández was born in Alcira Gigena, Córdoba (Argentina), and ordained a priest in 1985. He obtained a licentiate in theology with a specialization in biblical studies at the Pontifical Gregorian University in Rome, and a doctorate in theology at the Theological Faculty of the Pontificia Universidad Católica Argentina, where he was dean from 2008 to 2009; since December 2009, he has been rector of the same university. From 2007 to 2009 he was president of the Argentine Society of Theology. A former pastor and director of studies of the Seminary "Jesús Buen Pastor" of Río Cuarto, the diocese where he is originally from, he has served as expert on various committees of the Argentine Episcopal Conference, as well as member of the editorial committee of the General Conference Aparecida. He was professor of Scripture, hermeneutics, theological anthropology, homiletics, and spiritual theology in various theological centers of his country. In May 2013, he was appointed archbishop by Pope Francis and ordained in the cathedral of Buenos Aires. He took part in the Synod of Bishops in the assembly of 2014 and that of 2015. He has authored more than three hundred publications; among the most recent ones: *Conversión pastoral y nuevas estructuras* (Buenos Aires: Agape, 2010); *La fuerza sanadora de la mística* (Buenos Aires: Agape, 2012); *Il progetto di Francesco. Dove vuole portare la Chiesa* (Bologna: EMI, 2014); *Contemplativi nell'azione, attivi nella contemplazione. La preghiera pastorale* (Cinisello Balsamo: San Paolo, 2014); *Dar da mangiare, dar da bere. La carità è conveniente* (Bologna: EMI, 2015).

Contributors

José Mario C. Francisco, SJ, is a Jesuit from the Philippines and professor of theology and cultural studies at the Pontifical Gregorian University in Rome and the Loyola School of Theology Ateneo de Manila (Philippines). He is a founding member and representative for Southeast Asia Academy of Asian Christian Studies. He has held senior positions in various academic and religious institutions, and has taught courses in Asia, the United States, and Europe. He has published Filipino manuscripts of the seventeenth century and anthologies on Asian Christianity, the most recent of which bears the title *Christianity and Nation in Southeast Asia*. He is the author of several essays in *The Oxford Handbook on Christianity in Asia* (Oxford: Oxford University Press, 2014); *The Cambridge History of Christianity* (Cambridge: Cambridge University Press, 2006); *Christianities in Asia* (Malden, MA: Wiley-Blackwell, 2011); and of articles for international journals. He edited *Living Theology: The Intersection of Theology, Culture and Spirituality* (Manila 2001); and he coedited *Science, Religion and Culture in the Jesuit Tradition: Perspective from East Asia* (Hindmarsh, Australia: ATF Press, 2006).

Carlos María Galli is a priest and doctor of theology, and is full professor of ecclesiology at the Theological Faculty of the Pontificia Universidad Católica Argentina, where he was dean from 2002 to 2008. He is director of graduate studies in the Department of Systematic Theology, and coordinates the research group La teología en la Argentina. A former president of the Sociedad Argentina de theología, as well as an expert and collaborator of the editorial board of the General Conference of Aparecida, he is a member of the CELAM Reflection Group, corresponding member of the Pontifical Academy of Theology, and member of the International Theological Commission (for the period 2014–2019). He is the author of numerous publications in Italian, which include *Dio vive in città* (Vatican City: Libreria Editrice Vaticana, 2014). Among the many volumes he edited, on his own or in collaboration, the last to appear in chronological order is *La Eclesiología del Concilio Vaticano II* (Buenos Aires: Agape, 2015). Among the essays and studies published in books and journals, are "La teología pastoral de Aparecida, una de las raíces latinoamericanas de la exhortación *Evangelii gaudium*," *Gregorianum* 96, no. 1 (2015) 25–50; "La recepción del Concilio Vaticano II en nuestra incipiente tradición teológica argentina (1962–2005)," in *100 años de la Facultad de Teología*, ed. F. Ortega et al. (Buenos Aires: Agape, 2015), 341–87.

William Henn, OFM Cap, is a Capuchin, and after several years as a lecturer and educator in his own province in the United States, has been teaching ecclesiology and ecumenism at the Pontifical Gregorian University in Rome for more than twenty-five years. He took part in the bilateral dialogue between the Catholic Church and the Pentecostals, the World Communion of Reformed Churches, the Baptist World Alliance, the Lutheran World Federation, and the Mennonite World Conference. Currently he is vice moderator for the Catholic Church at the Commission of Faith and Order of the World Council of Churches. Since 2002, he is also a consultant of the Pontifical Council for Promoting Christian Unity. He is the author of *The Hierarchy of Truths according to Yves Congar, OP* (Rome: Pontificia Università Gregoriana, 1987); *One Faith: Biblical and Patristic Contributions toward Understanding Unity in Faith* (Mahwah, NJ: Paulist Press, 1995); *The Honor of My Brothers: A Brief History of the Relation between the Pope and the Bishops* (New York: Crossroad, 2000); and *Church: The People of God* (London: Burns & Oates, 2004), as well as several articles for theological magazines, dictionaries, and works in collaboration.

Hervé Legrand, OP, holds a licentiate in philosophy, a degree in canon law, a doctorate in theology, and is professor of theology for the Order of Preachers. Legrand has studied at the Faculty of the Saulchoir (France), Walberberg (at Bonn, Germany), the University of Strasbourg (France), St. Thomas Aquinas (Rome) and Athens (Greece). A professor emeritus at the Institut Catholique in Paris, where he directed the program of doctoral studies and the Institut supérieur d'études oecumeniques, he was also associate professor on the Faculty of Canon Law. He is a member of the International Commissions for Dialogue of the Catholic Church with the Pentecostals and the World Lutheran Federation and the international working group Saint Irénée for dialogue between Catholics and Orthodox. Consultant to the Council of European Bishops' conference, the synod of the Maronite Patriarchate of Antioch, the French episcopate Committee for Dialogue with the Orthodox Church and the Permanent Committee of the Lutheran and Reformed, he is also vice president of the Académie internationale des sciences religieuses. Among his publications are "Il primato romano, la comunione tra le chiese e la comunione tra i vescovi," *Concilium* 5/2013; "Les enjeux ecclésiologiques des réformes institutionnelles envisagées par le pape François," in *L'an I de la révolution du pape François*, ed. M. Dubost (Paris: Cerf, 2014); "La primauté romaine de Vatican I au pape François," in *Le Concile Vatican II et l'Église orthodoxe* (Geneva: Centre Orthodoxe du Patriarcat Oecuménique, 2015).

Angelo Maffeis is a priest of the diocese of Brescia and at the Brescia campus of the Catholic University of the Sacred Heart (Milan). In 1991 Maffeis received his doctorate in theology at the Pontifical Gregorian University in Rome. He is full professor of history of theology at the

Theological Faculty of Northern Italy (Milan) and teaches also at the Theological School of the Seminary of Brescia and at the headquarters of Brescia's Catholic University of the Sacred Heart. He was a member of the Faith and Order Commission of the World Council of Churches. Since 1995, he is a member of the International Commission for Catholic-Lutheran dialogue, established by the Pontifical Council for Promoting Christian Unity and the Lutheran World Federation; since 2002, he is consultant to the Pontifical Council for Promoting Christian Unity; and since 2012, he is president of the Paul VI Institute of Brescia. His publications include *Il Ministero nella Chiesa. Uno studio del dialogo cattolico-luterano (1967–1984)* (Milan: Glossa, 1991); *Giustificazione. Percorsi teologici nel dialogo tra le Chiese* (Cinisello Balsamo: San Paolo, 1998); *Il dialogo ecumenico* (Brescia: Queriniana, 2000); *Teologie della Riforma* (Brescia: Morcelliana, 2004); *Penitenza e unzione dei malati* (Brescia: Queriniana, 2012).

Mary Melone, SFA, is a religious of the Franciscan Angeline Nuns and is professor of trinitarian theology and pneumatology at Rome's Pontifical University Antonianum, where since 2014 she has held the post of rector. She received her doctorate in dogmatic theology with a study of the pneumatology of Richard of St. Victor. Since 2014, she is president of the Italian Society for Theological Research. Her publications include several studies of theology of the Holy Spirit in the Middle Ages: "*Donum in quo omnia alia donantur.* Aspetti di teologia dello Spirito Santo in Bonaventura da Bagnoregio," *Ricerche teologiche* 17 (2006): 51–75; "L'universalità dell'azione salvifica dello Spirito. Una prospettiva medievale," *Antonianum* 86 (2011): 237–58; 451–70); and in contemporary theology, "La pneumatologia contemporanea. Indicazioni in margine allo *status quaestionis*," in *Credo nello Spirito Santo*, ed. G. Giorgio and M. Melone (Bologna: EDB, 2009), 45–78.

Serena Noceti is full professor of systematic theology at the Istituto Superiore di Scienze Religiose "Beato Ippolito Galantini" in Florence, and teaches courses at the Theological Faculty of Central Italy. A founding member of the CTI (Coordinamento Teologhe Italiane), she is vice president of the Italian Theological Association. Her publications, which focus on ecclesiology, theology of gender, and catechesis, include S. Dianich and S. Noceti, *Trattato sulla chiesa* (Brescia: Queriniana, 2002, 2015^3); R. Battocchio and S. Noceti, eds., *Chiesa e sinodalità. Coscienza, forme, processi* (Milan: Glossa, 2007); M. Perroni, A. Melloni, and S. Noceti, eds., *"Tantum aurora est." Donne e Vaticano II* (Munster: LIT, 2012); S. Noceti and R. Repole, eds., *Commentario ai documenti del Vaticano II, II: Lumen Gentium* (Bologna: EDB, 2015).

John W. O'Malley, SJ, is a professor in the department of theology at Georgetown University. He received his doctorate in history at Harvard University, specializing in the history of the Church in modern times. He has received lifetime achievement awards from the Society for Italian History, from the Renaissance Society of America, and the American Catholic Historical Association. In 2016 he received the Centennial Medal from Harvard University, the highest honor awarded by the prestigious university. His major work is *The First Jesuits* (Cambridge, MA: Harvard University Press, 1993), which has received two awards for best book and has been translated into thirteen languages. He is the author of other volumes, winners of other similar awards and translated into many languages; among the most recent are *What Happened at Vatican II* (Cambridge, MA: Belknap Press of Harvard University Press, 2008); *Trent: What Happened at the Council* (Cambridge, MA: Belknap Press of Harvard University Press, 2012); "Trajectories and Hermenuetics" in *After Vatican II: Trajectories and Hermeneutics*, ed. J. Heft and J. O'Malley (Grand Rapids, MI: Eerdmans, 2012); "Vatican II Revisited as Reconciliation: The Francis Factor," in *The Legacy of Vatican II*, ed. M. Faggioli and A. Vicini (Mahwah, NJ: Paulist Press, 2015), 3–15.

Giancarlo Pani, SJ, is emeritus professor of the history of Christianity at the University "Sapienza" of Rome. His interests focus on early Christianity (Paul of Tarsus, apocalyptic literature) and biblical exegesis of both the early centuries and the sixteenth century. Since 2013, has been part of the collegium of writers of *La Civiltà Cattolica*. Among his publications are *Paolo, Agostino, Lutero: alle origini del mondo moderno* (Soveria Mannelli: Rubbettino, 2005); the Italian translation of Martin Luther's *Lectures on Romans (1515–1516)* (Rome: Publicazioni Agostiniani, 1983); *Studio e Sapienza. La passione per la verità e l'assoluto* (Palermo: Vittorietti, 2008); for the fourth centenary of the Galilean discoveries in 2010 he edited *Il caso Galileo. Il metodo scientifico e la Bibbia* (Palermo: Sigma, 2008). Among his most recent publications are "Il concilio di Trento e la modernità," in *L'uomo moderno e la Chiesa*, ed. P. Gilbert (Rome: Gregorian & Biblical Press, 2013), 147–75; "Matrimonio e seconde nozze al Concilio di Trento," *La Civiltà Cattolica* 2014/4: 19–32; "La Lettera ai Romani e Lutero," *La Civiltà Cattolica* 2016/1: 17–29.

Salvador Pié-Ninot was born in 1941 and is a priest of the diocese of Barcelona (Spain). He received his doctorate in theology at the Pontifical Gregorian University in Rome, with a thesis on *La Palabra de Dios en los libros sapienciales* (Barcelona, 1972). From 1971 to 2015, he was professor of fundamental theology and ecclesiology at the Faculty of Theology of Catalonia (Barcelona) and, from 1992 to 2013, also at the

Pontifical Gregorian University in Rome. As an expert, he participated in the Synod of Bishops of 2008 and 2012. His works, some translated into various languages, include *Sinodalitat Eclesial* (Barcelona: Facultat de Teologia de Catalunya, 1993); *Introduzione all'Ecclesiologia* (Rome: Gregorian & Biblical Press, 2013[5]); *La Teología Fundamental. "Dar razón de la esperanza" (1 Pe 3,15)* (Salamanca: Secretariado Trinitario, 2009[7]); *Eclesiología* (Salamanca, 2015[3]); *Che cos'è la Chiesa?* (Brescia: Queriniana, 2009); and, with Christopher O'Donnell, *Diccionario de Eclesiología* (Madrid: San Paolo, 2001).

Hermann J. Pottmeyer is a diocesan priest and received his doctorate in theology and philosophy. A professor of fundamental theology at the University of Bochum, he has also been a visiting professor at the University of Notre Dame. He is a member of the Académie internationale des sciences religieuses and member of the Scientific Committee of the Paul VI Institute of Brescia. Among his publications: *Il ruolo del papato nel terzo millennio* (Brescia: Queriniana, 2002); "Dialogstrukturen in der Kirche und die Communio-Theologie des Zweiten Vatikanums," *Communio* 41 (2012): 602–15; "Die konziliare Vision einer neuen Kirchengestalt," in *Kleine Christliche Gemeinschaften verstehen*, ed. C. Hennecke (Würzburg: Echter, 2009), 31–46; "Primato e collegialità episcopale nella ecclesiologia di J. Ratzinger," in *Primato e collegialità*, ed. R. La Delfa (Rome: Città Nuova, 2008), 71–90; "Le dogme de Vatican I et l'invitation œcuménique du pape Jean-Paul II dans *Ut unum sint*," in *Scio cui credidi*, ed. I. Ledwoń et al. (Lublin: Wydawnictwo, 2007), 421–34; "Dal Sinodo del 1985 al Grande Giubileo dell'anno 2000," in *Il Concilio Vaticano II. Recezione e attualità alla luce del Giubileo*, ed. R. Fisichella (Cinisello Balsamo: San Paolo, 2000), 11–25.

Andrea Riccardi has taught contemporary history, as full professor, at the University of Bari, University "Sapienza" of Rome, and the University of Rome III. In 1968, he founded the Community of Sant'Egidio. Since March 2015, he has been President of the Dante Alighieri Society. Among his numerous publications, many of which are translated into multiple languages, are *Il secolo del martirio. I cristiani nel Novecento* (Milan: Mondadori, 2000); *Il Partito Romano. Politica italiana, Chiesa cattolica e Curia romana da Pio XII a Paolo VI* (Brescia: Morcelliana, 2007); *Giovanni Paolo II. La biografia* (Cinisello Balsamo: San Paolo, 2011); *La sorpresa di papa Francesco. Crisi e futuro della Chiesa* (Milan: Mondadori, 2013); with Jean-Michel Di Falco and Timothy Radcliffe, *Il libro nero della condizione dei cristiani nel mondo* (Milan: Mondadori, 2014).

Gilles Routhier is the Monseigneur-de-Laval professor of theology and dean of the Faculty of Theology and Religious Studies at the Université Laval (Quebec, Canada). After his doctoral thesis on the reception and teaching of Vatican II on the synodality of the local church in the Quebec church, he continued his research by focusing on ecclesiology. Besides ecclesiology, his research interest is on Vatican II: its history, its interpretation, its teaching, and reception. He is the author of books and numerous articles on the subject in French, English, Spanish, German, and Italian, among which are *Il Concilio Vaticano II. Recezione ed ermeneutica* (Milan: Vita e pensiero, 2007); *Un Concilio per il XXI secolo. Il Vaticano II cinquant'anni dopo* (Milan: Vita e pensiero, 2014); *La réception d'un concile* (Paris: Cerf, 1993, 2012^2).

Léonard Santedi Kinkupu is a diocesan priest and doctor of theology at the Institut Catholique in Paris and of the history of religions and religious anthropology at the Sorbonne. Since 1993 Kinkupu has taught fundamental theology at the Université catholique of Congo and, since 2012, has been visiting lecturer at the Institut Catholique in Paris. Former member of the International Theological Commission, he is secretary general of the Congolese bishops' conference, scientific secretary of the Association of African Theologians, and member of the editorial board of the international journal of theology *Concilium*. Among his publications are *Dogme et inculturation en Afrique. Perspective d'une théologie de l'invention* (Paris: Karthala, 2003); *La théologie et l'avenir des sociétés. Cinquante ans de l'École de Kinshasa* (Paris: Karthala, 2010); editor of *Unité et Pluralité en Théologie. Mélanges offerts au professeur M. Ngindu* (Kinshasa: Ed. Croix du Salut, 2014). His recent articles include "Nouvelle évangélisation et catéchèse dans la perspective de l'Église famille de Dieu en Afrique," in *La catechesi e le sfide dell'evangelizzazione oggi*, ed. G. Routhier, L. Bressan, and L. Vaccaro (Brescia: Morcelliana, 2012), 91–101; "L'Église et la construction d'une nation en République Démocratique du Congo," *Spiritus* 213 (2013): 391–404.

Jorge A. Scampini, OP, is a Dominican priest. He obtained his doctorate in theology in Fribourg (Switzerland) and is a professor of dogmatic theology and ecumenism at the center of philosophical and theological studies of the Order of Preachers (Universidad del Norte "Santo Tomás de Aquino," Buenos Aires) and at the theological Faculty of the Universidad Católica Argentina. He has participated in numerous ecumenical and theological dialogue committees: The Faith and Order Commission of the World Council of Churches (1991–2013); with the Baptist World Alliance (2006–2010), and the World Communion of Reformed Churches and the World Methodist Council. A consultant to the Pontifical Council for Promoting Christian Unity, from 2010 to 2013 he was president of the Sociedad Argentina de teología. Among his most recent publications: with Carlos Schickendantz, *Itinerarios receptivos del Concilio Vaticano II* (Buenos Aires: Agape, 2015); "The Sacraments in the Ecumenical Dialogue," in *Oxford Handbook of Sacramental Theology*, ed. M. Levering and H. Boersma (Oxford: Oxford University Press, 2015), 675–91; "La jerarquía de verdades de *Unitatis redintegratio* a *Evangelii Gaudium,*" *Studium. Filosofía y Teología* 17 (2014): 137–79; "Perspectivas ecuménicas en y a partir de la exhortación apostólica *Evangelii Gaudium,*" in *Instauremos el reino del Padre y su justicia. Comentarios a la Evangelii Gaudium*, ed. E. Gómez (Buenos Aires: Docencia, 2014), 211–33.

Juan Carlos Scannone, SJ, was born in Buenos Aires in 1931, earned a degree in philosophy (University of Monaco of Bavaria), a licentiate in theology (University of Innsbruck), was president of Área San Miguel (University of El Salvador, Argentina) and dean of philosophy, as well as teacher and director of the Instituto de Investigaciones Filosóficas. He was guest lecturer at the universities of Frankfurt, Salzburg, and Vienna, at the Gregorian University of Rome, University Iberoamericana of Mexico, at the Hochschule für Philosophie of Monaco, the Institute Skt. Georgen in Frankfurt, the Institute Lumen Vitae in Brussels, and others. He received an honorary doctorate in philosophy from the Universidad Católica de Córdoba (Argentina); he is an honorary professor at the Universidad de San Marcos based in Lima (Peru), and member of the European Academy of Sciences and Arts. Among his most recent books are *Religión y Nuevo Pensamiento* (Barcelona–México, 2005); *Discernimiento filosófico de la acción y pasión históricas* (Barcelona: Anthropos, 2005); *Le Pape du Peuple. Bergoglio raconté par son confrère théologien, jésuite, argentin* (Paris: Cerf, 2015).

Silvia Scatena was born in 1970 and studied at the University of Pisa, University of Rome III, and at the Catholic University of America. Since 1995 she has collaborated with the Foundation for Religious Studies in Bologna and is professor of contemporary history at the University of Modena and Reggio Emilia. In the academic year 2014/15, she taught history of Christianity at the Catholic University of Louvain-la-Neuve (Belgium). She was a member of the editorial board of the international journal of theology *Concilium*. Among her publications are *In populo pauperum. La chiesa latinoamericana dal concilio a Medellín (1962–1968)* (Bologna: Il Mulino, 2008); *Taizé. Le origini della comunità e l'attesa del concilio* (Zurich: LIT, 2011); *1962–2012: la storia dopo la Storia? Contributi e prospettive degli studi sul Vaticano II dieci anni dopo la Storia del concilio*, the monograph issue *Cristianesimo nella storia* 34, no. 1 (2013); "Internationale, interconfessionnelle, œcuménique. La Communauté de Taizé et l'Église Réformée de France: l'affaire des frères pasteurs," in

Toward a History of the Desire for Christian Unity: Preliminary Research Papers, ed. L. Ferracci (Zurich: LIT, 2015), 121–37.

Carlos Schickendantz holds a doctorate in theology from Eberhard-Karls University of Tübingen (Germany), and currently works as a researcher for the Manuel Larraín Theological Center of the Universidad Alberto Hurtado in Santiago, Chile. He is working on a research project titled "The Historical Events as a Theological Place. A Contribution to the Methodological Renewal of Theology" (funded by the Fondecyt Program, 2015). His publications include *Cambio estructural de la Iglesia como tarea y oportunidad* (Córdoba: EDUCC, 2005); "Das II. Vatikanum als ein qualitativer Sprung in der Kirchengeschichte," in *Zukunft aus der Geschichte Gottes. Theologie im Dienst an einer Kirche für Morgen*, ed. G. Bausenhart, M. Eckholt, and L. Hauser (Freiburg i. Br.: Herder, 2016), 170–95; "Autoridad teológica de los acontecimientos históricos. Perplejidades sobre un lugar teológico," *Teología* 50/115 (2014): 157–83; "El Vaticano II como texto constitucional de la fe. Valor y límites de una interpretación del género textual," *Teología y vida* 56, no. 3 (2015); "Sinodalidad en todos los niveles. Teología, diagnóstico y propuestas para una reforma institucional," in *La Eclesiología del Concilio Vaticano II. Memoria, Reforma y Profecía*, ed. V. R. Azcuy, J. C. Caamaño, and C. M. Galli (Buenos Aires: Agape, 2015), 513–34.

Antonio Spadaro, SJ, was born in Messina, earned a degree in philosophy from the University of Messina in 1988, and a doctorate in theology from the Pontifical Gregorian University in 2000, where he was a visiting professor at the Faculty of Theology and the Interdisciplinary Center of Social Communication. From 2004 to 2009 he was a delegate for the cultural and intellectual activities of the Italian Jesuits. Since 2011, he has been editor of *La Civiltà Cattolica*, in which he has published about two hundred essays. Since then, he has been a consultor of the Pontifical Council for Culture; and he was also consultor of the Pontifical Council for Social Communications; he then was on the Vatican Media Committee. He is an advisor for the union of Italian Catholic publishers and booksellers (Uelci). He has published several volumes of literary criticism and theology in dialogue with contemporary culture, especially digital, such as *La grazia della parola. Karl Rahner e la poesia* (Milan: Jaca Book, 2006); *Abitare nella possibilità. L'esperienza della letteratura* (Milan: Jaca Book, 2008); *Svolta di respiro. Spiritualità della vita contemporanea* (Milan: Vita e pensiero, 2010); *Nelle vene d'America. Da Walt Whitman a Jack Kerouac* (Milan: Jaca Book, 2013); *Cyberteologia. Pensare il cristianesimo al tempo della rete* (Milan: Vita e pensiero, 2012) (translated into eight languages). He is the author of the first book of conversations with Pope Francis: *La mia porta è sempre aperta.*

Una conversazione con Antonio Spadaro (Milan: Rizzoli, 2013), which has been translated into multiple languages. He also edited the Italian texts that J. M. Bergoglio published before his election to the pontificate, his homilies at St. Marta, Francis's main pontifical documents (encyclicals, apostolic exhortations, etc.), and the texts of the two synods on the family, in which he participated as a pontifical appointee.

Dario Vitali was born in Edolo (Brescia), and is a priest of the diocese of Velletri-Segni and professor of ecclesiology at the Pontifical Gregorian University in Rome. Consultor of the Secretariat of the Synod of Bishops, he was secretary and member of the Italian Theological Association's steering committee. Among his recent publications: *Lumen Gentium. Storia, commento, recezione* (Rome: Studium, 2013); *Il Popolo di Dio* (Assisi: Cittadella, 2013); *In attesa della sua venuta* (Cinisello Balsamo: San Paolo, 2013); *Verso la sinodalità* (Magnano: Qiqajon, Comunità di Bose, 2014). Among recently published articles in scientific journals: "'La totalità dei fedeli non può sbagliarsi nel credere' (LG 12): il *sensus fidelium* come voce della Tradizione," *Urbaniana University Journal* 66, no. 2 (2013): 37–70; "Più collegialità: senso e portata di una richiesta," *Rivista del Clero Italiano* 95, no. 3 (2014): 182–206; "*Sensus fidei* e Magistero," *Revista Catalana de Teología* 39, no. 1 (2014): 97–128.

Myriam Wijlens was born in the Netherlands, has a licentiate in theology (Nijmegen, Netherlands), received her doctorate in canon law (Ottawa, ON, Canada) and her licentiate in canon law (Munster, Germany). Since 2005, she is professor of canon law at the Faculty of Catholic Theology of the University of Erfurt (Germany), where she was deputy head from 2008 to 2011, and is an honorary professor of Canon Law and Ecumenism at Durham University (UK). On behalf of the Pontifical Council for Promoting Christian Unity, Wijlens is a member of the Catholic Church Commissions for Dialogue with the Community of Protestant Churches in Europe (2012–2018) and the Commission on Faith and Order (2008–2022), where she is comanager of the project Moral Discernment in the Churches. She is also cochairwoman of the international group of the Peter and Paul Seminar research, which is interested in a reform of the Church in light of ecumenism. Her research focuses on the interaction between ecclesiology and canon law, with emphasis on ecumenical implications. Among her publications are coauthor, *Communion of Churches and Petrine Ministry: Lutheran Catholic Convergences*, ed. Gruppo di Farfa Sabina (Grand Rapids, MI: Eerdmans, 2014); "Supporting the Vision with the Help of Canonical Structures," in *Protestant Church Polity in Changing Contexts*, ed. A. Janssen and L. Koffeman, vol. 1 (Zurich: LIT, 2014), 191–204.